THE HAMLYN ENCYCLOPEDIA OF House Plants

THE HAMLYN ENCYCLOPEDIA OF
House Plants

Rob Herwig

HAMLYN
London · New York · Sydney · Toronto

Translated from the Dutch by Marian Powell

Jacket photography by the author

First published by Zomer & Keuning-Ede under the title
Herwig Kamerplanten Encylopedie

This edition published in 1984 by
Hamlyn Publishing,
a division of
The Hamlyn Publishing Group Limited
Bridge House, London Road, Twickenham,
Middlesex, England

Second impression 1985

ISBN 0 600 30561 9

Set in 8/9½ and 7½/8½ Palatino by
Page Bros (Norwich) Ltd, England
Printed and bound by Graficromo s.a., Cordoba, Spain

Contents

Introduction 7

The development of indoor gardening

What is a house plant? 9
Pot plants in history 9
Exotic plants 9
Developments in the twentieth century 10
Plants as friends 10

Situations for indoor plants

The window-sill 11
Free-standing plants 12
Plant containers and hanging baskets 14
Combinations – Planting – Types of container
House plants in summer quarters 17
Tub plants in summer – Tub plants in winter – Tub plants in spring
The conservatory or garden room 19
Building a conservatory – Suitable plants for a conservatory
The flower window 20
Plants to look for
The greenhouse 21
The best situation – Construction – Materials – Putting up a greenhouse – Lighting – Heating – Ventilation – Screening – Watering – Humidity – Choosing your plants
Glass cases, plant tanks and bottle gardens 26
Closed or open? – The various options – Maintenance – Choice of plants

The use of indoor plants

Buying plants 27
Which window? – Which room? – Deciding on size – Colour harmony – Variegated plants – Related plants
Disposable plants 29
Fashions in plants 30
The best situation 30
Plants as room dividers – Time for a change
Plants and containers 32
The importance of shape and colour – Antique containers – Problems of ornamental pots – The fashion in containers
Plants in the office 34
Status symbols – Losing the human factor – Personal care – Mixing plants – The importance of correct placing – Constant temperatures – Climate control – Office gardens
House plants in public places 37

House plants in the home 37
The bedroom – The bathroom – The kitchen – The attic – The garage – The cellar – Plants on board ship

Indoor plant groups

Flowering plants 38
Foliage plants 39
Palms – Ferns
Bromeliads 40
Hanging and climbing plants 40
Indoor trees 41
House plants from seeds 42
Succulents 42
Cacti – Other succulents – Exotic shapes – Finding a site
Bulbs and tubers 44
Orchids 44
Bonsai 44

Cultivation systems

Hydroponics 45
Ground roots and water roots – Clay granules – Ion exchange – Pros and cons of hydroculture
Self-watering systems 46
Simple methods

The importance of lighting

Special lighting 47
Daylight and darkness 47
Hints on installation 47

Care and cultivation

Introduction 49
Some botanical basics 49
How a plant grows from seed – Intake of nutrients – Assimilation and photosynthesis – Respiration – The flower – The leaf – The stem – The root
Light 52
What is light? – Measuring intensity – Screening – Errors in lighting – Day length and flowering
Temperature 54
Interpretation of symbols – Variations in temperature – Mistakes in temperature control – Standing your plants outside – Soil temperature – The effect on bud formation
Moisture 55
What the plant tells you – Watering for growth – Evaporation – A question of judgement – Moisture control – Water temperature – Methods of watering – Plastic pots – Mistakes in watering – Water quality – Clay pots – Replacing the top layer of compost – Improving the water – Domestic remedies – Rainwater
Atmospheric humidity 58
What is humidity? – Plant requirements – Explanation of the symbols – Heating methods and humidifiers – Increasing relative humidity
Rest periods 60
Day length and temperature – Winter quarters – Other resting places
Feeding 61
Varying requirements – Types of fertiliser – When to feed – Accumulation of salts
Potting composts 62
Different requirements – Man-made mixtures – Acidity – The symbols – Main proprietary mixtures – Home-made mixtures – Examples of useful mixtures – Repotting – When to repot – Choice of pot – Removing the plant – Protecting the root system – Drainage – Potting on – Aftercare
Daily care 64
Acclimatising the plant – Positioning – Watering – Screening – Spraying – Tying – Trimming – Cleaning the foliage – Pruning – Stopping
A home for plants 66
Built-in containers and flower windows
Holiday time 67
Caring for special groups 68
Bulbs, corms and tubers – Bromeliads – Orchids – Palms – Succulents – Ferns
Propagation 72
Special aids – Sowing – Division – Cuttings – Air-layering – Grafting
Pest and disease control 77
Diagnosis – Control – Drawbacks of chemicals – Less dangerous remedies – Biological remedies available – Chief pests and diseases

Identifying the plants

Nomenclature of cultivated plants 81
Family, genus, species, variety and strain – How to use the symbols – Arrangement of plant descriptions – Key to symbols
Plant descriptions in alphabetical order 82–272

Plant lists and tables

Plants for full sun and high temperature 273
Plants for full sun and moderate temperature 273
Plants for full sun and low temperature 273
Plants for half shade and high temperature 273
Plants for half shade and moderate temperature 274
Plants for half shade and low temperature 274
Plants for full shade and high temperature 275
Plants for full shade and moderate temperature 275
Plants for full shade and low temperature 275
Plants requiring high humidity 275
Plants requiring moderate humidity 276
Plants which tolerate dry air 276
Plants which thrive in standard potting compost 277
Plants which need an acid compost 277
Plants requiring special mixtures 277
Flowering plants 278
Foliage plants 278
Bromeliads 279
Palms 279
Ferns 279
Orchids 279
Cacti 280
Succulents 280
Bulbous plants 280
Tuberous plants 280
Trailing and climbing plants 281
Tub plants 281
Poisonous plants 281

Index 282

Bibliography 288

Acknowledgements 288

Introduction

I well recall how, in 1967, I called on a publisher with the proposal that I should write a new book on house plants. I felt that the three or four little books on the market provided insufficient choice. 'But surely there is already a book on house plants?' the Managing Editor exclaimed in amazement, and he quickly sent me packing.

Since then there has been quite a change. Not only did I compile the book I had planned, but I then wrote many more. Nor have other authors been idle, so that there is now a considerable choice.

However, the popularity of house plants is still on the increase and with it the need for more detailed information. Simple volumes describing 100 to 200 plants were soon followed by books on 200 to 400 species, and now the time has come for a book containing about 700 plants illustrated in colour, with approximately 1500 described.

This book consists of four parts. The first section, illustrated with colour plates, concerns the use of plants in the home, in the greenhouse and in the conservatory, as well as in offices and public places. The second section, illustrated with sketches, provides an extensive manual on all the practical jobs concerned with the growing and care of indoor plants.

The third part, again illustrated in colour, consists of the actual encyclopedia, describing a large number of house, greenhouse and tub plants which are more or less freely available and reasonably manageable. They have been arranged alphabetically under their botanical names. In spite of the extent of this book, absolute completeness is impossible to achieve. You only have to consider the many hundreds, indeed thousands, of cactus species which may be grown in the greenhouse by amateurs specialising in these plants to realise that it is not possible to describe and illustrate more than a very small part of such collections. However, those house plants that have been selected have been comprehensively dealt with, and in greater detail than in many other books on the subject. In addition you will find that many exotic and rare greenhouse plants have also been included.

The fourth part, following the plant dictionary, contains tables and lists of plants for different conditions. There is also an extensive index of botanical as well as popular names and their synonyms, so that it is easy to look up those plants whose botanical name has temporarily escaped your memory. Most important of all, you will also find listed here the synonyms by which some of the plants may be better known to you. For one of the difficulties of plant nomenclature is that names may vary between one authority and another, depending on how up to date they are. Names are sometimes changed and plants reclassified, which frequently leads to confusion – even among the experts.

The book contains a great deal of information which previously could only be supplied by professionals. Apart from the fact that these professionals may not appreciate such demands on their time, they are not necessarily the best people to ask for advice. Today the professional grower is a super-specialist. He knows everything there is to know about one particular method of cultivation. He may, for instance, grow azaleas or ferns, but as a rule his expert knowledge is confined to those species he grows himself. If you ask a grower of bromeliads something about cacti, you will no doubt receive an answer, but don't count too much on his being right.

Generally speaking, you will not find the same expertise in flower shops and garden centres as in a nursery: they do not grow their own plants, which are bought in from wholesalers. Their staff therefore seldom have the knowledge or experience of the professional grower. So unless you have access to a specialist house plant nursery, your best source of information is often the written word, such as articles in magazines, or books on the subject.

You may wonder whether it is really essential to examine all the conditions necessary for the health of house plants in such great detail. Are all these things really indispensable – these special composts, the rest periods, the prescribed temperatures? Wouldn't the plant grow just as well in ordinary soil with a little water every day?

Don't forget that this book is intended for people who genuinely *love* plants. In every case the conditions outlined are the conditions considered ideal for that particular plant. The care of plants is a serious hobby and genuine plant lovers require sound and detailed knowledge. So nothing but serious, honest information will do, even though some of it may at times seem rather difficult. There are, after all, more elementary books available for beginners, but I believe that only the best is good enough for our plants.

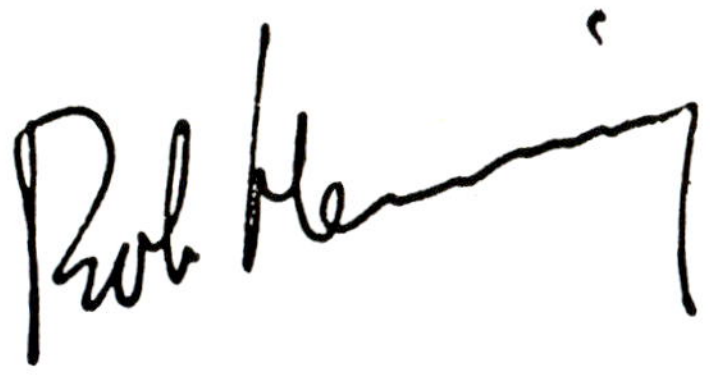

一筆齋
文調画

The Development of Indoor Gardening

A Japanese colour woodcut by Ippôtsusai Bunchô, made in 1777, and thought to represent a scene from the drama 'Senchai Hagi'. The plant is an ornamental cherry, cultivated as a bonsai

What is a House Plant?

Actually there is no such thing. There is not a single natural plant which would grow spontaneously indoors, unless you include dry rot, the fungus which attacks the beams under the floorboards – something you don't notice until your foot goes through the floor. Possibly an ivy shoot might penetrate the wall, but that's about all.

What we call house plants are those that have been introduced into the home by man and which survive reasonably well in the living room – or, more correctly, in any building.

In the course of the last century, by a process of crossing and selection, plants have been created for the express purpose of being grown in rooms or greenhouses. Consider, for instance, the many begonia hybrids, or the hibiscus strains cultivated by radiation. Commerce is the principle which governs these activities. Only rarely are plants crossed for non-commercial purposes.

Pot Plants in History

One of the essential characteristics of a house plant is that it does not grow in the open ground. We place these plants in bowls, pots, tubs, or any other suitable containers. This custom already existed among the Sumerians and in ancient Egypt, about 3500 years ago. Illustrations surviving from those times show plants, usually shrubs or trees, growing in stone pots and vases, and these were probably kept out of doors. During the reign of Ramses III in particular, many shrubs were planted in vases. But several of these plants are known in our climate as house or greenhouse plants: for instance myrtle (*Myrtus communis*), pomegranate (*Punica granatum*), palms, and probably also the popular Umbrella Plant (*Cyperus alternifolius*).

Of course all these plants had to be artificially watered, but this presented no problem, for the Sumerians already had irrigation systems and Egyptian gardens usually incorporated rectangular ponds, whose main function was that of water reservoirs.

The Chinese, too, were preoccupied with plants at a very early stage, but little is known about plants being grown in pots. The well-known Japanese bonsai, which in our climate must be counted as indoor plants, or rather plants for the unheated greenhouse, are not so very old.

The Greeks and Romans, who were in contact with late-Egyptian civilisation, simply adopted the custom of planting in pots and other containers. Two thousand years ago their patios were filled with pot plants, but it is not known whether they were kept indoors as well. These plants were mainly those which we now regard as tub plants.

Above In Seville a patio provides sufficient shelter for plants which we can only grow under cover. The foliage plants in the pots are aspidistras

Above right The study of the Dutch poet Staring (1767–1840), reconstructed in the Municipal Museum in Zutphen. Both the araucaria and the palm had been imported by that time

Below right A late 19th-century kitchen in The Netherlands, reconstructed in the same museum. The dracaena is a plant appropriate to the period

Exotic Plants

The Crusaders already imported plants from Asia Minor, though on a small scale, but early in the 15th century Italian seafarers began to bring large numbers of exotic plants home from Asia. Many of them could be grown out of doors, but true tropical species had to be protected to some extent in winter, even in Italy. It is logical that people would try to grow these plants indoors; these might therefore be called the first house plants.

Better methods, however, were developed soon after and in 1585 the first greenhouse was built in the botanical gardens in Padua. This was an octagonal building containing one single palm, *Chamaerops humilis*, which in our day has become a well-known house plant. Soon it became all the rage to grow exotic plants and in the 17th century greenhouses and conservatories appeared like mushrooms all over the place, not only in botanical gardens, but especially on the estates of rich landowners in England, France and Germany. By the early 18th century more than 5000 different exotic plants were beginning to be imported.

In a short time the fashion began to attain ridiculous proportions: people travelled all over the world and brought exotica from India, Africa, North and South America and even from Australia back to Europe. The names of many house plants remind us of these adventurous times. One example is the book *Description d'un voyage autour du monde*, published in 1772 by Louis Antoine, Comte de Bougainville, a French explorer who even at that early period sailed through the Straits of Magellan to Polynesia. His name survives in our house plant the bougainvillea. Dozens of similar examples might be given, each commemorating an adventurous voyage inspired by man's remarkable urge to explore.

Most of the efforts made in this respect, however, were aimed at financial gain, and most of the profits ended up in the pockets of large nursery owners in Europe, and later in the United States. Publicity created great enthusiasm among the general public and high prices were paid for exotic plants. Originally most of them were garden plants, but the proportion of 'stove plants' increased with the number of hothouses and conservatories erected. The well-known winter gardens date from this period (1750–1850); some of them developed into veritable Gardens of Eden. The heating of these large areas presented a serious problem, for strangely enough it was not until 1818 that someone discovered that hot water will circulate through a system of pipes. Before that, free-standing stoves were placed in the hothouses, with all the disadvantages these entailed. Once central heating had been invented, private hothouses developed fairly rapidly in the second half of the last century, especially in England.

In the Netherlands, where there were fewer hothouses, it became the custom to grow exotic plants indoors. As a rule they were stately foliage plants, satisfied with a modicum of light, such as palms, dracaenas and aspidistras. In those days small windows and heavy curtains restricted the light indoors, unlike our present-day sunny rooms. Few sun-loving plants were therefore grown, although even at that time there were, of course, already genuine plant lovers, who raised difficult plants in greenhouses and glass frames.

Developments in the Twentieth Century

By the 20th century house plants were no longer regarded as rare exotics but were considered a part of the interior. Initially they had a mainly decorative function, but as our society became more informal, plants were accepted more and more as living creatures.

Up to the second world war, keeping house plants was a relatively relaxed occupation, a pleasant hobby for the housewife, passed on from mother to daughter. Little information was available and the choice of plants did not vary much. Methods of cultivation did not change: the plant was simply put in a red clay pot, which in turn was placed in an ornamental pot, and that was all. Potting compost was brought home from the florist in a bucket; as a rule it consisted of rotted beech leaves mixed with rotted cow manure.

Today, faced with the many dozens of organic and inorganic tonic mixtures on the shelves of your garden centre and wondering which is the right one to choose for your plant, you will realise that far-reaching changes have taken place. Since 1965 plants in the home have become particularly important, especially in Britain where, until then, house plants were not so widely grown as on the Continent. The reason for the increasing interest in plants is generally explained by the growth of urbanisation: flat dwellers do not possess gardens. Personally I believe that it is also the increasingly hard and businesslike attitude that has crept into our lives which attracts man to plants and animals.

Two so-called Kirlian photographs made after leaves (in this case rose leaves) have been subjected to a strong current. This might be described as a plant's aura – one of the natural mysteries still to be solved. The leaves were photographed one hour after being picked. As the leaf dies, the aura disappears

They provide the counterbalance so badly needed.

Whatever the reason, our homes are now filled with plants. They create a warm and attractive environment and have without doubt improved our sense of well-being. We have made friends with our plants.

Plants as Friends

Each of the plants in our living-rooms tells its own story. One may come from a distant forest in New Zealand, where it grows by the side of a clear brook. Another winds itself around the branches of a tree, somewhere in a tropical jungle, sometimes to a height of dozens of feet. If we delve into the origin of all our house plants and try to imagine the atmosphere of their natural habitat, there is no doubt that the plants acquire an added dimension.

It has been said that most animals and certainly plants, on a lower level of creation, have a community soul – that is, not an individual soul, as in the case of man. According to this view plants can transmit 'feelings' from one to the other. It is a fact that genuine communication can be achieved. A few examples may tend to bear this out.

The investigations of the American Clive Backster are well known; he examines plants with the aid of a kind of lie detector. This apparatus measures the galvanic resistance of the skin in man, but Backster applies these measurements to plants. Fluctuations in resistance are noted by a pen on a moving paper roll.

Backster found that a plant under investigation reacted sharply whenever he destroyed another plant or threw a live shrimp into boiling water. Even the mere *intention* to do so resulted in a clear reaction from the plant, even at a distance. The communication thus established between man and plant, animal and plant, or plant and plant, is not interrupted by placing the plant in a Faraday cage (a screened-off space), or even in a lead box. The nature of the transference therefore lies outside the electro-dynamic pattern of radiation, just as do other forces, such as those used in telepathy.

In 1956 J. I. Rodale discovered that cuttings grow better if the mother plant is still alive. It seems as if the latter exudes something or other which protects and stimulates the cuttings. When he burned the mother plant, cuttings taken from it thrived far less well than those from a control group, in which the mother plant remained undamaged. The distance between mother plant and cuttings played little or no part in these experiments.

In the United States tests involving prayer meetings for plants were carried out by J. B. Rhine, a well-known personality in the field of parapsychological experiments, and the Rev. Franklin Loehr. Various seeds were sown in two separate groups. Daily prayers were said for one group; the other had to manage without these good offices. You've guessed it: the plants for which prayers were said grew better. The result is equally positive if prayers are said for the water used for the plants.

Dr Marcel Vogel, an IBM research chemist and radiographer, in 1971 stated that: 'Plants have a demonstrable psyche; they have thought processes and there are species which register every emotional reaction of human beings.'

An excellent plant for experimentation is the philodendron; species with incised foliage, such as *Philodendron bipinnatifidum*, *P. elegans*, *P. laciniatum* and *P. squamiferum* appear to be particularly sensitive.

You might try it yourself. Perhaps you have an electronically minded friend who could make a lie detector for you. Instructions may be found in hobby literature. Connect two stainless steel electrodes to the detector and attach it to the leaves of the plant. Resistance can be measured on the principle of the Wheatstone bridge, but considerable amplification of the ohms variations registered is essential. The result can be read from a millivoltmeter, or better still from a recording card.

Relax in a chair at a distance of about 1.50 m (5 ft) from the plant and concentrate your thoughts on the philodendron. Consider the beautiful structure of the plant, the practical form of the magnificent leaves whose divisions allow light to fall on the foliage below. Think how marvellously the plant will develop in your home into a miracle of perfection. After thus meditating for 20 to 30 minutes you should be aware of contact between the plant and yourself. You feel true affection for it.

Once communication has been established you will notice that the plant picks up your thoughts and that changes in the conductivity of the foliage transform them into electrical impulses which will be recorded by the needle of the meter or on the paper roll. For instance, you might be planning to give the plant a welcome dose of rotted cow dung to encourage its growth – and you will immediately note its reaction.

Another interesting field of experiment is aura-photography (see photographs, above left).

It is my personal opinion that all these experiments indicate that plants have a soul and that it is possible to communicate with them. There is nothing new in that: we used to call it 'having green fingers'. But now it is possible to explain it better and confirm it.

Situations for Indoor Plants

In the course of the years it has been found that house plants are capable of growing in the most unlikely places. Some of them are exceptionally hardy and need very little care; all they seem to require is some light, water and heat. But make no mistake: the large majority of plants are a great deal more particular in their requirements.

House plants in their natural habitat. **Above left** Bromeliads growing on a branch in Surinam; **Centre left** The epiphyte orchid *Miltonia flavescens*; **Below left** The Common Passion Flower with fruits; **Below centre** *Philodendron bipinnatifidum* climbing up a tree; **Below right** Terrestrial bromeliads in Curaçao. The large plate shows specimens of perennial *Pelargonium radens* near a sunny window, where they are obviously thriving

The Window-sill

The window-sill is probably a direct descendant of the embrasures which used to be built into thick walls. It forms an ideal situation for house plants and it is estimated that a large proportion of all plants cultivated indoors are kept on these ledges.

At one time the window-sill was a fairly narrow strip, just wide enough for a small flowerpot. Double glazing was unheard of, and the way the glass was fitted, especially in leaded windows, for instance, often encouraged draughts. There was no radiator under the window and often there would be no central heating at all. In winter, in particular, the plants were kept fairly cool, for even when there was a good fire in the room, the temperature near the window would rarely reach 20°C (68°F).

The choice of plants depends almost entirely on the conditions prevailing near the window. Plants which were kept successfully in former days were those that liked a cool situation in winter. To mention just one example: cyclamens were grown without any problems, for these plants appreciate a temperature of 10 to 15°C (50 to 59°F) in December.

Conditions are now very different. Insulation has been considerably improved; many houses have double glazing and draughts are (fortunately) a thing of the past. Radiators have been placed below the windows, forcing the hot air upwards and thus counteracting the remaining cold in the window area. As a result the window-sill is no longer cold in winter. On the contrary, the temperature may rise considerably, especially when the winter sun is making an effort. The warm air

flows round the leaves and dries them out, for in many cases the window-sill is too narrow. We try to keep the living-room temperature throughout the year at about 20°C (68°F), which is easier than it used to be. But many plants which require a cooler winter period have succumbed as a result. Cacti and other succulents rot or do not flower well; the cyclamen loses its flowers after a few days and the hibiscus flowers throughout the winter, but will be exhausted after a few years. Whole groups of house plants still on the market are quite unsuitable for this constant temperature of 20°C (68°F) throughout the year.

Fortunately there are also plants which do enjoy constant warmth, for instance the ficus plants, dracaenas, dieffenbachias and all other tropical plants which today are our favourite house plants.

Now that so much heat is being created under the window, the width of the window-sill has become an important consideration. Ideally it should be about 50 cm (20 in), which would protect the foliage from rising hot air. Unfortunately architects pay little attention to this point and narrow window-sills remain the rule rather than the exception.

Passionate plant lovers will not be daunted when confronted by such a narrow strip of tiles, stone or wood. They will quickly replace it with a more generous window-sill. A new window-sill may be constructed from tiles, natural stone, wood, formica or veneered hardboard, preferably without gaps through which the warm air might rise.

Instead of a level window-sill you could choose a wide, peat-filled trough into which the plants may be bedded. Such a solution is already beginning to look like a flower window (see page 20). Sketches of different window-sill treatments are found on page 66.

Naturally the part of the room nearest the window receives the most light. This is the main reason why the window ledge is such a good position for plants. The correct choice of plants is important however: a north-facing window entails an entirely different choice from a south-facing one. A free-standing plant, placed on the floor, can be moved forward or back to some extent, but this is not possible on the window-sill. The initial choice must therefore be the correct one.

When selecting your plants the symbols used in this book will be found very useful. For instance, plants marked with the symbol ◐ are particularly suitable for an east- or west-facing window, or for one with a southern aspect which is screened during the day by a sun blind, awning or some other form of protection. Needless to say the symbols referring to temperature and atmospheric humidity must also conform to the conditions of your room.

Gradually you will develop a plan for your window-sill. You might make a list of suitable plants for each window, consisting of foliage plants with a few flowering plants. Next, consider whether any of your existing plants fit into the scheme, move them around if necessary (unless they are doing particularly well in their old spot) and then buy the other plants on your lists. There are people who consider one window ledge per window is not enough and fit several, one above the other. This is a good solution if you possess a lot of smaller plants. Brackets must be fixed on either side of the window to carry the necessary number of shelves. If the window is a wide one it is advisable to drill a hole in the centre of the shelves, through which a thin steel cable is passed and attached to the ceiling. Fix a small clamp under each shelf and make sure that they are level. The shelves are best covered in formica or some other plastic material. Such a full window obscures the view and makes cleaning a formidable task, but these disadvantages do not weigh equally with everybody.

Free-standing Plants

Although for practically all house plants the best situation is near a window, there are a number of hardy species which will survive further back, for instance ferns, *Dracaena* species, the Swiss Cheese Plant, aspidistra, cissus and other species requiring little light. Early in this century such plants were often placed on pedestals which were easily knocked over. It is a miracle that these plants survived for any length of time, particularly when you consider how closely the windows were covered in net curtaining.

Today conditions for free-standing plants are much improved. The most important factor is the increased use of glass in modern houses. Many windows reach almost to the ceiling, allowing the light to enter much further into the room, which naturally benefits free-standing plants. With the aid of a light meter (see page 52) it is possible to determine exactly how far your chosen plant can be set back from the window. It is especially interesting to note how unexpectedly favourable the lighting conditions may be in winter. If a house faces a certain aspect, the sun can reach far into a room towards sunset – a great advantage to foliage plants for which adequate assimilation is difficult at that time of year when days are short.

Free-standing plants and plant troughs must be placed in a spot where they are not in the way, for people constantly rubbing against them can damage the foliage. In modern room settings pedestals and other unstable equipment are seldom used. Instead, low containers and pots standing directly on the floor are preferred and are much more stable, but care must be taken to ensure that water does not escape, since this would damage the floor covering. It is advisable to use either a saucer or a drip tray underneath, which can be ugly, or a watertight container, or an ornamental container round the clay or plastic pot.

Watertight plastic troughs and cylinders are becoming more and more popular. They are very suitable for growing plants, even if they are small in diameter. The idea that the walls of a pot must be porous to admit sufficient oxygen to the roots is a myth. On the other hand the correct watering of plants in these pots does present a problem. Tall, narrow cylinders are particularly deceptive: the top layer of compost may appear to be bone dry, but water can collect in the bottom without being noticed and this will cause the roots to rot. It is not surprising that great efforts have been made to find solutions to this problem. Several of them are described in this book, for example hydroponics and semi-hydro (pages 45–46), and the placing of a simple plastic tube in the pot, through which you can gauge the water on the bottom (page 56).

Free-standing plants have this advantage over mixed containers in that conditions are more easily controlled. Only one plant has to be considered, with fairly narrowly circumscribed requirements of light, temperature and humidity. In a subsequent chapter on plant containers it will be shown that we should aim at combining plants with approximately similar requirements.

Another problem in the planting of mixed containers is the question of shape. Opinions may vary on the combination of different types of plants in a bowl or container, but there can be no objection to a single specimen plant in a container. It is bound to look right, which unfortunately cannot be said of many plant combinations.

It can do little harm to introduce some ground cover under a large specimen plant growing in a generous container. *Soleirolia soleirolii* or *Ficus pumila*, for instance, might be used for this purpose. These little plants will cover the edge of the container; they are quite neutral in appearance and the total effect is attractive.

Nothing is more tempting than to move a free-standing plant from place to place, but you should try to resist this temptation whenever you can. Plants dislike this kind of treatment intensely and will react by showing inhibited growth or losing their leaves. It is quite another matter if a plant has to be moved aside for a few minutes, for instance when the room is being cleaned. As long as it is put back in exactly the same place it will

A good example of an ideal window-sill: wide and solid, so that the plants are not affected by rising heat

come to no harm. Nor is it harmful to move a specimen plant out of doors during a mild summer shower for an hour or so while it is still light enough, to refresh the foliage. In this case cover the compost with kitchen foil to avoid saturation.

The correct balance between pot and plant is particularly important in the case of specimen plants, not only because the roots should have sufficient room, but also for aesthetic reasons and to ensure stability. Too large a plant in a small pot cannot grow. It looks unstable and will soon be overturned. Do not, therefore, be afraid of repotting. Give your specimen plants a new container every year if possible and make sure that plant and pot are in proportion. Never forget that the container itself is an important visual factor, especially in the overall appearance of a specimen plant. It shouldn't be purely an object for holding the potting medium.

The *Monstera deliciosa* or Swiss Cheese Plant is very popular as a free-standing specimen. It can grow very large

Two well-branched examples of *Dracaena marginata* in a wide, low container, with a ground cover of plectranthus. The ground cover can easily be replaced if necessary

A magnificent, ceiling-high *Dieffenbachia amoena* in a restful, dark plastic cylinder. Anything added would spoil the effect

Three specimens of *Dracaena deremensis* 'Warneckii' carefully arranged in one container to achieve the most satisfactory visual effect

Ficus lyrata is a strong, reliable house plant, very suitable for a free-standing position. In this case, too, the container has been filled with a few smaller plants

Plant Containers and Hanging Baskets

The term 'plant container' covers receptacles of all shapes, sizes and constructions, in which various genera and species of plants may be combined, in contrast to the specimen plants described in the previous chapter.

There are quite small containers which can be kept on the window-sill, as well as very large, built-in ones. Where a plant container is constructed in front of a window it may be called a flower window (see page 20).

Combinations

The most difficult part of planting a container is deciding on the correct combination of plants. The plants have to share more or less identical conditions of light, temperature, watering, atmospheric humidity and soil. At most it may be said that in larger containers the lower plants in the centre and at the bottom receive slightly less light, while the relative humidity is fractionally higher as a result of evaporation. Apart from these two points, all the plants put into the container have to accept the same conditions.

It is remarkable how rarely this simple and readily understood fact is taken into account. Frequently plants are combined purely for their appearance, with the result that they remain in good condition for a few weeks at the most. After that some begin to fade. Regardless of how the container is moved about or is watered, it is impossible to keep all the plants healthy. It is particularly strange that so many florists and garden centres are guilty of this error: they ought to know better. Or are they perhaps interested only in the immediate profit?

Whatever it is, you can do better yourself, especially with the aid of this book, since all species are classified by symbols. By combining plants with similar symbols success is practically guaranteed. To make things even easier, plants with identical codes have been listed in the tables on page 273.

Starting off on this basis, you will find that not all plants with the same symbols will necessarily blend well together. You should therefore also be guided by your own taste.

Planting

There are two ways of filling a container. (a) Fill the entire container with potting compost, remove the plants from their pots and plant them directly into the compost. The advantage of this method is that it is easier for the roots to find nourishment, so that the plants will grow more rapidly and more luxuriously. A disadvantage is that, if you wish to remove or replace a plant, the roots will be found to be so entangled with each other that it is quite a job to separate them.

In system (b) keep the plants in their individual pots, and bury them to just over the rim in peat fibre. This has the advantage, up to a point, of enabling each plant to have its own special potting mixture. The plants are easily removed, so that flowering plants can be replaced when necessary. In the course of time some of the root systems will grow out of their pots, but they will never get into such a tangle.

If the container is to look its best from one particular side, the tallest plants should, of course, be put at the back and the lowest in front. If the container can be seen from all sides, the tallest species should be placed in the centre. As containers are often placed near a window (since otherwise they may lack daylight) the correct grouping of the plants is not as simple as might be thought. On the one hand it is necessary to consider the angle of the light, so that the lower plants should be nearer the window and the taller ones facing the room. All the foliage will then turn towards the light. On the other hand the spectators must be taken into account, and they, as a rule, see the plants from inside the room. Frequently they're out of luck, for all they can see is the back and the underside of flowers and leaves. To avoid this we can sit between the window and the container, or we can place the container to one side, which allows us to see at least part of the foliage turning towards the light. In both these cases the plants may lack light, since the strength of light decreases with the square of the distance from the window (2 × the distance from the window = 4 × less light).

Where the plants are left in their pots they may be turned temporarily with their best side towards the room. Most foliage plants will put up with this treatment. The main stem will at the same time grow straighter, making the plant look more attractive.

The problem is largely solved where it is possible to obtain a certain amount of light from the side of the room, for instance in the form of a strong artificial light source (see page 47), or when daylight can come in through a skylight, or when the room is small enough to receive light from two sides at once.

In this informal interior with its rough walls and bare wood floor the somewhat untidy plant trough shows to advantage. In these circumstances it should always be remembered that the plants must receive sufficient light. This trough is situated at a distance of about 2m (6ft) from the window, but fortunately there is a second window on the left (out of the picture), so that the light is sufficient. Because they are lit from two sides, the plants are not inclined to slant in one direction

Types of Container

Disregarding for a moment the alternative methods of watering, which will be discussed later, these are the different types of container to choose from:

(a) free-standing containers;

(b) permanently constructed containers built up of concrete or bricks;

(c) permanent floor-level containers;

(d) hanging baskets and containers.

Free-standing containers There is little difference between free-standing containers and specimen plants. In both cases we are dealing with containers varying in size between small and very large, filled with soil or a soilless potting medium. The only difference is that a plant container (in the present meaning of the word) can be planted with a variety of species or genera, while a specimen container holds only one main plant. To avoid trouble with water these containers are best without holes.

Small free-standing containers or bowls of mixed plants, often given as presents, may find a place on the window-sill. Because, as mentioned earlier, the combination of plants is often ill-chosen, they rarely last long. It is therefore advisable to repot the plants immediately you receive them so as to give each individual species a better chance of survival. Slightly larger containers, which may be placed directly on the floor, are now becoming more widespread. Plastic is a popular material for these containers, since it is inexpensive and impervious to water. More expensive are units made of polystyrene in carefully designed shapes. The question of colour presents no problem where plastic is used. Plastic pots and troughs can contribute to the colour scheme of your room or of the plants themselves, but, unless you are very careful, the effect may easily become too showy, particularly in the case of mixed plants. Preference should therefore be given to fairly neutral shades, such as white, dark brown and green. Plastic containers can be shiny or matt.

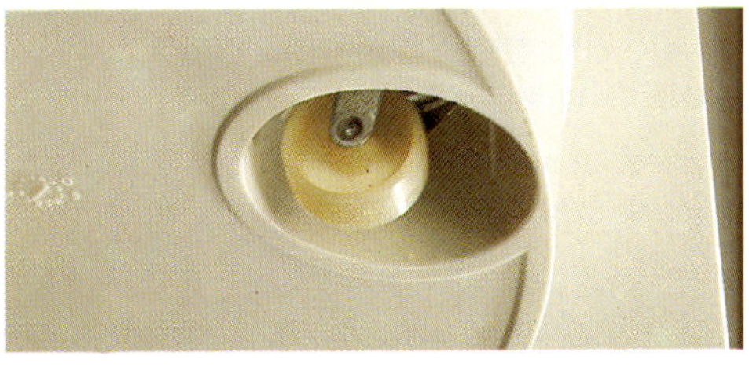

Left, top An enormous *Philodendron bipinnatifidum* planted in a free-standing container in a well-lit stairwell

Left, centre Free-standing container with a combination of plants with similar requirements. They are all *Ficus* species

Left, below Detail of a built-in castor beneath a container. These make it much easier to move

Above top A permanent concrete container serves as a room divider

Above A group of enormous yuccas in a permanent container. As a rule these plants survive for only a few years

Another good and inexpensive material for plant containers is cement compound. It does not leak, but it does sweat to some extent and such a container should therefore not be placed directly on the floor, unless it is equipped with legs or castors.

Wooden containers must be rot proofed and, if placed indoors, have to be made waterproof, which can only be achieved by the use of an impervious lining such as plastic or zinc.

Large containers may be fitted with castors so that they can be moved for cleaning purposes. Some people place these mobile containers near a window from time to time, to enable the plants to live in a fairly dark corridor for the rest of the time – a form of 'recharging the battery'. This does sometimes work, provided it is done regularly and the same side of the plant is turned to the light each time.

Permanent built-up containers Where the floor is sufficiently solid, permanent brick or concrete containers can be erected. As a rule this is done only on concrete floors, since wooden floors may warp, causing cracks in the masonry. The siting of a permanent container in relation to the light is of the greatest importance and must be chosen with care, since it cannot be changed afterwards. Daylight is essential, the more the better. Such a container should therefore be constructed at most a few feet from the window, unless the windows are so large that the light reaches far into the room – for instance in a large office or entrance hall. It is advisable to establish the best position with the aid of a light meter (see page 52).

A suitable spot for a permanent plant container is sometimes in the stairwell of an apartment building or an office block. In such places there is frequently a great deal of light coming from above or from one side, and where the stairs have been built on a generous scale the plants have room to grow upwards in the centre or hang down from above. A large container could be constructed on the ground floor, with smaller containers being distributed over the various floors, either centred round the stairwell or on the window side, thus turning the stairs into a veritable jungle.

The whole scheme would have to be thought out by the architect well in advance, but it would be a good idea to design it in such a way that the plants can be given a shower once a month, which would keep them clean at the same time. Naturally the wall finishes must stand up to this treatment and provision would have to be made for drainage.

It is a simple matter to incorporate a good-sized winter garden into the entrance hall of a large office block. In many cases the container can be several feet long and wide, but its height need not exceed 60 cm (2 ft). A pond can even be built into part of the container. A necessary condition for such a scheme is that the architect's design includes a frontage with a great deal of glass, so that the plants will receive plenty of light. An east-facing glass wall is the ideal.

It is advisable to waterproof such a built-in container with a lining of bitumen, polythene or other suitable material. The bottom must slope very gently to one point, where the water can drain away. The quantity of water will be fairly small and a plastic tube, such as is used for electric wiring, is usually adequate. The top should be covered with a piece of a plastic pan scourer, to prevent blockage. In this way excess water will always drain off, ensuring the survival of the expensive plants. The bottom of a permanent container may be covered with a layer of pebbles, possibly with a filter layer or a thin sheet of plastic

foam on top to prevent the compost being washed into the pebble layer.

In the larger containers the compost does not have to be replaced every year; regular doses of fertiliser will be sufficient. When after two or three years all the plants are fully grown, the whole planting can be dismantled and healthy plants may be used again. Today an automatic watering system is frequently incorporated in such large containers, or hydroponics are used instead. The savings on maintenance are considerable. You will find more on this subject on pages 45–46.

Permanent floor-level containers The lower the container, the more light the plants will generally receive. This is one of the most important reasons for building a plant container into the floor, besides which it looks very decorative as well.

As far as the light is concerned, the same principles apply as in the case of built-up containers. If too little light reaches the plants, they will 'stretch' or simply die. Artificial light is fairly expensive and should be used as an emergency measure only. Consider whether it would be possible to let in light through a skylight; this would be the best solution.

In an existing house it is no simple matter to construct a floor-level container. Breaking up a concrete floor is dangerous, since it may weaken the structure of the entire house. Always consult an expert before you undertake such a scheme.

To a lesser extent the same applies to houses with wooden floors, though the actual construction is somewhat simpler, at least for an experienced handyman. But again, it is essential to take the advice of an expert.

A tile floor is the most practical place for siting a built-in container, as the edge does not have to be finished. However, be careful that the soapy water with which the floor is cleaned doesn't soak into the compost for this would undoubtedly cause problems in the long run.

Floor-level containers such as these can easily be provided with a self-watering or hydroponics system. In that case it is essential that both the bottom and the walls of the container are porous.

Containers for hanging plants Everyone knows the simple hanging pots and baskets, with or without a saucer, which can be screwed to the wall. There are also attractive bowls and other small containers which can be suspended on a cord from the ceiling near the window. They are all useful for there are many hanging plants which can be shown in this way to their best advantage.

There are, of course, other means of growing hanging plants. One way is to put a number of such plants in a large free-standing or built-up container, where they will trail attractively over the edge.

Well-lit stairwells are ideal for trailing plants. All you have to do is to place a number of simple containers along the edge of an upper floor. You will be surprised by the lengths which the tendrils may reach. Make sure that the container is firmly fixed and cannot tumble down, plant and all, and it's important to see that the stems are not rubbed through on the edge of the pot. Sometimes they grow so long and heavy that you may have to give them some support halfway down.

Galleries, too, are suitable places for growing trailing plants, provided the light is good.

A very up-to-date method for growing hanging plants is to use a number of plastic tubes or cylinders grouped together. Other materials, for instance earthenware, are equally suitable. The cylinders may be brightly coloured and are entirely or partially filled with potting compost. By combining tubes of varying lengths a kind of organ pipe effect is created, from which the plants hang down in an elegant waterfall. With a little imagination you can create variations on this theme: you might, for instance, construct an artificial tree with holes for the trailing plants.

Left Floor-level plant trough near a south-facing window. The cacti must be moved to a cooler position in winter

Top centre Various modern hanging containers

Top right Make sure there is plenty of space at the top for water when planting hanging pots

Bottom A home-made arrangement of colour-sprayed plastic drainage tubes

This brings us to the epiphyte tree. This is also an artificial construction, but is made to appear as natural as possible. It is planted with orchids, bromeliads and various trailing and climbing plants. Such a tree is shown on page 40.

It is a remarkable fact that plants placed high up are often forgotten when the watering is done. But they enjoy a drink just as much as their colleagues closer to the ground. Try to think of a way to prevent these plants from drying out. Hydroponics might be a solution, or a self-watering system with its 'secret supply' may bridge a period of forgetfulness.

Hanging baskets and pots should have sufficient room allowed for water at the top, since overflowing water can cause bad strains on the walls. Choose pots which are a size larger than you would normally use, so that they will hold more water, and avoid unglazed red clay pots, from which the water evaporates through the sides. Trailing plants grown on blocks of tree fern or in baskets must be taken down and plunged into water – this is often the best method for pots as well.

House Plants in Summer Quarters

In the chapter on the development of indoor plants we referred to the fact that many of our house plants originally grew in a subtropical climate. The first orange trees (*Citrus aurantium*) were grown out of doors in England as early as the late 16th century. In the long run this proved unsatisfactory and a certain Sir William Temple suggested that the trees should be brought indoors in winter. It is therefore not surprising that such a frost-free storage place has ever since been called an 'orangery'.

Even today plants which live outside from May till late September and spend the rest of the year indoors at a temperature which need be only just above freezing point, are referred to as 'orangery plants' (or conservatory plants). In this book such plants are easily recognised by their symbols. Most of the orangery plants – often called tub plants, since at one time they were always grown in tubs to facilitate movement – are marked with the symbols ○ and ⊖. Plants marked ◐ and ⊖ may also be counted among the tub plants.

This special method of cultivation – cool but frost-free in winter and in summer placed in a sunny or half-shady, well-ventilated position – is the only correct one for all tub plants. The chapter on rest periods on page 60 deals with this subject in greater detail. The cool winter environment is essential for bud formation and the large amount of light is necessary for adequate photosynthesis. These simple facts will explain the failure of many fine house plants marked with the symbols indicated above. Often they are kept in the living-room at far too high a temperature in winter and are then kept in much too dark a place in summer. They also lack the fresh air which is so desirable, as well as the occasional summery shower to clean the foliage.

Tub plants in summer

It is not difficult to keep tub plants in good condition in our summers. The word 'tub' should not be taken too literally. The plants needn't be very large. A hibiscus will flower a year after a cutting is rooted, when it is still quite a small plant, happy in an ordinary pot. Nearly all tub plants can be kept within reasonable proportions if pruned every spring.

Let us take it that you have a sunny balcony, where you would like to grow a number of plants in summer. Start by constructing a windscreen to the height of the balcony rail, if it hasn't, in fact, already been incorporated in the original design. Put your plants in plastic pots with drainage holes and allow a good layer of crocks at the bottom, so that surplus water can drain away. Small pots have the disadvantage of being easily blown over. Try to stabilise them somehow (for instance by wedging them with large pebbles). Real teak tubs are particularly suitable; expensive, of course, but beautiful and indestructible. Here, too, drainage holes must be provided. Plastic cylinders, stone pots without drainage holes and similar containers are unsuitable, because rainwater will collect at the bottom.

If the plants have been kept indoors or in the greenhouse they must not be taken outside until the end of May or even later, and then only on a mild, windless day. The nights must not be too cold. Quite possibly you may have to wait until June for the weather to be favourable; better too late than too early. A too-sudden transition can cause a great deal of damage. Refer to this book

An attractive collection of tub plants placed out of doors in summer in the garden of the Cantonspark in Baarn, Holland. In September these plants, most of them growing in tubs or pots, are brought indoors to overwinter in a cool or unheated greenhouse. If you have an unheated room or other space where your plants can spend the winter, you could create a similar effect on a smaller scale in your own garden

to see whether a particular plant tolerates full sun and if not, provide some form of moderate shade – this might consist of narrow lattice work above the plants. Spray them frequently, especially in the first few weeks, and make sure that the compost never dries out too much. Small pots in particular have little water in reserve. An automatic watering system is, of course, also suitable.

In the garden conditions are generally more favourable than on a balcony. The chief reason is that the micro-climate is milder at ground level than at great heights, such as the 12th floor, say. A terrace is the best place of all for tub or orangery plants. Being close to the house they are clearly visible and this will remind you to water them.

Tub plants may also be buried out in the garden. For this purpose it is best to use 20-cm (8-in) deep plastic pots with a diameter of 30 cm (1 ft). The rim should be 5 cm (2 in) below ground level.

Tub plants in a royal environment.

Above A Japanese azalea in a magnificent urn outside the Rococo palace on Mainau, an island in Lake Constance

Below The well-known orange trees in the park of the Palace of Versailles. Note the style of the containers

Tub plants in winter

By the middle of September, before the first night frosts occur, tub plants must be taken indoors. As a rule it is then that problems arise, for who nowadays has a cool, frost-free, well-lit space available where orangery plants may be 'parked' for the winter? On page 60 you will find a suggestion for a useful addition to the garage – an idea many more people should follow. Greenhouse owners are also in a happy position. If the thermostat can be kept at 5°C (41°F), the weather will do no harm. Don't forget to open all the windows on mild days for maximum ventilation.

Few readers will be lucky enough to possess an old-fashioned orangery – one of those beautiful buildings with tall, south-facing windows.

Provided the temperature is kept down in winter, conservatories or garden rooms provide excellent storage areas for tub plants. They are discussed in detail on the facing page.

The same applies to a cool hall or stairwell. The pity of it is that these areas are often kept at quite high temperatures, as if fuel costs nothing. But plants would be perfectly happy there so long as the temperature is kept at between 5 and 10°C (41 and 50°F).

Deciduous shrubs grown in tubs may be buried in the garden in winter. This is sometimes done with fuchsias, among other plants, but it's worth trying with other shrubs, too. Wait until most of the foliage has dropped and lay the plants on their side in a large pit dug in a fairly dry spot in the garden and cover them completely. The hole should be about 20 cm (8 in) deep and in frosty weather the covering soil should be protected with a layer of bracken or straw. Don't wait too long before you dig them up, certainly no later than the beginning of March before they start making growth. This is not a very attractive method, but it is better than nothing. Evergreen shrubs must not be buried.

Tub plants in spring

Early in spring the temperature in your storage area may rise appreciably, especially where there is a great deal of glass on the south side, when the sun may rapidly increase the temperature to 20°C (68°F).

This will cause the plants to put out their shoots quite early – no problem if the weather were to continue warm, so that the tub plants could be taken outside early, but unfortunately our climate doesn't allow this. There they are, those plants with their young shoots: they can't be hardened off properly and, when the plants are finally moved, they won't be proof against wind and cold.

To be successful with tub plants it is therefore necessary above all to retard the shoots as much as possible. This can be done by keeping the air cool by means of ventilation and screening. Towards the end of April, and certainly in early May, the shoots can be held back no longer, but by then it will soon be possible to move your tub plants out of doors. In the South those that are proof against a light night frost can go out in mid-May, and the more sensitive species after the end of May or the beginning of June. Pick a cloudy, rainy and windless day for this operation.

Small orangery plants must be repotted every year, preferably in spring. Where the pots or tubs are fairly roomy, replanting can be restricted to every two or three years, but it is advisable to repot early rather than late.

At the same time all plants that flower on one-year old wood, that is, before July, may be drastically cut back. This is useful, for some plants are so vigorous that they may become difficult to handle. All dead wood can be removed at the same time.

Tub plants in a less exalted environment.

Top A fine orange tree on a terrace. It must be taken indoors in winter

Centre A remarkable construction filled with a variety of tub and bedding plants. A spray system at the top keeps everything watered

Bottom Tub plants on the balcony of a flat

The Conservatory or Garden Room

There was a time when many houses had a conservatory, structures consisting mainly of glass. Since deal or metal is used in addition, these conservatories need a considerable amount of maintenance, otherwise the frames will rot and leakages occur.

Often a conservatory has a glass roof, which is not only good for the plants but it also adds light to the adjoining part of the house. A disadvantage of so much glass is that it is often impossible to sit there in winter, for it is very expensive to heat such a space, the more so as a great deal of heat is lost through the – usually single – glazing. A modern form of conservatory is the house extension or garden room, much of which is often glazed and is therefore especially suitable for growing plants.

If the conservatory faces south, it can become quite hot on a sunny day, so some provision must be made for screening. Venetian blinds are ideal for the purpose, but rotproof net curtains are also suitable. The roof should preferably be made of wire-reinforced glass – safer in case a roof tile from the house comes crashing down. This kind of glass requires no screening.

As a rule a conservatory is ventilated by means of French windows and usually there is access from the adjoining room. A skylight or other form of ventilation in the roof can also be useful.

The best method of heating a conservatory or garden room is by connection to the main central heating system, using one or more thermostatically controlled radiators. This is the only reliable way to control the temperature in winter. If the conservatory is mainly used for tub plants (see page 18), a minimum winter temperature of 5 to 10°C (41 to 50°F) is enough. In that case it must be possible to shut the area off from the adjoining room. If, however, it is to be used as a living space in winter also the temperature will have to be kept much higher, around 20°C (68°F), and this is too hot for tub plants, cacti and other succulents.

Building a conservatory

There are complete pre-fab conservatories and room extensions on the market, but they do not always fit in with the design of your house.

You would do well to choose materials that are damp-proof and need little maintenance. Cedar (Western Red Cedar) is the best wood to use, as it warps very little and is absolutely rot-proof. It doesn't have to be varnished, but in the course of time it will turn an unattractive dull colour. Oiling helps to some extent. Most other types of hardwood are treated with varnish or some other preparation, but it is quite a job to keep the wood in good condition.

Aluminium is a great deal more convenient, especially if it has been anodised. This is particularly advisable if you live near the coast or in an industrial region, where untreated aluminium will quickly become stained.

Use glass in the windows rather than plastic – wire-reinforced glass for the roof and single or double glazing for the sides. Bear in mind that there must be provisions for ventilation and screening.

The rest of the construction can be made of concrete or brickwork. A concrete floor, sloping gently to a drainage hole, will be found useful for cleaning purposes. At a later stage the floor may be tiled. Some rot-proof form of floor covering should also be used; this will improve the acoustics. The walls may be built up to about 60 cm (2 ft), with the radiators placed alongside. Be sure to include very wide window-sills, for a conservatory or garden room is, after all, chiefly intended for plants. Large French windows, preferably also aluminium framed, offer easy access.

A word about the pitch of the roof. This should be fairly steep to allow rainwater to run down freely, taking most of the dirt with it. Have the roof constructed with a minimum of obstacles: in other words, with wide glass panes and smooth, narrow framework. Such a roof is easily cleaned with a garden hose. The roof should be surrounded with plastic guttering to catch the rainwater, which should be collected in a roomy water butt. You will then always have good water for your plants.

Above This conservatory forms an extension of the living-room. Growing conditions have been greatly improved by the transparent corrugated plastic roof

Below Added on to the house, the conservatory here is practically overrun by plants, creating a jungle-like atmosphere

On the inside the roof should be constructed in such a way that condensation cannot drip down. There is special indoor guttering for this purpose.

When furnishing the conservatory remember that the degree of humidity will usually be high. Furniture, curtains and other equipment liable to rot or mould should be avoided. Do not build in cupboards; these would become breeding places for insects.

Suitable plants for a conservatory

If the conservatory can be kept really cool in winter, it will be an excellent place for tub plants which will be moved out to the terrace in summer, and for cacti and other succulents. If you want to maintain a moderate temperature in winter, you would do better to choose plants marked ⊜.

As a rule a conservatory faces south, so the light should be suitable for plants marked ○ and ◐, but choose the latter only if they can be screened during the day.

The degree of atmospheric humidity will usually be relatively higher than indoors, so it will be easier to grow plants marked ⊛.

Watering and potting compost can be controlled as necessary – a conservatory provides no special advantages or disadvantages.

If you tick the plants described in this book on the basis of the above symbols, you will easily compile a suitable selection. You will be pleased to see that there are quite a few plants among them which are described as typical greenhouse plants. A well-built conservatory is almost as good as a greenhouse.

Above A built-in flower window forms a kind of cupboard with glass front and back

Left A particularly fine flower window with large sliding windows on the inside. There are rather too many poinsettias, but fortunately beautiful orchids, bromeliads and tropical foliage plants are also included

The Flower Window

It might be better to refer to a 'plant window', for such a window contains many foliage plants and certainly doesn't mean flowers for cutting. As 'flower window' is a translation of the German 'Blumenfenster' it might be supposed that it is a German invention, but this is probably not entirely true. There was already mention of a *hortus fenestralis* in England in Victorian times, when Shirley Hibberd, the well-known writer on flowers and plants, described such a construction made by leaving a space for plants between double windows as a miniature greenhouse. The second window could be added either outside or inside. In this century the flower window has so far had little success in England, but it became quite popular in the post-second war Germany. A large measure of technical perfection undoubtedly contributed to this. A well-constructed flower window provides excellent growing conditions for the plants it contains.

There are various types of flower window possible. The open flower window is actually a very large plant container. In principle it does not differ from the plant containers described previously, but its chief criterion is that it should be constructed next to a window. It can be built into the floor or to a height of 40 to 60 cm (16 to 24 in). The enclosed flower window is the actual construction which has given the 'flower window' its impressive name. Such a growing space is completely cut off from the room by means of a separate pane of glass, thus creating an indoor greenhouse through which can be seen the outside world. The flower window has its own climate: temperature and atmospheric humidity can be controlled independently from those of the room. Needless to say practically any hothouse plant can be grown in such an environment. Bromeliads, orchids, foliage plants from the tropical jungle – all these will flourish and you can enjoy them from the comfort of your chair.

An enclosed flower window is fairly costly to install and is best constructed when a house is being built or renovated. You will find a number of sketches and technical details on page 66. To construct a flower window in an existing house usually involves an enormous amount of demolition and construction work and as a rule it will not be possible to extend the window on the outside. In a new building this can be done more easily and the architect can adapt his designs accordingly.

Looking after a flower window will of course take up more of your time than a row of plants on the window-sill. Think of the daily upkeep of such an indoor hothouse, often 60 to 80 cm (2 to 2 ft 6 in) deep. It has to be watered, plants have to be tied up, dead flowers removed; you may have to allow at least an hour every day. Nor is it easy to clean the inside of the outer window, though a long-handled sponge mop will help. The inner windows can be made to slide over their full width and to be removable, so that they can always be kept clean. The side walls are best made in clean brickwork. The ceiling must be made of damp-proof material, which can be wiped clean with a wet cloth. The bottom consists of the container itself, but it is advisable to leave a 5- to 10-cm (2- to 4-in) space all round to improve air circulation. In that case glass and walls may be hosed down. The water will run down the sides of the container and drain away below (see the section sketch on page 66).

If the flower window faces due south it is essential that it can be screened. The most suitable method is with an aluminium Venetian blind controlled from the inside. Actually an east-facing position is even better, as screening is rarely necessary.

Since the sun can cause an enormous rise in temperature in a flower window, good ventilation is an absolute necessity. This can consist of a rust-proof grating. Often such a vent is not enough to keep the temperature within reasonable limits, in which case a thermostatically controlled electric ventilator must be incorporated.

The degree of atmospheric humidity required will depend on what plants are grown in the window and may easily be too low. It should be checked with a hygrometer. If hosing of the walls and possibly the floor is insufficient, an electric humidifier, perhaps hygrostatically controlled, must be introduced. The ventilation must also be adjusted to prevent the windows misting. A double-glazed outside window has the great advantage of not misting over so easily.

Plants to look for

In an open flower window which is not separated from the living-room, all those plants suitable for a warm room can be grown. Because the plants grow closer together and the container is a large one, the degree of humidity may be somewhat higher than on the window ledge, but the difference will not be great.

An enclosed flower window is an entirely different matter. The great advantage here is the high degree of humidity and obviously you would select those plants which would normally flourish only in a heated, humid greenhouse, such as bromeliads, preferably grown on an epiphyte tree (see page 40 on how to construct such a tree), orchids (many of them epiphytes as well), tropical foliage plants requiring humid air, and ferns. Occasionally an enclosed flower window is turned into a cactus garden. In that case double glazing is better used on the inside, since these miniature landscapes must be kept cool in winter and need not be insulated from the outside. Such a window should be particularly well ventilated, so that the winter temperature can never rise above 10°C (50°F). Succulents detest a high temperature in winter.

The Greenhouse

A greenhouse is a wind-proof, transparent structure, either heated or unheated, intended exclusively for growing plants. There are three main types of greenhouse: the warm greenhouse or hothouse, the temperate or moderate greenhouse and the cool or unheated greenhouse, in which temporary heating may be used at night during a cold spell to keep it frost free. The difference lies in the minimum temperature to be maintained in winter, and not in the construction of the house. In a cool or unheated greenhouse the minimum temperature is from 5 to 8°C (41 to 46°F), in a moderate or temperate greenhouse 12 to 15°C (53 to 59°F), and in a warm greenhouse or hothouse 18 to 20°C (64 to 68°F). In the descriptions of greenhouse plants the type of greenhouse in which they belong is usually indicated.

When you are thinking of acquiring a greenhouse you should remember that a well-built, solid, heated greenhouse involves a considerable outlay of money. The relatively cheap models on the market are usually quite small, and the price does not include the foundation, heating, staging, erection, and even the glass may be extra, so that the additional cost will be considerable.

The second-hand value of a greenhouse is low and if, later on, you should find that you haven't the necessary patience or time to look after the greenhouse properly, you will have wasted your money. But for a genuine plant lover, who is willing to spend at least an hour a day on his or her hobby, a greenhouse can be a constant source of pleasure and the considerable investment required is worthwhile.

The various technical aspects of owning a greenhouse are described in detail below. Advice on cultivation of the plants will be found in the descriptions of individual plants in the A to Z section of plant portraits.

The best situation

There are free-standing greenhouses and a type which is built against a wall, known as a lean-to. In the latter case the cost of one glass wall is saved. Your choice should depend entirely on the situation.

If possible, a free-standing greenhouse should be placed in an approximately north-south direc-

All house plants grow better in a moderately heated or temperate greenhouse. It is not difficult to achieve the rather overwhelming effect shown in the photograph. In this case the intention was to achieve the most colourful and varied selection of all kinds of quite common plants, but specialisation, for instance in cacti or orchids, is also possible

Above left A handsome amateur greenhouse dating from the beginning of this century. **Centre left** A Victorian structure providing space for the largest plants. **Above right** In contrast, a modern lean-to greenhouse, which takes up very little space. **Centre right** Another beautiful Victorian greenhouse. **Below** A large greenhouse divided into areas of separate climatic conditions

tion. This has the advantage that, when the sun is at its hottest, it will be directed to the smallest surface, whereas the milder morning and evening sunshine are caught by the larger surfaces. A particularly favourable aspect would be where a good-sized tree grew at a little distance to the south of the greenhouse, which would provide some natural shade at the hottest part of the day, between about 11 a.m. and 3 p.m.

Sometimes the shade cast by a tall building can be turned to good account.

A lean-to greenhouse is frequently built against a south-facing wall, but if heating is going to be provided in winter the south side is not really the best position. In summer the sun will raise the temperature considerably, so that a great deal of screening and ventilation will be required. In such a greenhouse the temperature fluctuations can be enormous. A lean-to greenhouse against an east-, west-, or even north-facing wall is therefore much more advisable.

The so-called balcony greenhouse takes up even less room. This is a small greenhouse, which may be free-standing or not, into which you cannot enter. There is room only for the plants, which are reached through a large sliding window. These miniature greenhouses may have the disadvantage of lack of air circulation, causing excessive temperature variations. They are also unsuitable for large plants, but they are perfectly all right for succulents. They should preferably be placed in a sheltered position.

Construction

Building regulations may vary according to whether you live in a conservation area. A greenhouse may be regarded as a permanent structure or as a movable object, depending on the nature of its construction. You would be well advised to check. One essential requirement will be that your greenhouse does not extend from the building line and does not interfere with traffic (for instance by light reflection). It is also sensible to ask your neighbours whether they have any objection to its erection if it is near the party boundary.

If the greenhouse is to be built against the wall of a house, the foundation must be of at least the same depth. If it isn't, the greenhouse foundation may freeze in a severe winter, and cause the structure to move in relation to the house wall, resulting in leakages or breaking glass. Free-standing greenhouses are often built on special concrete foundation blocks. A brick-built foundation is another possibility. The greenhouse must be firmly attached to the foundation, or it may blow over in a gale. Many greenhouses are fairly low, and building up the foundation may increase the height by 10 or 15 cm (4 or 6 in). You will soon get used to the high threshold.

Materials

Greenhouses are made of steel, aluminium, deal, cedarwood, redwood, possibly other types of hardwood, or of various kinds of plastic. The framework may be covered in glass, perspex, PVC or polythene sheeting. Here are some of the pros and cons of each of these materials.

Steel has the advantage of being solid and relatively inexpensive. Such a greenhouse should preferably be galvanised or otherwise treated, primed

A cedar wood greenhouse, practically indestructible, but difficult for an amateur to erect because of the glazing. It is also one of the most expensive

A modern aluminium greenhouse is relatively easy to erect; the glass is fixed by means of clips. The more expensive models are quite solid

Some galvanised metal greenhouses are still being made. Very solid, but impossible for an amateur to erect

and then sprayed with paint, before being glazed. Today this material is rarely used for greenhouses.

On the other hand, aluminium building kits have become very popular. Such a kit consists of a box containing a number of ingeniously worked out sections, from which any DIY man will be able to build a greenhouse in a weekend, once he has worked out the instructions. Aluminium is light in weight and very durable. In coastal or industrial regions the metal will turn a whitish colour, but as a rule this will not weaken the structure.

Deal, the cheapest of all materials, is now rarely used. Its chief disadvantage is the fact that it is not impervious to the weather and frequently needs to be waterproofed or painted. It also warps easily.

Most wooden greenhouses are now made of Western Red Cedar or redwood. These types of wood have the great advantage of being practically indestructible. They are affected neither by damp nor by heat, but they do turn an unsightly colour. The colour may to some extent be restored by oiling. Glass remains the most popular covering. Whereas formerly small window panes were used, it is now more usual to incorporate large windows, which let through the light better and look more attractive. Second-quality glass is used, so-called greenhouse glass, but preferably not too thin so that it will withstand hailstones. Sometimes the roof is made of opaque glass, and this does not need screening.

In wooden greenhouses the frames are sprayed with hot plastic putty in which the glass panes are laid – quite a difficult job for an amateur. Glazing an aluminium greenhouse is much easier: strips of neoprene are used for sealing and the panes are held in the frames by means of stainless steel clips.

Perspex is another good material, being durable and unbreakable, but it is several times more expensive than glass and this is the reason why it is not used more often.

PVC greenhouse panes are now guaranteed against discoloration, but these materials have few advantages over glass. One unique material is a double-glazed perspex consisting of two layers of a man-made material with air in between. These sheets give far better insulation than glass, as your heating bills will show, but the material is as yet rarely used for greenhouses. It diffuses the sunlight sufficiently well to make screening superfluous.

Polythene is very useful in a greenhouse for providing additional insulation in winter. The polythene lining is attached a few inches from the inside of the glass – there are special clips for the purpose. It takes a few hours to apply, but will save quite a lot in fuel.

Putting up a greenhouse

The structure consists of two vertical side walls, a front and a back wall and a sloping roof. The slant of the roof is usually between 20 and 45 degrees. In greenhouses made of polyester sheets roof and walls are usually one.

Formerly all four sides were constructed with a 50- to 80-cm (20- to 32-in) brick wall base, with glass to about 1.50 m (5 ft), covered by the glass roof. It is now more usual to see all four sides made entirely of glass, which has the advantage of allowing sufficient light underneath the staging to grow more plants.

The construction chosen should to some extent depend on your future plans. Orchid growers still favour a stone or wooden parapet, because they believe that the close atmosphere under the staging will encourage their plants to grow. It is pretty certain, however, that such places will form breeding grounds for a great many pests.

A small greenhouse – say about 2 × 2.50 m (6 × 8 ft) – will have a central path 70 to 80 cm (28 to 32 in) wide. Staging is placed on either or on one side at a comfortable working height. It should not be more than 1 m (3 ft) wide and can be filled with peat or potting compost. In greenhouses without a brick parapet you should make sure that the staging is not too heavy to hang on the walls. The best staging consists of free-standing tables on legs.

Some people prefer to grow their plants on slats, sometimes stepped at varying heights. These will hold a great many small plants, such as cacti. Orchids are sometimes grown in this way as well.

An additional narrow shelf or gutter may be built above the staging, providing space for many smaller plants and hanging baskets. If aluminium guttering is used for this purpose, it is very easy to water the plants. The gutters are filled with water which allows the plants to take up water from below. After half an hour all surplus water can then be drained off.

A number of stainless steel or plastic-coated wires may be attached to the roof for training climbing plants. Vine eyes are easily screwed into a wooden framework or special bolts are available for aluminium greenhouses.

A greenhouse must be high enough to enable you to stand upright, allowing for any fitments along the top ridge. As a rule a height of 2 m (6 ft) is acceptable. If necessary the path can be constructed at a slightly sunken level.

The rainwater running from the roof is best collected on either side in a metal or plastic gutter, which channels the water preferably to inside the greenhouse, where there should be a good-sized water butt with an overflow. You will then always have clean soft water at the correct temperature for watering your plants.

Condensation forming on the inside of the greenhouse should not be allowed to drip on to the plants. Condensation is most likely to occur in larger greenhouses where the guttering is constructed inside. In that case it is advisable to use double-walled guttering or to construct a special drip gutter underneath.

Lighting

If much of the work in the greenhouse has to be done in the evening, or if you would like to show your plants to guests at that time, you would do well to fit some form of lighting. For this purpose it is best to use fluorescent tubes with waterproof fittings installed at the highest point of the roof. In a small greenhouse two 40-watt tubes are enough.

If you wish to provide extra light for your plants, the tubes should be fixed underneath the upper shelves at about 40 to 60 cm (16 to 24 in) above the staging. Some people even fit lighting underneath the staging in order to grow more plants at ground level. Not a bad idea.

There are other reasons why it is useful to have electricity in the greenhouse (see Heating, below), so if at all possible, incorporate one of those heavy duty cables, buried underground. In many cases the current may be taken directly from your central meter. An electrician will install the wiring.

Heating

A greenhouse that is totally unheated is of very little use, especially for indoor plants. In winter it will have to be completely emptied because of the danger of frost. Fortunately there are several methods of heating a greenhouse.

The cheapest method is the blue-flame paraffin heater, better known as an Aladdin heater. If a paraffin tank is placed outside, the heater will continue to burn for a few months at a time. This kind of heater is inexpensive, but does not raise the temperature by more than 5°C (9°F), so that it is no good in a severe frost. It does not require an outlet.

Left An amateur's small greenhouse with free-standing staging on three sides

Below A slightly larger greenhouse with staging on one side only, heated by two paraffin heaters and screened

An ordinary oil heater without wick is also used in greenhouses. It may be necessary to introduce a ventilator to improve the draught. Special models are available for greenhouses and other damp spaces. Its heating capacity is greater than that of an Aladdin, but so is its fuel consumption.

Now that natural gas is in general use, its advantage in the greenhouse is obvious since it is non-toxic to plants. Special greenhouse burners are available, but an ordinary gas stove which is relatively rust-proof may also be used. An outlet is essential.

If the central heating system in your house has sufficient capacity, it may be possible to extend it to the greenhouse, where a number of radiators can be placed. The temperature in the greenhouse is best controlled by means of a mixer valve connected to the tank. The use of thermostatically controlled radiator taps is less expensive. The installation of this form of heating is rather costly, but in the course of time you will gain on the saving in fuel consumption and convenience.

A completely electric heating installation is extemely reliable and easy to control, but it is not very economical to use. If there is already electricity in your greenhouse, the cost of installation will be modest. There are special ventilator heaters for greenhouses on the market, which have a capacity of 3000 watts and are thermostatically controlled. A heater with a separate thermostat placed at a height of about 1.50 m (5 ft) is found to be most satisfactory. Electric ribbed heating tubes placed underneath the staging are also available. Since there is no ventilation, the distribution of heat is less satisfactory.

Electricity is also used for additional heating, for instance cables laid in a layer of sharp sand on the floor of the staging. The bottom temperature of your plants can then be thermostatically controlled, which is particularly useful, enabling part of the staging to be turned into a kind of 'incubator', and covered with a sheet of glass. Here all plants can be grown from seed or cuttings.

When something goes wrong with the heating in a greenhouse, it is bound to happen on a bitterly cold night, when the temperature outside is well below freezing point. If you do not spot the trouble in time your plants will all be frost bitten by the time you wake in the morning – that's how quickly things happen in a glasshouse. It would therefore be most useful to install a kind of alarm system to warn you when the temperature drops below the safety level. The bell of such an alarm system could be installed in your bedroom.

It is remarkable that in most private greenhouses the temperature is kept the same night and day. There is always only one thermostat and actually this should be adjusted every evening and every

A small natural gas burner, one of the most practical and cheapest methods of heating

A 3000-watt thermostatically controlled ventilator heater, large enough for a small hothouse

morning, but of course this is usually forgotten. It is a fact that more electricity is consumed at night, so turning back the thermostat by, say, four degrees, will save a great deal of money. Moreover, plants grow much better and stronger if the night temperature falls a little. It might therefore be worth considering putting in two thermostats, automatically switched. An even better system is one based on the intensity of the light. There are construction kits on the market from which any good handyman can make a light sensor switch.

Ventilation

You must allow excessively hot or moist air to escape by opening doors, windows or roof vents, or by switching on a ventilator. This may be vital to the plants. The greenhouse should be ventilated more frequently than usual at the time when various plants begin to ripen, for instance in the case of succulents towards the start of winter. The greenhouse must also be frequently ventilated – and this applies particularly to flowering plants, orchids and cyclamens, for example – if the air is too moist, particularly in autumn. At the same time the heating should be turned on to dry the atmosphere. If not, the flowers will be stained, or mould will occur.

Small greenhouses are usually equipped with two roof vents. Sometimes further ventilation is provided in the side walls, often by means of a grating or a louvred window. It is advisable always to allow a certain amount of ventilation when you are away from home, since otherwise the temperature may easily become too high. Automatic ventilation mechanisms, based on a cylinder in which gas or oil expands, are ideal, but unfortunately they break down quite often and the cylinders are expensive to replace.

An electric ventilator provides an entirely different method. It is built into the upper part of the front wall and is switched on when it becomes desirable to air the greenhouse. Naturally this, too, can be thermostatically controlled – a very reliable method of ventilation. A grating is built into the opposite wall at ground level, to allow fresh, cooler air to enter. The ventilator should be of the type which shuts automatically when not in use, or it will leave a hole through which too much cold air can enter at night.

Screening

If the roof of the greenhouse is made of clear glass, it must be screened when the sun is shining, or most of the plants will be scorched. How much screening is necessary depends entirely on the type of plants grown. Cacti and other succulents, for instance, nearly all tolerate full sun except early in spring when the sun is still an unknown quantity. Orchids, on the other had, require very dense screening, except possibly in darkest winter.

There are many screening systems available. Some are fitted on the outside, such as the well-known slatted roller blinds, usually made of teak or plastic. Others are hung on the inside of the glass, like the plastic curtains which are frequently used. All are suitable, but they share one disadvantage: you have to remember to lower or raise them in time. It's a job that only needs to be forgotten once to damage most of the plants. An automatic system is difficult to install, involving as it does small engines and transformers – expensive and apt to break down.

In my experience the best method of screening is to paint the entire greenhouse, with the exception of the north-facing wall, with a special liquid which is white when the sun shines, but transparent in rain. This preparation is brushed on in March (better than spraying) and removed in October. It is true that there will be a little less light inside the greenhouse, but it is a great advantage not to have to remember to adjust the screens.

If the roof is made of opaque glass, screening is less essential, although many a malicious sunbeam will enter through the walls. Greenhouses made of polythene or polyester sections need never be screened.

Above Ventilation in a greenhouse glazed with perspex

Below left Exterior plastic screening

Below centre Similar screening fitted inside the greenhouse

Below right A plastic water butt connected to the greenhouse gutters

Watering

In a small greenhouse watering is easiest if carried out with a watering can with a very long spout. On your daily round (more frequently in warm weather) each plant should be given its due. Sometimes it is possible to water with a hose, for a number of plants tolerate a fine spray. As a rule the floor is watered also.

Automatic watering systems are now becoming quite popular. Systems specially adapted for greenhouses are on the market. The best-known method is the capillary system, in which the staging is covered with porous matting which is kept constantly damp. The pots are pressed down firmly on the matting and if the contact is good, sufficient moisture will always rise up through the soil.

The drip system is another invention. Numerous fine plastic tubes are connected to a hose, each tube ending near a plant. Large plants need two or three. A drip of water reaches the plants every few seconds.

Humidity

Depending on the needs of the plants grown, the relative level of humidity in a greenhouse should be high, though naturally cacti, for instance, require less humidity than most orchids. Moist air is created by evaporation from the plants themselves and from the damp peat or compost on the staging. In addition there are often water reservoirs for watering purposes underneath the staging and these contribute to the evaporation.

When the greenhouse is being ventilated a great deal of humid air will escape, especially if the house is heated. This method is therefore used to get rid of excess moisture. If the relative degree of humidity is too low (measure it with a good quality hygrometer), an electric humidifier may be introduced (page 59). Keeping the floor constantly wet is also helpful.

Choosing your plants

Practically all indoor plants will grow much better in a greenhouse than in the living-room, if only because of the better light conditions.

In addition to the more common house plants, nearly all lesser known tropical plants can successfully be grown in the greenhouse. Many are described in this book. Many greenhouses are used for growing the popular cacti and orchids.

The greenhouse will serve very well as a refuge for plants which do not thrive for long in the living-room. They may be brought indoors when they are in flower or when their foliage is at its best and taken back to the greenhouse to 'recharge their batteries'.

Growing plants from seed or cuttings is in most cases best done in a greenhouse.

Glass Cases, Plant Tanks and Bottle Gardens

In the 1830s a London physician, Dr Nathaniel Ward, discovered that all kinds of exotic plants could be grown in a small, enclosed glass case. Soon the Wardian case, as it came to be called, became all the rage. At first only ferns were grown, but soon it was discovered that other plants, particularly tropical foliage plants, also thrived. Such a case is actually a cross between a hothouse and the flower windows already described. Here, too, the secret lies in the fact than in an enclosed space a high level of atmospheric humidity can be maintained. The temperature is the same, or slightly higher, than outside the case. Light may be the only problem, for if such a case or a bottle garden is kept too far from the window, the plants will cease growing.

Planting a narrow-necked bottle requires patience, but once done it will need little attention for several months

Closed or open?

Many people are surprised that such a case or bottle garden need never be ventilated. What happens is that the enclosed space forms a miniature world on its own. Water is absorbed through the roots and evaporates through the foliage. It condenses on the glass and runs back into the compost. Only if the plants grow very vigorously (and the foliage becomes dense) may it be necessary to add a little water. The same principle applies to the process of assimilation and dissimilation. During the day the plants produce oxygen and absorb carbon dioxide. At night this process is reversed. It is true that the quantities absorbed and produced are not entirely equal, but in practice this is hardly noticeable. It is therefore best to keep the case or bottle hermetically sealed.

The various options

Unless you happen to find such an old Wardian case in an antique shop, a terrarium is the best substitute. This is actually an ordinary aquarium, readily available. There are now all-glass aquaria on the market, in which bottom and sides are joined with silicone, avoiding solid corner pieces and bases. Such a case is an easy DIY job; instructions are given with the silicone kit.

The bottom of the case is covered with a 5-cm (2-in) drainage layer consisting of gravel, or better still, coarse charcoal, with a 5- to 10-cm (2- to 4-in) layer of compost on top. The case can be enclosed by a sheet of glass.

Large cases of firm, clear plastic are also available – actually an extended form of the indoor propagator. The more luxurious models are provided with heating and lighting and are almost small hothouses. It's hard to know where a plant case ends and a hothouse begins.

There are a number of free-standing cases on the market, provided with lighting. This means that such a terrarium or whatever it is called need not be placed near a window. However, built-in fluorescent lighting provides relatively little light, so that only plants with moderate light requirements are suitable for these installations.

A large glass bell jar or carboy, an aquarium tank or a laboratory tank may also be turned into a plantarium. As long as the glass is clear and the receptacle can be enclosed, plants will grow in it. Carboys made of clear glass are very popular; small plants will flourish in such a bottle. It is quite difficult to insert the plants through the narrow neck, but to some people this is part of the attraction. The trick is to use spoons, forks, hooks and razorblades tied to long sticks. The difficulty arises when the plants have outgrown the bottle and have to be removed. It is therefore advisable to use poor quality compost and no fertiliser in these bottles, in the hope of retarding the plants' growth.

Maintenance

As mentioned before, watering is practically unnecessary. Provided the moisture content is correct in the first place, there will always be some condensation on the inside of the glass. If there seems to be too much condensation, the cover or cork should be left off for a few days; if there is none at all, a little water should be added.

Feeding is necessary only if the terrarium provides enough space for growth.

On the other hand it is advisable to remove dead leaves, since in such a damp atmosphere mould will easily develop. The glass or plastic must also be regularly cleaned inside and outside, so that the installation always looks fresh.

Top A Wardian case, popular in the last century

Bottom A modern plant case with built-in lighting and heating. This is a small model – they are also available in much larger sizes

Algae can be troublesome, causing an unattractive deposit on the glass and the compost. This can be controlled by wiping the glass with cotton wool dipped in diluted Algimycin – a preparation which controls algae, is not readily harmful to plants and is safe for human beings.

A terrarium is soon filled to the brim by growth and it is therefore essential to remove some of the plants at regular intervals. Maintenance is quite time consuming, and this is the chief reason why many amateurs get rid of their glass cases and bottle gardens after a time.

Choice of plants

Plants suitable for a glass case, terrarium or bottle garden are marked with the following symbols: ●, ⊜, (‴), (⁂) and (◧). They are mostly ferns, tropical foliage plants, orchids and small bromeliads. Start with small-sized plants, especially in the case of bottle gardens.

The Use of Indoor Plants

There are many different ways of using house plants. You have probably thought of most of them, but there may be some ideas that have never occurred to you. And some plants are more suitable for certain purposes than others.

Buying Plants

Some people buy plants on impulse. They happen to be in a flower shop or pass through the market and suddenly see a plant they like, and they buy it without giving a thought as to whether they can give it a situation where it can flourish. It is not very likely that the happy owner will be equally happy at the end of six months.

You who are true plant lovers will, I am sure, be more sensible about it. You will first consider what is lacking in your collection before you start to look for a particular plant, knowing in advance where you want to put it. Chances are that the plant will then be as happy with you as you are with it.

Which window?
The amount of light in a room is determined by the direction in which the windows face. (For further details on this subject see page 53.) When you are buying a plant it is sensible to ask yourself in which window you are going to put it or, if you don't intend to put it on a window-sill, to bear in mind where the necessary light is to come from. The light symbols in this book will give you clear indications: ○ needs a south-facing window, unscreened; ◐ a screened south-facing window, or a window facing east or west; ● a north-facing window, or, if the plant is to be placed near a lighter window, further back into the room.

Which room?
The living-room has an even temperature for most of the year. Many other rooms, for instance the study, kitchen or playroom are also constantly

There is a wide choice of plants for most situations. The picture below shows a collection of codiaeums and cordylines, plants which enjoy a humid atmosphere

heated. Plants requiring a definite resting period (that is, at lower temperatures) are therefore unsuitable for these rooms, unless you can house them somewhere else while they are dormant.

It is an entirely different matter if you intend to buy a plant for a cool hall, for a weekend cottage which is practically unheated during the week, or for a conservatory. In that case select plants which like to keep cool in winter – the choice is large.

If the plant is intended for the bathroom or the kitchen, where the atmosphere is usually more humid than in the living-room, you could choose a plant needing moderate or even high relative humidity.

Deciding on size

All house plants start off small, so their size when you buy them bears no relationship to their eventual size. When you are buying a plant for a certain position you should therefore inquire how large it can become in the conditions provided. Will it be possible to restrict its size by pruning, or would that harm it? This kind of information will be found in the descriptions of individual species.

It is also possible to buy plants which are already enormous. There are growers who specialise in plants of great size, *Ficus* species, *Dieffenbachia*, *Dracaena* and other marketable species. Often they are magnificent examples of professional cultivation, but the price will certainly reflect the many years of tender care. These indoor trees may be recommended for special circumstances or events, but you have to be prepared for a certain amount of leaf loss in the early stages.

Colour harmony

It makes sense to choose plants with colours which will harmonise with each other and with their environment. This doesn't mean that one plant of the wrong shade will spoil your entire decor, but – as is the case in the garden – the total effect is improved if the colours are chosen with care.

As a rule the various shades of green found among house plants will not clash, but there certainly are variegated and multi-coloured species which should never be placed side by side. Even more often flowering plants can contrast badly with the wallpaper, the curtains or the furniture. It is, after all, easy enough to choose a harmonising colour. Cut flowers should also fit into your colour scheme if at all possible. With a little thought you can obtain striking results, since most flowers have quite definite colours.

Variegated plants

In variegated plants the foliage is partially white, red or yellow. These coloured sections contain little or no chlorophyll, and as a result variegated leaves assimilate or photosynthesise less well than all-green leaves. And yet such a multi-coloured plant looks so attractive in a dark corner of your room! Obviously there is a clash of interests here: *you* would like the plant to cheer up a dark spot, but the plant itself wants much better light. No doubt you will solve it with a compromise. You could experiment a little: if the foliage begins to turn green, the plant must be moved closer to the light.

Related plants

It is a fact that quite often various plants belonging to the same family require the same conditions. In other words, if your sinningia thrives in a particular spot, other members of the gloxinia family (*Gesneriaceae*) will probably do equally well there. Members of the same family generally blend well in appearance too. There are, however, exceptions to this rule. The vine family, to which well-known plants such as cissus and rhoicissus belong, also includes succulent species which require entirely different treatment. When in doubt you will be able to look up the facts very quickly, simply by comparing the symbols.

Above, left A collection of plants for a south-facing window: from left to right ananas, coleus, cereus, stapelia, pachypodium, cephalocereus and euphorbia

Above, centre Plants for an east- or west-facing window: from left to right calathea, maranta, saintpaulia, odontoglossum, peperomia, stephanotis, microcoelum and another saintpaulia

Above, right Plants for a north-facing window: from left to right sansevieria, asparagus, asplenium, pellaea and chlorophytum

Below When buying a plant you would do well to consider the size it may eventually attain. This *Ficus benjamina*, for instance, could reach the ceiling in a few years' time

Disposable Plants

The plants referred to on pages 27 and 28 are perennial plants, that is, those which in theory will survive for years in the living-room, or at any rate indoors. But you may acquire others, species whose survival is doubtful, and even some which you know will die after a few months. I call these by the disrespectful but realistic name 'throw-away plants'.

It depends entirely on your personal attitude whether you are able to regard a beautiful house plant as a 'throw-away'. Many people (fortunately) feel they would like to give the plant another chance. The drawback of this attitude is that their window-sills in the end have the appearance of a hospital ward: nothing but sad-looking, ailing plants which – if you ask me – would be much better somewhere else. Plants more suited to the conditions provided would have had a longer life than those poor wretches, and do better justice to their surroundings.

Seen in this light it appears less strange to regard a plant from the start as a throw-away plant. Instead of a long but sorry life give it a relatively short, but at least flourishing, one in the living-room.

There are, however, different kinds of disposable plants: in some cases acceptable, in others definitely unsympathetic and artificial. What about, for instance, the potted chrysanthemum, those mass-produced little plants in all sorts of bright colours, available all the year round? They have been brought into flower at completely unnatural times of the year by means of artificial light and imposed darkness; they are purposely prevented from growing to their naturally proud heights. In addition they are stuffed with the most dreadful chemicals – this is allowed since the plants are, after all, not intended for consumption. When they have finished flowering these little monsters may be planted out in the garden, where they might possibly reach their natural height. This would at least be something, although nothing can be done about their loud colours – but often the poor things are not fully hardy. It is therefore a hopeless struggle. (In spite of all this, these little potted chrysanthemums are enormously popular – obviously I am in a minority!)

Ferns, which require a high degree of humidity, rarely survive the winter in our living-rooms and might therefore be regarded as disposable plants. But once the central heating has been turned off, perhaps in April, they may be kept in good condition for several more months, provided they are properly looked after. Watering is a particularly delicate operation. In some homes they start dropping within a week or two. Although disposable plants, they still provide us with a challenge.

Other expendable plants are such annuals as *Senecio cruentus* (better known as cineraria, very popular at one time), *Thunbergia alata* (Black-eyed Susan) and exacum. It is practically impossible to keep these plants for another season and they are therefore finished when the last flower has died.

The large, festive begonias are other plants which do not easily survive – they are very subject to mildew. The cooler their position, the longer they will keep, but once they have finished flowering they may as well be thrown away.

Did you know that bromeliads are self-destructive? When the rosette comes into flower, the dying process has already begun. It is true that young shoots may be used to propagate the plant, but it is not easy to grow flowering plants and the process may take at least two years. If you have no intention of trying, please look upon the beautiful bromeliad as a throw-away plant and don't leave it standing about until it has become a kind of straw plant.

Above The flowering begonia is essentially a throw-away plant, but you will be able to enjoy it for many weeks, especially if it is kept fairly cool

Right A typical lasting plant, this syngonium has been placed near an east-facing window, where it will easily survive for five years

The great advantage of disposable plants is that you need pay little or no attention to the symbols. Provided a fern or a bromeliad is not placed in a pitch dark spot, the situation, temperature, humidity control and quality of the potting compost hardly matter. However, you should try to water it correctly, since this will certainly affect the length of its life.

It is a mistake to place hardy and disposable plants together in one container. This involves a great deal of extra work: just when the stayer begins to develop, the short-lived plant has to be removed. Better to keep non-permanent plants in separate pots, so that they can easily and inconspicuously be disposed of.

I strongly object to using plants as throw-aways which ought naturally to be regarded as stayers. I don't like the attitude of people who say: 'The yucca can go in the dark corner – when it dies we'll buy a new one.' Such people only consider the decorative aspect of their plants and show little understanding of their inherent nature.

Try to give it the most favourable position possible – in summer preferably out of doors, and in winter a cool situation – so that it will have the best chance of survival. There are many other plants which often die quickly, but which with a little care can take their place among the permanencies. Such unexpected successes can give enormous pleasure.

Fashions in Plants

Is the choice of plants a question of fashion? On the face of it fashion has little to do with it, for the primary consideration should be whether a particular plant will thrive in the position for which it is destined. But as soon as we start to consider whether the colour of a certain plant will harmonise with our environment (a sensible thing to do, after all), fashion begins to play a part.

In recent years interior decorators have gone even further. For instance, as soon as the style of the twenties became fashionable once more, it was fairly logical that the 'in' plants of that period should be selected to match. Palms, ferns, clivia, oleander, hydrangea, broom; ask your grandmother – she'll remember which plants she used to grow at that time. House plants which became popular at a later stage, such as bromeliads, Stag's Horn Ferns, philodendrons, Swiss Cheese Plants, Umbrella Plants and yuccas are quite out of place in this kind of decor. The conscious choice of the right kind of plants will make the style of the decor more authentic.

Sometimes a certain plant or group of plants becomes fashionable again regardless of the interior decor of our homes. In the first half of the 1970s the enthusiasm for cacti increased enormously, for no apparent reason. You might also follow your own instinct and suddenly discover that the old-fashioned aspidistra is actually a very decorative and extremely hardy plant with many possibilities. In no time many people will follow suit.

Publicity, too, can play a large part in the renewed popularity of a plant. This happened a few years ago in the case of *Pachystachys lutea*, described in the media as an 'entirely new' plant, which was to take the market by storm. Suddenly everybody started to write about it, and since it is quite an attractive plant its sales increased by leaps and bounds. In practice the plant is, however, not all that easy to grow and it is therefore quite likely that the pachystachys rage will die down after a time. A nine-day wonder, useful as fodder for the illustrated press.

Above Antique brass bowls and vessels, like this Spanish specimen, often make very attractive plant containers

Left A typical fashion plant, *Pachystachys lutea*. It is not easy to keep and many buyers will not be inclined to repeat the experiment

Below, centre A Peanut Plant in flower. There are times when everybody seems to be trying to grow plants from peanuts

Below, right A grafted gymnocalycium, another typical fashion plant, but unlikely to survive for more than a year

Another fashion phenomenon is the recurring popularity of certain methods of cultivation, for instance sowing house plants from pips. This trend may be combined with that of collecting all kinds of 'produce' plants. Coffee plants, tea, bananas, peanut plants, avocados – go and have a look in a botanical garden to see what can be done. Suddenly everyone wants to grow these plants, and although the experts may shake their heads, they are often surprised at the results that can be achieved.

Some of these fashions, of course, are commercially inspired. Meat-eating plants, for instance, snatched from their natural habitat can almost certainly be expected to die within a month or two in the living-room, but they constitute a neat profit for the importer. It's best to resist plants which are commercially pushed, for there may well be a catch in it. Since 1975 there appear to have been no barriers to the import of plants. If you were to believe the advertisements, your living-room could become a museum of biological curiosities.

The Best Situation

It is important that carefully chosen plants should also be given correct positions. Where should they be put and where will they show to best advantage? From a technical point of view the first question is easily answered: house plants should be placed where they will grow well. This position is determined by growth factors. These growth factors (indicated by symbols) are mentioned in the A to Z section describing the individual plants. Only where one or more growth factor can be artificially created (such as with artificial light, a glass case, flower window, or winter storage facilities), can the plant be placed in a position where it would not grow naturally.

The plants show to best advantage if they are well adapted to the atmosphere and the size of the room. A large room with a high ceiling demands good-sized plants with large foliage, but a smallish room would be made to appear even smaller by this kind of plant. For such a room lower-growing plants with smaller foliage should be selected.

There is also quite an art in choosing a plant which harmonises with the style of the decor. Plants with delicate, mainly green foliage look best in an old-style room, but in a modern interior with a great deal of glass, steel and white formica good results will be achieved with plants that have distinctly shaped, large and variegated leaves. A room with cane furniture requires mainly plants with long, narrow, striped leaves. Patterned wallpaper, chair covers or curtain material must also be taken into consideration. The colour is important, but you should also avoid foliage which resembles the patterns too closely or which is lost against such a background. It is therefore a good idea to use large leaves against a small design and the other way round.

The plant's best side also counts. As you know, the leaves will always turn towards the light in the course of time. There are, however, plants which have no leaves, or which develop small rosettes that do not grow to one side so easily. So what is its best aspect? An oblique view, from above? In that case it should be placed on the floor. Or from below? If so, it should be hung or placed at some height. From directly above? Make sure, then, that it is visible from the stairs, or from a gallery. Careful siting can greatly improve the effect of the plants.

Variation in the shape and colour of the foliage is very desirable. A room containing nothing but *Ficus* species, all more or less the same shade of green, is rather boring. I am by no means an advocate of an abundant variety of colour, but it is advisable to experiment a little with unusual shades. You will soon see where the emphasis should lie. Some plants with rosettes of linear leaves look well against a background of long stems with alternating leaves. But be careful: it is easy to make the mistake of creating combinations which would be impossible in a natural environment, and this is very noticeable. You should therefore also consider the plants' natural habitats, to see if they are similar.

It is logical that small plants should be placed on the window-sill and larger specimens on the floor. Many people go against this rule, with the result that large plants grown close to the window rob the smaller ones, further back, of light. Their positions should be reversed. It is frequently possible to place a small table near the window, to hold pots of small plants. They are then easy to care for, since they can be reached from all sides.

Difficult plants, for instance those requiring a high amount of humidity, may be combined in a glass case or a flower window, where favourable conditions can be created by means of artificial light. Provided the light is good enough, such a case can be placed literally anywhere. These (rather expensive) plant cases are particularly suitable for offices and public buildings. More about artificial light on page 47.

Plants as room dividers

Large areas can be made to appear smaller in an attractive way by introducing walls of green plants. Such a division is semi-transparent, and yet creates the impression of separate rooms. Unfortunately such room dividers often fail through lack of light. There is rarely a window or a skylight near the place where such a division is wanted, with the result that the plants wither away or become drawn and straggly. It is only the very strongest, such as the indestructible climber *Cissus rhombifolia* (syn. *Rhoicissus rhomboidea*) which can save such a dividing wall. When, therefore, you intend to install such a wall of plants, the first thing you should do is to measure the light very accurately. The correct way of doing so is described on page 52. If the available light is less than 700 to 1000 lux, you would do better to forget the idea of plants and to think of another way of dividing the space, unless you can provide some kind of artificial light, if only to supplement the natural daylight.

The room divider can consist of a permanent plant container, forming part of a built-in dividing wall, but it may equally well consist of a number of separate containers placed in a row or in a group. This last method has the advantage that it is interchangeable. If it should be found that certain plants will not thrive, they can often be saved simply by pushing them closer to the light.

In a room divider you should always use plants satisfied with little light, in other words those marked with the symbol ●. Quite a number of climbing and hanging plants belong to this category. Such plants will need some kind of support. The supports may vary from simple plastic-covered wires (laundry lines), strung between floor and ceiling, and semi-open walls made of concrete blocks or glass bricks. Try to choose a material which will enable you to spray the plants and do no damage when water is spilled. If stone or bricks are used it is a good idea to choose those with soft or rough surfaces to which the tendrils of climbing plants can cling easily.

A general rule, particularly applicable to room dividers, is that plants should be arranged in such a way that people do not constantly brush against them. No plant will tolerate this: the leaves will simply die. It is also important that the plants do not stand in a draught, for instance near an ill-fitting window. Such plants are easily affected by pests, or the foliage may dry up.

Time for a change

After a few years' experimentation you will have arranged the plants so favourably that they all thrive. The obvious thing would be to leave it at that and only continue the necessary maintenance. It is perfectly all right to do this for a couple of years, but if your indoor garden remains unchanged for too long, the effect will become rigid and dull. You may not notice it yourself, but your visitors will. Make up your mind one day to change the lot. Buy new plants, place them in different containers and start afresh. You will find that your whole environment benefits from the change.

Above An unused fireplace can often be used for growing ferns which require little light, but beware of draughts

Below A permanent plant container has been built behind the settee, with a dieffenbachia and a group of yuccas acting as a room divider

Above For a position near such an antique stove choose a plant container in approximately the same style. It is doubtful whether this dracaena is getting enough light

Centre If this philodendron is moved any further away from the window it will suffer from lack of light, but at night it could be pushed a little further into the room

Below Placed around the edge of this central fireplace, the ferns are receiving only just sufficient light

Plants and Containers

The chief characteristic of a house plant is that it grows in a pot, tub or other container. This is something that hasn't changed since the time of the Sumerians. In those days the containers were usually tubs made of fired clay, sometimes glazed, and this remained the case for a long time.

A few centuries ago wooden tubs were introduced for growing plants and a real teak tub is still the ideal container.

Fancy pots and other containers came into fashion in the last century. They couldn't be fantastic enough and it is often difficult to see the difference between a sculpture in ancient Greek style and a plant pot. Bird cages and aquaria were combined with gaudy jardinières to form objects which at that time were regarded as the height of good taste. Materials used were porcelain, terracotta, wood, brass and glass. It is easy to see that in these receptacles the plant only played a subsidiary role, the eye being blinded by the ornamentation of the container.

The Victorian excesses were followed by Art Nouveau, a style in which pots and jardinières were still highly decorated. Not until the Bauhaus period did the plant itself regain its importance; the pot was reduced to a functional object which did not have to be an ornament in itself.

Except for the numerous gaudy pots which might be considered as kitsch, but are still sold in large numbers, this is still the case: we like our pots to be inconspicuous, for the plant has become more important to us.

In the early part of this century pots were made mainly of ceramics, a material which can be used in a great many ways. Unfortunately hand-made pottery has become practically priceless, while most pottery manufacturers produce shapes which do not come up to the standard of other branches of modern interior decoration. So it is not surprising that after the second world war designers began to search for materials with other possibilities, and they came up with various forms of plastic and PVC.

At one time plastic plant containers were made from drainpipes, which were provided with bottoms and sprayed in various colours. This method of production was fairly cumbersome and the pots were quite expensive. Then plain pottery containers were imported from Italy, similar in appearance to the plastic cylinders, but much more fragile. Some beautiful containers arrived from the United States, made from polyester. These were slightly cone-shaped, with an inward-curving rim – convenient when potting a plant, but when it was time to repot after a year or two, it was impossible to get the soil ball past the rim, so that the plant had to be dug up. The Finns also concentrated on designing plant pots. The best-known result is the Arabian pot with matching saucer, made of a strong ceramic material and beautifully finished.

Once this trend got under way it could not be checked. Plastic plant cylinders were also pressed, a much cheaper process, but with less beautiful results. Cheap ceramic pots in all sorts of colours also came on the market and today there are even plastic imitations of the distinctive Arabian pots.

The importance of shape and colour

We are once more entering upon a period when plant and container may be seen as a whole, more attractive than its separate parts. This was also the case a hundred years ago, but at that time the accent was on the ornament. Modern pots are plain, but distinctive in shape and colour and can enhance the effect of a plant without being in any way obtrusive. Take a simple green foliage plant, a ficus, say, or an aspidistra. Such a plant looks good placed in a scarlet or a matt green cylinder, in the first place because of the contrast in colours or the effect of varying shades of the same colour, but in addition the shape of a tall, slender cylinder will present the plant in an entirely different way from when it is placed in a more traditional pot.

This can't be done with very tall-growing plants – these look better in solid, wide containers. On the other hand ferns such as the nephrolepis, with curving stems and practically corresponding in height and width, show to good advantage in a tall cylinder. A tree-shaped plant, for instance a dracaena or a Bay Tree, also looks good in a cylinder-shaped pot of the right height, diameter and colour. Flat, very wide containers, again, will create different effects, and are, for instance, particularly suitable for low-growing cacti.

Above, top A *Philodendron elegans* with its incised foliage harmonises well with the terracotta statue and the antique bronze container

Above, centre These Art Deco containers are still to be found. Plant a fern and you will have a magnificent ornament

Above, bottom Antique copper looks good in combination with a number of house plants, but this particular arrangement should not be regarded as permanent

Above, top An attractive arrangement in an antique plant table

Above, bottom It's a matter of personal taste whether you like these pottery ornaments or not. But they are fairly widespread

Antique containers
Provided they harmonise to some extent with the interior decor, antique pots, whether originally intended for plants or not, remain attractive. The material should be appropriate for use as a plant container. Antique Chinese bronze bowls are just as suitable as holy water vessels from a 19th-century church, and copper containers, preferably genuine antique ones, are always popular.

Where there is a risk of corrosion or rotting, a container may be waterproofed inside with polyester fibre glass, an easy job for a DIY-man. Grandmother's bowls, pots and jardinières are also becoming fashionable again, and even the chamberpot has found a new purpose.

Problems of ornamental pots
What exactly is an ornamental pot? In general this name is given to any container in which the ordinary (clay or plastic) pot can be placed. Copper kettles and antique bowls also become ornamental pots when used to hold plants in their separate pots.

The advantage of these ornamental pots is supposed to be that you can take out the plants at any time to make sure there is not too much moisture, that the plants are easily and quickly replaced and that it is possible to plunge the plants from time to time, for the ordinary pots have holes in the bottom, which is usually not the case with pot holders.

All this is true, but I can think of a number of disadvantages as well. To begin with it is an unattractive sight when you look down on such an ornamental pot, only to be faced with the mildewed, discoloured inner pots. Sometimes the plant pot does not fit and extends above the rim of the pot holder. In many cases a window-sill full of ornamental pots of mixed origins is an unattractive sight.

In addition excess water often collects in the bottom of these ornamental pots. It is not difficult to see when the plant is lifted, but this is easily forgotten. Between inner pot and pot cover there is an empty, damp space, an ideal breeding ground and living space for various insects such as springtails. Woodlice and earwigs also like these spaces.

There are two ways of avoiding these drawbacks: either place the plants on the window-sill in their ordinary pots, or plant them out properly into the ornamental pots. Ordinary clay pots on discarded saucers look quite pleasant in an informal room, but not everyone likes such an arrangement. Even a well-shaped plastic pot, preferably black, with a matching saucer would look better.

Planting out into an ornamental container has the disadvantage mentioned earlier in this book: the plant is easily over-watered. Fortunately there are also ornamental pots with matching saucers without this disadvantage, for the pots have holes in the bottom and excess water will drain into the saucer. The pots themselves can be exceptionally beautiful and it is surprising really that they are not used more often. Many of them appear in the illustrations in this book.

The fashion in containers
As already mentioned in the introduction, plant pots, or at least pot holders, are subject to fashion. But there are also short-lived crazes, for instance the sudden spread of spherical hanging pots about ten years ago. From time to time somebody thinks up something new or discovers that common everyday objects (aquarium tanks, for instance) may be used as plant containers – and immediately everybody follows suit. In most cases the market for these articles collapses within a few years, and you are left with the lot. You should be rather cautious therefore before following such waves of fashion.

Some time ago small, square pots covered in mirror glass appeared on the market. The effect is unusual, but whether they attract buyers is another question. Other designers began to cover plastic pots in cork or imitation panther skin. The day may come when we return to the Victorian fashion of over-ornamented pots in which the plant plays a secondary role.

When you are thinking of buying a new container, you would do well to weigh up all the pros and cons. It is possible that an aquarium tank, carefully filled with sand in two different colours (see photograph), may in the course of three months or so turn green with algae. By giving the matter some thought and not buying on impulse you will save yourself a great deal of expense.

Above An example of a modern cylindrical container carefully planted with three separate dracaenas

Below Pottery always looks attractive in a modern interior

Above, top Aquarium tanks filled with sand in two colours to form a pattern. Because of algae formation the sand has to be frequently renewed

Above, centre Plant holders in the form of pottery animals

Bottom A *Dracaena marginata* 'Tricolor' in a plain white plastic cylinder will fit into any environment

Plants in the Office

Perhaps it all started with the young seamstress, who took a cutting from her mother's Busy Lizzie to the workroom so that she might have something else to look at apart from all those lengths of dress material. This must have happened quite some time ago, for there always seem to have been plants in workrooms, factories, schools and offices. Quite logical – it is easy enough to look after a little plant on or near your desk or workbench. There is no need for the work to suffer and for a strong plant the growing conditions are adequate.

Today the simple cutting in the window has grown into something quite different. Since the sixties, especially, the office plant has become big business, involving millions of pounds. The homely saucers and plant pots have been replaced by enormous containers filled with shiny plants growing several feet high. What's the reason for this phenomenal increase?

Status symbols

One explanation is that as society becomes harsher, as offices and workrooms become more rectangular, starker and colourless, man's need to soften his environment increases. Managements have come to the conclusion that it makes sense to meet these needs to some extent and so a sum is allotted to supplying greenery in the next budget. A very pleasant development.

In many cases managements' choice of plants is for specimens which enhance the status of a firm, which usually means that large, imposing plants such as immense ferns, monster dieffenbachias and expensive ficuses are given preference. In this way two birds are killed with one stone: the fine entrance hall is seen to its best advantage and the fresh green of the plants blends well with the deep brown rosewood of the manager's desk.

And what about some plants in the factory workshop? True, the workers may push their cigarette ends into the compost. but at least the firm has proved that it is a modern concern which acknowledges the need for greenery.

The way I write about it sounds very cynical. You might almost think that I consider the decor of a reception hall or manager's office unimportant. Not at all. I only want to point out that this attitude, often the only argument thought to be valid, is to my mind the wrong motivation.

Losing the human factor

For in its zeal management has forgotten how it all started: with the milliner or typist who took a cutting to work because she liked it. She was motivated by the relationship between person and plant, a relationship based on liking or love, a subject which I touched on elsewhere (page 10).

In the example mentioned earlier, human beings play no part at all. The aim is a relationship between industry and plant, something that is not possible. In many places where masses of plants in fine containers have been introduced, the staff are only allowed to look at them. Watering, spraying, feeding, removing the dead leaves (all jobs a plant lover enjoys) is strictly forbidden. The staff are supposed to know nothing about plants (has anyone in management ever visited their homes?); the valuable plants are bound to be overwatered, incorrectly fed or pruned. Plant maintenance is supposed to be a job for the professional.

That was the beginning of maintenance contracts, planned, scientific, clinical care. And so he arrives one day, probably the most junior nursery employee, straight from horticultural college, with a handy little cart full of chemicals, foliage gloss, fertiliser pills, pumps for replacing the hydro-solution, and so on – a boy who has probably never taken any notice of the plants on his mother's window-sill. He'll show them, all those unmarried secretaries (probably the most devoted plant lovers of all) and the rest of the staff, how all that industrial greenery should be looked after.

Is it so surprising that the staff soon take a dislike to all those show plants: that they start to put out their cigarettes in the soil, empty their coffee cups, snatch cuttings and finally nick the last remaining decent plants when no one's looking? I don't think so. Plants should be cared for by the people for whom they are intended. Plants are living creatures and cannot live without love.

Personal care

Fortunately some firms, particularly the smaller ones, have a different attitude. There is no need for the window-sills of an office to be filled with languishing cuttings in discoloured pots on flowered saucers (although in certain environments this is quite acceptable). There is no reason why plants should not create a good impression while still being individually cared for. A good way to start is to form a small plant committee, consisting of staff members who are knowledgeable about plants. The committee should have meetings with the architect or interior designer to decide on the shapes of pots and containers. A florist or garden shop may be consulted on the material available and the choice between mixed containers and specimen plants should be discussed. The pros and cons of hydroponics and automatic watering systems must also be considered. The question of whether to order the plants from a wholesaler and have them arranged by members of the staff must be decided. Why should they not devote a little of their spare time to the project, when the firm is willing to spend a great deal of money on the plants and containers? A plant that has been planted by one individual is always better looked after than those treated impersonally.

There is no reason why impressive status plants shouldn't be introduced in the reception hall, the canteen or the boardroom, provided they are selected with care so that they will thrive in their allotted positions. A member of the staff could be given the task of looking after them. The care of a large, expensive plant requires no more expertise than that of a cheap little geranium. You need only take a walk through any town or village to discover how many people have green fingers. Any plant enthusiast will certainly be happy to extend his love for plants to the working environment.

Mixing plants

When plants are ordered by a large firm there appears to be a strong preference for mixed combinations. I am not sure whether it is the supplier or the client who expresses this preference, but that is beside the point. It is a fact that the arrangement of a mixed container, consisting of plants requiring the same growing conditions, is much more difficult than the introduction of specimen pots. Frequently mistakes are made, with the result that some of the plants will soon give up, spoiling the total effect. When a specimen plant is found to languish, a more favourable position may be tried, but in the case of an incorrectly mixed container no position is the right one (see page 14).

I should therefore like to advocate the use of more specimen plants in offices. There is no doubt that this would save a lot of plants and consequently money.

The importance of correct placing

In order to grow, plants require light and we should therefore start with the principle that they should be placed near a window to survive. This principle applies as much to offices as to the home, but it is remarkable how often this simple truth is overlooked. Dark corners, niches, corridors faintly lit by striplights – a plant is expected to cheer the place up. Far from it – it's more likely to languish for a few months and then die. If plants *must* be given a dark position, good artificial lighting is the only solution and one that is, moreover, very easy to provide in offices and factories. But this subject requires a chapter to itself (page 47).

Whatever he calls himself – florist, plant contractor or whatever – a serious expert must first go round the building with a light meter. He will mark on the floorplan those places where plants may be expected to thrive, noting the average strength of the light. Measurements should be repeated at various times of the day. Only then will he be able to design a planting scheme likely to be successful. There are many who just deliver a number of containers and mistakenly think they have the right to call themselves professionals. It is important that the client should take note of these details, for plants are rarely guaranteed for long. And the plant contractor should be equally careful, since his reputation is at stake.

In most modern offices there is fortunately plenty

Facing page This enormous pandanus enhances the atmosphere in a large study. It is, moreover, a very strong plant

Right A view of a tree-lined canal and in addition a fine philodendron – few people are lucky enough to work in such an attractive environment

Below In this smart boardroom the plants have been placed between two glass windows, about 40 cm (16 in) apart. The effect is unusual

of light. On the upper floors of tall buildings the light enters freely. As a rule the windows are fairly high and wide and it all makes a difference.

The tinted windows now frequently used require special consideration, however. It is of the greatest importance that such windows do not exclude exactly those rays necessary for the process of photosynthesis. A laboratory report will settle this. The client, or better still, the architect, should on no account overlook this detail, for otherwise the result may be a project costing millions where no plant will grow – and this might not be acceptable.

Constant temperatures

In modern offices the temperature is usually kept at an even 20°C (68°F) wherever possible. As explained earlier, most plants will not appreciate such conditions, and all plants that need a dormant period, such as succulents and many tub plants, are therefore unsuitable for such buildings. The symbols and plant descriptions in this book will show clearly that the choice of plants tolerating an all-year-round temperature of 20°C (68°F) is very limited.

Then there is the possible lowering of the temperature at night. For reasons of economy the heating is often turned low. Other firms, on the other hand, are extravagant over energy and keep the temperature high day and night. If the plants' needs were considered, the temperature would fall by a maximum of 6°C (10°F) at night. Lower temperatures might be harmful. The change-over from day to night temperature and vice versa should ideally synchronise with dusk and dawn. In the middle of winter the heat should be kept up a little longer, since darkness comes very early. A combination of time clock and photo-electric cell provides the best form of control.

Climate control

In some buildings the indoor climate is controlled in such a way that both atmospheric humidity and temperature are kept constant. It is a well-known fact that dry air is unpleasant to man and increases the risk of catching colds. Practically all plants profit from a reasonable degree of humidity in winter. Details of relative humidity are found on page 58. Try to keep the humidity at a level which is agreeable to man, although an extra degree can do no harm to plants.

Office gardens

This is a fairly new expression, simply meaning that there are so many plants in the office that it resembles a garden. Office landscape is another term. I should also like to include indoor workshop and factory gardens.

In general an office garden consists of a fairly large space, divided into smaller areas by means of numerous or large plant containers. In many cases the containers are built into the design, but this is not essential.

As mentioned in the chapter on room dividers, the angle of the light is the main problem. Unless the windows are enormous or there is light from above, it is useless to install botanical space dividers: everything would die through lack of light. Such an office garden can therefore only be successful where the area resembles a tall greenhouse. However, it would get very hot in such an area in summer and some form of cooling is therefore essential – ventilation or double glazing for instance. In other words, the concept of an ideal office garden must be incorporated in the original design of a building, by an architect who knows something about growing conditions. For this reason the creation of an office garden in existing buildings is not always the success that is hoped.

Correct planning can, of course, lead to wonderful results. Usually the containers are very large, so that the root systems can find plenty of nutrients. As a rule an automatic watering system is included, or hydroculture is selected, since it is practically impossible to carry thousands of gallons of water

Top, left An indoor garden in a bank. High-pressure mercury lamps may be used in the spherical shades, to make up for the lack of daylight

Top, right In this office, plant containers decorate the bannisters

Above This bank in a magnificent old canal house has been discreetly modernised and is furnished with plants

Right In a canteen, plants are almost indispensable. This is a simple, but unusual, example

about every day. Evaporation will greatly contribute to the relative atmospheric humidity. After a few years it may be necessary to use the pruning knife to good effect, to avoid the garden growing into a jungle. All the foliage will be concentrated at the top, and at eye level all you'll be able to see is a forest of bare trunks – not an attractive sight. The people who look after an office garden should therefore not be afraid to prune or even to remove a plant and replace it by a young specimen.

House Plants in Public Places

Among public places can be counted, for instance, the entrance of a town hall, the stairwell of an apartment building, or shopping arcades and precincts.

It is a well-known fact that there is a great deal of vandalism in places where anyone can enter. This bad habit seems to be especially stimulated by neglect. The healthier the plants, the less likely they are to be damaged. Nevertheless disappointments are to be expected. In any case the damage should immediately be made good.

A great deal can be done to save the quite expensive plants. Where there is plenty of space, veritable indoor trees may be planted in large containers. A good example is the departure hall of Schiphol Airport, where a *Ficus benjamina* spreads its leaves high above the public. Similar trees could find a place in modern railway stations. It is practically impossible to break off a branch.

Another solution is to place the plants at higher levels, on balconies, indoor window-sills, or on walls which cannot be reached by the public. This will include the person who looks after the plants, so automatic watering is essential. Preferably the architect should recognise these problems when he draws up his design.

The stairwells of apartment buildings are often a sad sight. Frequently plants are lacking altogether. Surely if the inhabitants got together with the architect something could be achieved? These areas are often unheated, but they are frost-free, providing ideal conditions for many house plants, for instance climbers and members of the vine family, not to mention innumerable fine tub plants. As long as light and space are adequate and the plants are watered from time to time, nothing can go wrong. I am talking about built-in containers with a large soil capacity. It might be possible to create a link with the area outside the building (for instance by extending the container on the exterior of the window), so that moisture enters through capillary action of the soil). Drip-watering systems as well as other self-watering methods are also easily installed.

House Plants in the Home

As a rule house plants are kept in the living-room, sometimes in the hall, the porch or on the landing. But there are many other places in the home where plants could be grown successfully.

The bedroom
For a long time plants were banned from the bedroom because it was thought that they exuded too much carbon dioxide at night, harmful to our health. The quantity however is minimal, and out of all proportion to the amount we produce ourselves. In any case a bedroom should always be well ventilated, and a little extra carbon dioxide will make no difference at all.

So long as there is good daylight in the bedroom, plants will thrive there. An east-facing bedroom is of course ideal (sun on waking in the morming, cool in the evening) both for ourselves and for many plants. Install a wide window-sill or large containers placed on the floor, and your plants will give you great satisfaction.

If you like your bedroom permanently cool, or if you have a rarely used spare room, you could use it for winter storage of your plants. In that case the temperature should preferably never rise above 10°C (50°F). A thermostatically controlled radiator is ideal. Should the temperature have to be increased for a few days (for instance when you have guests who don't appreciate a cold bedroom) the plants will not be harmed, provided the heating is turned down or off afterwards.

The bathroom
It's a pity that in older houses the bathroom is often so badly lit. The windows were kept small to avoid the room being overlooked. Today this can be achieved by other means (moisture-proof curtains and louvres, for instance) so that bathrooms may have normal-sized windows, very suitable for plants, which can be successfully grown in this environment. The more water is spilled in a bathroom, the more humid the atmosphere and most plants enjoy this. Ferns, for instance, always thrive in such a room.

The kitchen
Here too the atmospheric humidity is relatively high. The less effective the cooker hood and the more cooking is done, the better for the plants. A great deal of greasy steam, however, is harmful, and in that case plants with large, leathery leaves which are easily washed should be chosen. Having to clean a small-leaved ficus is an irritating job.

Naturally the light must be good enough to grow plants successfully. Have a permanent container built in the window, or a wide window-sill. You might also add a window-box outside where you can keep pot-grown herbs in summer which may be brought indoors in winter to be kept a little longer.

The attic
Growing plants presents a problem if the attic is lit only by a dormer window. In many cases the window-sill is very narrow or is lacking altogether. In a corner house a window has often been constructed in the side wall as well and the possibilities are greater. There are also houses with a flat roof above the second floor, or some other construction which allows large vertical windows to be installed. Such a house is very favourable to plants.

Too dark an attic may be improved by the construction of a large sloping skylight, but remember that it must be possible to screen it, for the sun entering through such a window can be very hot.

The garage
Elsewhere in this book it has been said that a garage provides excellent winter storage, provided light can enter through a skylight, or windows, and provided the temperature does not drop below 5°C (10°F). The same applies to a shed where there is room for a few plants. This storage space could also be used in summer, especially for annuals.

The cellar
No plants can grow in a cellar, but some species can be overwintered there – geraniums, for instance. As a result of lack of light the plants will form long white shoots, and although this may occur, geraniums are sufficiently strong to make new shoots in spring, if they have been pruned. Naturally much depends on the temperature in the cellar. Bulbs and tubers can also be kept there, provided they do not moulder or rot. This may be prevented by keeping them in very dry peat, which must be renewed every time it has absorbed too much moisture. Remember that some bulbs and tubers must not be kept at too low a temperature. The minimum temperature is generally indicated in the plant description.

Plants on board ship
It should be mentioned that plants can also be grown on board large ships. The air conditioning now mostly in use creates many possibilities. In general the best results are achieved with fairly strong, simple plants, placed near a porthole. There are enthusiasts who manage to grow the more difficult plants, such as orchids. It appears that plants do not get seasick! The main problem is the constant change in the angle of the light, which of course depends on the ship's course.

In this well-lit bedroom the multi-stemmed dracaenas may thrive for years

The asparagus fern will not last for ever in this dark bathroom, but it will certainly keep for a couple of months

Indoor Plant Groups

A beginner in the field of house plants may find his mind boggles on entering a well-stocked garden shop or florist's. Which plant should he choose and for what reason? House plants may be divided into a number of groups, each with their individual advantages and disadvantages, their varying applications, their secrets and their problems. Once you learn to which group a plant belongs, your understanding of its needs will improve.

An example of an epiphyte tree so thoroughly overgrown that it is difficult to distinguish the branches. It grows in a large hothouse on the island of Mainau and is covered with all sorts of plants, all of more or less epiphytic habit. Most of the species can be kept only in a greenhouse

Flowering Plants

It is important to distinguish between plants which flower only once and are then thrown away (potted chrysanthemum, cineraria, Black-eyed Susan) and plants which may flower year after year (azalea, hydrangea, stephanotis).

Plants in the first group should be regarded as pure show plants; the owner wants to introduce a little colour into the room and prefers a living plant to a bunch of flowers. Both actually have the same function, but a plant takes a little longer to die than cut flowers. Such flowering plants are frequently added to plant combinations; others are placed individually on the window-sill. As a rule their colours are quite striking. It is important to select the various shades with care, since the total effect of the plants in the room may be greatly enhanced in this way. On the other hand, if not chosen carefully, such flowering plants may overwhelm the other house plants.

An attractive way of using small plants that flower only once is to place them in groups of between six and twenty, preferably all of the same colour, for instance in an antique container, a large bowl or a beautiful basket.

The second group consists of plants for the true plant lover; they have a totally different function. The essential factor is not the immediate colour effect, but the fact that the owner has sufficient knowledge and love to bring the plant into flower again. The more difficult this is supposed to be, the greater the satisfaction if it succeeds. Quite frequently these plants are not very interesting

when out of bloom. The foliage may be rather unattractive and the plant becomes lanky. No matter – you will soon forget that when the delightful moment arrives and the flowers appear again.

These hobby plants can rarely be kept in the warm living-room throughout the year, for as a rule they require a period at a lower temperature and/or in a drier atmosphere before they can flower again; it might be said they need a rest. Azaleas and hydrangeas may be moved out of doors in summer, while plants which flower in summer need a period of rest in winter.

Below Coleus is available in a wide variety of foliage tints

Bottom, left Green with cream or white and green with pink or red are the usual colours of variegated foliage

Bottom, right Palms (this one is *Washingtonia filifera)* have leaves which separate only when fully opened

Foliage Plants

The majority of plants belong to this group. As the name implies, they are plants whose ornamental value lies mainly in the beautiful shape or colour of their leaves. Mainly, for many foliage plants flower as well, but they are called foliage plants if the ornamental value of the leaves exceeds that of the flowers.

There are plants with all-green foliage, but other species available have red foliage, white-striped leaves, marbled leaves in varied colours or other variegations. As already mentioned in the section on light, the white parts of a leaf are incapable of photosynthesis, and variegated strains must therefore always be placed in better light than green varieties of the same species. The very large group of foliage plants may be further sub-divided, which makes things easier.

Palms

For a time palms were considered old fashioned, but in the last few years they have once more become popular. Rightly so, for most palms are very strong and tolerate an environment with little light and a dry atmosphere. For vigorous growth, however, a palm needs good light, but not full sunlight.

Palms have a woody stem, which is as a rule unbranched. The large leaves grow in a fan shape at the top of each stem (fan palms) or they are pinnate (feathery), occasionally single and incised at the tip. Except for *Chamaedorea* species, which readily produce pendulous racemes of yellow or orange flowers, palms rarely flower indoors.

Palms like to grow in deep pots and the modern plastic cylinders are therefore very suitable. The ideal method would be to use two cylinders, one inside the other, the inner one having plenty of holes at the bottom and draining well. In this way the plant may be plunged without danger of excess water gathering at the base. Because palms can survive in the dark for a long time, they were at one time often used as seasonal plants. After a few months in the entrance hall of an office or hotel they were then moved to the greenhouse to recover condition. Anyone who possesses a small greenhouse or a winter garden might adopt this method. In the 1920s palms were often available on hire, but this rarely happens now.

Ferns

Unlike other plants, which produce seed, ferns are grown from spores. Seed requires fertilisation, but spores are the cells of embryo plantlets and do not need to be fertilised. The spores are always found on the underside of the leaves. Not all the leaves produce spores, in which case we distinguish between fertile (that is, spore-bearing) and sterile (infertile) leaves.

Another characteristic of most ferns is that the leaves are usually composite and, more specifically, pinnate. A pinnate leaf is one incised right down to the centre vein. Some ferns are doubly pinnate – each frond is individually incised. Some are even tripinnate.

Ferns enjoy a humid atmosphere and a soil ball which is kept constantly moist. In a heated room the air is sufficiently humid only when there are many other plants or when a humidifier has been installed. Watering is not easy. The fern dislikes stagnating water, but a dry soil ball is even more harmful. These plants are therefore best grown in well-drained plastic pots with plenty of crocks at the bottom and should be liberally watered twice a day. A self-watering system is of course much more reliable as well as convenient and will give excellent results.

As a rule ferns are regarded as annuals, for they rarely remain in good condition for more than six months. They may be used in a fairly dark spot, for instance in a draughtproof unused fireplace (but first close off the chimney), and in corners of the room where other plants would succumb within a few days. Ferns may last for months in such places. Carefully looked after, and with timely repotting and adequate light, a fern may in fact be able to survive in good condition for years. This is proved by the Stag's Horn Fern (*Platycerium bifurcatum*), protected from the dry living-room atmosphere by its waxy layer. Provided it hangs in not too dark a spot it may grow into an immense plant.

Ferns are plants which harmonise easily with both modern and traditional interiors. The delicate green of most species looks well with various shades of brown, for instance those of wood.

Most ferns are disposable plants, but for a few months they may be a magnificent sight, like this nephrolepis

Platycerium bifurcatum, the Stag's Horn Fern, is one of the hardy ferns. A waxy layer protects the foliage from a dry living-room atmosphere

Bromeliads

As explained on page 69 in the chapter dealing with the cultivation of bromeliads, most species must be regarded as one-year house plants, in fact, throw-away plants, since the mother rosette starts to die after flowering and the plantlets should really be raised in a greenhouse. Regarded in this way, bromeliads can decorate our living-rooms for quite a time; the dying process can take more than a year. Green-leaved, but especially variegated, bromeliads are frequently used in mixed plant containers. In my opinion they look attractive only if the plants with which they are combined grow under approximately similar conditions in their natural habitat. The combination of a bromeliad with a desert cactus in one container, something I saw the other day, gives a very bizarre effect.

Bromeliads are very popular in tropical flower windows, for the high level of humidity achieved in such an enclosed space will allow the plants to thrive. The family embraces several interesting species. In a hothouse, where many of them may be grown on blocks of fern root, they will give a great deal of pleasure. In this environment propagation is little problem, so that progeny is almost assured.

The few hardy bromeliads, such as *Billbergia nutans*, which produces one rosette after another and flowers regularly, make attractive indoor plants, highly valued by the amateur. Unfortunately they are not often available.

A so-called bromeliad or epiphyte tree, suitable for a flower window or a large greenhouse, is easily constructed. A real tree is the most attractive, but a good-sized branch is usually adequate. Take for instance an old, gnarled acacia which branches so attractively, or a mature rhus. The tree should be attached to a heavy base, made of iron or concrete. Tufts of fern root, or possibly of sphagnum moss, are then attached where the tree branches. The plants are bound on with copper wire (rustproof). The tree can be watered by means of a spray incorporated in the ceiling of the flower window or the roof of the greenhouse.

Artificial epiphyte trees can be made of PVC drainpipes, with a diameter of 32, 40 or 50 cm (12, 16 or 20 in). Matching bend sections, triple sections and connection pieces are available, which a handyman can combine into any desired shape. The trunk, of course, should be made of wider piping than the branches.

When ready, the 'tree' should be covered entirely in cork or moss. If it has been properly glued, it will be watertight and may be connected to the water supply, with a tap for control. It is necessary to experiment to find where tiny holes should best be drilled. In this way the moss and the plants can be kept moist automatically or semi-automatically, saving you a lot of work. It is also possible to attach bundles of drip-tubes, covered in moss to hide them from view.

Hanging and Climbing Plants

Hanging and climbing plants are a great asset in the living-room. Bare brickwork has become quite popular in modern architecture, to the benefit of climbers. If your walls are covered in expensive wallpaper you wouldn't dream of spraying your climbing plants every day, but brickwork stands up to this treatment very well. Moreover, foliage looks very attractive against a brick background.

There are actually innumerable climbing plants which cling to the wall without support, although they do not necessarily all develop firm climbing roots like the ivy. As a rule it is necessary to give the plants some support in the shape of wires attached to hooks in the wall, or by some other method. In this way the plants often reach the ceiling.

Hanging plants, of course, are ideal for stairwells, galleries and other elevations so popular in modern homes. Sometimes the stems do not trail for more than a few feet, but other plants easily reach 5 m (16 ft). In that case make sure the container is standing firm and cannot crash down.

Small hanging or creeping plants can successfully be used in large containers, where they act as ground cover or trail attractively over the rim of the container. This applies to mixed containers as well as to specimen plants, which sometimes look a little unnatural all by themselves in a pot.

When placing your hanging and climbing plants you have to take into account that at higher levels, that is, over 2 m (6 ft), it is a great deal warmer than on a wide window-sill behind single glazing,

Top *Aechmea fasciata* is a fine example of the bromeliad family. As soon as the flower opens the rosette starts to die

Bottom In their natural habitat many bromeliads are epiphytes. Several of them can be tied to an old tree trunk, together with a number of hanging and climbing plants

Top This *Cissus rhombifolia* (syn. *Rhoicissus rhomboidea*) looks particularly attractive against the wall not just because of its shape, but even more so because of the colour contrast

Bottom On this gallery plants have been used to good advantage. Provided there is sufficient light they will thrive

especially in winter when the heating is on and the warm air collects at the top of the room. You will notice this if you climb a step-ladder to wipe off a mark on the ceiling. The plant will notice it as well, and in such cases you should therefore only use plants marked with the symbol ⊜. For stairwells, which are kept at a much lower temperature, suitable plants are marked ⊖ or ◯.

When plants are being watered those placed at higher levels are frequently overlooked, and for that reason it is a good idea to use fairly large pots with room for reserve water. Special hanging pots with matching saucers are available – useful, because the water does not run out at the bottom. But often their shapes leave much to be desired.

Indoor Trees

Several house plants are capable of growing so large that we might call them indoor trees. Good effects can be achieved with such trees, but they have their individual problems, as we shall see. No doubt you are familiar with the enormous *Ficus* species, of which *Ficus benjamina* is one of the best known.

Indoor trees are best planted in a large tub, without the competition of other plants – or at most with some low-growing ground cover. For young plants a smaller pot will do, but they must be repotted in good time, since they grow very rapidly. They may in fact have to be repotted three times within one year.

In the living-room such plants quickly reach the ceiling and it is useful if they will then curve, so that they need not be stopped. Not all plants will do this: *Ficus elastica*, for instance, will grow very tall, but does not easily branch, so that it does not grow into a well-shaped tree. Better to plant three to five young plants together in one container and to pinch out the tips from time to time, when they are 50 to 100 cm (18 to 36 in) tall. This will make for a more attractive plant.

Once the indoor tree has reached a height of a few feet and occupies a tub approximately 80 cm (32 in) in diameter, it is no longer necessary to repot it every year. However, it must be regularly fed in summer and watered very carefully. A hygrometer would be a great help in checking the humidity and you might consider hydroculture or an automatic watering system.

It is not always possible to prune indoor trees in such a way that their natural shape is retained. When they become *too* large, it may be possible to sell them and start again. But if you do decide to prune them, be careful to keep their shape intact.

Not many plants are suitable for use as indoor trees. They have to be very vigorous and must, in addition, tolerate a more or less even temperature of around 20°C (68°F) both in summer and in winter. They must also be satisfied with a moderate amount of light, for a sunlit position cannot always be guaranteed. Suitable species are found particularly among ficus plants. *Sparmannia africana* or House Lime is another plant that needs space, but it has to be moved out of doors in summer, so that its application is limited.

For spaces kept cooler in winter, such as stairwells, indoor trees can be found among the tub plants. Here the choice is a little greater. Take note of the symbols, however, when selecting one, for many plants recommended as indoor trees, such as the yucca, are totally unsuitable for this purpose, since too little sun enters the living-room, and especially since they will not tolerate a constant temperature of 20°C (68°F) although such a plant comes into the category of tub plants. Understandably, incorrect advice may lead to enormous disappointment.

A large container with a number of dracaena stems – the quickest way to grow a good-sized indoor tree

One of the best known, and probably the finest, indoor tree available: *Ficus benjamina*

House Plants from Seeds

Practically any house plant can be grown from seed, if you prefer this form of propagation. In some cases they are not easy to sow and make little progress, unless you have an indoor propagator. However, there are plenty which are easy to grow, even on the window-sill. Dozens of species are found in the better seed catalogues, for instance abutilon, asparagus, begonia, browallia, cacti, and right through the alphabet up to streptocarpus. An indoor propagator is always a useful aid.

Many plants can be grown from the pips of tropical fruits such as fresh dates, avocados, mangoes, lychees, peanuts (unroasted) and many more. They are not all described in this book, because they do not all produce lasting house plants. When sowing the pips of oranges, lemons, grapes or apples, it must be remembered that the plants they produce are not the same as those bearing edible fruit. The latter are propagated by grafting: they do not grow satisfactorily on their own root systems. Orange pips will produce a 'wild' orange plant, bearing no fruits, or at most inedible ones. Only the pips of an indoor orange plant (*Citrus microcarpa*, syn. *Citrus mitis*) will develop true to type, although its fruit is also inedible.

In general you cannot expect tropical fruit plants to flower or bear fruit in the living-room. An avocado pip (*Persea americana*) will grow into quite an attractive plant, but it will never bear fruit.

Better results are obtained with a number of vegetables grown in the living-room if you haven't got a garden. Tomatoes, gherkins and cucumber are easily grown indoors. Use good-sized pots, for these plants are enormously vigorous. However, the descriptions of these vegetables are beyond the scope of this book.

Succulents

Succulent plants are capable of storing moisture to enable them to survive in the dry season. Cacti are distinguished from other members of the succulent family by their protruberances, called areoles, usually bearing thorns.

Cacti

All cacti belong to the same family. A number of species look like ordinary foliage plants, the pereskia being the best known example. The *Opuntia* group, or pad-cacti, as they are sometimes called, are also distinguished. The original leaf shape may still be recognised; the areoles not only bear thorns, but also tiny barbed spines, known as glochids. Anyone used to handling these plants will know how easily these spines may catch in your skin (for instance when the cacti are being repotted), and how difficult it is to remove them.

The most typical cacti are those in which the leaf shape can no longer be recognised. These have columnar or spherical bodies, covered in ribs or warts, which bear the areoles, and these in turn bear the thorns. Some species are also covered in white hairs to protect them from the sun and prevent excess evaporation.

Cacti which in their natural habitat grow in forests, such as the epiphyllum and the Christmas Cactus, again are quite different in appearance. The long jointed stems are flattened and have the same function as leaves. A few rudimentary thorns grow along the edges.

Many house plants are easily grown from seed. Below are just a few examples, with their seeds. From left to right: the Coffee Plant, yucca, Tea Plant, cordyline and *Ficus benjamina*

Other succulents

Although, as we have seen, cacti belong to the succulent family as well, the name 'succulents' is usually given to plants which have no areoles, but nevertheless store moisture in their tissue. In some cases their succulent character is obvious – a number of species look exactly like spherical cacti.

Sometimes we find a transitional shape, for instance in the well-known peperomia, which some people count among succulents while others do not. In some cases the water is stored only in the leaves, sometimes only in the stems, often in both. Many succulents branch normally, while others develop rosettes.

Exotic shapes

The strangest shapes may occur among cacti and other succulents, for instance the cristate forms, in which the ordinary cactus can hardly be recognised. These plants are not suffering from a disease: it is simply a freak of nature, the cause of which is still largely unknown. Fasciation – its scientific name – also occurs among many other plants.

Then there are the grafted cacti, often in shades of yellow or red, which are grown on short green stock from another cactus species. Some people believe that the yellow or red globe at the top is a 'flower', but this is not the case: it is the cactus itself which lacks chlorophyll and cannot therefore grow on its own root system. It lacks the power of assimilation and lives on the nutrients provided by the stock.

The long-tailed Rat's Tail Cactus, the strangely thorned *Euphorbia* species, the remarkable spheres and globes from which a few green leaves may appear if you wait long enough – all these are forms of succulents which can create great interest as room decoration or to amateurs specialising in these plants.

Finding a site

As you will see on page 70, where the care of succulents is discussed, nearly all these plants require a resting season. During this dormant period the plant's metabolism should come to a complete standstill and it is then that the flower buds for the coming season are developed. In 95 per cent of cases this dormant period, during which the temperature must be reduced, falls in winter. Succulents are therefore unsuitable for the heated living-room, with the exception of a few very hardy species which ignore the temperature but will rarely flower in such conditions.

Because people are not always aware of these simple facts the purchase of a succulent plant frequently results in disappointment. How many of those colourful, grafted little cacti die a miserable death because of excess heat, lack of light and often too much water! And think of the number of valuable melocacti that must have come to grief in European living-rooms. Fortunately the import from the Antilles is now restricted. These magnificent plants have very long roots, which are left behind when they are lifted, and in our climate they will not grow new ones. Cacti, especially, die after a short time, but among other succulents there are a number which might be considered permanent house plants.

On the other hand, all succulent plants are particularly suited to the moderately heated greenhouse. They will also do well if grown on a sunny window-sill in summer and moved to a frost-free garage, shed or unheated bedroom in winter. To keep a beautiful succulent permanently in a warm, dark place is like committing murder and is unworthy of a genuine plant lover.

Succulent plants vary enormously in shape. **Top left** An attractive collection of parodia in an amateur's greenhouse

Top right A seed tray in which species of lithops, all different, have been picked out

Above The succulent *Haworthia fasciata* with its typical 'windows', through which light reaches the inner cells

Right A group of columnar cacti, in this case espostoa, with striking hair formation

Below, left *Pachyveria* 'Clavata', an obvious foliage succulent

Below, centre A group of conophytums, outstanding succulents for the amateur collector

Below, right Another succulent, the Crown of Thorns (*Euphorbia splendens*). It stores large amounts of water, mainly in its stem and branches

Bulbs and Tubers

As you will see on page 68, where the care of these plants is discussed in more detail, they are divided into two groups: spring-flowering and summer-flowering species.

Spring-flowering plants, such as tulips, hyacinths, amaryllis, daffodils and narcissi, are temporary house plants. They are planted in the form of dry bulbs, which will flower in the course of a few months and decorate the window-sill for a week or two, then as a rule are discarded afterwards. The attraction of these plants lies chiefly in the pleasure of preparing them and watching them grow and this is no doubt the understandable reason why pots with flowering daffodils rarely come on the market. There is no fun in buying them already in flower.

The same applies to some extent to summer-flowering species, except that these plants can more easily be kept through the winter, especially if cultivated in a greenhouse. In that case a gloriosa tuber or an amaryllis bulb (more correctly, hippeastrum) may increase in size from year to year, enhancing the joy of cultivation. Practically all bulbs and tubers have a dormant period, during which the foliage dies. Only very few species keep green foliage throughout the winter.

All these different bulbs and tubers, of which a large selection is available, are ideal plants for the plant lover. Many of them are of recent origin, producing a striking effect when you suddenly have a magnificent array of exotic blooms in your window. As a rule a bulb or tuber guaranteed to flower is much less expensive than an ordinary house plant, so try the experiment.

Orchids

Orchids are typical plants for specialist collectors, who have a separate greenhouse for the purpose, which in winter can be kept at a minimum temperature of 18°C (64°F) and is heavily screened. There are also orchids for the moderate greenhouse, minimum 12°C (53°F). Practically all orchids require a special compost and a high degree of humidity.

One would therefore be inclined to say that they are not suitable as indoor plants. However, there are a few exceptions which will do reasonably well or even thrive in the living-room. The odontoglossum is the most hardy, but there are people who always grow cattleyas, coelogynes, epidendrums or miniature cymbidiums, lycastes, oncidiums, paphiopedilums and phalaenopses in their living-room, especially on an east-facing window-sill, with apparent success.

Naturally an enclosed flower window, which has the same climate as a hothouse, is highly suitable for growing orchids, provided there is not too much sun. In such plant cases orchids are often attached to a fine epiphyte tree. The species must be carefully selected so that they can all receive the same care.

The orchid has very characteristic flowers. There are three sepals, the upper one frequently being called the dorsal sepal. Of the three petals one deviates in shape and is called the 'lip' or 'slipper'. The centre of the flower consists of a column to which style, pistil and stamens are attached. The flower stems of orchids may be several feet long.

Orchids are rather expensive, but the more common species described in this book are fairly reasonable. Few as a rule will be available at the florist's or garden centre. To purchase plants you would do best to contact a specialist nursery, who will have a catalogue to choose from. They will reach you through the post.

Above, top Bulbs are often brought into flower in spring

Above Orchids, a group of plants for a specialised hobby

Below Various forms of bonsai, a Japanese method of cultivating miniature trees. They are not really indoor plants

Bonsai

The word 'bonsai' actually means pot plant, and that is what this entire book is about. However, the Japanese, who adopted the system of growing outdoor plants in pots or containers from the Chinese, give a different meaning to the word. In the early stages small wild trees or shrubs of unusual shape were collected from hill slopes. Subsequently these plants were grown from seed and tied and pruned until they acquired the desired shape. This is still being done in Japan.

In this country numerous bonsai, complete with container, are imported from Japan. Mature trees are very expensive. They are also being grown here from seed. There is no reason why you should not sow the seed of practically any shrub you might like. It is not essential to take original Japanese plants, such as *Pinus thunbergia*, the Japanese Black Pine. Many shrubs suitable for growing as miniatures are widely available in this country in the form of garden plants – *Cryptomeria japonica*, for example, the Japanese Cypress; hornbeam, wistaria, laburnum, ornamental cherry, elm and juniper. In principle practically all hardy woody plants are suitable, provided their foliage is not too large, for this would cause problems.

Bonsai must live out of doors in unrestricted light and fresh air whenever possible. As the small plants are easily upset by gusts of wind and heavy rain might flood the containers, they are frequently grown in a sheltered spot. In many cases a special rack is constructed and placed preferably against a west-facing wall which protects the plants from an easterly wind. Sometimes the rack is made of heavy bamboo and has four or five shelves, topped by a sloping roof to prevent the plants getting drenched. In bad weather roller blinds are lowered on all open sides to protect the bonsai from extreme weather conditions.

Most species are entirely hardy and can be kept out of doors throughout the year, but in a sharp frost the bowls and containers might crack and in that kind of weather the plants must be carefully covered. This presents no problem in the case of deciduous plants: a thick layer of straw will keep out the frost. Evergreen bonsai must be kept in the light and for them a frost-proof container, or possibly an unheated greenhouse, is ideal. On no account should the plants be kept too warm in winter. In a high temperature the shoots appear too early and the plants become susceptible to late frosts.

There are various types of bonsai, such as the cascade shape, the rock-based tree, the stiffly erect form, the windswept form and the miniature copse – they all have magnificent Japanese names. The eventual shape must appear natural, although it is largely the work of human hands, achieved after years of bending and pruning. Young branches, which are still malleable, are wound with copper wire and bent into the desired shape. As the wood matures it becomes hard and the wire can be removed.

The correct choice of pot or bowl is as important as that of style. For details get in touch with a bonsai club.

Bonsai need water and food just like any other plant, and they even have to be repotted from time to time. They should not grow too rapidly, but growth must not cease altogether or their powers of resistance will be affected. Genuine bonsai lovers will have to forget about holidays – in summer especially the bowls must be watered at least twice a day. This operation requires care and cannot be left to just anyone.

Cultivation Systems

To be able to grow vigorously, practically all house plants must be rooted in a medium containing sufficient moisture, air and nutrients. For centuries ordinary garden soil or compost was used for this purpose, generally mixed with matter such as rotted leaves, pulverised clay and numerous other ingredients (see page 62). The crumbly nature of such mixtures ensured ventilation for the root system, retained moisture and contained nutrients.

When it became too complicated to make all these mixtures, growers changed over to what is called 'soilless compost', which as a rule consists of peat fibre, turves and sharp sand. All nutrients are artificially introduced. Such a mixture, too, is sufficiently heavy to support the plant.

Hydroponics

In the last century Von Liebig discovered that plants can grow in a glass of water, provided the necessary nutrients are added. In this way he was able to establish exactly which nutrients a plant requires. At that time the commercial applications of this new system were thought to be negligible.

It was not until the 1930s that renewed experiments were made with hydroculture, as the system was called. By 1938 my brother, G. P. Herwig, had already converted dozens of square metres of our father's greenhouses to tomatoes grown by hydroculture. In the second world war the Americans on Ascension Island introduced so-called hydroponics: growing vegetables for the troops stationed there using the hydroculture method.

After the second world war, lovers of house plants also began to grow their favourites in water. Some of you may remember the green glass pots with insets filled with ground basalt. The young plant's roots grew partly in the basalt, partly in the nutrient solution. This system gradually became more popular, partly because of the novelty of this form of cultivation. Hydroculture was also found to be very useful for people who were often away from home.

Below, left A bunch of water roots. These are noticeably different from ground roots

Below, right An example of the hydroculture sets now generally available. Cuttings rooted in water may be directly transferred to these pots

Bottom A large hydro-container in an office building

Ground roots and water roots

After a time it was discovered that a plant can develop two kinds of roots, ground roots and water roots, with a number of physiological differences. A cutting from a Busy Lizzie grown in a bottle of water has water roots. If the same cutting is grown in potting compost, it will develop ground roots, that is, normal roots which take in oxygen directly from among the particles of the soil. Moving a plant with water roots to compost, and vice versa, always involves a period of transition, during which the plant is particularly sensitive. It is rather as if it has to start off from scratch. The younger the plant, the easier it will adapt.

Once this was thoroughly understood, growers began to raise special plants for hydroculture, in order to save their customers the transitional period. The results were excellent. From the start, plants grown in water made much better progress in hydroculture than plants which had been started off in compost.

Clay granules

At approximately the same time a clever grower discovered that the filling (basalt or pumice) could be replaced by lightweight clay granules. These granules absorb practically no water, they are chemically inert and give good support to the plants.

It soon appeared that offices and public buildings were particularly suitable for plants grown by the hydroculture method. The Swiss-German company Luwasa was one of the first to go into business on a large scale. They introduced large containers, in attractive colours, filled with clay granules in which the hydroplants are set out. The nutrient solution reaches approximately halfway up the container, so that part of the root system can grow below the surface of the water, and the remaining part in the drier granules above. This combination appears to ensure a balanced intake of both nutrients and oxygen.

A free-standing water level meter is placed in the container, so that it is easy to see when more water has to be added. Smaller hydrosets working on the same principle are also available. Lately other forms of filling material have appeared on the market, which may to some extent replace clay granules, for example small black plastic bars, 4 cm ($1\frac{1}{4}$ in) in length and with a diameter of 2 mm ($\frac{1}{10}$ in). As long as the material is chemically inert and provides adequate support it doesn't really matter what it is made of, but clay granules are more attractive to look at because of their fairly natural appearance.

Ion exchange

The nutrient solution used in hydroculture can be obtained by dissolving tablets in water, or by diluting a concentrated liquid. The water evaporates and must be regularly topped up, and after a few months it is necessary to pump or pour out the solution to get rid of the waste products of the plants, rinse the container with clean water and introduce fresh nutrient solution. The rising lime content is particularly harmful to the plants.

All in all it takes a fair amount of time to look after hydroplants and it was therefore found to be a considerable improvement when the well-known firm of Bayer introduced a feeding system based on ion exchange, namely Lewatit HD5. This product, available both in litres and in 25-ml capsules, contains all necessary nutrients and trace elements, chemically bound in synthetic resin. The nice thing about it is that harmful ions are absorbed. In fact the water must contain some calcium and salts, since otherwise no nutrient ions would be released. The exchange continues until all the nutrients have been replaced by the plant's waste products. The process takes about six months, after which new Lewatit HD5 is added and the whole thing starts all over again.

For smaller plants one 25-ml capsule is sufficient; larger plants need two. Large plant containers are satisfied with 500 ml Lewatit per square metre (about 1 pint per square yard). All you now have to do is replenish the water lost by evaporation.

Pros and cons of hydroculture

Many people assert that plants grow better in hydroculture. If a comparison is made with the same plants grown by the traditional method of soil cultivation in optimum conditions, I don't believe this assertion is true. The difficulty is that plants grown in compost do not always receive the best possible care. This is especially true of plants grown in modern, non-porous containers which are frequently given far too much water and in those circumstances hydroculture is preferable. Should it therefore be considered simply as an emergency method for people unable to look after their plants in the proper fashion? In some cases this may be so, for instance in offices. Naturally moisture reserves which are sufficient for at least a week, often even for as much as a month, cannot fail to benefit a plant, and here hydroculture has the advantage. Long weekends and reasonably short holidays are thus easily bridged.

A disadvantage is that hydroculture is much more expensive. To begin with, you have to choose plants raised by the hydroculture method and at present this treatment still makes them more expensive than compost-grown plants (about 25 per cent more). Clearly, too, the choice of hydroplants available is far more restricted. You also need special, fairly expensive, containers, with water-level indicators and adequate nutrient supplies, pumps to remove the solution, and so on. The dealer claims that the extra costs are soon recovered because the plant will keep much longer but he may not always get his sums right.

Top Plant containers with self-watering systems in an office block. Though the watering is taken care of, it is doubtful whether they are getting enough light in this position

Centre Smaller containers with self-watering systems, suitable for the living-room

Bottom The 'mushroom', useful for ensuring an adequate water supply to a pot during holiday periods

Self-watering Systems

The term 'semi-hydro' which is occasionally used is somewhat confusing. What does a self-watering system do? The plant grows in compost in the normal way, even though a well-aerated mixture is preferred. There is a water reservoir at the bottom of the pot, connected to the compost by means of a wick or some other cunning device. As the compost dries out the wick will draw water from the reservoir. Provided the system has been correctly calculated (and as a rule the manufacturer will have seen to that), the compost will never be either too dry or too damp. The pots contain an opening through which the reservoir can be topped up, and an indicator for the water level. It is quite possible to mix liquid fertiliser with the water in the reservoir, so that the plant is fed through the wick as well.

Between the bottom of the plant pot and the water reservoir is a layer of air and extra oxygen can reach the root system by way of the topping-up device. Once you have read the section on the degrees of moisture on page 55, you will realise that the use of a self-watering system makes any differentiation between 'fairly dry', 'moderately dry' and 'constant moisture' impossible. The moisture level of the compost depends on the suction of the wick and naturally no manufacturer can provide three different degrees of moisture. The average is aimed at and plants whose needs correspond with this average will do best in this kind of pot. The average may vary from one make to another, but in my experience the compost in pots with a self-watering system is generally on the damp side. It follows that plants marked with the symbol (''') are most suitable for these automatic pots and experience confirms this.

However, with a little cunning it is possible to make plants marked ('') thrive in a pot with a reservoir as well. All one has to do is to wait for a week before refilling an empty reservoir. During that time the compost will dry out and absorb a lot of air, greatly appreciated by the plant.

Plants from the category marked (') will be less happy with a self-watering system. You could try using a thinner wick, or less absorbent compost (plenty of sand in the mixture), but it all becomes too complicated and you would do better to grow the plant by the orthodox method.

When plants require a dormant season, the water reservoir should be left empty as soon as they start their resting period and at the same time the pots should be moved to a cooler situation. To prevent complete drying out, a little tepid water may be given from the top from time to time. If the water level indicator shows that water has run into the reservoir, the plant has been overwatered. At the end of the resting period the plant should be returned to a warmer position and the water reservoir refilled.

Thirsty plants will empty the reservoir within a week. If you are going on holiday for longer than a week some provision must be made. This is easily achieved by applying the laws of suction.

Connect the reservoirs of the various pots by means of aquarium tubing. Make sure there is no air in the tube, only water, and insert the other end in a larger reservoir (a bucket or basin) filled with water. Try out the system in advance.

I believe there is a future for self-watering systems. They are easier to set up than hydroculture and have the same advantages. The plants need to be repotted only when they grow too large, and they are easily fed through the watering system.

Naturally it is important that pots with a self-watering system (as well as hydropots) should look as attractive as possible. In the early stages these pots, mainly of French manufacture, were absolute eyesores. It would seem that professional designers are now involved in the process, with the result that there are many very acceptable pots and containers available. Some are recommended for use out of doors as well.

Simple methods

Practically all self-watering systems depend on capillary action. Three systems are useful for emergency use in the holiday season (see page 67). The first consists of wool threads running from a basin of water to the pots, on the principle of a wick.

Porous threads drawn through the pot, with their ends in a dish of water, are more reliable, but then how large should the dish be? The third method is the 'mushroom' made of porous clay, which sucks up water from a reservoir through plastic tubing. This is not a cheap method, but I have found that it works extremely well (see photograph). For two or three plants you will certainly need a bucketful of water.

The Importance of Lighting

Light is an indispensable factor in the growth of plants. On page 52 you will see how light can be measured with the aid of a light meter, or even with the exposure meter of a camera. For the hardiest plant approximately 1000lux, measured in winter, is the minimum. There are authors who give the figure 700lux, but in that case the plants must really be exceptionally hardy.

If you want to grow plants in positions where there is not enough daylight, there is nothing for it but to give them artificial light.

Special Lighting

As explained on page 52, a plant's spectral sensitivity differs from that of the human eye. An ordinary light bulb is fine to read by, but whatever its strength, it does not enable a plant to grow properly. It is therefore necessary to use different sources of light, for instance fluorescent tubes, special plant lamps, high-pressure mercury lamps, high-pressure mercury-iodine lamps or high-pressure sodium lamps. The first three may be considered for amateur use in the home or in offices.

Although the lamps appear to give a fair amount of light, this is somewhat deceptive and they must therefore be placed close above the plants. A 32-watt fluorescent tube hung 1m (3ft) above a plant, for instance, provides only 250lux, a 160-watt Philips plant lamp about 700lux and a 125-watt high-pressure mercury lamp 1200lux. At this distance these lamps are therefore barely adequate, or even inadequate, if they are the sole source of light. The area lit by a lamp at a height of 1m (3ft) is moreover quite small, at most 1m (3ft) in diameter. Outside this area the strength of light is considerably less.

Where plants are entirely dependent on artificial lighting a veritable battalion of lamps must be used to provide overall light of 1000lux. And that is the minimum requirement of the most vigorous foliage plants, not to mention flowering plants or such lovers of light as cacti.

Where artificial lighting is used as a supplementary light source, that is, where there is some, though insufficient daylight, results may be better.

Daylight and Darkness

As you know, the photosynthetic process in a plant is set going by good light. With darkness, respiration, or breathing, begins. Both are necessary to keep the plant in good condition. Tests have shown that a plant must be kept in the dark for at least 6 hours in every 24 (though there are exceptions to this rule). This means that they may be in daylight or artificial light for 18 hours.

This information will enable you to control the artificial light as required. Daylight and artificial light may be combined at one and the same time, but the artificial light source may also be used to lengthen the day. For instance, in winter (when more artificial lighting is required), you might have the lights on between 4 and 8 in the morning and between 5 and 10 in the evening. In this way artificial light and daylight will be more or less continuous; the plant will not need a rest in between but can sleep for exactly 6 hours at night.

In a living-room used in the evening, plant lights may be disturbing. No matter – you can allow the plant to sleep from about 5p.m., when it gets dark outside, until 11p.m. The subdued lighting in your room will not interfere with its breathing. You then switch on the plant light source and leave it on until the arrival of daylight. In this way, too, artificial light and daylight are continuous and the resting period remains at 6 hours.

Hints on Installation

Plant lamps are best hung from their flex, which must naturally be tension protected. The lamps are often supplied with special fittings which direct the light straight down. As the plant grows, the flex may be shortened, but very tall plants really need light sources placed at various levels.

Where the plants to be lit are standing in a row it is an advantage to have a light track fixed to the ceiling. With the aid of adaptors a number of lights can then be plugged in, as many as the circuit will carry.

Of course, the lights can be switched on and off manually, but experience has shown that this is often forgotten. During the weekend there is nobody in the office, and people are often away for a day or two as well. The plants' habitual rhythm is disturbed and this appears to be very harmful. It's better therefore to install a simple time clock; they are quite reasonable and very durable.

Lately, so-called plant lamps of Chinese manufacture have come on the market. The packaging promises miracles, but the low wattage will tell you that they can never provide sufficient light. You will be able to measure the strength of the light to some extent, but not the spectrum. I strongly advise against the purchase of such lamps.

Above Special plant lamps enable these dracaenas to thrive even in a dark corner

Right Artificial lighting above hydro-containers in an office block. The spotlights consist of large mercury lamps which are kept on for part of the night

Care and Cultivation

Introduction

This section of the book is intended to teach you some of the secrets of success which you will find particularly useful in the care of your house plants.

Starting with a certain amount of theory about the way a plant functions, the purpose of the root system, the foliage and the flowers, we shall then go on to consider in depth the ideal growing conditions of plants – that is to say, the requirements essential to their health. This description of the growth factors will also contain a detailed explanation of the symbols used throughout the book.

In addition you will learn all you need to know about composts and pots, about daily care, the construction of built-in containers and flower windows, and about the problems which can arise when you are on holiday. A number of important plant groups are dealt with separately, all aspects of propagation are described and the most common plant pests and diseases examined.

A certain amount of basic botanical knowledge makes it easier to read and understand a book such as this one. You will, moreover, be more successful in growing house plants if you know a little bit about their main functions. The information in this book is confined to the basic principles, which you may already have learned at school, so that it will simply refresh your memory.

The process of germination can easily be seen in a large seed, especially if the method shown is used. This avocado stone contains sufficient reserve food to enable the root and the stem and leaves to grow. This doesn't apply to smaller seeds, in which far less food can be stored and where the seed lobes have to be raised in order to act as temporary leaves. Usually the root is formed first, followed by the stem and then the leaves

Some Botanical Basics

How a plant grows from seed

Many indoor plants are easily grown from seed. Ferns produce spores instead of seed, but in practice this makes little difference in propagation. In seed-bearing plants seeds with one seed lobe can be distinguished from those with two or more. The difference is obvious when the seeds germinate: one-lobed seeds put forth one leaf, others two. Bromeliads, orchids, lilies, palms, plants belonging to the arum family and a few others produce one-lobed seeds, but the large majority of house plants are double lobed. Plants with double-lobed seed are botanically classified as *Dicotyledones* (dicotyledons); those with single-lobed seed as *Monocotyledones* (monocotyledons). Seeds of conifers (a separate class) have more than two lobes.

If we dissect a fairly large seed – say an avocado stone – we find two seed lobes protected by the brown seed coat. The embryo of the plant is found at the point of junction; with some difficulty it is possible to discern the construction of root and stem.

If a number of sharpened matchsticks are inserted into the pip so that it can be suspended above the surface of water in a glass, it can be seen how, first of all, the root begins to pierce the seed coat. Next the two seed lobes separate and the embryo begins to develop into a stem.

An avocado stone has large seed lobes containing an enormous amount of reserve food, sufficient to allow a number of leaves to develop on the stem. This is not the case with smaller seeds where the seed lobes raise themselves on the stem to act temporarily as leaves in order to supply the assimilation products necessary for the growth of stem, roots and foliage. Where the seed lobes remain below ground we speak of 'hypogeal germination'. As soon as the true leaves are able to assimilate properly, the seed leaves disappear; they have accomplished their task.

Intake of nutrients

Food is absorbed through the roots, mainly in the zone near the tip of the root which is usually covered in very fine root hairs. These hairs or fibrils are extended cells of the epidermis and as a rule their average life is no more than a fortnight. Meanwhile new fibrils develop as the root grows so that water and food are constantly absorbed at different levels. When house plants are grown in clay pots a felty layer is often to be found on the outside of the soil ball, consisting of root tips and root hairs which are trying to absorb water and food from the porous wall of the pot. It goes without saying that if this layer is removed when repotting, considerable damage is done to the plant. And yet some plant books seriously advise you to do this!

Mineral salts are contained in the water between the soil particles or in the pores of the pot. But how do they become absorbed through the cell walls to reach the interior of the root? This question has been answered in several ways in the course of time.

At one time it was thought that absorption was simply due to the fact that the roots contained a stronger solution than the water outside, and in accordance with the laws of natural science the liquid moves in the direction of the strongest concentration – a phenomenon called 'osmosis'. If the concentration outside the root system is greater than inside, the process is reversed and the plant voids itself. We call this 'root scorch'. It is easily caused by giving too much food at once.

Subsequently it was proved that temperature also played a part: at 0°C (32°F) osmosis practically ceases. This is the reason why evergreen orangery plants must often be given warm feet. When the sun comes out in winter, the water in the leaves evaporates, but if the tub is standing on a cold floor the roots cannot absorb water, so the plant dries out and loses its foliage. There is also a connection between a plant's respiration (see below) and the water absorption. The conclusion is that the root tips must act as a kind of pump. The bleeding of a birch tree or a vine may be ascribed to this fact. The pressure from the roots is further increased by evaporation through the leaves of the plant above ground. This is why the sap rises.

How the mineral salts enter the roots is a question that is still hard to answer. What is certain is that they do not simply flow into the cells. The minerals are absorbed by the living protoplasm, chiefly in the form of ions. It is interesting to note that different plants absorb different amounts of salts from the same soil. In other words, every plant chooses its own diet. Acidity also plays a part: some plants like acid soil, others an alkaline medium. The symbols employed in the plant descriptions will indicate whether the plant loves or hates a calcareous growing medium.

Assimilation and photosynthesis

Assimilation is synonymous in this context with 'equalisation'. Nutrient materials are converted in the leaves of a plant into products similar to those of which the plant already consists, for only in this way can the plant grow.

Plants can absorb an enormous quantity of carbon dioxide from the atmosphere through their pores. It has been calculated that in the course of a summer day one sunflower plant stores 25 g (1 oz) of carbon dioxide. This is the quantity contained in 120 cu m (4238 cu ft) of air. Since the plant utilises only about one third of the available carbon dioxide, it means that in one day about 360,000 litres (79,180 gal) of air have passed through the foliage. On the other hand a cactus, which has few pores and grows very slowly, probably doesn't absorb more than one or two litres (2 or 3 pints) of air on a warm day; it needs very little carbon dioxide.

When the pores are open (in good light), carbon dioxide from the air enters the leaf cells and from there passes into the chloroplasts. The light stimulates the chlorophyll molecules and as a result the water molecules absorbed by the roots can be split into hydrogen and oxygen. This is known as a photochemical reaction. In combination with the hydrogen the carbon dioxide is converted into carbohydrates and the oxygen is given off as waste product.

We all owe our lives to this process, which is called photosynthesis. Animals use oxygen and release carbon dioxide. A fire cannot burn without oxygen and a fuel engine would be no use without oxygen. The amount of oxygen generated in a good-sized greenhouse full of plants refreshes a person who has just been exposed to heavy traffic fumes on the road. Indoors the effect is relatively small, since the number of house plants is usually restricted, and most house plants do not assimilate to the same extent as those growing out of doors. A 100-sq m (120-sq yd) lawn will release 1.2 kg (2½ lb) of pure oxygen in the course of twelve hours – that is the amount contained in 6 cu m (212 cu ft) of air. Measured throughout the growing season, such a lawn – provided it is properly maintained – will release sufficient oxygen to supply two people for a whole year.

The carbohydrates (starch and sugars) are produced in the day time. (A simple test will show that in the evening a leaf is heavier than early in the morning.) During the night the process ceases and the foodstuffs produced continue to be transferred, so that in the morning the leaf is empty. The carbohydrates are transferred to all the living parts of the plant where they serve as fuel, but also to storage organs, such as bulbs or tubers. In a potato field of 60 sq m (72 sq yd) nearly 500 g (17½ oz) of starch is stored every day.

The nitrogen assimilation, eventually leading to the production of proteins, is even more complicated. Nitrogen compounds (nitrates) contained in the soil undergo bacterial changes to enable them to be absorbed by the roots. Nitrates are reduced mainly in the leaves. Enzymes convert the resulting ammonia into amino-acids, which eventually produce proteins.

Respiration

The respiration of a plant is to some extent the reverse of photosynthesis and might therefore be thought of as a process of 'dissimilation'.

In respiration energy is released. The process is a particularly complicated one and we shall spare you the details. It requires oxygen, which is withdrawn from the air (or from the potting compost). This also partly consists of the oxygen produced in the photosynthetic process. It is therefore a mistake to regard photosynthesis and respiration as two separate processes. A plant's metabolism consists of a chain of processes, a characteristic of the living cell.

By comparing photosynthesis and respiration it is possible to stress the differences in order to obtain a better insight into the functions of a plant. In respiration oxygen is taken in; in photosynthesis it is released. Fortunately the amount released is much the greater of the two.

At night photosynthesis stops, but respiration continues. This is the reason why house plants used to be removed from hospital wards at night, a fairly useless custom, since the amount of oxygen used by a few plants is quite small in relation to the size of the room.

In photosynthesis sugars are produced; they are partially burnt up in respiration.

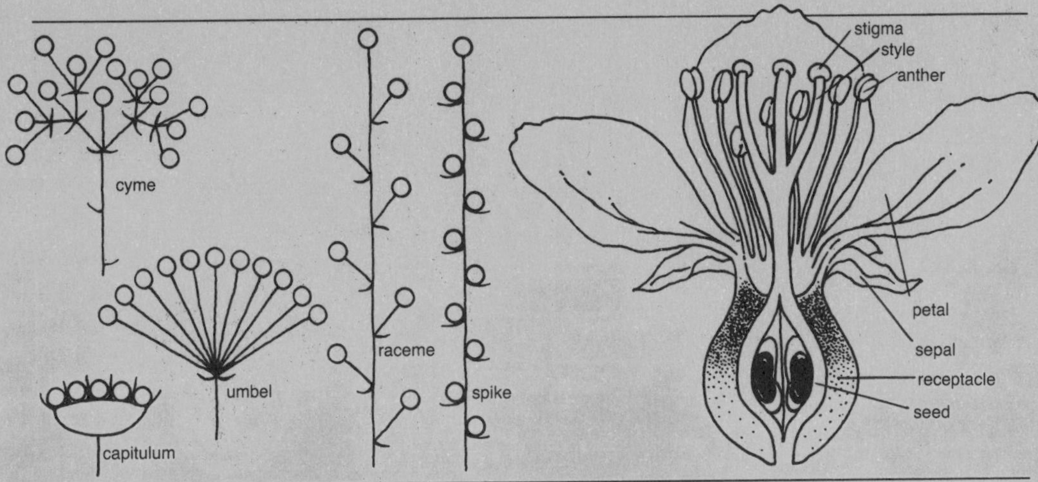

The flower may be regarded as a modified shoot in which the transformed leaves are placed close together. The flower contains the reproductive organs of the plant: stamens (male) and pistils (female). Usually they are protected by the crown (generally coloured) and the sepals, which as a rule are green.

There is tremendous variation in the structure of flowers, which is the reason why the systematic classification of plants is based on the flower structure. It is unusual for a plant to bear only one flower. Where the flowers occur in groups, we speak of racemes, spikes, umbels and heads. In composite flowers (*Compositae*) the variously shaped florets – the rays (outer) and the tubular florets (inner) – share a common receptacle.

The leaves are arranged on the side of the stem, the youngest growing at the tip. The leaves are positioned in a certain way and are limited in size. Within these limits practically anything is possible.

The amount of water given off by leaves varies. Evaporation is partly determined by the pores (see adjoining sketch), organs which are usually found on the underside of the leaf. These are capable of opening or closing. In some cases there might be several hundreds per square millimetre.

In forest plants the leaves are shaped and positioned in such a way that they receive the maximum amount of light. Although encouraging evaporation, this is no drawback in a shady wood. Desert plants do everything in their power to restrict the surface of their leaves to a minimum. They may, for instance, adopt a spherical shape, such as with cacti.

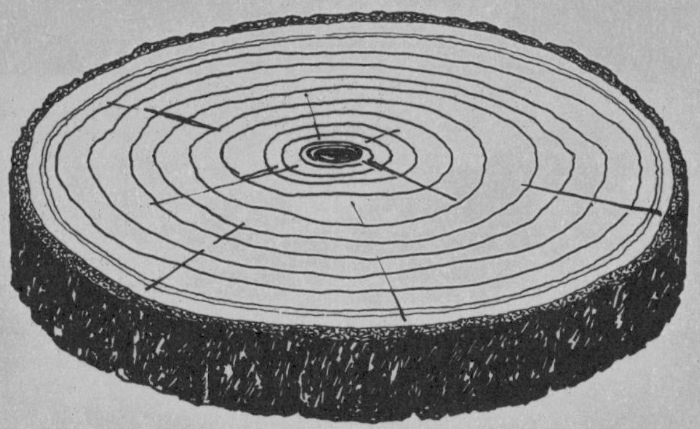

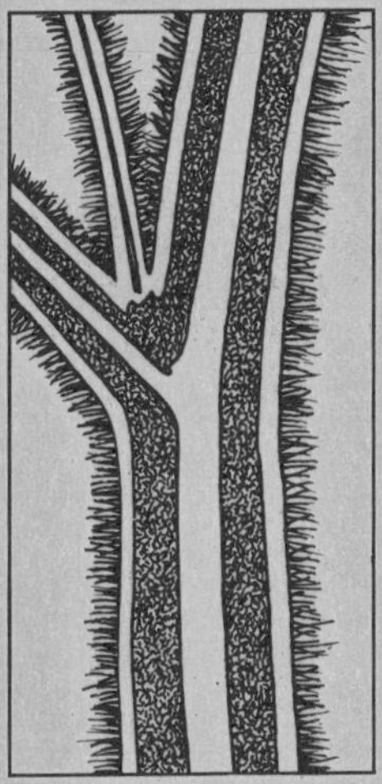

The stem of house plants may be woody or herbaceous. On the left you see a section of a mature woody stem. It is protected by its bark, under which is the bast, which looks after the transport of the descending sap. The next layer is the cambium. This layer is only one cell in depth, but it forms the heart of any woody plant, for it produces new bast on the outside and new wood on the inside. This explains the thickening of stems.

Nearer the centre is to be found the sap wood – young wood formed in most recent years. Rising sap moves mainly through the vascular bundle of last year's wood. The very centre consists of a dead core which supports the older plants.

In herbaceous plants (see adjoining sketch) the firmness of the stems is determined mainly by the cell tension (turgor). No wood is formed; the stems are annual.

The root anchors the plant and absorbs the nutrients. Roots never have leaves and always grow in accordance with gravity, occurring in all shapes and sizes. A well-developed mature plant has a very long root system – perhaps up to a few kilometres (a mile or two) in length! Plants which are obliged to search for their water and food at great depths have a long, straight taproot.

Far left on this page you see the kind of root system possessed by many house plants. Next to it a bulb, not a root in itself, but actually an abbreviated stem with underground leaves. Third from left, a rhizome or rootstock, that is, a thickened horizontal underground stem with roots on its lower side. Right, a corm, the swollen extremity of the stem (begonia, caladium) or an enlarged root (gloriosa). Annual corms are swollen stem bases each producing only one bud (crocus, gladiolus).

Light

The external conditions essential to the life of a plant are called growth factors. They are light, temperature, water, humidity, periods of rest and nourishment. The first four factors are reflected in the symbols found in the plant descriptions. In the case of house plants the growth factors can be controlled to a large extent. It is therefore important to know something about them and for that reason we shall deal with them in some detail.

Light is indispensable to the life of all green plants. On the preceding pages you have read about the function of light (photosynthesis), and on page 47 you can see how plants will grow under artificial light. In the following paragraphs we shall study what can be achieved with daylight.

What is light?

Light is a form of energy. This energy may be transformed into heat – for example, with mirrors or with lenses. From the point of view of physics, light is a wave motion with a very small wavelength, measured in nanometres: one millionth of a millimetre. The wavelength of visible light varies between 380 and 780 nanometres.

Daylight is usually perceived as white light, but in the morning and in the evening more of the red content is visible. White light is composed of all the colours of the rainbow, between infrared and ultraviolet. The bluer the light, the shorter the wavelength.

Thus the composition of light varies in the course of the day. Nor is the energy of light evenly distributed over the spectrum. The human eye is especially sensitive to yellow-greenish hues, but for the purpose of photosynthesis plants depend chiefly on the red rays, although all wavelengths in the visible spectrum are necessary for good and regular growth.

Measuring intensity

Nature is somewhat wasteful with sunlight. At most 3 per cent of the total light energy is used for photosynthesis. The rest is lost in reflection (a good thing, too, because otherwise we would not be able to see anything in nature!), or is transformed into heat or passes through the leaf.

The light falling on a certain area is measured in lux. This unit is based on the sensitivity of the human eye. The spectral sensitivity of plants is entirely different. To the human eye an orange-red neon light has a low light yield. Measured in lux the quantity of light is low. But this neon light is very suitable for plant irradiation. The energy value is consequently much greater than might be concluded from the number of lux. If, therefore, the illumination power of various light sources (sunlight, incandescent bulb, fluorescent tubes or sodium light) is compared, this point must be taken into account. So the lux measurement gives incomplete information about the energy which the plant can draw from the light source.

This chapter will be restricted to determining the strength of daylight and we shall therefore continue to use lux as the unit of measurement. Around noon on a sunny day in May or June between 160,000 and 320,000 lux may be measured near the window. The minimum at which an exceptionally strong house plant can survive in winter in a dark corner of the room is 700 lux. The level of light with which we have to deal in practice lies between these two values: 1000 lux in winter to 5000 lux in summer. Evidently a wide range, but it should be borne in mind that the level of light diminishes with the square of the distance from the light source. This means that at twice the distance from the window the light decreases four

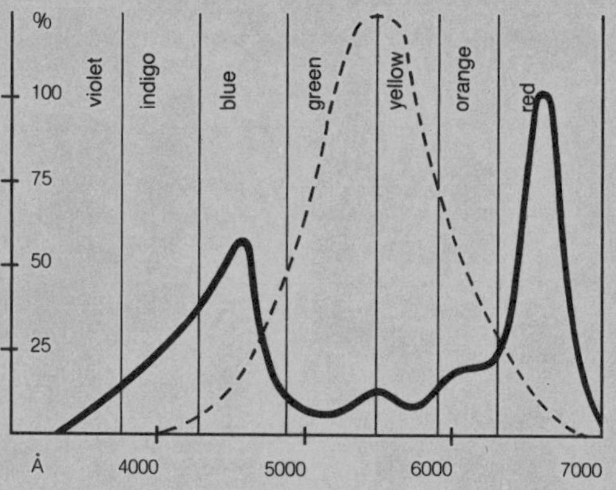

Sensitivity of the human eye (dotted line) and of the plant (solid line) to various wavelengths of light are not identical

Full sun. This plant tolerates unscreened sunlight as it passes through a south-facing window

Screened sunlight. Plenty of light is desirable, but between 10 a.m. and 5 p.m. the plant must be screened from bright sunlight

Less light required. This plant can grow without sun, but should not be put in too dark a position

The intensity of light decreases as the square of the distance to the light source. So if you move a plant twice as far from the window, say from 1 to 2 m (3 to 6 ft), it will receive only one quarter of the original light

An exposure meter (which may be built into a camera) can be used to check the strength of light more accurately than the human eye. Adjust the exposure meter to 50 ASA and 1/125 second. Measure the light reflected by a piece of clear white cardboard held close to the plant. The result is given as an opening of the diaphragm. The scale is approximately as follows:
f 16–22: full sun (approx. 160,000 to 320,000 lux)
f 8–11: screened daylight (approx. 40,000 to 80,000 lux)
f 4–5.6: less light (approx. 10,000 to 20,000 lux)
f 2.8: little light (approx. 5000 lux)
Take measurements in May or June, at noon on a clear day

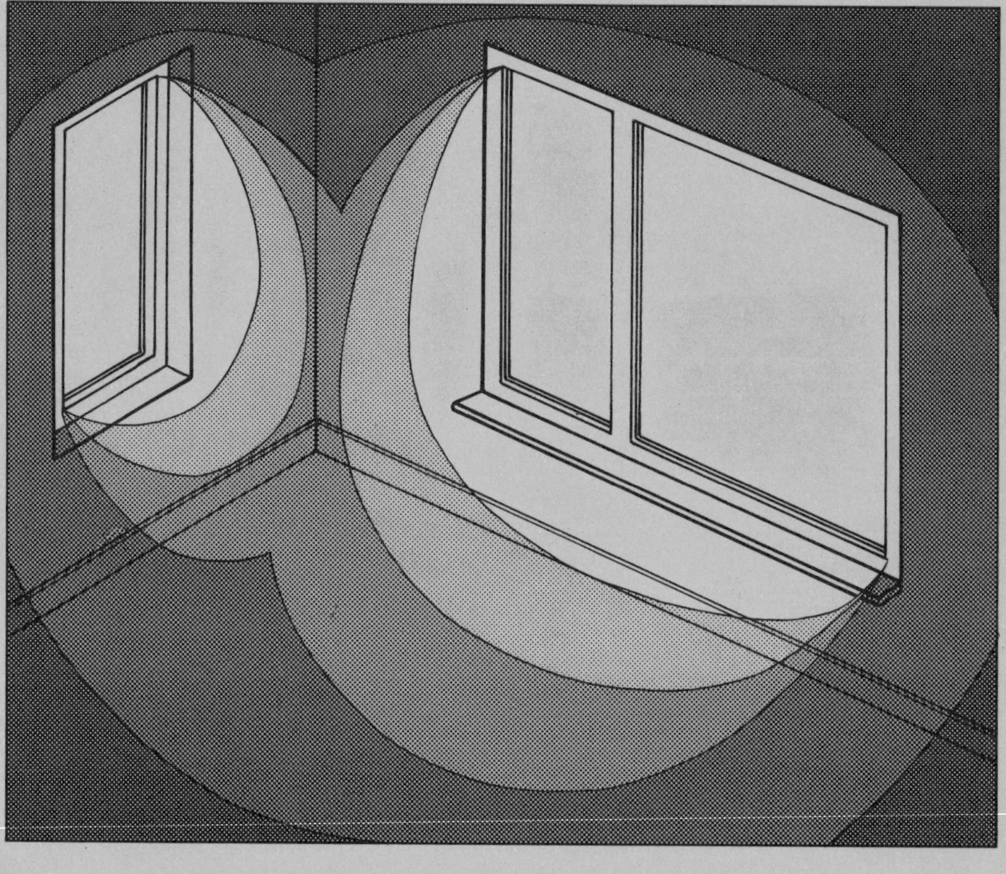

times. Because of the correcting effect of the iris this is not obvious to the eye, but this law of physics is easily demonstrated with a light meter or an exposure meter.

Screening

The light can be too strong only if there is direct exposure to the sun. Plants marked ◐ or ● cannot tolerate it, especially between 10 a.m. and 5 p.m. when the sun is really hot. Sunlight may be tempered in several ways. The popular Venetian blind with adjustable horizontal slats is very satisfactory. Awnings on the outside of the window have the advantage of keeping out much of the heat at the same time.

Net curtains also form a good protection, the effectiveness varying with the density of the weave. Small plastic screens are available, which can be inserted between the plant and the window.

The use of tinted or other protective glass is not so good for plants. In winter or in dark weather they cause light deficiency for plants at some distance from the window. It is also important to make sure that tinted glass does not filter out that portion of the spectrum which plays a part in photosynthesis.

In cloudy weather and in winter screening is unnecessary, but since the clouds may disappear while you are away it is better to be safe than sorry and to close the blinds or the net curtains.

It would be ideal for the plants if automatic screening was installed. Net curtains can, in fact, be closed automatically by means of a switch activated by a photocell.

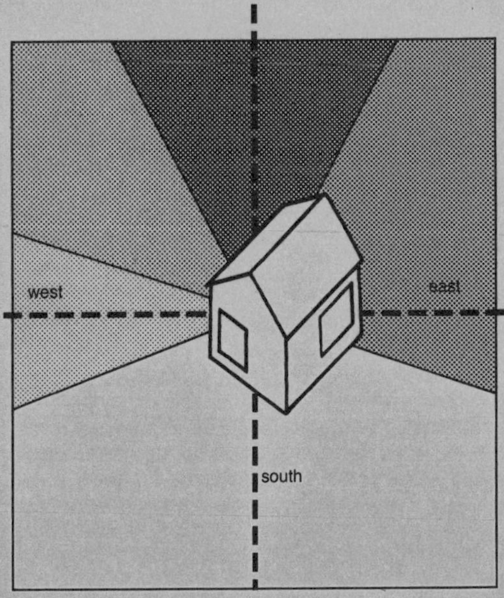

An unscreened window with southern exposure is only suitable for plants marked with the symbol ○. If screening is provided between 10 a.m. and 5 p.m., plants under category ◐ may also be grown here

An east-facing window is quickly heated in the morning. It will receive sunlight until about 11 a.m. and remains reasonably light for the rest of the day. Ideal for plants marked with the symbol ◐, but plants marked ● should be placed at a short distance from the window

A west-facing window receives approximately the same amount of light as one facing east, but it is a disadvantage that the sun only arrives towards the evening. Suitable for plants marked ◐

A north window is ideal for all plants with the symbol ●, provided there is no large tree nearby. Two metres (6 ft) from the window the light is insufficient for practically all plants

Variations of the astronomical length of the day for a latitude of 37 degrees north. The long day begins in April (more than 12 hours of light) and the short day does not begin until the end of September (less than 12 hours of daylight)

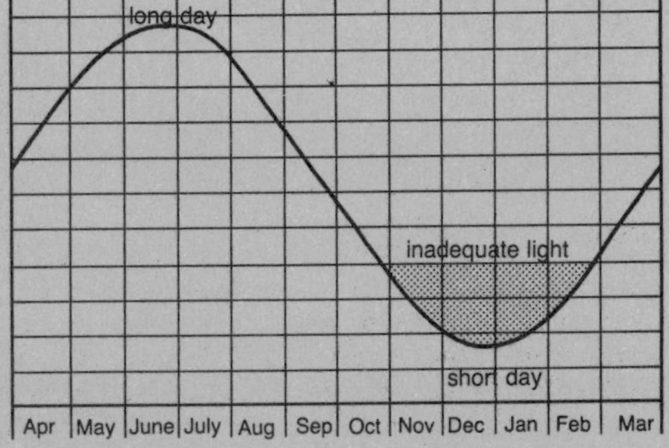

Errors in lighting

House plants are often placed in a position where there is too much light or it is too dark. To help clarify this, each plant description is accompanied by a symbol indicating the level of light required, and a method for measuring the light is suggested. It may be a good idea to look at a few examples.

Poor light It is a mistake to position a plant merely for its decorative effect. It is important to consider whether the plant feels happy in a certain place; if it does, it will look right there. For uninhabitable corners you can use disposable plants, such as ferns, which may survive there up to four months. Never put your beautiful permanent house plants in such a position, for they will wither away.

As noted above, a light value of 1000 lux in winter and 5000 lux in summer is about the minimum for a very strong foliage plant such as an aspidistra or *Cissus rhombifolia*. Flowering plants and most other foliage plants – certainly the variegated species – need considerably more light. If a plant is placed in poor light immediately after purchase, it will usually lose its leaves. The remaining leaves turn darker; the plant attempts to form more chlorophyll in an effort to increase photosynthesis. You will also notice that the leaves stretch towards the light. That they turn towards the window is normal, but something is wrong if they really become drawn out. When a plant behaves in an unusual manner, measure the illumination to see if light deficiency may be the cause.

Strong light Only excessive sunlight can be harmful to a plant. This becomes obvious when the foliage turns a much paler green, in extreme cases even yellowish. Very few plants tolerate full sunlight without being damaged. Even cacti can scorch in spring on unexpectedly bright days. Later, when they have become accustomed to the light, most cactus species can remain in full sun. On the whole other succulents also support sunlight well. Check with the sun symbol given for each species. When you suspect sun damage, move the plants a little further from the window, or – even better – provide adequate screening in the form of Venetian blinds, net curtains or awnings.

Turning the plant Certain plants won't tolerate being turned. They are used to a certain light angle, and if it suddenly comes from a different direction, the stems have to stretch to such a degree that the buds drop. Such problems occur only when plants bear flowers or buds. Leaves have a much greater facility to twist and turn. By marking the pot with a matchstick or a pencil mark it is easy to remember which side normally faces the light. Azaleas, camellias, gardenias, hoyas and jointed cacti are particularly sensitive in this respect.

Day length and flowering

Like chickens who go to roost when the day has ended, plants also have a built-in mechanism which keeps them informed about the length of the day. In many cases this – that is, the number of hours of light – determines whether or not flower buds will be formed. Three groups may be distinguished:

Short-day plants These form flower buds when they have had up to 12 hours of light a day over a certain period.

Long-day plants These flower when light has been available over a certain period for more than 12 hours a day.

Indifferent plants The length of day does not affect the formation of flower buds.

If you want a short-day plant to continue to grow because it is thought to be too young to flower, you must see that it gets at least 12 hours of light per day. As soon as the plant has developed sufficiently, the light supply can be reduced to a maximum of 12 hours per day (usually only 10 hours), and after a week or so it will form flower buds. Once these have appeared the length of the day no longer matters.

Well-known short-day plants are Indian azaleas, large-flowered begonias, indoor chrysanthemums, kalanchoes, Christmas Cacti and zygocactus.

The following plants will flower when they have had at least 12 but preferably 14 hours of light per day: *Campanula isophylla* (Star of Bethlehem), epiphyllum (leaf cactus), pelargoniums (geraniums), sinningias (gloxinias), stephanotis and many others. It is interesting to know that the kind of light is unimportant. Incandescent lamps are of little use for photosynthetic purposes (see page 49), but they are quite satisfactory for lengthening the day. Thus you may find that a simple Star of Bethlehem, which during December and January has received each evening about 8 hours of light from a small bedside lamp (30 lux is sufficient), will come into full flower in March. It is true that the leaf will be yellowish, because in this type of light the plant cannot photosynthesise properly, but the effect of the lengthening of the day on early flowering has been clearly demonstrated.

The flowering of both long-day plants and short-day plants may be affected by a slight interruption of the darkness at night. There is a story about a chrysanthemum grower who never succeeded in inducing his plants to develop buds. It turned out that the street lighting, although weak, was strong enough to lengthen the day artificially and keep his chrysanthemums in the vegetative state.

In commercial plant growing the determination of the moment of flowering by means of darkness or artificial illumination has become very important. Millions of potted plants and enormous quantities of cut flowers are cultivated in such a way that they flower at times different from those intended by nature. Everyone knows the small potted chrysanthemums. A well-planned schedule makes it a simple matter to induce them to flower in spring or summer. The same applies to poinsettias, which are now grown in large numbers at all times of the year. Numerous other plants will no doubt follow.

Whether this should be regarded as progress or as a shameful squandering of energy is a matter of personal opinion.

There is evidently a direct connection between the length of day and the periods of rest, a subject which we shall examine in more detail. Temperature also plays an important part in the formation of flower buds. When the plant will flower is not only determined by the length of the day. To achieve the desired results certain temperature requirements must also be met. For some plants the temperature must be high and the day short; others require the reverse, and there are many permutations in between. It is the task of research institutes to find the exact requirements of each individual plant.

Temperature

The plants we grow in our homes or in the greenhouse originate in very varying climatic regions. Many of them come from the tropical rain forest, where the temperature is relatively high and constant. Others originate in mountainous regions, where it may be very hot during the day, while the temperature drops sharply at night and in winter. In addition there are other extremes in temperature in native environments.

In general it may be said that a plant grows and flowers best where the natural conditions can be imitated as far as possible – and this applies not only to the temperature. Everyone knows that a Flamingo Flower (*Anthurium scherzerianum*) cannot be grown in an unheated conservatory, but errors are frequently made with plants which actually like a cool environment. They are placed in too warm a position.

Throughout this book a great deal of attention has been paid to the ideal temperatures at which individual plants can be grown. To begin with the original habitat of practically all the plants is mentioned, and in addition one or two of the symbols accompanying each of the plant descriptions refer to the temperature.

Interpretation of symbols

It was not easy to establish the correct temperature criteria, for in its natural habitat no plant enjoys a constant degree of warmth. It is for instance logical that the temperature is higher when the sky is clear, except, of course, at night, when the temperature everywhere is nearly always lower than during the day. Then there are the seasons – winters are always colder than summers. And finally there are the marginal temperatures: the extremes between which plants will thrive. So there are really three scales to take into account:

day – night
summer – winter
minimum – maximum.

From among these options we have selected the minimum night temperature in summer (which is usually the growing season), and that for the following reasons.

Daytime temperatures are unpredictable especially in summer, since they are so greatly dependent on our climate. In full sun, during a heatwave, you might find the temperature among your plants behind the window to be as high as 40°C (104°F). Most plants will tolerate this, especially because in such conditions there is sufficient light to allow them to photosynthesise, a process which is at a high pitch in such circumstances. But on a cool, overcast summer's day, the temperature in the living-room will not exceed 20°C (68°F) – a 100 per cent difference. And yet the plant will continue to thrive, so great are its powers of adaptation. Thus day temperature is an unsatisfactory standard.

In winter many plants require a cooler environment than in summer. In general this applies to plants which grow only in plenty of light (that is, in summer). Other plants, on the other hand, continue to grow in winter, although more slowly.

The minimum night temperature in summer is therefore the best choice. The temperature symbols are interpreted below.

You may wonder whether a minimum night temperature of 3°C (37°F) occurs in our summers, but if you interpret the word 'summer' as 'growing period' you will realise that in May or September this level is often reached. The plants included in the last category will cope with this temperature.

Warm conditions. Minimum night temperature in summer 16 to 20°C (60 to 68°F).

Moderate warmth. Minimum night temperature in summer 10 to 16°C (50 to 60°F).

Cool conditions. Minimum night temperature in summer 3 to 10°C (37 to 50°F).

Variations in temperature

In general excessive temperature fluctuations during the day are bad for plants. They grow better in an even temperature.

However, they often appreciate a slightly cooler environment at night. The needs of various plants vary to some extent but there has not been sufficient research done on this subject. Probably a drop in temperature assists the changeover from photosynthesis to respiration (see page 50), resulting in healthier plants. It is a fact that nearly all house plants will *tolerate* a lower temperature at night, so it is possible to make considerable economies in the heating of rooms and greenhouses (see also page 24). The thermostat may safely be turned down by 4 to 6°C (7 to 11°F) or more – see the interpretation of the symbols. It will be obvious that plants marked ⊖ will tolerate a greater drop in temperature than those marked ⊜.

In winter the difference between day and night temperature may at times be too great, especially for plants which require a cool environment in winter – say at 5°C (41°F). If the sun shines in the day time, the room must be ventilated to prevent the mercury rising to 15°C (59°F) or more, otherwise the plants might think that their resting period has come to an end and put out new shoots, which will only shrivel up at a later stage.

In winter some plants may suffer from the cold at night. Although the thermostat may safely be turned down a few degrees, if curtains are drawn and a plant is left behind them beside a single-glazed east-facing window, the temperature surrounding it may fall to as low as 5°C (41°F) and this may be altogether too much. If this could happen in your house, remember at least to move warmth-loving plants, such as an anthurium, away from the window at night, inside the curtains, or at least provide some form of insulation (such as foil or newspaper). As a general rule plants which require a high night temperature in summer shouldn't be kept too cold in winter, either.

Mistakes in temperature control

Many plants are kept at the wrong temperature with the result that they do not flower well or – even worse – pine away. Perhaps in the first place the temperature is too high in winter. This point is dealt with under the heading 'Rest periods' on page 60. Then there are the numerous plants which should not be grown in a warm living-room at all, but are intended for cool corridors, entrance halls, stairwells or even the garden (aucuba is one such plant). This cannot be easily deduced from the symbols and so this important point is included in the text. A plant will not usually suffer from too high a temperature; it will only die if the interior temperature reaches 44°C (111°F). As long as there is moisture for evaporation, this will not easily happen.

At night, the temperature on a narrow window-sill behind closed curtains may fall sharply, especially in winter. It will depend on the plant species whether this may be harmful. If the window is double-glazed, the temperature variation will be far less

A plant is more likely to be damaged by cold. The hardiest indoor plants will tolerate a few degrees of frost. In that case it is important to thaw them out slowly, for instance by dousing them with ice-cold water until the temperature has risen to just above zero. Then there is the category of plants which must be kept just above freezing point. This is a very large group to which nearly all succulents belong.

The minimum temperature tolerated by the most sensitive greenhouse plants may be as high as 18°C (64°F); hence the minimum temperature indicated for a hothouse is at that level. For many well-known house plants the critical level is 10 to 12°C (50 to 53°F); a pandanus kept for 48 hours at below 11°C (52°F), for example, will not survive, even though it may be two months before it finally dies. An anthurium may in fact be damaged if it is transported in an unheated van in winter.

Standing your plants outside

Whether your plants can safely be put outside is determined in the first place by the minimum night temperature. In general only those plants marked with the symbol ⊖ can be placed outside without problems. However, they should not be moved too early: about the beginning of June, provided the weather is mild. They must be brought indoors before the onset of night frosts, which may be as early as mid-September. All tub plants not only can, but in fact should, live out of doors in summer in order to thrive.

Soil temperature

When checking the temperature you should, for the sake of interest, occasionally take the temperature of the compost as well. If the pot is placed near a single-glazed east-facing window you will be amazed how low it is. And since (note above) the absorption of water through the roots is proportionate to the temperature of the compost, it is advisable to keep an eye on it. In a clay pot, in which water evaporates through the wall, the temperature of the compost will always be one or two degrees lower than in a plastic pot. To keep the compost a little warmer some form of bottom heat might be provided, for instance by extending the window-sill out over the central heating radiator, as is often done. At one time tub plants, such as the oleander, were sometimes placed over a heating grill in winter. Today it is easier to supply bottom heat, possibly by means of an electric soil-warming cable.

The effect on bud formation

It is not only the length of the day which may affect bud formation, temperature also plays an important part. Some plants, for instance succulents, develop buds when exposed for a certain length of time to a low temperature. If cacti are kept too warm in winter they will produce few if any flowers in summer. Chrysanthemums, on the other hand, will not develop buds unless kept at a minimum temperature 16°C (60°F). Once the flower buds have formed at a low temperature, as in the case of the Easter Cactus (*Rhipsalidopsis gaertneri*), more warmth may be provided, after which the flowers will develop further.

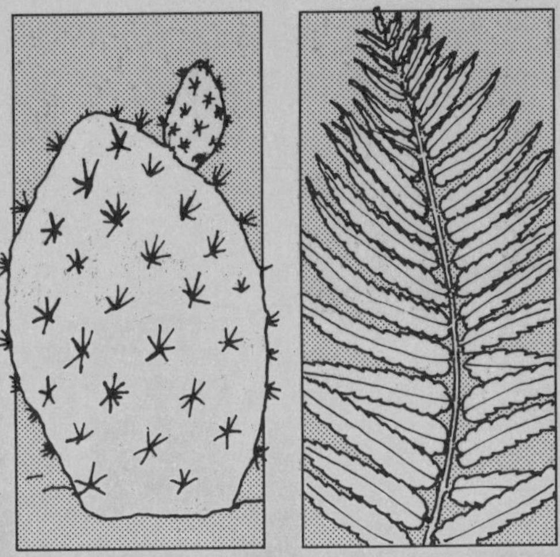

Two extremes of evaporation. **Left** A cactus with its protective epidermis and water storage capacity, entirely adapted to minimum water requirement. **Right** A fern with its large leaf surface and no water storage ability; a structure which ensures maximum evaporation

Constantly moist. The compost must never be allowed to dry out, but must contain some air. No water should therefore be left at the bottom in the saucer or pot cover and the pots should be well drained. Plastic pots are preferable to clay

Moderately damp. Allow the soil to dry out between watering, but do not allow it to become so dry that the foliage droops. Should this happen, the pot must immediately be plunged in water and the foliage will then revive. Use plastic or red clay pots, well drained

Fairly dry. Water moderately and only when it is warm. Many plants in this category are kept entirely dry during the dormant season (winter). Plastic or red clay pots must be exceptionally well drained

Moisture

No plant can live long without water. As we have seen, a plant only absorbs nutrient elements if diluted with a great deal of water. The plant itself, moreover, consists largely of water.

To absorb water it is practically always necessary for parts of the plant, usually the roots, to be in contact with it. One well-known exception to this rule is the tillandsia which hangs rootless from trees and 'lives on air'.

Water evaporates from the plant mainly through the pores in the leaves. Other parts are protected against drying out by a cork membrane, the cuticle. The plant is capable of controlling its own evaporation by opening or closing its pores. Plants growing in dry areas have fewer pores than those in wetter regions, and are also constructed in such a way that little moisture is lost. On the other hand they can absorb and store a great deal. Take, for instance, a cactus.

When the amount of water lost through evaporation is greater than that which the roots can absorb, the turgescence (tension) of the cells decreases, with the result that the various parts of the plant will droop and wither. This occurs especially in plants requiring a lot of water, such as the hydrangea.

What the plant tells you

The appearance of a plant often indicates how much water it needs. With a little experience you will soon be able to judge. It is, for instance, obvious that most cacti, being desert plants, need very little water. Overwatering is the easiest way to kill them. As a rule plants with thick, leathery leaves are also satisfied with little water, but where the foliage is delicate, pale green and feathery, for example in ferns, you may be sure that a great deal of moisture will be lost through evaporation and will have to be replenished.

Watering for growth

It is also apparent that the water consumption of a plant is dependent on its growth. Dry bulbs and tubers which have not yet started into growth need no water: in fact, it might cause them to rot. Take, for instance, an amaryllis bulb. In the first few days after potting the compost must be kept just slightly moist, so that the plant will realise that its resting period is at an end and will start to put down roots. As the flower stem develops, however, evaporation begins, and since the plant is usually kept in a very warm position during this time, some degree of evaporation will also take place through the pot-wall and the compost, so a little more water will be needed. Once plenty of foliage has developed, the factory will really get going and several cupfuls of water will be needed every day.

The opposite applies when we drastically cut down a plant, such as, for instance, a *Begonia semperflorens*. A great deal of foliage is lost in the process, considerably reducing the evaporating surface. If you continue to water as before the compost will soon become a morass. The balance between the root system and the foliage must always be maintained. Once this balance has been disturbed you must adjust the watering accordingly.

Evaporation

Evaporation is directly related to the surrounding temperature. We drink more water on a warm day, and the same applies to plants. On a rainy day, plants near a window may need only half a cupful of water, but when the sun comes through they may lose so much moisture through evaporation that the pot will easily take three cupfuls. Any system in which a plant receives the same amount of water every day is therefore wrong in principle. Watering should always be in accordance with the plant's needs. It is because these needs are frequently misunderstood that so many errors in watering are made.

A question of judgement

Based on touch it is possible to distinguish five stages between dry and wet compost: cork dry, fairly dry, moderately damp, very damp and soaking wet. It is difficult to establish these terms as standard, since practice has shown that everybody has different ideas about what constitutes 'moderately dry' compost.

However, some form of classification is essential for there is no doubt that, while one plant likes moderately moist compost, another prefers to be kept fairly dry. In this book therefore standard terms are expressed in symbols accompanying each plant description. Since the extremes of cork-dry and soaking wet compost are rarely wanted, only three symbols have been chosen. For the explanation of the symbols see above.

But there are a few cases where cork-dry and soaking wet compost is applicable. During their resting period in winter most cacti and other succulents are kept completely dry at a temperature not exceeding 10°C (50°F). It is in fact possible to leave these plants without a drop of water from the end of October to the end of February, provided the temperature is kept very low. Various semi-succulents, for instance geraniums (*Pelargonium* species and varieties) tolerate this treatment as well. Some people remove these plants from their pots, shake off the soil and hang them in bundles in a cool, frost-free dark cellar. In February the plants prove to have survived.

Soaking wet compost is also required in a few cases, such as a number of water plants grown as house plants. The well-known Umbrella Plant (cyperus) is an example. The pot must be kept in a saucer constantly filled with water, something that would mean certain death for nearly all other plants. These exceptional conditions are always indicated in the text.

Moisture control

The important question is how to establish with certainty whether the compost in the pot is on the dry or the damp side. Clearly for many people this presents a difficulty. The best test of all is your own forefinger, which is always to hand! If you push it into the compost to a depth of about 1 cm (½ in) you should, with a little experience, be able to determine the degree of moisture there fairly reliably.

Another method is to estimate the weight of the pot holding the plant. Lift it up: if it feels lighter than usual it probably means that it needs watering. This method requires familiarity with the weights of individual plants and is not really a very reliable system.

Where clay pots are used, you can hear if it is dry by rapping the pot with a hard object. The colour of the pot will also betray whether it is damp or dry.

A great deal less subjective, and much more practical in use, are the hygrometers, now more generally available. These instruments work on the principle of the different degrees of electric conductivity of wet and dry soil. The drier the compost, the lower its conductivity. The dial of the instrument indicates dry – moist – wet, values which conform fairly well to the terms used in this book.

Another gadget ticks softly when the pins are inserted into the compost. The faster it ticks, the wetter the compost.

If after some practice you find you are still quite unable to gauge the moisture content of a pot with a forefinger, you could invest in an aid of this kind. Even if you save only a few plants the expense is soon recovered.

In the deep plastic plant cylinders now sometimes used the dampness of the compost can be difficult to establish. Water can easily collect in the bottom, especially when the pots are tall, which is very harmful to the root system. You can, of course, cover the bottom with a layer of crocks, but this only works so long as the water level doesn't rise above them. Deceptively, the compost in such impervious containers quickly appears dry on the surface, and the pins of a moisture meter are only about 10 cm (4 in) long so do not indicate the situation lower down.

A solution has been found for cylinders of this kind, too. First of all a 5- to 10-cm (2- to 4-in) layer of gravel or crocks is placed at the bottom of the container, and a plastic tube stood on top of it, reaching just to the top of the container. The pot should now be filled with compost and the plant inserted. By looking into the tube or by inserting a stick you will be able to establish whether water has collected at the bottom over the level of the crocks. If this is the case, you should immediately stop watering until the compost at the bottom has dried out. A clever handyman could insert a small cork float at the bottom of the tube, attached to a length of firm red flex. Then when the cork floats, you are warned by the flex appearing at the top of the tube.

Water temperature

The minimum temperature at which plants are capable of absorbing water from the soil varies considerably between individual species. For most tropical plants it lies between 10 and 15°C (50 and 59°F). Reindeer moss, on the other hand, which grows in polar regions, can absorb water at a temperature far below zero. For the more common house plants the minimum temperature usually lies between 5 and 10°C (41 and 50°F). The cooler the compost, the more difficult it is for these plants to absorb water. When the compost is too cold, the roots do not work, even when the moisture content is adequate.

When house plants are kept on the window-sill of a heated room, the water will quickly attain the temperature of the compost in the pot. It is advisable, however, not to give them ice-cold water; better to use tepid water.

Plants kept in a cool environment, for instance during their dormant period, require more attention. Here the water should definitely be on the warm side, up to 40°C (104°F). By the time it has reached the roots it will have cooled down considerably. The maximum temperature tolerated by the root system is approx. 45°C (113°F).

Methods of watering

Because the watering of plants can present quite a few problems, several ingenious systems have been invented to automate the process. The most important are hydroculture and semi-hydroculture systems, described on page 45. The drip system is sometimes used in greenhouses and yet another method is the capillary mat. These two procedures are dealt with on page 25.

The remaining method, the simple domestic way, is best carried out with a fairly large watering can with a long spout. Normally the plants are watered from the top, a few drops, a dash or a

Press your finger into the compost to test for dryness

Tap a clay pot lightly: the sound will indicate how dry the compost is

A moisture meter with an indicator to show how much water the compost contains

One type of moisture meter makes a sound to indicate the degree of moisture

Using a plastic tube and float to indicate an accumulation of surplus moisture in deep plastic plant cylinders, which rarely have drainage holes.

The bottom is covered with a thick drainage layer consisting of gravel or crocks. A plastic tube is inserted to about 1 cm (½in) from the base. When water collects in the pot it can be seen through the tube. If a small cork is introduced attached to a rigid wire or flex the length of the tube, it will be easily noticed when the flex rises above the level of the tube.

This method has the additional advantage that it may be used to feed the plant in a more natural way. Remove the float and fill the tube with a nutrient solution. The root system can now absorb the nutrients directly from the bottom, without their first having to penetrate a thick layer of compost, and no harmful substances can collect in the upper layer of the pot. Be careful not to give too much fertiliser, since this would do more harm than good. Half an hour later the tube should once more be dry at the bottom

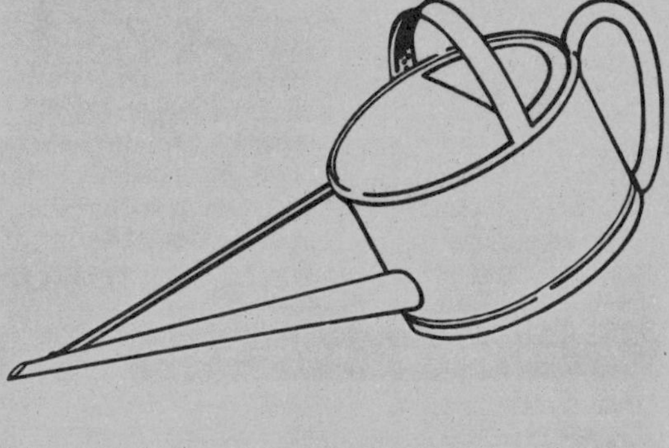

Good watering cans are difficult to find. This well-balanced model has a long spout, so that plants at the back are easily reached

Right Plants may be plunged in the kitchen sink

good dose, according to their needs (see page 55).

Water may also be given from the bottom. This method is used for plants which tend to rot (cyclamen and cacti, for example). After 15 minutes all surplus water collecting in the saucer must be poured away.

Plants requiring moderate or constant moisture may be plunged from time to time. This is a particularly useful method of watering, in which the whole soil ball is kept under water for a quarter of an hour. Numerous bubbles will rise from the top, indicating that the air in the compost is being driven out by the water. Afterwards the pot is left to drain, making room for fresh air. Plants which are given this treatment must be grown in well-draining pots with holes at the bottom, since otherwise the water cannot escape. Plunging must only be done during the growing season, when the plant can quickly dispose of excess water by evaporation.

A little fertiliser may be mixed with the plunging water. In this way nutrients rinsed away in the process are immediately replenished.

Plastic pots

Although it is generally realised that plastic is an impervious substance, a lot of plants were 'drowned' when plastic pots were first introduced. The fact that a red clay pot could cause a considerable loss of water through evaporation, sometimes even more than the plant itself, was often overlooked. A plant in a clay pot which habitually requires two cupfuls of water should perhaps need only one cupful or less when it is transferred to a plastic pot.

We are gradually getting used to the plastic pot, but it still happens only too often that plants potted in plastic are overwatered. The use of a moisture meter will avoid this error.

To be on the safe side, incorporate a good drainage layer in the pots, so that excess water can at least soak away, and be on the mean side when you water. Too much water still kills more plants than too little.

If you really cannot get used to plastic pots, go back to the good old-fashioned clay pots. Plants from category (') and possibly those from category ('') might be grown in clay pots, whereas for group (''') (constant moisture) a plastic pot is nearly always preferable.

Mistakes in watering

It cannot be too often stressed: overwatering is the error most frequently committed. Either the moisture content in the compost is not checked, or the fact that water has collected in the bottom of the pot is overlooked. This often happens when pot covers are used, but it is easily checked by lifting the inner pot from time to time. A way of checking excess water in plastic cylinders has been described on page 55 (Moisture control).

Another mistake is to water too regularly, almost automatically. If you do the rounds with the watering can every morning after breakfast, giving the same dose of water to each plant, this is fatal. All plants from groups ('') and (') like their compost to dry out occasionally. These plants should be passed over until they are ready for it. This does not mean that they should be left to dry out altogether! There may be occasions when it gets so hot in the course of the day that a little water in the afternoon is very desirable.

The above example is only one among dozens which might be mentioned. The obvious conclusion is that a genuine plant lover, living in a hard-water area (which is likely), will take some precautions.

Of course it also happens that a plant gets too little water. Again this is due to inadequate moisture checks. Sometimes the compost has become so dry that there is a space between it and the side of the pot, so that when it is watered, the water is seen to run out at the bottom. The soil ball is too dry to absorb water easily. If this is overlooked for long the plant's days are numbered. The remedy is immediate plunging to saturate the compost.

Some plants react badly to water spilled on the foliage, for instance the African Violet. The leaves will become covered in white spots. Plants with leaf shoots close to the soil must never be watered in the centre (clivias, sansevierias and aloes) for the heart will rot. Exceptions to this rule are the tubular bromeliads, which may have water poured into the tube.

Water quality

As if watering plants is not difficult enough, we also have to consider the quality of the water. The days are long past when you could cheerfully give all your plants ordinary tap water brought to room temperature. It *can* be done, of course, but most plants will not thank you for this uncharitable treatment, for very often tap water is harmful. The drinking water we carelessly consume is fine for us, but it may well be fatal to plants.

Our drinking water consists largely of waste water purified at great expense. The purification processes are only partly successful and tap water therefore still contains large quantities of salts and poisonous substances even more harmful to plants than to us. The degree of hardness is an especially serious problem, and is mainly determined by the lime and magnesium content of the water. This is clearly seen in old red clay pots which have often been watered with calcareous water, creating a thick white crust of calcium bicarbonate around the edge.

The degree of hardness of the water supply is normally expressed in parts per million (ppm), that is, parts of lime and magnesium per million parts of water. A certain degree of hardness is tolerated, and even appreciated, by most plants, but in the case of sensitive or acid-loving plants the problems start at a hardness of over 150 ppm, although a much higher degree is popularly thought to be quite acceptable.

Damage caused by tap water may show itself in increased alkalinity in the compost, particularly harmful to plants which cannot grow in alkaline soil (with a high pH value).

This is especially marked in plants indicated by the symbol (◉) which will have difficulty in absorbing iron, resulting in lack of chlorophyll in the foliage (chlorosis). It may also be seen in too high a concentration of salts in the soil ball, which causes the roots to become 'scorched', and certain chemical substances, such as phenol or fluoride, can poison the plant.

The degree of acidity is discussed in greater detail on page 62. Here we shall only give a simple but representative example. An azalea likes an acid soil with a low pH value, approximately 4 to 4.5 pH. This is why this plant is sometimes grown in pine needle compost, which is very acid. Even if the azalea is watered for five months with relatively 'soft' water with a lime content of 'only' 110 ppm, the pH of the compost will still have increased by 1.5. Since a pH value of 6 is already critical for an azalea, it will be obvious that the poor plant is on the point of dying. Imagine how quickly such a plant will be killed if given even harder water, which in many regions is no exception! (The answer is: in about two months.) This would not matter if the azalea could be regarded as a typical throw-away plant, but it is in fact an ideal plant to keep.

Excess mineral salts and calcium will be deposited on the outside of a clay pot

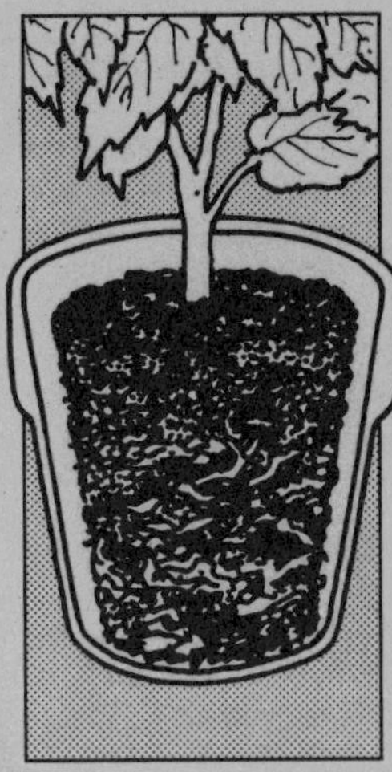

The new pot should be large enough to allow a finger to be inserted between the soil ball and the side of the pot

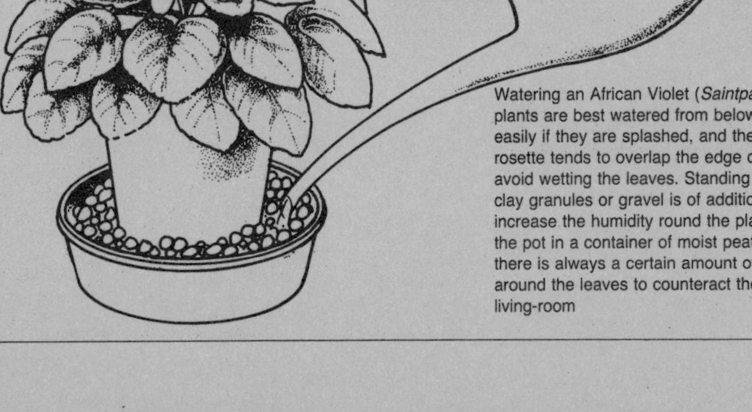

Watering an African Violet (*Saintpaulia ionantha*). These plants are best watered from below, as the hairy leaves stain easily if they are splashed, and the way in which the foliage rosette tends to overlap the edge of the pot makes it difficult to avoid wetting the leaves. Standing the pot in a saucer of inert clay granules or gravel is of additional benefit, as it helps to increase the humidity round the plant. An alternative is to bury the pot in a container of moist peat, which will ensure that there is always a certain amount of atmospheric moisture around the leaves to counteract the damaging dry air of a living-room

Clay pots

In regions where there are problems with the quality of the water, red clay pots should be banned whenever possible. Too much water is evaporated, entailing much more frequent watering and the more water that passes through the compost, the more pollution will occur. In this case therefore the plastic pot has obvious advantages, especially for acid-loving plants. Fortunately these plants usually come within the category marked (constant moisture), so the additional water-retentive powers of a plastic pot are an added advantage.

Replacing the top layer of compost

When a plant is watered from the top, harmful mineral salts will collect in the upper layers of the compost. It is in these layers that the roots frequently start to die as a result of too much salt concentration. The remedy is easy: the top layer may be removed as far as the root system, and replaced by a fresh layer of compost (or better still, peat fibre). Complete repotting, of course, is even better.

Improving the water

Many problems may be avoided by improving the quality of the tap water. Several methods are available, some of them unsuitable, but most of them yielding good results.

Let's start with the unsuitable ones. These include all those domestic water softeners which have to be rinsed with a kitchen salt solution from time to time. In the course of the softening process all 'hard' calcium and magnesium ions are replaced by sodium ions contained in the kitchen salt. This doesn't lessen the so-called carbonate hardness – the most harmful factor for sensitive plants; on the contrary to some extent it can only increase it. A great deal of misunderstanding exists on this point. There are even watering cans on the market with a built-in softener which works on this principle. They only help to kill the plants.

The best way of lowering the carbonate hardness of the water, while at the same time removing all harmful substances, is to use a demineralisation apparatus. In its simplest form this consists of a perspex tube filled with millions of minuscule grains of a synthetic material. The filtering process is based on the principle of ion exchange and provided the water passes through sufficiently slowly (about 20 litres [36 pints] an hour), the result is at least as good as once-distilled water. After a time the filling discolours and has to be replaced.

On the other hand pure distilled water is not good for your plants either. It should be mixed with ordinary tap water, the proportions depending on the desired hardness. For many plants equal parts of distilled water and tap water is satisfactory, but for very sensitive plants such as orchids 2 parts demineralised water should be mixed with 1 part tap water. The distilled water may also be used in tropical aquaria, for rare cage birds and for making tea or coffee.

Domestic remedies

If water is boiled for five minutes, the lime it contains is deposited in the form of scaling. This method can therefore be utilised for softening hard water. Pour the boiling water into a container, leave it for 24 hours and carefully pour off the clear water. Using cold tea for watering plants is based on the same principle.

There are also chemicals on the market which will cause lime to be deposited. Adding oxalic acid (which is poisonous!) or superphosphate to the water will create a cloudy, whitish deposit; the clear water may then be poured off.

Filtering water through a thick layer of ordinary peat will also remove a considerable amount of lime.

The ice deposited in refrigerators and deep freezers is practically equal to distilled water. When thawed and warmed it may be mixed with tap water and used to water plants.

Rainwater

Rainwater is soft water and in theory is therefore excellent for your plants. However, as a result of air pollution it may contain harmful elements other than mineral salts.

Unfortunately it is not easy to determine whether rainwater has been polluted or not. Occasionally an oily layer is seen on the surface, but that is not the end of it. The direction of the wind may affect pollution of the rainwater. After a long dry period the rain filling your water butt may bring down a lot of rubbish from the roof.

Provided you don't live in an industrial area it is well worth catching the rainwater coming from the roof gutters in one or more water butts. Insert a replaceable filter in the drainpipes, consisting of old nylons and plastic foam. The water butt must have a lid, and of course an overflow for surplus water. You might be able to buy an old 200-litre (44-gal) barrel. In winter the rainwater should first be warmed.

Water from a clear (that is, a biologically balanced) garden pond is also useful for watering plants. The pond is best refilled from the drainpipes. Maintaining the water level with tap water will usually encourage algae, because it contains more nutrients (phosphate among others).

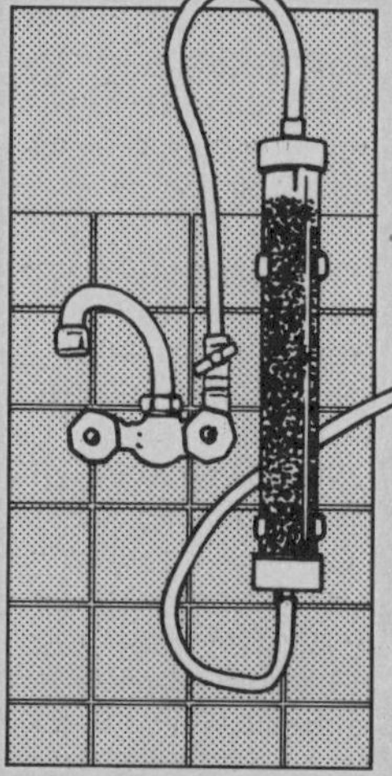

An ion exchange apparatus placed next to the tap can provide distilled water

A chemical water softener may be used to encourage lime to collect at the bottom

Atmospheric Humidity

It is not always easy to find a perfectly lit spot for a plant, but it can be done. Maintaining the correct temperature presents even greater problems. Next comes watering: as can be seen, you practically need a water factory of your own. But the most difficult factor of all is how to provide sufficient atmospheric humidity in a dry living-room. Nearly every heated room is too dry for plants and it is therefore important that something is done.

What is humidity?

When the air is saturated with water vapour, we speak of a relative humidity of 100 per cent. According to physical law, the amount of vapour which the air can contain is in direct relation to the temperature. For instance, at a temperature of 5°C (41°F), air with a relative humidity of 100 per cent contains exactly 6.8 g ($\frac{1}{4}$ oz) of water per cubic metre (cubic yard), but at a temperature of 17°C (62°F) it can hold 17.4 g ($\frac{1}{2}$ oz) of water.

This means that the relative humidity in a heated

A wooden rainwater butt, made of an old beer barrel, connected to the roof drainage and equipped with an overflow

room is lowered when cold air is admitted from outside. The relative humidity of the cold air is high, but the absolute humidity is low. (You might like to make a calculation expressed in grams.) It sounds complicated, but it is a scientific fact.

Human beings enjoy a relative humidity of between 40 and 65 per cent; for plants the range is between 40 and 90 per cent. Succulents, for instance, require a low humidity, whereas plants from tropical rain forests feel happiest when the atmospheric humidity nears the point of saturation.

Plant requirements

Whether or not a plant can live in dry air depends largely on the size and the number of its stomata (pores). If the number of stomata is large, the plant has been accustomed to live in a humid environment. Desert plants have very few pores and are, moreover, capable of closing them. Little moisture is evaporated, and that is just as well, for otherwise they would soon perish.

Most of the problems arise from our desire to grow plants which originate in a climate with a 60 to 90 per cent atmospheric humidity in a room with a humidity of 40 to 50 per cent. The structure of these plants doesn't allow them to adjust to such conditions; they are unable to close their stomata sufficiently, lose too much moisture through their foliage and shrivel up.

You can save yourself a lot of touble by not attempting to grow such plants in a warm living-room. If, however, you are determined to do so, you must increase the relative humidity, especially in winter.

Explanation of the symbols

In the plant descriptions each species is marked with a symbol indicating its humidity requirements. The symbols are explained below.

Heating methods and humidifiers

Some people maintain that in the past the atmospheric humidity in our living rooms was more favourable because moisture is released when coal or oil is burned. However, this was of little benefit to plants, for an ordinary stove takes in air at the bottom and discharges it up the chimney. The moisture released in combustion disappears together with the smoke. The greater humidity was mainly due to the fact that near the window, where most plants are kept, the air was cooler, and the relative humidity therefore higher.

Modern methods of heating, usually based on the circulation of warm water, generally mean that radiators are placed under the windows and the warm air rising among the plants is relatively dry.

Another system used in homes and offices is hot-air heating. A small amount of the air in the building is usually exchanged for outside air to provide ventilation. This may be agreeable for human beings, but it is unpleasant for plants, because the available air becomes drier and drier. Fortunately humidifiers may be incorporated in this system (see next column) and the use of such an apparatus is highly advisable.

Increasing relative humidity

There are many ways in which relative atmospheric humidity can be increased.

A large number of plants in one room will together cause a relatively great amount of moisture to evaporate. Be careful not to lose the moisture by over-ventilation!

Big plant containers with a substantial area of damp moss or peat will also create a certain amount of evaporation, especially when there is warmth at the bottom, such as with a large container placed above a radiator.

A plate filled with water placed under the plants, or a large, water-filled bowl will provide increased humidity in the immediate vicinity. The plate must not be too small and the plant must not have its feet in water. This system is sometimes called the deep-plate method.

Wiping the foliage with a damp sponge will help for a short time, until the water has evaporated.

Spraying is better, especially if done frequently. There are plant lovers who spray as often as ten times a day and the result is soon visible. Use very soft water for this purpose, for otherwise unsightly blotches of lime deposit will stain the leaves.

Water containers hung on the radiators are somewhat out of date; it is now realised that they have practically no effect. In a normal-sized room 5 to 10 litres (1 to 2 gal) of water should evaporate in the course of the day, which means a lot of containers! And unless they are filled with distilled water ugly lime deposits will be formed, difficult to remove.

Air conditioning through the hot air system is ideal, especially when the moisture content of the air can be regulated by a hygrostat. The only disadvantage is that all rooms will be equally humid.

Water on the floor is possible where the floors are tiled, such as in a conservatory or garden room. Every evening the floor should be watered with a watering can. Where there is underfloor heating the effect will be doubled, since the water will evaporate all the quicker.

With a humidifier a rapidly revolving wheel releases the water in a very fine spray. Unfortunately the mineral salts are distributed at the same time and are deposited as a white powder on the furniture and the walls. Only distilled water should therefore be used. This kind of apparatus is electrically driven and makes a fair amount of noise.

Evaporators are stainless steel bowls, open at the top, and heated to about 90°C (194°F). Using 300 watt electricity they are capable of vaporising about 400 cc (14 fl oz) of water an hour, more than sufficient for a normal living-room. There are no moving parts and they are therefore silent in use. No harm is done if the apparatus boils dry. The mineral salts will still be deposited, but can be removed once a month with chemicals supplied with the apparatus. Since humid air feels slightly warmer than dry air, the central heating thermostat may be turned down a little if a humidifier is used, and the running costs and even the price of the apparatus are therefore soon recovered by the fuel saved.

In isolated areas the atmospheric humidity is easily increased; see the section on greenhouses on page 25. In glass plant cases and enclosed flower windows (pages 20 and 26), too, the atmosphere remains more humid, provided there is not too much ventilation.

High relative atmospheric humidity (above 60 per cent) can really only be achieved in a hothouse, a glass plant case or a flower window

Moderate relative humidity (50 to 60 per cent) can be created in a heated room provided a humidifier is used or if the plants are frequently sprayed

Low relative humidity (below 50 per cent). Plants marked with this symbol need no special treatment

A flat dish of water, with a saucer placed upside down to hold the pot just above the surface, is quite effective for small plants. The water evaporates and creates a higher degree of relative humidity around the leaves of the plant

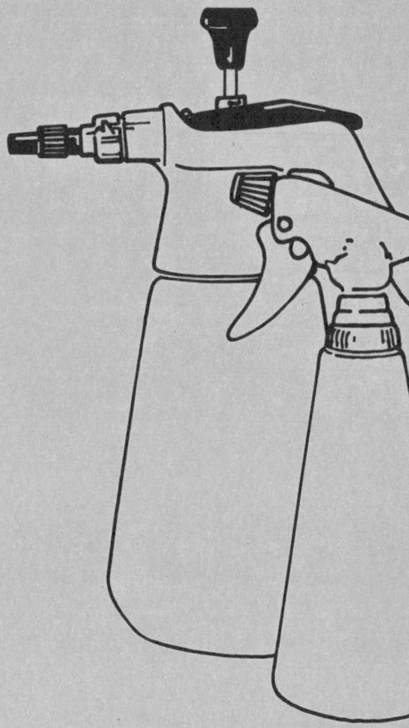

Sprays are available in all sorts of shapes. Do not use them too often on plants with hairy foliage and use softened water to avoid leaving lime deposits on the leaves

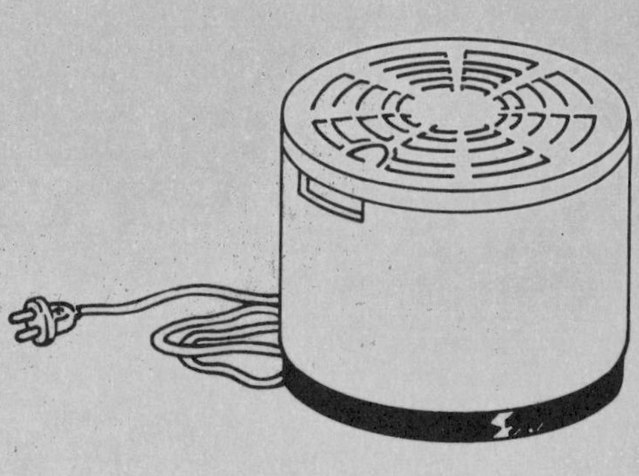

Evaporators are becoming increasingly popular. This is the most effective form of humidifier in centrally heated rooms

Rest Periods

Many of the plant entries in the dictionary section mention that a resting period is necessary. During that period to all intents and purposes growth ceases. The chief factor which leads a plant to enter upon its dormant season is the shortening day length. The number of hours of daylight is related to the process of photosynthesis (see page 50) and with it to the absorption of water and nutriments. The plant should therefore be given less water and certainly no food during its dormant period.

Since the living processes of the plant are slowed down during this time, the environment may be cooler, a few degrees in the case of some plants, dozens in others. Plants should not be kept warm during their resting season, since this would stimulate premature growth which would then be aborted by lack of light, causing the plant to become exhausted.

In general it may be stated that plants which *can* enjoy a resting period, *should* in fact have one. To mention one example: the apple tree, which during its dormant season will tolerate frost. If such a tree were transplanted to the tropics where it would not encounter frost, it would certainly continue to grow for a time, but the yield would be most unsatisfactory. All plants with leaves that fall in winter have a strict dormant season. The hydrangea, for instance, a deciduous shrub, must have a rest in winter. The fact that bulbs and tubers have organs for storing food indicates in itself that they will tolerate a resting period and they should therefore be given one, since otherwise they will gain no advantage from this capacity. Succulents also show from their fleshy stems or leaves that they may temporarily enjoy a rest (doing without water) and they should therefore be allowed one. Orchids have pseudobulbs (also a kind of reservoir) which indicate the same requirement.

If a plant which naturally needs a dormant season is denied one, undesirable leaf growth will be produced, the plant will become exhausted and bud formation will suffer. Most complaints about plants which refuse to flower may be put down to the fact that they have not been given a resting period, usually because of too high a temperature in winter.

Day length and temperature

As can be seen in the sections on 'light' and 'temperature', these two growth factors play an important part in the growing cycle of the plant. Lack of light, or rather, shortening hours of daylight, indicate to long-day plants that it is time to stop flowering and start their dormant period. Short-day plants, on the other hand, flower when there are fewer hours of daylight; these plants flower in winter and have their growing season in spring or summer.

Temperature has a similar effect on the development of flower buds. Some plants develop buds at a high temperature, others when it is cooler. By controlling these two factors, length of day and temperature, we can initiate the dormant season ourselves. However, it is more usually left to nature.

If a certain plant requires a resting period at some time or other, when it should be kept cooler and drier, this will be indicated under the plant description.

Winter quarters

Modern, centrally heated houses are less agreeable to plants than homes heated by more old-fashioned methods. Because the temperature is constant in all parts of the room, it is impossible to find a spot where the plants may be kept cool for a time. To save fuel, and to make ourselves more comfortable, we are constantly improving the insulation of our houses, to the disadvantage of our plants. At one time it was possible to grow a cyclamen in the living-room, at least near the window, for it likes a cool environment. Double glazing combined with central heating has increased the temperature near the window – fine for us, but fatal to the cyclamen. It is extraordinary that, in a period when people are so interested in house plants, architects seldom consider the requirements of plants. Provisions for a cool, well-lit spot need not cost a lot if incorporated in the original design. It is much more difficult – and expensive – to make changes at a later stage.

If it is impossible to provide a special resting place for plants in the living-room, an unused bedroom or attic might be used for the purpose. It must be well lit. If there is a radiator in the room it would not be expensive to install a thermostat, which would enable you to control the temperature in the room fairly accurately. A thermometer will tell you whether the temperature is the correct one for the plants which spend the winter in the room.

A conservatory which is not heated in winter is an ideal spot for your plants in the dormant season, especially if it is lit from above as well as from the sides. But be sure to keep it frost free.

Other resting places

Cacti and other small house plants might spend the winter in a small lean-to greenhouse on the balcony, but the compost must be kept above freezing point with the aid of an electric soil-warming cable.

Plants can also be kept in a shed or garage, so long as there is sufficient light. With perspex skylights and extra windows such a situation becomes ideal. How marvellous it would be if this was taken into account before the house was built! An excellent 'orangery', as shown in the sketch, could be provided at little extra cost.

For some plants the cool and fairly dark environment required in winter may be provided by digging them in. This is occasionally done with fuchsias and geraniums. A large pit is dug in October and the bottom covered with a deep layer of stones to provide drainage. After the plants have been cut back a little, they are buried in the hole. They must be covered with at least 30 cm (1 ft) of soil, possibly

This adaptation of an orangery, built against a garage, is very suitable for keeping tub plants and succulents in winter. Some form of heating is necessary to keep the temperature above 5°c (41°F) and it must be possible to open the windows and the roof vents to provide ventilation

with dry leaves or bracken on top. The soil should not be damp – the drier the better. This sounds rather barbaric treatment, but in spring, at the beginning of March, most of the plants will be found to have survived. Once potted up and pruned they will soon put forth new shoots.

Plants which have their resting season in summer are best planted out in a shady spot in the garden, or left on the balcony. Remember to bring them indoors in good time. A special greenhouse is the best place for them to spend the winter where the temperature can be kept at a minimum of 5°C (41°F) (see also page 21). A greenhouse provides plenty of room and light and the temperature can be controlled as required.

Feeding

The chief nutrients necessary to enable a plant to grow are nitrogen, phosphorus, potassium and in some cases calcium. In addition minute quantities of trace elements are required, for instance iron, magnesium, zinc, molybdenum, copper, boron and chlorine. Most species require sufficient nourishment in the soil, although, unlike human beings, they absorb food from the air as well. To begin with you will usually not have to worry about lack of nutrients when you first buy a plant, but after some time the nutrients contained in the small quantity of compost will be exhausted and you will have to replenish them. The nutrient which is present in the smallest quantity will be the one to affect the growth of a plant. If it lacks nitrogen, no amount of extra phosphorus or potassium will help. Since without the necessary laboratory apparatus it is impossible to determine the food content of the compost, a composite fertiliser is generally used, in the hope that it will restore the balance between the various nutrients. And it usually does.

Above A small lean-to greenhouse on the balcony will provide a cool winter environment for quite a few plants. A small, thermostatically controlled electric heater will keep it frost free

Below A thermostat on the radiator will keep the temperature in an unused bedroom at about 5°C (41°F)

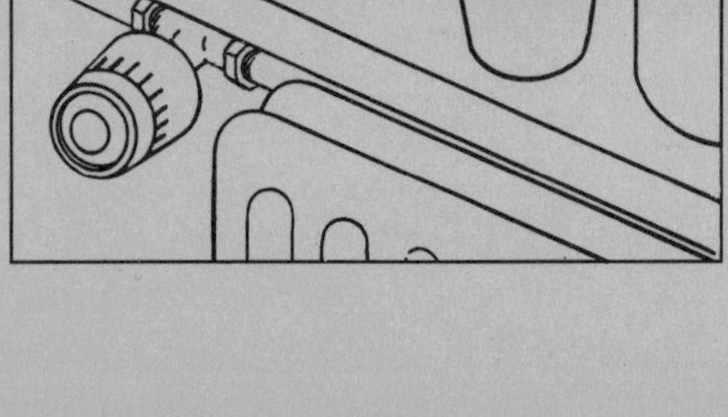

Varying requirements

The proportions of nitrogen, phosphorus and potassium present in a fertiliser are indicated by three figures; 6:4:6, for instance, provides a satisfactory balance for the average house plant. Succulents will flower better if they receive less nitrogen and the proportions should preferably be 4:7:9. There are many different combinations on the market and naturally each manufacturer maintains that his is the best.

Types of fertiliser

The preparation of a fertiliser may vary in principle, as well as its composition. There is a distinction between chemical products, usually called artificial or inorganic fertilisers, and nutrients based on organic substances (both animal and vegetable), which might be called natural or organic fertilisers. Both artificial and natural fertilisers are available in liquid as well as in solid form.

Which, you may wonder, is better for house plants, artificial or natural fertilisers? Even an advocate of 'biological gardening' who might be expected to advise using only natural manure will have to admit that where house plants are concerned there is not a great deal of difference between the two. To begin with the compost used by the grower is already saturated with chemical fertilisers. The pre-packed compost on the market is, as a rule, also based on artificial manure. But if you wish to prepare your own biologically balanced mixture (see page 62), it would be logical to use organic manure.

It is more sensible to be guided by the results achieved. It is important that the nutrients mentioned above should be present in the correct proportions and that the fertiliser should contain no harmful substances (for instance, too much chlorine), though this can occur in natural as well as in artificial fertilisers. The latter contain far more nourishment per gram than natural manure and are therefore at least ten times more economical in use. Liquid manure is more expensive than fertiliser in powdered form, for a bottle consists of more than 50 per cent pure water. It looks better, that's its only advantage.

In addition to mineral salts, natural manure also contains organic substances, favourable in themselves, but again of little importance, since most composts already have a large organic content. There is therefore little point in adding more.

To sum up, it could be said that the cheapest (that is, powder) form of artificial fertiliser is best for most house plants. Never use too high a concentration and follow the instructions. If your plants grow in biologically prepared compost, or if you dislike artificial fertilisers, then use natural manure.

Natural manure Dried cow dung is usually sold in the form of a powder or in tablets. A better product is made of dried blood, hoof and horn and bonemeal. Don't forget that this natural manure will slightly increase the pH content of the compost and should therefore not be used for pronounced acid lovers (azaleas, heaths, anthuriums and camellias). The same applies to chicken manure.

In some countries fertilisers based on seaweed are often used. In addition there is fish manure, especially popular among orchid growers.

Natural manure releases the nutrients fairly slowly. Although this is on the one hand a good thing as the roots are not easily scorched, it should be remembered that the effect on growth is delayed to some extent.

Special fertilisers Artificial fertilisers also include slow-acting types. Special chemical formulae, or fertiliser supplied in the form of slowly dissolving capsules, ensure that the effect is spread over a longer period. In this way the compost may be nourished for a whole growing season (three to four months) in one operation.

There are also liquid foliar feeds. It is true that nourishment can be absorbed through the leaves, but you must not expect miracles. The same fertiliser will also act through the root system.

When to feed

Feeding is necessary when
(a) The plant is grown in a fairly small pot.
(b) It grows very fast.
(c) You think it lacks food.

The latter usually occurs three months after repotting. Plants which have their active season in summer must be fed from June onwards. Feeding must stop in August, when the plant begins to prepare for its dormant season. Plants which grow in winter must be fed with great care. The short day enables them to assimilate little food, since they need light for the process.

To avoid root scorching always give plenty of water with the fertiliser. If the soil ball is dry, water it well before applying the fertiliser dissolved in water. With artificial fertilisers the risk of scorching the roots is greater than with slower acting natural manure.

Greedy plants, such as sinningias (gloxinias), like a little fertiliser in the water every day (half the recommended concentration or less). Slow-growing plants should be fed once a fortnight and the really slow ones once a month. Any departure from the normal, fortnightly rhythm of feeding will be indicated in the individual plant descriptions.

Needless to say, no food should be given to plants during their dormant season.

Accumulation of salts

At one time a plant might be kept in the same pot for years on end. Provided it was fed from time to time it managed very well. Today we are faced with the problem of hard or polluted water, which introduces many harmful substances into the compost. Artificial and natural fertilisers also contain harmful elements (for instance chlorine), which accumulate as well. Feeding therefore frequently aggravates the damage already caused by an accumulation of mineral salts.

The sensible plant lover will repot sooner rather than later (see the appropriate section on page 63). Removing the upper layer of the compost helps to get rid of a lot of poison. The new compost contains fresh nutrients, enabling the plant to continue for a time. The modern tendency is therefore to repot more often and to feed less.

Potting Composts

On page 49 you will have seen how food is absorbed through the root hairs, and it was clear that the following conditions are essential to make this possible: a good supply of air (oxygen); sufficient water; adequate nourishment.

All potting soils (or rather, growing mediums or composts, for they need not contain soil) have to meet these requirements. In addition the medium serves to support the plant.

Different requirements

The chapter on 'soil mixtures' in old-fashioned books on house plants describes dozens of different combinations in an endeavour to allot to each plant the kind of soil in which it grew in its native habitat.

Today it seems as if all plants have to be satisfied with the same standard compost. Both views appear to me to be exaggerated. There is no doubt that some plants prefer certain combinations, while others like their compost to be based on a different formula.

Man-made mixtures

Natural soil is now rarely used. At one time a certain amount of garden soil was used in potting mixtures, but even then leafmould and rotted turves played a large part. Analysis of the requirements of the root system (see above) has established that a satisfactory medium only needs humus, such as peat, so that it will retain plenty of water as well as the necessary air. Grains of some inert material (sand, plastic foam, perlite) may be added to improve drainage. As a rule the necessary nutrients are then added in the form of artificial fertiliser.

Acidity

It is of the greatest importance that the degree of acidity of the compost should suit the plant. The fact that house plants vary considerably in this respect must be taken into account. A large group of indoor plants will flourish when the pH lies between 5.5 and 6.5, in what we would call moderately acid soil. On the other hand there are several plants which prefer a more acid mixture, mainly because they are unable to absorb sufficient iron when the pH is high. Among this group are azaleas, brunfelsias, calceolarias, hydrangeas, primulas and sinningias. For these plants the most favourable pH lies between 4.6 and 5.4.

Orchids like very acid compost and cacti feel most comfortable at a pH of between 4.5 and 6.5.

Special mixtures are available for the most important groups, such as orchids. These can be obtained from specialist growers.

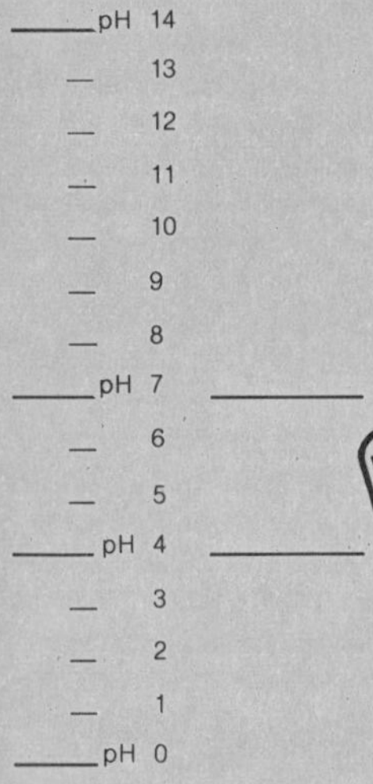

Above The degree of acidity, or pH, establishes the concentration of hydrogen ions. A neutral solution contains 10,000,000 hydrogen ions per 1 gram of water; in other words, the concentration is 10^{-7}. The pH is its logarithm, that is, 7.

The complete scale (sketch above, left) covers pH 0 (normal acid) to pH 14 (normal alkali). House plants will only grow at a pH of between 4 and 7

Above right A simple instrument to determine soil acidity, a Hellige pH meter, which is not readily available. Discoloration of the liquid indicates the approximate pH, but laboratory tests are necessary to obtain exact measurements.

There are various other soil-testing kits on the market which are widely obtainable and very easy to use. These will give an approximate pH reading against a colour chart, a method that is sufficiently accurate for most purposes

The symbols

To enable you to find out at a glance the kind of compost required, each plant description in the dictionary section is accompanied by the appropriate symbol. To avoid complications two symbols are used to indicate particular mixtures. About 75 per cent of the plants described in this book can successfully be grown in these composts. The best mixtures for the remaining 25 per cent are given in the plant descriptions and are indicated by a third symbol.

Use standard potting compost, generally available

Use an acid compost, easily made by mixing equal parts of standard potting compost and peat fibre

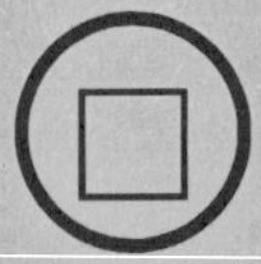

Use a special mixture; the appropriate formula is given under the individual plant descriptions

Main proprietary mixtures

The largest manufacturers of potting compost have got together to establish standard potting mixtures (■). These may be either soil based or peat based (soilless). Special mixtures are offered for acid-loving plants.

Cactus compost, an extra-porous mixture, is not often available. On page 70 you can read how to mix it yourself.

Other mixtures available are special seed composts and composts for rooting cuttings. Ordinary mixtures are too rich for the purpose of propagation and the special composts contain very little nourishment.

Many such standard composts have been available for a long time, for instance the well-known soil-based John Innes composts offered by different manufacturers but made up to a standard recipe. There is also a wide range of peat-based composts with added nutrients, marketed by various manufacturers.

Home-made mixtures

Many plant lovers like to mix their own compost. These mixtures are often far better than commercial potting composts, if only because of the love that has gone into making them. The following ingredients may be used:

Leafmould Beech leaves are best, but leaves from other trees may also be incorporated. However, it's best not to use oak leaves. If fairly fresh, the foliage should be left to rot on the compost heap for a few years and then sieved. Do not allow it to get dry.
Rotted turves Turves taken from an old lawn or from a meadow preferably grown on clay are stacked until they are completely decayed and the soil is then sieved.
Garden compost Composted garden and kitchen refuse is useful in a potting mixture, but it can contain a lot of weeds!
Stable manure Cow dung must be left to rot for two years before it is pulverised for use, or it can be bought ready prepared.
Peat fibre This is also used in commercial mixtures. It must not contain too many mineral salts.
Garden soil This can be quite useful.
Sphagnum or peat moss Some florists and garden shops still sell it, but it is becoming very hard to obtain. Useful for very light mixtures.
Conifer needles Semi-rotted soil from pine forests.
Clay or loam This can be very useful, though you will have to collect it yourself.
Sharp sand or river sand This must not contain too much lime and is therefore washed before use. Coarse sand is best.
Perlite A kind of expanded rock, very light and porous; it is sold in bags. Make sure you get the 'horticultural' variety, which is neutral.
Charcoal Sold for barbecues, charcoal is sometimes used to lighten the potting mixture.
Lime A necessary addition to achieve the required pH level. Most humus substances are too acid.
Dried blood, hoof and horn and bonemeal All these are good alternatives to artificial manure. They contain nitrogen, potassium and phosphorus, as well as quite a lot of lime. They should therefore not be used in mixtures for acid-loving plants.

There are numerous other possible ingredients, such as those for orchids (see page 69) and various kinds of fern roots and tree bark.

Examples of useful mixtures

Mixture for common plants (■):
4 parts sieved leafmould;
1 part sharp sand;
1 part rotted cow manure.
To each litre (quart) add 5g (¼oz) of lime or Dolomite limestone powder and 5g (¼oz) of dried blood, hoof and horn and bonemeal.

Mixture for acid-loving plants (◧):
3 parts conifer needle compost;
2 parts peat fibre or garden peat;
1 part rotted cow manure.
To each litre (quart) add 1 to 2g (a pinch) of lime or Dolomite limestone powder and 2g (a pinch) of mixed fertiliser 12:10:18, in pulverised grains.

Seed compost:
1 part standard potting compost;
1 part pure peat fibre.
To each litre (quart) add 2g (a pinch) of lime or Dolomite limestone powder.

Recipes for other compost mixtures are found in some of the plant descriptions. See also pages 69 and 70 for orchid and cactus mixtures.

Repotting

A house plant is kept in a relatively small amount of compost. In a natural environment the roots can grow wherever they want in order to obtain their nourishment, but the roots of an indoor plant have to go round and round in one small area. Their food supply thus quickly becomes exhausted – within six weeks in the case of fast-growing plants. There are two remedies: feeding and repotting. On page 61 it was explained when a plant must be fed and mention was made of the damage caused by salts, which is aggravated when the quality of the tap water deteriorates. Mineral deposits are therefore one of the reasons for repotting, for these are just as harmful as lack of food.

When to repot

As a general rule, plants should be repotted when the roots have entirely filled the compost and are starting to wind round in the pot. Repotting is essential when the outer edge of the soil ball consists of a felty mass formed by the root hairs. Repotting is also necessary when lime deposits appear on a clay pot or when a layer of green algae grows on top of the compost. In addition repotting will often be found effective when a plant is ailing or when it is attacked by pests, whether in the compost or on the foliage.

Plants may be repotted at any time of the year, although spring is the best time for practically all species. It will do no harm to take the rootball out of the pot for a moment to examine the state of the root system. As long as the roots are not damaged the plant will continue to grow as before.

The frequency at which plants should be repotted varies between once a month and once every two years. A vigorous young abutilon, for instance, may easily want a larger pot every six weeks between April and September, when it produces one shoot after another. A shrubby begonia, which may also grow very fast, may be saved from a mildew attack by frequent repotting. On the other hand a 50-year-old agave, perhaps an heirloom from Grandmother's time, which decorates the terrace faithfully every summer growing in its teakwood tub, will require fresh compost at the most every two years. In other words, the frequency at which plants are repotted depends on their vigour.

Choice of pot

The difference between plastic and red clay pots has already been mentioned on page 57 in the section on watering and various ornamental pots and containers are discussed on pages 14 and 32. Hydroponics and self-watering systems are also dealt with on pages 45 and 46. The most satisfactory all-round pot is the ordinary plastic pot with saucer – cheap and practical. Ornamental versions are also available.

In principle the new pot must be a little larger than the old one, normally an inch larger in diameter. But when you are repotting a young plant which you know to be a rapid grower, there is no reason why you should not transfer it to a considerably larger pot, to avoid having to start all over again within a few weeks.

The roots of some plants like to go deep, while others have a more shallow root system. Attempts have been made to adapt the shape of pots to these tendencies. You will have seen the narrow, deep palm pot and the wide, more shallow azalea pot, for instance. The use of such pots is of importance mainly to growers, who have to make the best use of their available greenhouse space and of expensive potting compost. In other words a palm pot must be deep but need not be narrow and an azalea pot must be wide, but the depth is not important.

New, and therefore dry, red clay pots must first be thoroughly scrubbed. Do not use cleansers; they would be absorbed by these pots and be difficult to remove. Most them are harmful to roots.

Removing the plant

It will be easy to remove the soil ball from a smooth, non-porous pot, but red clay pots, in which the root hairs have firmly attached themselves to the pot wall, are a different matter. Plunging the pot in water for a time will help to some extent. If it is still impossible to remove the soil ball, the clay pot will have to be very carefully smashed. The resulting pieces will always come in useful as crocks for drainage.

Plants which have been buried in their pots in the garden will often have long roots growing through the hole in the bottom. These roots should on no account be cut off, for they serve to feed the plant. In this case, too, the pot must be smashed (or with a plastic pot, cut away), to preserve the root system.

Some ornamental pots have an incurving rim – very attractive, but a nuisance when you have to repot. The only thing you can do is to remove as much loose compost as possible and push the roots to the centre to free the soil ball, which will then no longer be intact.

Protecting the root system

This must be your main consideration when repotting, and for that reason the soil ball must be pushed about or cut as little as possible. If you think 'I'll just get rid of that ugly felty mess', you are robbing the plant of much of its capacity to absorb food.

When the plant is grown in a red clay pot most of the roots will in fact be found around the edge, where they suck nourishment from the pot sides. In the centre you may find nothing but compost. This may be removed, but it is much simpler to leave it. The old compost will do no harm, for the roots grow elsewhere. In plastic pots the roots fill the whole soil ball to a much greater extent. Here, too, it is unnecessary to remove the old compost. Only the upper layer, usually free of roots but saturated with salts, must be changed if possible.

Drainage

Pots with holes in the bottom are always preferable. Stagnating water at the bottom of a pot is fatal for practically all plants. Fortunately there are now also ornamental pots (in plastic and ceramic) with drainage holes and a matching saucer. Drainage holes may become obstructed, sometimes by a root, but this can be avoided by inserting a drainage layer consisting of crocks, charcoal or pebbles. Plants which are very sensitive to stagnant water, for instance orchids, often have a crock layer reaching halfway up the pot. This is a little exaggerated, but it is important to ensure that the water can drain away freely.

In cylinders, or other containers without drainage holes in the base, there is little point in introducing a drainage layer of crocks. As soon as the water covers the layer, the roots will get wet again. A layer of crocks is only useful if you have inserted

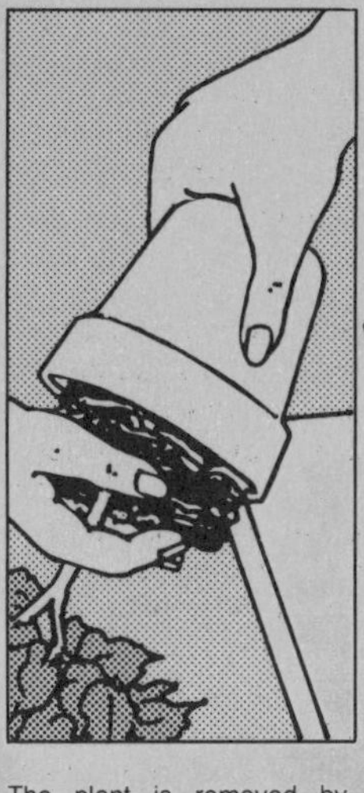

The plant is removed by gently knocking the pot against the edge of a table

Where a tangle of roots has grown through the drainage hole, the pot must be smashed to save the roots

a tube (see also page 56) to gauge the amount of water that has collected at the bottom.

A drainage layer is not necessarily advisable in every case. For instance, if you intend to water the plant from the base, there should be very few crocks in the bottom of the pot, otherwise the water will not reach the compost. The plant would dry out, for the crocks lack sufficient capillary action. This applies particularly to all pots grown on a capillary mat or where other self-watering systems are used. In such cases the compost must reach right down to the bottom of the pot to be able to draw in the water.

Potting on

The drainage layer should be covered with a few inches of potting compost. The old soil ball is placed on top and surrounded with fresh compost, firmly pressed down with the fingers or with a stick. Room must be left at the top of the old soil ball to allow a few inches of fresh compost to be added (if necessary choose a larger pot), but it must not be taken right up to the rim of the new pot, or this would make watering difficult. At least 1.5cm ($\frac{5}{8}$in) should be left at the top so that water does not spill over the edge.

Aftercare

The root system is bound to suffer to some extent when being repotted and may therefore have a little more difficulty at first in absorbing water and food. In addition the root hairs are now confronted with a much richer food supply in the fresh compost (sometimes too rich, in fact). Because of the new demands made on the plants they should be treated gently for a few weeks after repotting – not kept in a draught, nor in full sun, nor put immediately out of doors and certainly not fed.

To counteract the concentration of mineral salts it is advisable to water the plant generously immediately after repotting, but not so much that water can collect at the bottom of an ornamental pot. After being repotted a plant does not usually need feeding for six weeks.

Daily Care

From what has been said, you will have gathered that it is important to give your plants daily attention. Here, in more detail, is a reminder of what has to be done on these occasions.

Acclimatising a new plant. Place the pot in a plastic bag to protect the leaves from the dry air of the living-room. If the bag is lowered a little each day, by the time the plant is fully exposed it will have become more accustomed to the dry atmosphere

Acclimatising the plant
When a new plant is brought into your home the odds are that it has been grown in a greenhouse, where the atmospheric humidity was probably a good deal higher than that in your living-room. The plant must gradually grow accustomed to the drier air – a process of acclimatisation. Actually this should have been done for you up to a point, for the plant should have been kept at a lower degree of relative humidity for a time before being sold. However, this is often not done for long enough. You would do best to harden plants marked ❂ by spraying them more frequently than usual during the first few days. You could also place them in a plastic bag, open at the top, and push it down a little further each day until the plant is standing in an open atmosphere.

Positioning
House plants should be kept in a permanent position whenever possible. There are plants which will flourish on board a moving ship, but in general they like to stay put. The position should be the correct one from the start, for once the plant is growing well it should not be moved – in many cases that is the beginning of the end.

Plants such as ivy must be attached to the wall at several points

Soft-stemmed climbers, like this Passion Flower, are usually trained round a wire hoop

Watering
Little more need be said on this subject, which has been covered in detail on page 55. It is important to inspect all plants growing in ordinary pots (that is, not provided with a self-watering system) at least once a day, even more often on sunny days. If a plant suddenly starts to wilt, the situation may yet be saved. Always water with great care. Make sure the plant really is thirsty before you give it any and try not to turn your daily round into an automatic routine.

Screening
All plants marked ◐ or ● must be protected against scorching sunlight. Unless permanent provisions have been made, someone must remember to adjust the net curtains or to lower the Venetian blinds. In conservatories and greenhouses, in particular, scorching and drying out can easily occur.

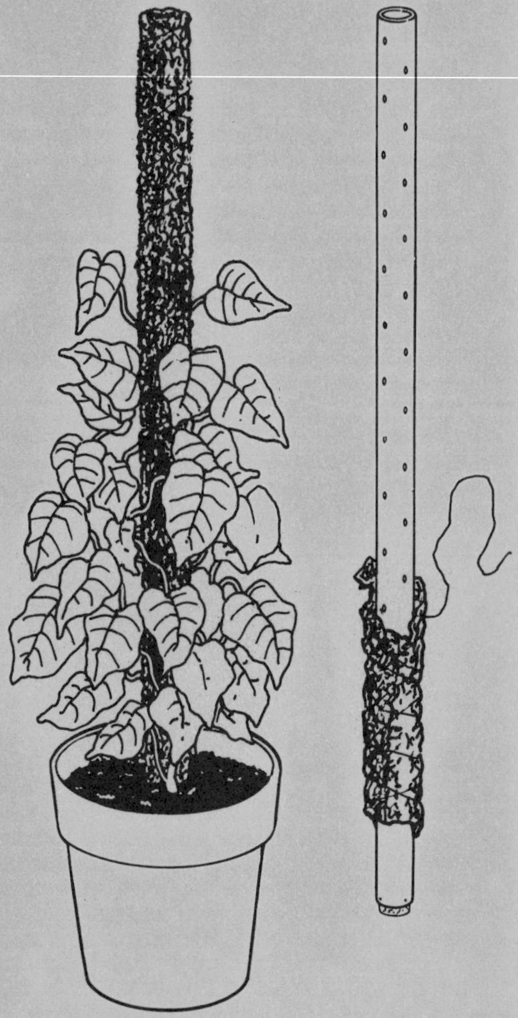

A home-made moss pole. Water poured into the top will run out through the numerous tiny holes, so that the moss is kept damp. The part of the plastic tube that is buried in the pot should not be drilled and the bottom end should be sealed off

Left When plants are placed out of doors to enjoy a mild shower, the surface of the compost must first be covered in plastic to prevent it becoming saturated

Spraying
When there are no provisions for increasing the atmospheric humidity (for instance by the use of a humidifier), sensitive plants should be sprayed several times a day, especially in winter when the heating is on.

Tying
Plants with long, winding or climbing stems must be tied in from time to time. When they are growing against a wall, brass eyelets may be screwed into rawlplugs. Brass does not rust, is not conspicuous and can be left for years. The tendrils can be tied to the eyelets with dark plastic-coated wire.

If a plant has to be movable, a wire hoop or a framework may be inserted in the pot to which the young tendrils can be tied at intervals. Several plants, including the dipladenia and the Passion Flower, are sold in this form. Climbers originating in the tropical jungle, for instance *Philodendron* species, are often sold growing up a moss-covered post. Such a post is easily made by closely covering a section of PVC tubing in moss and tying it on firmly with black thread, but it is quite difficult to keep the moss damp without saturating the compost. By drilling a large number of holes in the pipe before it is covered, you can water by filling the tube from the top; the water will be absorbed by the moss through the holes. The damp moss encourages the development of aerial roots. Unfortunately such moss-covered posts are not always easily obtainable sold separately.

Trimming
In the case of flowering plants dead flowers must regularly be snipped off. Unsightly leaves should also be removed.

Fast-growing house plants, for instance an abutilon, which have become too large, may be drastically cut back. They will soon put out new shoots so you need not be afraid to use the knife from time to time

Above, left The right way to prune. Always cut above an eye, but not immediately above, as in the upper sketch. In the second sketch the cut is too far above the eye. In the third the cut slopes the wrong way. The fourth sketch shows the correct method.

Above Three sketches showing how to stop a plant. **Left** The plant before the tip has been pinched out; **Centre** After tip cutting; **Right** The plant with its new growth: several of the eyes in the axils have developed, creating a well-branched plant

Left Detail of the stopping operation. This is the second time it has been done and therefore it is now the sideshoots which are pinched out. Always cut just above an eye

Cleaning the foliage

Both assimilation and breathing take place through the leaves and it is therefore important that the foliage is kept clean, since dust and grease may obstruct the stomata.

Only smooth, shiny leaves are cleaned. Hairy leaves should never be polished – it would destroy the hairs. Where leaves are covered in a waxy layer, as is the case, for instance, with the Stag's Horn Fern, this must on no account be removed in your passion for cleanliness, for it is this layer which protects the plant from drying out.

Chalk deposits on foliage are easily removed by wiping the surface with a mild vinegar solution. Always use lime-free water for rinsing and spraying foliage, for otherwise the spots will soon return. Various sprays are available which certainly remove the chalk deposit, but which at the same time give the foliage an unnaturally shiny appearance. Rinsing with a little tepid milk gives excellent results.

Areas difficult to reach, such as the spaces between the ribs of a densely thorned cactus, may be cleaned with baby's cotton buds dipped in milk.

Plants with innumerable small, shiny leaves may be placed out of doors in a very mild shower; this will greatly improve their appearance. If there are no drainage holes in the pot, cover the compost with foil to prevent it becoming swamped. Some people put their plants under the shower, but this is advisable only if the water is lime free, or it will leave chalky deposits.

Pruning

There are two reasons for pruning house plants. In the first place it is done because a plant may have grown unsightly and requires shaping and in the second place because a plant has grown too large for the living-room.

Pruning should preferably take place when growth is at its minimum (the dormant season), usually just before the plant starts into growth again. It therefore often coincides with repotting, which should be done at approximately the same time. It makes sense that these operations should coincide. When a plant is repotted part of the root system is often (accidentally or purposely) destroyed and it is not good for the plant if the part above ground is left untouched. New growth is encouraged if the evaporating surface is reduced proportionally to the roots.

Pruning is best done with sharp pruning shears. It will promote good development and a more regular shape. If there are too many branches on one side of the plant, remove more of them than on the other side. Branches crossing each other in the centre of the plant should be cut back, for damage might be caused where they rub together.

In some plants, among others those of the *Euphorbia* family, the cuts discharge a milky liquid; this can be checked with charcoal or ash.

Stopping

This is a special method of pruning, in which the tips of young plants are pinched out or cut to encourage branch formation. To achieve a really bushy plant, the process may be repeated after a few weeks. Many more growing points will be created in this way, and at the same time more flowers.

Sometimes the tips are removed to delay flowering. In a fuchsia, for instance, or a chrysanthemum, the flowering season may easily be put back by constantly removing the tip up to a certain time. This is a useful process when plants are being grown for an exhibition. An experienced amateur will know exactly when to stop removing the tips and when the plant may be expected to flower.

A Home for Plants

Built-in containers and flower windows

The advantages of installing a built-in plant container or a flower window have been referred to on page 20. In this section you will find the technical outline necessary for building your own container or instructions which can be passed on if you are going to get someone to do it for you. Flower windows, in particular, must be very carefully planned, preferably when the house is being built. To install such a window in an existing house is a costly business and involves a great deal of demolition. Hence the detailed sketches, which you might like to discuss with your architect.

A plant container or flower window should preferably be built where it will receive plenty of light from outside. Additional lighting (see page 47) is easily installed, but if the plants are to be entirely or largely dependent on artificial light, problems arise. Not only will the installation and running cost of extra lighting be very high, the enormous amount of artificial light required will also have a disturbing effect.

It is a pity that so few flower windows are built in this country. Most builders have no idea of what is meant when they are asked to construct such a window. There seems to be a general lack of expert knowledge. If, however, you decide you would like to have a flower window built you may be guided by the photographs in this book and by the sketch on the right, which gives a good idea of the principles involved in an enclosed flower window, if not the exact proportions. Make sure that only rustproof materials are used, for instance stainless steel or aluminium, for as a result of the humid atmosphere in such a window other materials will soon rust or warp. It must also be easily accessible so that it can be properly cleaned.

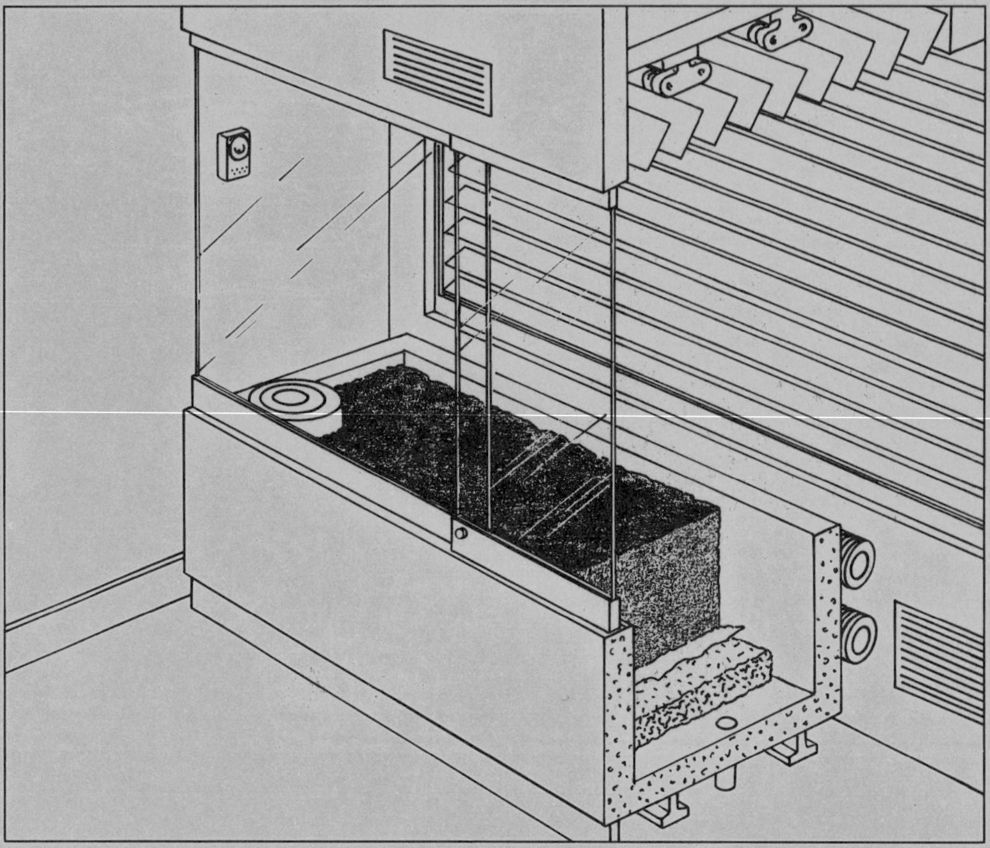

Section of a well-designed flower window, equipped with artificial lighting, heating, ventilation and a humidifier. The measurements are not drawn to scale

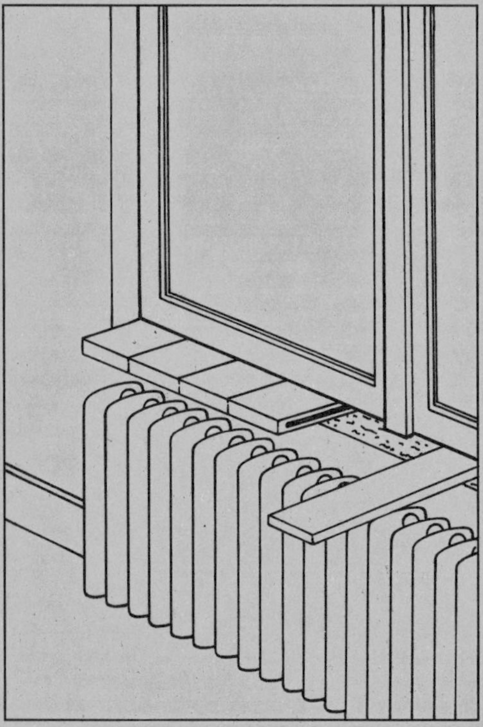

Many houses are built with a very narrow window-sill, hardly worthy of the name and no good for your plants.

Where there are tiles, these can be removed with a hammer, after which planks of the appropriate thickness are inserted in the gap at 50-cm (20-in) intervals. If necessary they can be levelled with the aid of wedges. They need not be glued or nailed in place

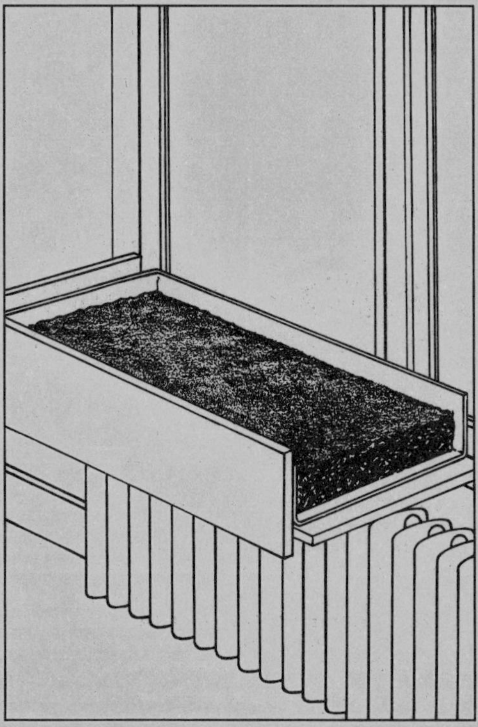

A zinc or other suitable container may now be placed on the planks. When filled with peat fibre and watered, the container will be quite heavy but firm as a rock. To make the container more attractive it can be finished with a veneered edge, coloured hardboard or similar material

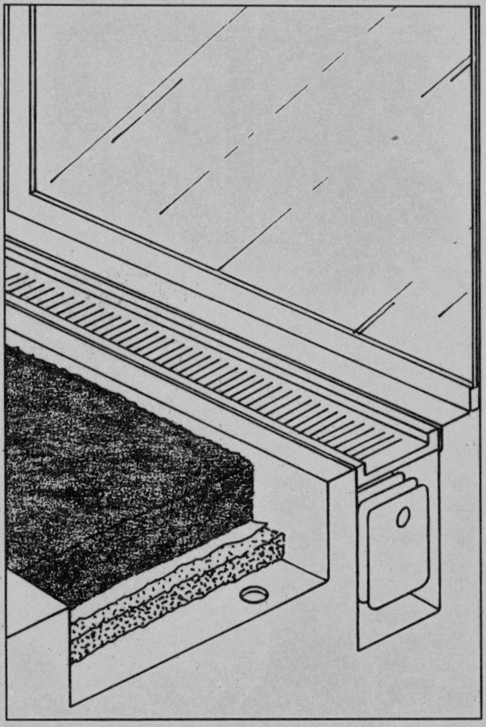

An example of a flower container built into the floor. You will save yourself a lot of expense if the idea is introduced before the house is built. Note the drainage layer and the waste pipe. The convector heater supplies warmth, but the plants are kept away from the hot air current

Holiday Time

Problems can arise when you decide to go on holiday.

The best solution is to ask a good friend or a relative to come and water your plants while you are away. Place them in a spot where they cannot get scorched, for you can hardly ask your friend to race to your house every time the sun comes out.

If some of your plants require special treatment, leave a note. You can't expect everyone to learn the instructions in this book by heart! The Umbrella Plant, for instance, should have a label 'Keep the saucer full of water'. That sort of thing may help, but don't get upset if something goes wrong in your absence. There are plenty more plants at the garden shop.

If you possess pots with self-watering systems or grow your plants in hydroponic pots (see pages 45–46) the whole thing is much simpler, but you must find out in advance how long the water supply will last. During the summer months, especially, this may be shorter than you think. There are a few useful systems based on capillary action. The best-known one consists of porous threads or wicks. These are passed through the compost with their ends coming out of the drainage hole. The pot is raised above the water level in a bowl and the threads hang down into the water.

A slightly more expensive gadget is shaped like a mushroom and is made of porous stone, hollow inside. It is filled with water, and when the mushroom is pushed into the compost, water will be released through the porous wall. The water level inside the apparatus will drop, but if it is connected to a bowl of water by means of narrow plastic tubing, the liquid will be constantly replenished.

Both these systems work very well so long as the reserve supply is adequate. It is wise to test the system for a few weeks before you go on holiday.

Plants which do not easily rot – this applies to most plants with woody stems – can be covered entirely by a plastic bag to prevent evaporation. The compost should be moderately damp and the plant must on no account be placed in the sun. This is a slightly risky method, but many people swear by it. A less drastic system is to cover only the pot in plastic. Even this will help, especially with red clay pots.

Then there is the tub method known of old. Take a large old-fashioned bath-tub (if you can find one!) or some other large receptacle – the bath if necessary – and place a double layer of porous bricks on the bottom. Fill it with water to just below the upper level of the bricks, and place the plants on top. Red clay pots are, of course, best since they will readily soak up water. Put some damp moss or wads of wet newspaper between the pots. The water will rise through the porous bricks and the plants will remain in good condition for about a fortnight.

Some house plants, marked ⊖, or possibly ⊜, may be buried, pot and all, in the soil in the garden. Choose a shady spot where the sun cannot reach between 9 a.m. and 6 p.m. and out of the wind. First plunge the pots (preferably clay pots) in water, then dig them in and cover the surface of the pot with a layer of leaves or mown grass. Get your garden sprinkler out and ask your neighbour to turn on the tap occasionally when there is a drought.

If you go on holiday in winter, the thermostat may be turned back to about 12 to 14°C (53 to 57°F). Practically all plants will survive in this temperature, provided they are not near a draughty window. Even at this temperature they should be watered from time to time, but ask your stand-in not to drown your plants. That would be just as bad as letting them dry out.

At one time it was possible to leave your plants in a nursery during the holidays. Perhaps there may still be places where this can be done, but it's more usual to ask good friends or neighbours to look after your plants in their home or greenhouse while you are away.

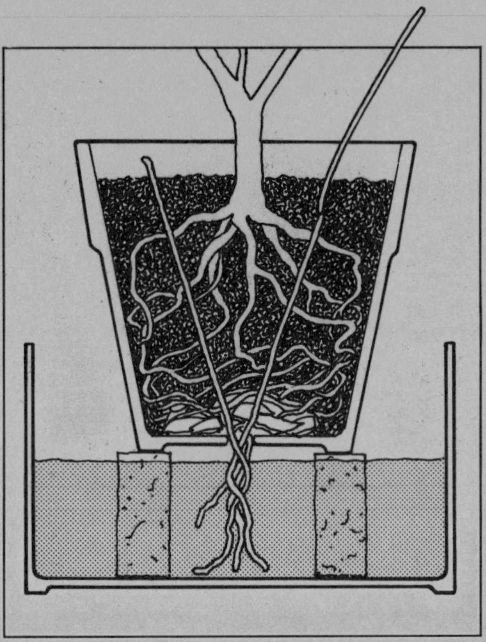

Action of porous threads: the part extending above the compost is cut off. A satisfactory system, though of course the water in the dish or bowl is exhausted fairly soon

This ceramic mushroom filled with water slowly releases the water through its porous red clay shaft. When the pressure in the mushroom drops, fresh water is supplied from the reservoir through the narrow plastic tube. If you use a large bucket, you can go on holiday for a whole month. Larger plants should have more than one mushroom with an equal number of buckets

A good old-fashioned way of keeping plants in clay pots watered in your absence is to stack porous bricks in the bath, with the clay pots placed on top in such a way that they are just out of the water. The pots soak up the water through the bricks

Plants which can normally be placed out of doors may be dug in for the winter. Cover the soil with some loose material such as straw, leaves or bracken to prevent drying out and choose a shady spot

Caring for Special Groups

House plants may be divided into groups, usually according to family, but occasionally also because of their special requirements. A number of the most important groups are referred to in this book, because a certain amount of skill is required for successful cultivation. The tips below should be read in conjunction with the individual plant description which will tell you all you need to know.

Bulbs, corms and tubers

This group of plants has the ability to store food for the lean (that is, the dry) season. The usual sequence therefore is that they have a growing season during which foliage and flowers are developed, and a very strict resting period in which all growth above ground dies, while the remaining bulb, corm or tuber remains and is kept completely dry, either in or out of the pot. There are only a few tuberous plants which have a less strict dormant season, and this will be indicated in their descriptions. Bulbs and tubers for indoor use may be divided into two groups: spring-flowering and summer-flowering plants.

Spring-flowering species, such as tulips, hyacinths, crocuses, daffodils and narcissi, are potted in the autumn in wide, shallow bowls, in groups of about 12. The bowls or pots must be well drained; the soil should be a sandy mixture – garden soil if necessary. It need not contain a great deal of nourishment.

If you have a garden, the best method is to dig a pit in a fairly dry corner with good drainage. No water must collect in the bottom of the hole in the course of the winter; this would cause the bulbs to rot. Nor must the soil be dry as dust, for this would inhibit root formation. The pit should be 40 to 50 cm (16 to 20 in) deep. To improve drainage, the bottom of the pit should be covered by a layer of crocks or gravel. The pots are then arranged on top in tidy rows. Put a few sticks among them; this will make it easier to dig them up. Fill the pots with friable light garden soil but do not press it down. In times of frost it helps to cover the pit with a thick layer of bracken or straw – not to keep the bulbs frost free, but to make it possible to dig them up in a hard frost if necessary.

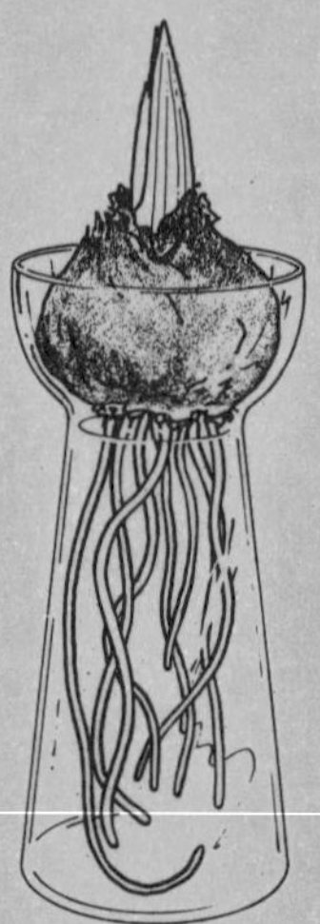

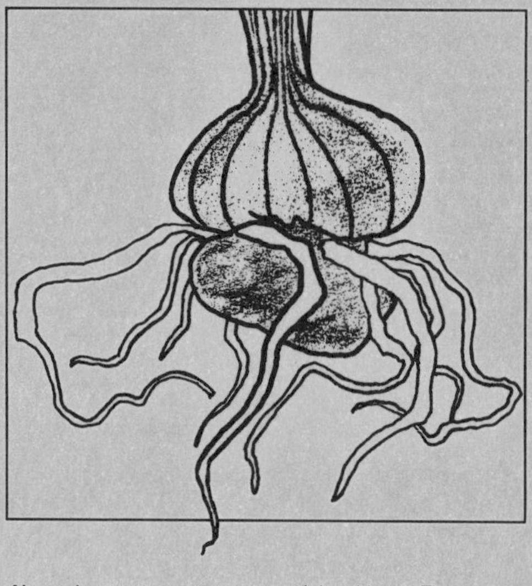

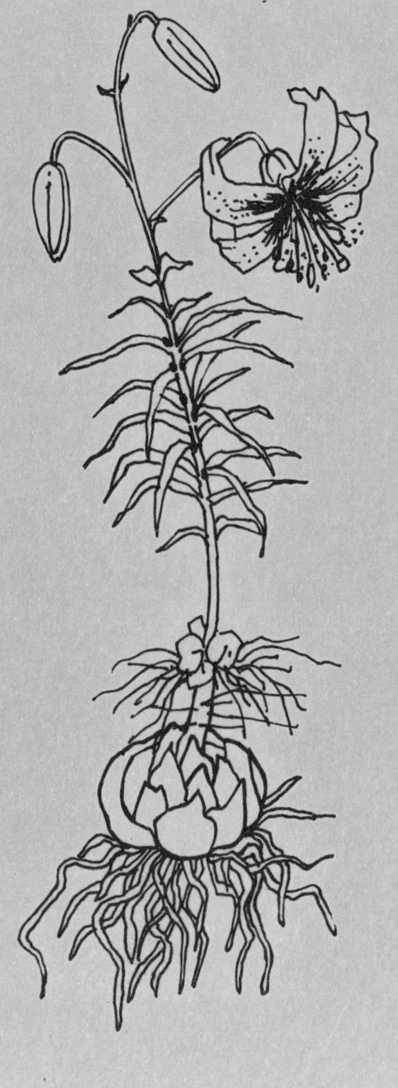

Right Daffodils, narcissi and hyacinths are sometimes grown in special glasses. The water should reach to just a few millimetres below the bulb

Burying spring-flowering bulbs. Choose a spot in the garden which is neither too wet nor too dry

Winter storage suitable for a balcony. The filling consists of peat fibre, which is an excellent insulator

Summer-flowering bulbs are always planted near the surface in order to give the roots more space to develop. Make sure that they have good drainage

Above A new corm grows on top of the old one. The process is repeated every year

Left Many lily species develop roots both at the top and at the bottom of the bulb. This must be taken into account when planting the bulbs: they must be placed fairly deep in the pot and extra tall pots are usually best

If the pots are buried in late October, a few of them should be lifted in late January to check if the shoots are long enough. When you can feel the flower bud in the shoot the pots may be brought into the light.

If you have no garden, a storage place may be constructed on the balcony, consisting of a wooden box filled with reasonably damp peat fibre in which to bury the pots. The box should preferably be kept out of the sun, for the best temperature at which the bulbs will root is 9°C (48°F).

Bulbs will also root in a cool cupboard or storage room. They need not necessarily be covered in soil, but must be kept completely in the dark. The bulbs are planted in such a way that their nose appears just above the soil; a second pot with the drainage hole sealed off can be inverted on top. Another method is to wrap the pots in black polythene; this will also prevent them drying out. It goes without saying that bulbs kept in the warmer atmosphere of a cupboard or storage room must be watched, for the soil must be kept moist.

Sometimes bulbs such as hyacinths and narcissi are forced in hyacinth glasses or in gravel. In both cases the water must reach to about 2 mm below the bulb but not touch it to prevent rotting. This capacity of bulbs to grow in clean water is, of course, due to the fact that they store all the nutrients necessary to develop flowers and leaves. The roots serve only to take in moisture.

All spring-flowering bulbs must root in a cool and dark environment, with the exception of two narcissi, 'Grand Soleil d'Or' and 'Paperwhite', which can go straight into the light and into the heated living-room. As soon as you can feel the flower buds of bulbs kept in the dark, they can be brought into the light. The shoots will soon turn green. It depends on the kind of bulb as to whether room temperature will immediately be tolerated. As a rule it is advisable to keep the plants in a fairly cool situation to begin with, preferably not above 16°C (60°F). Grape Hyacinths, snowdrops, Glory of the Snow and many other attractive small bulbous flowers dislike artificial heat. It is for that reason that this book only deals with those bulbs which can be forced in the living-room without too many problems.

While the bulbs are being forced, the degree of atmospheric humidity must be as high as possible. New shoots must frequently be sprayed. Sometimes a plastic bag can be put over the plant to prevent it drying out.

Summer-flowering bulbs, corms and tubers intended for the living-room or the greenhouse are planted in spring, usually in March–April. Stone or plastic pots with a deep layer of crocks at the bottom are used. In most cases ordinary commercial potting compost (■) is suitable; the addition of a little extra sand can do no harm.

These bulbs do not have to be put in the dark. They can go straight on to the window-sill or into the greenhouse, at temperatures varying between 15 and 25°C (59 and 77°F), depending on the species. Thoroughly moisten the soil immediately after potting, but be careful to water sparingly until the foliage has appeared.

Some summer-flowering plants will die after flowering. In that case the bulbs, corms or tubers should be kept, either in or out of their pots, at not too low a temperature. Although species which retain their leaves do have a dormant season, the foliage should not be allowed to die entirely. All these details are dealt with under the individual plant descriptions. The bulbs, corms and tubers mentioned in this book will be found in the tables on page 280.

Bromeliads
This name is frequently used for various members of the *Bromeliaceae* family. As a rule it will not refer to the true *Bromelia* genus, which is rarely grown since it becomes far too large for the living-room. However, since the collective name is so well known, the following general remarks will apply to the entire family.

Bromeliads may be divided into two groups:
(a) Terrestrial bromeliads. These are species which all grow at ground level. They have a normal root system which is best grown in ordinary potting compost. The ananas, or pineapple, is a well-known example.
(b) Epiphytic bromeliads. These species grow at higher levels, on the trunks or branches of trees. The roots are far less developed and grow in small amounts of humus collected in the axils of trees. Cultivated species enjoy a very light mixture of sphagnum moss, fern roots or pieces of tree fern.

The structure of all bromeliads has this in common: that the long, usually strap-shaped leaves always form a tube-shaped rosette. Reserve water collects in the tube. The plants are so constructed that in periods of drought this water can be absorbed by the leaves. The most pronounced tubes are found in the epiphyte species. Terrestrial species have less need for such reserves, because the soil retains moisture longer than air.

The light requirements of different bromeliads varies considerably. Many terrestrial species grow in full sun, but their epiphyte colleagues live largely in the shade of the trees and must therefore not be grown in too bright a light in cultivation. In a natural environment the atmospheric humidity is at its highest in places where epiphytes grow.

It is perfectly possible to grow epiphytic bromeliads in pots filled with a mixture of sphagnum moss, rotted leafmould, peat fibre, rotted cow manure and some sharp sand, but they look more attractive grown on an artificial tree. The plants are put in handfuls of the mixture described above, held in place with copper wire. Watering and feeding present a few problems, but they are not insoluble.

Unfortunately the pleasure of growing a fine, flowering bromeliad is short lived, for every rosette dies after flowering. It is a strange thought that when you buy a vriesea in flower, it is already dying. But this is a fact. The bromeliad must be regarded as a disposable plant and if you can't afford to bother too much about the correct position, light or the humidity required by your plants, this is the kind you should choose. Even a dedicated plant lover, who will grow the plant in ideal conditions, will be unable to induce a rosette to survive after flowering.

However, your bromeliad will not leave you without a successor. One or more plantlets always develop at the foot of the parent rosette. As soon as the old plant shows clear signs of dying (and this may take as much as a year), the plantlets should be carefully removed together with their roots and individually potted. Whether you will be able to bring them into flower depends entirely on the way they are treated. The chance of success is greatest in a heated greenhouse, where the degree of atmospheric humidity is higher than in the living-room.

Young bromeliads should flower when they are two years old. Unfortunately this does not always happen, but never mind: growers have discovered that acetylene gas encourages bud formation. This gas can be introduced through the water in the funnel; another method is to put a tiny piece of carbide in the tube. The same gas is exuded by ripe apples and one way of inducing flowering is to put the entire plant into a plastic bag for a day, together with a couple of apples. The temperature must not drop below 20°C (68°F). The most up-to-date method is to introduce a few drops of a special liquid (Ethrel), but this could be difficult to obtain.

Bromeliads may also be grown from seed, which is usually imported. It must be germinated under glass at a temperature of 30 to 35°C (86 to 95°F).

The table on page 279 shows which bromeliads have been included in this book.

Orchids
Like bromeliads, orchids may be divided into terrestrial and epiphytic species. Those belonging to the second group have storage organs, but in orchids these consist of pseudobulbs, not tubers. In some cases the pseudobulbs are very conspicuous, in other species the rootstock is only slightly thickened. Occasionally the leaves are also capable of storing moisture. These epiphytes – the group most frequently grown by amateurs – are best cultivated in a greenhouse, for in general a high degree (±80 per cent) of atmospheric humidity is essential. There are, however, a number of exceptions which will do reasonably well in the living-room, provided they are properly cared for.

The temperature at which orchids must be cultivated varies from one genus to another. Some species like to grow in a moderately warm greenhouse, others prefer a hothouse. These details are indicated in the individual plant descriptions. Direct sunlight is rarely tolerated and orchid houses are therefore always sprayed all over with white paint, while in the living-room orchids are best kept near a north-east facing window.

Orchids are extremely demanding over their water supply. Only clean rainwater or demineralised tepid water may be used.

Potting compost The compost mixture may consist of chopped fern roots (osmunda fibre), chopped sphagnum moss or pine bark chippings. The correct mixture is always indicated in the plant descriptions. The fern roots chosen for the purpose are usually those of *Polypodium vulgare* (Oak Fern) and *Osmunda regalis* (Royal Fern). After cleaning, the fern roots are chopped, finely or coarsely, depending on the requirements of the species. For terrestrial orchids rotted beech leaves, turf loam or peat fibre may also be used. The mixture should have a low pH. The latest development is to grow orchids in bark; many species will do well in this medium.

Hanging orchids are sometimes grown on blocks cut from the aerial roots of tree ferns. The little plants are carefully tied to the blocks with copper wire and suspended in the greenhouse. They are watered by taking the whole arrangement down and plunging it in tepid water.

Above Tillandsia, a bromeliad growing as an epiphyte. It develops extended rosettes from which the flower stalks emerge

Right Epiphytic orchids develop pseudobulbs in which moisture is stored. As a rule the appearance of pseudobulbs in orchids indicates that a resting period is required

Resting periods Orchids, especially those with pseudobulbs, must have a strict resting period, during which they are kept practically dry. Sometimes the temperature may also be lowered a little. New flower buds are developed during this period. Some species may lose all their foliage during the dormant season.

Repotting The best time to repot orchids is immediately after the dormant season. It is usually done every second year. Carefully rinse the roots to remove the old rotted humus, remove dead roots and cut back diseased roots carefully. A thick layer of crocks should be put in the bottom of the pot, for orchids react very quickly to stagnant water. In the growing season the plants may be generously watered, provided the water can easily drain away. If you find that an ordinary pot retains too much water, orchids may be grown in special orchid baskets.

Fertilising Feeding orchids is not an easy matter. Though like all plants they need certain substances to survive, it appears that they are able to absorb most of them from the air. It is therefore not essential to feed orchids, but nevertheless very weak doses of organic as well as of artificial manure may give good results. Some amateurs use the most bizarre concoctions, such as fish emulsion or the urine of a pregnant cow – all naturally in very weak solution. Advice on composts and feeding requirements can be obtained from specialist growers.

Propagation Orchids are reproduced by division of the pseudobulbs, sometimes from cuttings, but most frequently from seed. The latter method is extremely complicated and is really outside the scope of this book. It is very easy to cross different forms of orchids and there are numerous hybrids bearing the strangest names. It is quite impossible to enumerate them all, even by approximation. Amateurs who would like to know more about these plants should refer to specialist literature on the subject.

Pests and diseases Orchids are prone to attacks by greenfly, woodlice, thrips and mealy bug. Red spider mites will appear if the air is too dry. Occasionally they are also subject to attacks by scale insects and they are attractive to slugs. Mites are the pests most difficult to deal with; they are minute, almost invisible insects living on the lower surface of the leaves or eating the flowers, and they are very persistent. In commercial cultivation virus diseases may also occur. See also page 77.

Palms

In the last decade palms have once more become very popular. This is not surprising, for they make excellent house plants, able to take some hard knocks.

Their requirements for light are modest. Bright sunlight is undesirable; palms prefer a spot away from the window. However, a minimum of 1500 lux is necessary in winter.

For most palms the living-room temperature is on the high side. They feel more comfortable at temperatures between 12 and 16°C (53 and 60°F), so a corridor or stairwell which is kept fairly cool would probably be a better situation.

It is advisable to keep the compost constantly moist, and to plunge the plant from time to time. However, except in the case of the Dwarf Coconut Palm, *Microcoelum weddellianum*, no water should be left in the saucer.

Moist air will do no harm, but fortunately the firm foliage will also tolerate fairly dry conditions. The leaves should, however, be regularly sponged, and in summer the palm may be put out of doors in the rain.

Practically all palms have composite foliage, fan shaped in some species, pinnate on others. The stems are woody and rarely branch

Palms like tall pots with good drainage, and standard potting compost (■) may be used. A mixture of turf loam, rotted cow manure and a little sand is even better. When the plants are repotted (only once every three years in the case of mature plants – provided they are given water of the correct pH degree), the mixture must be pressed down very firmly. In the growing season extra feeding is advisable.

Occasionally palms may be propagated by division, but they are usually grown from seed. The seeds are germinated at a high temperature, and afterwards the young palms have to remain in the hothouse for at least a year. This is therefore not a simple process.

A frequent complaint is that the leaves suffer from brown tips. This can never be entirely avoided, since palms are actually born with brown-tipped foliage. The points are originally fused and break off when they unfold. The brown tips may be cut off, but a 2-mm edge of brown must always be left, for otherwise the cut itself will turn brown. The damage will be increased by people rubbing against the plant, by too low a degree of humidity and by lack of water.

Palms are frequently attacked by scale insects; these can be removed with the aid of a matchstick. Other pests are thrips, red spider mite, mealy bug and mites. For pest control see page 77.

Succulents

Cacti and other succulents are cared for in practically the same way and are therefore treated under one heading. The common denominator of these plants is their capacity to store water – cacti in their bodies, other succulents in their fleshy leaves or in the stems. All plants possessing storage organs require a resting period (as described in the case of bulbs and tubers, bromeliads and orchids), and succulents are no exception.

As a general rule cacti and other succulents will tolerate full sun, but early in spring they need to adapt themselves gradually. A few species require slight shade: this certainly applies to all jointed and leaf cacti. Though the temperature may rise appreciably when the sun shines in summer, the structure of succulents allows for this. On the other hand it is harmful if the temperature should rise when the light is bad, as can happen in this country in winter. Watering would start the plants into premature growth which could not come to anything for lack of light.

Succulents are not thirsty plants, but in a warm summer spell they will appreciate a drink every two or three days. Take care, however, that certain plants, less capable of evaporation than other species, are not given too much water. A cactus may survive after being kept too dry for months on end, while two days of overwatering will be fatal. It is advisable to use rainwater, since cacti dislike chalky soil.

Most succulents do not need a humid environment, and this may be a problem in itself. For the air may sometimes be *too* moist – in a greenhouse, for example – which will cause the plants to rot.

Cacti and other succulents require a porous, but moisture-retaining mixture. They certainly will not grow in a pot of sand. Good results are achieved by adding 30 to 50 per cent perlite to standard potting compost (■). This lightweight silicate will ensure good drainage, but at the same time retains a minimum amount of water for long periods and it is this attribute which protects the cactus roots from drying out. Most succulents prefer a pH value of 4.5 to 6.5 and the above mixture meets these requirements.

The pot must not be too small (the tiny pots in which they are frequently sold are simply an economy for the grower). A plastic pot is excellent, provided you water with care.

Resting periods are of the greatest importance to all succulent plants. The large majority have their dormant season in winter, but some succulent genera have their resting period in summer (*Rebutia*), in autumn (*Zygocactus*), or in spring

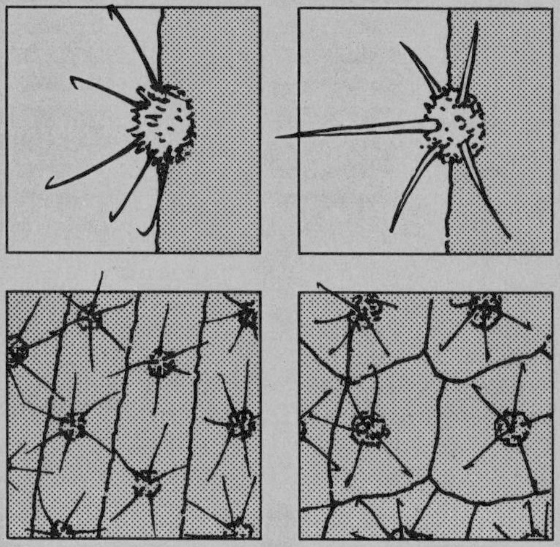

Top, left Thorns grow from the areoles of a cactus. In this case the thorns appear around the edge of the areole only; the point is curved

Top, right In this cactus the centre thorn is clearly different in structure

Above, left Example of a cactus with ribs bearing the areoles

Above, right A so-called wart (or nipple) cactus. The warts are often arranged in spirals

From left to right A columnar cactus, a pad cactus and a spherical cactus

Kalanchoe tomentosa has an elongated rosette of fleshy leaves, covered in woolly hairs, and capable of storing a quantity of moisture. It has beautiful reddish-brown leaf tips

Sedum rubrotinctum has practically spherical leaves, closely arranged in a rosette. These exceptionally fleshy leaves drop easily and will root rapidly

The very succulent lithops (Living Stones) form pebble-like bodies (corpuscula), annually renewing themselves from the centre outwards. In some cases light can enter the interior of the plant through little 'windows'

The leaf rosette of the well-known succulent echeveria. The close-growing leaves are a few millimetres thick and store a fair amount of water. The sunnier its position, the finer the colour of its leaf rosettes, which often become tinged with red

(*Rhipsalidopsis*). A rest means little or no water and a low or very low temperature. The two conditions are linked: the cooler the environment, the less water is required. Many cactus lovers purposely allow 1 to 2°C (2 to 3°F) frost in their greenhouse. Most cacti will tolerate this treatment, but in that case it is essential that they are kept absolutely dry from November onwards. If the plants still retain too much moisture, they will perish. It appears that this treatment is a great help in promoting flowering.

If succulents are left without water for long periods, they will shrink to some extent. In cacti this is not easy to observe. As soon as the plants are seen to shrink, they should be very lightly sprayed, or a few drops of water should be poured down the edge of the pot. If the temperature rises during the resting period in winter, ventilation is required. As a general rule a minimum temperature of 5°C (41°F) is specified. Only a few species of cacti or other succulents must be kept at a slightly higher temperature. Favourable positions for the dormant season are suggested on page 60.

If a succulent stops growing in summer, the water supply should be reduced then as well. Resting periods at other times of the year are always mentioned in the plant descriptions.

Once growth has started, succulents could use a feed, but the fertiliser should contain little nitrogen, since otherwise the plants would grow too rapidly and become prone to disease, especially to rotting. In a good cactus fertiliser the nitrogen content (the first figure indicated) must not exceed 20 per cent of the total: 5:10:10 would just be acceptable. As long as the plants continue to grow, they may be fed every fortnight, but feeding is usually stopped around August 1, to allow the plants to ripen.

Succulents are grown from seed, from cuttings or by grafting. The various methods are described on page 72.

Succulent plants may be attacked by woodlice, slugs, root lice, mites, scale insects and red spider mites and are particularly sensitive to rotting and cork formation: The last two conditions are always due to too high a degree of atmospheric humidity at too low a temperature.

All the cacti and other succulents mentioned in this book are included in the tables on page 280.

Ferns

Ferns are often treated as disposable plants, because it is difficult to keep them in good condition in the living-room. A fine, large *Nephrolepis exaltata* is not very expensive, and reasonably cared for will last for two months or more. To keep the plant for a year or more you'll have to be an expert.

Although ferns can be kept in poor light for a certain time, they need a good deal of light to make them grow. Bright sunlight is, of course, harmful. Depending on the species, the minimum temperature during the growing season is between 15 and 18°C (59 and 64°F).

Ferns need a fair amount of water, since the large surface of the foliage contains numerous pores. In species with shiny, leathery foliage, such as *Cyrtomium falcatum*, the Holly Fern, less water is evaporated, and these can therefore be grown more easily in the living-room. Other species appreciate a high degree of humidity.

Nearly all ferns may be grown in standard potting compost (■). Since they are very vigorous, they may need repotting twice a year. Use well-draining plastic pots and keep the compost constantly moist.

Ferns are at their most attractive in their growing season. You may therefore start regular feeding six weeks after repotting, using a weak solution of artificial fertiliser.

If in spite of all your good care a fern stops growing, you might try to give it a rest. Temporarily reduce the water supply, put the plant in a slightly cooler environment and cut off all the old foliage. After six weeks repot it, return it to a warmer position and try to bring it into growth again.

Ferns do not flower, and therefore produce no seed. Instead, spores are formed on the backs of the leaves; these are, as it were, plants in embryo, from which new ferns may be grown. Great care is needed for this operation. Seed trays and compost must be sterilised, the bottom temperature must be kept at 25°C (77°F) and the trays must be covered with glass. The young plants can only be raised in a hothouse.

Ferns are not very susceptible to pests, but there may be attacks by mealy bug, scale insects, thrips, eelworm and the larvae of the sciarid (see page 79).

The ferns described in this book are mentioned in the table on page 279.

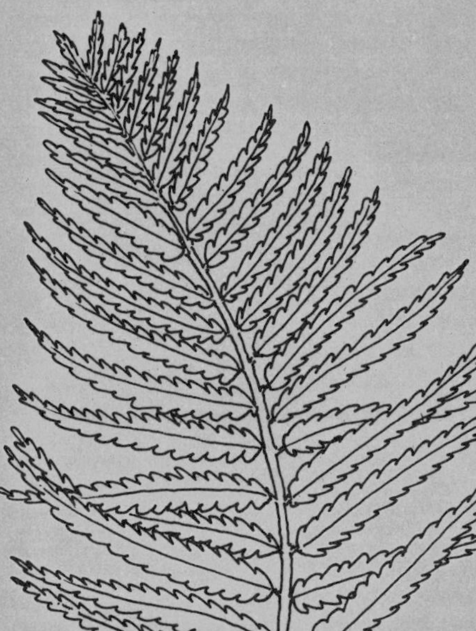

Ferns are spore-bearing plants. New plants are grown not from seed, but from spores – tiny cell structures found on the backs of the leaves

Propagation

Most house plants are relatively easy to increase. This is probably one of the reasons for their popularity. A fine, large plant, grown from a cutting, gives far more satisfaction than a specimen bought from the florist or garden centre.

Anyone can put cuttings in a bottle of water, but not all plants will root in this way. Some cuttings must be grown in a high temperature. Other plants are grown from seed, by air-layering, or by grafting – a range of options all within the capacity of the indoor gardener. All these different methods are described here, starting with a few simple aids.

Special aids

Seed and cutting compost A light, damp medium, containing a small amount of nutrients, is required to root seeds or cuttings. This may consist of a special seed and cutting compost, but in many cases rooting will succeed in damp sphagnum moss, in water, or in a porous artificial medium.

You can make your own seed and cutting compost by mixing equal parts of peat fibre and standard potting compost, thus halving the nutrient concentration in the potting compost, which would be too high for the tender roots. The mixture should be thoroughly moist.

Small pots made of compacted dry peat are available on the market. These swell when put in water and can be used for sowing seed or for cuttings. You can also buy small compost-filled plastic bags, in which you cut slits to insert cuttings, on the same principle as growbags. Add a little water and once the cuttings have rooted, just remove the bag. Growers use all sorts of artificial media for their cuttings. The principle remains the same: the roots must receive sufficient moisture and air.

Flower pots Cuttings are best rooted in small plastic pots with good drainage. It is also possible to start them, several at a time, in larger bowls or trays and prick them out into individual pots when they have rooted. Compressed peat pots, too, are very useful. Once the plants have started into growth, the roots will pierce the walls of the pots and the whole thing can then be planted in a larger pot. The peat pot will be absorbed into the new compost.

Humidity Cuttings have as yet no roots, but they do have leaves. They must be protected from drying out by evaporation being reduced to a minimum. Young seedlings, too, must not lose too much moisture by evaporation. The whole container may be put in a plastic bag, or a plastic bag can be inverted over the top of the pot, supported by bent wire.

A small indoor propagator is even more useful: this is a plastic tray with a transparent cover. The height of the cover should provide sufficient room for the tallest cuttings. Everyone ought to have such a propagator – they are very inexpensive and can be used over and over again.

Warmth Many cuttings and seeds will develop roots only if the soil temperature is raised, usually to 20 to 30°C (68 to 86°F), though difficult plants require a soil temperature of 35°C (95°F). You can achieve this temperature by placing the indoor propagator on a warm window ledge, but in that case the temperature level cannot be controlled. A propagator equipped with a small electric soil-warming cable is better. Ideally it should be thermostatically controlled. Make sure that the heated compost is always kept moist. Propagators heated by an electric element are also available.

Jiffy-7 is a flat disc which swells in water to form a seed pot. When the roots outgrow the pot, the whole thing can be planted in a larger pot

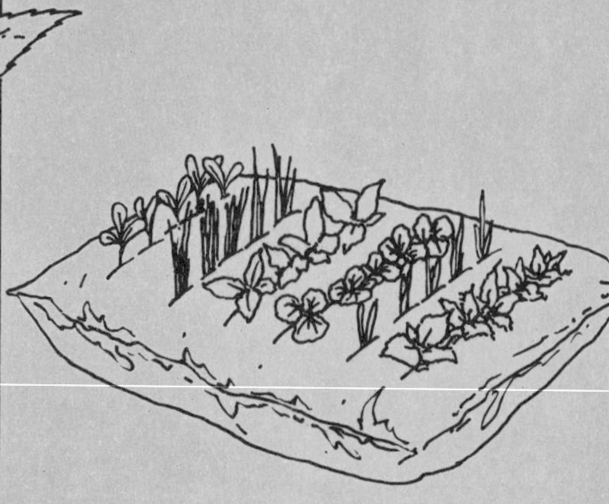

Growbags for seedlings or cuttings are now available, and contain the correct seed and cutting compost. Cuttings and seedlings are inserted through splits made in the plastic, and water is then added

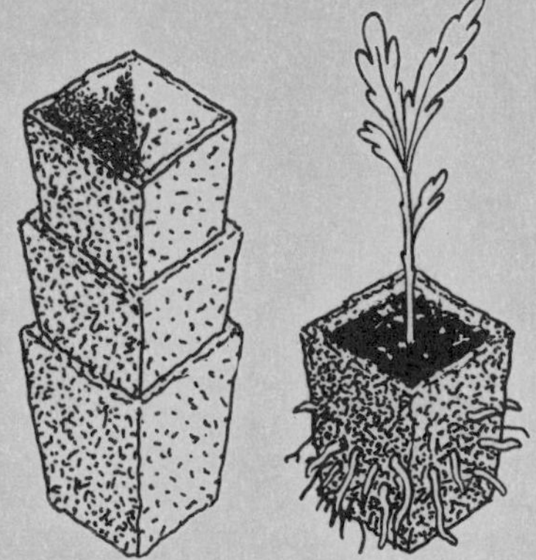

Peat pots must be filled with suitable seed or cutting compost. When the roots have developed, the young plants may be transferred, pot and all, to larger pots

To protect cuttings or seedlings from drying out, the pot may be covered with a plastic bag. The sketch shows two different methods

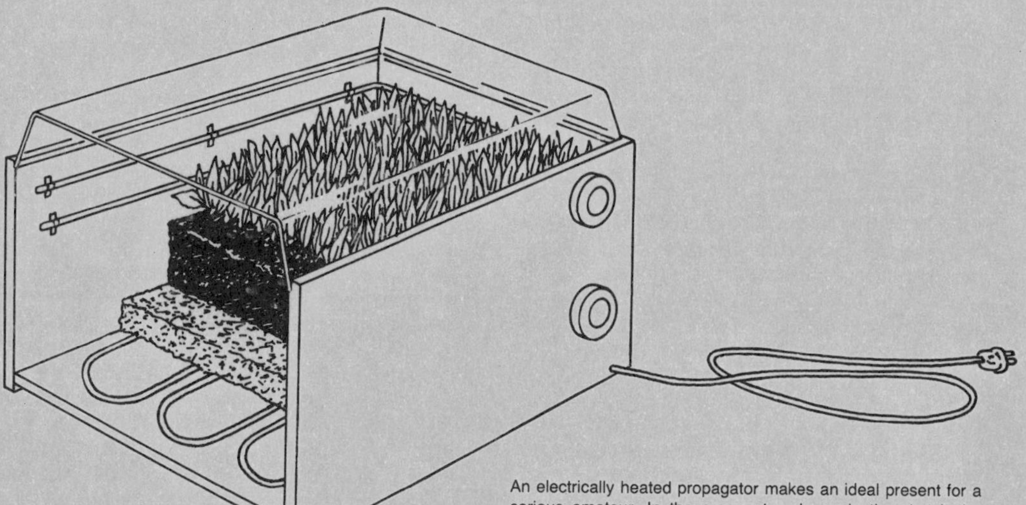

An electrically heated propagator makes an ideal present for a serious amateur. In the propagator shown in the sketch the temperature of the compost and the air are separately controlled by two thermostats. The bottom must always be covered with a layer of white sand, for if laid directly in the potting compost the cable will burn out

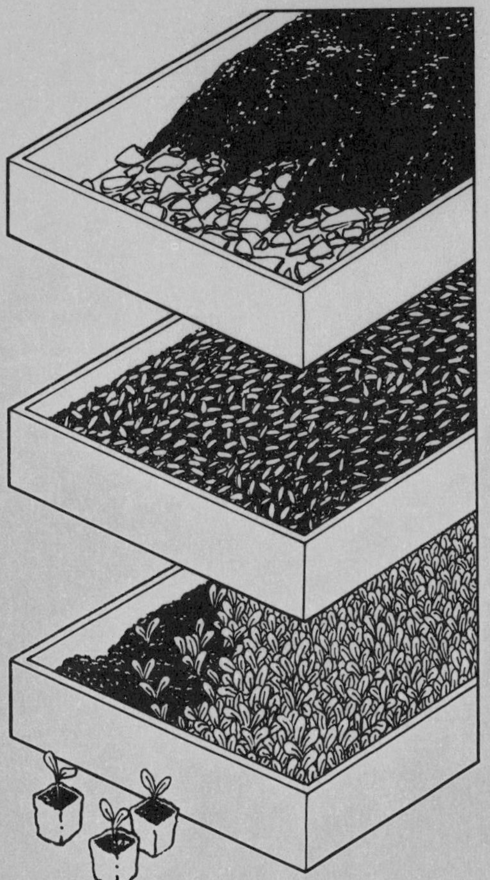

Sowing

Many house plants can be grown from seed, which may either be bought or collected from old plants. If you collect your own it is advisable to plant the ripe seeds immediately. Some hard seeds, which do not easily germinate, should first be soaked in water for 24 hours. Sometimes the hard skin can be filed off a little, but take care not to damage the germ.

The seed compost should be pressed down reasonably firmly in a pot or a seedtray and the seeds scattered on top. Be careful not to sow fine seed too densely, for this will create difficulties when the seedlings appear. A thin layer of clean white sand can be scattered on top to prevent the surface of the compost turning into a hard crust, which would keep out oxygen.

Drainage holes are essential, and to moisten the compost all over it is best to plunge the pots or trays in water until the white sand layer changes colour. This indicates that the mixture is moist throughout. If the pots or trays are now put in an enclosed propagator, no further watering will be necessary until the seeds have germinated.

Most seeds germinate without light and the seedtrays can therefore be put in the dark. However, as soon as the seedlings appear they must be placed in good light, or they will stretch, but keep them out of direct sunlight. When watering becomes necessary, use the plunging method described above.

Some seeds, for instance those of the primula, first need cold treatment. The moistened pot or tray is wrapped in aluminium foil and placed in the freezer compartment of the refrigerator, where it is left for two weeks. The seeds can then be allowed to germinate at a very low temperature – 5 to 10°C (41 to 50°F).

Seeds or spores which germinate very slowly must be sown in sterilised seed compost, since otherwise algae will grow in it. Put the seed compost in a casserole or baking tin with a raw potato on top, cover it with a lid and place the whole thing in the oven at 150°C. By the time the potato is cooked the compost may be considered sufficiently sterile. Quickly transfer it to the seed tray and cover it with glass. When the compost has cooled, sow your seed in the normal manner. A glass cover, initially covered with paper to keep out the light, is essential.

Above left Preparing a seedtray. A layer of crocks on the bottom ensures good drainage. This is then covered by seed compost which may or may not be sterilised.
The seeds then germinate. In the bottom tray the first true leaves have appeared and the seedlings are now ready to be pricked out

Left The seedlings are transferred singly to peat pots, either with the aid of an incised plant label, or with your fingers. Moisten the compost thoroughly.
At a later stage the peat pots can be transferred to larger plastic pots

Pricking out

Seeds do not all germinate at once. If you sow a mixture, you will notice that some seedlings develop ahead of the others. Usually the quickly germinating seeds belong to one group, for instance those of one particular colour. When a mixture of cactus seeds is sown, some of them will germinate months after the others. Seed trays should therefore not be cleaned out too soon, and do not use only the largest seedlings from a mixture.

Giving the seedlings more room is called 'pricking out'. This is done as soon as the seedlings can be handled or have two true leaves. The seedlings may be pricked out into separate pots, or spaced out in a seedtray. A tiny fork, dibber or an incised plant label may be found handy for the purpose. Use potting compost with a little extra peat added.

Hardening off

When seeds have germinated in a heated propagator and have been pricked out, they must be maintained in warmth until they are seen to start into growth. They can then be hardened off, that is to say, the vents in the propagator are opened a little, or the glass covering the seedtray is raised an inch or two. The moisture will now evaporate much more rapidly and you should therefore check regularly to prevent the compost drying out. If the young plants have a tendency to grow leggy, they should be stopped once or twice to induce bushy growth.

Division

Numerous house plants are very easily increased simply by being divided when they are being repotted. Each section is then potted separately, but it is essential that the roots remain intact. Use only young, vigorous sections and throw the older, damaged ones away.

Some plants develop long runners, from which plantlets appear. If these plantlets are pegged down in compost-filled pots, they will speedily root, and their link with the parent plant may then be cut. This method of propagation is called 'layering'.

Tubers are best divided immediately after their dormant season. Place them in a warm and humid place, until a little growth appears. The tubers may then be cut into sections, but remember that each section must have at least one shoot, otherwise it will not produce a plant. To prevent rotting the cuts should be treated with charcoal powder.

Bulbs often develop offsets at the base. These may be removed and grown separately, but they must be given the best possible conditions. These cannot often be provided in the living-room and the method is therefore rarely successful indoors. Greenhouse owners, however, will be able to increase their stock fairly easily.

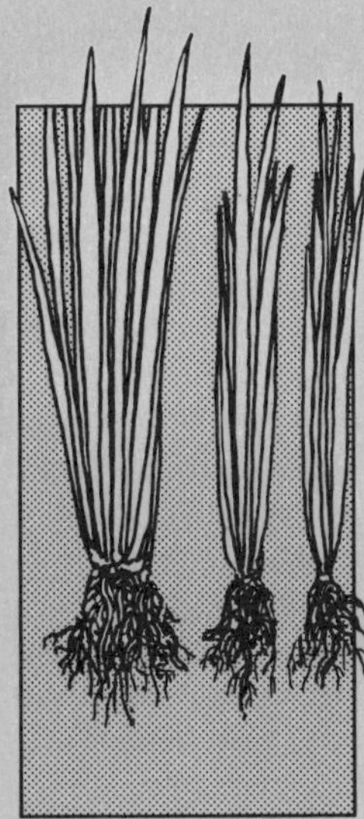

The easiest way of increasing plants is by division

Layering shoots frequently yields good results

A tuber can be cut into as many sections as it has eyes

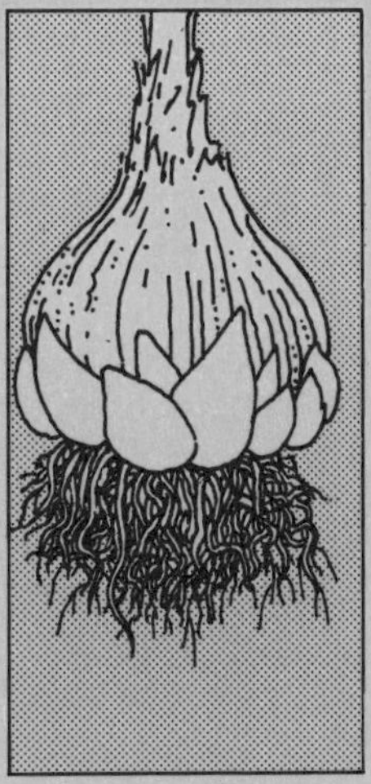

Bulbs develop offsets which may be removed and planted separately

Propagation from cuttings

Parts removed from a plant to be rooted are called 'cuttings'. They may be taken from various parts of the plant; there are shoot or tip cuttings, eye cuttings, leaf cuttings and root cuttings.

A shoot or tip cutting is usually taken from a non-flowering young or just-ripened shoot, which has grown the same year. The growing point is situated at the tip and a few leaves must be left on the cutting. The lower leaves are removed and this section is inserted in the growing medium.

An eye cutting is an undeveloped growing point in the axil of a leaf. The leaf and the leaf stalk are retained and the stem is cut above and below the eye.

A leaf cutting consists of a leaf inserted upright or laid flat on the compost. Roots and shoots will develop from the veins.

A root cutting is a non-developed eye of the root system. Each cutting needs to have only one eye.

Rooting medium

Cuttings strike best in a light, moisture-retaining medium, which must not be too rich in nutrients. Damp sphagnum moss, peat fibre, leafmould – all these retain sufficient moisture, while at the same time admitting air. In some cases (where the cuttings are soft and fleshy) it is undesirable for the mixture to be too damp, for this would cause rotting. To prevent this, clean sharp sand is added. An all-purpose mixture in which practically all cuttings will root consists of equal parts of peat fibre and sharp sand. Nutrients are almost entirely lacking and as soon as roots have developed the plantlets must be transferred to another medium.

Many amateurs root their cuttings in water, interesting to watch, but otherwise without special advantages. In this method the cuttings develop water roots, which will be of benefit if the plants are to be grown on under the hydroponics system. If, on the other hand, the plant is to be grown in compost, the water roots have to transform themselves into ordinary roots and it would therefore be better for the plant if the cuttings were started in a cuttings mixture.

Evaporation

Cuttings which still bear some foliage are particularly sensitive to evaporation. Water is lost through the leaves, but there are as yet no roots to supply new moisture. Evaporation may be reduced to a minimum by covering the pot with a plastic bag, or an indoor propagator with a transparent cover is even better. A certain amount of skill is required to maintain the humidity at such a level that the cuttings neither rot nor dry out, for this varies from plant to plant. Large leaves (such as might be taken with an eye cutting) are sometimes rolled up and held in place with a rubber band, in order to reduce evaporation. Another method is to cut or tear off part of the leaf, but this can only be done in the case of plants which do not 'bleed'.

When to take cuttings

Spring is a good time to take cuttings, but it can usually be done in summer as well. Where it is indicated that the cuttings should be taken from mature wood, this means that it should be done after August. Leaves for leaf cuttings must be fully grown.

Temperature

A high temperature always encourages rooting. The electrically heated indoor propagator is therefore excellent for this purpose also. The correct temperature varies from one plant to another, but always lies between 18 and 35°C (64 and 95°F).

Taking a shoot or tip cutting. The lower leaves are removed. After the cutting has been inserted in the compost, roots will develop from the lower eyes

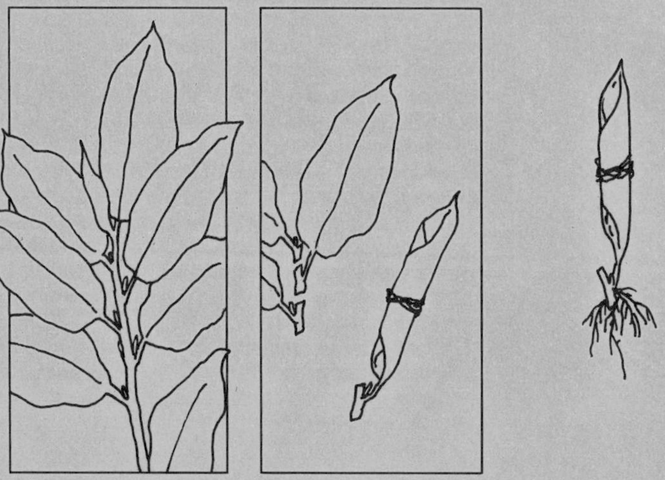

An eye cutting – the example is that of a ficus. The leaf is rolled up to minimise evaporation

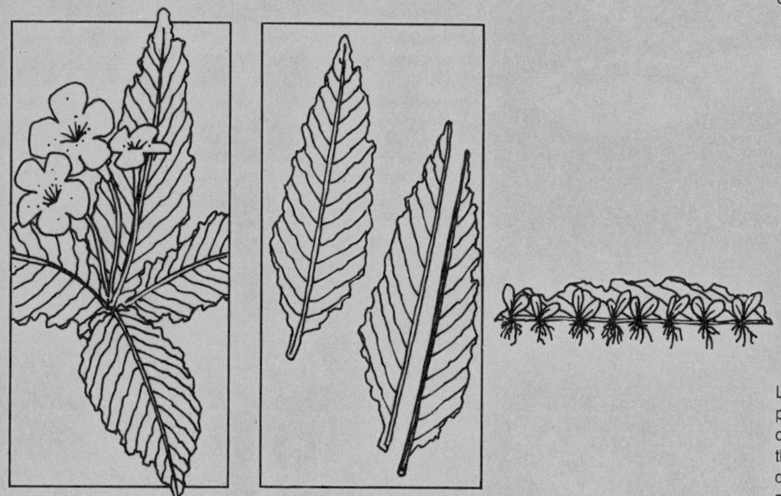

Leaf cutting of a streptocarpus. The leaf is cut along its central vein and inserted into the compost on its side. In the course of time a whole row of plantlets will develop

Stem cutting of an anthurium: in a warm and humid environment a piece of stem will develop roots and shoots from the dormant eyes

Leaf cutting from a sansevieria. Each section is approximately 7 cm (2¾ in) long and is inserted to a depth of 2 to 3 cm (¾ to 1⅛ in). Make sure they are planted the right way up. The variegated *Sansevieria trifasciata* 'Laurentii' will revert to green when grown from a cutting

Leaf cutting of a foliage begonia. Every leaf may be cut into very small pieces, which will each form a new plant. The trick is to keep the pieces flat on the compost; this can be done with the aid of small hairpins

Difficult cases

Cuttings which do not easily root are frequently taken with a heel, that is, a piece of the bark at the base. Rooting powder is also often used into which the cuttings are dipped, but when inserting them into the compost be careful to ensure that the powder is not rubbed off. Make a hole, insert the powdered cutting and press the compost down.

Leaf cuttings

Leaves of sansevieria are simply cut into 7-cm (2¾-in) sections, which will root in sandy soil. They must, of course, be the right way up – no roots will develop if the pieces are inserted upside down. Cuttings of variegated forms will revert to green. These can only be propagated by division.

Leaves of a foliage begonia can be cut in 1-cm (½-in) pieces. These are placed flat on the surface of the cutting compost and covered with a few grains of white sand, in such a way that they just remain visible.

The long leaves of the streptocarpus are divided along the centre vein and inserted on their side into the growing medium. Dozens of new plantlets will develop along the vein.

Saintpaulia leaves with a short piece of stem can be inserted upright into the cutting compost. This plant is easy to grow from cuttings; roots will develop even in water.

Fleshy cuttings

Broken-off joints of a number of succulents, cactus cuttings, the foliage crown of a pineapple with a little of the fruit attached, the fleshy stem cutting of a geranium – all these are examples of cuttings which must first be left to dry out for a few days (sometimes for as long as a week), or they will rot when planted. The drying-out process should take place out of the sun – a dry and draughty spot in the shade is better. Allow the tissue to shrivel up before inserting them in the growing medium.

Mist-spraying

The advanced amateur will install a mist-watering apparatus in his greenhouse, consisting of an automatically controlled sprayer which distributes the water in a fine mist. Cuttings which are very difficult to root such as conifers, rhododendron and other woody plants should be kept within reach of the spray and the compost warmed. If a large number of plants are required the costs of installation will soon be recovered. The system will also benefit cuttings of some house plants.

In the case of woody plants a cutting is frequently taken with a heel at the base. The cambium will increase the chances of root formation

If the crown of a pineapple is cut off, left to dry for a few days and then potted up, it will develop a new plant

Mist-watering apparatus suitable for an amateur's greenhouse. Even the most difficult cuttings will strike under mist-spraying

Air-layering

Like layering, this is a method in which the cutting is left on the plant. The plant continues to grow, but a bunch of roots is induced to develop somewhere along the stem.

To achieve this, the plant must be cut, for roots can only grow from the wound tissue. Such a wound can be created by removing a strip of bark, making an upward-slanting incision halfway through the stem or by removing a ring of bark halfway round it. The sap supply to the upper part of the plant must be maintained, but to a lesser extent.

Roots will develop only if the wound is surrounded by a light, damp medium. The cut stem should be wrapped in damp sphagnum moss and covered with a piece of plastic to keep it from drying out which is bound to the stem above and below the moss ball. From time to time check that the sphagnum moss is still damp.

Root formation may take several months, but can be speeded up by a little rooting powder sprinkled in the cut and also by the compost being watered very sparingly, while at the same time the moss ball is kept moist.

As soon as roots develop in the moss ball the stem is severed just below it and the new plant is potted. It must be frequently sprayed at first, or some of the leaves may be removed to restrict evaporation.

This system is often applied to woody plants which have grown too tall, for instance a Rubber Plant (*Ficus elastica*), when the upper 50 cm (20 in) are air-layered. It is a safe method, but it should be pointed out that it is usually easier to take eye cuttings, for which, however, a heated indoor propagator is required.

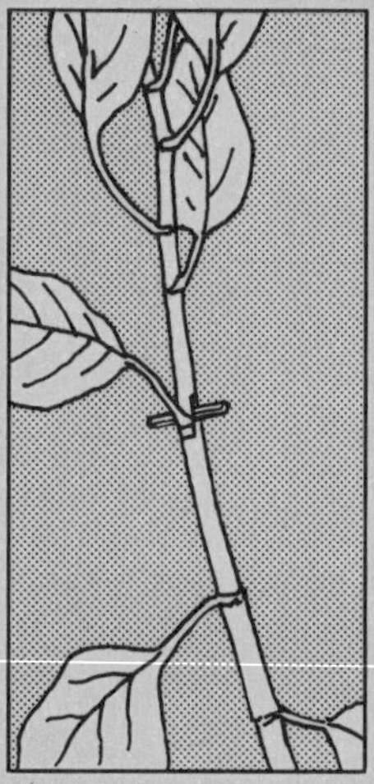

In air-layering a cut is made just below an eye and held open by a matchstick

The cut is wrapped in damp sphagnum moss

The moss ball is wrapped in plastic and bound to the stem

After rooting, the upper section is removed and potted separately

Grafting

Grafting is a method of propagation in which two different plants are bound together with their cambium layers touching to induce union. The species must be closely related – it is not possible to graft a cactus on to a hibiscus stock, for instance. The method is often used in the cultivation of cacti, because in our climate the light is often insufficient for many cactus species to flourish. Red and yellow cacti, in fact, are altogether incapable of photosynthesis because they lack chlorophyll. The weakling may be encouraged by grafting it on to vigorous green cactus stock, which shares its abundant living matter. In other words, the stock is the donor and the scion the recipient.

There is a second motive for grafting. Some hanging plants are shown to better advantage when growing on a stock. To mention just a few, azaleas look very attractive grafted on a stock and a waterfall of Christmas Cactus flowers grown on stock is also a beautiful sight. Standard geraniums and fuchsias are as a rule not obtained by grafting on a stock, but by tying the main shoot tightly upright until the desired height is reached. The plant is then topped to encourage a bushy crown.

Eriocereus jusbertii is frequently used as stock. This species is easily grown from seed and once the plants have reached a good size, the stem is cut straight across at a height of 5 to 7 cm (2 to 2¾ in) and the scion is placed on top. The disadvantage of this stock is that it frequently dies in a low winter temperature. *Trichocereus spachianus*, another cactus species described in this book, is hardier, but often the scion absorbs so much of its living matter that the stock dies.

A plant used as stock must be between four and eighteen months old. Immature stock will usually die. The scion is also cut straight across, and its cut surface may be somewhat smaller than that of the stock to prevent it sliding off. The sections are joined immediately after cutting and held together by rubber bands or a weight on top.

The union may take several weeks to form and is shown to be successful when the scion starts into growth. Grafting must always take place in the growing season.

A Christmas or Easter Cactus can also be turned into a standard by grafting it on *Eriocereus jusbertii*. In this case the stock must be about 30 cm (1 ft) tall. The top is cut off and a 2- to 3-cm (¾- to 1-in) incision is made in the cut surface. The scion, a small shoot of a jointed cactus, is tapered with a razor blade over a length of 2 to 3 cm (¾ to 1 in) and is inserted into the incision in the stock, where it is kept in place with a large cactus thorn. When the scion has started into growth it is stopped a couple of times to achieve a fine, branched crown.

Grafting shrubs for indoor cultivation is a job for the expert.

Above When grafting a cactus the stock must be of sufficient size. It is severed at the desired height and the edge is slightly rounded.
The scion is cut straight across and immediately placed on the stock. The sections are held in place with rubber bands or string until union has taken place

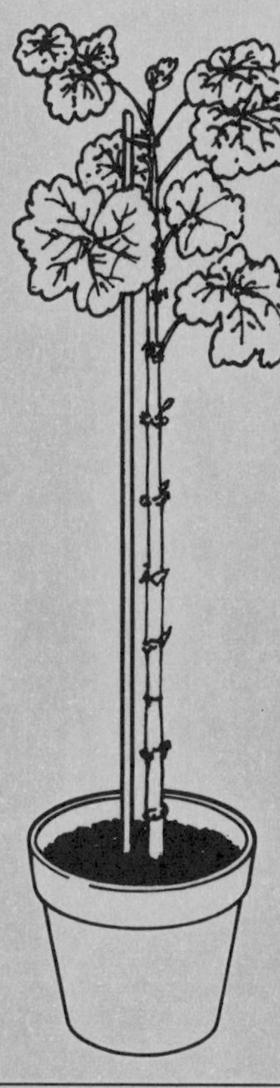

Right Standard forms of geranium or fuchsias may be created by removing all sideshoots and tying the centre shoot to a stake. Once the desired height is reached the plant is left to grow normally, though it may be pinched to encourage it to bush out

Pest and Disease Control

The term 'disease' includes not only the ailments of the plant itself, but especially attacks by fungi, virus infections and bacteria. Some diseases are due to a lack of certain nutrients. Diseases nearly always indicate that the plant's powers of resistance have weakened. It is often thought that a healthy plant may be infected by a diseased specimen, but this only happens when the apparently healthy plant itself is no longer in top condition. Tests have proved that mildew from an affected begonia, transferred to a thriving plant, had no effect. It would therefore appear that a plant in perfect condition develops a kind of defence mechanism (possibly a certain scent?) to keep attackers at a distance.

There can be many reasons why a plant does not thrive. To find the answer to this question the first thing to do is to consider its native habitat, for the conditions of its natural environment are almost certainly the ideal ones. As soon as these conditions are changed the plant may become diseased.

Fortunately this standard need not be too strictly adhered to, otherwise practically no house plant would survive, for no climate in the world can be exactly recreated in our living-rooms.

In this book climatic conditions are indicated by means of symbols representing degrees of light, temperature, moisture and atmospheric humidity. In addition the plant's growth is dependent on the correct balance of the potting medium. And finally it is of the greatest importance that the appropriate resting periods are allowed for.

Diagnosis

In 90 per cent of all cases plant ailments are due to an attack by insects. These cannot always be clearly seen, and you will need a good magnifying glass if you want to observe the minute creatures. They are usually found on the lower surface of the leaves. Where you see tissue formation or a sticky substance (honeydew), you may be sure there are insects present. Holes in the leaves indicate that the insects are eating the foliage. During the day the guilty ones may be in hiding.

Fungus diseases such as botrytis, mildew and rust are easily diagnosed by the white, grey or other coloured spots on the leaves, which can be rubbed off.

Leaves turning yellow or brown indicate errors in care and will be dealt with in the sections on diseases.

Wilting may indicate insufficient watering or root rot, which in turn could be caused by overwatering.

Deficiency diseases caused by lack of certain nutrients occur only when the plant has not been repotted or fed for a long time and are recognised by discoloured foliage or stunted growth.

Virus diseases cause blotches on the foliage and on the flowers.

Control

When a plant begins to ail, start by checking whether its position and the way it is cared for are in accordance with the symbols in this book. Also check whether the correct potting compost has been used. If you are not sure about this, repot the plant in the mixture indicated in the individual plant descriptions. In 90 per cent of all cases repotting and improving the conditions will be enough to cure the plant. The measures described below should only be resorted to if actions yield no result, or when the plant is so far gone that more drastic treatment is necessary.

Removing pests Insects which can be seen can often be removed by hand. Scale insects, for instance, can be rubbed off with a matchstick. The same applies to small numbers of greenfly, but other methods must be used where tiny pests occur in large numbers.

Luring Several pests may be trapped with bait. Earwigs hide in the daytime; provide them with a dark refuge near the plants they attack and empty it daily. Other pests, such as slugs, can be lured with poisoned bait.

Chemical remedies Spraying with chemicals is the method most often used. A liquid product is diluted with water and a spreader is added to increase the efficiency of the spray, or a ready-mixed aerosol spray is even easier. Chemicals in powder form are shaken over the plants. Greenhouses are frequently fumigated with smoke tablets incorporating pest controls, and vaporised sulphur against fungus diseases is also commonly used.

Systemic chemicals This method has become increasingly popular in recent years. A small insecticide spike is pressed into the compost. The poisonous substances it contains are dissolved when the plant is watered and are absorbed by the roots. The plant itself does not suffer, but pests eating the plants will be poisoned.

Biological remedies These are products of vegetative origin and far safer than most chemical controls. The two best known are derris and pyrethrum. Another form of biological pest control is the introduction of the pests' natural enemies. The whitefly parasite, for instance, *Encarsia formosa*, is sometimes introduced in greenhouses badly affected by whitefly. The larvae of this very small wasp feeds on the pupa of the whitefly. But amateur plant growers may find it difficult to obtain these predators.

Drawbacks of chemicals

In recent years many very poisonous remedies have been taken off the market. They had been in unlimited use for many years and experts are now asking how much damage has already been done to the ecology of the world in general and to the health of human beings in particular. It is quite possible that the products generally used today will be banned tomorrow. Serious doubts about them have already been raised.

It is for this reason that I have decided to recommend no chemical remedies in this or future books. If you still wish to use them, you do so at your own risk.

The odds are that the house plant you have bought from the garden centre or supermarket is already stuffed with chemicals, for growers use them a great deal. You will have to wait for some time and repot the plant before it will be biologically pure. Practically all the plants described in this book will grow very well without remedies, provided they are cultivated in the best possible conditions. And that is both the art and the attraction of plant care.

Less dangerous remedies

Before all those complicated chemical compounds were invented, parasites were combated with simple, natural products or with domestic remedies. Now that such serious objections have been raised against chemicals, we are gradually returning to the old-fashioned remedies. The following are some of them.

Spirit and soap 20g (¾oz) green soap and 10g (⅓oz) methylated spirit are dissolved in 1 litre (2pints) water and sprayed over the plant. An excellent remedy against greenfly, but also against other pests if regularly repeated.

Pure spirits Apply the spirits with a small paint brush to scale and other insects.

Tobacco infusion Pipe tobacco or shag (or a demolished cigarette) is left to infuse in water. The solution, which will contain a certain amount of nicotine, is then strained and sprayed over the plants. Take care not to use too high a concentration.

Infusion of quassia wood with green soap Boil 10 to 15g (⅓ to ½oz) of quassia wood (obtainable from a herbalist) for several hours in 1litre (2pints) water; the liquid is then strained. Add 10g (⅓oz) soft green soap as spreader.

Infusion of wormwood with green soap Prepare in the same way as the last remedy, using dried wormwood instead of quassia wood. This can also be bought from herbalists. (If you have a garden you can grow it yourself. It will keep parasites away.)

Stinging nettle manure Leave fresh or dried stinging nettles in water for several days. Add 1 per cent green soap as a spreader and spray the plants with the strained liquid. It does not have a very pleasant smell, but has the advantage of acting as foliar fertiliser at the same time as keeping pests away. If your plants are sprayed with this concoction twice a week throughout the summer, you will rarely be plagued by pests.

Equisetum tea Equisetum; better known as horse tail. Boil 300g (11oz) of the dried herb in 1litre (2pints) water for 30 minutes. Cool and strain, then dilute 5cc of the liquid with 1litre (2pints) water and use as a spray. Effective against fungus diseases such as mildew, but only as a preventative measure.

Rhubarb spray Chop up 1kg (2lb3oz) of rhubarb leaves and boil them for half an hour in 2litres (3½pints) water. Strain and add 25g (1oz) soft soap. A remedy against greenfly.

All these remedies can be applied by means of the practical plant sprays available. The cheaper models work on the principle of a suction pump; the more expensive have a pressurised reservoir to distribute the liquid evenly.

Biological remedies available

Pyrethrum, made from the flower heads of a chrysanthemum species (*Chrysanthemum cinerariifolium*), is available in aerosols or as a liquid for use in plant sprays. Look out for possible non-biological additives. It is effective against greenfly, young caterpillars, thrips and capsid bug.

Rotenone is the active ingredient of derris roots, available in powder form and as a liquid. It is sometimes included in the contents of aerosols, and is effective against greenfly, caterpillars, thrips and whitefly.

Sulphur is successful in combating many fungus diseases, especially mildew. Available as flowers of sulphur or in powder form for dusting the plants. The liquid form, to be diluted in water for use in sprays, is more convenient. Sulphur powder is used in vaporisers. Although not pleasant to use, sulphur is believed to be harmless to our health (think of the volcanic sulphur springs).

Chief pests and diseases

On pages 78 to 80 inclusive you will find a survey of the most important pests and diseases which may attack house and greenhouse plants in general. Diseases which affect only certain genera are discussed under their appropriate headings.

Ants
Ants occasionally nibble plants, but usually they make for the sweet secretion of greenfly, the so-called honeydew. Greenfly control will at the same time check the ant infestation. The ants themselves may be combated with derris powder.

Aphids
These are the best-known parasites. They are usually green or yellow in colour, sometimes winged. They live in groups, often on young shoots. They secrete a sticky substance on which the black fungus downy mildew will subsequently grow.

A mixture of soap and methylated spirits is the best remedy, also derris, pyrethrum or rhubarb soap.

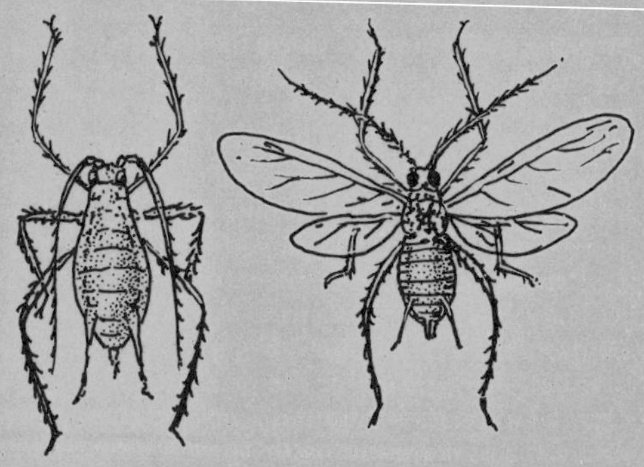

Basal rot, see Wilting.

Botrytis, see Grey mould.

Brown patches on the leaves
This usually occurs because the plant has temporarily been kept at far too low a temperature. Check the minimum temperature required. Another cause may be lack of potassium (q.v.). Pale blotches on hairy leaves are caused by drops of water.

Capsid bugs
Most capsid bugs possess wings, but in some they are lacking entirely. The insects have flat heads and wide, flat bodies with six legs and long feelers. The colour is green or brown; their maximum length is 8mm (⅓in) and they move rapidly. They are sucking pests and make small holes in parts of plants. Growing shoots and flowers become misshapen.

Control by dusting or spraying with derris products or with pyrethrum.

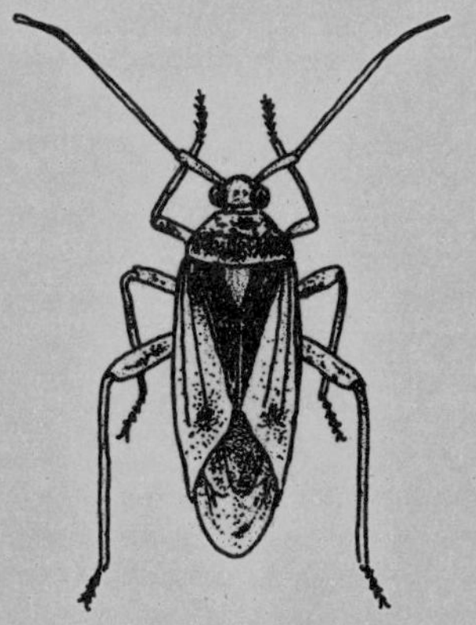

Chlorosis or iron deficiency
This usually occurs in acid-loving plants grown in excessively chalky soil. At too high a pH level these plants are unable to absorb the iron essential for the production of chlorophyll. Initially a network of paler tissue appears between the darker-coloured veins and subsequently the entire leaf turns yellow. Manganese deficiency produces practically the same symptoms, but this rarely occurs in indoor plants.

Spraying with iron chelate may help for a time, but the best solution is to repot the plant immediately in a more acid compost.

Cockroaches
Large insects, similar to beetles, but with a flatter body, up to 4cm (1½in) long. Feelers and legs are exceptionally long. They are found almost exclusively in hothouses, where they feed mainly on young shoots and seedlings. They are nocturnal insects.

They may be trapped in glass jars or jugs containing a little beer, syrup or cheese.

Comma scale, see Scale insects.

Cut worms
These are the larvae of moths. The grey caterpillars nibble the plants both below and above ground level.

You can control them by picking them off or by repotting the plant. During the day they curl up underground.

Damping off fungus
Caused by various fungi. Seedlings or cuttings rot near the soil and collapse. Always use fresh compost and if this does not stop the trouble, sterilise the compost. Infected plants must be removed immediately.

Downy mildew
This mould is greyish white and occurs chiefly on the reverse of the leaves.

Control by decreasing the amount of humidity and by spraying or dusting with sulphur products.

Earwigs
Dark brown, jointed insects with a pincer-shaped tail. During the night they feed on flower buds and young leaves but they also like greenfly.

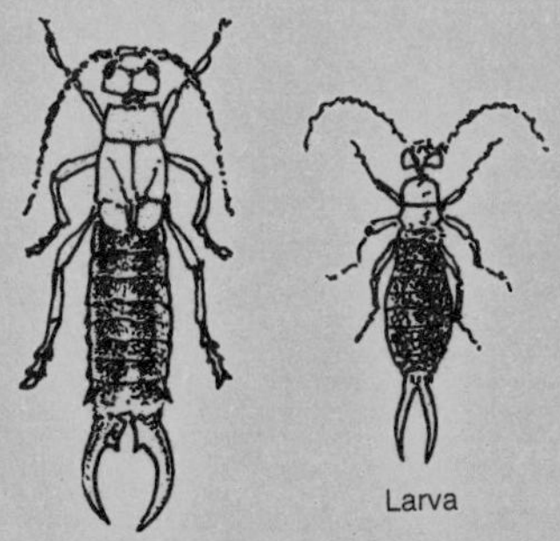

The pests may be trapped in inverted flowerpots filled with woodwool or straw in which they will hide during the day. Empty the pots every day.

Eelworms
Eelworms are minute creatures, usually invisible to the naked eye, living either in the compost or in the foliage of plants, where they can cause damage.

Aphelenchoides species are the most harmful. They cause distortion and gradual dying of the foliage, often bit by bit, starting at the oldest leaves. Buds and stems may also be damaged. Professional growers sterilise the compost by chemical means, but amateur growers are advised to discard infested plants. Always use fresh potting compost, which will be free of eelworms.

Excessive chlorine
This is damage caused by mineral salts when the water contains too much kitchen salt. Use demineralised water or rainwater. The foliage will be dark green, but the plant does not grow.

In older leaves the edges may turn brown, as in potassium deficiency.

Flea beetle
Small metallic beetles, sometimes striped with yellow. They skip around and nibble windows and, later, holes in the leaves, especially attacking seedlings.

The remedy is to dust with derris powder, or spray repeatedly with pyrethrum.

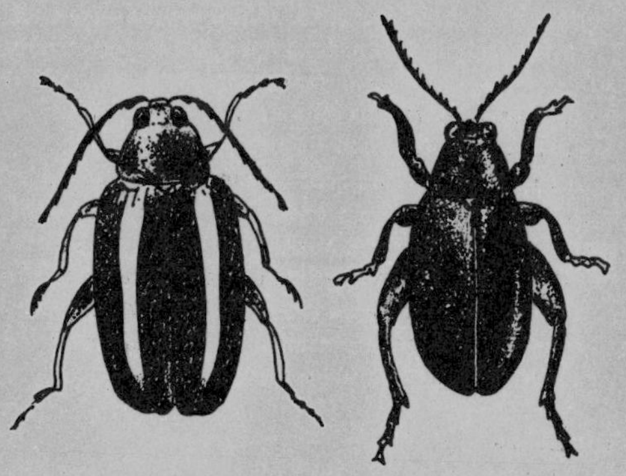

Leaf-blotch eelworms, see Eelworms.

Greenhouse grasshopper
Brown-marbled grasshoppers, about 3cm (1in) long, with exceptionally long feelers. They occur in hothouses, where they remain hidden during the day and feed on both young and more mature plants.

The best method of control is to fumigate the hothouse. Special tablets are available for the purpose, but these generally contain very poisonous chemicals.

Grey mould
Botrytis cinerea is a brown-grey mould developing on dead or damaged plants in particular, occasionally on seedlings. To prevent it, provide plenty of ventilation and do not keep the compost too moist.

Iron deficiency, see Chlorosis.

Leaf fall
If a plant is abruptly moved to a different position it will frequently lose some of its foliage. Other causes may be dryness or unbalanced feeding.

Leaf frog hopper, see Leafhopper

Leafhopper
Slender, somewhat boat-shaped insects, green or brown in colour. They jump away when the plant is touched. Leafhoppers suck the leaves, creating tiny white spots. An infestation by leafhoppers is easily recognised by the fact that the yellow-green nymphs cover themselves in a layer of foam (cuckoo spit).

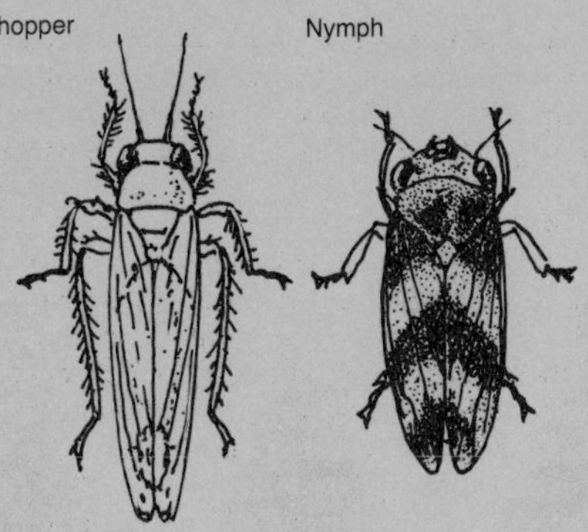

Lice, see Aphids.

Mealy bug
These sluggish pests are pink or orange in colour and are covered with a white mealy wax. They always live in colonies.

Control by dabbing the colonies with alcohol in the form of methylated spirits or gin.

Mice
These animals rarely feed on plants, but they may become a nuisance in the greenhouse, where they like to make their nests on the staging. Keep the greenhouse as humid as possible, for mice choose dry, warm spots. Trapping is often the most effective remedy. The use of any form of poisoned bait is dangerous unless it can be guaranteed that children and domestic animals cannot reach it.

Mildew
A fungus disease occurring in a variety of plants. The leaves become covered with white, powdery patches, which can be rubbed off.

Sulphur remains the best remedy, to which few objections can be raised. The product is available in powder and in liquid form. However, when a plant such as a begonia is covered entirely in mildew, even sulphur will not help.

See also Downy mildew.

Millipedes
These resemble centipedes to some extent, but have a more cylindrical body, more or less flat at the bottom. Each segment has one pair of legs. They have no poison glands. Unlike centipedes, they are harmful to plants: they feed mainly on soft parts of the plant or on young roots. They frequently occur in damp, dark places and are nocturnal.

There are three possible remedies: place hollowed-out, halved potatoes, cut side down, on the soil. Cut a notch in the side through which the pests can enter. Towards morning the millipedes will seek shelter in the potatoes, which can then be thrown away. Or try surrounding the plants with peat fibre soaked in paraffin, or sprinkle tobacco among the plants. The pests will be deterred by the smell.

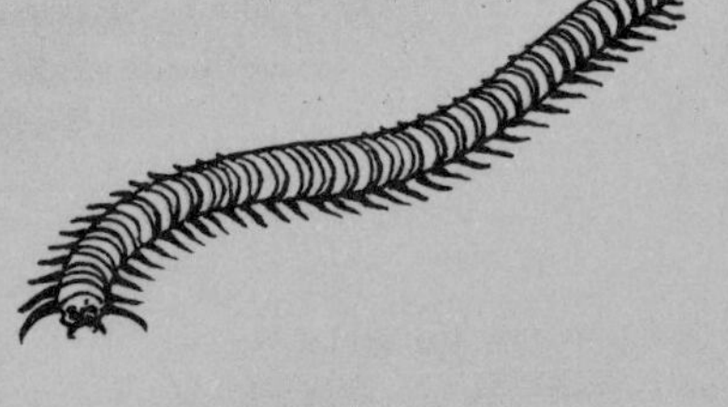

Mites
Minute pests, hardly visible to the naked eye. They suck the leaves and can do enormous damage. Red spider mites (q.v.) also belong to this family.

Control is difficult, because mites are only affected by the most poisonous substances. You may therefore be forced to use chemicals, especially in the greenhouse. The best method is to use fumigant tablets, usually containing lindane.

Nitrogen deficiency
Young and mature leaves turn pale yellow and growth is retarded.

The condition will immediately be improved if the plant is fed with a composite fertiliser.

Oyster shell scale insects, see Scale insects.

Phosphorus deficiency
The leaves turn dark to bluish-green, sometimes shading to purple or red on the reverse.

Feeding with a composite house plant fertiliser will help.

Potassium deficiency
The edges of old foliage turn yellow and subsequently wither, while the rest of the leaves turns a bluish-green. The condition rarely occurs in house plants. Feeding with a composite fertiliser will help.

Red spider mite
These insects are barely half a millimetre long, yellow when young, later turning red. They are hardly visible to the naked eye, but observed through a magnifying glass they resemble tiny spiders.

Red spider mite is always found on the undersides of leaves. They suck the tissue and manifest themselves in small white spots on the upper surface of the foliage, which subsequently join up, giving the leaves a grey and faded appearance. Very fine but dense webbing hiding the colonies appears on the underside of affected leaves.

Red spider mites like dry air. Frequent spraying (daily or more) under the leaves is therefore a good remedy. Dilute a little methylated spirit and soap or a pyrethrum solution in the water. This is a very persistent pest, difficult to control. Root pesticide spikes may be used as a last resort.

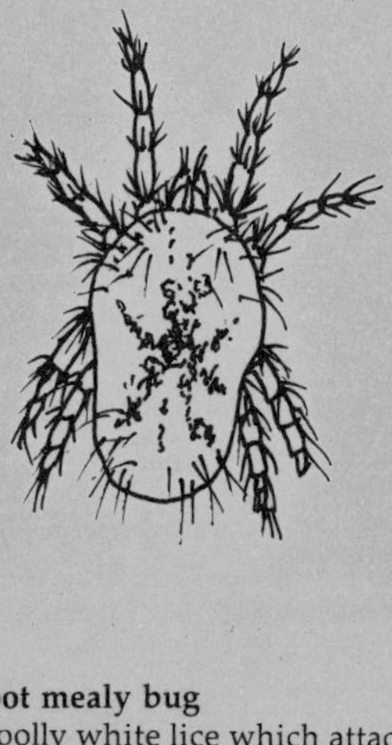

Root mealy bug
Woolly white lice which attack the roots and cause stunted growth.

For control see under Root millipede.

Root millipede
Rapidly moving white millipedes with one pair of legs per segment. They eat roots. Water with liquid derris diluted as appropriate. Another method is to plunge the plant repeatedly and for long periods in fairly warm water, but not above 45°C (113°F). And, finally, wash the roots, remove all millipedes and repot.

Root rot
The roots turn brown and rot and the plant stagnates and dies. This may be due to bacteria, fungus disease or root eelworm. Fungus disease is the most likely cause; it occurs when the soil is far too wet or too cold. Improve conditions and repot the plant.

Salt damage
If you were to sprinkle ordinary kitchen salt around a plant it would die. Sensitivity to common salt varies considerably from plant to plant and is greatest in orchids, followed by anthuriums, *Rhododendron simsii*, sinningias and others.

If the tap water contains too much salt, other water must be used for watering plants (see pages 57–58).

In most cases salt damage amounts to excess chlorine (q.v.), but other salts can also be harmful. In doubtful cases repot immediately.

Scale insects
There are four kinds: the comma scale, the oyster shell scale, *Eulecanium* species and the mealy scale. They all hide under shield-shaped shells and so it is difficult to control them with chemicals. The only real solution is to poison the plant itself and the root pesticide spikes are therefore an effective remedy. The scales may also be removed with a matchstick or they can be dabbed daily with alcohol in the form of methylated spirits or gin. As a rule they will finally give up the struggle.

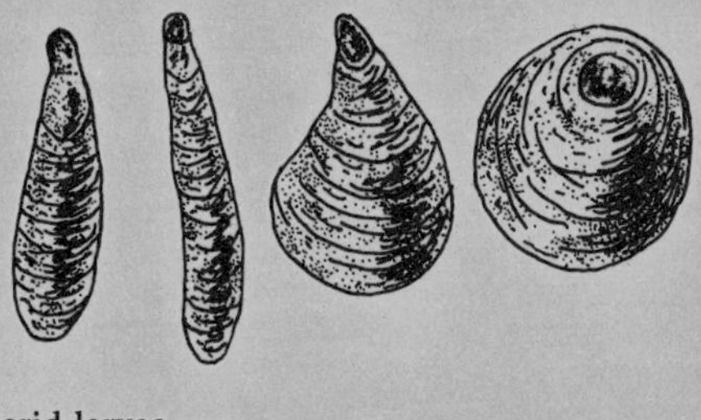

Sciarid larvae
These 3- to 4-mm ($\frac{1}{4}$-in) larvae have the appearance of tiny glass rods. They live in the soil and feed on seedlings, pricked-out plantlets and cuttings.

Control by watering with liquid derris. The midges themselves are harmless but should be destroyed by spraying with pyrethrum products or by fumigating the greenhouse.

Scorching
This is not a disease, but is the result of overfeeding, usually leading to excess nitrogen. The leaves dry out at the edges and curl up. As soon as these symptoms appear the plant should be removed from the pot and repotted after the root system has been rinsed clean.

See also page 61 for an explanation of the symptom.

Slugs
Molluscs which feed off young plant shoots. They rarely occur indoors, but only too often in greenhouses.

Control by spreading slug pellets made of bran mixed with the poison metaldehyde. But be sure to keep these safely out of the reach of children and domestic animals.

Sooty mould

A fungus disease in which the foliage is covered with a black deposit which can be rubbed off. It always forms on the syrupy secretion known as honeydew of aphids or scale insects.

Remove or spray the aphids and thorougly wash the foliage with tepid water.

Springtail

Tiny, usually white, wingless insects, 1 to 4mm ($\frac{1}{16}$ to $\frac{1}{4}$in) in size, jumping and living in damp places. They are frequently found between pot and pot cover or in wet saucers. Cleaning the pot and keeping the plant drier will help to control them. As a rule the damage they cause is slight, although the white species may feed off roots.

Control with pyrethrum products in places where they have been observed.

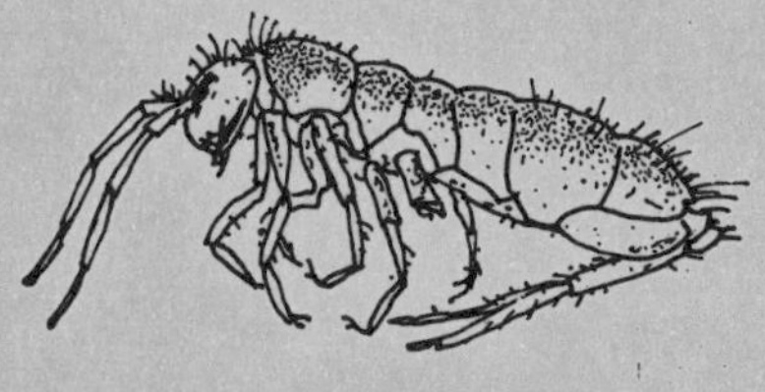

Sun scorch

When a plant which prefers shade is placed in the sun, or when any plant is suddenly moved to a sunny spot after having stood in the shade for a long time, strong sunlight will damage the foliage. The leaves develop paler patches and wilt.

Plants which have been kept in a dark environment during the winter must be gradually accustomed to the sun in spring by being screened. Even cacti do not tolerate direct sunlight immediately after their winter rest.

Tarsonemid mites

Tarsonemus pallidus occurs not only on cyclamens, but also on African violets and other plants. The leaves become distorted and the edges curl up. The flowers, too, become distorted and dark patches occur.

This pest can only be controlled by the use of very poisonous substances.

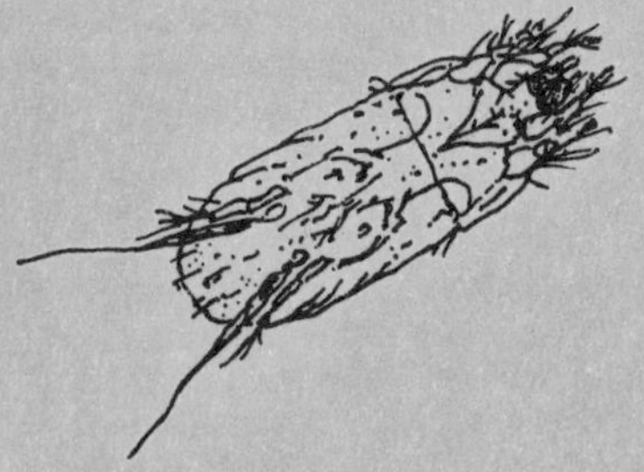

Thrips

Adult insects are only 1 to 2mm ($\frac{1}{16}$in) long, dark brown, red towards the tail. They suck the leaves, causing pale spots which may become so numerous that the entire leaf appears silvery. Eventually the leaves turn yellow and drop.

Thrips are not easily controlled. They hatch best in a high temperature. Frequent spraying with a pyrethrum solution will help to some extent. Derris is another reasonably effective remedy. An infusion of pipe or shag tobacco sprayed on to the plant should give good results. Try it first on a few leaves to ensure that the solution is not strong enough to damage the foliage; if it is, dilute it further. Root pesticide spikes will kill the thrips while the plant will survive.

Vine weevil

There are two kinds, black beetles and brown beetles. They occur on other plants as well as on vines. The legless larvae are particularly harmful in house plant cultivation; they live in the compost and feed on roots.

The beetles can be caught in wads of woodwool or straw put in flower pots placed among the plants. The beetles will hide in the woodwool, which can then be discarded. Beetles or larvae which are visible can be dusted with derris powder. If the larvae are buried in the soil, repot the plant, carefully check the rootball and use fresh compost.

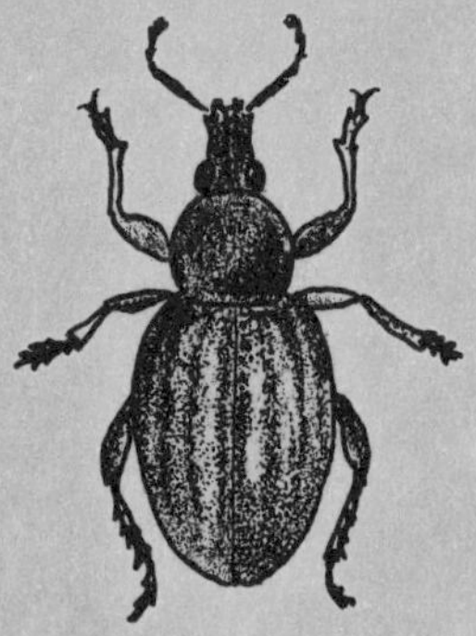

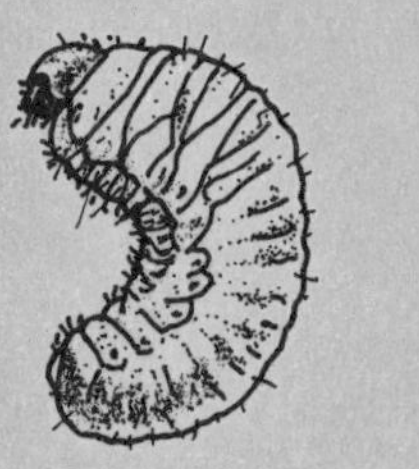

Larva

Virus diseases

Strange yellow bands or circles may appear on the foliage. Sometimes the stems suddenly turn red, and the leaves do not grow to their normal size.

Virus diseases occur mainly in commercial cultivation and can only be avoided by creating the most hygienic conditions. Once they do occur, the affected plants should be discarded immediately.

Whitefly

A much-feared insect, especially in greenhouses, but also in the home. They are tiny white moths which fly out when the plant is touched, but quickly land again. They feed on the lower side of the foliage. Like greenfly, whitefly secretes honeydew. Control by repeated spraying with a soap and methylated spirits mixture or with a derris preparation. The eggs will not be killed and it is therefore essential to repeat the operation after four days. In practice you will find that you will have to continue spraying almost throughout the summer. Biological control is possible by introducing the whitefly parasite *Encarsia formosa*, but this is a practical proposition only in greenhouses and in any case the whitefly parasite is not very easily obtainable.

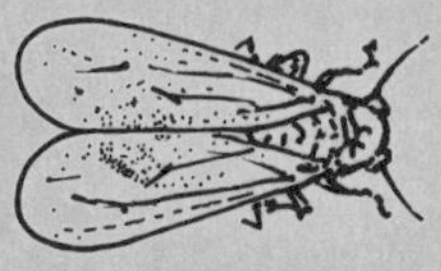

Wilting

A plant is described as 'wilting' when it is insufficiently watered, but wilting may also be the result of a fungus infection. One fungus causes the plant to rot at the base. Such diseases are promoted by the use of old, unsterilised potting compost, or by growing plants too often in the same compost. Always use fresh potting compost.

Woodlice

Flat grey insects with numerous legs, living in damp places. At night they feed on fleshy parts of plants.

They may be caught under hollowed-out potatoes or beetroot or by being lured with bran, sugar or rolled oats. Remove them daily, together with the bait.

Worms

Sometimes common earthworms are discovered in the potting compost. As a rule they do no harm, in fact they help aerate the soil. If there are too many, clean the roots and repot the plant.

Yellowing leaves

It is quite normal if some of the leaves of evergreen plants occasionally turn yellow or drop. If the problem becomes too serious check whether the plant is kept too wet or too dry and improve the conditions.

IDENTIFYING THE PLANTS

In this section the plants have been alphabetically arranged, using the botanical names at present employed.

When looking for a plant which you know only by an older name (synonym) or by its popular name, you will find all the names in the index at the end of the book and this will refer you to the correct page.

Plants for which you do not know the name may be identified by looking at the illustrations.

Nomenclature of cultivated plants
People often wonder whether it is really necessary to use the difficult Latin names. Why not use popular names?

The answer is that many plants have more than one popular name, varying not only from one country to another but sometimes between regions. For this reason, as well as because many plants simply do not have a popular name, they can only be arranged alphabetically under their correct – that is, botanical – names.

Just to make it a little more difficult: what *is* the correct botanical name? You may already have noticed that many of the names in this book differ from those found in other books or in certain catalogues. The reason – which may come as a surprise – is that the botanical nomenclature is not irreversible. Names are being changed every year, which doesn't help and simply adds to the confusion.

The problem is that we are bound by the so-called rule of priority, introduced by the Swiss A. de Landolle (1806–1893), which lays down that the oldest written name is the correct one. From time to time a very old plant description is unearthed, which must then replace the familiar, but more recent name.

In the second place the systematic classification is sometimes modified, which occasionally results in certain genera being moved to different families. It is likely that this irritating confusion will continue for a time, but thanks to improving communications in the course of the centuries, there should be an end to it one day.

In some scientific works the most recent names of practically all plants are mentioned. For the purposes of this book the authority used is the generally accepted *Handwörterbuch der Pflanzennamen* by Zander, 10th edition. This edition appeared over six years ago, which means that some of the names mentioned here, although by now perfectly familiar, are no longer correct. I have decided to leave them until a new edition of Zander or another reliable register is published.

In order to allow for comparison of the names in this book with those used in other works, periodicals or in common usage, the most familiar synonyms are also given.

The best-known popular names are included in the headings or in the text. These names are also found in the index, so you should have no difficulty in finding the plant you are looking for.

Family, genus, species, variety and strain
Each plant is indicated in the first place under its generic name, followed by its specific name. This is the system also used in official registers of people, for example *Smith* (generic name), *John* (specific name). Thus the correct name for the well-known Chinese Rose is *Hibiscus* (generic name) *rosa-sinensis* (specific name).

Where more than one species are mentioned only the initial letter of the generic name is given, for instance: *H. rosa-sinensis*. This entirely natural *Hibiscus* species has single, rose-pink flowers. In the course of the last hundred years growers have succeeded in cultivating a number of varieties with as a rule much larger, often double, flowers in the colours orange-red, yellow, and cherry-red. Some mutations were the result of atomic radiation. These cultivated varieties must on no account be confused with naturally growing varieties of certain species and the former are therefore referred to as cultivars (abbreviated to cv.) which simply means strains or breeds. The names of strains are printed in roman type, not in italics; they have a capital initial and are placed in inverted commas.

Example: *Hibiscus rosa-sinensis* 'Anita Buis' has large, single, deep yellow flowers.

Hundreds of such strains are described in this book, for many plants are the outcome of crossing or selection. This applies even more to garden plants.

In the case of natural varieties, the (botanical) name is printed in italics.

Occasionally you will find a reference to a subspecies, abbreviated to ssp. and very rarely, below variety, to a form, abbreviated to f. The basic form of a modern indoor hydrangea, for instance, is called *Hydrangea macrophylla* ssp. *macrophylla* f. *otaksa*.

On some occasions two species belonging to the same genus are crossed to produce a new species. In such cases we speak of hybrids, not of strains. Crossing is indicated by an × in front of the new specific name. For example the broom *Cytisus* × *racemosus* is a cross between *Cytisus canariensis* and *Cytisus maderensis* var. *magnifoliosus*.

It happens more frequently that two different genera are crossed. A well-known example of such an intergeneric hybrid is × *Fatshedera lizei*, the result of crossing *Fatsia japonica* with *Hedera helix*. This was achieved in France in 1910. In the alphabetical classification this 'artificial' genus is placed under F. Orchids are easily crossed and this family therefore contains an enormous number of hybrids.

How to use the symbols
The five main requirements for growth have been expressed in five groups of three symbols. They are explained here and on the jacket flap.

In the alphabetical section individual species are alphabetically arranged in their turn. The name of the first species described is always followed by the appropriate symbols. Where subsequent species are not accompanied by symbols, those mentioned under the previous species apply. If, on the other hand, the requirements of growth differ, however slightly, the whole series of symbols is repeated.

In many cases two symbols from one group are shown. Where, for instance, you see the symbols for warm conditions and for moderate warmth printed side by side, you may assume that both conditions are acceptable or that the correct temperature lies somewhere between the two. Where the symbols for standard potting compost and special soil mixture appear side by side, it means that the plant prefers a special mixture, but will grow in standard compost as well.

Arrangement of plant descriptions
The following paragraphs are intended to give you a better idea of the way in which the plant descriptions in this book have been arranged.

Every genus is classified under a heading starting with the botanical generic name. Next comes another botanical name indicating the family to which the genus belongs. This is followed by the popular or common name. Many plants are known by dozens of different popular names and it would of course be impossible to mention them all. Frequently no popular name exists.

A heading might therefore appear as follows:

Hibiscus
Malvaceae
Chinese Rose

Basic information concerning the entire genus is always classified under the same headings:

- Name
- Origin
- Description
- Position
- Care
- Watering
- Feeding
- Repotting
- Propagation
- Pests and diseases

The last heading appears only where there is a real likelihood of the plant being affected by pests or diseases.

Next come the descriptions of individual species, alphabetically arranged under their botanical name. They start with the correct specific name, followed by the symbols applying to the species (and possibly to subsequent species). If a botanical synonym exists (that is, a well-known alternative but obsolete name), it will appear with the prefix 'syn.' on the third line. The species under discussion may have an individual popular name, in which case it will be shown. The species is then briefly described as far as possible. It is not easy to recognise a plant merely from its description and it is for this reason that all the more important species are illustrated, which will be of much more help. Important strains of the species described are always mentioned. House plant strains are more often identified by colour alone than garden plants. If you cannot immediately find a particular species, reference to the synonyms (possibly through the index) may lead you in the right direction.

Key to symbols

Requires direct sunlight when available

Requires plenty of light, but must be screened from the sun between 10 a.m. and 5 p.m.

Tolerates less light

Warm conditions; minimum night temperature in summer 16 to 20°C (60 to 68°F)

Moderate warmth; minimum night temperature in summer 10 to 16°C (50 to 60°F)

Cool conditions; minimum night temperature in summer 3 to 10°C (37 to 50°F)

Constantly moist; the compost must never dry out

Moderately damp; allow the compost to dry out between watering

Fairly dry; water moderately and only when it is warm

High degree of relative atmospheric humidity (above 60 per cent)

Moderate relative atmospheric humidity (50 to 60 per cent)

Low degree of relative atmospheric humidity (below 50 per cent is acceptable)

Standard potting compost, acidity between pH 5.5 and 6.5

Acid potting compost, acidity between pH 4.5 and 5.5

Special compost mixture required (described in the text)

Abutilon striatum 'Thompsonii', with fine variegated foliage

Abutilon megapotamicum

Abutilon hybrid 'Golden Fleece'

Abutilon striatum 'Thompsonii'

Abutilon

Malvaceae

Name The Arabic name of this or of a related genus is *aubutilun*.
Origin Chiefly the tropical and sub-tropical regions of South and Central America.
Description Slightly tender evergreen herbaceous shrub or small tree. It has slender, more or less arching branches and leaves which are usually heart shaped. In a number of species these are variegated as a result of a virus infection. It bears striking bell-shaped flowers in white, yellow, orange and red, sometimes with contrasting darker veining. Properly cared for, the plant can grow several feet high even in your living-room.
Position In summer keep it in a half-shady, sheltered spot in the garden or on a balcony. If kept indoors it likes sun in the morning, but screen it from the sun in the afternoon. It needs the lightest possible situation in winter.
Care From September to February abutilons need a resting period at a temperature of 12 to 15°C (53 to 59°F). If kept in the living-room, the plant will drop some of its leaves. In spring, when it will have lost some of its beauty, it should be cut back and repotted, after which it will start into growth once more. Flowering usually starts in early summer and may continue throughout the winter, provided the plant is then kept in a very light, well-ventilated and cool position. Don't hesitate to open the windows – abutilons love fresh air. When growing fast the plant develops soft shoots which must be tied in.
Watering Water freely during the growing season; tall plants 2 to 3 m (6 to 9 ft) high will need water several times a day in warm and sunny weather, for the soil ball must be kept moist. In winter the plant will tolerate dry air fairly well, but prefers moderate humidity. Water sparingly while the plant is kept cool in winter.
Feeding From March to September the plant should be fed weekly with a standard solution.
Repotting Use a commercial soil-based potting compost or a mixture of equal parts leafmould, clay and rotted cow manure. Frequent repotting will prevent attacks by mealy bugs.
Propagation Hybrids are sown in January or February in light soil at a temperature of 20°C (68°F). When it is a question of maintaining special colours or variegated species, the plants are grown from cuttings. The earlier these are taken, the stronger the plants will be that same year. Use strong shoots without flower buds and root them under glass or plastic in a mixture of leafmould and sharp sand and at a bottom heat of 22 to 25°C (71 to 77°F). Once the cuttings have started into growth they should be potted in groups to provide bushy plants. *Abutilon megapotamicum* is sometimes grown as a standard tree. To do this, remove sideshoots until the stem has reached the desired height. If you then take out the tip, the plant will rapidly form a crown.
Pests and diseases Scale insects, mealy bug, or red spider mites may occur.

Abutilon darwinii
Up to 1 m (3 ft) in height, with bell-shaped, red-veined, orange-red flowers throughout the year. The heart-shaped leaves, growing on stalks, are covered in soft hair and are felty to the touch.
***Abutilon* hybrids**
Resulting from crossing *Abutilon darwinii* and *Abutilon striatum*. The hand-shaped foliage has three or five lobes. The bell-shaped flowers are white, yellow, orange or red, or a mixture of these colours. 'Ashford Red', for instance, is salmon-red, 'Boule de Neige' white with orange stamens, 'Canary Bird' yellow, 'Fire Bell' red and 'Golden Fleece' deep yellow. They flower from May to October.
Abutilon megapotamicum
Syn. *Abutilon vexillarium*. An evergreen shrub with slender, drooping stems and crenate, pointed oval leaves without lobes. The pendulous flowers grow separately and differ in shape from other abutilon species: they consist of a five-sided red calyx and yellow petals with protruding dark purple stamens. 'Variegatum' has yellow and green mosaic-patterned foliage.
Abutilon striatum
Syn. *Abutilon pictum*. Bell-shaped orange flowers are produced from August to November. The strain 'Thompsonii' has smaller, yellow-blotched leaves.

Acacia

Leguminosae

Mimosa Tree, Wattle

Name Derived from the Greek *akakaia*. The tree we generally call acacia is really the False Acacia, and its botanical name is *Robinia pseudoacacia*.
Origin A large genus with over 800 species, belonging in the tropical and sub-tropical regions of Africa and Australia.
Description All acacias are trees or shrubs. The tallest may attain heights of 12 m (40 ft). The African species have feathery foliage. In some Australian species the foliage has been reduced to flattened stalks called phylloclades. From January to March very small flowers appear, growing in compact groups. Every flower has ten or more protruding stamens, giving it a spherical, woolly appearance. Some species bear thcrns or thorny stipules.
Position In summer acacias should be placed in a sunny, sheltered position in

Acacia armata, the Kangaroo Thorn

the garden or on the balcony. Bring them indoors in October and keep them in a light and distinctly cool place in winter.
Care Keep at 4 to 6°C (39 to 43°F) in winter. Very long shoots may be shortened after flowering.
Watering If your plant arrives from the garden shop in January, bearing very small buds, it must be sprayed daily with tepid water to prevent the buds drying out and dropping. Stop spraying as soon as the little balls turn yellow and fluffy. Don't be too mean with water in winter. In summer the well-rooted soil ball must be kept damp. A surprising amount of water is evaporated by these rather dry-looking plants.
Feeding Each fortnight the plant should be given a feed at normal concentration.
Repotting Repot in spring, in humus mixed with a little sand and clay. When damaged, the roots frequently give off a disagreeable smell.
Propagation Increase from seed, which must first be soaked in warm water, since otherwise germination will be very slow. The best time to take cuttings are April or July–August. The cuttings should be rooted in a mixture of sand and peat, with bottom heat.

Acacia armata

Syn. *Acacia paradoxa.* Dark green branching shrub, up to 1.5m (5ft) in height. It flowers freely; the pale yellow flower heads grow on separate stalks and are delightfully scented.

Acacia baileyana

This has pale, bluish foliage and small, deep yellow flower plumes.

Acacia dealbata

Syn. *Acacia decurrens* var. *dealbata.* A tall shrub with sulphur-yellow flowers. This is the plant from which the well-known mimosa branches sold by florists are taken. It tolerates 5 to 6°C (9 to 11°F) of frost.

Acalypha hispida, Red-hot Cat's Tail

Acalypha
Euphorbiaceae

Name *Akalephe* is the Greek name of a species of nettles. The foliage of acalypha resembles that of the stinging nettle to some extent.
Origin The majority of species originate in the South Sea Islands belonging to the Australian archipelago, and in New Guinea. In other words they come from tropically humid, warm regions.
Description The genus contains 430 species of herbs, shrubs and even trees. The flowers usually appear in composite spikes or racemes. The foliage is green or coloured in shades of red or bronze, and sometimes the leaves have mosaic-like markings.
Position They require a warm position with a high degree of humidity and plenty of light, essential for fine coloration, though full sunlight should be avoided. Without good light variegated leaves will revert to green.

Acalyphas will give most pleasure if placed in a heated greenhouse. In summer they may be brought indoors for a time, or may even be planted out in a warm, sheltered position in the garden.

Acalypha wilkesiana 'Musaica' has fine variegated foliage, but inconspicuous cat's tails

In winter they must be kept in a well-lit, warm and humid environment.
Care To obtain a bushier plant pinch out the tips of the longer shoots once only. *Acalypha wilkesiana*, which is chiefly grown for its foliage, may be topped two or three times.

Dead flowers should be removed regularly. The minimum desirable temperature in winter is 16°C (60°F).
Watering During the growing and flowering season the compost must be kept constantly moist, though the pot shouldn't stand in water. Provide a high degree of humidity by means of the deep-plate method (see page 59), and spray the foliage daily, using tepid water, to discourage red spider mite.
Feeding During the growing season give a dose of fertiliser at normal strength once a week.
Repotting You would do best to make a porous, nutritious mixture, rich in humus, consisting of leafmould, rotted cow manure, sharp sand and powdered clay or loam.
Propagation Cuttings should be taken in early spring and rooted with bottom heat at a minimum of 20°C (68°F) under glass or plastic, either in a standard potting compost or in a mixture of equal parts of sand and leafmould or peat.

The cutting may lose its leaves, but if it is kept warm and moist the bare stem will soon put out new shoots. To obtain bushy plants remove the tips from time to time and when potting on combine three or more cuttings in one pot.

Young plants are the finest. Older plants may be cut back in January or February and will soon recover their attractive appearance.
Pests and diseases Red spider mite and aphids will occur if the air is too dry, also thrips, and grey mildew.

Acalypha hispida

Syn. *Acalypha sanderi.* Red-hot Cat's Tail; Chenille Plant. It owes its popular names to the striking red inflorescence which may grow to 50cm (20in) in length. It is a dioecious shrub, but only the female form is generally cultivated. The long, pointed leaves grow on hairy stalks. The flower tails grow in the axils and soon start to curve, extending beyond the leaves. The cultivar 'Alba' has a whitish inflorescence.

Acalypha wilkesiana

A monoecious shrub, in which male flower spikes are longer and female spikes shorter than the leaves, which have a maximum length of 20cm (8in). These are oval in shape and frequently variegated in a range of beautiful red shades. There are some magnificent cultivars, for instance 'Godseffiana', with oval to lancet-shaped leaves, pale green, roughly crenate; 'Hamiltoniana', similar to the previous form, but with irregularly shaped leaves, often ending in a tail and 'Musaica', with leaves in a mosaic of bronze, red and brownish-orange. 'Marginata' has olive-green, pink-edged leaves, sometimes with red veins; and there is also 'Obovata', in which the leaves are initially olive green with an orange-yellow margin, but later change to bronze-green and carmine.

Acanthocalycium violaceum flowers readily

Acanthocalycium
Cactaceae

Name The Greek word *akantha* means thorn or spine and *kalyx* is our word calyx.
Origin All nine known species are natives of Argentina.
Description Spherical to short cylindrical bodies with sharp ribbing. The medium-sized flowers open during the day. These cacti bear membranous scales, spiny at the top. Long woolly hairs grow in the axils of the scales.
Position They like plenty of light, but in general they do not tolerate direct sunlight at midday, when the sun is at its hottest. They enjoy fresh air and may therefore be taken out of doors in summer. Keep them cool and dry in winter.
Care Like most other cacti, acanthocalyciums require a temperature of 5 to 10°C (41 to 50°F) in winter.
Watering Water moderately in summer; keep practically dry in winter. On a warm summer's day indoor cacti may appreciate a fine spray.
Feeding From May to mid-August give a special cactus fertiliser.
Repotting Repot every spring in a well-drained soil-based potting compost. Special cactus mixtures are available, or you can make your own mixture from 5 parts standard potting compost, 2 parts coarse sand and 1 part clay or loam.
Propagation Sow seed in early March, with bottom heat of 20 to 30°C (68 to 86°F).
Pests and diseases Red spider mite, mealy bug and root aphids are the pests to look out for.

Acanthocalycium spiniflorum

Syn. *Echinopsis spiniflora.* Forms a matt green, spherical body with between 17 and 20 sharp ribs. It has needle-sharp yellowish-brown thorns and bell-shaped, pale pink flowers, 4cm (1½in) in length.

Acanthocalycium violaceum

Grows at a level of 1000m (3280ft) near Córdoba in Argentina. It resembles both echinopsis and the species above, but the 10 to 20 thorns are longer and somewhat curved. This cactus grows to 20 cm (8in) in height, with 15 ribs and a diameter of 15cm (6in). The clear mauve-pink flowers may attain 7cm (2¾in) in length and 6cm (2¼in) in width. The species flowers easily.

Acanthus montanus, the best indoor species

Acanthus
Acanthaceae

Name From the Greek *akanthos*. This was the Greek name for *Acanthus mollis*, the leaves of which were used as a design for the decoration of capitals of columns.
Origin The native habitat of the 20 species is in the warmer regions of Africa, Asia and the Mediterranean.
Description Thistle-like herbs or shrubs, often with very large incised pinnate leaves. The flowers are white, bluish-purple or blue, with thorny bracts, and grow in terminal spikes.
Position The acanthus requires a well-lit position, where it can be screened from strong sunlight. The plants are rather prickly, so be careful with your curtains. Where there are small children in the house, the plant is best placed out of their reach.
Care Acanthus is happiest when it has plenty of space both for its roots and for its upper parts.
Watering Well-rooted plants in full growth must be generously watered. Keep moderately moist in winter and in warm weather provide plenty of humidity. Spray regularly.
Feeding Give a fortnightly dose of a standard fertiliser solution.
Repotting If you want to mix your own compost, take 3 parts standard potting compost, 1 part powdered clay and 1 part peat, and use large pots.
Propagation Towards the end of winter, take tip or eye cuttings and root them under glass or plastic at 25 to 30°C (77 to 86°F) bottom heat. They will root within two or three weeks.

Acanthus ilicifolius
Grows in coastal regions in the tropics, in areas with brackish water. It has feathered leaves, up to 30 cm (12 in) long and 10 cm (4 in) wide with a spiny or a smooth edge. The surface of the leaves is smooth and shiny, never blistered.
Acanthus montanus
This is the best-known indoor species. It is an evergreen shrub which in tropical West Africa may grow to as much as 2 m (6 ft) in height. The branches are green and in maturity develop many aerial roots. The feathered leaves are held horizontally and are spiny, blistered and curved at the margin. The 5-cm (2-in) long flowers are pinky white in colour.

Achimenes hybrid 'Rose'. This cultivar flowers abundantly for long periods

Achimenes
Gesneriaceae

Name Derived from the Greek *acheimenos*. 'A' indicates a negative and *cheimon* means storm or wintry cold. The plant certainly dislikes cold, for after all, it is a native of the tropics.
Origin Central and South America. The majority of the approximately 50 species originate in Brazil, Mexico or Guatemala.
Description Deciduous, perennial greenhouse plants, erect growing and usually hairy. The achimenes has a bushy habit, usually with unbranched stems. The dark green leaves are oval to lancet shaped and crenate. The flowers consist of five linked petals ending in a tube. The colours vary from white through pink to purple, but yellow species also exist. The plant has a scaly underground rhizome, white, pink or lilac in colour.
Position Like all *Gesneriaceae*, the achimenes dislikes direct sunlight. To avoid scorching it should be given a situation in good light, but out of the sun. In poor light the stems will grow long and leggy and no flower buds will form. Be careful to keep the plant out of a draught and provide sufficient warmth.
Care After the foliage has died, the rhizomes should be removed and kept dry in peat fibre or sand during the winter, at a temperature of 10 to 15°C (50 to 59°F). Between January and April the rhizomes may be replanted in fresh compost at a depth of 1 to 2 cm (½ to ¾ in). Keep the compost moist and provide bottom heat of 18 to 20°C (64 to 68°F). Give only water with the chill off it and preferably keep the pot under glass or plastic. Young shoots will soon appear, and these may need some support. In the flowering season dead flowers must be removed.
Watering In the growing and flowering season water regularly, using tepid, softened water. Do not let the soil ball dry out, or the leaves and flowers would soon shrivel up. When the flower buds appear provide a high degree of atmospheric humidity by frequent spraying. Once the plant is in flower stop spraying, but use the deep-plate method. In September or thereabouts the achimenes begins to drop its leaves and flowers and starts its resting period. Gradually decrease the water supply and allow the plant to die off undisturbed.
Feeding During the growing and flowering season give a lime-free fertiliser solution at normal strength once every ten days. Alternatively the plant may be plunged into tepid water to which fertiliser has been added.
Repotting Use a lime-free mixture, rich in humus – for instance equal parts of peat fibre, leafmould and sharp sand, adding a little rotted cow manure.
Encourage drainage by placing a few crocks in the bottom of the pot.
Propagation This can be done from the rootstock, from cuttings or from seed. Large rhizomes may be split in spring before being repotted. Each rhizome may produce as many as six new plants in every growing season. The advantage of reproduction from cuttings is that growth is usually more vigorous. Tip cuttings, 5 cm (2 in) long, will root in peat fibre. Cuttings from rhizomes which have just started into growth are best, since they root more readily. Provide bottom heat of 20 to 24°C (68 to 75°F). After three or four weeks the plantlets should be potted up and given a fertiliser solution at one third of the normal concentration every fortnight. Propagate from seed only if you wish to add new species to your collection. Sow in January or February in a heated greenhouse, using equal parts of peat and sharp sand.
Pests and diseases Common pests are greenfly, thrips and eelworms. A virus causing spotted wilt is often transmitted by eelworms. It manifests itself by yellowish-green rings or V-shaped streaks on the leaves. Affected plants are best discarded. Yellow blotches which later turn brown indicate either too strong sunlight or too cold water.

Achimenes erecta
Syn. *Achimenes coccinea; A. rosea; A. pulchella*. The plant grows to 45 cm (18 in) in height and is covered in soft hairs, with reddish, slightly blotched stems. The veins of the green leaves are red on the underside. The plant produces an abundance of scarlet flowers. Cultivars have pale red to red flowers, sometimes striped.
Achimenes grandiflora
Syn. *Trevirana grandiflora*. Height to 60 cm (2 ft). The underside of the foliage and the stems are frequently red. The flowers are reddish purple and numerous. 'Leibmannii' is smaller in all its parts and has pinkish-purple flowers.
***Achimenes* hybrids**
The best known strains are 'Ambroise Verschaffelt', white with violet veins; 'Camille Brozzoni', lilac with a white centre; 'Little Beauty', carmine pink, small-flowered; 'Paul Arnold', purple, large-flowered; 'Purple King', purple, and 'Rose': the name speaks for itself.
Achimenes longiflora
In this species the tube of the corolla, white or red, is up to 6 cm (2¼ in) in length and the petals are violet. This is the ancestor of many hybrids.
Achimenes patens
A hairy plant, up to 15 cm (6 in) in height. The stems are green to brown. The leaves are roughly serrated, and the petals finely serrated.

Achimenes 'Little Beauty', with small flowers

Achimenes 'Paul Arnold', with large flowers

Acorus gramineus 'Variegatus'

A fine example of a fully grown *Adiantum raddianum*, of which there are many cultivars

Acorus
Araceae
Sweet Flag

Name From the Greek *akaron*, a plant name of which we do not know the meaning.
Origin The house plant *Acorus gramineus* comes from Japan. Another member of this genus, *Acorus calamus*, is known in Europe as a water and bog plant. Its fragrant rootstock was used in Babylon, Egypt and Greece for its medicinal qualities.
Description At first sight the grass-leaved Sweet Flag seems more like a grass than a member of the arum family, but when it flowers (I have never seen a plant do this when kept indoors), the relationship is unmistakable. The plant grows to 40 cm (16 in) in height and has a creeping rhizome. In the species the foliage is green, but variegated cultivars also exist.
Position The green form, in particular, tolerates a fair amount of shade. The variegated strains should be kept in a slightly higher temperature and better light, but keep them away from full sunlight.
Care Provided the temperature is kept low, the Sweet Flag provides few problems in the home. Make sure it has good ventilation on warm days.
Watering The compost must never dry out. This plant likes plenty of moisture at the roots and it is therefore best kept in a bowl of water. As a rule the normal living-room atmosphere is sufficiently humid, but occasional spraying will be appreciated.
Repotting Acorus will thrive in commercial potting compost, but a good mixture can be made up of sand, peat, leafmould and clay. It should be sandy to peaty and moisture retaining.
Propagation Both the species and the variegated strains are easily propagated by division, preferably in spring.
Pests and diseases Red spider mite is the chief hazard.

Acorus gramineus
A stalkless, clump-forming plant. As can be seen from the photograph, the grass-like leaves are placed in two rows, and appear to grow from the rootstock in the shape of a fan. The finest forms are 'Argenteostriatus', with white-striped leaves, and 'Variegatus' with variegated striped foliage. *A.g. pusillus* grows to only 10 cm (4 in) in height.

Adiantum
Adiantaceae
Maidenhair Fern

Name *Adianton* was the Greek name of a fern which, after spraying, did not look wet because the drops of water did not spread, but lay intact on top of the leaves or fell off.
Origin This genus of ferns consists of more than 200 species, originating in tropical and sub-tropical regions all over the world, but especially in Central and South America, where they grow in the humid rain forests. *Adiantum pedatum* is found as far north as the Arctic Circle and *Adiantum capillus-veneris* is a cosmopolitan plant found practically anywhere in the world.
Description The chief characteristics of these elegant ferns are their thread-like, brown-black leaf stalks and their composite feathery foliage. The sporangia are usually found along the curving margins of the fronds. This fern has hard, woody roots.
Position When choosing a position for your Maidenhair Fern, bear in mind that the tropical forest was its native habitat, so it will prefer a warm, shady situation with a high level of atmospheric humidity. Draughts are fatal. It will not be easy to provide the necessary conditions in the living room.
Care If, after momentary carelessness, some of the leaves have dried out, cut the stalks back to just above the soil level. The plant will probably put out new shoots. If, in spite of all your tender care, your adiantum loses some of its attraction in the autumn, it means that it would like a rest. Temporarily reduce the water supply and cut down old foliage, but don't let the temperature drop below 18°C (64°F). Two months' rest is enough. Give it some bottom heat if you can; this fern dislikes cold feet.
Watering Regular and generous watering is essential to prevent the compost drying out. Be particularly careful when the plant is fully rooted, for by then the soil ball will not hold much water. Once the compost dries out it is difficult to moisten it again, for the water will run down along the woody roots without being absorbed. In addition to watering it is therefore advisable to plunge the plant once a week. Always use soft, tepid water for watering, spraying and plunging. The degree of humidity required can be achieved by spraying or by adopting the deep-plate method.
Feeding During the main growing season, from March till August, feed once a fortnight with strongly diluted liquid fertiliser – for instance, half or one third of the recommended concentration.
Repotting Mix 2 parts of standard potting compost with 1 part peat fibre and 1 part sharp sand.
Propagation The most favourable month for sowing spores is March. The method is described on page 71. A much easier way is to pull the rootstock apart; this must also be done in spring. Make sure that each section has a growing point and plant the sections in relatively small pots in a mixture of equal parts of leafmould, sand and pulverised clay.
Pests and diseases Ferns weakened by incorrect treatment may be attacked by greenfly, scale insects, root aphids, thrips and eelworm.

Adiantum caudatum
Syn. *Adiantum ciliatum*. Leaf stalks are 10 to 15 cm (4 to 6 in) long, and practically recumbent.
Adiantum formosum
A vigorous fern, up to 1 m (3 ft) in height. There are purplish-black leaf stalks and masses of pale green, almost triangular leaves, with numerous conglomerations of spores.
Adiantum macrophyllum
Foliage 40 cm (16 in) in length, slightly curving. The leaves are often reddish in colour at first. The sterile fronds are somewhat narrower than the fertile ones. The hard leaf stalks are brown-black.

Adiantum tenerum 'Scutum'

Adiantum raddianum 'Goldelse'

Adiantum raddianum
Syn. *Adiantum cuneatum*. The variety 'Decora' was at one time called *Adiantum decorum*. It grows up to 50 cm (20 in) in height. The young fronds grow erect, but later curve, and the leaves are wedge-shaped at the bottom. There are many cultivars, such as 'Goldelse', with slightly pink leaves at first, later turning golden yellow; propagate by division. 'Brilliantelse', cultivated from the former cultivar, is even more vigorous and can be grown from spores. 'Fragrantissimum', to 75 cm (30 in), is fragrant where a number of plants are grown side by side. 'Fritz Lüthi' has a more erect and firmer habit.
Adiantum tenerum
Even more delicate and airy foliage than *Adiantum raddianum*. In 'Scutum' the young leaves are green, and in 'Scutum Roseum' rose red.

Other strains, all resembling each other, have been cultivated by growers.

Adromischus trigynus has a spherical habit

Adromischus
Crassulaceae

Origin This genus of succulents consists of more than 50 species originating in South West Africa and in the Cape Province.
Description Most species remain small – up to 10 cm (4 in) – but some grow a little larger, with short trunks. They frequently produce aerial roots and beautifully coloured or blotched leaf rosettes. The insignificant flowers are rectangular, the points of the petals spreading in the form of a star. However, adromischus is chiefly grown for its beautifully marked foliage.
Position Very suitable plants for combination with other succulents or cacti in bowls or other containers. They should be placed in a sunny position on the window ledge or in the greenhouse.
Care Minimum temperature in winter should be 5°C (41°F). Giving it a resting period at low temperature will prevent leggy growth, attack by aphids, and leaf loss. The drier the plant is kept and the poorer the compost, the more vivid will the foliage become, but at the same time the risk of the lower leaves dropping off increases.
Watering Water with great care, for the roots of *Adromischus* species are very sensitive to overwatering. Root rot can be prevented by watering very sparingly throughout the year and by keeping the plant practically dry in winter.
Feeding Provided the plant is repotted once a year, no further feeding is necessary.
Repotting Make a porous mixture from sand, loam and leafmould and provide an adequate drainage layer in the bottom of the pot or bowl.
Propagation Increase from cuttings, in summer. The plant may also be divided or grown from leaf cuttings. They are easily detached from the stem and will root in a mixture of sand and peat.
Pests and diseases This plant is rarely subject to disease. Too high a temperature in winter may occasionally precipitate an attack by aphids.

Adromischus cooperi
○ ⊜ ◐ ⊛ ◼
The thick, fleshy leaves, up to 4 cm (1½ in) in length, are often wavy. They are covered in a grey-green waxy layer with reddish-purple patches. The flowers are red with white points to the petals.
Adromischus festivus
This species has grey-white foliage, which makes the purple patches more conspicuous.
Adromischus trigynus
Compact habit and silver-grey foliage with reddish-brown marking.

Aechmea
Bromeliaceae

Name From the Greek *aichmê*, meaning spearhead or point. With a little imagination you might say that the pointed, spined bracts prick like a lance.
Origin This genus incorporates about 150 species originating in tropical and sub-tropical Central and South America.
Description In their native habitat most aechmeas grow as epiphytes, but terrestrial plants also occur. The roots of the epiphytes living in the jungle serve as support rather than to take in food. For the former purpose they also have little suckers at the bottom of the rosettes. The leaves often bear thorns. They are curved like gutters to catch the water and end in sheaths forming a funnel to hold the water.

After flowering the rosettes die, but meanwhile young plants will have developed at the base of the parent rosette; these can be used for propagation. *Aechmea fulgens* and *Aechmea miniata* have fairly thin foliage; *Aechmea fasciata*, on the other hand, has stiff, hard leaves. Aechmeas are well worth growing for their inflorescence, which may vary from blue, violet, red, white and green to yellow, sometimes changing colour in the course of the season, usually between May and October. They are occasionally confused with *Billbergia*. The difference is that in aechmeas the flowers are erect, whereas in billbergias they droop. Aechmea flowers are usually also a little smaller. The plants have striking fruits as well: white, yellow, purple or black. The bracts often retain their fine colouring even after flowering has ceased.
Position Keep in a well-lit, warm place, but away from direct sunlight. In a greenhouse they may be grown as epiphytes, on blocks of wood.
Care In the dormant season the temperature must not drop below 15°C (59°F); in the flowering season the minimum temperature should be 18°C (64°F), but in summer preferably 18 to 22°C (64 to 71°F). Too cold a situation results in rotting and leaf damage. If your aechmea grows well but refuses to flower, try the following domestic remedy: enclose two ripe apples with the plant in a plastic bag for a few days. The gases exuded by the apples will encourage flowering.
Watering Soft, tepid water with a pH of 4.1 to 4.5 must be used for watering and spraying. Rainwater is excellent. If the water is too cold, or if the plants are still wet in the evening, there is a risk of rotting. In summer it is advisable to pour water into the funnel as well, but in the dormant season only the soil ball should be watered. If the plant is kept warm in winter – about 22°C (71°F) – the water remaining in the funnel may be left, but at a temperature of 16 to 18°C (60 to 64°F) it is better to empty the funnel. The degree of atmospheric humidity must not be too high. Spray only on hot days. Water freely in the growing season, but do not let the compost become saturated. Keep only just moist in winter.
Feeding During the growing season pour a weak solution of liquid fertiliser into the funnel – half the concentration recommended on the bottle. Once every five weeks rinse the funnel with clean water. Foliar feeding is also possible.
Repotting Since the plant is thrown away after flowering, it never needs repotting. However, it may take as much as six to eight months for the old plant to die. The new plantlets are best potted in a compost which ideally consists of sphagnum moss, chopped fern or orchid roots and well-rotted beech leaves. A little sharp sand and rotted cow manure may be added. Use relatively small pots.

Aechmea recurvata benrathii

Aechmea fasciata, the best-known species

Aechmea weilbachii

Detail of a flower cluster of *Aechmea fulgens*

Propagation The young rosettes may be removed when they are half the length of the parent rosette. Before that they will not have developed their own roots and should on no account be removed. Start pouring water into the small funnels two weeks before they are cut off. Try to retain as much of the root system as possible – of the parent plant as well as of the young rosette.

Pests and diseases A combination of too high a temperature and too low a degree of humidity may lead to attacks by scale insects and thrips. Aechmeas affected by wilt are better destroyed to prevent infection.

Aechmea bromeliifolia

This forms a funnel-shaped rosette. The 60-cm (2-ft) long leaves are rounded at the tip and have brown thorns. The upper surface is green, the lower has white scales. The greenish-white flowers soon turn brown.

Aechmea calyculata

A green rosette of 50-cm (20-in) long leaves with a scarlet, cylindrical inflorescence with yellow florets.

Aechmea caudata

This species is a vigorous grower. The point of the green leaf ends in an incurving thorn. It has a pyramid-shaped inflorescence with orange-yellow bracts and deep yellow flowers. 'Variegata' has green leaves banded with cream.

Aechmea chantinii

The dark olive-green leaves have pinkish-white stripes at regular intervals. The flower plume has reddish, curved bracts and yellow florets.

Aechmea coelestis

This has a funnel-shaped rosette with finely serrated, prickly leaves, 50 cm (20 in) long. The upper surface is green, the lower surface frequently has zebra-stripe markings. Pinkish leaves sheathe the flower stalk. The inflorescence consists of a hairy, yellowish spindle with sky-blue flowers.

Aechmea fasciata

The 50-cm (20-in), 6-cm ($2\frac{1}{4}$-in) wide curved leaves form a funnel-shaped rosette. They are spined along the margin and have a blunt tip bearing a thorn. The foliage is grey-green, beautifully striped and blotched. The compact pyramid-shaped inflorescence has pink bracts and small blue flowers fading to lilac. This is one of the most popular bromeliads, a very strong plant which will flower for months on end. Cultivars on the market vary mainly in the width and colour of their leaves. 'Silver King' and 'Superauslese' have striking silver-grey foliage.

Aechmea fulgens

This forms a loose rosette consisting of 40-cm (16-in) long, 6-cm ($2\frac{1}{4}$-in) wide leaves. They are green, bloomed with white, especially below the middle line, and fairly widely serrated. The erect-growing inflorescence extends beyond the foliage and bears a pyramid-shaped cluster of bright red flowers, tipped with blue in mature plants. The variety *discolor* is more striking, because the leaves are bloomed on the underside in purple and grey, forming a beautiful contrast to the olive-green upper surface.

Aechmea lindenii

Syn. *Aechmea comata*. The grey-green leaves may be as much as 1 m (3 ft) long. The inflorescence consists of a spike producing yellow florets from the centre outwards. The most frequently cultivated form is the variegated strain 'Variegata', which has wide, cream-coloured longitudinal stripes.

Aechmea marmorata

The rosette consists of only four to six olive-green serrated leaves marbled in brown. The erect-growing or drooping inflorescence has red bracts and white flowers, soon changing to blue.

Aechmea miniata

This consists of a dense rosette of narrow green leaves, at most 40 cm (16 in) in length, with a red inflorescence. 'Discolor' has shiny leaves, purplish brown underneath, and blue petals.

Aechmea tillandsioides

The 40-cm (16-in) long, 2-cm ($\frac{3}{4}$-in) wide leaves form rosettes only 15 cm (6 in) in height. The serration is not coloured. It has yellow flowers growing in two bands along the flower stalk. The bracts are red.

Aeonium arboreum with its shrubby habit is the best-known species

Aeonium tabuliforme

Aechmea weilbachii

A funnel-shaped rosette consisting of leaves up to 60 cm (2 ft) long, serrated at the bottom, but smooth along the upper margins. The inflorescence is frequently a little shorter than the foliage. The narrow flower plume has red bracts and a rose-red corolla. The cultivar 'Leodiensis' is more attractive. It has coppery leaves, wine red at their base.

Aeonium

Crassulaceae

Name From the Greek *aioon*, meaning persevering, eternal, indicating that these plants never entirely lose their foliage.

Origin The genus includes 40 species, 34 of which are native to the Canary Islands, where they grow in dry, rocky places. *Aeonium arboreum* originates in Morocco. The other species have their natural habitat in the Cape Verde Islands, Madeira and the southern Mediterranean countries.

Description They are succulents, developing rosettes at the extremities of their fleshy stems. The lower part of the stem is often bare, because the leaves continually drop. Most species have green to golden-yellow flowers, but brick-red and cream-coloured racemes also occur. The flower stalk arises from the centre of a rosette and develops several side-shoots. After flowering the rosette which has produced the flower stalk dies. *Aeonium* species are easily crossed and it is therefore difficult to distinguish pure species. They produce many-seeded fruits.

Position In summer aeoniums prefer a sunny spot in the garden, but if this is not possible it should have a sunny but cool position indoors. Like all other succulents, it must be kept cool in winter.

Care In order to maintain the characteristic shape of the leaf rosettes the plant should be kept at 10°C (50°F) in winter. If it is kept in a warmer environment it will grow limp and leggy.

Watering In the dormant season it should be given only just enough water to prevent the roots from drying out. The cooler the position, the less water it will need. Many of the leaves will turn yellow and shrivel up during this period. Frequently only small, leafy balls are all that remain of the rosettes. The same thing happens in their natural habitat, so there is no need to worry. In March or April resume watering normally.

Repotting Repot in spring, in nutritious, porous compost: 2 parts leafmould, 1 part sharp sand and 1 part pulverised clay.

Propagation Increase by vegetative reproduction only, because plants raised from seed are rarely true to type. Allow the shoot or leaf cutting to dry out for a few days first.

Pests and diseases Leaves that have shrivelled up in the dormant season may occasionally harbour mealy bugs and must therefore be removed in good time.

Aeonium arboreum

Branched shrubs with bright green foliage and yellow flowers. 'Atropur-

Aerides lawrenceae

pureum' has brown foliage, especially in summer. 'Zwartkop' has dark brown leaves throughout the year.

Aeonium haworthii
These have blue-grey to green leaves with red margins. The flowers are pale yellow.

Aeonium tabuliforme
Unbranched, with conspicuously flattened, multi-leaved rosettes, pale green and covered in soft hairs, and sulphur-yellow flowers.

Aerides
Orchidaceae

Name From the fact that *Aer* means light it can be seen that this is not a terrestrial orchid, but grows 'in the air', that is, on trees.
Origin These orchids come from the tropical forests of Asia. They are found from India to Japan, where rotted leaves and bird manure in the trees provide pockets of nutritious matter.
Description Most epiphytic orchids have pseudobulbs, surface organs in which to store food, but these are lacking in aerides. This orchid has a central, leafy stem growing to 1.5m (5ft). In all species numerous beautiful and fragrant flowers appear on a pendulous stem.
Position It likes as much light as possible, but protect it from bright sunlight. An indoor propagator or enclosed flower window are essential for the cultivation of the more sensitive species.
Care The temperature requirement varies from one species to another. It is best to experiment with temperatures between moderate and very high.
Watering In the growing period the plants need a high degree of humidity and should therefore be sprayed frequently.
They need only be watered two or three times a week, but make sure that they have good drainage. In winter water only once a week.
Repotting Use orchid compost from a specialist grower or make your own mixture from fern roots, sphagnum moss, charcoal and peat. Good drainage is essential.
Propagation Raise from seed.

Aerides japonicum
Fragrant flowers, greenish white with reddish purple markings. The flowers appear in summer.

Aerides lawrenceae
Fragrant, summer-flowering species with waxy white and purple flowers.

Aerides multiflorum
The white with pink and purple flowers appear in summer.

Aerides vandarum
This is the best-known species, with white, delightfully scented flowers in spring.

Aeschynanthus
Gesneriaceae

Name From the Greek *aischyne*, meaning shame, and *anthos*, flower.
Origin These epiphytes, of which more than 170 species are known, are found in the humid forests of Asia, from the Himalayas to Indonesia.
Description These herbaceous hanging plants closely resemble the related genus *Columnea*. Properly cared for, they may flower in profusion. The flowers are scarlet, orange, yellow or greenish and grow either terminally or in the axils of the leaves. The shortened calyx consists of five sepals. The tube of the corolla is extended, bulging or spreading at the top, often incurving. The edge of the crown is double lipped, often slanting. The upper lip is divided and is either erect or curves backwards. The lower lip is divided into three spreading points, of which the centre one may curve back. The four stamens nearly always extend beyond the petals. The leaves are opposite, fleshy or leathery, green or marbled.
Position A warm, half-shady humid situation is best. The plants are therefore very suitable for flower window or hothouse cultivation. However, they can give you a great deal of pleasure in the living-room, where they may be placed on high shelves, or in containers forming a room divider. Shifting temperature variations and changes in the level of humidity may cause the buds to drop. They should therefore be left in the same spot whenever possible.
Care The minimum temperature tolerated in winter is 18°C (64°F). It is thought that a temperature of 12 to 15°C (53 to 59°F) during the last four weeks of the dormant season will encourage flowering, but the plant will often flower even without this drop in temperature.
Watering In summer water generously, using tepid, softened water (pH 4 to 4.5). In winter reduce the water supply, but continue to spray the foliage, for the aeschynanthus requires a high degree of humidity throughout the year. The water used for spraying must also be tepid and soft.
Feeding Give a weekly dose of lime-free fertiliser in normal concentration. To ensure rich flowering, the plant should be given little nitrogen.
Repotting The compost must be friable and well draining. A good basic mixture consists of equal parts of leafmould, sphagnum moss, loam and sharp sand. The addition of some extra leafmould, sphagnum moss, compost and rotted cow manure will promote profuse flowering. A little perlite may be added to make the mixture even more friable. Put a drainage layer in the bottom of the pot to avoid root rot. Good results may also be achieved if you grow your plant in standard peat-based potting compost.
Propagation Artificial pollination will readily produce numerous seeds. They must be sown in a heated propagator. Leaf or stem cuttings with an eye may be taken in February; they will root fairly easily under glass or polythene at a temperature of 25 to 30°C (77 to 86°F). Combine a few of the rooted cuttings in one pot to create a bushy plant.
Pests and diseases Growth and flowering are retarded if the compost contains too much lime, and spraying with cold or hard water causes spotting of the foliage. Aphids or thrips may occur if the plant is kept too dry.

Aeschynanthus javanicus is one of the finest species

Aeschynanthus speciosus, a species with large, erect-growing flowers

Aeschynanthus boscheanus
Syn. *Trichosporum boscheanum* and *Aeschynanthus lamponga*. Grows to 30cm (1ft). The leaves are oval to elliptical, with blunt tips. The flowers grow in clusters in the axils of the leaves. The calyx is cylindrical and smooth, the corolla is double the length of the calyx, up to 5cm (2in), scarlet, and downy to the touch. The main flowering season is from June to August.

Aeschynanthus javanicus
Syn. *Trichosporum javanicum*. A hanging plant with oval, lightly toothed leaves. In some parts of the world it is called the Lipstick Plant. At first only the brownish-purple tubes, that is, the calices, are visible, and the scarlet tubular corolla which appears later completes the lipstick effect. The corolla also contains a little yellow, especially on the lower lip. Both calyx and corolla are hairy.

Aeschynanthus lobbianus has flowers in terminal clusters

Aeschynanthus lobbianus
Syn. *Trichosporum lobbianum*. This has curving stems with leaves in groups of two or three, dark green, fleshy, elliptical, with practically smooth edges. The flowers appear in terminal clusters. The calices are brownish purple, with downy hairs. Initially the corolla forms a small ball at the bottom of the calyx. In full flower, usually in early summer, the blooms are about 5cm (2in) long, a beautiful red with yellow patches on the three lower lobes.

Aeschynanthus marmoratus
Syn. *Trichosporum marmoratum*. The lanceolate pointed leaves, up to 10cm (4in) in length, grow in pairs along the trailing stems. The upper surface is dark green and marbled and the reverse is dark red. The leaves are waxy and vaguely dentate. The tubular flowers are up to 3cm (1⅛in) in length, green with brown patches, growing singly in the axils of the terminal leaves. The sepals are long and narrow and separated right down to the base.

Aeschynanthus parasiticus
Syn. *Trichosporum grandiflorum* and *Aeschyanthus grandiflorus*. A plant with fleshy leaves, up to 10cm (4in) long and 1cm (½in) wide, growing on branching stems. The flowers grow in terminal clusters. The stamens extend fairly far beyond the downy red corolla, of which the lips are more or less compressed. It tolerates a slightly lower temperature.

Aeschynanthus pulcher
Syn. *Trichosporum pulchrum*. Fleshy, leathery leaves, up to 6cm (2¼in) long and 2cm (¾in) wide. The veins are depressed, and the edges are smooth or vaguely dentate. Flowers are scarlet with a yellow centre in summer. The calyx is greenish yellow.

Aeschynanthus speciosus
Syn. *Trichosporum speciosum*. Lanceolate, fleshy green leaves, up to 10cm (4in) in length. The downy corolla is yellow-orange-red from base to top. The stamens and the style extend beyond it.

Agapanthus
Liliaceae

Name Derived from the Greek *agape*, love, and *anthos*, a flower.
Origin The ten species originate in the southern tip of Africa.
Description Herbaceous perennials with fleshy stems. The elegantly curved long and narrow leaves grow in rosettes. The white or blue flowers have the shape of a narrow funnel and grow in circular umbels at the tip of long stems. They are used as cut flowers and the seed heads are frequently incorporated in dried flower arrangements.
Position In summer a sunny and sheltered position in the garden or on the balcony is preferred. In winter agapanthus should be kept in a cool but frost-free spot: the garage, a cool greenhouse or an unused bedroom. If the greenhouse is becoming overcrowded in April, the plant may be temporarily moved to the warm living-room.

It is even possible to keep this plant in a cold frame in winter, provided it is protected by rush mats in periods of frost.

In coastal areas and in a few really sheltered regions the agapanthus may sometimes be kept outside for several years on end, although it should be given a protective cover of leaves or bracken. It should on no account be grown in a damp position, for this would cause the roots to rot. Sudden severe or unexpectedly early winter weather will generally kill the plant.
Care The cooler an agapanthus is kept in winter, the less water it will require and the better it will flower the following summer. If the temperature can be kept between 1 and 5°C (34 and 41°F) it will not suffer if kept fairly dark. As a general rule, the warmer the environment, the more light is required. Yellow and rotting leaves must always be removed. After flowering cut down the flower stalks as close to the soil as possible.
Watering Water generously in the growing season. Give very little water in winter and ventilate in frost-free weather.
Feeding Give a weekly dose of fertiliser solution at normal concentration.
Repotting The fleshy roots are damaged fairly easily and the plant should therefore not be repotted more than once every two years, in fact only when the root system fills the pot. Agapanthus should be cultivated in large tubs or pots, in a nutritious, loamy compost.
Propagation Increase by division, in the autumn, after flowering. Young plants may flower in a year or two. They may also be grown from seed, sown in April in a temperature of 13 to 15°C (55 to 59°F), but the seeds germinate very irregularly and plants grown from seed will take a long time to flower.
Pests and diseases If the plants are kept out of doors beware of slugs and woodlice. An agapanthus will rot if kept too damp in winter.

Flowers of the agapanthus, a tub plant

Agapanthus africanus
Syn. *Agapanthus umbellatus*. Blue African Lily. This is smaller than the following species in all its parts. The leaf rosettes are less dense, the foliage is narrower and less smooth and grows more erect, and there are fewer flowers at the tip of the stalk.

Agapanthus praecox* ssp. *orientalis
Syn. *Agapanthus orientalis*. This is the best-known species. It has large leaf rosettes; the leaves are up to 60cm (2ft) long and 3cm (1⅛in) wide, and there are magnificent blue flowers growing in clusters. In 'Albus' and 'Maximus albus' the flowers are white. 'Variegatus' has variegated foliage.

Agave
Agavaceae

Name From the Greek *agauos*, meaning proud. These large, vigorous plants with their enormous inflorescences dominate the landscape wherever they grow.
Origin The 300 species originate in the desert areas of America. After the discovery of this continent they were brought to Europe and they have now also established themselves in countries bordering the Mediterranean.
Description Many people count agaves among the succulents, but they actually belong to the group of xerophytes, plants able to survive in areas where the water supply is scanty. In our climate they rarely flower and are cultivated solely for their fine, sword-shaped leaves, usually short stalked and arranged in rosettes. The inflorescence, which in the tropics may appear after 10 to 15 years, but will take half a century in our regions, consists of a plume of tubular or bell-shaped flowers. The inflorescence will supersede the growing point and after flowering and seed formation the rosettes will die.

The tall inflorescence of *Agave americana* may well be familiar to many, since it occurs profusely in popular holiday regions on the Continent. Its common names, Century Plant and American Aloe, are both inaccurate, the first because the plant never reaches that age, since it flowers and dies off much sooner, and the second because the aloe belongs to the lily family or *Liliaceae*.

In Central America the agave used to be of great economic value. The Incas and the Aztecs made sisal from the long, tough leaves. Sugar, honey, vinegar and wine were obtained from the sap of the stem of the young inflorescence and to this day the Mexican national drinks tequila and pulque are made from the fermented juices. The sharp thorns at the tip of the leaves were used as needles or nails.
Position The smaller species are very suitable for indoor cultivation on the

Agave americana 'Mediopicta', a handsome cultivar with cream centre bands

Agave americana, the common green species, grown here in a tub on the lawn

window-sill. They like full sun and may be placed out of doors from the end of May until mid-September. The larger species are grown as tub plants and are very suitable for an orangery. Place them outside on the balcony or the terrace in summer, but beware of the thorns. They are not suitable plants to grow if there are small children about, though you could stick tiny pieces of cork on the spines to prevent accidents. In the case of large specimens, lack of a suitable winter place is frequently a problem. All species must be kept in a cool, but frost-free, environment in winter. A cool greenhouse is the best place, but, provided they are kept absolutely dry, they will be satisfied with a darker position: the attic, the garage or near the cellar window. A few leaves may drop for lack of moisture, but in spring the plant will soon recover.

Care In winter they must be kept in a well-ventilated, fairly dry place at a temperature of 4 to 6°C (39 to 43°F).

Watering In sunny summer weather, plants may be watered freely, but if it rains continuously, it is advisable to bring them inside for they are unable to withstand a flood of water. Good drainage is in any case essential. Hard water is acceptable. In winter, watering depends on the amount of light: do not water at all if the light is poor, but give an occasional small dose if the plant is kept in good light. Dry air is tolerated well.

Feeding In the growing season feed once a fortnight, using a fertiliser solution at normal concentration.

Repotting Repot annually, early in spring, carefully removing the compost from between the roots and cutting off dead roots. Use a mixture of 2 parts commercial potting compost and 1 part sharp sand, placing a layer of crocks in the bottom of the pot. After repotting gradually increase the water supply, but water sparingly in the first few weeks.

Propagation Seeds readily germinate, but it may take a long time before the plants are of reasonable size. A simpler method is to root the runners, or to use the plantlets which some plants develop. The shoots should be left to dry for a few hours before they are inserted in a sandy mixture.

Pests and diseases Scale insects, mealy bug and root aphids are the most common pests.

Agave americana

This is the species known as the Century Plant. The grey-green or grey-blue leaves grow up to 1.75m (5ft) in length and 20cm (8in) wide. The leaf spines end in an incurving point, initially brown, later grey. The terminal spine is up to 3cm (1in) long. The flower stalks may grow to 6m (20ft) and the inflorescence, which has yellow-green flowers, to 3m (10ft). In the cultivar 'Marginata' the margins of the leaves are pale to golden yellow. 'Marginata Alba' has white margins, pink in young plants. In 'Marginata Aurea' the edges of the leaves are greenish yellow and in 'Marginata Pallida', pale green. In 'Medioppicta' the leaves have a central, cream-coloured band.

Agave applanata

Syn. *Agave schnittspahnii*. Pale grey to white foliage, 1m (3ft) long, 10cm (4in) wide.

Agave attenuata

A mature rosette consists of grey-green, untoothed smooth leaves, wider in the middle than at the base.

Agave ferdinandi-regis

Spreading leaves, which form a gutter on the upper side and are sharply angled on the reverse. The terminal spine is black. The leaf edges eventually turn grey-white.

Agave ferox

An open rosette, consisting of 1.30-m (4-ft) long, dark grey-green and fleshy leaves. Dark brown spines develop on the triangularly dentate edges and the teeth are linked by horny tissue.

Agave filifera

A spherical rosette of stiff, pointed leaves, curving upwards. Lines of horny tissue appear on the upper surface and along the edges of the leaves. These break up and form thin threads.

Agave geminiflora

A dense rosette consisting of as many as 200 dark green, linear leaves, only 5mm (¼in) wide and up to 50cm (20in) in length.

Agave ghiesbreghtii

This species develops runners, and consists of a stalkless rosette of dark green leaves. Immature leaves have a slightly paler band down the centre.

Agave stricta

Agave ferdinandi-regis

Agave ghiesbreghtii

Agave parrasana with its magnificent red spines is one of the finest species

Agave parrasana

The Sierra de Parras is its natural habitat. Leaves are up to 30cm (1ft) in length, grey-blue, stiff and fleshy, with wavy edges interspersed with red spines. The terminal thorn may be up to 25cm (10in) long.

Agave parryi

Leaves are 30cm (1ft) long, 10 to 15cm (4 to 6in) wide, pale grey-blue with a sharp brownish-grey point. This is one of the hardiest species and may be kept out of doors in a mild winter.

Agave striata

The grey-green leaves have darker stripes and are up to 45cm (18 in) long.

Agave stricta

These form dense rosettes of very narrow green leaves, up to 35cm (14in) long and bearing 2.5-cm (1-in) terminal spines. The rosette does not die after flowering. The edges of the leaves are dentate and horny.

Agave victoriae-reginae

A semi-spherical dense rosette of dull green leaves with white lines along the margins and a keel-shaped lower surface. 'Variegata', as the name implies, has variegated foliage. The minimum temperature tolerated in winter is 10°C (50°F).

Aglaonema commutatum develops shiny red berries

Aglaonema

Araceae

Chinese Evergreen

Name From the Greek words *aglaos* and *nema*, meaning brilliant thread. This is thought to refer to the stamens.
Origin The 50 species originate in southern Asia, mainly in Indonesia, Malaya, Thailand, the Philippines, and Sri Lanka (Ceylon), where they grow in the humid, heavily shaded tropical forests.
Description The evergreen shrubby or tree-shaped hardy plants are suitable for cultivation in the greenhouse or the living-room. They are erect in habit. The large majority have beautifully marked variegated foliage. As is usual in the arum family the inflorescence consists of a spathe and a spadix. The flowers are small in proportion to the foliage. After pollination some species develop magnificently coloured fruits.
Position A warm, humid spot, perhaps a flower window or a hothouse, is preferred. However, some people do manage to keep these difficult plants in good condition in their living-rooms. Place them in a shady position, except the variegated species which should preferably be in half shade.
Care In winter the soil and air temperature must not drop below 15 to 18°C (59 to 64°F).
Watering Use only tepid, softened water for both watering and spraying. Water freely in the growing season, moderately in winter. The plants are bound to flourish if you use the deep-plate method. Spray regularly. In some species spots will occur on the foliage and these should therefore only be mist-sprayed.
Feeding From April to August give a lime-free fertiliser solution at normal concentration every ten days.
Repotting Repot in March–April in friable compost. Carefully remove the old compost from the fleshy roots and put a layer of crocks or pebbles in the bottom of the pot. Use wide, shallow pots or bowls and a commercial potting compost mixed with sphagnum moss, peat fibre and sharp sand.
Pests and diseases They may be subject to scale insects and mealy bug. The appearance of red spider mite is usually the result of too much light.

Aglaonema brevispathum hospitum

Aglaonema commutatum
This has dark green foliage with grey markings along the veins, greenish-white spathes and shiny red berries. 'Pseudobracteatum' has yellow-white flower stalks. 'Treubii' has a smaller habit.
Aglaonema costatum
Dense foliage, up to 30 cm (1 ft) tall. The dark green foliage has numerous white patches and a white centre vein.
Aglaonema crispum
Syn. *Aglaonema roebelinii*. A tall stem, up to 1 m (3 ft) high, is covered in 30 long leaves, green with grey patches. The berries are red.
Aglaonema pictum
Leaves up to 15 cm (6 in) long, velvety green with greenish-grey patches. In addition the form 'Tricolor' has silvery patches.
Aglaonema treubii
This closely resembles the species *commutatum*, but the leaves are narrower and have pale grey markings along the veins. 'Silver King' and 'Silver Queen' are well-known forms of this species, with more white in their markings. The former strain has spotted leaf stalks, but in 'Silver Queen' they are plain green.

Aglaonema treubii 'Silver Queen'

Allamanda

Apocynaceae

Name Named after the Swiss botanist Allamand, who worked in Leyden, Holland, during the second half of the 18th century.
Origin About 15 species are known, most of them native to Brazil. The species described here is the best-known one.
Description Tropical shrubs, trees or trailing plants with magnificent large flowers, yellow or violet. The long oval leaves, pointed at both ends, usually grow in groups of three or four.
Position These plants rarely survive for long in the living-room. Their native habitat is in the tropical jungle and they therefore require a high level of humidity. In addition their growth is often too exuberant for indoor cultivation. A warm greenhouse or conservatory is the most favourable environment, although some people do manage to keep them in good condition in the living-room. They should be placed in good light, but screened from bright sunlight in summer.
Care In the dormant season keep the temperature above 18°C (64°F). At lower temperatures or in poor light the foliage will drop. In November or December the plant should be cut back to encourage new growth. Long shoots can be grown round wire hoops or given support on the wall, or if you want a bushier shape you can cut them back.
Watering Water generously during the growing season from April to September and spray frequently, preferably using rainwater. From September to February water sparingly and only occasionally spray with tepid water.
Feeding Give a weekly measure of fertiliser solution at normal concentration.
Repotting In spring, repot in equal parts of pulverised clay, rotted cow manure and leafmould, adding a little sharp sand.
Propagation Increase from cuttings, in leafmould and sharp sand with bottom heat.
Pests and diseases Pests include mealy bug and scale insects, red spider mites and whitefly.

Allamanda cathartica
A bare climbing shrub with oval leaves growing in whorls of three or four. The edge of the leaf is wavy and the leaf stalk is up to 5 mm ($\frac{1}{4}$ in) long. Flowers appear in clusters. The corolla is up to 8 cm (3 in) across, yellow, with pointed lobes. 'Hendersonii' has larger flowers, orange-yellow, and brownish when in bud, and 'Grandiflora' is a weaker climbing strain, but with lemon-yellow flowers up to 12 cm (4$\frac{1}{2}$ in) across.

Allamanda cathartica 'Hendersonii'

Alloplectus capitatus

Alocasia lowii

Alloplectus

Gesneriaceae

Name From the Greek words *allos*, other, and *plectos*, braided.
Origin The approximately 70 known species originate in tropical regions of America.
Description Erect-growing and hanging shrubs and semi-shrubs, living partly as epiphytes. The leaves are opposite. The calyx of the flower has five sepals, dentate or with smooth edges, usually red, and the corolla is yellow or white. The fruit is berry shaped and the roots are fleshy.
Position A half-shady situation is preferred, warm and humid.
Care In the dormant season the temperature must not drop below 18°C (64°F). The plant will indicate when it needs a rest by looking less flourishing in spite of your tender care.
Watering Most species have hairy leaves and must not be sprayed. You will have to depend on the deep-plate method or a humidifier to keep up the atmospheric moisture. Water regularly in the growing period and make sure that the compost does not dry out. Water somewhat less in winter. Always use tepid water.
Feeding Feed once a fortnight during the growing season, with a solution at normal concentration.
Repotting Use proprietary potting compost or a mixture rich in humus.
Propagation Increase from cuttings with a bottom temperature of 25 to 30°C (77 to 86°F), and from seed. If you sow in January the plants will flower the same summer.

Alloplectus capitatus

Fleshy, more or less square stems, up to 80 cm (32 in) tall. The opposite oval leaves are up to 20 cm (8 in) long, dark green and velvety on the upper surface, reddish on the underside, growing on red leaf stalks. The flowers appear in dense, round clusters; the calyx is red, the corolla yellow.

Alloplectus vittatus

Fleshy stem, up to 60 cm (2 ft) tall. The leaves are up to 15 cm (6 in) long, bronze to moss green with silver bands along the centre vein and at the base of the side veins. The calyx is red; there is a yellow corolla and black fruits.

Alocasia

Araceae

Origin The 70 species are natives of tropical Asia.
Description The alocasia is one of the finest foliage plants. It is erect in habit, herbaceous, with a thick stem, above or below ground, and shield- or arrow-shaped leaves on long leaf stalks. The foliage is often variegated. The inflorescence consists of a spathe and a spadix.
Position The hothouse and the enclosed flower window are the most ideal surroundings for these tropical plants. Fortunately they may be kept in good condition for a few months in the living-room as well, especially *Alocasia sanderiana*. Give them a half-shady, warm and humid position.
Care All variegated species require a more or less strict resting period in winter. The minimum temperature should be 18°C (64°F).
Watering In the active season the compost must be kept moist. Water sparingly in winter, just enough to prevent the foliage dropping.
Feeding From May to August a nutrient solution should be given at normal concentration once a fortnight.
Repotting In late winter, repot in a mixture of rotted leafmould, peat, sphagnum moss and pieces of charcoal. A proprietary mixture is also suitable.
Propagation Increase from seed, from runners, or by division of the rootstock. Dust the cuts with charcoal powder and keep moderately moist until the shoots appear.

Alocasia lowii

The dark green leaves have eight or nine white veins. The base lobes are joined along half their lengths. In 'Veitchii' the leaves are olive green along the veins with irregular white patches. The margins are whitish.

Alocasia metallica

Syn. *Alocasia cuprea*. Copper-coloured leaves with darker veins; the lower lobes are joined almost along their entire length. The lower surface is purple.

Alocasia plumbea

Large arrow-shaped leaves, purple to green. The lower lobes are hardly joined at all. The leaf stalks are up to 2 m (6 ft) long.

Alocasia sanderiana

This has shiny, metallic leaves, green and pendulous, with white veins and wavy white margins.

Aloe

Liliaceae

Name The Greek word *aloe* means bitter. In ancient times the bitter juices of the aloe were used as a pain killer and a laxative. The active ingredient is called aloin.
Origin Many of the 400 species originate from South Africa, and others come from Malagasy, Arabia, south-west Asia and tropical regions of Africa.
Description To some extent they resemble the agave, but the rosettes of the aloe do not die after flowering. The inflorescence of these succulents develops in the axils of the leaves. In many cases the flower stalks are long and the flowers are tubular or bell shaped. The rosettes consist of thick, pointed leaves, often spined along their edges; in some species the foliage is marked. They are tree or shrub shaped, with or without a stem.
Position Place them in a sunny, sheltered spot out of doors in summer. The sunnier their position, the finer the foliage and the richer the flowering will be. In winter they should be kept in a well-lit, cool place, for instance in a cool greenhouse or in the attic.
Care A temperature of 5°C (41°F) in winter promotes bud formation.
Watering As long as it rains from time to time they need not be watered when kept outside. Water moderately in periods of dry weather and in winter water sparingly. If they are kept in the living-room they should be watered once or twice a week, depending on the temperature, but they will accept a dry

A young plant of *Aloe arborescens*

atmosphere. Never put water on the plant itself. Moisture collecting near the base will rapidly cause rot.
Feeding Feed once a fortnight in the growing season.
Repotting This is required only once every two or three years, in April. Mix 1 part pulverised clay and 1 part leafmould with sand and perlite to obtain a porous mixture. Do not start watering

Aloe × *principes* is a cross between *A. arborescens* and *A. ferox*

Aloe mitriformis, with densely thorned leaf rosettes

Ampelopsis brevipedunculata maximowiczii 'Elegans'

Aloe ferox

until there are signs of new growth.
Propagation Sow in March in a sandy mixture at a temperature of 21°C (70°F). If you want to grow the plant from offsets, these should be cut off carefully, with as much of the root system as possible. Leave them to dry for two days and pot them in a sandy mixture.
Pests and diseases Look out for mealy bug and root aphids.

Aloe arborescens

The foliage sap has a healing effect on burns and cuts. The plant can develop stems up to 3m (10ft) tall. The rosette consists of thorny, curving and pointed green leaves, and it bears orange-red flowers.

Aloe ferox

Syn. *Aloe supralaevis*. The edges and the surface of the thick, succulent, bluish-green leaves are covered in reddish-brown spines. The inflorescence is branched, with red flowers.

Aloe humilis

This forms low-growing, dense rosettes of blue-green, spiny leaves, often with an incurving tip, and bears tubular red flowers.

Aloe mitriformis

Leaves are up to 15cm (6in) long, plain blue-green to green, with pale, horny spines. It has dense clusters of red flowers in summer.

Aloe saponaria

Syn. *Aloe disticha; Aloe umbellata*. Dense rosettes of 25-cm (10-in) long leaves with white patches in irregular rows, and horny spines along the margin. The flowers are yellow to red.

Aloe striata

Syn. *Aloe cincta*. This has dense rosettes of grey-green, red-bloomed spotted leaves, and coral-red flowers in spring.

Aloe variegata

Up to 30cm (1ft) in height. The leaves grow in rows in rosettes. They are dark green with white cross-banding and are V-shaped in section. Red flowers.

Amaryllis
Amaryllidaceae
Belladonna Lily

Name In a work by Virgil this was the name of a beautiful shepherdess.
Origin This bulbous plant, of which only one species is known, has its native habitat in a fairly small area along the south-west coast of South Africa.
Description When we are talking about an amaryllis, we are usually referring to the genus *Hippeastrum*. The following information will enable you to distinguish between the two. The *Amaryllis* has a solid flower stalk with six to twelve flowers. The plant flowers in autumn, after the foliage has dropped. New leaves develop in late winter and early spring. The *Hippeastrum*, on the other hand, has a hollow flower stalk with four to six slightly larger flowers which appear in winter and spring, before or at the same time as the leaves appear. The seeds are brown-black, whereas in the amaryllis they are green.
Position The most ideal spot is a sunny greenhouse, which is kept frost free in winter. If you treat them as tub plants, you can put them outside in summer. They do best if they are kept in the same place year after year. They provide excellent and long-lasting cut flowers. If the bulb is kept in the greenhouse, you could cut the flower and keep it in a vase indoors.
Care Keep them at a temperature of 5°C (41°F) in winter. Dead flowers, stems and leaves must be removed.
Watering Water moderately in growing and flowering seasons and very sparingly during the winter. Spraying is unnecessary.
Feeding Give a fortnightly feed at normal concentration in the active season.
Repotting The round bulbs with their long necks must be planted quite deeply, the largest as much as 20cm (8in) below the surface. Repot every five or six years in proprietary compost.
Propagation The quickest way to increase them is to grow them from seed, but even so it will take at least three years before they will flower.

Amaryllis belladonna 'Carina'

Amaryllis belladonna

Narrow green leaves and fragrant pink flowers, trumpet shaped and pendulous. 'Hathor' is white with a yellow throat. 'Parkeri' is the most profusely flowering strain. The flowers are deep pink with a yellow throat.

Ampelopsis
Vitaceae

Name As the name indicates, the plant resembles (*opsis*) a vine (*ampelos*).
Origin About 20 species are known. Their native habitats are in the Atlantic regions of North America, in Mexico, western, southern and especially eastern Asia.
Description They are woody climbers, ascending with the aid of their trailing stems. The single or composite long-stalked leaves are scattered along the stems. The small, greenish flowers usually have five petals. The fruits contain one to four seeds. The plant resembles the wild vine parthenocissus, but lacks the suckers at the end of the tendrils.
Position The plant needs good light, but keep it away from the bright midday sun. In summer it may be put outside. It is essential to keep it cool in winter, perhaps in a cool greenhouse or in the hall. To avoid the tendrils strangling your other plants, it should be given a free-standing position.
Care Keep at 5 to 10°C (41 to 50°F) in winter.
Watering It loses all or part of the foliage in autumn and this is when the resting period begins, during which the plant must be kept fairly dry. Water moderately at other times of the year.
Dry air in the living-room is tolerated fairly well.
Feeding Give it a fortnightly dose of liquid manure at normal concentration.
Repotting This should be done annually, in spring, in a proprietary potting compost.
Propagation Cuttings, taken in July or August, can be rooted in equal parts of sand and peat litter, in a temperature of 15 to 18°C (59 to 64°F).

Ampelopsis aconitifolia

Syn. *Vitis dissecta, V. vinifera*. A vigorous climber with fresh green leaves up to 7cm (2¾in) long, palmately lobed or divided. The berries are blue, later turning orange.

Ananas comosus 'Aureovariegatus'; a mature rosette with offset

Detail of the offset growing from the fruit

Ampelopsis brevipedunculata
Syn. *Cissus brevipedunculata.* The variety *maximowiczii* and its cultivar 'Elegans' are the forms most frequently cultivated for indoor use. Initially the young shoots are hairy, but later they become smooth. The foliage is roughly serrated, pointed and incised, and the leaves are marbled in pink, white and green. They grow on pendulous stems and are shed in winter. In the species the leaves are dark green and larger, up to 12cm (4½in) long.

Ampelopsis japonica
Syn. *Ampelopsis serjaniifolia.* An elegant creeper, originating in Japan and China. The leaves are three to five lobed, pinnate or pinnately divided, dark green and shiny, and there are blue fruits.

Ananas

Bromeliaceae

Pineapple

Name *Ananas* is the Brazilian name for this plant.
Origin It is a native of all tropical and sub-tropical areas of America. Once it had been brought into cultivation, the edible pineapple was also introduced in Africa and Asia, where it became established and now also grows wild. Today the islands of Hawaii are the largest suppliers of pineapples – they supply more than half the total world yield. In recent years the pineapple has become more and more popular as a house plant. They are imported, among other places, from the Azores, but they are also grown in this country.
Description The original ananas has rosettes up to 2m (6ft) across and 1m (3ft) high. The leaves are fairly narrow, spiny and dark green on the upper surface. Cultivars grown as pot plants are frequently somewhat smaller. In all species the cylindrical inflorescence appears just below the tip of a straight stem. The inflorescence may bear as many as 100 florets. Each of these will form a berry and at the same time the central axis will swell and become fleshy and juicy. The fruit is the result of the coalescence of all the bracts, the ovary, flower stalks and axis. This axis ends in a tuft of stiff, small leaves. The typical pineapple smell is caused by ethylbutyrate.
Position The plant can stay in the living-room throughout the year, preferably in a light, warm and sunny spot. The beautiful marking of the variegated species will be further improved by the sun. If you keep the plant on the window-sill, be careful with the curtains and net curtains, for the leaves are edged with curved thorns.
Care Minimum temperature in winter should be 15 to 18°C (59 to 64°F). In summer the temperature may rise to 25 to 30°C (77 to 86°F), but in that case the room must be well ventilated.
Watering Water generously in the active season in summer and pour water into the leaf rosette as well. Allow the compost to dry out between waterings. Keep it a little drier in winter. In very warm weather spray with tepid water.
Feeding From May to September, give a solution at normal concentration every fortnight.
Repotting When a cutting has rooted, pot in standard potting compost, perhaps mixed with sharp sand and leafmould or conifer needle compost.
Propagation Like all other bromeliads, the rosette dies after flowering. Shoots developing at the base of the plant may be used as cuttings. They should preferably be taken from the parent plant in March or April.

It is also possible to root the crown of leaves at the top of the fruit. You can even grow a plant from a pineapple bought from the greengrocer. Choose a specimen with an undamaged fresh green tuft of leaves. Cut the crown with a section of the fruit, remove the flesh and leave the rosette to dry for 24 hours. Pot in damp peat fibre mixed with plenty of sand. Covered with a plastic bag, it will root in a warm place.

Ananas comosus
This forms a dense rosette of 30 to 50 sword-shaped leaves, dark green above, grey-green on the reverse. The flower raceme is pink. 'Variegatus' has lengthwise yellow banding.

Rose of Jericho, open

Rose of Jericho, closed

Anastatica

Cruciferae

Rose of Jericho

Name The Greek word *anastasis* means resurrection. A dried Rose of Jericho will be resurrected if laid in water.
Origin The desert areas stretching from southern Iran to Morocco. The plant is frequently confused with *Selaginella lepidophylla*, which resembles it closely, but which is a native of Central America.
Description When you buy the plant, it looks like a dry rosette of claw-like stems and leaves, about 8cm (3in) across. The plants have been collected in the wild and have been left to dry. However, they are capable of absorbing water in this state. The rosette will then unfold and show a fresh green interior.
Position In their natural habitat the plants grow in deserts, where the moisture is only sufficient to allow vegetation for short periods. At that time the Rose of Jericho is green. With the arrival of the dry season it curls up and may be blown to another place by the wind. If it should happen to fall in a moist spot, it will revive again.
Care Anastatica is an annual. Laid in a bowl of water in the living-room it will remain green for quite a long time. The plant can rarely be rooted again.
Propagation Anastatica can be grown from seed in March in warm conditions, but it may prove difficult to obtain the seeds.

Anastatica hierochuntica
Low-growing annual plants with leaves arranged in rosettes; they have a taproot. They are brown in their dry state, but a fresh green when they open in moisture.

Angraecum

Orchidaceae

Origin Africa and Malagasy.
Description Most species are fairly large and decorative, with ivory-white or greenish-white spurred flowers. An angraecum seed weighs 0.7y (y is a millionth of a gram). Frequently the fruits contain millions of seeds and this is no coincidence, nor is it needless waste, for in the wild the chances that the minute seeds will land in a spot where they can germinate without difficulty are minimal.
Position To provide them with the warmth and humidity they need, they should really be kept in a hothouse, though an enclosed flower window is,

Angraecum sesquipedale, a hothouse plant

The best known Flamingo Plant is *Anthurium scherzerianum*, of which only hybrids are in cultivation. They flower profusely

of course, also suitable. Place them in a shady spot, or screen them against bright sunlight from April to September.

Care In summer the night temperature must lie between 18 and 21°C (64 and 70°F), and 21 and 28°C (70 and 82°F) during the day. When the sun is shining, even higher temperatures will be tolerated. The minimum temperature in winter is 16°C (60°F).

Watering In summer water freely, especially in high temperatures, and provide a high level of humidity. Moisten the plants with a fine spray before ventilating the room in the morning, and spray again in the afternoon when the windows are closed. In winter the plants must not be sprayed directly, but the level of humidity should be adapted to the temperature. In too high a degree of humidity the flowers easily become stained. There is no actual dormant season, but at the end of the growing season the plants should be kept a little drier.

Feeding In general these plants require little feeding, but in summer they may be given a fortnightly solution of fertiliser at normal strength.

Repotting Mix finely chopped fern root or beech root and sphagnum moss in equal parts. Repot in spring.

Propagation This is a job for a specialist grower, who can provide sterile conditions.

Angraecum eburneum

◐ ● ⊜ ⓞ ⊛ ⊡

This has fairly long stems with linear leaves and up to 15 fragrant white flowers in racemes. The spur is up to 8 cm (3 in) long.

Angraecum sesquipedale

Racemes consist of six white flowers; December till February. The flowers can only be pollinated by a single nocturnal species of butterfly – *Xanthopan morgani praedicta*. The length of its tongue corresponds to that of the orchid's spur.

Angraecum* × *veitchii

This is a cross between the two previous species.

Anthurium

Araceae

Flamingo Plant

Name From the Greek *anthos*, meaning flower, and *oura*, a tail. The inflorescence consists of a spathe and a spadix which resembles a tail.

Origin The 500 species originate in the tropical rain forests of Central and South America. The physician and botanist Karl von Scherzer discovered the first species in 1850, and in his honour it was called *Anthurium scherzerianum*.

Description These members of the arum family are grown both for their fine foliage and for their flowers. In recent years the long-lasting flowers are encountered more and more as cut flow-

Anthurium andreanum

Anthurium magnificum, a hothouse plant

Aphelandra aurantiaca roezlii

ers. The inflorescence is composed of a spathe, often strikingly coloured, and a straight or curved spadix, on which the minuscule florets appear. The spathe varies between red through pink to white, or may be bicoloured. Species with a less conspicuous spathe may develop bright red berries on the spadix. There is a great variety in foliage: sometimes the leaves are heart shaped, and sometimes spear shaped. There are species with dark green leathery leaves and others with velvety leaves with magnificent marking. In general they are erect in habit, with or without a stem, but there is also the epiphyte climber *Anthurium scandens*.

Position It requires plenty of light but does not tolerate direct sunlight. The plant should therefore be placed near a north- or east-facing window. *Anthurium scherzerianum* hybrids are the strongest and therefore most suitable to be used as house plants. *Anthurium andreanum* enjoys a heated flower window and *Anthurium crystallinum* will probably only thrive in a tropical greenhouse or flower window, since this is the kind of environment which most closely resembles its native habitat.

Care In winter *Anthurium* hybrids require a temperature of at least 15°C (59°F), with bottom heat of 18°C (64°F). *Anthurium crystallinum* demands 18 to 20°C (64 to 68°F). Keep the temperature at 20°C (68°F) in the active period. Higher temperatures will do no harm, provided the atmospheric humidity is kept at a high level. The plants will grow best if not subjected to temperature fluctuations. Foliage anthuriums require more warmth and shade than species grown for their flowers.

Watering To encourage profuse flowering, keep the plants a little drier than normal for six to eight weeks in winter. During the growing season water generously with completely demineralised water (pH 4 to 4.5), or tepid rainwater. A high degree of humidity is also desirable, and it is best to use the deep-plate method. Spray the foliage with tepid water, but never spray the flowers, or they would become stained. Another method is to place the pot in a large ornamental pot holder and to fill the space between the two pots with damp sphagnum moss. Be careful about drainage. Stagnating water will rapidly cause rotting of the thick roots.

Anthurium scherzerianum hybrids are very suitable for hydroculture.

Feeding During the growing season give a weak solution (half strength) of a lime-free fertiliser every week.

Repotting Every two or three years, in spring, repot in an open, peat-based compost bearing in mind that the plant is very sensitive to mineral salts. You can make your own mixture from pine needle compost or leafmould, peat, a little perlite to aerate the soil, and some rotted cow manure to provide nutrients. Sphagnum moss could have too high a salt content. Do not press the compost down too firmly; this would prevent aeration.

Propagation When large specimens are being repotted they may at the same time be divided, or some of the rooted shoots may be removed and potted up separately. If your plant has ceased to flourish you can increase it from stem cuttings. Remove all the leaves, taking care not to damage the invisible eyes in the axils, and insert them upright in equal parts of sand and peat fibre, covering them almost entirely. An electrically heated indoor propagator is necessary to maintain a bottom temperature of 25 to 35°C (77 to 95°F). Leaves and roots will develop after a few weeks.

Propagation from seed is another possibility, but it is a rather complicated process. The stigmata of the bisexual flowers ripen before the stamens and it is therefore best to cross-pollinate. This must be done around noon on a sunny day. Using a small paintbrush or a piece of cottonwool, move pollen from the spadix of one plant to the ripe stigmata of another. (The stigmata are ripe when they exude a sticky substance.) The seed will ripen after about nine months, when it should immediately be sown in a mixture of sand and peat. Just press it down, do not cover the seed. The bottom temperature should be 25°C (77°F). Germination will follow in two or three weeks. Prick out after four months and pot up three to four months later.

Pests and diseases Eelworm, aphids, scale insects, mites, red spider mites, slugs and thrips are possibilities. Mistakes in cultivation may result in root rot, leaf spotting and discoloration.

Anthurium andreanum

Of this species only hybrids are in cultivation. It has short stems and long leaf stalks with heart-shaped leaves. The spathe is very large and shiny, with colours between red and white.

Anthurium crystallinum

Large, dark green leaves with a velvety surface and white veins.

Anthurium magnificum

Pendulous, pale green foliage with white veins. This is a hothouse plant.

Anthurium scherzerianum

Of this species also only hybrids are in cultivation. It has lanceolate leaves on fairly short leaf stalks and a profusion of red or orange 'flowers'. The spadix is spiralled.

Aphelandra

Acanthaceae

Name From the Greek words *apheles*, simple, and *andros*, man. This indicates that the plant has simple anthers with one pollen sac.

Origin The 200 species originate in tropical and sub-tropical regions of America, especially Mexico, Brazil and Colombia, where they grow in the jungle.

Description These are shrubs or perennial herbaceous plants. They have simple shiny foliage, often large and beautifully marked. The inflorescence consists of simple or branched spikes, terminal or borne in the axils of the leaves, with fairly large bracts, frequently beautifully coloured and overlapping like roof tiles. The double-lipped corolla is yellow, orange or red. The calyx has five sepals and is generally smaller than the bracts. There are four stamens and a maximum of four seeds.

Position It must be kept moist, warm and in half shade. In a hothouse fantastic effects can be achieved, but with a little extra care you will be able to keep the plant in good condition for several months in the living-room as well.

Care In the growing season the ideal temperature lies between 18 and 25°C (64 and 77°F), in the dormant season between 10 and 14°C (50 and 57°F). Of their own accord the plants rarely branch, but you can induce them to do so by stopping, although such specimens frequently bear smaller flowers. After flowering the flower spikes should be cut off and following the resting period, which lasts for six to eight weeks, the aphelandra may be cut back to three axillary buds. It should then be repotted, placed in a warmer position and given more water.

Watering A great deal of water evaporates through the large leaves and the plant should therefore be watered generously from the time the new shoots appear until flowering. The water must be softened. Spray frequently and rinse the leaves with tepid water. During the dormant season water and spray more sparingly.

Aphelandra squarrosa

Feeding In the active period give a weekly dose of fertiliser solution at normal strength.
Repotting In March, repot in a well-aerated mixture rich in humus, possibly a commercial potting compost with some extra peat added.
Propagation Root shoot or eye cuttings can be taken under glass in a mixture of 4 parts peat to 1 part sand, at a temperature of 25°C (77°F). The best time is between November and April.
Pests and diseases These include scale insects, mealy bug, thrips, mites and eelworm. Too much sun or too cold an environment will cause the leaves to drop.

Aphelandra aurantiaca
Dark green foliage and yellow to orange flowers. The variety *roezlii* is more compact in habit and has silver-marked leaves.
Aphelandra blanchetiana
Syn. *Aphelandra amoena*. Green foliage; the centre vein and part of the lateral veins are white. The stems are red at the joints, and it bears deep yellow flowers with red bracts.
Aphelandra chamissoniana
Syn. *Aphelandra punctata*. It has a silver band along the centre and lateral veins. Bracts are yellow and dentate, with green tips, and the flowers are yellow.
Aphelandra fascinator
This has olive-green leaves, white along the centre vein, violet on the reverse, and magnificent red flowers.
Aphelandra liboniana
Orange bracts and small yellow petals. The foliage is variegated.
Aphelandra nitens
This species has bronze-coloured foliage which looks as if it had been laquered, green bracts and a red corolla.
Aphelandra squarrosa
Yellow inflorescence and dark green leaves, up to 30 cm (1 ft) long, with white veining. The variety *leopoldii*, with red stems, and 'Louisae' are better known; both have fine markings. The best-known strains are 'Dania', 'Superdania', 'Fritz Prinsler' and 'Uniflora Beauty'.

Aporocactus
Cactaceae
Rat's Tail Cactus

Name Derived from the Greek *aporos*, entangled.
Origin The six species originate in Mexico, where they are frequently found growing at high altitudes.
Description These are undemanding cacti and they are therefore very suitable for a novice cactus collector to gain experience. They are branched, with long, slender, pendulous branches. They may be used as hanging plants, but can also be grafted on stock. They produce an abundance of pink to red flowers. The areoles are covered in fine spines.
Position Small specimens can be grown on a sunny window-sill; large specimens are better used as hanging plants. They dislike bright sunlight in the afternoon. In summer they may be put out of doors. Keep them in a cool, well-lit place in winter.
Care In the dormant season maintain a minimum temperature of 5°C (41°F). Never turn the plant when it is in bud or flowering, or the buds will drop.
Watering Water generously in summer, but keep fairly dry in the resting period. Spray in warm weather or when the air is dry. When the buds are forming and when flowering the plant must be kept moist.
Feeding A lime-free feed at normal strength should be given once a fortnight.
Repotting Use special cactus compost or leafmould and clay.
Propagation Increase from seed or cuttings.
Pests and diseases Mealy bug, root aphids and red spider mites are possible pests.

Aporocactus flagelliformis
Syn. *Cereus flagelliformis*. This has red flowers, up to 10 cm (4 in) long, in spring; they keep for about four days. The green stems are about 12 mm ($\frac{1}{2}$ in) across, and covered in small thorns.
Aporocactus flagriformis
Syn. *Cereus flagriformis*. This species has stronger stems and thorns, yellow to red buds and violet-edged scarlet flowers up to 9 cm ($3\frac{1}{2}$ in) long. It is less well known than the previous species.

Aporocactus flagelliformis, Rat's Tail Cactus

Arachis
Leguminosae
Peanut Plant

Name This ancient Greek plant name belonged to another leguminous plant.
Origin The 12 known species originate in tropical South America, chiefly in Brazil. Peanuts are now cultivated in many countries: China, India, tropical regions of Africa, the southern United States and even in Europe, in Spain and Italy.
Description Low-growing to recumbent tropical plants, herbaceous annuals with green, often feathery leaves. They are being sold more and more, grown in bright plastic pots. It is less expensive to grow your own from unshelled raw peanuts – the plants will be equally beautiful.
Position A well-ventilated sunny, moderately warm position in the greenhouse or on the window ledge is the best situation.
Watering The Peanut Plant is very sensitive to too much moisture. Always water sparingly and keep an eye on the temperature, but it likes moderately high atmospheric humidity (50 to 60 per cent).
Propagation In spring put three seeds in a pot. They will germinate in a temperature of 20°C (68°F) and you will have flowering plants within about three months.
Pests and diseases They are very prone to whitefly. Check the underside of the leaves regularly.

Arachis hypogaea
Grows to between 25 and 45 cm (10 and 18 in) high. The leaf consists of two pairs of oval leaflets. The yellow flowers, which soon fade, open just above the surface of the soil. After pollination the flower stalk lengthens and pushes for an inch or two into the compost, where the fruits ripen.

Arachis hypogaea, the Peanut Plant

Araucaria heterophylla, the Norfolk Island Pine

Araucaria
Araucariaceae
Norfolk Island Pine

Name Named after Arauco, a southern province of Chile, or after the Araucani, a Chilean Indian tribe.
Origin The best-known species, *Araucaria heterophylla*, has its native habitat in Norfolk Island and other islands between eastern Australia and New Caledonia; the majestic trees are also found in the forests of southern Brazil and on the mountain ranges of Chile.
Description In their native habitat these conifers may reach heights of up to 60 m (amost 200 ft). The leaves are always arranged in a spiral around the branches.
Position It makes an excellent specimen plant in all kinds of interiors. Keep it away from other plants in a quiet corner, where people do not constantly bump into it. It must have a half-shady position in a cool, well-ventilated environment. In summer it can go outside, perhaps in a half-shady spot under a tree. Bring it indoors in September and put it in a very cool, frost-free and fairly well-lit place. If it is kept permanently in a shady and cool greenhouse, it will grow very tall – tall enough, in fact, to outgrow the greenhouse within a few years.
Care The transition from summer to winter treatment and vice versa should be gradual. The plant dislikes extremes. From October onwards the ideal temprature is between 5 and 10°C (41 and 50°F).
Watering To keep your araucaria in

good condition regular watering is vitally important. If the soil ball dries out, the lower levels of the foliage will drop. This may also result from over-watering in the dormant season or from excessively dry air. This is why, with the introduction of central heating, the plant is now rarely used indoors. Fortunately the sale of humidifiers is on the increase, which will improve conditions. Only tepid, soft water should be used.
Feeding Give a dose of lime-free fertiliser at normal strength once a fortnight.
Repotting Do not plant the araucaria too deeply. The point where the upper roots develop should lie just below the surface, for otherwise the plant will become diseased. Ideally use a mixture of leaf-mould and moorland soil, to which a little turf loam and sharp sand has been added. Repot every two or three years only, to prevent the plant growing too rapidly.
Propagation Increase only from tip cuttings. This is really a job for an expert and few amateurs will succeed in growing a worthwhile plant from a cutting.
Pests and diseases Mealy bug and occasionally thrips may occur. If some of the branches die or wilt in winter it is practically always the result of too high a temperature and not enough light.

Araucaria heterophylla

Syn. *Araucaria excelsa*. Norfolk Island Pine. Where it grows wild, this is a stately tree which may grow up to 40m (135ft), but in the living-room it will remain a small tree, with branches growing in a symmetrical circle. The bright green leaves, or needles, are up to 1.5cm ($\frac{5}{8}$in) long, sharp and curved. In 'Glauca' they are blue-green. 'Gracilis' is more compact in habit than the species.

Ardisia
Myrsinaceae
Spear Flower

Name From the Greek *ardis*, meaning spearhead.
Origin There are about 250 species, occurring mainly in tropical southern and eastern Asia, where they grow in the shady jungle or in mountain forests.
Description Evergreen, low-growing shrubs or small trees with alternating leaves. The inflorescence is terminal or borne in the axils of the leaves and is unisexual, or dioecious. There are usually five petals and five stamens. The berries are globular with one seed; they are white, red, blue and black.
Position A well-lit, sunny spot is best, in a moderately warm room. In summer screen the plant against bright sunlight. It needs good ventilation, especially in the flowering season.
Care In winter the most favourable temperature lies between 12 and 16°C (53 and 60°F). In a higher temperature the berries will drop, and if the air is too dry they will shrivel up. When the plant is in flower you can give nature a helping hand by transferring a little pollen to the pistil with the aid of a small brush. Keep the foliage free from dust. Frequently little nodules are found along the edges of the leaves. These contain bacteria and should be left alone. If they are removed, the plant's vigour will diminish appreciably.
Watering Keep the compost moist in summer. If the plant is kept in a warm room, spray throughout the year, except in the flowering period, when pollination and fruit formation would be inhibited. Always water and spray with tepid water. Keep moderately moist in winter.
Feeding In the growing and flowering seasons feed once a fortnight, following the instructions on the label.
Propagation Increase from cuttings or from seed in bottom heat. As a rule the berries ripen towards the end of December. The seeds should be removed and left to dry before being sown in peat and sand. The same medium can be used for cuttings.
Pests and diseases Scale insects and mealy bug can be troublesome.

Ardisia crenata

Syn. *Ardisia crenulata*. In Japan and in southern Asia the plants may grow up to 1m (3ft) in height. The spreading branches bear shiny, dark green, leathery leaves, up to 10cm (4in) long, with nodules along the lower edges. These 'bacteroids' contain *Bacillus foliicola*. The fragrant flowers are white, sometimes pink, and appear in terminal, pendulous racemes. The magnificent red berries stay on the plant for a long time. 'Albo-marginata' has variegated foliage.

Ardisia malouiana

Syn. *Labisia malouiana*. Pointed, lanceolate leaves, up to 25cm (10in) long, dark green and velvety with whitish markings along the centre vein. The reverse is red. The flowers are pale pink, the berries red.

Ardisia crenata with a crop of new berries, though it still bears some of last year's fruits

Arequipa
Cactaceae

Name Called after the town of Arequipa in southern Peru.
Origin About 10 species occur in Peru and northern Chile.
Description Initially spherical in shape, sometimes putting out shoots. Subsequently the cactus becomes more columnar and finally it becomes recumbent. The crown is frequently lop-sided and the cactus body is densely spined. The flowers are zygomorphous, which means that the flowers are symmetrical about one plane. The tube of the flower is usually curved and hairy.
Position The best place for these cacti is a cool greenhouse, where there is plenty of light in summer, while it is nice and cold in winter. The temperature may drop to 5°C (41°F) – this will promote healthy growth and flowering.
Care In summer the plants may be kept quite warm. They tolerate full sun, except perhaps early in spring when it is sometimes necessary to accustom them slowly to the light. It will do no harm to give them some fresh air from time to time, or even to grow them in

Arequipa paucicostata

a cold frame. As long as the temperature is high enough during the day, the night may be cold.
Watering In summer water very sparingly, if possible using rainwater or demineralised water. In winter they may be kept completely dry if the temperature is low.
Feeding In the growing season give a dose of nitrogen-free fertiliser once every three weeks.
Repotting The well-known cactus mixture, consisting of equal parts of commercial potting compost and perlite, is very suitable. Use plastic pots and repot in spring, older plants every two or three years.
Propagation Species which put out shoots can be grown from cuttings. After having been left to dry these cuttings may be rooted, or they can be grafted on to suitable stock (in which case they are not dried first). It is also possible to grow them from seed. Good-quality seed can be sown in February–March, under glass, at a bottom heat of 20–25°C (68 to 77°F). Germination may take a long time.
Pests and diseases Mealy bug and root aphids are the chief enemies. If the plants are kept too damp in winter they will rot.

Arequipa rettigii

Syn. *Borzicactus leucotrichus.* Initially spherical, later becoming columnar, this cactus has a maximum of 20 ribs, grey-green and densely covered in thorns growing from thick, felty, pale yellow aeroles. The longest thorns are up to 5cm (2in). The flowers are carmine to scarlet, up to 7.5cm (3in) long; the pistil is pale red and the stigma yellow.

Arequipa paucicostata
This species has few ribs.

Arisaema

Araceae

Origin The 150 species originate mainly in South and East Asia and in North and South America.
Description They are herbaceous perennials with thick tubers. The American species are called Jack-in-the-pulpit; the spadix represents Jack and the spathe is supposed to resemble the type of canopied pulpit sometimes found in old churches.

The Indians used to dig up the tubers to use them as food which is why they are sometimes called Indian Carrots. If you bite into a raw tuber, it leaves a disagreeable stinging feeling in your mouth and throat. The Indians got rid of the oxalates by first boiling the tubers, then peeling them, leaving them to dry, grinding them, heating the flour and leaving it outside for several days.
Position Choose a half-shady position, out of the draught, in a moderately warm environment.
Care Pot the tubers in October and bury the pots in a pit in the garden. Dig them up in spring and bring them indoors.
Watering Always keep the soil ball moderately moist. To prevent it drying out, mix a little extra peat fibre and leafmould with the potting compost. Provide moderate humidity – in centrally heated rooms spray at least once a day.
Feeding During the growing season feed every ten days, using a fertiliser solution at the recommended strength.
Repotting In October the tubers should be potted in a proprietary potting compost, preferably mixed with some extra peat fibre and leafmould.
Propagation When the plant starts into growth in March or April, carefully remove the shoots and pot them separately.

Inflorescence of *Arisaema candidissimum*

Arisaema candidissimum

This species has large dark green leaves with flowers up to 7.5cm (3in) long which appear in June. The photograph shows their beautiful white, pink and green colouring.

Asparagus

Liliaceae

Asparagus Fern

Name The Greek word *asparagos* referred to the edible asparagus.
Origin The majority of the 300 known species come from East, West and South Africa, especially from the Cape Province and Natal; Malagasy, and from Sri Lanka.
Description Hardy and non-hardy, very graceful shrubs, climbers or hanging plants with tubers or thickened rootstock. They have fleshy or woody, often strongly branched stems. The actual leaves are tiny, often no more than scales, spurred at the base. The pseudo-leaves, or phyllodes, are needle or leaf shaped, growing singly or in tufts, occasionally in a circle round a twig.

They usually produce racemes of small white flowers early in summer, growing from the axils of the leaves. Sometimes these are followed by berries.
Position A half-shady position is preferred, but a strain such as *Asparagus densiflorus* 'Sprengeri' can tolerate a great deal of shade. In summer they enjoy fresh air. The following species are very suitable as hanging plants: *Asparagus asparagoides, A. crispus, A. densiflorus* and *A. scandens deflexus. Asparagus falcatus* may grow to more than 1m (3ft) in height and is therefore not exactly the best plant for the window-sill. It also bears spines, so you have to be careful with your curtains and net curtains. But don't let these disadvantages stop you from buying the plant – it is extremely strong and exceptionally decorative.
Care It is advisable, though not essential, to give the plant a resting period at 8 to 10°C (46 to 50°F) in winter. If you spray regularly, few needles will drop. *Asparagus setaceus* should be kept at 12 to 15°C (53 to 59°F) in winter.
Watering In summer a great deal of water evaporates through the numerous tiny leaves and generous watering is therefore essential. It is advisable to allow the plant a resting period in winter, when it is watered more sparingly. However, *Asparagus densiflorus* may be kept in the living-room in winter, so long as the compost is kept moist. Regular spraying will be necessary to maintain moderate humidity, and rainwater is preferable both for spraying and watering. *Asparagus setaceus* is sensitive to dry air and must be sprayed very frequently. Nearly all asparagus species have very thick roots in which water is stored, so that it need not be a disaster if you occasionally forget to water them.

Too dry a soil ball will shrink and this is especially the case with asparagus plants. The water will run to the gap between pot and compost and the plant will not benefit. When the compost has reached this stage only extended plunging will do any good; this will make the soil ball swell up again.

Asparagus densiflorus 'Meyeri'. The flowers in the foreground belong to a begonia

Asparagus asparagoides

Asparagus densiflorus 'Sprengeri'

Feeding From May to September well-rooted plants should be fed every week. Follow the instructions on the label. If the plant is kept in the warm living-room in winter, it must be fed once a fortnight with a solution at half the strength of that used in summer. If you give a teaspoon of fertiliser per litre ($1\frac{3}{4}$ pints) water in July, it should be reduced to half a teaspoonful in January.
Repotting Young specimens should be repotted every year in April, and older plants every second year. When the plant becomes pot bound, the roots will exert pressure on the pot until it breaks. When repotting, thin the root system out a little. Always remember to place a crock over the drainage hole, or the roots will soon grow out of the pot. Use a proprietary compost or a mixture of equal parts of leafmould, pulverised clay and rotted cow manure. *Asparagus setaceus* likes light soil and will benefit from the addition of a little extra leafmould and peat. *Asparagus densiflorus* 'Sprengeri' prefers a loamy mixture, so some extra clay should be added.

If, at the time of repotting, the plant has many yellow phyllodes, this is a suitable time to cut it back a little. Cut the stems at the base; the plant will soon develop new shoots.
Propagation In March or April the plants can be divided and the sections potted separately. April is also a good month for sowing. Properly cared for, *Asparagus densiflorus* 'Sprengeri' occasionally produces red fruits containing seed capable of germination at 16°C (60°F).
Pests and diseases Common pests are aphids and scale insects, thrips, red spider mites and root millipedes. Healthy plants, properly looked after, are rarely subject to disease. However, if they are attacked, drastic measures are needed: all diseased shoots must be cut out at the base and destroyed.

Asparagus asparagoides

Syn. *Asparagus medeoloides.* An attractive trailing plant with widely branched stems up to 2m (6ft) long. This is one of the few species with heart-shaped leaves, up to 3cm ($1\frac{1}{4}$in) long, single, fairly thin and leathery. They are green and shiny. The scent of the greenish-white little flowers is reminiscent of oranges. The berries are purple. At one time the plant was called *Medeola asparagoides*, and mature tendrils were used in bridal wreaths and for table decoration, because they remained fresh and green the whole day.

Asparagus setaceus, better known as *A. plumosus*, used for cutting

Asparagus densiflorus 'Sprengeri' by the bath

Asparagus densiflorus 'Myriocladus'

Asparagus falcatus, a vigorous species

Asparagus crispus
Syn. *Asparagus decumbens*. A tuberous plant, like the previous species. The stems clearly zigzag. Phyllodes grow in groups of three or four, usually sickle shaped. The single flowers have relatively long stalks and are white and fragrant. The berries are white or pink.
Asparagus densiflorus
Syn. *Asparagus myriocladus*. Of the various strains of this species 'Sprengeri', at one time called *Asparagus sprengeri*, is probably the best known. It is one of the strongest forms for indoor cultivation. It is a semi-shrub with soft stems, which will become more and more pendulous as the plant grows older. The phyllodes always appear in small groups. They are up to 3 cm (1¼ in) long, fresh green, often slightly curved. The thread-like stems also bear small curved thorns. The white or pink flowers have a pleasant scent and are followed by red berries with black seeds, which may be sown. A more compact and slower growing form is 'Meyeri', which is erect in habit. In 'Myriocladus' the phyllodes grow in dense clusters. They are needle shaped and bright green.
Asparagus falcatus
This species can grow to over 1 m (3 ft) in height. It has erect, but soft, green stems with hard spines and firm linear or sickle-shaped foliage.
Asparagus scandens
A climber with round green stems and flat, pale green linear phyllodes, up to 2 cm (¾ in) long and curved. The variety *deflexus* has curving, zigzag stems.
Asparagus setaceus
Syn. *Asparagus plumosus*. These plants do not climb while they are growing, but they do when mature. The very thin, threadlike pale green phyllodes, up to 6 mm (¼ in) long, and the terminal branches spread horizontally or are slightly curved. They resemble a number of fern species. The flowers are white, the berries purple. 'Nanus' is smaller in all its parts, and 'Cristatus' has a cyprus-like habit.

Aspidistra
Liliaceae

Name From the Greek words *aspis*, shield, and *astron*, star.
Origin All the eight known species have their natural habitat in Asia, in the eastern Himalayas, China, Japan and Taiwan.
Description Evergreen herbaceous plants without a stem. The leaves grow directly from the rootstock. Plants were brought to Europe from China as early as 1800 and are among the oldest of our house plants, largely due to the fact that they tolerate a great deal of shade and temperature variations.
Position They will grow in a half-shady spot as well as in the centre of a room, rarely reached by the sun. The variegated species naturally require more light. It is one of the few house plants which will not be harmed by draughts.

As you can see from the illustration below, this is one of those plants which can be used effectively to enliven rooms other than the living-room. There is no reason why you should not keep it in the bathroom, the kitchen or the bedroom, provided you pay attention to the information given under the headings 'watering' and 'care'.

Aspidistra elatior 'Variegata'

Care In winter the most suitable temperature lies between 7 and 10°C (44 and 50°F). If the plant is not regularly cared for, older leaves may tear. Otherwise they stand up to anything except sun and compost which is too moist.
Watering Keep moderately moist. Stagnating water in the pot leads to root rot. Although the leaves are large, the surface is leathery, so that relatively little water evaporates, and dry air is therefore well tolerated. If the foliage gets dusty you can put the plant under the shower or sponge the leaves.
Feeding In spring and summer give the plant a fertiliser solution at normal strength once a month.
Repotting Leave the plant in the same pot for several years. Repot in a cylindrical container, slightly larger than the original pot, but do not feed that year.
Propagation The plants may be divided in March or April. Gently shake the soil from the roots and divide the rootstock into several sections, using a sharp knife. Care should be taken not to damage the roots, however strong the plant.
Pests and diseases The plants are subject to attacks by red spider mites and scale insects.

Aspidistra elatior
The dark green leaves are up to 70 cm (28 in) long and 10 cm (4 in) wide. They

Aspidistra elatior, so vigorous that it may be grown almost anywhere in the house

are long stalked and grow directly from the rootstock. Mature specimens may flower in winter. The single flowers are whitish, tinged with purple inside. They grow from the rootstock and flower just above or below ground level. 'Variegata' has green foliage with creamy linear marking.

Asplenium
Aspleniaceae
Spleenwort

Origin This plant is found in all continents, but most of the species grow in the rain forests of Asia, in Africa and in Australia.
Description A few of the 700 species are suitable for the rock garden; the rest are greenhouse and indoor plants. In tropical forests some of them live as epiphytes, collecting their nourishment in the funnel-shaped leaf rosettes. Others are terrestrial plants. The leaves are pale to dark green, undivided, pinnate or finely divided, often firm and leathery. The spore cases on the reverse of the leaves stand at right angles to the centre vein, to one or other side of the side nerves.
Position A tropical window or an enclosed flower window with bottom heat are the most suitable places. These ferns require little light. They are rewarding plants for the living-room, provided the level of humidity is adequate.
Care Aspleniums must be kept moderately warm in winter. The minimum temperature should be 12°C (53°F). For *Asplenium nidus* the minimum temperature in winter is 16°C (60°F). This species must always be kept slightly warmer than the others. If the edges turn brown feed and spray more frequently. Possibly it has been too cold. The ugly edges may be cut off, but be careful not to cut into the green part, for this would turn brown in its turn.
Watering All species should be watered with rainwater or softened water. During the growing season water freely and plunge the plant regularly. For the rest of the year the compost should be only just moist. Dust must be removed. A high degree of humidity is essential to keep the plants in good condition. Use the deep-plate method, spray the plant every day and if necessary buy a humidifier.
Feeding Feed once every 10 or 14 days, following the instructions on the label. Properly fed, the plant will develop plenty of new foliage.
Repotting Most species will grow in a proprietary potting compost, but they will definitely do better in a mixture of 1 part pulverised clay, 2 parts beech leafmould or peat fibre and 1 part clean sharp sand or perlite. Grown as an epiphyte, *Asplenium nidus* will grow best in a very light mixture, which may consist of coarse peat, rotted leafmould and a little rotted cow manure.

The pots must be particularly well draining, as for orchids, among other plants. In the greenhouse or in a flower window the Bird's Nest Fern may be grown on an epiphyte tree.
Propagation Increase from spores, in March, July or August. *Asplenium bulbiferum* and *Asplenium daucifolium* produce plantlets on mature leaves and these are easily removed. Wait until roots have formed and pot them in a sandy mixture rich in humus.
Pests and diseases Scale insects, root aphids and slugs are the chief enemies, and broad ferns may suffer from cockroaches. Check at night by suddenly shining a torch on to the plant – you will see them jump.

Asplenium bulbiferum
This species can grow to almost 1 m (3 ft) in height. The greyish leaf stalks are 15 to 30 cm (6 to 12 in) long. The frond is 30 to 60 cm (1 to 2 ft) long, 20 to 30 cm (8 to 12 in) wide and bi- or tripinnate. The foliage is dark green and fleshy. Small plantlets develop on the upper surface of mature leaves, and these can be removed and potted up separately. 'Laxum' with its more pendent habit is the most frequently cultivated form.
Asplenium daucifolium
Syn. *Asplenium viviparum*. As you can see in the photograph, this fern, too, develops plantlets on its mature leaves. At first all that can be seen are small nodules, but these soon grow into recognisable small ferns. The species is firmer and more erect in habit than the previous one. The fronds are up to 60 cm (2 ft) long and 20 cm (8 in) wide. The leaf stalks are fairly short and gracefully curved. It is a very suitable species for use indoors, but is rarely cultivated.
Asplenium dimorphum
Slightly larger than *Asplenium bulbiferum*, in this species the fronds may grow to 1 m (3 ft) in height and 50 cm (20 in) wide. They are dark green, gracefully curved and tripinnate. The sterile leaves may have a size of up to 4 by 2 cm ($1\frac{1}{2}$ by $\frac{3}{4}$ in). They are an oblique lozenge shape, blunt at the point, and are irregularly bidentate. The fertile leaves are divided into linear lobes, the spore cases occurring along the upper edge. In this species the sterile and fertile leaves are therefore easily distinguished. The difference does not appear in ferns bearing plantlets.
Asplenium nidus
The Bird's Nest Fern. An epiphytic fern with a short, vertical rhizome. It collects humus in its leaf rosette. Its undivided foliage makes it look quite different from other ferns. The leaves, which may grow to 1 m (3 ft) in length and 20 cm (8 in) wide, but in cultivation always remain smaller, are shiny and of a beautiful bright green. They form a tube, at the bottom of which a tangle of dark fibres may be seen, which is the origin of the plant's popular name. The midrib is shiny, and darker towards the base. Mature leaves have spore cases along the side veins on the reverse, but the spores do not readily germinate. The variety *australasicum* has narrower leaves and an almost black midrib.

Detail of *Asplenium daucifolium*

Asplenium nidus

Asplenium nidus, the Bird's Nest Fern, dislikes dry air

Asplenium daucifolium

Astrophytum myriostigma, a magnificent cactus, better known as Bishop's Cap

Astrophytum

Cactaceae

Name From the Greek *astron*, star, and *phyton*, plant. Seen from above the star shape is obvious.
Origin The four species all orginate in Mexico.
Description Spherical to cylindrical ribbed cacti, with or without thorns, and usually covered in tufts of woolly hairs. The funnel-shaped flowers are yellow, occasionally red in the centre, and scaled. The flowering season is usually in summer. They are nearly always grown singly. Only mature plants occasionally develop a sideshoot.
Position Species with a dense covering of white hair and thorny species should be given a warm situation in good light, but they must be screened against bright sunlight. Green species without thorns can be put in a semi-shady spot. Keep them in a cool, dry and well-lit place in winter, in a greenhouse if possible. A cool environment in winter is essential if the plant is to flower.
Care In summer these cacti should be kept warm with a temperature at night of 16 to 20°C (60 to 68°F). Keep cool and in good light in winter at a temperature of 5 to 10°C (41 to 50°F).
Watering Always water sparingly. From early March until late October water only when the compost dries out. In winter practically no water should be given. At that time the air must be dry, for in a cold and humid environment ugly yellow and brown patches will appear and in many cases the cactus will rot. *Astrophytum asterias* is particularly sensitive in this respect: it prefers a low level of humidity. Occasional spraying is only permissible if the temperature in the greenhouse becomes very high in summer.
Feeding Hardly necessary, but from May to August a small dose of fertiliser may be given every three or four weeks. Follow the instructions on the packet.
Repotting Every spring, repot in special cactus compost or in a mixture of 2 parts clay, 1 part rotted leafmould and 1 part

Astrophytum asterias, the Sea Urchin Cactus

Astrophytum ornatum

sharp sand, with the addition of a little bonemeal and gravel. The soil must contain more minerals than humus. Large specimens do not require repotting every year, especially if they are always watered with soft water.
Propagation Since *Astrophytum* species rarely put forth shoots, new plants are usually grown from seed. The fairly large, dark brown seeds are sown in spring in a temperature of 21 to 25°C (70 to 77°F). They will germinate within a few days, but are very sensitive to grey mould (q.v.). They will grow more rapidly if temporarily grafted on to stock such as *Pereskiopsis*. After a few years they may be removed from the stock and grown on their own roots. *Astrophytum asterias* never develops sideshoots, but should other species do so, they may be cut off in summer and rooted in sand. They strike within about three months and may then be potted.
Pests and diseases Root aphids may occur, and old plants may become discoloured at the base. The same thing happens in the wild, but it can be avoided if you cover the soil with a layer of fine gravel.

Astrophytum asterias

The Sea Urchin Cactus. The cactus body, 4 cm ($1\frac{1}{2}$ in) tall, is symmetrically divided into eight sections. Every flat section bears a row of woolly tufts on the widely separated areoles. Daisy-like yellow flowers appear from June to August. It is a slow grower and is therefore frequently grown on stock.

Astrophytum capricorne

This has a spherical stem, turning cylindrical in the course of time. It grows to 25 cm (10 in) in height. It usually has eight sharp ribs with a variable number of white woolly tufts and brown-black, 7-cm ($2\frac{3}{4}$-in) long twisted thorns on the areoles, and it bears shiny yellow flowers with a red throat.

Astrophytum myriostigma

Bishop's Cap. Growing to 15 cm (6 in) high, this species has a spherical to columnar body, usually with five or six ribs. The specific name means 'with ten thousand marks' and this refers to the numerous woolly white tufts. It readily produces silky, pale yellow flowers. A four-ribbed variety, *A.m. quadricostatum*, also exists, as well as a form called 'Nudum', which is plain green, without white tufts. In addition there are many hybrids in cultivation, the results of crossing natural forms and varieties.

Astrophytum ornatum

A spherical to columnar cactus with eight ribs, green, and covered in white scales in a feathery pattern. It has yellow to brown thorns, up to 5 cm (2 in) long and large yellow flowers. A number of deviating forms exist of this species as well, for example *A.o. glabrescens*, practically tuftless, and 'Mirbellii', one of the finest, with golden yellow thorns.

Aucuba

Cornaceae

Name The Japanese name of this plant was *aokiba*.
Origin There are three species. Their native habitat is in eastern Asia and in the Himalayas.
Description Evergreen shrubs, with opposite, stalked, smooth-edged or denticulate leaves, sometimes covered in large or small spots. They are dioecious and have small reddish flowers, from which berry-like stone fruits may develop. Aucubas are ornamental plants for the unheated greenhouse, the garden or the living-room. The fact that they are hardy and adaptable and require little light to thrive may explain their popularity, though naturally the ornamental value of their foliage and berries also contributes.
Position Indoors the plant grows best in a cool environment. In summer it may be brought into the living-room, but in winter it would suffer from the high temperature and the dry atmosphere. Cool entrance halls, unheated rooms, attics and garages are ideal in that season. Used as a tub plant it can stand on the terrace or in a half-shady position in the garden in summer and in a well-ventilated spot in an unheated greenhouse or a cool place indoors in winter.
Care This is a very easy plant to grow. Provided it is kept cool you will always have success with it, but indoor strains must spend the winter in a cool environment. The variegated strains will need slightly better light than the green forms.
Watering In summer keep the compost moderately moist. Be sparing with water in winter; the amount should depend on the temperature. If the plant is kept fairly warm in winter, it should occasionally be sprayed. It has stiff, leathery leaves, through which little water evaporates, so it never needs much water.
Feeding In the growing season, from April to August, give it a fertiliser solution at normal strength.
Repotting Repot in spring, in nutritious compost, rich in humus. Unsightly branches may be removed at the same time.
Propagation Increase from seed or cuttings. Take cuttings in February or in August, preferably using half-ripe wood. Rooting will be most rapid in a temperature of 20°C (68°F) but will also succeed at 15°C (59°F).
Pests and diseases Scale insects will be a problem if the temperature is too high in winter.

Aucuba japonica

In the wild this shrub grows to 2 m (6 ft), but in cultivation it remains smaller. It has leathery, dark green leaves, oval to lanceolate, up to 20 cm (8 in) long and coarsely dentate, with insignificant red flowers and red fruits. The variegated forms are the ones most often grown in the living-room: 'Crotonifolia', foliage with tiny yellow tips; 'Limbata', large, yellow-edged foliage; 'Picturata', green leaves with yellow patches in the centre, surrounded by smaller spots; and 'Variegata', leaves densely covered in yellow spots.

Aucuba japonica

Beaucarnea
Liliaceae

Name This genus is often called *Nolina*; the nomenclature is not entirely clear and the two plants are frequently confused.
Origin About 20 different species occur in Texas, California and Mexico.
Description The stem of this plant is thickened at the base and the narrow leaves are arranged in rosettes. It closely resembles the better known yucca.
Position They are tub plants and, as with the yucca, like to be kept out of doors in summer and in a cool, frost-free and well-lit place in winter.
Care From the end of May onwards put the plant in a sheltered, sunny position outside, or possibly on a sunny window-sill indoors. In October they must be moved to a cool place, where they can spend the winter at a minimum temperature of about 5°C (41°F). During this time the beaucarnea must not grow. An unheated but well-lit hall or stairwell might be a good spot. In their natural habitat the plants may grow several feet tall and in Los Angeles they are used as trees to line the streets.
Watering Always keep the compost moderately moist in summer and practically dry in winter.
Feeding While growing, the plant may be fed every three weeks.
Repotting Use a mixture of pulverised loam or clay, rotted beech leaves and sharp sand in equal parts. Cultivate in tubs or other containers with good drainage.
Propagation When the plant puts out sideshoots, these may be used as cuttings, but it is easier to grow new plants from seed.

Beaucarnea recurvata
Syn. *Nolina recurvata*. Initially the leaves develop from the tuber-shaped base, but later a stem is formed, which branches at the top and bears the rosettes of curving green leaves.
Beaucarnea stricta
Syn. *Nolina stricta*. Similar to the previous species, but the leaves stand away from the stem and are slightly rough along their margins.

A young plant of *Beaucarnea recurvata*

Begonia limmingheiana is one of the finest hanging begonias

Begonia
Begoniaceae

Name Charles Plumier, a French botanist and monk, who described the first begonia in 1690, named the genus after Michel Bégon, his patron, who lived from 1638 to 1710. He was an official in San Domingo and later governor of Canada and encouraged the science of botany.
Origin The more than 1000 species are widely distributed over the tropical and subtropical regions of Asia, Africa and America, but many of the individual species are restricted to one area only. They grow not only in warm, humid and wooded regions such as the Amazon district and tropical West Africa, but also in forests at higher altitudes in the Andes and the Himalayas, where the temperature and the level of humidity are lower. Many species have adapted themselves to a drier and colder climate by developing corms.

Begonia minor (syn. *Begonia nitida*) was probably the first species to be grown in a greenhouse in Europe (1770). In 1880, Professor Balfour, Curator of the Botanical Gardens in Edinburgh, introduced a begonia from the island Socotra, which was named *Begonia socotrana* and had a most important characteristic: it flowered in winter. This was the ancestor of the *Begonia lorraine* and *Begonia elatior* hybrids. In the course of the last century many new forms have become known, many imported, others the result of crossing.
Description This genus includes many very different species, some suitable for garden cultivation, others only for a heated greenhouse or the living-room. Some are not hardy; others are annual, perennial, erect growing or pendent, usually evergreen, semi-shrubs or herbaceous plants. They not only vary considerably in height, habit, colour of flowers and foliage and size, but also in the shape of the leaves, although most begonias may be recognised by the asymmetrical foliage. They have imitated the leaves of oak, ivy, maple, palm, elm, water lily, fern, holly and many others. The botanical name is often an indication. One thing they have in common is that their flowers are unisexual, though usually male and female flowers occur on one plant. The latter may be recognised by the inferior, almost triangular and winged ovary, filled with innumerable minuscule seeds. They usually have five, sometimes six to eight, petals, whereas male flowers have two or four, with numerous stamens. The most common colours are white, pink, red and yellow to orange. The inflorescences are compound umbels growing in the axils of the leaves.

Botanically, begonias may be divided in several ways, among others in three groups: fibrous rooted, tuberous, and those with rhizomes. They may also be divided according to their methods of cultivation or their appearance: foliage begonias, whose ornamental value depends on the leaves; winter-flowering begonias, which include forms capable of flowering in other seasons, such as *Begonia elatior* hybrids; tuberous begonias, of which single and double, large-flowered and small-flowered types are known and which also include hanging begonias; the summer-flowering *Begonia semperflorens* hybrids; and botanical species.
Position Most begonias require plenty of light, but not full sun. In poor light the stems become limp and the plant will become susceptible to mildew. Foliage begonias should be given a fairly warm, half-shady spot, whereas begonias grown for their flowers may have more light and like some fresh air. *Begonia semperflorens* hybrids tolerate sun. The only species described here which demands sun in order to flourish is *Begonia venosa*. Move or turn your begonias as little as possible and make sure that they are never in a draught. When buying a winter-flowering plant, allow it to become acclimatised somewhere at a temperature of 12 to 14°C (53 to 57°F) before bringing it into the living-room, where the atmosphere is so much drier and warmer than at the florists's or nursery.
Care Begonias which have a resting period in winter like to spend this time

Hanging tuberous begonia 'Aphroditis'

Begonia hydrocotylifolia

Begonia hispida cucullifera

Begonia lorraine hybrid

in a moderately heated room at around 15°C (59°F). The heated living-room is frequently too warm for them, causing leaf curl and blotches on the foliage. They will also be more prone to pest attack.

Foliage begonias are best maintained at a temperature of 15 to 18°C (59 to 64°F) in their dormant season. During this time they are distinctly less attractive, as no new leaves develop and they may lose a few of the old ones. After being repotted in spring they will start into growth again and if they are not crowded by other plants and if the foliage is not touched, they will soon recover.

Begonia semperflorens hybrids are used as bedding plants as well as house plants. Try to keep the temperature at below 20°C (68°F) in summer. As a rule they are grown each year as annuals.

Tuberous begonias must be kept cool throughout the year: in summer below 20°C (68°F) and in winter around 10°C (50°F). To prevent the tubers shrinking during this fairly cool and dry period, the peat fibre in which they are stored should be moistened from time to time. If, when repotting, you are uncertain which is the top (in theory the hollow side), keep them in a warm and humid environment until they put out shoots. This has the added advantage of encouraging more rapid growth.

Winter-flowering begonias prefer a temperature of 18 to 20°C (64 to 68°F) while they are in flower. In a higher temperature they will soon stop flowering. It is very difficult to keep them for another year, and most people discard them after flowering. If, however, you want to try, keep them a little drier for at least a month after flowering and prune them severely. After this period of rest they may be repotted and brought into growth. Make sure that in summer the temperature does not fall below 15°C (59°F), for this would cause them to react as long-day plants. Normally they are short-day plants, that is to say that they flower in less than 12 hours of light per day. These begonias can be induced to flower outside the winter season by artificial light treatment.

Shrubby begonias which have grown too tall or bare should be cut back before they start into growth in spring and before they are repotted. They will soon develop new shoots. In *Begonia albopicta*, *Begonia corallina* and *Begonia maculata* two- and three-year-old stems are removed. Vigorous growers such as *Begonia metallica* should occasionally be thinned out.

Watering In the growing season water regularly, using tepid, demineralised water with a pH of 4.5 to 5. It is fatal if the soil ball dries out, and it is advisable to grow them in plastic pots to reduce the risk of drying out to a minimum. If, on the other hand, the plant is kept too damp, root rot will occur. A moderately high level of atmospheric humidity is best, as dry air often causes the male flowers to drop. Foliage begonias and botanical species require a higher degree of atmospheric humidity than tuberous begonias and *B. semperflorens* hybrids. Never spray directly on to the foliage or the flowers as this will encourage mildew or grey mould. For most begonias winter is the dormant season, and species that have rhizomes or a stem should be watered very sparingly. For tuberous begonias the water supply should gradually be reduced after the growing season and wilting stems cut off. The tubers are kept dry in peat fibre throughout the winter. Winter-flowering plants are usually kept slightly drier at a somewhat lower temperature when flowering has ceased, to give them a rest.

Feeding During the growing and flowering season all species should be given a fortnightly feed at half the concentration indicated. A lime-free fertiliser is preferred.

Repotting Give them a light and nutritious mixture, rich in humus. A proprietary compost mixed with an approximately equal quantity of extra peat and some sharp sand is best. A little rotted cow manure may be added. Always use pots which are wide rather than deep and insert a drainage layer. The plants should usually be repotted

In the foreground, *Begonia imperialis*

The best-known form of Begonia boweri is 'Nigramarga'

once a year in April. Young begonias are sensitive to salts; composts containing mineral salts should be avoided.

Propagation Begonias are able to develop adventitious buds on parts that have been cut, such as leaves, shoots or tubers, and these will produce new plants. This is of particular importance where crossed forms are concerned, since they do not grow true to type from seed. Tuberous begonias may be sown in January or February in porous seed compost. In spring the tubers may be cut into sections and potted separately. Allow the cut surfaces to dry and dust them with charcoal powder to prevent rotting. Shoot cuttings, 5 to 6 cm (2 to $2\frac{1}{4}$ in) long, taken from tubers can be rooted in sand.

To grow foliage begonias from cuttings take leaf stalks with fully developed leaves in summer. Using a sharp knife, make a number of incisions on the underside of the leaves where the main veins branch. Insert the stalk in porous cutting compost and lay the leaf flat on the surface. Make sure that the incisions remain in contact with the compost, perhaps by weighting them with a few pebbles. Maintain the temperature at 20°C (68°F) and keep the soil damp. Plantlets will soon develop, and they can be removed when they have formed three leaves.

Botanical species are easy to grow from shoot cuttings throughout the year, either in water or in compost, but they can also be grown from leaf cuttings or from seed. *B. semperflorens* hybrids are sown at 20°C (68°F) in a mixture of sharp sand and leafmould. The seeds are minute: 1 gram contains 75,000 seeds! Do not cover them, merely press them down very gently. Double-flowered species are grown from cuttings. With the winter-flowering species, *B. lorraine* hybrids and Rieger forms can be increased from leaf cuttings and *B. elatior* hybrids from tip cuttings. Cuttings taken between November and January will soon root in a peat and sand mixture at 20 to 22°C (68 to 71°F). After two months they develop shoots which, because the days are short, immediately produce flowers. Vegetative growth only begins from the end of March onwards. *B. lorraine* hybrids may also be grown from shoot cuttings in summer.

Pests and diseases Begonias are subject to attacks by eelworms, aphids, begonia mites, grey mould, weevils, mildew, thrips, root rot and virus diseases. Bacterial diseases manifest themselves by watery, glassy patches along the leaf margins and on the underside of the leaves. Affected leaves will turn brown and dry. The stems become lead coloured and contain a purulent substance. These diseases are very infectious and affected plants must immediately be destroyed. Do not pour water on the plants.

Begonia corallina

Begonia × *erythrophylla*

Begonia conchifolia

Begonia heracleifolia, with deeply incised foliage

Begonia albo-picta

A semi-shrub, up to 1.5m (5ft) high, with short leaf stalks and up to 7-cm ($2\frac{3}{4}$-in) long, narrow green leaves with numerous silver spots. It has pendulous greenish-white flower racemes.

Begonia boliviensis

An erect-growing tuberous begonia with bright green leaves on smooth, branched stems, a pendulous inflorescence and orange-red bell-shaped flowers with pointed petals.

Begonia boweri

Low-growing foliage plant with dark red rhizomes, from which fairly small, fresh green leaves develop. The edge of the leaves is brown, lightly incised and hairy. In 'Nigramarga' the dark markings occur along the veins as well. Small white flowers with red blotches are borne on long stalks.

Begonia conchifolia

This has fairly thick, shield-shaped and pointed leaves, dark green and shiny; the reverse is brown and hairy. The small pale pink flowers are on hairy stems up to 25cm (10in) long.

Begonia corallina

A climbing plant or shrub up to 2m (6ft) tall. It has lanceolate foliage, usually plain green, and pendent racemes of large red flowers practically all the year round. 'Lucerna', with bronze-green white-spotted leaves, 'Bismarckiana' and 'President Carnot' are some of the well-known hybrids.

Begonia crispula

A low-growing plant with round to broad kidney-shaped leaves, grey-green with a wrinkled surface. The small flowers are pink on the outside, and white inside.

Begonia diadema

Up to 1m (3ft) tall, the five- to seven-lobed leaves with silver patches are deeply incised; the underside is red. There are pale pink flower racemes.

Begonia dregei

Up to 80cm (32in) high, this has fleshy red stems and bronze-green leaves with purple veins, and small white flowers in racemes.

***Begonia elatior* hybrids**

These are the result of crossing *Begonia socotrana* with botanical tuberous begonias from South America. These large-flowering winter begonias will flower in other seasons as well. Well-known forms are 'Nelly Visser', orange red; 'Exquisite', bright pink, very large single flowers; 'Man's Favourite', white. Rieger begonias belong to the *B. elatior* hybrids, but are much less sensitive to mildew and bud fall. Well-known strains are 'Lachsorange', profusely flowering, salmon pink; 'Schwabenland', large, orange-red flowers; 'Aphrodite', double, cherry red.

Begonia × erythrophylla

The result of crossing *Begonia manicata* with *Begonia hydrocotylifolia*. The creep-

Begonia foliosa, a fine hanging plant

Begonia masoniana (Iron Cross)

Begonia elatior Rieger hybrid

Begonia manicata may flower profusely

Begonia manicata 'Aureomaculata'

ing rhizome may spread outside the pot. It has shiny oval to shield-shaped foliage, hairy along the edges and red on the reverse, on stalks covered in red scales. The upper surface of the leaves is olive green with paler veining, and there are pink flowers.

Begonia foliosa
As they grow older, the branching shoots often become pendent. Numerous 1.5-cm (¾-in) long, serrated leaves, green and shiny; the bracts are retained. Insignficant white flowers appear in the axils of the leaves.

Begonia fuchsioides
A bushy shrub, up to 1 m (3 ft) tall with slightly curving stems; the leaves are red at first, later dark green, and edged with short hairs. The bracts drop. There are red flowers.

Begonia goegoensis
Bushy plant with a short, thick, reddish trunk and round to oval green leaves with bronze-coloured patches and dark red veining underneath. There are small rose-red flowers. This is a hothouse plant.

Begonia grandis
Syn. *Begonia discolor*. This often has small tubers in the axils as well as underground. The variety *evansiana* has shiny green, oval leaves with red veining on the reverse and terminal racemes of pale pink flowers.

Begonia heracleifolia
Fleshy leaf stalks grow from thick brown rhizomes and bear deeply incised brown-green leaves, sometimes fading to red, with paler veining. The underside is reddish with green-lined veins. Both surfaces are hairy. Long flower stalks carry white or pink flowers. In 'Punctata' the leaves are not so deeply divided.

Begonia hispida cucullifera
Fairly large oval leaves, pale green and hairy; adventitious buds develop on the main veins, resembling tiny plantlets. It bears white flower racemes.

Begonia hydrocotylifolia
Round to heart-shaped green leaves, smooth and shiny on the upper side. The underside is red and hairy. There are numerous rose-red flowers in summer.

Begonia imperialis
A low-growing species, having a short, creeping stem with broad, oval leaves, dark or brown-green, densely haired, with silvery green marking in the centre and along the veins. The reverse is red, with green veins, and there are white flowers. 'Smaragdina' has plain emerald green foliage.

Begonia incana
Thick, erect growing, with stems not readily branching; like the shield-shaped foliage they have a white felty surface. The leaves are thick but very fragile. The small bracts drop, and there are white flowers.

Begonia incarnata
A shrubby plant, up to 1.5 m (5 ft) tall. It flowers profusely from autumn to spring, the rose-red flowers growing in pendulous racemes.

Begonia limmingheiana
Because of its limp stems, this 80-cm (32-in) tall plant is suitable for use as a hanging plant. The leaves are almost symmetrical, 12 cm (4½ in) long and 5 cm (2 in) wide, and it bears pendulous racemes of rose-red flowers.

***Begonia lorraine* hybrids**
A cross between *Begonia socotrana* and *Begonia dregei*. The first strain that was cultivated was called 'Gloire de Lorraine'. These small-flowered winter begonias have pink or white flowers and usually green marbled foliage.

Begonia luxurians
The shield-shaped divided foliage consists of 10 to 20 small lanceolate leaves, green to red and serrated, and there are cream-coloured, fragrant flowers.

Begonia maculata 'Picta'

Begonia metallica, a shrubby plant which may grow to 1 m (3 ft)

Begonia rex hybrid, a foliage begonia

Begonia socotrana, with shield-shaped foliage

Foliage of *Begonia serratipetala*

Begonia maculata
Syn. *Begonia argyrostigma*. Shrubby plants, up to 2 m (6 ft) tall. They have lanceolate leaves, up to 25 cm (10 in) long, green with silver spots and purple to red on the reverse and produce white or pale pink flowers in pendulous racemes. 'Lucerna' has broader leaves and enormous flower racemes. In 'Picta' the white spots on the foliage are larger.

Begonia manicata
The leaf stalks and the underside of the green leaves are partially covered in hairy red scales, and these also surround the upper part of the leaf stalk. In winter it bears a veil of small pink flowers. 'Aureomaculata' has yellow-blotched foliage and in 'Crispa' the edges of the leaves are frilled.

Begonia masoniana
The bright green, distinctly blistered leaves have hand-shaped dark markings which have given the plant the name of Iron Cross. It has greenish-white flowers.

Begonia metallica
A shrubby plant, strongly branching, growing up to 1 m (3 ft) in height. The foliage is dark green, asymmetrically heart shaped with a metallic gloss, darker along the sunken veins, which are red on the reverse. There are pink-white flowers.

Begonia pearcei
◐ ⊖ ◎ ✻ ◙
Low-growing, it has softly haired stems with pointed leaves, green with paler veins on the upper surface, dull red underneath. This is the only yellow-flowering tuberous begonia and so it is often used for crossing.

Begonia rajah
◐ ⊜ ◎ ✻ ◐
This species has a creeping rhizone and brown-green foliage with pale green veins, enclosing blistered areas. It bears racemes of pale pink flowers.

***Begonia rex* hybrids**
Descendants of *Begonia rex*, mainly grown for the magnificent foliage, which may include the colours black, pink, red, silver and green. The flowers are usually pink.

Begonia schmidtiana
◐ ⊖ ◎ ✻ ◙
A spreading, bushy and hairy plant with dull green foliage and an abundance of white to pink flowers.

***Begonia semperflorens* hybrids**
Descendants of *Begonia semperflorens*. Bushy plants with fleshy green or dark green, shiny leaves and white, pink or red flowers.

Begonia serratipetala
◐ ⊜ ◎ ✻ ◐
A shrubby plant with shiny, bidentate olive-green leaves with blood-red patches, and pink flowers.

Begonia socotrana
This has shield-shaped leaves, forming a funnel in the centre. The base of the leaf stalk is thickened like a tuber. It bears dark red flowers in winter and for that reason is often used for crossing.

Tuberous begonias
◐ ⊜ ⊖ ◎ ✻ ◐
The assortment presently available consists of hybrids which are the result of crossing various botanical species. All begonias which die in the autumn and whose tubers are kept dry in winter belong to this group. The large-flowered forms are divided into single, semi-double and double types. In addition there are medium-sized and small-flowered begonias and hanging begonias, such as 'Aphroditis', with double pink flowers.

Begonia venosa
○ ◐ ⊜ ◎ ✻ ◐
The slanting heart-shaped foliage has a felty surface. The large, reticulate bracts remain on the plant and it bears fragrant white flowers.

Beloperone
Acanthaceae
Shrimp Plant

Name From *belos*, meaning projectile or arrow, and *perone*, point or spine.
Origin A native of Mexico.
Description A genus consisting of 60 species of tropical shrubs and semi-shrubs, only one of which is regularly found on sale, *Beloperone guttata*. The decorative value of the plant lies chiefly in the green to brownish-red bracts. The small white flowers soon drop.
Position Light, air and sun encourage the fine colouring of the bracts, but in summer it should be screened from very strong sunlight.
Care Maintain a temperature of 15 to 25°C (59 to 77°F) in summer; in winter keep the plant at 12 to 15°C (53 to 59°F). To maintain a fine, bushy shape, it should be cut back by one third every year in spring, when it is repotted.
Watering Water generously from the time it starts into growth. Decrease the water supply in mid-August, but make sure the compost does not dry out, and maintain a moderate level of atmospheric humidity.
Feeding Feed every week from May to September.
Propagation Increase from seed or cuttings in spring and summer, under glass at 20°C (68°F).
Pests and diseases Watch out for red spider mites and whitefly. The plant is also liable to rotting.

Beloperone guttata
○ ◐ ⊜ ◎ ✻ ◙
Both the stems and the leaves are hairy. The small white flowers, the lower lip purple spotted, grow in pendulous spikes and have reddish-brown bracts, overlapping like roof tiles. The fruits spring open in the sun and scatter their seeds over an area of several square yards.

Beloperone guttata, the Shrimp Plant, is at its best in really good light

Bertolonia marmorata 'Bruxellensis'

Bertolonia marmorata

Bertolonia
Melastomataceae

Name Named after the Italian botanist Antonio Bertoloni (1775–1869).
Origin All 10 species come from southern Brazil.
Description Herbaceous or semi-shrubby plants. Leaves three to nine veined, often with five veins and variegated. Its chief ornamental value is provided by the foliage. The red or pink flowers have five petals; the ovary is trilocular.
Position Preferably keep it in a hothouse or an enclosed flower window. In the living-room it will only remain in good condition if kept among other plants in a container, in adequate humidity. Put it in a shady spot and try to sustain a constant temperature.
Care Maintain a temperature of 20 to 22°C (68 to 71°F); in summer it may rise to 25°C (77°F). Only young plants are beautiful.
Watering Water moderately throughout the year, and ensure there is a constant and high level of humidity.
Feeding Rarely necessary.
Repotting This is usually only a question of potting up. They grow best in coarse moorland soil or conifer needle compost with peat fibre.
Propagation Increase from seed, which a correctly cared-for bertolonia produces in large quantities. Sow in a heated indoor propagator.

Bertolonia maculata
The velvety green, spotted and hairy leaves have white or grey bands along the centre veins, and it bears pink flowers.
Bertolonia marmorata
Short, creeping stems with green foliage with a white band along the centre vein. The underside of the leaves is purple and there are lilac-pink flowers. 'Bruxellensis' has silvery leaves with green spots arranged in rows between the main veins.

Billbergia
Bromeliaceae

Name Named after the Swedish botanist, Billberg.
Origin The 60 species are natives of the tropical jungle from Mexico to southern Brazil and northern Argentina.
Description The billbergia is a terrestrial bromeliad. There are foliage and flowering plants for the living-room, the hothouse and for a moderately heated greenhouse. Only two species are commonly cultivated: *Billbergia nutans* and *Billbergia* × *windii*. The first one, especially, is an indestructible indoor plant. The photograph shows that mature plants will form an attractive foliage rosette interspersed with flowers. The time of flowering depends on the temperature at which they are kept in winter. If the plants are kept rather cold at that season, they will flower late in summer, but kept in the living-room they will flower in spring.
Position These plants tolerate plenty of light and even full sun, but in a half-shady position the foliage colouring will show to better advantage. In summer billbergias may go outside, provided they are given a very sheltered position, free from draughts.
Care After flowering cut off the flower stalk. In winter the plant likes a temperature of around 16°C (60°F), and will be damaged if it drops below 12°C (53°F).
Watering In summer water may be poured into the leaf rosette, as well as on to the compost. In winter it is better to water the compost only, especially if the plant is kept cool. Water freely in summer, but in winter the water supply should depend on the temperature. Use tepid water; it need not be soft. Dry air is tolerated fairly well.
Feeding Give a nutrient solution at normal concentration once every 10 days. Continue to feed after flowering has ceased, for it will now put out four or five new shoots at the base.
Repotting Use a proprietary potting compost or a mixture of 2 parts leafmould, 1 part rotted cow manure and 1 part sphagnum moss. The pots should be wide rather than tall and have a good layer of crocks in the bottom to provide drainage.
Propagation Separate the new shoots when they have reached half the height of the parent plant. Remove the plant from the pot, shake the soil off the roots and make sure that each plantlet has a few roots.
Pests and diseases Scale insects are the chief hazard.

Billbergia nutans
This species forms funnel-shaped rosettes of prickly linear leaves. The flower stalk initially grows straight up from the centre, but curves at a later stage. A spike of blue-edged yellow to greenish flowers will appear from the rose-red bracts.
Billbergia × windii
One of the many hybrids resulting from crossing *Billbergia nutans* and *Billbergia decora*, it is larger in all its parts. The 3-cm (1¼-in) broad, crossbanded leaves are covered in grey scales. The corolla is yellow-green, and the sheath red.

The flower and bracts of Billbergia × windii

Billbergia nutans, an extremely industrious bromeliad, flowering readily

Blechnum
Blechnaceae

Origin Most species originate in moderate climates in the southern hemisphere, especially South America and New Caledonia.
Description These ferns either have a stem or are low-growing with a creeping rhizome. The foliage is pinnate or pinnately divided, usually leathery, green and shiny, arranged in funnel-shaped rosettes.
Position Best placed in a flower window without bottom heat, but well cared for it has great decorative value in the living-room. Give it a shady, but not too dark position, moderate temperature and good ventilation.
Care Maximum soil temperature in winter should be 16 to 18°C (60 to 64°F), when the air temperature should be between 13 and 25°C (55 and 77°F), whereas in summer it may be between 20 and 35°C (68 and 95°F)
Watering Water generously from May to July, when growth is at its most vigorous. At other times water moderately, but never allow the compost to dry out. Maintain moderate humidity. Do not

Blechnum gibbum

spray directly on to the leaf surfaces.
Feeding During the main growing period give a strongly diluted feed once a fortnight, a quarter of the concentration indicated on the label.
Propagation Increase by division or from spores sown in bottom heat.
Pests and diseases Plants weakened by incorrect treatment are frequently attacked by aphids, scale insects, mealy bug, eelworm, thrips and red spider mites.

Blechnum brasiliense
The stem may grow to 50 cm (20 in). Young leaves are brown-red, mature foliage is green, pinnate, and up to 1 m (3 ft) long, with a striking centre vein. 'Crispum' has curly-edged leaves.
Blechnum gibbum
May develop a 1-m (3-ft) long stem. It has short leaf stalks, covered in black scales at the base. The leaves are up to 1 m (3 ft) long, the leaflets are wavy, densely arranged, up to 10 cm (4 in) long.
Blechnum occidentale
Leathery leaves form rosettes up to 40 by 10 cm (16 by 4 in) in size, slightly curved, separated.

Borzicactus
Cactaceae

Name Named after Antonio Borzi, 20th century, Curator of the Botanical Gardens in Palermo, Italy.
Origin At least 11 species occur from Ecuador to northern Peru.
Description A little known, but extremely beautiful genus of small, columnar cacti, which branch readily and sometimes have a more recumbent habit.
Position These plants should not be kept as cool in winter as other cacti. Experts recommend a minimum temperature of 10°C (50°F), slightly lower than in a moderate greenhouse. A cool room might be suitable.
Care In summer these columnar cacti require full sun, either in a greenhouse or in a cold frame covered in rainy weather.
Watering In summer water sparingly to moderately and in winter do not let them dry out completely. Because the temperature is relatively high, the plants will continue to lose some moisture.
Feeding In summer give a cactus feed every three weeks.

Borzicactus samaipatanus

Repotting Standard potting compost is suitable, but it is advisable to add a little extra clay.
Propagation Cuttings may be taken from mature, branched specimens, but it is really a pity to do so. Seedlings grow rather slowly. For that reason young plants are frequently grafted after a few months on *Pereskiopsis* stock, when they will grow much more rapidly. After a time, when the plants grow too large for the thin stock, they are either used as cuttings or newly grafted on to *Trichocereus spachianus*. This is the best way of obtaining large flowering plants within a reasonable time.

Borzicactus samaipatanus
Syn. *Bolivicereus samaipatanus*. Small, branched columns to 70 cm (28 in) in height, with eight to twelve ribs covered in firm white thorns. It flowers at an early age, producing large flowers with protruding stamens.
Borzicactus sepium
Syn. *Cleistocactus sepium; C. roezlii*. Up to 1.5-m (5-ft) columns with nine to twelve flattened round ribs covered in golden-yellow to red-brown thorns and bearing carmine flowers.

Bougainvillea spectabilis 'Orange Queen'

Bougainvillea
Nyctaginaceae

Name This plant was discovered in the second half of the 18th century by an expedition led by the famous French navigator Louis Antoine de Bougainville.
Origin We know about 15 species, occurring in tropical and semi-tropical regions of South America, especially in Brazil. They were introduced into Europe in the first half of the 19th century and thrive in Mediterranean countries.
Description Shrubby or herbaceous plants, evergreen or deciduous, and usually climbing. In the wild they grow to 4 m (13 ft) in height. They have thorny twigs and insignificant little flowers encased in strikingly coloured, long-lasting papery bracts.
Position Give them plenty of sun, light and air, whether indoors or in the garden. The same applies in winter, except that they should be kept cool to encourage flowering.
Care During its dormant season the plant must be kept at 8 to 10°C (46 to 50°F). The flowers develop on one-year old wood and the plant must therefore be pruned only after flowering.
Watering In summer water generously, but sparingly in winter when the plant often sheds much of its foliage. Take care, however, that the soil ball does not dry out entirely. Spray frequently, to prevent the leaves dropping and the wood drying out. The other period when you should not water too often is in spring, when the new shoots are about 30 cm (1 ft) long. Overwatering and overfeeding at that time will retard flowering.
Feeding In summer give a normal fertiliser solution every week.
Repotting Repot young plants every year, later every two or three years.
Propagation Increase from cuttings. Unfortunately this is not easy, for a very high bottom temperature – 30 to 35°C (86 to 95°F) – is essential. Use rooting

Bougainvillea spectabillis

powder and make an attempt in spring.
Pests and diseases Aphids, red spider mites, thrips and mealy bug may appear. Yellow leaves are the result of iron or nitrogen deficiency.

Bougainvillea × buttiana
A hybrid of *Bougainvillea glabra* and *Bougainvillea peruviana*. The best-known form is 'Mrs Butt', with scarlet bracts.
Bougainvillea glabra
A vigorous climber, with thorny branches and rose-red bracts in summer. 'Sanderiana' is less vigorous, but flowers profusely at an early age. In 'Alexandra' the bracts are bright purple to violet, and 'Variegata' has variegated foliage.
Bougainvillea spectabilis
This thorny climber is the most vigorous species. It has dark green, elliptical leaves and the small white to cream-coloured tubular flowers are enclosed in the three reddish-purple bracts. White, yellow-orange, pink and red strains also exist, such as 'Orange Queen', shown in the photograph.

Bouvardia hybrid 'Mary'

Bouvardia
Rubiaceae

Name Named after Charles Bouvard, personal physician to Louis XIII and Curator of the Jardin du Roi in Paris.
Origin This genus originates in Central America, especially Mexico, and includes several dozen species.
Description They are usually shrubby plants, rarely herbaceous, and are evergreen. The oval or lanceolate leaves are arranged in threes or fours round the stalks, or are opposite. Terminal flowers, often delightfully scented, come in white, pink, red or a combination of two of these colours. There are a number of hybrids cultivated for cutting.
Position Place in a well-lit, sunny spot, which is well ventilated, and in a moderate temperature. In summer they may be put in a sheltered position out of doors. If kept indoors in summer, they should be screened only from the strongest sunrays. In the dormant season the temperature should be kept at 5 to 10°C (41 to 50°F). In many cases they thrive in a greenhouse rather than in the living-room, because the level of humidity is higher.
Care In winter maintain a temperature of between 5 and 10°C (41 and 50°F). Repot in February, shorten the plant and gradually get it accustomed to higher temperatures. Mature specimens of species flowering in July and August should be stopped twice, between April and late May.
Watering Water freely in the growing season and especially when the plant is in flower. At other times ensure that the compost does not dry out and water sparingly but keep the humidity high.
Feeding Feed weekly from May to September at the normal concentration.
Repotting Use a potting compost based on loam, with added rotted cow manure.
Propagation After two or three years the plants lose some of their beauty and cuttings can then be taken in spring. They should be rooted at 21°C (70°F) and grown on at 12 to 15°C (53 to 59°F). Root cuttings can also be taken.
Pests and diseases Look out for mealy bug and scale insects.

***Bouvardia* hybrids**
Single forms include 'Mary', with a white corolla and rose-red tubes; 'President Cleveland', red corolla with paler tube; 'Rosalinde', red corolla. Double-flowered forms are 'Alfred Neuner', white, and scented; 'Bridesmaid', pink; and 'Thomas Meehan', scarlet.
Bouvardia longiflora
Up to 80 cm (32 in) tall. It bears large, white, scented flowers, to 10 cm (4 in).

Brassavola perrinii

Brassia maculata

Brosimum alicastrum

Brassavola
Orchidaceae

Origin This genus of epiphytic orchids originates in Central America, in the climatically moderate regions of Mexico, Venezuela, Colombia, Brazil, Surinam and the islands of Costa Rica, Jamaica and the West Indies.
Description This orchid has pseudobulbs, from which as a rule only one leathery leaf appears, which is cylindrical or flat. The inflorescence is very graceful and the flowers are often delightfully scented. They are usually greenish white in colour.
Position They demand plenty of light, but do not tolerate direct sun. Since they require a high degree of humidity, an enclosed flower window or a greenhouse is the ideal situation.
Care Day temperature in summer should be 18 to 22°C (64 to 71°F); 16 to 18°C (60 to 64°F) at night. When the sun shines the mercury may rise a little. In winter keep at 16 to 18°C (60 to 64°F) during the day and at 13 to 16°C (55 to 60°F) at night. In a severe frost both day and night temperature may drop by 5°C (9°F).
Watering Water generously in the growing season, copiously in hot weather. Water with care in winter: allow the plant to become fairly dry before watering. Spray in summer, but very little in winter.
Feeding Give a monthly dose of orchid fertiliser from May to September.
Repotting These orchids may be tied to fern blocks or tree bark, but they can also be potted in a mixture of 2 parts osmunda fibre and 1 part sphagnum moss, with the possible addition of some charcoal. Fill the pot up to a third with crocks.
Propagation Increase by division of the pseudobulbs and from seed.

Brassavola cucullata
Every pseudobulb produces a leaf. It bears fragrant, creamy-white flowers from September to December.
Brassavola nodosa
This has yellow-green flowers with a white lip in autumn and winter.
Brassavola perrinii
The pale green flowers have a heart-shaped white lip.

Brassia
Orchidaceae

Origin About 40 species have been found in Central America, from Mexico to southern Brazil, and also on the islands of Costa Rica, Jamaica and in the West Indies.
Description All species have fairly large pseudobulbs, growing close together. These serve to store water and nourishment. Every pseudobulb produces two leathery leaves. These epiphytes have small, very graceful flowers. They are rewarding and unusual plants, and fairly easily cultivated in the living-room.
Position Choose a half-shady spot in the living-room or a moderately heated greenhouse. Put them in a position where they can be sprayed frequently.
Care Keep fairly warm in summer. In winter keep the temperature at 17 to 20°C (62 to 68°F) during the day and at 13 to 17°C (55 to 62°F) at night.
Watering Keep them moist in summer, using soft water, and frequently spray throughout the year. Shrivelling pseudobulbs indicate inadequate watering. In winter the plant needs little water.
Feeding In summer give a weak dose of lime-free fertiliser once a fortnight, using half the concentration indicated on the label.
Repotting Repot in a mixture of sphagnum moss and osmunda fibre, preferably in lattice baskets, to allow maximum aeration of the roots. They must be kept in the same container for at least two years.
Propagation Increase by division of the pseudobulbs or from seed.

Brassia maculata
Syn. *Brassia guttata*. Every pseudobulb has one tongue-shaped leaf. The yellow-green, waxy and brown-spotted flowers grow in pendulous racemes. There is a red-spotted white lip.
Brassia verrucosa
Ribbed, oval pseudobulbs with two linear leaves. There are greenish-white flowers with purple patches at the base and a white lip with dark warts. This is the best-known brassia, and the one most suitable for living-room cultivation.

Brosimum
Moraceae

Name Derivation unknown.
Origin Not known, but it probably comes from the tropics.
Description This is one of those remarkable mystery plants, which are by no means rare. Occasionally they are found in quite small flower shops in the provinces, where they may be sold as 'a kind of ficus'. They are indeed related to the ficus, but should not be given that name. The strange thing is that the plant is not mentioned in any other plant book. Its existence is hidden and nobody recognises the plant as a brosimum. All the more reason to include it here.
Position As to its favourite position, the plant may, in fact, be compared to a ficus: it enjoys being kept throughout the year in a warm room and tolerates a fair amount of shade. I have grown it for several years near a sunless window.
Care The brosimum requires little care. Rinse the foliage from time to time, and cut back lanky stems – that is about all it needs.
Watering The plant must be watered with care – too much water in the pot makes the foliage turn yellow. On the other hand the soil ball must never dry out.
Feeding From April onwards, when the new shoots develop, feed every fortnight.
Repotting Standard potting compost is a good medium for the brosimum. It does not need fresh compost every year. But make sure it has good drainage.
Propagation Very easily grown from cuttings, which are nearly always successful. Use tip shoots, provide some degree of bottom heat and root them under glass.

Brosimum alicastrum
A widely branched, erect-growing shrub with hairy brown twigs. Alternate lanceolate leaves, 15 to 20 cm (6 to 8 in) and 3 to 5 cm (1 to 2 in) wide, sharply pointed, plain green. The leaf stalk is 3 to 4 cm (1 to 1½ in) long.

Browallia
Solanaceae

Name Named after the Lutheran bishop Johan Browallius, professor of physics and theology. Originally a friend of Linnaeus: they later came into conflict.
Origin Tropical South America.
Description Eight annual herbaceous plants and one semi-shrub, *Browallia speciosa*, are known. The five-petalled flowers are blue, violet or white. The leaves have smooth edges and are sometimes sticky.
Position Keep in a fairly cool room, where the plants can get plenty of light but no direct sun. They are not very sensitive to the temperature and may therefore also be kept in a heated room. In summer they can be put in a sheltered position outside.
Care Faded flowers must be removed immediately.
Watering Keep the compost moderately moist, and atmospheric humidity at between 50 and 60 per cent. Dry living-room air is tolerated better than

Browallia speciosa, a plant which is usually grown from seed

their appearance leads us to suppose.
Feeding Feed every two weeks, following the instructions on the label.
Repotting Repot in proprietary potting compost or in loamy garden soil rich in humus.
Propagation Increase from seed. You may expect to have a plant capable of flowering approximately four months after sowing. Sow in a temperature of 20 to 25°C (68 to 77°F). Combine four young plants in one pot for a bushy effect and pinch out the tips to encourage branching. They can also be grown from cuttings.
Pests and diseases Aphids are the chief problem.

Browallia speciosa

Syn. *Browallia major*. A semi-shrub, growing to 50 cm (20 in), with oval green leaves and trumpet-shaped, single-growing flowers, blue-violet with a white throat. 'Major' has larger flowers. They flower practically all the year round.

Browallia viscosa

A 30- to 60-cm (1- to 2-ft) tall annual. All its parts are covered in sticky hairs. The corolla is violet coloured, with a white centre. 'Compacta Saphir', up to 30 cm (1 ft) tall, flowers profusely.

Brunfelsia

Solanaceae

Name From the German botanist and theologian Otto Brunfels, compiler of the first large book of herbs.
Origin Central and South America.
Description Thirty species of evergreen shrubs and trees with large white, yellow or violet-blue flowers, flattened, with a long tube. The seeds are fairly large and the fruit is leathery or fleshy.
Position They need a well-lit situation throughout the year but screen against sun in summer. They do best in a greenhouse or a flower window, but if you have neither, you could try the living-room. Ensure a constant temperature. They may be put out in the garden in summer.
Care Low temperatures encourage bud formation. Give the plant a rest from November to January at a temperature of 10 to 12°C (50 to 53°F); provide fresh air. When the buds become visible, move the plant to a slightly warmer position and increase the water supply. After the flowering period, in May–June, they require a second resting period. After a few weeks, prune and repot.
Watering Keep moderately moist by watering regularly in the growing and flowering seasons. Keep slightly drier in the resting periods. They require a fairly high degree of humidity.
Feeding During the autumn–winter resting period an occasional dose of nitrogen fertiliser will prevent discoloration of the foliage. During the growing and flowering periods feed weekly, following the instructions on the label.
Propagation Well-grown tip cuttings, about 7 cm ($2\frac{3}{4}$ in) long, may be rooted under glass at 30°C (86°F). They do not strike readily, and the operation must be carried out under glass, that is, in the greenhouse.
Pests and diseases Aphids and red spider mites may be encountered.

Brunfelsia hopeana

Syn. *Franciscea hopeana*. Dark green, lanceolate leaves, paler on the reverse. The flowers are smaller than in any other species, but very numerous. As in the following species their violet colour fades to white.

Brunfelsia pauciflora calycina

A spreading shrub, up to 60 cm (2 ft) tall, with lanceolate leaves, green on the upper side, pale green underneath. The flowers have a violet corolla, with a white ring in the throat.

Brunfelsia pauciflora calycina

Caladium bicolor hybrids, showing a few of the dozens of different markings

Caladium

Araceae

Angel's Wings

Name Derived from the Malay word *keladi*, which means plant with edible roots. This applies to other members of the family as well.
Origin Tropical South America, especially Brazil and the Amazon region, where they grow in the jungle.
Description Fifteen species of foliage plants with tuberous rootstock. The foliage is heart or arrow shaped, finely veined and magnificently coloured: white, silver, green, pink and red. They have the characteristic inflorescence of all *Araceae*: a fairly inconspicuous spathe and spadix on a flower stalk. The leaves die off in autumn.
Position This should be warm and shady, preferably in a flower window or a heated greenhouse with sufficient humidity. If you want to bring your plant into the living-room for a time, put the pot in a larger pot holder and fill the space between with damp peat, to increase the level of humidity around the leaves.
Care In the autumn the leaves become unsightly and die and the plant spends the winter in this state. Put the tuber, pot and all, in a warm spot, or keep the tuber in dry sand with a minimum temperature of 18°C (64°F). If the temperature is too low the tubers will rot or become corky. In February–March repot them in fresh compost at a temperature of 22 to 24°C (71 to 75°F) and in a humid atmosphere. When the foliage develops gradually harden the plant by lowering the temperature, but not the humidity.
Watering Water generously in spring and summer, then gradually decrease the water supply. Most species require a high level of humidity, but do not spray directly on the leaves.
Feeding Feed weekly during the growing period; follow the instructions on the label.
Repotting Remove old roots and compost. Use a sandy, porous mixture: 3 parts potting compost, 2 parts sharp sand and 1 part sphagnum moss, or equal parts of leafmould, peat fibre and rotted cow manure.
Propagation At the end of the winter the tubers may be increased by division. Wait until they have started into growth, so that you can see the eyes – every section must have at least one eye. Dust the cut surfaces with charcoal powder, let the sections dry and plant them in a mixture of peat fibre and sharp sand at a temperature of 22 to 25°C (71 to 77°F). As soon as roots have developed the plants must be repotted in normal compost, as indicated above. Needless to say, cultivation must take place under glass in a high degree of humidity.

Artificial pollination will produce seed, which ripens after two months.

***Caladium bicolor* hybrids**

Arrow-shaped leaves in a variety of sizes grow on long leaf stalks. There are many strains with magnificent colouring.

Caladium humboldtii

Syn. *Caladium argyrites*. A low-growing plant with green, arrow-shaped leaves with transparent white patches, very suitable for living-room cultivation.

Calanthe

Orchidaceae

Name From the Greek *kalos*, beautiful, and *anthos*, flower.
Origin The 150 species are native of eastern and southern Asia, Central America, tropical regions of Africa, and Australia.
Description This genus includes epiphytes as well as terrestrial orchids. They may also be divided into two groups: deciduous species, with rhizomes and a leafy central stalk with the flower stalk beginning at the base of the rhizome or the leaves, and evergreen species, with fairly large pseudobulbs bearing two or four short-stalked leaves, from the base of the pseudobulb.
Position Keep in a moderate to warm greenhouse or in an enclosed flower window. Evergreen species must be screened more heavily in summer.
Care The minimum temperature in winter for deciduous species is 13°C (55°F) and evergreen species 16°C (60°F).
Watering Give adequately in the growing season, but keep a little drier when the plant is in flower. Deciduous species must not be watered in winter, and evergreen species should be watered

Calanthe hybrid 'William Murray'

sparingly, although they do not actually have a dormant season. Atmospheric humidity should be high in the growing period, moderate in winter.
Feeding From May to August give a little cow manure solution every fortnight.
Repotting Deciduous species should be removed from their pots towards the new year, kept dry and repotted around April in a mixture of sphagnum moss, sand and leafmould plus an equal quantity of peat fibre. The same mixture is suitable for evergreen species.
Propagation Increase from young tubers or from seed.
Pests and diseases Red spider mites are the most likely threat.

Calanthe triplicata

Syn. *Calanthe veratrifolia; C. furcata*. An evergreen species, in which the flower stalk is 1m (3ft) tall and bears small snowy white flowers with a yellow-orange centre in summer.

Calanthe vestita

Easier to grow than the previous species, it is deciduous, bearing white flowers with an orange-yellow spot on the lip; they appear in winter. 'William Murray' is one of the many hybrids; it has white and carmine flowers.

Calathea

Marantaceae

Name The Indians used the long leaves for weaving baskets. The Greek word for basket is *kalathos*.
Origin Mainly in South America, but some of the 150 species are natives of tropical Africa and of the archipelago between Indonesia and Australia. They grow in the tropically humid jungle and are cultivated accordingly.
Description Evergreen perennials, with short or long stems and leaf stalks which grow from the root and bear magnificent, usually fairly long leaves. They vary in colour and have characteristic markings. The genus *Calathea* may be distinguished from *Maranta, Stromanthe* and *Ctenanthe* by its trilocular ovary. The calathea moreover has one staminodium (a sterile stamen) while the maranta has two. There are also differences in the foliage, but they are not very obvious. In spring or summer small baskets of flowers appear. There is only one species in which the flowers are the major attraction, and that is *Calathea crocata*.
Position Preferably they like a hothouse or an enclosed, tropical flower window. It is not easy to keep these plants in good condition in the living-room, for as usual the atmospheric humidity forms the greatest stumbling block. Put them in good light, but out of the sun. They tolerate a fair amount of shade, and are very suitable for use in mixed containers.
Care Keep them warm in summer, and in winter at between 13 and 16°C (55 and 60°F). Clean the leaves regularly either with water or with a little leaf gloss on cotton wool.
Watering Water freely in spring and summer, using tepid, demineralised water. Make sure that the entire soil ball remains constantly moist. Both dry and excessively moist compost will cause damage. Water moderately in winter. A high level of atmospheric humidity is essential, especially when the leaves

Calathea crocata, known for its inflorescence

Calathea lancifolia

begin to appear. Spraying alone is not enough. You should use the deep-plate method as well, or a roomy pot holder filled with damp peat, or a humidifier.
Feeding During the growing period give a fertiliser solution once a fortnight, using half the concentration indicated.
Repotting The plants must be repotted at least once a year for they soon exhaust the compost. They have a fairly shallow root system and should therefore be grown in wide rather than in deep pots. Use porous, slightly acid compost, for instance a proprietary compost mixed with extra peat fibre, some clay and some sharp sand.
Propagation Increase from tip cuttings, or an easier method, suitable for all species, is by division. This should be done in spring, in a bucket of lukewarm water. Divide the plants in such a way that every section has a number of leaves and healthy roots. A temperature of 18°C (64°F) is needed to promote rooting and growth.

Calathea bachemiana

Syn. *Maranta bachemiana*. Grows up to 50cm (20in) tall. It has lanceolate, pointed leaves up to 25cm (10in) long and 5cm (2in) wide. The upper surface is pale grey-green with a narrow dark green margin and midrib and almond-shaped dark green patches on either side of the latter, and green underneath.

Calathea crocata

The only species cultivated for its flowers. The foliage is green with a dark red bloom, obtuse oval in shape. The plant has a magnificent and striking orange flower spike, which lasts for a long time.

Calathea lancifolia

Syn. *Calathea insignis*. The lanceolate leaves, up to 50cm (20in) long, are pale green with a slightly darker margin and alternating large and small dark green patches parallel with the side veins. The reverse is brown to purple.

Calathea leopardina

The oval leaves are up to 20cm (8in) long, pale green with dark green patches. The reverse is bronze to purple.

Calathea lietzei

Syn. *Maranta lietzei*. An uncommon species, developing erect-growing shoots which bear offsets. It has oblong leaves, up to 16cm (6½in) long and slightly wavy. The upper surface has a metallic sheen, and white bands running from the centre vein are parallel with the side veins. The underside is purple.

Calathea lindeniana

Oblong to oval leaves, about 15cm (6in) long, dark green with three emerald green zones: one along the centre vein and two just inside the dark green margin. The reverse has similar, but purple, marking.

Calathea louisae

This species does not produce offsets. The shape of the leaves is broad oval; they are up to 20cm (8in) long and 10cm (4in) wide. Feathery dark and pale markings are visible along the midrib and the reverse of the leaf is green or reddish.

Calathea makoyana

Syn. *Maranta makoyana*. Grows up to 60cm (2ft) tall. The leaves usually reach 20cm (8in), but may be longer in mature plants. Because of the feathery marking of patches and streaks running from the centre vein to the margin, it is sometimes called the Peacock Plant. The background is pale green, the marking dark green; the reverse is purple with similar marking.

Calathea medio-picta

This has pointed oblong leaves, up to 20cm (8in) long and 9cm (3½in) wide. The upper surface is dark green with a fairly wide, irregularly toothed, whitish band along the centre vein, and the underside is pale green. The leaf stalk is no more than 4cm (1½in) long.

Calathea ornata 'Sanderiana', a fairly well-known house plant

Calathea makoyana, the Peacock Plant

Calathea ornata
In cultivation it may grow to over 1m (3ft) in height. The leaf stalks may be very long. It has rounded oval to lanceolate leaves, dark green, with pairs of ivory streaks between the side veins; in young plants the streaks are pink. The underside is dark purple. 'Sanderiana' has broader foliage.
Calathea picturata
About 35cm (14in) tall; the leaf is an oblique oval shape, pointed and dark green with white and yellow-green streaks along the midrib and near the margin. The reverse is dark purple. 'Vandenheckei' has long-stalked leaves with silvery streaks in the centre and on either side.
Calathea roseo-picta
Leaves 20 by 15cm (8 by 6in) long with leaf-shaped pink streaks, parallel to the side veins, against an olive-green background. The streaks later fade to silvery white. The centre vein is red.
Calathea rotundifolia
Round to short-oval green leaves, up to 9cm ($3\frac{1}{2}$in) long. 'Fasciata' is most attractive; it has fairly wide silver-grey streaks along the side veins of the rather thick, leathery green foliage. The underside is grey with a purple tinge.
Calathea veitchiana
A striking species, up to 80cm (32in) tall. The shiny leaves are up to 40cm (16in) long and 25cm (10in) wide, oval to oblong, firm and leathery. They have feathery markings starting from the centre vein, beginning with yellow to pale green, next a band of dark to brown-green, a narrower band of pale green to white, and finally a bright green band. On the reverse the same marking occurs in purple on blue-green.
Calathea warscewiczii
Up to 1m (3ft) tall with oblong, velvety dark green foliage, yellow-green along the midrib and some of the side veins. The underside is wine red.
Calathea zebrina
Up to 60cm (2ft) tall with oblong leaves with a velvety sheen, soft green with crosswise dark green patches. The underside is grey-green, later sometimes reddish. 'Binotii' is smaller in all its parts. It has pale green leaves with black-brown streaks.

Calceolaria hybrid, the old-fashioned Slipper Flower

Calceolaria
Scrophulariaceae
Slipper Flower

Name Derived from the Latin *calceolus*, which means small shoe or slipper.
Origin The 500 species are natives of the cool and humid mountain regions of South America. Two species occur in New Zealand.
Description Annuals or perennials, herbaceous plants or small shrubs. The inflated, pouch-shaped lower lip is common to all. The flowers are multicoloured, but the largest part is usually yellow to purple and brown. They either grow in the axils of the leaves or are terminal and as a rule grow in umbels. The leaves encircle the stem or are opposite. Annual hybrids are usually available between January and May. They die after flowering, and may then be discarded.
Position Keep in a well-lit position in the living-room, out of the sun and not in a draught, otherwise your plant will almost certainly be attacked by greenfly.
Care The Slipper Flower prefers a moderate temperature, between 10 and 12°C (50 and 53°F). Always remove dead flowers.
Watering The compost must always be kept moderately moist. Remember their mountain forest habitat and maintain a fairly humid atmosphere by occasional spraying, and by using a roomy pot holder filled with damp sphagnum moss or peat. When the plant is in flower mist-spray only.
Feeding Apply a fertiliser solution at half the indicated concentration once a fortnight.
Repotting Always use a lime-free potting compost.
Propagation In July, increase from cuttings. Some strains can be grown from seed as well. In both cases cool conditions should be provided. Screen against the sun and ventilate in good weather. At 8 to 10°C (46 to 50°F) plants will develop flower buds in about four to six weeks. Flowering can then be brought

A yellow-flowered *Calceolaria* hybrid

forward by using fluorescent lighting.
Pests and diseases You may have trouble from eelworm and aphids, grey mould, and whitefly. Yellowing foliage is the result of iron deficiency, which in turn results from the wrong kind of potting compost or too high a mineral concentration. Virus disease and rotting may affect plants; the foliage wilts because the base of the stem rots. Avoid too much moisture, do not plant too deeply and use clean compost.
Calceolaria hybrids
Syn. *Calceolaria × herbeohybrida*. These are annuals. In the 'Grandiflora' group the flowers are up to 6cm ($2\frac{1}{4}$in) across. In 'Multiflora' they are up to 4cm ($1\frac{1}{2}$in) in diameter. Both groups comprise plain-coloured, striped, blotched and speckled flowers. The foliage is dentate.
Calceolaria integrifolia
A semi-shrub with wrinkled foliage and sticky yellow plumes of flowers up to 1.5cm ($\frac{1}{2}$ to $\frac{3}{4}$in) across which is suitable for balconies.

Calliandra tweedyi

Calliandra
Leguminosae

Name From the Greek words *kallos*, beautiful, and *aner* or *andros*, man.
Origin From Central America, especially Mexico, and from South America, mainly southern and south-eastern Brazil, Bolivia, Ecuador and Surinam.
Description Evergreen shrubs with very graceful pinnate or bipinnate foliage and unusual, but very striking, magnificent flowers; the conspicuous thin threads are the stamens.
Position A well-lit – in autumn and winter even sunny – position in the heated living-room. In spring and summer they must be screened on sunny days. They also thrive in a warm greenhouse or hothouse, where the level of humidity is much higher than in the living-room.
Care Minimum winter temperature should be 15°C (59°F). If the plants grow too large they may be cut back a little in spring.
Watering Keep the compost moderately moist throughout the year and in summer water generously on warm days. Provide an atmospheric humidity of 50 to 60 per cent. In the living-room spray at least once a day.
Feeding During the growing season feed once a fortnight, using the recommended concentration.
Repotting In spring, repot in standard potting compost, possibly with the addition of a little humus.
Propagation Increase from cuttings, under glass and with bottom heat.
Pests and diseases The fairly delicate foliage is prone to attacks by whitefly.

Calliandra tweedyi
The photograph will probably remind you of *Mimosa pudica* – not surprising, for they both belong to the family of *Leguminosae*. However, the bipinniate leaves of the calliandra do not fold when touched. The innumerable leaflets are practically linear in shape and silky to the touch when young. The long stamens are red to purple, with yellow anthers.

Callisia elegans

Callisia

Commelinaceae

Name The Greek *kallos* means beauty; *lis* means lily.
Origin Of the 12 species originating in Central and South America, three are cultivated over here. The best known of these is *Callisia elegans*, a native of northern Mexico, which has only been grown in the United States since 1943.
Description Herbaceous plants with a recumbent or erect habit. They are usually grown for their graceful appearance and attractive foliage. The flowers are usually white, but they are very inconspicuous.
Position In their native habitat they grow as ground cover in the forest and so they need a shady position. In too much light the leaves will fade and remain small.
Care Kept at a temperature of 16°C (60°F) or higher, callisias grow rapidly. When they become too lanky or lose their beauty they can be cut back to the second or third pair of leaves.
Watering While the plant is growing keep the compost fairly moist, but in winter allow it to dry between watering. Spray from time to time to keep the atmospheric humidity at 50 to 60 per cent.
Feeding Feed weekly in spring and summer.
Propagation Take 7-cm (2¾-in) long tip cuttings – they will root in a temperature of 20°C (68°F) either in water or in a sandy mixture. Cover with a plastic bag to prevent drying out. After about ten days, when roots will have formed, cut holes in the plastic to accustom the plants to the dry living-room atmosphere. As soon as the plantlets have started to develop new leaves, the bag can be removed.

Callisia elegans
◐⊜⊘⊛◙
Syn. *Setcreasea striata*. Recumbent stems with oval, sheathing leaves, downy. The colour is dull green with white stripes, and white flower racemes are borne on erect-growing stalks.
Callisia fragrans
Syn. *Spironema fragrans*. This has an erect stem with green foliage and small, fragrant white flowers.

Callistemon

Myrtaceae

Bottle Brush Tree

Name From the Greek words *kallos*, beauty or beautiful, and *stemon* meaning stamen.
Origin This genus embraces about 25 species, all natives of Australia and Tasmania.
Description In Australia these evergreen shrubs or small trees grow to between 1 and 3 m (3 to 10 ft) in height. Grown in pots or tubs they will reach about a third of this size. The leaves are firm and leathery, frequently with sharp tips and conspicuous veining. They are green and lanceolate in shape. In summer the plants produce magnificent 5- to 10-cm (2- to 4-in) long flower spikes. What we see are the scarlet, sometimes yellow, filaments which appear in a cylinder around the tip of the flower stalk. They are reminiscent of the brushes which were at one time used to clean the glass chimneys of oil lamps. They are, in fact, spirals of flowers which lost their sepals and petals as soon as the buds opened. After two months these flaming torches drop their stamens as well. From the ovaries hard, woody grey fruits develop, triangular or square, pressed close to the stem. The stem continues to grow beyond the inflorescence and develops new leaves.
Position This plant has been grown for a long time in unheated greenhouses and orangeries, but you can also grow it if you have a well-lit room and a balcony. Keep the plant in good light and an airy place in the living-room. A sunny situation and fresh air are both essential if the plant is to develop and flower.
Care To achieve a bushy plant, or to reshape it, you may cut it back in spring, before it starts into growth, or even better, when it has ceased to flower in summer. When pruning, remember that the plant flowers on stems developed in the previous year.
Watering Always use demineralised water, and very little in winter. From spring onwards keep the compost moist. When it is kept outside in summer it must also be watered regularly. When the buds appear, make sure that it is not too warm indoors, or spray regularly to maintain a high level of humidity, otherwise the plants will dry out.
Feeding From April to early August give a dose of lime-free fertiliser every fortnight.
Repotting Young plants should be repotted every two to three years, older plants every five to six years in March, preferably in woodland soil rich in humus, or perhaps in conifer needle compost.
Propagation From August to March, 5-cm (2-in) long cuttings can be rooted in sand in a temperature of 18 to 20°C (64 to 68°F). Cover with glass or plastic, and they will root in about five weeks and can then be potted up. They do not tolerate lime. Ideally, use a mixture of leaf-mould and conifer needle compost, with peat fibre and sand, and keep them under glass at 15°C (59°F) for a time. In the second year they may go outside. Regularly pinch out the tip, and give them sufficient light, water and food.

Callistemon citrinus, an unusual tub plant

Camellia japonica 'Beatrice Burns'

Callistemon citrinus
○⊜⊘⊛◐
Syn. *Callistemon lanceolatus*. The only species to flower at an early age and for that reason the only one in cultivation. At one time it was called *Callistemon lanceolatus*, because of the lance-shaped leaves which are lemon scented when bruised.

Camellia

Theaceae

Name Called after George Joseph Kamel, 1661–1706, who compiled an illustrated book of the plants growing on the island of Luzon.
Origin The 82 species originate in eastern Asia. *Camellia sinensis*, the Tea Plant, is the best known. The house plant *Camellia japonica* is a native of the cool mountain forests of Japan, Korea, northern China and Taiwan. It has been cultivated on a large scale since 1800 and in the course of time many magnificent hybrids have been developed.
Description A slow-growing evergreen, woody shrub with shiny, leathery leaves. The cup-shaped flowers occur in red, pink, white or are bicoloured. They also vary in size from 5 to 12 cm (2 to 4½ in) and in form: single, with numerous stamens, semi-double, and double with overlapping petals. Both the petals and the stamens are fused at the base.
Position Many people complain that the camellia is a difficult plant to grow indoors, but if you can find a favourable position for it you will have gone quite a long way towards success. In summer it prefers a sheltered, half-shady situation outside. If you want to keep it indoors all the year round, give it a spot near a north-facing window in a cool room. It is important not to move the plant, for the buds turn to the light and if the light should suddenly come from a different direction, the short stalk would break and the bud drop. If a camellia becomes too large for use indoors, plant it in a sheltered position out of doors and cover it in frosty weather.
Care From the above it can be seen that the camellia enjoys a regular existence. When the plant is brought indoors in September, the change in temperature must be as gradual as possible. Keep it at 8 to 10°C (46 to 50°F) in winter, then at 10 to 12°C (50 to 53°F) until the buds open. When the plant flowers the maximum temperature should be 16°C (60°F).

Camellia japonica 'Yours Truly'. In a mild climate this is a garden plant rather than a house plant

After flowering keep it at 6 to 10°C (43 to 50°F) and stand the plant outside again at the end of May or beginning of June.
Watering Keep the compost constantly moist and always use demineralised water, for camellias dislike lime. In winter pour tepid water into the saucer and remove the surplus after 15 minutes. Make sure there is a constant atmospheric humidity as well. Plants which arrive in your warm, dry living-room straight from the florist's or nursery are sure to drop their buds.
Feeding In the growing season give a lime-free feed every two weeks but don't feed after the buds have formed, for the new shoots would push out the buds.
Repotting Repot as seldom as possible, using lime-free compost. It is better to feed regularly or to replace the top layer with porous humus once a year.
Propagation In January or August you can take tip cuttings with three leaves or eyes. Dust with rooting powder and root them in a mixture of peat and sand with a bottom temperature of 18 to 22°C (64 to 71°F).
Pests and diseases Trouble from scale insects, aphids and mealy bug, as well as bud fall and foliage diseases, is often caused by incorrect cultivation.

Camellia japonica
◐⊖⊘⊛◐
The leaves are up to 10 cm (4 in) long, with edges which often curve inwards. The plant flowers between November and March, depending on the cultivar. There are numerous cultivars: 'Chandleri Elegans' is the strongest, with double rose-red flowers.

Campanula isophyllia 'Mayi', the blue Star of Bethlehem

Campanula
Campanulaceae
Bellflower

Name The Latin word *campanula* means 'little bell'. All the flowers of this genus are bell shaped.
Origin Grows wild in the chalky mountains of Europe and Eurasia and also in Mediterranean regions such as the Italian province of Liguria.
Description Most of the species belonging to this large genus are garden plants. Only two are used as house plants: *Campanula fragilis* and *Campanula isophylla*. They are very rewarding, easily cared for perennials with soft, very fragile, usually pendulous stems, containing a milky liquid. The white or purplish-blue flowers are bell shaped.
Position In the living-room the campanula will flower both on a north-facing window-sill and in a sunny window, though in the latter case it must be screened against excessively bright sunlight at midday. From the end of May onwards it can be placed on a draught-free balcony or in the garden. It is very sensitive to frost, so bring it indoors early in September to avoid risks and keep it in a well-lit, cool place in winter. It makes an ideal hanging plant.
Care Before the onset of winter the old flower stalks should be cut back to an inch or two above the rim of the pot. Keep at 6 to 8°C (43 to 46°F) in winter. Remove dead flowers regularly, for they rob the plant of nourishment.
Watering This depends very much on temperature and position. On a warm

Campanula isophylla 'Alba'

summer day a plant kept near a south-facing window may have to be watered three or four times a day, but in a north-facing bedroom three to four times a week is enough. Hard water will do no harm. Water sparingly in winter. Keep a moderately high level of humidity. In a greenhouse the air may be too humid, causing ugly black spots on the foliage. *Campanula fragilis* is particularly sensitive to drying out of the compost.
Feeding From spring onwards, when the plants start into growth until mid-August feed every week with a solution at normal concentration.
Repotting In spring, repot in a nutritious mixture, rich in humus, for instance equal parts of leafmould, rotted cow manure and clay.
Propagation *Campanula fragilis* is usually grown from seed. This is sown between February and April and germinates in 10 to 14 days. *Campanula isophylla* can be grown from cuttings taken in spring. The parent plant, which has been kept cool in winter after having been pruned, is repotted. The water supply is slightly increased and it is kept at a temperature of 10 to 15°C (50 to 59°F), but no more than 15°C (59°F) or the shoots will grow limp. Tip cuttings of 5 to 7 cm (2 to $2\frac{3}{4}$ in) will root in a mixture of peat and sand, though it may take quite a long time. Rooting powder will help.
Pests and diseases Red spider mite and thrips are possibilities, and leaf spot and grey mould occur when the atmosphere is too humid. When rooting cuttings, the level of humidity should also be kept low to moderate. Thrips transmit a virus disease which causes yellow rings, spots or streaks on the foliage. Affected plants should be discarded.

Campanula fragilis
○⊖⊘⊛◙
A hanging plant with 30-cm (1-ft) long, unbranched stems bearing small, smooth green leaves, and blue flowers in June, July.
Campanula isophylla
Star of Bethlehem. A recumbent to trailing plant with hairy stems. Soft blue flowers appear from July to September. 'Alba' has white, 'Mayi' purple, somewhat larger, flowers.

Canna

Cannaceae

Indian Shot

Origin All species probably originate in tropical and subtropical regions of America.
Description Herbaceous, rhizomatous plants, very sensitive to frost. The leaves are often broad, the flowers brightly coloured. Species are rarely available, but there are many hybrids on the market.
Position Canna is a garden plant in origin, but dwarf forms of *Canna indica* are also very suitable for the living-room, where they must have plenty of light. They need not be screened from the sun. They enjoy fresh air and can be stood outside in summer. Plant them out in a sunny, sheltered spot in a hole filled with nutritious soil, where they will develop better than in a narrow pot. In autumn move them indoors in good time.
Care Keep the plant warm in the growing season. In autumn reduce the water supply. The foliage will then wither and the rhizomes should be kept at a temperature of 15°C (59°F) in moderately damp peat fibre, since otherwise they would dry out too much. Repot them in early spring.

Canna indica hybrid 'Lucifer'

Watering Water moderately. In warm weather a great deal of moisture will evaporate through the large leaves and the plant will then have to be watered generously. Dry living-room air is tolerated reasonable well.
Feeding In the growing period give a weekly dose of fertiliser solution.
Propagation You can increase from seed, but they will not grow true to type. Soak the seeds for 24 hours, or scratch the surface. They can also be increased by division of rhizomes bearing more than one shoot after they have started into growth in spring.
Pests and diseases Aphids, slugs, red spider mites and virus disease may cause problems.

***Canna indica* hybrids**

Dwarf forms for indoor cultivation grow up to 60 cm (2 ft). They have tuber-shaped rhizomes, fairly large, sessile leaves, with parallel side veins and large flowers on irregular, dense spikes. The stamens are like undeveloped petals. 'Lucifer' has yellow-edged red flowers; 'Alberich' is salmon pink; 'Perkeo', red; 'Puck', yellow.

Capsicum annuum, the Red Pepper

Capsicum

Solanaceae

Red Pepper

Name Probably from the Latin *capsa*, which means box. This is thought to refer to the fruit, the capsule.
Origin The 50 species originate in Central and South America.
Description Deciduous or evergreen shrubs and semi-shrubs with a limited lifespan. They are not hardy. The flowers are small and insignificant, and the plants are cultivated chiefly for their shiny, colourful, egg- or cone-shaped fruits – the largest are eaten as paprikas. The smaller fruits are chillis. Most Red Peppers are sold around Christmas time.
Position If you buy the plants in autumn, they must be given the maximum amount of sun and light to colour the fruits. Plants sown from seed must be screened from the brightest sun. Indoors they should be given a cool, well-ventilated position in a temperature of 15°C (59°F). In summer they can be put in a sheltered and sunny spot outside.
Care If they are kept too dry or warm, the fruits will shrivel up. They will keep in good condition if given a cool situation and kept moderately moist. When the last fruits have withered, the plants may be discarded. When buying a plant, check for pests on the underside of the leaves.
Watering Keep the compost moderately damp. In the flowering season spray regularly to promote pollination. Dry living-room air is tolerated fairly well.
Feeding Normally give a dose at standard concentration only once every three weeks. As soon as the fruits appear, feed every ten days at half the concentration, until the fruits colour.
Propagation Sow in March at 15 to 18°C (59 to 64°F). Prick out after three or four weeks and keep at 15°C (59°F).
Pests and diseases Aphids, leaf and frog hoppers, red spider mites, thrips and whitefly are likely pests. Grey mould will occur if the plants are kept too wet.

Capsicum annuum

Not to be confused with the solanum. In this country the Red Pepper is always grown as an annual. The leaves are up to 10 cm (4 in) long and 4 cm ($1\frac{1}{2}$ in) wide, oval to lanceolate, and smooth edged. The yellow flowers grow singly or in pairs. Depending on the strain, the fruits vary in shape (egg to cone shaped) and colour (usually yellow to red, sometimes cream or aubergine).

Carex

Cyperaceae

Sedge

Name This is an ancient Roman name, of which the exact meaning is not known.
Origin The 1100 *Carex* species form the largest genus in the family, occurring in all parts of the world. *Carex brunnea*, the only species suitable for indoor cultivation, is a native of southern Asia and Australia.
Description An easily grown, grass-like perennial. Both the green species and the variegated form usually obtainable are particularly graceful and make a valuable acquisition.
Position Put them in good light; the sun will do no harm. These plants are very suitable for combining with others in a container.
Care Keep them at 8 to 16°C (46 to 60°F) in winter, moderately warm for the rest of the year. They do not like too warm a room.
Watering The compost should be kept constantly moist, but must never be soaked as in the case of the cyperus. Excess water in the saucer must be poured away. Maintain a moderate degree of humidity by occasional spraying.
Feeding Feed sparingly: a solution at normal strength once every three weeks in enough.
Propagation Plants grown from seed will revert to green and the more usual method is division of the root ball. Do not shake the soil from the roots.

Carex brunnea

Also on the market under the name *Carex elegantissima*. A clump-forming plant, to 30 cm (1 ft) tall, with long, thin, erect-growing leaves. The flower stalks are a little longer and bear a few brownish-beige flower spikes at the tip. In 'Variegata' the leaves have two lengthwise stripes.

Carex brunnea 'Variegata' planted in marble chips

Catharanthus roseus, often known by its former name *Vinca rosea*. This is the form 'Ocellatus'

Cattleya labiata, one of the finest orchids

Catharanthus

Apocynaceae

Name From the Greek *katharos*, meaning pure, faultless, and *anthos*, flower.
Origin The genus consists of five species, known more or less all over the tropics. The only species suitable for indoor cultivation, *Catharanthus roseus*, is a native of Malagasy.
Description Annual or perennial herbaceous plants. *Catharanthus roseus* is a perennial in its natural habitat, but is cultivated here as an annual. The flowers betray its relationship to the genus *Vinca*, the Periwinkle. However, they are easily distinguished, because the foliage of the vinca is quite different and smaller. In addition vincas develop tendrils which attach themselves to the soil and form a veritable carpet, while the catharanthus is erect in habit. Finally a small detail: in a catharanthus the throat of the corolla is practically filled with brush-like hairs.
Position Keep it in a light, sunny position in not too warm a room. In spring and summer it must be temporarily screened against bright sunrays.

In the garden it may be kept in full sun in a sheltered position during the summer.
Care If you want to keep the plant through the winter in order to take cuttings in spring, you must provide a temperature of 12 to 18°C (53 to 64°F). However, this plant is usually grown as an annual, because this produces better results.
Watering Water regularly to keep the compost constantly, but moderately, moist. In winter water somewhat more sparingly. The catharanthus enjoys a humid atmosphere, but will also tolerate normal living-room conditions. It is advisable to spray the foliage regularly with tepid water and it is best if the plants can be watered with tepid water as well.
Feeding Feed once a fortnight with a solution at the recommended strength.
Propagation You have a choice between sowing seed and taking cuttings. The advantage of growing from cuttings is that the plants will be capable of flowering at an earlier stage. Seeds are sown in February in a heated tray. When they are pricked out, pot them in groups.

Take cuttings in August if you want to keep rooted cuttings through the winter. If you have more space, keep the parent plants through the winter and take cuttings in spring. Pinch out the tips after the sixth leaf has appeared to obtain a bushy growth.

Catharanthus roseus

Catharanthus roseus

Syn. *Vinca rosea*. Pink Periwinkle. Erect-growing, bushy and fleshy plant with up to 9-cm ($3\frac{1}{2}$-in) long and 3-cm (1-in) wide leaves, green with a white vein. The flowers are short stalked, growing singly, 3 cm (1 in) in diameter, flat, pink with a much darker eye. In 'Albus' the flowers are white and 'Ocellatus' has a white corolla with a red centre. They flower from early in summer to late autumn.

Cattleya

Orchidaceae

Name Named after the English orchid collector William Cattley.
Origin The 60 species of this genus originate in South America.
Description Epiphytes, usually with long, cylindrical pseudobulbs, which may be thick or thin. Two long oval or short sword-shaped leaves appear from the top and remain on the plant for more than one season. The flower stalk grows from the sheath at the base of the leaf. The number of flowers varies between two and fifteen; in small-flowered species even more. Many of the species and strains are very suitable as cut flowers. In addition to the frequently bright colouring, cattleya flowers are characterised by their broad, tongue-shaped lip, frequently frilled at the edge.
Position They require a well-lit position, where they can be screened from bright sunlight between April and September. The best place is in a moderate or temperate greenhouse.
Care During the growing period the minmum temperature at night should be 15°C (59°F). In winter 12°C (53°F) should be taken as the minimum. The dormant season usually occurs after flowering, and at that time the temperature should be lowered by 2 to 3°C (3 to 5°F). The lower the temperature, the higher the level of humidity required.
Watering During the growing period cattleyas require a fair amount of water, depending on the temperature. This should be demineralised. Regular plunging is very helpful. Afterwards wait until the compost is on the dry side before watering again. In the dormant season give less water, but do not allow the pseudobulbs to shrivel up, and always provide good drainage. A high level of humidity can be maintained by means of indirect mist-spraying.
Feeding Plants should be fed once a month at one third concentration.
Repotting Repot after flowering, in 2 parts osmunda fibre to 1 part sphagnum moss, with a thick layer of crocks in the bottom of the pot. The greater part of the rootstock must be visible.
Propagation Increase by division of the rootstock. Each section must have at least two pseudobulbs and a growing point.
Pests and diseases Aphids and scale insects, mites, woodlice and slugs are pests to be reckoned with.

Cattleya bowringiana

Pale, pinkish-purple flowers with a darker lip, white at the base and with a brown band across. The flowers in autumn are up to 8 cm (3 in) across.

Cattleya dowiana

This hothouse species flowers in summer. The petals are yellow, streaked with purple on the reverse, and the lip is purple and yellow. The variety *aurea* flowers later. It has pure yellow petals with more yellow veining on the lip.

Cattleya gaskelliana

Flowering in summer, it has lilac-pink petals and a pink lip with a dark purple patch near the tip.

Cattleya labiata

Appearing in the autumn, the flowers are up to 15 cm (6 in) long, pink-purple, with a trumpet-shaped lip in pink, yellow and purple. 'Candida' is white.

Cattleya mendelii

Flowers after the resting period, in May–June. It has white to pink petals and fringed lip in purple, yellow and crimson.

Cattleya mossiae

Fragrant violet-pink flowers appear in May-June. They have a large, wavy lip, and are purple and yellow with a very pale margin.

Cattleya skinneri

Violet-purple flowers in spring. The lip is dark violet with a white throat.

Cattleya trianae

Flowers in winter, with soft pink to purple petals. It has a slightly frilly purple lip and orange-yellow throat.

Cattleya warscewiczii

Summer flowering; it bears fragrant, lilac-pink flowers with a large, crimson to purple lip, frilly at the edge, and two yellow spots in the throat.

Celosia
Amaranthaceae
Coxcomb

Name From the Greek *kelon*, which means a dry piece of wood, or from *kelis*, bloodstain. The first would refer to the dry membrane covering the flowers; the second to the red stain occurring on the leaves of some species.
Origin The 60 species originate in tropical regions of Africa, America and Asia.
Description Long-flowering annual plants used as bedding plants as well as for indoor cultivation. The inflorescence is plume or beard shaped, usually very striking, and the colours vary mainly between yellow and violet-red. If you cut the flowers and let them dry quickly

Celosia argentea cristata

– but out of the sun – the colour will be preserved for several years, so they make excellent dried flowers.
Position A sunny to slightly shady spot is preferred.
Care A combination of an air temperature as low as 16°C (60°F) and a high bottom temperature of 20°C (68°F) will produce magnificent colouring.
Watering Water moderately. The compost must not be moist for long periods, or this would cause the plants to rot just above the soil level. Regular spraying of the foliage will promote growth and induce a larger inflorescence.
Feeding Give a fortnightly dose of fertiliser at recommended strength.
Repotting Too rich a compost – that is, a mixture rich in nitrogen – will lead to less attractive colouring.
Propagation Sow seed in February – April at 20 to 25°C (68 to 77°F). The minimum at night should be 18°C (64°F), and if possible provide extra bottom heat.
Pests and diseases They may be affected by rotting and root rot, and attacked by aphids.

Celosia argentea
◐ ⊜ ⓦ ⊛ ◙
The variety *cristata* is a compact plant with pale green foliage and a broad inflorescence composed of large, wrinkled coxcombs. 'Jewelbox' and 'Nana' are well-known strains; they grow to only 30cm (1ft). *Celosia argentea plumosa* has pyramid-shaped flower spikes. There are many strains, such as 'Thompson's Magnifica', reaching up to 60cm (2ft). 'Golden Plume' and 'Red Plume' are dwarf strains, up to 30cm (1ft) in height.

Cephalocereus senilis, Old Man Cactus

Cephalocereus
Cactaceae

Name A combination of the Greek word *kephale*, meaning head, and the generic name *Cereus*.
Origin Mexico is the country of origin, where these imposing cacti can grow to 15m (50ft) tall.
Description Multi-ribbed columnar cacti, rarely branching. They do not flower until they are 5 to 6m (16 to 20ft) tall, and the flowers, usually white, then appear at night. They are very decorative cacti which produce their shocks of white hairs at an early age.
Position They need plenty of light; a sunny spot on the window-sill is best of all, but they do not tolerate draughts.
Care Keep them warm in summer and in winter give them a rest at a minimum temperature of 15°C (59°F).
Watering They enjoy humid warmth, which means that you should mist-spray at regular intervals. Water moderately in summer and keep dry in winter.
Feeding In the growing season give a measure of fertiliser once a fortnight, following the instructions on the label.
Repotting Use a porous mixture containing plenty of pulverised clay, and pots that are only slightly larger than the old one. Leave the soil ball intact and support the cactus with sticks for some time.
Propagation Increase by shallow sowing of seed in a finely sieved sandy medium.
Pests and diseases Insufficient humidity in summer encourages red spider mite and mealy bug, but too high a humidity in winter leads to mould and root rot.

Cephalocereus chrysacanthus
○ ⊜ ⓦ ⊛ ▢
Syn. *Pilocereus chrysacanthus*. Grows up to 4.5m (15ft) tall. It has a green body with a yellow woolly top and nine to fourteen ribs covered in amber-coloured thorns. There are thread-like white radial spines and reddish flowers.
Cephalocereus senilis
Syn. *Cephalophorus senilis*. Old Man Cactus. This is the best-known species. Columnar, rarely branching, but sometimes branching at the base, it is covered in 12-cm (4½-in) long, grey to white, slightly twisted hairs. In its native habitat it has pink flowers.

Cereus
Cactaceae
Torch Thistle

Name The Latin word *cereus* means wax taper or wax torch.
Origin The 25 to 30 species known originate in South America, especially in northern Argentina, Uruguay, Paraguay and eastern and southern Brazil. At one time the genus *Cereus* was the largest in the cactus family and, in addition to the columnar cacti, included shrubby, creeping and hanging types. Scientists have drastically changed the classification and the genus now only includes columnar cacti.
Description These very vigorous cacti are easy to grow in the living-room. In many cases the body is covered in a whitish, sea-green or bluish waxy layer, which helps to minimise evaporation. The flowers open at night. The tube of the corolla is practically unscaled and the fruits are smooth. Because these cacti are such vigorous growers they are often used as stock.
Position To ensure vigorous growth they should be given a light and sunny position. In summer they can be put on the terrace or in a sheltered position in the garden, together with your tub plants. They are also very suitable for combination with other cacti in a mixed container.
Care This is one of the few house plants which does not immediately react to neglect by a deteriorating appearance. In summer it must be kept warm, in winter cool, like your other cacti and tub

A young specimen of *Cereus peruvianus*. Older plants grow much taller

Cereus peruvianus 'Monstrosus'

plants. Minimum temperature in winter should be 3°C (37°F).
Watering During the growing period in summer water moderately. Occasionally spray the plant to remove the dust and open the pores. Water very sparingly in winter to discourage the column from growing lanky. A low level of humidity is sufficient throughout the year.
Feeding Cereus rarely needs feeding, least of all in the year in which it has been repotted. In other years it may be given an occasional dose of fertiliser.
Repotting Repot in a normal or calcareous porous compost. The plant certainly does not need to be repotted every year. Although most of the species are not very particular about the growing medium, it is advisable to cultivate beautifully spined species in a slightly heavier mixture containing clay, because this will promote development of the thorns.
Propagation It is very easily grown from seed as well as from cuttings, which must first be left to dry out a little.
Pests and diseases Mealy bug and scale insects may occur.

Cereus azureus
○ ⊜ ◌ ⊛ ◙ ▢
Azureus means sky blue. This refers to the waxy layer which covers the cactus body. It is a slender plant, not readily branching, up to 3m (10ft) in height and with a blue-green bloom. New shoots have a pale blue bloom. The columns have six or seven ribs more or less pronounced, and felty brown areoles. The thin black thorns grow in groups of 10 to 18. The 20- to 30-cm (8- to 12-in) white flowers open during the day; they are brown on the outside.
Cereus chalybaeus
The specific name means steel blue and connoisseurs believe this to be the bluest of all cacti. It grows to 3m (10ft) in height and the columns have a diameter of up to 10cm (4in). Usually there are six sharp ribs with ridges radiating from the areoles. Seven to nine radial thorns and three to four stronger centre thorns are black. The flowers, up to 20cm (8in) long, are pink to red on the outside, white inside, and the fruit is yellow.
Cereus huntingtonianus
This species usually branches at the base and has cylindrical, jointed stems. Growing to 2.5m (8ft), the branches may be up to 25cm (10in) thick. Young plants are blue bloomed and practically thornless. Later they develop three radial thorns and a strong central thorn. Red flowers with a yellow throat appear in the daytime.

Cereus jamacaru
This is a fast-growing cactus with four to six ribs. Originally the columns are blue bloomed; they are covered in strong yellow to brown thorns. Its white flowers appear at night. Because of its rapid growth it is often used as stock. 'Monstrosus' looks malformed as a result of a disturbed growth point.
Cereus peruvianus
This is the best-known species. It has five- to eight-ribbed blue bloomed columns. Sharp brown thorns grow in groups of seven or eight; the centre thorn grows to 2cm (¾in). Mature plants may produce large flowers, 12cm (4½in) across, red on the outside and white inside. 'Monstrosus', the Rock Cactus, develops strange freak forms as a result of a disturbance in the growth point. It has short, brown thorns.
Cereus validus
Initially bluish columns, usually five ribbed and so densely covered in areoles that the black-brown thorns become entangled. There is one centre thorn of 4cm (1½in) and five radial thorns up to 2cm (¾in) long.

Ceropegia
Asclepiadaceae
Hearts Entangled

Name A combination of the Greek words *keros* and *pege*, respectively meaning wax and source.
Origin The 160 species are found in south-east Asia, India, Malagasy, tropical Arabia, the Canary Islands and various parts of Africa. The family also has a representative in New Guinea and in Australia.
Description Two main groups may be distinguished within the genus: species with fleshy, erect-growing stems, often leafless; and the species that are best known – those with trailing, threadlike stems with pairs of opposite leaves at the joints. Many of the species in this genus are succulent plants. Most species have a tuber-shaped rhizome. In trailing plants those rhizomes may be as much as 5cm (2in) across. They also form tubers in the axils of the leaves, but these remain much smaller. The photograph gives a good idea of the very unusual shape of the flowers. They consist of a long, fairly narrow tube, ending in five petals fused at the tip, or, in some cases, recurved. When the petals are narrow, the flower resembles a small lantern; when they are broad, the flower is shaped like a parasol. The base of the tube is often broadened. The flowers grow in the axils, usually singly.
Position These are easy house plants; they thrive both in the sun and in a half-shady spot. They may be kept in the living-room throughout the year, but it would be even better to winter them in an unheated or cool greenhouse.
Care Ceropegia prefers to spend the winter in a sunny spot at a temperature of 10°C (50°F). Spindly stems may be cut back in spring. Cuttings can be rooted.
Watering Water sparingly throughout the year – once or twice a week, even less if kept cool in winter. It tolerates dry air.
Feeding Feed sparingly once a fortnight in the growing season.

Ceropegia woodii flower detail

Tuber-shaped roots of *Ceropegia barkleyi*

Ripe seeds of *Ceropegia woodii* ssp. *woodii*

Repotting Use a light mixture, rich in humus, with a little added chalk, or a standard potting compost mixed with an equal amount of sharp sand.
Propagation Increase from seed, by division or layering, or from cuttings. Take sections of stem with an axil tuber and let the cut surface dry before planting the cutting.

Ceropegia africana
○ ◐ ⊜ ⊖ ◌ ⊛ ▢
Closely related to *Ceropegia barkleyi*. It has winding stems with smooth, fleshy little leaves, which are oval, elliptical or spear shaped. The flowers are green and dark purple. The tube is 2.5cm (1in) long, with 12-mm (½-in) long petals fused at the tips.
Ceropegia barkleyi
This has thin, climbing or trailing stems without axil tubers. Leaves are pale green, 2 to 5cm (¾ to 2in) long, with white veining; they are fleshy, oval to spear shaped with a sharp point, either sessile or short stalked. Half of the round, tuberous rhizome grows above the soil. The green and purple flowers, up to 5cm (2in) long, appear in groups.
Ceropegia radicans
○ ◐ ⊜ ⊖ ◌ ⊛ ▢
Fairly thick, succulent and creeping stems carry almost circular but pointed leaves, 1 to 4cm (½ to 1½in) long. The flowers, growing singly in the axils of the leaves are up to 10cm (4in) long with a long, narrow tube, broadening slightly at the base. The five erect lobes are narrow, striped in green, white and purplish red.

Ceropegia sandersonii
Winding stems with oval to heart-shaped leaves and a yellow-green flower tube, broadening to a funnel shape at the top. The flower looks like a parachute.
Ceropegia stapeliiformis
Thick, erect-growing, winding stems, thinning towards the tip and bearing rudimentary leaves. Funnel-shaped flowers, up to 6cm (2¼in) long, appear in groups of two to four. They are white with dark brown spots.
Ceropegia woodii
Ceropegia woodii debilis has practically sessile, linear leaves on very thin stems. The flowers are greenish, with purple marking. *C. w. woodii* has 1- to 2-cm (½- to ¾-in) short-stalked, marbled, kidney-shaped leaves on thin stems. The corolla is flesh coloured with brown-black lobes, hairy inside.

Chamaecereus
Cactaceae

Name From the Greek *chamai*, which means dwarf, low; *Cereus* was the genus

Chamaecereus silvestrii, the Peanut Cactus

among which it was at one time classified.
Origin It inhabits the Argentine highlands, growing on shrub-covered slopes at a certain altitude, where the light conditions are most favourable.
Description The genus has only one representative. It is quite a popular cactus which, provided it is properly cared for, may produce masses of flowers. It grows fairly rapidly and branches readily.
Position The main condition for satisfactory growth and flowering is a well-lit, not too sunny, position. In poor light the shoots grow lanky, thin and pale green and too much sun will turn them brown.
Care It is essential that a chamaecereus is kept cold in winter – at night it is best if the temperature is a few degrees below zero. The plant will then shrivel, but it will flower all the more profusely.
Watering In summer water regularly but sparingly; in winter keep perfectly dry.
Feeding From April to August give a little nitrogen-free fertiliser once a fortnight.
Repotting Use a light, nutritious compost. Commercial cactus mixtures are satisfactory.
Propagation Break off a shoot, allow the wound to dry and insert the cutting in a sandy mixture. You will find it will root fairly rapidly. These cacti may also be grown from seed without much difficulty. Cover the seeds with a very thin layer of fine sand.
Pests and diseases Lack of light and air in summer may lead to attacks by red spider mites. In winter too high a temperature and humidity are fatal.

Chamaecereus silvestrii
◐ ⊜ ⊙ ⊛ ▢
Syn. *Cereus silvestrii.* A clump-forming, recumbent or hanging cactus, with finger-shaped stems, to 1.5cm (½in) thick, usually eight ribbed, and densely covered in white spines. It has funnel-shaped bright red flowers.

Flowers of *Chamaedorea elegans*

Chamaedorea
Palmae
Parlour Palm

Name From the Greek words *chamai*, dwarf, low, and *dory*, spear.
Origin The 120 species originate in Central and South America. The best-known species, *Chamaedorea elegans*, is a native of Mexico.
Description A graceful small palm, without spines. It has a tubular stem and pinnate foliage, occasionally undivided and split only at the tip. The dioecious flowers, and later the berry-like fruits, grow on single or erratically branched stems, appearing under or among the foliage.
Position Stand it in plenty of light, but never in direct sun.
Care From October to February the plant requires a resting period at a temperature which must not exceed 12 to 14°C (53 to 57°F), especially at night.
Watering In summer the plant should be plunged once a week and in addition generously watered. In winter the compost should only just be kept moist. Dry air in a warm room is harmful. The plant appreciates an occasional rain shower or a spray with demineralised water.
Feeding From March to August feed weekly, using a third of the concentration recommended on the label.
Repotting It will need repotting when the roots grow through the hole in the bottom of the pot. Use a tall, narrow pot and preferably a mixture of clay, leaf-mould, rotted cow manure and sharp sand.
Propagation After division plants do not root easily. The best method of propagation is to sow seed in a temperature of 24 to 26°C (75 to 78°F). Germination is often slow, because the seeds are hard and thick coated.
Pests and diseases Scale insects and red spider mites can be a nuisance.

Chamaedorea elegans
◐ ⊜ ⊙ ⊛ ▢
Syn. *Neanthe bella.* Up to 1m (3ft) tall, it has bright green, pinnate, curving foliage, with 12 to 15 leaves on either side. The upper pair is usually fused at the base. The inflorescence consists of tiny yellow balls. 'Bella' is smaller in all its parts.
Chamaedorea metallica
This has a short stem with single, densely veined leaves, incised at the tip, and orange flowers.

Chamaerops
Palmae
Fan Palm

Name From the Greek words *chamai*, low and *rhops*, shrub.
Origin It is the only palm growing wild in Europe.
Description Chamaerops is one of the fan-shaped palms and this characteristic foliage always makes a graceful house plant. It shows to good advantage against a plain background in an unfussy modern interior. The best-known species is *Chamaerops humilis*, which may grow up to 7m (23ft) tall.

An immense specimen of *Chamaerops humilis*, growing in southern Germany

Used as tub plant, it will, however, rarely exceed 1m (3ft), while spreading widely.

Position This palm may be placed outside from May to September, in a not-too-sunny spot, but in good light. In winter it accepts a fairly dark position, but may also be kept in a light spot. Make sure there is plenty of ventilation and do not let the temperature drop below zero, though provided the compost is thoroughly dry, it will even tolerate a few degrees of frost. A cool hall is a very suitable environment, and if the light is good enough the plant may be left there in summer as well.

Care It can be seen from this that the chamaerops must be kept cool in winter, at a temperature between 0 and 10°C (32 and 50°F). The palm requires fresh air throughout the year. Dirty foliage cannot carry out its function and the plant should therefore be rinsed regularly with soft water.

Watering In summer the palm must be watered generously. In winter the compost should be kept fairly moist, the degree of moisture depending on the temperature. When the mercury drops to around zero, it must be kept perfectly dry. A 50 to 60 per cent level of humidity is enough. The plant much appreciates regular spraying.

Feeding During the growing season it should be given a weekly dose of fertiliser at the concentration recommended on the label.

Repotting The compost should preferably be prepared well in advance and consist of nutritious loam, leafmould and sharp sand. To bring the plants into growth, extra bottom heat should be provided. This palm, too, can be grown in a tall, narrow pot, but give it a good drainage layer, for the brown leaf tips which often occur are usually the result of bad drainage. When cutting off the brown tips always leave a narrow edge of brown tissue, otherwise the trouble will recur after a few days.

Young plants need repotting every second or third year, but older plants can wait a little longer. If necessary some of the root system may be removed to fit the palm into the pot. At this period the plant is a little more sensitive and it is therefore advisable to keep it in a humid, enclosed space for a time. April is the best time for repotting; by then the central heating may have been turned down a little, and the air is somewhat more humid.

Propagation Increase from seed, sown in February or March in a light compost. The seedlings must be kept out of the sun for the time being. Good-sized plants may be obtained within two years. When after three or four years the plant has outgrown the pot, possible sideshoots can be removed and potted up separately.

Pests and diseases May be affected by red spider mites, mealy bug and other scale insects and occasionally thrips. Yellow, slightly greasy, patches on the leaves indicate leaf spot. Affected leaves are best removed immediately. Cut them off at the base with a sharp knife or scissors. Small yellow spots are the result of inadequate light or too high a level of atmospheric or soil humidity.

Chamaerops humilis
◐ ⊜ ⓜ ⊛ ⊖
In its natural habitat the plant's trunk is surrounded by brown fibres. Fan-shaped leaves on spiny stalks appear at the top of the trunk and yellow flower racemes among the leaves. In cultivation the trunk is nearly always missing.

A young plant of *Chlorophytum comosum* 'Variegatum'

Chlorophytum
Liliaceae
Spider Plant

Name From the Greek words *chloros*, green, and *phyton*, a plant.

Origin The 200 species occur in the tropics. The popular house plant species is a native of South Africa, where only the green species occurs.

Description Low-growing, herbaceous plants, often producing runners. The roots are fleshy or thickened like tubers and the oblong leaves grow directly from the roots. The flowers appear in more or less dense racemes, on tall or short, single or branched stalks.

Position This a very strong house plant, tolerating both sun and shade. It will thrive even in offices, where plants often suffer a measure of neglect. The variegated species require a little more light than the all-green plants.

Care The chlorophytum is satisfied with the most diverse conditions, but in winter it should not be kept in less than 7°C (44°F). A resting period is not essential.

Watering In the growing period water normally to plentifully, depending on the temperature, but give a little less water if it spends a resting period in a cool place. It will accept dry living-room air, but occasional spraying is beneficial.

Feeding Every week, from March to September, give a fertiliser solution at normal concentration.

Repotting The fairly thick roots retain a great deal of moisture and occasionally burst out of the pot. It should then (if not sooner) be repotted in a wide, fairly shallow pot, in a loamy mixture.

Propagation Increase from seed, by division or by removing the offset plants, which will root rapidly.

Pests and diseases The chief problem is brown leaf tips, which may be the result of too dry a compost, draughts or over-generous feeding.

Mature chlorophytums develop many runners

Chlorophytum capense
○ ◐ ⊜ ⊜ ⓜ ⓘ ⊛ ⊖
Syn. *Chlorophytum elatum*. Linear green leaves, up to 4cm ($1\frac{1}{2}$in) wide, often gutter shaped and curving. The flower stalk is occasionally branched, with a small rosette at infrequent intervals and star-like small flowers. In 'Mediopictum' the central band is cream-coloured; in 'Variegatum' the margin.

Chlorophytum comosum
Syn. *Chlorophytum sternbergianum*. Linear green leaves, up to 2cm ($\frac{3}{4}$in) wide. The flower stalk is initially short and erect. Later it lengthens and curves, and is usually covered in young rosettes. 'Variegatum' has a white band.

Chrysanthemum
Compositae

Name From the Greek *chrusos*, meaning gold, and *anthemon*, which means flower; a 'golden flower'.

Origin This large genus comprises more than 200 species. The potted chrysanthemum differs in many respects from the species; it belongs to the *Chrysanthemum indicum* hybrids originating in China.

Description The chrysanthemum, which at one time was the symbol of long life, is now cultivated as an all-year-round, disposable plant. They are marketed throughout the year, because the grower exploits the fact that they are short-day plants: they flower when the day grows shorter, which in natural circumstances is in autumn. With the aid of artificially controlled lighting plants can be brought into flower at any desired moment. In addition, certain substances are used to retard growth, in order to obtain more compact and profusely flowering plants. These manufactured plants are available in white, yellow, pink, orange, red and purple.

Position Keep them in good light, but out of direct sunlight. In a cool place they will flower longer than in a warm environment.

Care Regularly remove dead flowers. When flowering has ceased the plants are best thrown away. If they are planted in the garden they will grow to normal height but quite possibly freeze to death in winter. If you keep them indoors, cut them back to 5cm (2in) and maintain a temperature of 4 to 6°C (39 to 43°F). In spring they may be brought into growth again, but the results will rarely justify the trouble.

Watering Water moderately, but take care not to let the compost dry out. Potted chrysanthemums accept dry air fairly well.

Repotting This is seldom necessary; otherwise pot in standard compost.

Propagation Growers propagate these plants from cuttings.

Pests and diseases They can suffer attack by eelworm, aphids, grey mould, mildew, red spider mites, thrips, wilting, capsid bug, whitefly and root rot.

***Chrysanthemum indicum* hybrids**
◐ ⊜ ⓘ ⊛ ▣
Different hybrids are available in a large variety of flower shapes and colours.

Chrysanthemum indicum hybrid

Chysis

Orchidaceae

Name Derived from the Greek *chysis*, melting.
Origin These orchids originated in Central America, especially in Mexico, but they also occur in Guatemala, Colombia and Venezuela.
Description Epiphytic orchids with long pseudobulbs, each bearing two leaves. They frequently have pendulous racemes of fairly compactly shaped flowers.
Position They belong in a moderately heated greenhouse, which means that in summer a living-room temperature of about 20°C (68°F) is acceptable. Since their demands for atmospheric humidity are not exorbitant either, they can be grown indoors in summer without problems.

Chysis aurea

Care In winter the night temperature should be from 13 to 16°C (55 to 60°F) and the day temperature from 16 to 18°C (60 to 64°F), or slightly lower when it is freezing outside. From April to September screen against bright sunlight. Never spray directly on to the foliage, for this will cause ugly stains of lime deposit.
Watering Water freely in the growing season, especially when the temperature is high. The dormant season generally starts in August when the plants should then be kept drier and cooler with an atmospheric humidity of between 50 and 60 per cent.
Feeding If you want to feed them use only a very weak solution, preferably of organic fertiliser or special orchid food.
Repotting Use a compost consisting of 2 parts coarsely chopped fern roots and 1 part sphagnum moss, and include a good drainage layer. They may also be grown in lattice baskets or on pieces of tree fern. The plants are repotted after new roots have been developed, in March; *Chysis bractescens* as early as January–March.
Propagation Increase from seed.

Chysis aurea
This has pendulous flower racemes bearing three to seven flowers, each up to 4cm (1½in) across; the colour is golden yellow, with red-brown streaks. Flowers appear in May–June.
Chysis bractescens
The flower stalks bear three to eight creamy white flowers, up to 8cm (3in) in diameter. They have a white lip, and are yellow with red streaks inside. Flowers come in March–May.

Cissus

Vitaceae

Cissus rhombifolia 'Ellen Danica'. More familiar perhaps is the synonym, *Rhoicissus rhomboidea*

Name The Greek word *kissos* means ivy. The plant's habit explains its name.
Origin Nearly all the 350 species originate in the tropics. They are found all over the world. A few species also occur in sub-tropical regions.
Description The plants belonging to this genus vary considerably in appearance. About ten succulents as well as woody, green or multicoloured climbers belong to the genus *Cissus*. Some of these typical succulents are climbers; others develop a thick, succulent trunk which may grow to 4m (13ft) in height. Collectors like these succulents chiefly because of their strange shapes. The vine-like trailing plants are grown for their magnificent foliage and some species, such as *Cissus rhombifolia* (syn. *Rhoicissus rhomboidea*), because they are indestructible. All species have four petals, and the leaves are trifoliate, quinquefoliate or single. Unlike the grape vine, the fruits are usually inedible.
Position Succulents like to stand in the sun in summer. The climbers have varying requirements: *Cissus antarctica* likes a light spot, out of the sun; *Cissus striata* also likes light shade and *Cissus rhombifolia* may be put in a slightly shady position, but will grow amazingly well even in deep shade. Species such as *Cissus discolor*, *C. gongylodes* and *C. njegerre* are hothouse plants which require plenty of light, but must be protected from bright sunrays. These last species grow to enormous size and you must have plenty of space to show them to good advantage. *Cissus striata* remains small and is an excellent plant for small houses.
Care It is advisable to keep your cissus plants cool in winter. At that time the minimum temperature for succulent species is 5°C (41°F), for house plants 8°C (46°F) and for hothouse plants 15°C (59°F). *Cissus antarctica* should be cleaned once a month to remove dust and chalk deposits.
Watering A simple rule-of-thumb guide is to water moderately in summer, and in winter to let the water supply depend on the temperature. If the succulent species are kept cool in winter, then they may be kept practically dry. *Cissus discolor* requires a fair amount of water in summer and an atmospheric humidity level of 50 to 60 per cent is ideal. If *Cissus antarctica* is kept in a heated room in winter, it must be sprayed regularly to ward off leaf curl and red spider mite.
Feeding From the time the new shoots appear until mid-August, feed weekly with a fertiliser solution at normal strength.
Repotting Like the vine, all other members of this family appreciate porous, calcareous soil. Standard potting compost is on the acid side. An ideal mixture is a compost based on a mixture of leafmould, rotted turves or clay, with some sand and rotted cow manure.
Propagation Succulents can be grown from seed. They can also be grown from cuttings, but this would spoil their characteristic shape. Other species are grown from cuttings, which will readily root if they have sufficient bottom heat, say 25 to 30°C (77 to 86°F). Insert the cuttings in groups of three to five to obtain bushy plants. As a rule ripened tip cuttings are used, possibly taken in August, with the leaf surface reduced by half to prevent evaporation. The cuttings should be rooted in peat fibre mixed with an equal part of sand (or less).
Pests and diseases Brown spots, mildew and other moulds are caused by excess water, especially in winter. Red spider mite and other mites and thrips sometimes cause damage.

Cissus antarctica
This is a climber with hairy, woody stems and shiny dark green leaves up

Cissus antarctica

Cissus striata

Cissus discolor, a hothouse plant

The common *Cissus rhombifolia*

to 10 cm (4 in) long, sharply pinnate, oval and somewhat leathery.

Cissus discolor

◐ ⊜ ⦶ ⊛ ▢

Characteristics are red tendrils and twigs with heart-shaped, pointed leaves up to 15 cm (6 in) long, velvety violet to red, with silver grey and olive green. The leaves are purplish red underneath.

Cissus gongylodes

Syn. *Vitis gongylodes*. A very rapid grower with angular stems and long, red aerial roots. It has trifoliate, wrinkled leaves up to 30 cm (1 ft) long.

Cissus njegerre

A tall-growing climber with green leaves in threes, densely covered in violet to red hairs. The leaf stalks are up to 10 cm (4 in) in length. The leaves are elliptical to diamond shaped.

Cissus quadrangularis

○ ⊜ ⦶ ⊛ ▢

A climber, with succulent, square, winged stems, pinched in at the joints. It has small, thick, three-lobed leaves which drop soon after their appearance.

Cissus rhombifolia

◐ ● ⊜ ⦶ ⊛ ▢

Syn. *Rhoicissus rhomboidea*. A very strong plant with dark green leaves growing in threes on long leaf stalks. The underside of the leaves and young shoots are covered in reddish hairs. The centre leaf is bigger than the two others, which are asymmetrical in shape. In the course of time the plant may produce small, inconspicuous flowers, developing into small berries.

Cissus striata

Delicate trailing plant with thinly haired twigs and leaves in groups of five.

Citrus

Rutaceae

Orange Tree

Name *Citrus* is Latin for a citron tree.

Origin Most of the species originate in eastern Asia. The grapefuit is a native of the West Indies. In the early years of the Renaissance the first specimens appeared on the estates of West European noblemen. In summer they decorated the magnificent garden and in winter they were kept in orangeries.

Description The genus includes 12 species of evergreen, prickly trees and shrubs. They have shiny green, oval to elliptical leaves and racemes of delightfully fragrant, usually white, flowers with five long, outward-curving petals and protruding stamens. In sub-tropical countries many species are grown for their edible fruit – tangerine, orange, lemon and grapefruit. The seeds of these fruits are easily cultivated to form attractive little shrubs, though they will rarely flower or bear fruit. They will only provide a profusion of flowers and fruit if they have been used as stock on which a superior species has been grafted.

In addition to the edible fruits, these plants also bear the orange blossom which at one time was widely used in bridal bouquets.

The most popular ornamental orange tree for indoor cultivation is *Citrus microcarpa*, which flowers and bears fruit at an early age. The fruits may be made into marmalade.

Position When purchasing a plant, choose one with fruits that are beginning to colour and put it in a light spot, out of the sun and not too warm. In summer you can move it to the balcony or the garden, where it may stand in the sun. It is important that it should be kept cool in winter, in a cold, well-lit attic, or in a cool greenhouse.

Care During the winter rest it needs a temperature of 4 to 6°C (39 to 43°F) and must be ventilated from time to time. Prune in spring, but only if absolutely necessary, for a few flower buds are bound to be sacrificed.

Watering Water very sparingly during the cool winter period. The compost should only just be kept moist. Water freely in summer and regularly spray the plant, except when it is in flower. Because of its leathery foliage it accepts dry air tolerably well.

Feeding After repotting do not feed for six to eight weeks, then feed weekly until August, at the concentration recommended on the label. If the foliage turns yellow give the plant an infusion of rusty nails or a solution of iron sulphate, 1 teaspoonful to 1 litre ($1\frac{3}{4}$ pints) of water.

Repotting Use a mixture of leafmould, loamy rotted turves and a little sharp sand. The root system is rather delicate, and if you do not want to repot the plant just yet, it is sufficient to replace the top 5-cm (2-in) layer of compost by a mixture of clay and rotted cow manure.

Propagation Increase from cuttings, rooted in a mixture of peat and sand in a moderately warm and humid frame. If pips are sown they will produce attractive wild plants.

Pests and diseases Scale insects and mealy bug, red spider mite and thrips may attack the plants if they are incorrectly cultivated.

Citrus limon, the Lemon Plant

Flowers of *Citrus microcarpa*

Citrus microcarpa develops fruit at an early age

Citrus aurantium

○ ◐ ⊜ ⦶ ⊛ ▢

This produces acid, bitter oranges. Subspecies *aurantium* var. *myrtifolia* (syn. *C. a. sinense*), the Chinese Dwarf Orange Tree, is cultivated as a house plant. It has deep green, firm leaves, up to 2 cm ($\frac{3}{4}$ in) and waxy flowers, with small, bright orange fruits.

Citrus limon

Lemon Plant. This has short-stalked elliptical leaves and waxy flowers, tinged with rose red. Correctly cultivated, these plants will produce lemons, which will take a year to ripen.

Citrus microcarpa

Syn. *Citrus mitis*; × *Citrofortunella mitis*. Calamondin Orange. Flowers profusely and forms fruit while still at an early age. Lanceolate, dark green foliage and small racemes of three or four fragrant white flowers, about 12 mm ($\frac{1}{2}$ in) in size. Orange-yellow fruits, 4 cm ($1\frac{1}{2}$ in) across.

Citrus sinensis

Larger in all its parts. A slightly prickly plant with oblong to oval leaves and large, white, scented flowers.

Cleistocactus

Cactaceae

Name From the Greek *cleistos*, meaning closed. This refers to the flowers which never entirely open.
Origin Their native habitat is in South America, mainly in western Argentina, central Bolivia, Paraguay and Peru, where they grow in rocky areas with a fairly high level of humidity.
Description The genus includes about 30 cacti. They are slow growing, columnar, with slender bodies branching at the base. There are creeping as well as erect-growing species. As a rule the stem is slightly ribbed and very densely hairy or spiny. The flowers appear singly, growing from the upper areoles, and usually remain for four or five days. They are orange or red, tubular, frequently bent in an S-shape. The petals do not spread, so that it appears as if the flower does not entirely open, and the stamens frequently extend beyond the petals.
Position In summer stand it in a light and sunny position in the living-room, or in the garden. If you do put it outside, take care that it is not subjected to too

A cleistocactus showing the tubular flowers

much rain, for this is harmful to all densely hairy and spiny *Cleistocactus* species. In winter it must also be kept in a well-lit place, as well as cool.
Care In winter the temperature should ideally be kept at 10 to 12°C (50 to 53°F), with a maximum of 15°C (59°F). Tall plants must be staked.
Watering Water moderately from February to October, a little more freely in warm weather. This cactus is an exception to the rule that cacti must be kept dry during their winter resting period: it won't tolerate completely dry compost or a dry atmosphere. In spring and summer, especially, it is advisable to spray frequently, preferably in the evening.
Feeding In the growing season give it a dose of nitrogen-free fertiliser once a fortnight.
Repotting Repot in March or April in a mixture of clay, leafmould, sharp sand and fine gravel or perlite, in the proportions 4:3:2:1, and add a pinch of bonemeal at the rate of 3g (less than ⅛oz) per litre (1¾ pints) of compost.
Propagation Increase either from seed or cuttings. Cuttings must be left to dry for a few days before being potted.

Cleistocactus baumannii

Syn. *Cereus baumannii*. Develops a slender, pale green stem, 2 to 4cm (¾ to 1½in) in diameter, with 14 to 16 ribs. The areoles are placed close together and bear 15 to 20 yellow-brown thorns. The upper ones are 2 to 4cm (¾ to 1½in) long. The flowers, orange to scarlet and 8cm (3in) long, are slightly curved in an S-shape. They are easy to grow and mature plants may flower profusely.

Cleistocactus smaragdiflorus

This has a cylindrical, unbranched stem with 12 to 14 ribs. The areoles bear numerous thin thorns and a few harder, dark brown central thorns, up to 2cm (¾in) in length. In summer up to 6-cm (2¼-in) long flowers are produced with a bright red tube and emerald green petals. They bear conspicuous bright red fruits at a later stage.

Cleistocactus strausii

Syn. *Cereus strausii*. A columnar cactus with as many as 25 ribs; it does not branch readily. The ribs are inconspicuous, because the areoles are densely covered in white thorns. In mature plants the yellow central thorns may be as much as 5cm (2in) long. There are 7.5-cm (3-in) carmine tubular flowers.

Clerodendrum

Verbenaceae

Name The Greek word *kleros* means chance or fate; *dendron* means tree.
Origin The 400 species originate in Africa and Asia, chiefly in the tropical regions.
Description Woody trees, shrubs or climbing plants. There is one fairly hardy species for garden cultivation, and the rest are greenhouse and indoor plants. The leaves are opposite or grouped in threes. The flowers appear in terminal racemes. The calyx is more or less bell shaped and brightly coloured. There is a long flower tube with four or five petals, four protruding stamens and a berry-like stone fruit.
Position All the species mentioned below are greenhouse plants which need only be protected from the brightest sunrays. Only *Clerodendrum thomsoniae* can be grown in the living-room, where it must be stood in very good light. The long tendrils may be trained along the window frame.
Care In winter a dormant season in a temperature of 10 to 12°C (50 to 53°F) is essential. Most of the foliage will drop. Prune the plant at the end of February and start it into growth once more.
Watering Keep the compost constantly moist, but in winter keep the plant a little drier. Spray the foliage frequently to provide a high level of atmospheric humidity.
Feeding In the growing season feed weekly, using a fertiliser solution at normal strength.
Repotting Before the plant starts into growth, repot it in equal parts of leafmould, clay and rotted cow manure.
Propagation Increase either from seed, from root cuttings or from cuttings taken from ripened shoots, under glass and with bottom heat.

Clerodendrum philippinum

An easily cultivated plant, which may

Clerodendrum thomsoniae, a climber which may flower at an early age

Clerodendrum speciosissimum

Flowers of *Clerodendrum thomsoniae*

Cleyera japonica 'Tricolor'

display its magnificent flowers at any time of the year. It is erect growing and covered in felty hairs. It has broad oval leaves, up to 25cm (10in) long and hairy on the reverse, and upright flower heads, strongly scented, white shading into pink.

Clerodendrum speciosissimum

An erect-growing shrub with felty grey stems and leaf stalks. It has hairy, closely veined, heart-shaped foliage, up to 30cm (1ft) long, and scarlet flowers in an upright inflorescence.

Clerodendrum splendens

A shrub with erect-growing or climbing stems and pointed, heart-shaped leaves, up to 15cm (6in) long, with a wavy edge. The main flowering season occurs between December and May, when it produces dense, usually pendulous, bright red flower plumes. The calyces are small.

Clerodendrum thomsoniae

Climber with bare stems and opposite, dark green, pointed oval leaves. The inflorescence is terminal or axillary. The flowers consist of a white calyx, which remains on the plant for a long time, and a red corolla which soon drops.

Cleyera
Theaceae

Name Named after Andreas Cleyer, a 17th-century Dutch physician and botanist.
Origin The genus includes around 20 species, some originating in South America. *Cleyera japonica*, the only species generally cultivated, was brought to Europe by East Indiamen. Perhaps they expected this member of the tea family to have other uses than merely serve as an ornamental plant. *Cleyera japonica* has a wide area of distribution in Asia: the Himalayas, parts of China, Korea, Japan and Taiwan.
Description Evergreen trees or shrubs with smooth-edged or dentate leaves. The small bisexual flowers are stalked and grow singly or in groups in the axils of the leaves. The calyx has five sepals and the five petals are fused only at the base, and there are approximately 25 stamens with rough anthers. The multi-seeded berry does not spring open.
Position Very suitable for cool rooms. In summer it may be put in a sheltered position outside. Give it good light, but always keep it out of direct sunlight. If you intend to use it in a mixed container, make sure that its fellow plants all grow in similar conditions.
Care The cleyera feels happiest if kept throughout the year in a cool room. In spring and summer the temperature may vary between 8 and 18°C (46 and 64°F); in winter it prefers 10 to 12°C (50 to 53°F).
Watering The root system of a cleyera is very finely divided and quickly dries out. It is therefore essential to prevent the compost drying out by watering very regularly, using softened water or rainwater if possible. In winter, too, the compost should be kept constantly moist. The foliage must be rinsed from time to time to remove the dust; you may like to use some leaf shine. Because of its leathery leaves it does not require a very high level of humidity, but occasional spraying is greatly appreciated.
Feeding From January to August give a dose of absolutely lime-free fertiliser at the recommended strength every fortnight.
Repotting Cleyeras grow so quickly that it is by no means necessary to repot them every year. Before they enter your house they will have been growing in the nursery for two or three years. Use ordinary potting compost, or a mixture of rotted moorland soil or leafmould, with the addition of some rotted turves. The soil must be pressed down well.
Propagation Increase in spring, from tip cuttings. These should be rooted in bottom heat of 18 to 20°C (64 to 68°F) under glass or plastic. They will root considerably faster if mist-sprayed.
Pests and diseases Too high a temperature in winter and incorrect treatment weaken the plant and make it vulnerable to pest attack.

Cleyera japonica
◐ ⊖ ⊖ ⓞ ⊛ ◼ ▢
A small, evergreen tree or shrub with elliptical to reverse-oval stalked leaves, pointed, smooth edged, and up to 10cm (4in) long and 4cm (1½in) wide. The yellow to white, delightfully scented flowers grow singly in the axils and are followed by globular to egg-shaped red fruits. In 'Tricolor' the foliage initially shades into pink and the margins have irregular yellow marking and green marbling along the centre vein.

Clivia
Amaryllidaceae
Kaffir Lily

Name The plant is named after Lady Charlotte Florentine Clive, Duchess of Northumberland and governess to Queen Victoria. A number of species of the genus were brought into flower for the first time on her estate at Alnwick.
Origin All species are natives of South Africa. The first to be introduced in Europe was *Clivia miniata*. It comes from Natal, where it grows in valleys with nutritious, loamy soil, rich in humus and with a porous subsoil.
Description The genus includes three species. Although they belong to the amaryllis family, they do not possess a bulb. Instead, the rootstem is built up in layers and develops fleshy roots from the centre. The strap-shaped leaves are dark green and shiny and grow directly from the root. New leaves are developed in pairs and in the course of a few years they form a thick stem consisting of layers of foliage, growing to 60cm (2ft) in height. The firm flower stalks bear terminal clusters of 10 to 20 trumpet-shaped flowers.

Normal inflorescence of *Clivia miniata*

Position It is important to find the correct situation where the plant can be left alone, for it dislikes being moved. However, to meet its requirement of fresh air, it may be planted out in a sheltered, half-shady position in the garden in summer. Indoors it should also be stood in a slightly shady spot, for instance a window where the morning sun enters. Too much sun will cause the leaves to turn yellow.
Care In the dormant season the plant should be kept in a cool position in a temperature of 8 to 10°C (46 to 50°F). When the flower has withered, cut the flower stalk as low as possible. When the remaining stump has dried out it is easily removed. It is advisable not to allow seed to form, as this exhausts the plant too much.
Watering The secret of successful clivia cultivation lies in correct watering. In many cases the flower stalk remains strangely short; in others no flowers develop at all. These problems can be avoided by following the rules. Clivias have to be goaded into flowering. This is done by giving them a resting period, starting in October, during which very little water is given, only just enough to keep the compost slightly moist and to prevent the foliage drying out. At this time the plant must not, of course, be fed. Sponge the leaves from time to time. A flower stalk will appear in the early months of the year. Curb your enthusiasm and do not immediately increase the temperature and the water supply, for this would result in the flowers developing between the leaves. Do not begin to give more water until the flower stalk is at least 15cm (6in) long.

While the plant is in flower and for some time afterwards, water freely. Make sure that no water can collect in the bottom of the pot or the fleshy roots would quickly rot and the plant would

Clivia miniata 'Citrina'

die. It is advisable to withhold water until the surface of the compost is dry. Spray when new leaves or flower stalks are developing. Yellow patches on the leaves are frequently the result of too much water, and especially of water that is too cold.
Feeding From February to August feed every fortnight, using a solution at the strength recommended on the label. From then until the dormant season, feed once a month.
Repotting This may be done immediately after flowering has ceased. Great care is needed, since the fleshy roots are easily damaged. Cut away rotting patches and dust them with charcoal powder. Young plants should be repotted every year. In the intervening years the upper layer of the pot soil should be scratched out and replaced with fresh compost.

The best potting mixture for clivias consists of rotted turves, rotted beech leaves and rotted cow manure, with 2 tablespoonfuls of dried blood, hoof and horn and bonemeal added to each potful of compost.
Propagation If you possess a great deal of patience these plants can be grown from seed, but it will be at least three years before they flower. The seed which may be produced will take a year to ripen and another three to four years will elapse before it will germinate in bottom heat and eventually develop flowering plants.

The plant can also be increased by carefully removing offsets with at least four leaves from the parent plant. On the other hand they may be left where they are, and in time a large family will develop, which will take up a great deal of space.
Pests and diseases Keep a look out for scale insects and mealy bug.

Clivia miniata
◐ ⊖ ⓞ ⊛ ▢
Strap-shaped leaves, up to 6cm (2¼in) wide, grow on two sides. The flowers are orange to red with a yellow sheath. 'Citrina' is one of the hybrids, with cream-coloured flowers. 'Striata' has white-striped foliage.
Clivia nobilis
Leaves 4cm (1½in) wide. It bears racemes of pendulous red flowers in summer, more numerous and smaller than those of *Clivia miniata*.

The flower of this *Clivia miniata* is stunted because the plant was watered too soon

Coccoloba uvifera

Coccoloba
Polygonaceae

Name From the Greek words *kokkos*, berry or fruit, and *lobos*, lobe.
Origin A native of tropical and sub-tropical regions of Central and South America, including the archipelagos: the Bahamas, the West Indies and the Antilles.
Description This genus includes at least 125 species of evergreen trees, shrubs and climbers. The foliage is usually leathery. The corolla is fused and becomes more or less fleshy when the fruit ripens, and in some species it is then edible. One example is *Coccoloba uvifera*, the Seaside Grape, which grows in practically pure sand along the coasts of Central America. The small tree has fine, heart-shaped leaves, so large that they can serve as picnic plates. In a gale they do not mind being sprayed with salt water. The flowers appear in graceful racemes on curving stalks. The corolla turns into berry-like red fruits, about 2cm (¾in) across, from which the local population makes a delicious jelly.
Position They require good light, but do not tolerate direct sun. They need a warm environment and plenty of room. Species such as *Coccoloba pubescens* may present some problems, however – in its natural habitat the leaves may attain a diameter of 110cm (3ft 8in)! Because of this unusual characteristic it is sometimes grown in botanical gardens. But if you have got plenty of space available, you will find it can be grown without difficulty by an amateur. In a pot it will remain smaller than if planted out. Mature plants which have grown too large may be cut back, or you could just keep young plants, grown from cuttings.
Care The plants should be grown in a warm environment. In winter the minimum temperature must be 12°C (53°F). Always aim at a temperature of 14 to 18°C (57 to 64°F) at night.
Watering Keep the compost moderately moist. More water may be given if the temperature in a greenhouse becomes too high in summer. Because many species have leathery leaves, they tolerate dry air fairly well, but occasional spraying will do no harm.
Feeding During the growing season give a fertiliser solution once a week, following the instructions on the label. Mature specimens, in particular, can take plenty of nourishment.
Repotting A loamy, nutritious mixture is best, for instance compost based on domestic refuse with the addition of some dried blood, hoof and horn and bonemeal.
Propagation Take half-ripe tip shoots and root them under glass or plastic in a temperature of 30 to 35°C (86 to 95°F) bottom heat. You can also increase from seed, grown in bottom heat, or by air-layering. The roots will take many weeks to develop.

Coccoloba pubescens
◐ ⊜ ⓞ ⊛ ⊛ ▢
Syn. *Coccoloba grandiflora.* Enormous, perfoliate leaves, up to 110cm (3ft 8in) across, downy, reddish underneath.
Coccoloba uvifera
The Seaside Grape. In cultivation it is a shrub with leathery, circular to kidney-shaped leaves, with red, later ivory-coloured veining. The flowers are white and the fruits purplish red, but it does not flower in cultivation.

Cocculus
Menispermaceae

Name From the Greek diminutive of *kokkos*, berry.
Origin The genus includes more than 10 species originating in the tropical and sub-tropical regions of North America, eastern and southern Asia, Africa and Hawaii.
Description Erect-growing or climbing shrubs with evergreen or deciduous leaves, sometimes incised. The flowers are inconspicuous and the plants are cultivated for their foliage. They are fairly easy to grow and make attractive indoor plants, provided the temperature can be kept moderate.
Position Full sun is tolerated, but they will also grow in a well-lit spot which is shady for part of the day. They may also be grown in tubs and placed outside in a sheltered position from the end of May or beginning of June to early September.
Care Allow the plant a resting season in a cool greenhouse at 4 to 10°C (39 to 50°F) from October to March. Ensure good ventilation in winter as well as in summer.
Watering In summer water generously in warm weather and moderately at other times, but very sparingly in the dormant season. Atmospheric humidity between 40 and 60 per cent is best. From time to time clean the foliage with a damp cloth, for dust restricts photosynthesis.
Feeding During the growing period feed once a fortnight with a solution at the recommended concentration.
Propagation Increase from seed, stem or root cuttings.
Pests and diseases Mealy bug is the most likely predator.

Coccolus laurifolius

Cocculus laurifolius
○ ◐ ⊜ ⓞ ⊛ ▣
In its natural habitat this may grow into a 5-m (16-ft) shrub, but in cultivation it remains considerably smaller. It is an evergreen plant, with smooth, magnificently glossy leaves, oblong, lanceolate or narrow elliptical, with three conspicuous veins, and axillary racemes of insignificant flowers.

Cocos
Palmae
Coconut Palm

Name From the Greek word *kokkos*, which means fruit or berry.
Origin The genus is represented by only one species. The Coconut Palm is found in all tropical regions, especially in countries bordering the sea. It is no longer possible to establish its original habitat, though it is thought that it originated in Polynesia. The fruits may be carried over large distances by the sea and may spontaneously germinate on the beaches where they are eventually deposited.
Description This feathery palm is sometimes called the jewel of the tropics, because its various parts yield hundreds of useful products. However, it is chiefly cultivated for its fruit, the coconut.

On plantations the palms are capable of producing fruit from their tenth to their sixtieth year, sometimes even until they are a hundred years old. They yield about 300–450 coconuts a year. The trees may grow to 30m (100ft) tall. Often the lower part of the trunk grows obliquely, while the upper part is vertical.

About seven months after pollination the coconut has reached the stage where the milk can be drunk. While the shell gradually hardens, the milk forms an increasingly thick layer of pulp inside, reaching its maximum in two months' time. At that stage the coconuts are picked to be dried, if they are to be eaten. To produce oil, the fruits must be left on the trees for another three or four months; they are usually left to drop spontaneously. The kernel is turned into copra, which is pressed to produce oil. A large part of the oils and fats sold all over the world is derived from the coconut. The remaining pulp is turned into cattle fodder, and other by-products. A very rare and unique product is the coconut pearl, globular and cream coloured, with a very fine-grained surface. Practically nothing is known about its origin.

In the living-room the plant is unfortunately short lived, keeping for only one, or at the most two, years. Germination takes six months; the small roots and the first few leaves appear from the same eye. The nut contains a tissue which transports the nutrients from the flesh to the germ.

Cocos nucifera, the Coconut Palm

Position It needs a well-lit spot, where the plant can be screened from direct sunlight in summer.
Care Keep the temperature at 20 to 23°C (68 to 73°F). The minimum temperature in winter should be 16°C (60°F). Ventilate frequently, particularly in summer.
Watering From May to October water freely, moderately in autumn and sparingly in winter. Coconut Palms require a high degree of humidity, which presents problems in the living-room. Spray frequently with rainwater.
Feeding Feed once a fortnight in spring and summer, using half the concentration recommended on the label.
Propagation You could buy a fresh coconut and wait until it begins to sprout, or occasionally you might find an unmarketable, sprouted nut in the shop. Put the fruit in damp sphagnum moss at a temperature of 20 to 25°C (68 to 77°F) and pot it up when the root is clearly visible.

Cocos nucifera
◐ ⊜ ⓞ ⓞ ⊛ ▣
A feathery palm, 30m (100ft) in height in its natural habitat, bearing a crown of leaves at the top. The fronds can be up to 6m (20ft) long. It bears flower racemes in yellow sheaths and at a later stage stone fruits with three weak spots in the shell.

Codiaeum

Euphorbiaceae

Croton

Name There are two opinions on this point. The first holds that *Codiaeum* is a Latin corruption of Kodiho, a plant name from the island of Ternate-Tidore in the Moluccas. According to the other view *Codiaeum* is derived from the Greek *kodeia*, meaning the head of a plant.
Origin The 14 species are natives of South East Asia, especially Indonesia and Polynesia.
Description Magnificent evergreen trees and shrubs, which in the tropics grow to 3 m (10 ft) in height. The leaves may be broad or narrow, and are beautifully coloured in pink, yellow, orange, red to almost black, and, of course, green. They have veined or blotched marking, or coloured margins. The insignificant flowers grow in long racemes in the axils of the upper leaves. Since they were introduced in Europe they have been crossed many times and the resulting plants are classified as *Codiaeum variegatum pictum*.
Position The Croton was originally a greenhouse plant, but hybridisation and rigid selection have produced plants which will give a great deal of pleasure in the living-room as well. Put them in the best possible light, but do not expose them to bright sunlight. The better the light, the finer will be the coloration.

They prefer a window-sill with south-eastern or south-western exposure, but they are sensitive to draughts and severe temperature fluctuations. Try to maintain a constant atmosphere.
Care Keep the temperature at a minimum of 18 to 20°C (64 to 68°F) both in summer and in winter if you can, though the hardiest species will tolerate 16°C (60°F) in winter – if necessary even a few degrees lower for a short time. Keep the temperature as constant as possible.
Watering Crotons usually have a great deal of foliage, so that a lot of water is evaporated. From March to September water generously, preferably with tepid water. Excess water must be poured away after half an hour, for having wet feet causes root rot. Water moderately at other times of the year, but never let the compost dry out.

When the air is too dry, leaf fall, mildew, red spider mites and thrips may occur. Spray regularly, especially in the morning and early in the afternoon, but never after 4 p.m. You might possibly use the deep-plate method or buy a humidifier. In addition the plant should be regularly sponged with tepid water.
Feeding Young plants should be given a feed at normal strength every two or three weeks. Older plants are better fed every week. Feeding is begun when the plant has started into growth and no longer drops its leaves, and is continued until August.
Repotting This is necessary only if the plants outgrow their pots. Leafmould, rotted cow manure, rotted turves or pulverised clay in the proportions 2:2:1 make a good mixture. Provide a drainage layer in the bottom of the pot.
Propagation Take cuttings from ripe shoots and insert them in a mixture of equal parts sharp sand and peat fibre with a bottom heat of 25 to 30°C (77 to 86°F) under glass or plastic. If they are kept at a constantly high temperature rooting will take less than three weeks. Since the plants belong to the spurge family, the stems will secrete a white fluid when cut. Stop the bleeding by dusting the cut with charcoal powder. The plants may also be grown from seed or increased by air-layering.
Pests and diseases Crotons are particularly prone to attacks when the air is too dry, and may be plagued by scale insects, mealy bug, mites, thrips and red spider mites.

Codiaeum variegatum 'Spirale'

Inflorescence of a codiaeum

Narrow-leaved and broad-leaved forms

Young leaves of a broad-leaved codiaeum

Codiaeum variegatum pictum, with flower. This can be seen on the left

Codiaeum variegatum pictum

Syn. *Codiaeum pictum*. Shrubby foliage plants with narrow or small, shiny and leathery leaves in numerous shapes and colours. Inconspicuous flowers are borne in axillary racemes.

All the hybrids on the market – there are several hundreds – are classified under this name. Most cultivars have names of their own, but they are rarely used.

Codonanthe

Gesneriaceae

Origin Central America, especially Costa Rica and Panama, and the northern countries of South America.
Description An attractive addition to your collection of hanging plants, particularly useful when you find that other plants are unable to cope with the low level of atmospheric humidity in your home. As the name suggests, *Codonanthe crassifolia*, the only representative of the genus, has thick, slightly succulent leaves, which enables it to put up with dry air. Unfortunately you will rarely find it available.
Position A slightly shady position is excellent, for it dislikes direct sunlight.
Watering Water moderately during the growing season. Only water when the surface of the compost looks dry and make sure it has good drainage, for rotting will occur if it remains damp too long. Low to moderate atmospheric humidity is sufficient.
Feeding In the growing season give a fertiliser solution once a fortnight, using half the concentration recommended on the label.

Codonanthe crassifolia

Repotting Ideally use plenty of conifer needle compost in the potting mixture.
Propagation Increase from seed sown with bottom heat. Propagation from cuttings is easier. Take a long shoot and cut it into sections, each of which must bear three pairs of leaves. Remove the two lower leaves and insert the cutting in damp peat fibre. Cover the pot or tray with glass or plastic and provide some bottom heat. They may also be increased by division.

Codonanthe crassifolia

Herbaceous plant with fairly thin, branching and creeping stems which easily root at the joints. Firm, waxy, elliptical leaves; the underside is speckled with red. Small, trumpet-shaped white flowers with a few red speckles in the throat appear in the axils of the leaves. In time red berries, 1 cm (½ in) across, will develop.

Coelogyne flaccida

Coelogyne

Orchidaceae

Origin About 120 species are known. They occur over a wide area in East and South Asia.
Description The genus includes terrestrial as well as epiphytic species. Most of the species bear rather uninteresting flowers which die soon after being cut, and these are therefore not cultivated. The only species which is highly suitable for cultivation in a centrally heated living-room is *Coelogyne cristata*, an epiphyte. These orchids grow on rootstock with oval pseudobulbs, each bearing two leaves. The flower stalks grow either from the base or from the top of the pseudobulbs, and the flowers vary in size as well as in colour.
Position They need a well-lit situation, where the plants can be screened from the midday sun from March onwards. They are really orchids for a moderate or temperate greenhouse, in fact some are hothouse species. *Coelogyne cristata* is best placed in an east-facing window.
Care For *Coelogyne cristata* and other species for the moderate greenhouse, the temperature must not drop below 12°C (53°F); 16 to 18°C (60 to 64°F) in the day time. In winter hothouse orchids must be kept at 16 to 18°C (60 to 64°F) at night and 18 to 21°C (64 to 70°F) during the day.
Watering In their growing period these orchids require plenty of water, which must be free of minerals and lime. In December, just before the plant flowers, *Coelogyne cristata* should be kept a little drier. After flowering the plant has a dormant season lasting one or two months, when it should be watered moderately. Species grown in a moderate greenhouse usually have a six- to eight-week dormant season. Hothouse orchids continue to grow practically throughout the year and only have a short rest in autumn. During the resting season the pseudobulb may shrivel up a little. The plant should be sprayed in the dormant season, but never when it bears flowers, which stain easily. At other times try to achieve the highest possible level of humidity.
Feeding A little orchid fertiliser may be given in the growing season (see page 70).
Repotting As many of these orchids have pendulous flower stalks, they can be grown in lattice baskets. They may also be grown in pots filled to a third of their depth with crocks. Use a mixture of equal parts of sphagnum moss and osmunda fibre, to which a little rotted cow manure and turves may be added. The plants are often set back by repotting.
Propagation Increase from seed and by division. Care must be taken that each section of rootstock bears at least three pseudobulbs.
Pests and diseases Scale insects and red spider mites are the chief pests.

Coelogyne cristata

Oval pseudobulbs with two lanceolate to linear leaves, up to 3 cm (1 in) wide. The pendulous racemes appear from January to well into March bearing five to seven fragrant white flowers with yellow-crested lips.

Coelogyne flaccida

Thinner, spindle-shaped pseudobulbs. Flowers appear in March–April; there are five to eight on each pendulous stem. Creamy-white corolla, to 4 cm (1½ in) across and the lip has yellow and orange to brown markings.

Coelogyne massangeana

Pear-shaped pseudobulbs with two narrow, folded leaves. There is a pendulous flower stalk and numerous scented, ochre-yellow flowers with white and brown markings on the lips. The main flowering season is from May to July.

Coffea

Rubiaceae

Coffee Plant

Name Goes back to the Arabian *khawa*, which refers to the drink.
Origin The genus includes approximately 40 species, mainly originating in tropical regions of Africa. *Coffea arabica* is a native of Ethiopia and was introduced in Arabia a long time ago.
Description It is not generally known that the Coffee Plant makes an excellent house plant. It is evergreen and may grow to a height of 2 m (6 ft). From its third or fourth year onwards it may even bear flowers and fruit. This does not mean that you will never have to buy coffee again, for before the beans are ready for consumption they must be roasted, which is really a job for a professional, for unless it is done correctly your health may be damaged. When the beans are roasted, sugar turns into caramel; this gives the coffee its brown colour. The delicious smell is also produced by this process.
Position These plants must be placed in a well-lit, well-ventilated but warm spot, though out of direct sunlight which would scorch the foliage. The plant may grow quite large, so you will need plenty of space.
Care The dormant season occurs between October and March. During this time the temperature should be kept between 16 and 20°C (60 and 68°F), or, in a cool room, between 12 and 15°C (53 and 59°F). Avoid temperature fluctuations. Another general rule: the younger the plant, the higher the temperature should be.
Watering Water generously in summer, using tepid, demineralised water. Remove excess water after half an hour. In winter water carefully, depending on the temperature in the room. The com-

Young coffee beans, still green

Foliage of *Coffea arabica*

post must be kept fairly moist. Try to maintain the highest possible degree of atmospheric humidity by frequent spraying with tepid water. If the air is too dry the edges of the leaves will turn brown.
Feeding During the active season the plant should be given a weekly dose of lime-free fertiliser at the concentration recommended on the label.
Repotting Early in spring, repot into a mixture of rotted turves, leafmould, compost and some sharp sand, using roomy pots.
Propagation Increase from seed. Since their germinating power is restricted, the seeds must be sown immediately, in bottom heat. Cuttings rarely strike.
Pests and diseases The main enemy is scale insects. Yellowing leaves indicate iron or magnesium deficiency.

Coffea arabica
An evergreen shrub with shiny, dark green elliptic leaves, somewhat undulate, up to 15 cm (6 in) long and 6 cm ($2\frac{1}{4}$ in) wide. It carries fragrant white flowers in axillary umbels, followed by red fruits up to 15 mm ($\frac{1}{2}$ in) long, with two seeds containing caffeine. 'Nana' is a dwarf form.

Dry-flowering *Colchicum autumnale*

One of the finest of the *Coleus blumei* hybrids

Colchicum
Liliaceae
Meadow Saffron

Name From the Greek *kolchikon*, derived from the regional name Colchis, on the eastern shore of the Black Sea.
Origin The genus contains at least 50 species. Those originating in western and central Asia and in North Africa are suitable for indoor cultivation.
Description This bulbous plant contains colchicine, a poison which, strongly diluted, has healing properties and is used in remedies for gout. It also affects cell division and is used in the improvement of agricultural produce. The flower resembles the crocus, but the bulb is larger and the leaves are wider.
Position Dry-flowering species can be set without water in a saucer in August or September and placed in a well-lit, or even sunny, position. After flowering they should be planted in the garden. In indoor cultivation the colour of the flowers is unfortunately appreciably paler than when grown in the garden.
Care The term 'dry flowering' indicates that they need no care of any kind: no water, no spraying – they will put out shoots of their own accord. After flowering bury them in the garden, 10 cm (4 in) below the surface, to allow them to put down some roots before the onset of winter. In spring leaves will appear; these must not be cut off until they are yellow. In or around July the bulbs may be lifted for use indoors.

Colchicum autumnale
In Europe this plant, up to 20 cm (8 in) tall, grows wild. It flowers in late summer and early autumn. The pastel-coloured flowers resemble the crocus. Foliage is developed in the following spring and will die before the flowers appear. Various strains are obtainable with white, red and double flowers.

Coleus
Labiatae
Flame Nettle

Name From the Greek *koleos*, sheath. The filaments are joined at the base, forming a kind of sheath.
Origin The 200 species have their native habitat in tropical Asia and Africa.
Description Tropical herbaceous plants and semi-shrubs, some grown for their fine foliage, others for their attractive flowers.
Position For really effective colouring they must be given the best possible light. Sun is tolerated, but they should be screened from the brightest midday sun. In poor light the Flame Nettle will turn green and pale.

In mild climates coleus can be successfully grown out of doors in summer, where they may develop into magnificent specimens. In colder climates this can be achieved only on a very sheltered and roofed-in balcony.
Care It is useless to keep the plants for longer than a year, as two-year old specimens grow lank and bare. As soon as they lose their foliage in autumn, when heating is turned on, they should be placed in a cool position, out of sight but in good light so that cuttings can be taken in spring. *Coleus pumilus* must first be cut back to produce strong shoots. Always remove the flowers of plants grown for their foliage.
Watering The sunnier its position, the more water will evaporate from the plant and the more generously it must be watered, otherwise it will soon droop. Always use demineralised water and plunge the pot at least once a week. Use every means available to maintain the highest possible degree of humidity, for instance by spraying, using the deep-plate method, and possibly by installing a humidifier. Spray frequently, especially in high temperatures. For foliage plants the growing period occurs between spring and summer and this is the time for especially liberal watering.

Winter-flowering species require different treatment. They have their dormant season in summer and must then be kept somewhat drier than between November and April, when they require generous watering and spraying. Dry compost is fatal to both categories.
Feeding During the growing season give the plants a weekly dose of lime-free fertiliser in the concentration recommended on label.
Propagation Sow in March in bottom heat to obtain a colourful mixture of seedlings. It is essential to prick them out in good time and to keep the young plants under glass for a while. The finest specimens may be grown from cuttings. Few house plants strike as readily as the coleus. Tip cuttings and eye cuttings will root quickly in water as well as in any soil mixture. In view of the fact that the plants are beautiful for a short time only, it is a good idea to take cuttings fairly frequently.
Pests and diseases Coleus may be affected by aphids and mealy bug, thrips, whitefly, mites and mosaic virus.

Coleus blumei hybrid

Another example of a *Coleus blumei* hybrid

***Coleus blumei* hybrids**
The species is a perennial semi-shrub growing wild in the tropics. The hybrids have erect-growing, angular stems and graceful, nettle-like leaves, oval with a sharp point and toothed. The leaves occur in a fantastic variety of colour combinations and there are insignificant white and blue flower umbels. Heights are between 30 and 60 cm (1 and 2 ft) depending on the strain.
Coleus frederici
An annual which may grow to 1 m (3 ft) in height. It is strongly branched and has pale green foliage. Long racemes of deep blue flowers appear in December.
Coleus pumilus
Syn. *Coleus rehneltianus*. Up to 20 cm (8 in) tall, with small, green-edged dark brown leaves on recumbent stems, this hanging plant develops blue flower racemes, up to 20 cm (8 in) long, from November to February. It can be kept for several years.
Coleus thyrsoideus
Growing to 1 m (3 ft) tall, this has an erect habit, and an unbranched hairy stem with roughly toothed, oval leaves, up to 15 cm (6 in) long. There are branching pale blue terminal flower racemes.

Colletia

Rhamnaceae

Name Named after the French botanist Philibert Collet, 1643–1718.
Origin The 17 species originate in South America, mainly in the non-tropical areas.
Description Entirely or nearly leafless shrubs. The twigs grow opposite, in the shape of crosses, often thickened or compressed and assume the functions of the non-existent leaves. Where leaves do occur, they are very small and grow opposite. Flowers appear below the thorns, either singly or in small groups. The calyx is tubular or bell shaped, with four to six divisions. The petals are lacking. There are four to six stamens. The fruits burst and separate into three parts. These very individual plants may be grown without too many problems, but they are very seldom available. You could try to obtain a cutting from a friend or grow them from seed.
Position In winter keep the plant, together with your other tub plants, in a cool, well-lit place. At the end of May it can go outside, where it should be given a sunny spot, perhaps against a warm, south-facing wall.

The colletia may temporarily be kept in the living-room, and naturally you will want to do this when it bears its delightfully scented flowers. Keep the thorny plants out of children's reach.
Care Colletias are really plants for a cool greenhouse. In winter it prefers a temperature of 4 to 6°C (39 to 43°F), but will tolerate one slightly higher.
Watering Water sparingly, and moderately in adequate temperatures only. It readily tolerates a dry atmosphere.
Feeding If the plant is repotted every second year, feeding is not really necessary.
Repotting Repot into a mixture of proprietary potting compost to which some extra loam has been added.
Propagation When mature plants produce seed, this may be used for propagation. If not, cuttings can be taken from half-ripe twigs. As a rule this will affect the beauty of the parent plant, so do not be too generous with your cuttings. In any case they take a long time to root. Young plants should be stopped once or twice to encourage branching.

Colletia cruciata in flower

Detail of *Colletia cruciata*

Colletia cruciata

In the wild it grows to a height of 3 m (10 ft). It is a thorny, grey-green shrub with flattened branches bearing flat triangles on either side; these are actually shoots. The small leaves soon drop and are succeeded in winter by fragrant white flowers, resembling Lilies of the Valley. Seedlings and young plants bear round green thorns instead of the characteristic flattened shoots.

Columnea

Gesneriaceae

Name Named after Fabio Colonna, an Italian botanist who lived from 1567 to 1640.
Origin Most of the 160 species have their native habitat in the damp jungle of Central America.
Description These are shrubs, semi-shrubs and herbaceous plants. They include evergreen, hanging, climbing or creeping plants, perennials and epiphytes. They are not hardy, but are grown as hanging plants for their cheerful tubular flowers or for their fine foliage. Smooth-leaved species are hardier than those with hairy foliage. The leaves grow opposite and quite often one of the pair is larger than the other. The flowers grow singly or in groups in the axils of the leaves. The most common colour is orange-red, but the yellow and pink species are also worth growing. The berries are usually white.
Position Hang or place them in a lightly shaded position. They must be kept out of direct sunlight, for which their native habitat in the jungle has made them unsuited. In too strong a light *Columnea hirta* will develop yellow patches on its foliage.
Care The maximum temperature is between 18 and 22°C (64 and 71°F), except during the dormant season, when a temperature of between 14 and 16°C (57 and 60°F) is desirable. As soon as the buds appear you can allow the temperature to rise to 18 to 20°C (64 to 68°F). *Columnea × banksii* is satisfied with 10 to 15°C (50 to 59°F) in winter. *Columnea microphylla* 'Stavanger' requires 18°C (64°F).

Columnea plants flower on their new shoots and must therefore be pruned immediately after flowering. If they are not pruned flowers will appear only at the tips of the pendulous stems. Pruning has the added advantage of encouraging the plant to branch. After being pruned and possibly branching it will take a while before the plant starts into full growth once more and during this period it should be pampered with warmth and moderate watering.

Columnea linearis

Watering Keep the compost moist with tepid, demineralised water or rainwater. In high tempratures, when a great deal of water evaporates, the plant must be watered generously but do not water when the surface of the compost is still moist to the touch. Profuse flowering is encouraged by giving the plant a resting period in December and January, keeping it slightly cooler and giving it little water. A high degree of atmospheric humidity must be maintained at this time as well as during the rest of the year. If you supply the humidity by spraying, it is best to mist-spray around the plant and preferably not on the leaves. Direct spraying is definitely harmful when the buds are starting to colour or when the plant is in flower, and species with hairy foliage should also not be sprayed directly, since this will cause yellow patches or rings. The deep-plate method may be used as well. Columnea species usually do well in the kitchen, where the air is slightly damper.
Feeding During the active season feed once a week or every ten days, using a lime-free fertiliser solution at the recommended strength.
Repotting Since they are epiphytes, columneas do best in a loosely packed mixture, rich in humus, such as woodland and moorland soil with some sphagnum moss or chopped fern roots, mixed with a little charcoal and rotted cow manure. They may be grown on tree bark or in orchid baskets, but in that case they must be kept in the greenhouse: in the living-room such a compost mixture would dry out too quickly.
Propagation When the plant is pruned, cuttings may be taken from the parts removed.

Alternatively, a healthy stem can be cut into sections, each with three pairs of leaves, of which the lower pair is removed. The cuttings are then rooted in peat fibre with bottom heat, at about 20°C (68°F), under glass or plastic. New plants may also be grown from seed, but this is rarely done.
Pests and diseases Aphids and thrips can be troublesome, and leaves will drop if the plant is kept in a draught.

Columnea × banksii

Firm, pendulous or creeping stems with small, glossy leaves, dark green on the upper surface, reddish below. The two-lipped flowers are orange-red with vague yellow streaks in the throat.

Columnea gloriosa

This has long, limp trailing stems with small, egg-shaped green leaves covered in red hairs. The scarlet flowers have a yellow spot in the throat.

Columnea microphylla should be grown in a hanging pot or basket

Columnea gloriosa

Columnea × banksii

Columnea teuscheri with seeds

Columnea hirta
The creeping to trailing stems develop roots on the nodes, and the entire plant is covered in stiff short hairs. Leaves are elliptical to oblong and there are single red flowers, 10cm (4in) long, in spring.
***Columnea* hybrids**
Several species have been crossed and it is not always certain that a plant is true to type.
Columnea linearis
A bushy, trailing or erect-growing epiphyte with long and narrow, glossy dark green leaves. Two-lipped, tubular pink flowers grow in the axils.
Columnea microphylla
The long and thin hairy stems up to 1m (3ft) long carry tiny, practically circular leaves covered in coppery hairs. Two-lipped, orange-red flowers are produced in spring or summer. 'Stavanger' is more robust and larger in all its parts. A strain with variegated foliage also exists.
Columnea schiedeana
Erect-growing hairy stems bear oblong to lanceolate opposite leaves, up to 10cm (4in) long, thick and green, and often with red veins. The flowers grow singly or in pairs; the corolla is 4 to 6cm ($1\frac{1}{2}$ to $2\frac{1}{4}$in) long, orange-yellow with dull red streaks and spots. This is a hothouse plant.
Columnea teuscheri
This has thin, hairy, branched stems with opposite leaves of different size. The flowers, appearing in winter, are unusually shaped: they are long stemmed, hairy, tubular, brown-violet with feathery sepals covered in red hairs, and the throat is yellow.
Columnea tulae
Erect-growing or curving stems carry opposite oval green leaves. There are single red flowers, to 5cm (2in) long. 'Flava' has yellow flowers.

Conophytum

Aizoaceae

Cone Plant

Origin About 300 species are known, all originating in South and South West Africa.
Description Succulent plants, at first sight reminiscent of lithops. They resemble the stones among which they grow in their natural habitat. The sessile leaves have grown into spherical bodies – corpuscula – with a narrow split in the centre, through which the flowers appear. The corpuscula may be speckled or otherwise marked. They grow in small groups, few species beyond 5cm (2in) in height. The flowering season occurs between mid-August and November. They bear daisy-like flowers in white, yellow, pink, red, purple and all shades in between. Conophytum bodies are often smaller and greener than those of lithops.
Position Put them in a sunny spot on the window-sill or in a moderately heated greenhouse.
Care In winter the temperature must not drop below 5°C (41°F).
Watering With a few exceptions, conophytums have a resting period from December to July, during which they should be given practically no water. On a warm spring day they may be given a generous supply to prevent the bodies shrivelling. From July until the end of the flowering season the plants should be watered when the compost feels dry to the touch, but from late October onwards water sparingly. The bodies will shrivel up, but new corpuscula will grow through the epidermis of the old. Conophytums tolerate a dry atmosphere and love fresh air.
Repotting Repot only once every three years in a sandy compost, rich in humus, mixed with a little powdery loam.
Propagation Seeds may be sown in May in a temperature of 21°C (70°F). Do not cover the very fine seed. Cuttings with a little old tissue attached may be taken in July and rooted in sand at a temperature of 20°C (68°F). The easiest method of propagation is by division in summer.
Pests and diseases Mealy bug and root mealy bug can cause damage. If the soil is kept damp for a long time, the plants will rot.

Conophytum bilobum
Grey-green bodies, 3 to 5cm (1 to 2in) tall and up to 2cm (¾in) wide; the colour gradually changes to red. The short-stalked yellow flowers, 2.5cm (1in) across, appear in September and October.
Conophytum calculus
Pale green spherical bodies, up to 5cm (2in) high. They have a shallow lengthwise split in the upper surface, and brown-tipped yellow flowers.
Conophytum mundum
Spherical corpuscula, flattened at the top, they are dull green with darker green patches and yellow flowers.
Conophytum scitulum
Conical grey-green corpuscula with a reddish bloom and marked with red lines. The flowers are 2cm (¾in) across and appear in October–November.
Conophytum wettsteinii
Fairly large bodies, flattened at the top and a pale grey-green. The red flowers are up to 3cm (1in) across.

Conophytums flower profusely

Conophytum wettsteinii with its unusual flattened corpuscula

Convallaria
Liliaceae
Lily of the Valley

Name The Latin word *convallis* means 'enclosed valley' and the plant was given the name because it was frequently found in such places.
Origin Temperate zones of Europe, Asia and America.
Description The genus contains only one species, a herbaceous perennial which may be grown in the garden as well as indoors. They are not really house plants, but they are an attractive way of brightening up the living-room around Christmas time.
Position Place them in a cool, well-lit spot out of direct sunlight.
Care In order to have flowering Lilies of the Valley at Christmas you have to obtain crowns which have been retarded by refrigeration. These are plants which have for some years produced foliage only and could have flowered in the previous spring if they had not been moved to cold storage just before flowering. As soon as they are brought into a warmer environment the flowers will appear.

Convallaria majalis, Lilly of the Valley

If you wish to use crowns from your own garden, take only the plumpest, lift them early in spring and bring them into growth in pots. This avoids the cold storage treatment.

Insert the crowns in a mixture of equal parts of clay and leafmould and make sure they are well drained. The tips, which must be visible above the surface, should then be covered with a thin layer of sphagnum moss. Keep the pots in the dark at a temperature of 25°C (77°F) and do not move them to the window-sill until the shoots are about 9 cm ($3\frac{1}{2}$ in) long. In a normally heated room they will flower for a few days only.
Propagation Increase by division and from seed.
Pests and diseases When growing retarded plants, check for mould. If this should occur, ventilate and keep the plants a little drier.

Convallaria majalis

A medicinal rootstock plant, with elliptical leaves growing from the rootstock, usually in pairs, up to 20 cm (8 in) long. The white flowers are bell shaped, five to eight to a flower stalk. 'Fortin's Giant' is a popular strain.

The variegated plant in the foreground is *Coprosma baueri* 'Marginata'

Coprosma
Rubiaceae

Name From the Greek words *kopros* and *osme*, respectively: manure and scent. You will know why if you bruise it.
Origin The genus originates in New Zealand.
Description Evergreen ornamental shrubs with decorative foliage. They are very suitable for moderately heated interiors.
Position The variegated species, in particular, demand plenty of light, but none of them will tolerate direct sunlight. They should be kept in good light during the dormant season as well.
Care Ensure a moderate temperature throughout the year, though in the dormant season in winter the temperature should be lowered, perhaps to 5 to 10°C (41 to 50°F), but always above zero.
Watering In summer the plants should be kept moderately moist. Allow the compost to dry between watering. Water generously in warm weather. If your coprosma is kept in a cool spot indoors or in the greenhouse in winter, it must be watered very sparingly. Dry air is tolerated fairly well, but the plant prefers a moderate degree of humidity and appreciates being sprayed from time to time.
Feeding In the growing period give a fertiliser solution at recommended concentration once every ten days.
Repotting Repot in spring after the resting period, mature specimens once every two years only. Use standard potting compost and make sure they have good drainage.
Propagation In March cuttings with a heel may be taken from the previous year's shoots. They can be rooted in a heated indoor propagator, in a mixture of sharp sand and peat fibre, at a temperature of 20 to 25°C (68 to 77°F). Cuttings of short sideshoots may be rooted in a cold frame in July or August.
Pests and diseases If the plant is kept too warm it will be vulnerable to diseases.

Coprosma baueri

An evergreen shrub with blunt, leathery, glossy dark green leaves, 7 cm ($2\frac{3}{4}$ in) long and 5 cm (2 in) wide, and an axillary inflorescence of small greenish flowers. The fruits are orange-red, at most 1 cm ($\frac{1}{2}$ in) across. 'Variegata' has creamy-white blotches or margins and in 'Marginata' the green leaves have a cream-coloured margin.

Coprosma repens

Recumbent shrub with grey, rooting branches and bright green oval leaves. The flowers are greenish white and are followed by orange-red berries.

Cordyline terminalis in flower

Cordyline
Agavaceae

Name The Greek word *kordyle* means club. The roots of the plant bear club-shaped tubers.
Origin The 20 species have their native habitat over a wide area stretching from south-east Asia to New Zealand.
Description Tropical and sub-tropical trees, shrubs and semi-shrubs. Stemless species grow to about 2 m (6 ft), those with trunks may reach as much as 15 m (50 ft). The evergreen plants are grown for their magnificent foliage; they resemble palms. There are species with stalkless, often sword-shaped pointed leaves and others have stalked leaves, broader and conspicuously marked. Mature specimens produce flower clusters which are usually rather insignificant. The plant is closely related to the dracaena and many people find it difficult to distinguish between the two. However, when cut, the dracaena proves to have yellow roots whereas in the cordyline they are white. At one time cordyline roots were eaten by Maoris.
Position *Cordyline terminalis* should be given a well-lit position, out of direct sunlight. Since it loves humid air it prefers a greenhouse or an enclosed flower window and in the living-room the tips of the leaves are unfortunately apt to turn brown. This species is very suitable for mixed plant containers, where its unusual colouring provides a cheerful note.

Most species, however, such as *Cordyline australis*, *C. rubra* and *C. stricta*, do not belong in a warm environment. They require a well-lit to sunny situation and may be put outside in summer. Mature specimens of *C. australis* grow very tall. They are attractive plants for offices.
Care Unheated greenhouse species must be overwintered in a well-lit, frost-free spot, preferably at between 4 and 7°C (39 and 44°F). Hothouse species require a minimum winter temprature of 10 to 13°C (50 to 55°F).
Watering Hothouse species demand a

Cordyline terminalis 'Tricolor'

Cordyline terminalis, the green species

high degree of humidity. If kept in the living-room, they should be mist-sprayed at least once a day. Excessively dry air leads to leaf drop. Bare plants can be air-layered. Put the plants out in the rain from time to time. In summer water freely, using tepid water, and ensure that the compost does not dry out. In winter water moderately, depending on the temperature. Species kept in an unheated greenhouse may be watered generously in summer, but in winter, when they are not growing, the compost should only just be kept moist. These species are satisfied with a degree of atmospheric humidity of 50 to 60 per cent.
Feeding 'Cold' species need only one dose of fertiliser a month, others should be fed every fortnight. Follow the instructions on the label.
Repotting Use a standard potting mixture and repot only when absolutely necessary. For *Cordyline australis* a little extra loam may be added to the mixture. *Cordyline terminalis* will also do well in conifer needle compost.
Propagation Increase from seed, from offsets, or from cuttings. Sections of stem with at least three eyes each also root readily. In the case of *Cordyline terminalis* tip cuttings should be rooted under glass, with a bottom temperature of 30 to 35°C (86 to 95°F).
Pests and diseases Cordylines are subject to virus diseases.

Cordyline australis
Syn. *Dracaena australis.* A slow-growing plant, which may reach 2m (6ft) in height. It has a branching stem with sword-shaped grey-green leaves, 2 to 4cm (¾ to 1½in) wide and 1m (3ft) long. There are yellow- and red-striped strains. They have terminal white flower plumes.
Cordyline indivisa
Syn. *Dracaena indivisa.* In its natural habitat it may grow to 6m (20ft), but as a pot plant it will not exceed 1.5m (5ft). The stem is unbranched; the leaves grow in rosettes and are narrow, lanceolate, very thick and leathery, with a long point. The central veins are red or yellow and blue-green underneath.
Cordyline rubra
Syn. *Dracaena rubra.* In the wild it grows to 4m (13ft). It has firm, dark green leaves, broadest above the mid-line, 40cm (16in) long and 4cm (1½in) wide. The leaf stalk is up to 15cm (6in) long. Axillary, jointed flower stalks bear plumes of lilac flowers.
Cordyline stricta
Syn. *Dracaena stricta.* Grown as a house plant it is low growing and unbranched. The leaves grow in loose rosettes and are up to 50cm (20in) long and 3cm (1in) wide, wider at the base and strongly curved. The veins are inconspicuous, and there are violet-coloured flower plumes.
Cordyline terminalis
Syn. *Dracaena terminalis.* In young plants the foliage develops from a central growing point. The palm-like shape does not occur till a later stage. Lanceolate green leaves, to 50cm (20in) long and 10cm (4in) wide, gradually change to red and it carries lilac plumes and red berries. There are many strains with magnificently coloured foliage, such as 'Amabilis', which has wide oval leaves, dark green and glossy, with white or pink patches; 'Firebrand', curving, oval, purple-red leaves with paler veins, and 'Tricolor', with green, yellow and red-streaked leaves.

Corynocarpus
Corynocarpaceae

Name From the Greek words *koryne*, club, and *karpos*, fruit.
Origin The genus includes five species, natives of New Zealand and of some of the smaller islands in the Pacific.
Description Bare trees which may grow to over 30m (100ft), but remain considerably smaller in cultivation. They have grey-brown bark and round branches and twigs, smooth-edged, alternate, oblong to reverse oval leaves, and small flowers, succeeded by stone fruits. They arc decorative shrubs for the unheated greenhouse or other cool spaces and have the advantage of being immune to pest infestation.
Position They will thrive both in the sun and in a slightly shady spot. Treat them as tub plants, which means that in May they can be moved to the garden where they will spend the summer, to be returned to the cool greenhouse before the onset of night frosts. Make sure they have good light in winter.
Care In winter the temperature must be between 3 and 14°C (37 and 57°F). Young plants must be supported to encourage good shaping. Mature plants may be cut back a little in spring.
Watering In warm summer temperatures water liberally, moderately at other times. If the plants are kept below 6°C (43°F) during their dormant season in winter, they hardly need watering, but if they are kept at a higher temperature, make sure that the compost does not entirely dry out and provide moderate humidity.
Feeding When the plant is in growth, give a dose of fertiliser at normal concentration every 10 days.
Repotting Repot in a proprietary compost with some added loam and rotted cow manure.
Propagation Increase from half-ripe cuttings in spring or summer with bottom heat at 18 to 20°C (64 to 68°F).

Corynocarpus laevigatus
A small evergreen tree with thick, leathery, shining green leaves, up to 20cm (8in) long. It bears bitter, very poisonous fruits.

Corynocarpus laevigatus

Coryphantha
Cactaceae

Name Derived from the Greek: *koryphe*, skull or top, and *anthos*, flower. The flowers do, in fact, appear at the top of the cactus.
Description Small, spherical cacti, related to the mammillaria. They may produce enormous flowers at an early age.
Position A cool greenhouse is best – put them in full sun in summer and keep them cool in winter. Any temperature above zero is tolerated.
Care The genus may be divided into two groups: the densely spined desert species must be kept very dry, and the less thorny and more fleshy prairie species prefer damper compost and more humus.
Watering In summer they must be kept dry to moderately moist, depending on the species (see above), and in winter they should be kept absolutely dry at a low temperature. Always use rainwater.
Feeding In summer give a dose of cactus fertiliser solution once a month.
Repotting The desert species require a sandy, very porous mixture with plenty of perlite added. Include some loam and leafmould in the potting compost used for prairie species. After repotting sprinkle some fine gravel on the surface of the compost.
Propagation Increase mainly from seed but also by grafting.

Coryphantha cornifera
Spherical, grey-green cactus with large areoles bearing yellowish radiating thorns and a 1.5-cm (½-in) red-brown central thorn. The flowers are lemon yellow, with red stamens. This is a prairie species.
Coryphantha elephantidens
A large spherical cactus with conspicuous areoles bearing six to eight curved thorns. The flowers are rose red and brown, and up to 10cm (4in) across.
Coryphantha pseudonickelsae
Egg-shaped cactus, invisible under its long white radial thorns and its large black central thorns. The flowers are pale yellow, 3 to 4cm (1 to 1½in) across. A desert species.

Coryphantha cornifera

Costus
Zingiberaceae

Name *Costus* is a very ancient plant name.
Origin The approximately 140 species discovered to date have their native habitats in tropical regions all over the world.
Description The genus is not yet well known. It consists of herbaceous plants with a thick rootstock, often spiralled stems and sessile on short-stalked leaves.

A number of species bear remarkably fine flowers; however, these do not last for long.
Position Plants for the hothouse or the moderate greenhouse. They have a dormant period in winter, but do not entirely die down. They are very suitable for use in flower windows, especially the species with beautifully marked foliage. Direct sunlight must be avoided.
Care Provide a temperature between 18 and 22°C (64 and 71°F) coupled with a high degree of humidity. If possible, plant them out directly on to the staging and they will grow all the better.

In winter the temperature may fall to 12°C (53°F). The appearance of the plants will suffer, but if they are drastically cut back in spring they will recover. One disadvantage is that most species grow rather large and in small greenhouses only *Costus igneus* can be grown.
Watering In summer the compost must be kept moderately, but constantly, moist, preferably with rainwater. Keep the plants a little drier in winter.
Feeding Feed from time to time in the growing season, but do not give too much: the plants will in any case grow quite large.
Repotting Costus will thrive in standard potting compost, but the addition of loam or clay is even better. A mixture of conifer needle compost, rotted cow manure and perlite is also recommended. Use large pots (or plant out on the staging) and ensure that they are well drained.
Propagation Increase from tip cuttings as well as from stem or eye cuttings. The cutting medium must be warm and the cuttings must be kept under glass or plastic for several weeks. Mature plants may be propagated by division.

Costus igneus
A plant with an erect growing habit and reddish stems bearing a large number of leaves, especially at the top. The leaves are oval to lanceolate, up to 15cm (6in) long and 5cm (2in) wide, pointed, fleshy, dark green without hairs. They grow in a spiral round the stems. The dense flower spikes end in sharply pointed bracts. The orange-red flowers are 4 to 6cm (1½ to 2½in) across, and the petals are set horizontally. They look like tiny Japanese parasols.
Costus lucanusianus
A plant growing to 2m (6ft) in height. The leaves are up to 30cm (1ft) long and 10cm (4in) wide, grey-green on the upper surface, silver-green underneath. The very large flowers grow on much shorter stalks and are fragrant and the spikes are up to 9cm (3½in) long. They have white petals and a carmine lip with yellow patches.
Costus malortieanus
Leaves are round to reverse oval, a velvety green with darker marking among the veins, and hairy. Flowers grow in 6-cm (2¼-in) long spikes, and are yellow, with an orange-red striped corolla. The lip is streaked yellow to orange-red.
Costus speciosus
A species with lanceolate green leaves up to 20cm (8in) long, hairy on the lower surface. The flower spikes are up to 12cm (4½in) long, with fringed red bracts and flowers 10cm (4in) across. The calyx is red, the corolla white, and the lip is yellow at the base.

Costus igneus, a fairly rare but beautiful greenhouse plant

Cotyledon undulata 'Silver Crown', detail of the inflorescence

Cotyledon
Crassulaceae

Name The Greek work *kotyle* means bowl or navel. At one time the Navelwort was included in this genus, but it has now been reclassified under the genus *Umbilicus*.
Origin There are nearly 50 species, of which the majority originate in South Africa. One species has its native habitat in Eritrea and southern Arabia.
Description The genus may be divided into two groups: one group consists of shrubby plants with evergreen, opposite foliage, and the other has a thickened or fleshy stem with alternate leaves, shed once a year. Some succulents are grown for their beautifully coloured foliage, others for their flowers, which usually grow in pendulous racemes and do not appear until the second or third year.
Position They thrive in full sun, both on the window-sill and in a temperate greenhouse.
Care Do not touch the plants: this would damage the white bloom on the leaves. In winter they must be kept cool and dry, at a minimum temperature of 10°C (50°F).
Watering Water sparingly throughout the year and very carefully – do not let the foliage become wet. After the leaves have dropped, deciduous species should be kept dry until new leaves appear. Cotyledons are satisfied with a moderate to low degree of humidity.
Feeding During the growing period feed once a fortnight at a normal concentration.
Repotting Repot when necessary, in spring, using a light compost consisting of equal parts of sand, clay and leafmould.
Propagation It is possible to increase from seed, but more easily done from cuttings, which must not be woody. Allow the wound to dry before inserting the cutting in the medium. *Cotyledon undulata* is grown from leaf cuttings.
Pests and disease Mealy bug is a possibility.

Foliage of *Cotyledon undulata*

Cotyledon orbiculata
An evergreen, erect-growing, branching shrub, with leaves covered in grey-white bloom and with a narrow red margin. It has yellow and red tubular flowers up to 2cm (¾in) long in summer.
Cotyledon paniculata
Syn. *Cotyledon fascicularis*. A slow-growing, deciduous plant. The fleshy brown stem, swollen at the base, has branches bearing pale green, spoon-shaped leaves at the tips only, and there are green-striped red flowers in summer.
Cotyledon reticulata
Like the previous species, which it resembles, it is deciduous, but this plant branches at the base of the stem. Erect-growing, yellow-green tubular flowers appear in summer.
Cotyledon undulata
A small evergreen shrub with very thick, fleshy, bloomed and waxy leaves, undulate at the edges. In sunlight the colour occasionally turns to red. It bears orange-yellow, tubular flowers in summer.

Crassula portulacea, one of the most vigorous species

Crassula
Crassulaceae

Name The Latin word *crassus* means thick or solid. Many of the species belonging to this genus have thick, fleshy foliage.
Origin The majority of the approximately 300 species originate in the Cape Province. Others have their native habitat in tropical regions of Africa and Malagasy. In addition a number of divergent species are known, encountered all over the world as water and marsh plants.
Description There is an enormous variety of habit among plants of this genus. There are tree-like species which may grow to several metres, low-growing clump-forming species, and all forms in between. For that reason they are very suitable for use in mixed succulent arrangements. Some species flower only once; other herbaceous plants, semi-shrubs or shrubs may flower every year. The leaves, placed opposite, are frequently covered with a fine white powder or with hairs. The fairly small, five-petalled flowers frequently grow in terminal racemes. All species form a useful addition to an amateur collection.
Position They like a light and sunny situation. In summer they should preferably be planted out in a sheltered position in the garden, perhaps from the end of May to mid-September. They may, of course, also be left on the window-sill, but should then be ventilated from time to time. White-bloomed and pale green species must be protected against strong direct sunlight. In winter they are best kept in a cool greenhouse, but they can remain indoors.
Care In the dormant season, which in our climate occurs in winter, they must be kept cool, that is to say, at 6 to 10°C (43 to 50°F). Place them in a well-lit position. If the temperature exceeds this level, lanky growth and leaf fall may occur, and they could be attacked by aphids. A low temperature in winter moreover encourages flowering. Too high a degree of humidity may cause mildew. It is advisable not to prune the plants, since this would to some extent affect their characteristic habit.
Watering Crassula species must always be watered sparingly. Depending on the temperature, in the dormant season they should either not be watered at all, say at 5°C (41°F), or once a week (in a moderately heated room). Only the largest species, which are unable to contain sufficient moisture for the entire resting period, should be given a little more. All species tolerate a low degree of humidity and should be sprayed only when they become very dusty.
Feeding Once a month is sufficient. Use a diluted solution at half the concentration indicated on the label.
Repotting The plants should be repotted annually after the dormant season. Carefully remove the compost from the roots and repot in a mixture of leafmould, clay or loam, with added sand for good drainage, using pots which are wide rather than deep. After repotting, water as little as possible to prevent rotting of damaged roots.
Propagation Increasing from seed produces a very mixed group of descendants. Unless you intend to add new species to your collection, plants are better grown from cuttings, for which the tips of shoots or leaf cuttings are used. Always allow the wound to dry before inserting the cuttings in a mixture of equal parts of peat and sand. New plants may also be grown from offsets.
Pests and diseases Incorrectly cultivated plants are prone to mealy bug and aphids, red spider mites and thrips.

Crassula conjuncta

Crassula turrita

Crassula tetragona

Crassula falcata

Crassula arborescens
Syn. *Cotyledon arborescens.* Silver Jade Plant. A tree-shaped plant with thick foliage and a shrubby habit, reaching 2m (6ft) tall. It has a thick, strongly branching stem, with thick, ringed branches. Fairly flat, grey-bloomed leaves are speckled with fine dark spots and surrounded by a narrow red margin. Initially white flowers, later fading to pink, are borne in June–July.
Crassula barbata
A perennial plant with a leaf rosette and stalkless leaves growing in four rows. They are edged with white hairs which spread in damp weather, but at other times curve inwards. White flower heads are borne on limp stems.

The tree-shaped *Crassula arborescens*, which grows up to 2m (6ft) high

Crassula rupestris

Flowers of *Crassula rupestris*

Crassula perforata

Crassula columnaris

An egg-shaped grey sphere, columnar in a more humid atmosphere, with blunt, fleshy leaves with curved edges. They grow so close one above the other that it appears as if the thick upper edges have been pressed outwards.

Crassula cooperi

Syn. *Crassula bolusii.* Lanceolate to spatulate, opposite leaves, forming a rosette at the base, and producing a profusion of white or pale pink flowers in spring.

Crassula cordata

A semi-shrub, nearly 1 m (3 ft) in height, with stalked, heart- to kidney-shaped, smooth-edged succulent leaves, with a dense white bloom and a reddish margin. It has loose, tripartite, long-stalked flower racemes; the white or reddish flowers frequently appear throughout the summer. Occasionally small plantlets grow on the inflorescence.

Crassula falcata

Syn. *Rochea falcata.* Sickle Plant. A semi-shrub, 1 m (3 ft) tall, with unusual sickle-shaped fleshy grey-green leaves growing in alternating rows to right and left of the stem. Profusely branched racemes of scarlet to orange-red flowers are borne in summer. It is at its finest when it does not grow too tall.

Crassula lycopodioides lycopodioides

Watch Chain Crassula. The stems are completely covered in rows of minute, scale-shaped leaves, overlapping like roof tiles. It grows to 25 cm (10 in) tall, and produces insignificant white flowers with a disagreeable smell.

Crassula obliqua

Syn. *Crassula argentea.* Jade Plant. This resembles *Crassula arborescens,* but the foliage is green and glossy and not widened at the base. It has pink flowers.

Crassula perforata

A perennial, up to 60 cm (2 ft) high. Erect-growing stems are covered in pairs of triangular leaves joined at the base. It appears as if the grey-green leaves have been perforated and threaded on strings. Insubstantial white flower clusters appear in April–May.

Crassula pyramidalis

A low-growing perennial with triangular to oval dark green leaves growing in four rows so close together that the stem is entirely covered. The base of the leaves bears hairs which in one night absorb more dew than the plant is able to evaporate in a whole week. In a drought the foliage folds up, enclosing the hairs, so that no water can evaporate.

Crassula rupestris

Syn. *Crassula perfossa.* Closely resembles *Crassula perforata,* but it has yellow flowers in an umbel-shaped cluster.

Crassula schmidtii

Syn. *Crassula impressa.* A clump-forming plant with green, sometimes slightly reddish leaves. It flowers for months on end. The flowers are small and rose red.

Crinum

Amaryllidaceae

Name From the Greek *krinen,* lily, the plant bears lily-shaped flowers.
Origin The genus includes about 130 species, found in tropical and sub-tropical areas all over the world, often in coastal regions. The species used as indoor plants originate in the Cape and belong in an unheated greenhouse.
Description They have bottle-shaped bulbs, which may grow very large and can weigh as much as 10 kg (22 lb)! The 'neck' of the bottle may grow to 50 cm (20 in). The strap-shaped green leaves grow in a rosette, with an erect-growing, firm stem in its centre bearing graceful, often delightfully scented lily-shaped flowers.
Position In winter they are happiest in good light in an unheated greenhouse, but in summer they can go outside in a sheltered, sunny position.
Care They must be given a resting period in the unheated greenhouse in winter.
Watering Gradually start watering in spring. Increase the water supply as they start into growth and decrease after flowering. Give very little water in winter.
Feeding During the active season feed once a fortnight, using the concentration indicated on the label.
Repotting Repot once every three years, in March. Be careful not to damage the fleshy roots. In the other years only the top surface of the compost should be renewed. Make sure that the larger part of the bottleneck is below ground, although this may be difficult.
Propagation Increase from seed germinating at 21°C (70°F). Alternatively the small offset bulbs can be removed and potted up separately in spring. Offset bulbs can flower after three years, plants grown from seed after five years.
Pests and diseases Look for bulb mites.

Crinum × *powellii*

Crinum* × *powellii

A spherical bulb with a fairly short neck. It has pale green, sword-shaped leaves, to 1 m (3 ft) long and about 10 cm (4 in) wide at the base. The flower stalks bear about eight pink, slightly pendent flowers.

Crocus

Iridaceae

Name From the Greek *krokos,* saffron. This yellow substance, which is used to colour rice, was originally made from the stigmata of *Crocus sativus.*
Origin There are nearly 80 species, originating in the countries to the north and east of the Mediterranean, Asia Minor, southern Russia and Persia.
Description The crocus is a bulbous plant with grass-like leaves clearly marked with a central white stripe. The differences between the various species are mainly in the colour and the flowering period. The flower consists of a slender tube, growing directly from the bulb and unfolding six oval petals. Practically half the tube remains below ground. The genus may be divided into two main groups: spring-flowering

Crocus neapolitanus, forced for indoor flowering

species and those flowering in the autumn. Dry-flowering species belong to the first category.
Position Give them a well-lit position, but not in full sun, since this would cause the colour of the flowers to fade and that would be a pity.
Care Dry-flowering species should be set in dry sand or gravel in August. Good bulbs will flower after a time. Pot suitable bulbs of spring-flowering species in October and bury the pots in the garden. Carefully cover the soil, so that the pots can be lifted in January when the noses are 6 to 7 cm (2¼ to 2¾ in) tall. They may also be kept in a cool cellar. Water moderately. In January they may be brought into the light, but should be kept cool until more than a third of the flower bud is visible. Keep them moist by mist-spraying or by half-covering them with a plastic bag. They can be forced into flower in soil as well as in water and gravel.
Watering Water moderately, to avoid root rot. If, on the other hand, they are kept too dry they will not put down roots.
Propagation Increase from seed or from the small offset bulbs.
Pests and diseases They may be a prey to aphids, virus diseases and rotting if they are kept too damp.

Crocus neapolitanus

Syn. *Crocus vernus.* Flowers early in spring. This is the species most suitable for indoor cultivation. It comes in a variety of colours, but never yellow. Strains with large bulbs are 'Jeanne d'Arc', white; 'Queen of the Blues', soft blue; 'Vanguard', striped white and lilac.

Crocus speciosus

This has pale violet flowers, 12.5 cm (5 in) long, in autumn. They have yellow stamens and red stigmata. 'Albus' is a white form; 'Cassiope' blue with a yellow heart and 'Oxonian' has dark violet-blue flowers.

Crossandra infundibuliformis 'Mona Wallhed'

Crossandra
Acanthaceae

Name The Greek word *krossos* means fringe, *aner* or *andros* is man.
Origin Evergreen tropical semi-shrubs with usually hairless, smooth-edged leaves and magnificent white, yellow, orange to red flowers in square spikes. The flowers will keep for a fairly long time. They are difficult plants to grow in the living-room because they require a very high degree of humidity.
Position In summer they should be kept in a half-shady situation, and in winter in the best possible light, but out of direct sunlight. The plant really belongs in a hothouse, but it can temporarily be kept in the living-room. An enclosed flower window is, of course, ideal, but you may be successful if the plant is kept in a mixed plant container, where the atmosphere is always somewhat more humid than elsewhere in the room.
Care The plant should be kept in a warm environment indoors throughout the year. In winter the temperature must not fall below 13°C (55°F). When you first buy it, check the underside of the foliage for pests. After flowering it is advisable to throw the plant away and grow new specimens from cuttings. Mature plants are vulnerable to aphids.
Watering Water copiously in the growing season, keeping the compost constantly moist, and always use tepid, demineralised water or rainwater. During the dormant season, from October to February, water moderately. As stated, the plant will only thrive in a high degree of atmospheric humidity. Either mist-spray frequently, using tepid, softened water, and use the deep-plate method, or if necessary buy a humidifier. Try to keep water off the flowers; this would cause staining. Too low a degree of humidity will result in leaf curl and non-flowering of the plant, even if it has reached you in bud. Remember that at the florist's or nursery the atmospheric humidity is generally higher than in your home.
Feeding From the time the first shoots appear until flowering has ceased give a fertiliser solution (preferably lime free) at the recommended concentration once every ten days.
Repotting In spring repot in light, slightly acid, compost with plenty of humus. A proprietary potting compost is quite satisfactory.
Propagation Increase from seed, which germinates fairly readily in a temperature of 16°C (60°F). Alternatively take soft cuttings in May or June and root at 20 to 25°C (68 to 77°F), first dipping the cuttings in rooting powder. Plant in groups of three to five in a pot. Young plants should be stopped from time to time to produce bushy specimens. The shape of mature plants may be improved by pruning.
Pests and diseases Aphids, red spider mites and whitefly may appear.

Crossandra infundibuliformis

Crossandra flava

An evergreen perennial with smooth-edged green foliage. Its main flowering season occurs between December and June, but it can flower at other times of the year as well.

Crossandra infundibuliformis

An evergreen, herbaceous semi-shrub, 30 to 50 cm (12 to 20 in) tall. It has opposite-growing, oval to lanceolate, pointed and slightly blistered leaves, 7 to 12 cm (2¾ to 4¾ in) long; they are dark green and glossy, with a wavy margin. The base is abruptly contracted into the stem. The square, axillary flower spikes, 10 cm (4 in) long, are densely covered in green bracts. Flowering starts in April and may continue until autumn. The flowers are yellow, salmon coloured to orange-red, and trumpet shaped with a tubular corolla, up to 3 cm (1 in) long, and an asymmetrical, five-lobed disc, to 3 cm (1 in) across. The seeds are covered in feathery scales. A Swedish strain, 'Mona Wallhed', has a more compact and vigorous habit, with very dark green foliage and a dense, brick-red inflorescence.

Crossandra nilotica

An evergreen semi-shrub, up to 60 cm (2 ft) tall, with hairy, elliptical leaves 10 cm (4 in) long, narrowing at either end, blunt, on equally hairy stems. Pale red or orange flowers develop in dense, long-stalked spikes, up to 6 cm (2¼ in) long, growing in the axils of the leaves, and there are softly haired bracts. The tube of the corolla is nearly 2 cm (¾ in) long, and the three lower petals form a lip. The main flowering season is from May to August.

In the foreground *Cryptanthus lacerdae*, with *Cryptanthus zonatus* 'Zebrinus' behind

Cryptanthus
Bromeliaceae

Name From the Greek words *kryptos*, hidden, and *anthos*, flower.
Origin The 22 known species all have their native habitat in Brazil and Guyana.
Description In the wild it is an epiphyte as well as a terrestrial-growing plant. Most species are suitable for growing in shallow containers or bowls. They form flattened rosettes, but these are not intended to collect water in the tubes, as is the case with other bromeliad species. The foliage is often beautifully coloured and sometimes strikingly marked. As may be gathered from the name cryptanthus, the flower remains hidden among the leaves; it is very small and insignificant, and usually white. After flowering the plant dies. In tropical regions some cryptanthus species grow as ground cover in the wild. This indicates that it is a tough plant well suited for indoor cultivation, and is easily cared for.
Position A well-lit situation is best, possibly with some sunlight. In too dark a position the foliage will quickly lose its fine colouring and marking.
Care In winter the temperature must be kept high. For variegated species it should be between 20 and 22°C (68 and 71°F). Other species are satisfied with 18°C (64°F).
Watering During the growing season water regularly, keeping the compost moist. Water should only be poured into the centre of the rosette in summer. In winter water sparingly, but do not let the compost dry out. Always use tepid water for watering and spraying and maintain an atmospheric humidity of 60 to 70 per cent.
Feeding In the growing period a plant should be given a diluted fertiliser solution once a fortnight, using half the recommended concentration. The solution may be poured on to the compost, or the plant can be fed through the foliage.

Cryptanthus beuckeri

Repotting The cryptanthus has a small root system and is therefore best grown in shallow pots or containers. Standard potting compost is satisfactory but you would do even better by adding some extra sphagnum moss and leafmould, plus some sand for good drainage. For the same reason a layer of crocks should be placed in the bottom of the pot or bowl. These plants may also be grown as epiphytes in hanging baskets or on tree bark.
Propagation By the time the plant is in flower and about to die in the near future, it will as a rule have produced progeny in the shape of young rosettes. These can be separated from the parent plant, but in the course of time they will detach themselves spontaneously and it is better to wait for this to happen. The young rosettes should then be potted up in pure conifer needle compost in shallow bowls.

Cryptanthus acaulis
Small rosettes of narrow, pointed leaves, up to 15cm (6in) long, with strongly undulating thorny margins. The upper surface is green, the underside is covered in grey scales. It has white flowers.

Cryptanthus beuckeri
These form fairly flat rosettes of spreading leaves, pointed and finely toothed, up to 15cm (6in) long. Just above the base they narrow like stalks. The green foliage is marbled in hues of white and pink.

Cryptanthus bromelioides
Large rosettes, 40cm (16in) tall, without offsets, made up of long, slightly wavy, pointed leaves of dark green. 'Tricolor' has smaller foliage with cream stripes, red or pink tinged at the base and margins.

Cryptanthus fosterianus
Large, flat rosettes of long, thick and fleshy leaves, wavy and toothed and copper coloured, with irregular cross-banding consisting of grey scales.

Cryptanthus lacerdae
The rosettes grow to only 10cm (4in) across. The foliage is dark green with two lengthwise silver stripes and white scales on the reverse. It bears whitish flowers.

Cryptanthus zonatus
Fairly flat rosettes of undulate leaves up to 20cm (8in) long and 4cm (1½in) wide, with fine thorns along the margin. It has irregular silvery-grey crosswise marking against a dark green background and white scaling on the reverse.

Ctenanthe
Marantaceae

Name Derived from the Greek words *ktenis* meaning a comb, and *anthos*, a flower or inflorescence.
Origin The original habitat of the 20 species is in the tropical rain forests of South America. The majority come from Brazil.
Description The ctenanthe is grown for its magnificent foliage which clearly shows its relationship with the Prayer Plant, *Maranta leuconeura*, and the calathea. The underside of the leaves is purple or green. The flowers are insignificant, but it may be of interest to know that, as far as monocotyledons are concerned, the detail of the flower structure is exceeded only by grasses and orchids.
Position These plants grow best in a tropical environment, which is easiest to provide in a hothouse or an enclosed flower window, but they can also be grown in plant groups in warm rooms, where the atmosphere is often fairly humid. To maintain the fine marking plenty of light is necessary, but no direct sunlight. Although they will grow in less favourable light conditions, their foliage will lose its attraction.
Care In winter a daytime temperature of 18 to 20°C (64 to 68°F) and 16°C (60°F) at night is recommended.
Watering It is important to use only tepid and demineralised water, and to water regularly. Do not water when the surface of the compost is still damp. In winter the compost should only just be kept moist. A high degree of humidity is essential. If the plant is kept in a centrally heated room, spray or mist-spray several times a day, preferably again using tepid and demineralised water. If the plant is grown singly in a pot, use the deep-plate method as well.
Feeding In the growing season feed the plant once a fortnight, ideally with a lime-free fertiliser, at the concentration

Ctenanthe lubbersiana

Ctenanthe oppenheimiana 'Variegata'

Ctenanthe rubra

which is recommended on the label.
Repotting Ctenanthes develop a spreading root system and are therefore best grown either planted out or in a shallow container or bowl. In a mixed plant container they will also have room to spread. Ensure good drainage, for they dislike wet feet. Plant them in a mixture of coarse leafmould and peat, with some rotted cow manure and possibly a small quantity of sharp sand. They need only be repotted once every two or three years.
Propagation The plant develops offsets which may be carefully removed from the parent plant and potted separately. Give them a humid environment, especially in the early stages, to avoid excessive evaporation.
Pests and diseases Too low a degree of humidity may cause the leaves to curl or turn brown.

Ctenanthe compressa

A bushy plant with waxy green leaves, asymmetrical in shape, oblong and leathery, grey-green on the reverse. They grow at an angle on thin leaf stalks. The plant has the unusual characteristic of developing bare, erect-growing stems which carry two to four plantlets at the tip.

Ctenanthe kummeriana

Syn. *Maranta kummeriana.* A bushy plant, 40 to 60cm (16 to 24in) in height. The leaves have dark green streaks on a white background and the underside is purplish. The leaf sheath is hairy.

Ctenanthe lubbersiana

May reach a height of 60 to 80cm (24 to 32in). The sheathed leaf stalks bear leaves up to 20cm (8in) long, oblong and ending in an abrupt point. The upper surface is marbled in yellow and dark green and the underside is pale green. This is one of the finest and most robust species.

Ctenanthe oppenheimiana

The Never-never Plant. A densely leaved shrub which may grow to 1m (3ft) in height. The leaf stalks are partially encased in red sheaths. The leaves are up to 40cm (16in) long and 12cm (4¾in) wide, oblong and leathery, dark green on the upper surface, with silver bands to either side of the main veins. In some cases these bands are incised with green at the base. The reverse is purple-red. This is the most robust species.

Cuphea

Lythraceae

Cigar Flower

Name The Greek word *kyphus* means curve or hump. The flower tube is frequently lumpy or spurred.
Origin About 250 species occur in North and South America.
Description The genus embraces annuals, herbaceous plants, perennial shrubs and semi-shrubs. In many cases the stems are round; the leaves grow opposite or in whorls. There are axillary, stalked flowers, in which the petals are sometimes lacking. The tube of the corolla is frequently brightly coloured, curved or lumpy, with an oblique margin.
Position A light and sunny situation is best, but if it is kept indoors in summer, it should be protected against the midday sun, to prevent the leaves turning yellow. This need not be done if the plant is grown in the garden. All species appreciate fresh air.
Care If you want to keep them through the winter, they must be kept at a temperature of 7°C (44°F). Cut them back in late autumn. These plants are rarely kept for more than two seasons.
Watering Keep them moist throughout the growing season but water very moderately while they are in cooler conditions in winter. They need only a moderate degree of humidity.
Feeding Feed weekly in the growing season.
Propagation Increase from cuttings in March or April, or in autumn. They may also be grown from seed sown in February at a temperature of 13 to 16°C (55 to 60°F). To obtain bushy plants pinch out the tips several times.

Cuphea ignea

Syn. *Cuphea platycentra.* An evergreen plant, 30cm (1ft) tall, with smooth, lanceolate green leaves up to 5cm (2in) long. It has bright red tubular flowers, 2.5cm (1in) long, with a purple-black mouth and a white throat, from April to November.

Cuphea ignea

Cussonia

Araliaceae

Name The plant is named after the French botanist P. Cusson, 1727–1783.
Origin The genus contains 25 species, originating in southern Africa and also occurring in Malagasy and the Comore Islands.
Description These are evergreen small trees and shrubs with long-stalked, palmately divided leaves. In cultivation they rarely flower.
Position These plants tolerate a great deal of shade. They will thrive in a cool or temperate environment, such as stairwells and entrance halls. Make sure that they are not in a draught. In summer they may be kept in a sheltered spot in the garden or on the terrace.
Care The cussonia may be treated as a tub plant. It should preferably spend the winter in a cool greenhouse at a temperature of 3 to 10°C (37 to 50°F). The dormant season lasts from October to March. A moderate degree of humidity must be provided throughout the year. As a rule the plant is most attractive in its natural shape, but it may be pruned a little in spring.
Watering Water copiously in the growing season, especially in warm weather. If kept cool in winter, water moderately.
Feeding During the growing season feed once every 10 or 14 days with a fertiliser solution at the concentration recommended on the label.
Repotting Young plants should be repotted every year, mature specimens every two or three years, in a nourishing mixture of standard potting compost, rotted turves, and some rotted cow manure.
Propagation Increase from seed, which will germinate in a temperature of 13°C (55°F).
Pests and diseases Scale insects and red spider mites are likely problems.

Cussonia spicata

This is an evergreen tree with leaves 40cm (16in) across, palmate and composed of five to nine incised leaflets.

Cussonia spicata can only temporarily live indoors

Cycas
Cycadaceae
Sago Palm

Name The name is derived from the Greek *kukas*, palm, or from *kukeoon*, a drink which used to be made from the starch found in the pith of the palm.
Origin These plants were already in existence in the carboniferous age. The majority have died out in the course of time, but a number of species have survived. They are natives of eastern and south-eastern Asia.
Description Although the cycas closely resembles a palm, botanically the plants are only remotely linked. They belong to the order of gymnospermous plants and are therefore more closely related to conifers and ferns. As a rule they grow to only a few feet in height, very occasionally to about 20m (65ft). Once every one or two years they develop a crown of new leaves, which unroll like ferns. The central stem and the individual leaflets uncurl from the base to the tip. At this time they are very delicate and easily damaged. Mature leaves were frequently used at one time on graves or for palms on Palm Sunday, because they are able to survive in great heat. The reason is that the stomata lie deep within the foliage, while the leaves are covered with a waterproof epidermis and the leaf stalk possesses a system of mucus tubes capable of closing the vascular cells, so that moisture is retained in the cut leaf.

The plants are unisexual, dioecious; they flower very irregularly. There are underground as well as surface stems, usually rough as a result of broken-down old leaf crowns. The fleshy pith may contain farina, but before this is recovered, the pith has to be washed very thoroughly because it also contains a poisonous substance which protects the cycas from pests. This imitation sago has never acquired great economic importance, since the cycas grows very slowly and must be destroyed before the starch can be reached.
Position It needs a well-lit, sunny position and a moderate – in summer fairly high – temperature. Screen against strong direct sunlight.
Care In winter the cycas should be moved to a cool position, about 12 to 15°C (53 to 59°F). In summer considerably higher temperatures are tolerated, so long as there is some shade and a higher degree of humidity.
Watering The cycas needs little water. In winter, especially, if it is left in a cool situation it should be kept fairly dry. When new leaves develop it is advisable to increase the water supply. The water must be at room temperature.

The fact that it thrives in an office environment indicates that the atmosphere does not have to be very humid, but it will do no harm to spray from time to time. Occasionally sponge the foliage to remove dust.
Feeding When a crown of leaves develops and uncurls the plant requires more water and a feed at normal concentration every ten days.
Repotting Repot every two or three years in a proprietary mixture or in equal parts of clay and leafmould, mixed with some rotted cow manure. Mature plants develop root nodules which must on no account be removed.
Propagation Ripe seeds – usually imported – should be sown immediately. Give them a bottom temperature of 25 to 30°C (77 to 86°F). Germination may take several months.
Pests and diseases Scale insects can be common pests.

Cycas revoluta

The thick stem may grow to 3m (10ft). The feathery leaves vary between 50 and 200cm (20in and 6ft). The individual leaflets are small in proportion to the total size of the foliage; they are narrow, stiff and dark green.

Cycas revoluta, an exceptionally decorative house plant, which must be kept cool in winter

A *Cyclamen persicum* hybrid with frilled flowers

Cyclamen
Primulaceae

Name Derived from the Greek *kuklos*, circular. Young corms are spherical, though later they flatten, still remaining round.
Origin The 15 species grow wild in Mediterranean countries, Asia Minor and Iran.
Description All the species belonging to this genus resemble each other and are instantly recognisable. The rootstock is tuberous and most of the roots develop from the centre on the underside. The leaves grow from the top. They are long stalked and are usually heart or kidney shaped, dark green with silvery marking and reddish on the reverse. The flowers emerge from the foliage and are shaped like badminton shuttlecocks without the cap. They often have five petals, of which one is pendulous. Occasionally they have a slight, but delightful, scent. A large number of strains have been developed and all shapes and colours are now available: smooth edged, fringed, striped, small flowered, in pastel shades as well as in pure white and bright red.
Position In general they will do best in a lightly shaded position, but there are cyclamens which, contrary to all the rules, bear a profusion of flowers throughout the year on a south-facing window-sill. However, a cool environment is essential. In the nursery they are grown in cool conditions and if they are suddenly brought into a warm room the foliage will droop, and that will be the end of your beautiful plant.
Care The ideal indoor temperature for flowering cyclamens is between 10 and 16°C (50 and 60°F). Faded flowers and yellow leaves must be removed by twisting the stem and pulling sharply. If a little of the stem does remain behind, it must be cut off close to the corm with a sharp knife to prevent rotting.

It is quite feasible to bring cyclamens into flower another year. After flowering gradually reduce the water supply. The sap in the leaves will be absorbed by the corm and the foliage will fade. Leave the corm in the pot and keep it throughout the winter in a cupboard. This resting period – during which the corm is kept cool – will last for one to two months. During the resting period give a little water from time to time, to prevent the corm shrivelling up. The corm should then be repotted in fresh compost and the water supply gradually increased, but continue to keep the plant cool. When not in flower cyclamens may be put out in the garden in summer.
Watering Cyclamens require plenty of water, especially when they are in flower. In a warm environment it is better to give a little water several times a day than a whole lot at once. In cool rooms it is sufficient to water two to four times a week. Water from underneath by pouring it into the saucer, especially when the corm is buried deep in the compost. When the corm is visible it will do no harm to water the surface of the compost, but avoid getting water in the heart of the plant, since this would cause rotting, and always pour away any excess water left in the saucer after half an hour.

It is beneficial to plunge the pot once a week. Always use tepid, demineralised water or rainwater.

Ensure a moderate degree of humidity. Excessively moist air will stain the flowers, but when the plant is not in flower it should be regularly sprayed and mist-sprayed.
Feeding During the growing and flowering period give a dose at normal concentration once a fortnight.
Repotting Remove the old compost and dead roots and plant the corm in a nutritious mixture, such as equal parts of clay, leafmould and rotted cow manure. Standard potting compost with a little clay added is also satisfactory. Older specimens do not require repotting every year. Leave a little of the corm above the surface. A number of cyclamens, especially 'Wellensiek' strains, grouped in a bowl are an attractive sight.
Propagation Increase from seed. Exceptionally healthy plants may occasionally be allowed to drop a few seeds, but in

Large-flowered *Cyclamen persicum* 'White'

Small-flowered type, the so-called 'Wellensiek'

Large-flowered *Cyclamen persicum* 'Bonfire'

general this puts too great a strain on the plants. Sow in a temperature of 16 to 18°C (60 to 64°F) in January–February or in August–September. Germination will take at least a month. Grow the seedlings on at a temperature of 12 to 14°C (53 to 57°F).
Pests and diseases Cyclamens are vulnerable to aphids, crown and leaf rot, grey mould, black leg, mildew, cyclamen mite, red spider mite, thrips, virus disease and root knot eelworm. Early yellowing of the leaves is the result of too much water or water which is too cold, or too dark a position. Don't be deterred by this depressing list; a well-cared for cyclamen will not suffer.

Cyclamen persicum

A bare plant, reaching 25 cm (10 in) in height, with a large, flat corm. The leaves are oval to heart shaped, dark green with white or grey marking, often red on the underside and long stalked. It bears singly growing, long-stalked white or pink flowers, sometimes with a differently coloured eye. This is the ancestor of the selection now available, which is mainly classified by colour, shape and size of the flowers. The strains may be grouped as follows:

1. Smooth-edged strains. This is the most important group, large flowered, available in a variety of shades: rose pink, salmon pink, pure red and purple. 'Bonfire' is a well-known red-flowered strain.
2. Small-flowered strains. Wellensiek crossed large-flowering plants with botanical cyclamens to produce fragrant, small-flowered strains such as 'Sonja', white with a red centre, and other pastel-coloured cyclamens.
3. Frilled strains, in which the edge of the petals is finely incised. Many of the strains belonging to the first category also occur in frilled forms.
4. Rococo strains. The petals are always frilled, but in these strains they stand out horizontally.
5. Victoria strains. These have a coloured eye and a fringed margin in the same colour.
6. Cristata strains. In these rarely cultivated forms the petals are partially covered by a feathery crest or beard.
7. Double-flowered strains. 'Vermilion' and 'Mauve' are examples.

Cycnoches
Orchidaceae
Swan Orchid

Name Derived from the Greek words *kuknos*, swan, and *aichen*, neck. In these orchids the style is long and curved, like a swan's neck.
Origin They originate in tropical Central and South America.
Description The genus includes epiphytes with long pseudobulbs bearing three or four folded leaves; these are later shed. Swan orchids have a unique shape: the lip is curved upwards and the style is unusually curved. The flowers are unisexual, and male and female flowers are easily distinguished. At least four to ten flowers develop on each flower stalk.
Position It is of the greatest importance that these orchids should be given the best possible light conditions, both in a greenhouse and in the living-room. They are really plants for the temperate greenhouse or hothouse, but they will, of course, also thrive in an enclosed flower window. If sufficient humidity can be maintained, they can also be kept in the living-room, but direct sunlight in spring and summer must be avoided.
Care Correctly treated, a Swan Orchid may flower twice a year. The minimum winter temperature is around 14°C (57°F). When the time has come to rouse the plant from its winter sleep, slightly increase the water supply and the temperature in March. A small shoot will appear at the base of the pseudobulb, showing that the plant has started into growth.
Watering Water liberally during the growing season, which usually starts in March. There is no need to spray. When the foliage falls the plant enters its dormant season, during which it should be kept fairly dry. The pseudobulbs must not be allowed to shrivel up.
Feeding For three months from the moment this orchid has started into growth it should be given doses of orchid fertiliser, following the instructions on the label.
Repotting Repot in spring, when the new shoot is about 5 cm (2 in) long. Use a mixture of 2 parts osmunda fibre and 1 part sphagnum moss and add some pulverised crocks or charcoal. The orchids may be grown in pots or lattice baskets, or be tied to tree bark.
Propagation Increase from seed.
Pests and diseases Red spider mite is the most likely pest.

Cycnoches chlorochilum

Elongated pseudobulbs, 20 cm (8 in) long, with five to eight elliptical leaves. The stems bear three to five yellow-green flowers 15 cm (6 in) in diameter with a green patch on the lip.

Cycnoches pentadactylum

An interesting species, with spindle-shaped pseudobulbs and gutter-shaped leaves. The large flowers are yellow-green in colour with brown cross-banding, and the hand-shaped lip is whitish with red spots.

The Swan Orchid, *Cycnoches chlorochilum*

Cymbidium
Orchidaceae

Name Possibly from the Greek *kumbos*, boat. The lip is boat shaped.
Origin The 50 species occur in large areas of Asia and in Australia. Species for the cool greenhouse have their native habitat in the high mountains from India to Vietnam. Those for the temperate greenhouse occur in China, Japan, Taiwan and Australia, and hothouse species originate in Indonesia and the Philippines.
Description Most of them are evergreen orchids, epiphytes or semi-terrestrial. They have a creeping rootstock, with large pseudobulbs encased in leaf sheaths and long and narrow curved leaves. The inflorescence is erect growing or pendulous. There are a large number of hybrids in a variety of soft colours, large-flowered and miniatures. In water the flowers will last for weeks.

'Zuma Beach', a small-flowered cymbidium

'Norma Talmadge', one of the innumerable cymbidium hybrids in cultivation

Position Give them plenty of light, air and room. Species grown in the cool greenhouse may be placed outside in summer, but bring them indoors when the temperature threatens to drop below 8°C (46°F) at night.
Care Cool greenhouse species should be overwintered at 7 to 12°C (44 to 53°F) at night and 13 to 16°C (55 to 60°F) during the day.
Watering Give plenty of lime-free and mineral-free water at room temperature in the growing season. After flowering, decrease the water supply and during the dormant season give only sufficient water to prevent the pseudobulbs shrivelling up. A moderate degree of humidity is usually enough.
Feeding In the growing season give a fortnightly dose of orchid fertiliser.
Repotting This depends, among other factors, on the plant's natural habitat. A mixture of osmunda fibre, sphagnum moss, conifer bark and beech leaves in the proportion 3:2:2:1 is satisfactory. A mixture of peat, beech leaves and some sharp sand is also good. Mature cymbidium plants need repotting only once every three years.
Propagation Increase from seed.
Pests and diseases Look out for red spider mite and scale insects.

Cymbidium lowianum
◐ ⊖ 〃 ⊛ ⊚
A vigorous grower. It has greenish-yellow flowers with a red-marked cream lip from February to May.
Cymbidium* × *tracyanum
Large greenish-yellow flowers with brown streaks are produced in winter. The lip is hairy, streaked with yellow, with red patches.

Cyperus
Cyperaceae
Umbrella Plant

Name From the Greek plant name *kypeiros*.
Origin The genus includes more than 600 species, occurring in most tropical and subtropical countries. A number of species also grow in temperate zones. The Egyptians already knew *Cyperus papyrus* in 2700 B.C. and used the plant to make papyrus for their book rolls, as well as for matting, string and sandals. Other consumer plants are *Cyperus esculentus*, with an edible tuber, and *Cyperus rotundus*, a native of Indonesia, which also produces edible tubers.
Description Decorative, rush-like ornamental grasses with long stalks bearing star-shaped umbrellas or crowns of leaves which may be needle thin. Among these moisture-loving plants the non-hardy species are used as house plants. Small, usually insignificant flower spikes grow in symmetrical flower heads with leaf-like bracts.
Position Put them in a well-lit position out of reach of the strongest sunrays in spring and summer. They prefer a fairly warm environment. They often show to good advantage in a modern interior, possibly grown in glass tanks filled with coarse gravel and stones.
Care Although these plants may be kept in the heated living-room throughout the winter, it is better to allow them a resting period from October to March. At this time *Cyperus alternifolius*, *C. argenteostriatus* and *C. haspan* should be kept at a minimum temperature of 12°C (53°F), the other species preferably a few degrees higher. Variegated species always rapidly revert to green. Try to retain the marking by planting them in poor soil and slightly reducing the water supply. Old, fading stems should be cut off. If you wish to cut brown tips from the leaves, always leave a narrow margin of brown, for the cut green surface would soon turn brown as well. If you have a cat you may have noticed that they regard some species of *Cyperus* as a delicacy. All you can do is to replace them frequently or to keep the plants out of the cat's reach.

The true *Cyperus papyrus* is an exceptionally decorative plant, but lack of light may prevent it from surviving the winter. In that respect *Cyperus haspan*, which looks like a miniature papyrus, is very much easier to grow. Put it near a south-facing window from November onwards and return it to a lightly shaded position in April.
Watering *Cyperus alternifolius* and

Cyperus diffusus

Cyperus haspan, a miniature version of the enormous *Cyperus papyrus*

Cyperus papyrus, the true Papyrus Plant, may easily grow to 2 m (6 ft) in the living-room

Cyrtomium falcatum, the Holly Fern

Cyperus papyrus are among the few plants which need never present watering problems: they require a permanent footbath. The water may reach to the top of the soil ball, but the stems must be kept dry. Other species require moist compost, but dislike being kept constantly wet. Use tepid water and on warm days, especially, spray regularly to create a damp atmosphere.

Feeding During their growing season these plants need plenty of nourishment. Feed weekly from April to September, using a fertiliser at normal concentration. It is advisable to use an organic fertiliser from time to time.

Repotting Repot every spring. If you make your own mixture, you can use equal parts of clay and leafmould plus a little rotted cow manure and some sharp sand. If you grow them in a glass tank it is easiest to keep them in their pots, filling up the tank with gravel, stones or marble chips.

Propagation All species may be propagated by division or from seed. *Cyperus alternifolius* and *C. haspan* may also be grown from cuttings. The latter develops offsets after flowering. Take well-shaped, fully-grown umbrellas, cut off half the foliage to reduce evaporation and leave 5 to 10 cm (2 to 4 in) of the leaf stalk. Place them upside down in water, that is, with the stalk upwards; after a few weeks roots and new leaves will appear. The cuttings may also be inserted in damp sand, with the leaf tips appearing just above the surface. If the temperature is maintained at 20°C (68°F), results will be rapid.

Cyperus alternifolius

◐ ⊜ ⓦ ⊛ ⊛ ▢

A tall, slender, decorative plant, reaching 1 m (3 ft) in height. Stiff stalks end in sword-shaped pointed leaves, up to 25 cm (10 in) long. The form 'Variegata' has leaves with lengthwise white stripes.

Cyperus argenteostriatus

This species has more root leaves and a more compact habit, growing to 50 cm (20 in), and it flowers more readily than the previous species. The name refers to the three whitish lengthwise veins. It is very robust.

Cyperus alternifolius

Cyperus diffusus

◐ ● ⊜ ⓥ ⊛ ▢

It has many leaves growing from the roots and few stalks, 50 cm (20 in) high. The leaves are fairly wide and it flowers readily.

Cyperus gracilis

◐ ⊜ ⓦ ⊛ ⊛ ▢

Syn. *Cyperus alternifolius* 'Gracilis'. Resembles *C. alternifolius*, but is smaller in all its parts. It seldom grows beyond 40 cm (16 in) in height.

Cyperus haspan

This looks like a miniature Papyrus Plant. Up to 50 cm (20 in) tall, it has stiff stalks bearing tufts of stiff, thread-like leaves. It requires a little more light than the other species, and produces downy flower heads in summer.

Cyperus papyrus

Egyptian Paper Plant; Papyrus Plant. This will grow to 2 to 3 m (6 to 10 ft) in the living-room. It has triangular stalks with crowns of linear leaves and radiating, pendulous spikes.

Cyrtomium

Aspidiaceae

Holly Fern

Name From the Greek *kyrtos*, curved. The plant owes its name to the slightly curved foliage.

Origin Most species have their natural habitat in China and Japan, but originally they also occurred in South Africa, Indonesia, Hawaii and Sri Lanka.

Description Ferns with simple, pinnate, glossy and leathery dark green leaves. They are easily grown from spores and tolerate a great deal of shade. They make graceful and robust house plants.

Position Excellent plants for mixed containers in cool spaces, such as entrance halls, corridors and stairwells. In a lower temperature, and among other plants in a container, the air is naturally somewhat moister, a circumstance appreciated by all ferns. They require very little light and will even thrive below the staging in a greenhouse. When the foliage is not yet dark green, the plants may be placed in even deeper shade.

Care These ferns prefer to spend their dormant season at a low temperature: 7 to 10°C (44 to 50°F) is the ideal. The resting period lasts approximately from October till February. Try to find a cool place for the purpose, such as a frost-free garage, an unheated bedroom, or, best of all, an unheated or cool greenhouse.

Watering Water freely in summer, preferably using softened water, spray regularly and occasionally put the plant outside in a shower. Monthly plunging is also recommended. Always mix a little fertiliser or liquid manure in the water in which the pot is plunged, thus killing two birds with one stone. If the plant is kept cool in winter, water sparingly.

Feeding In summer feed regularly. Use a solution at one third of the concentration recommended on the label. If the plant is growing vigorously, old leaves with lots of spores can be removed, which in turn promotes growth.

Repotting Repot in a commercial potting compost with a little extra sand and peat, or, better still, in a mixture of leafmould or conifer needle compost and some rotted cow manure. Provide good drainage.

Propagation Increase from spores sown in damp, warm peat, and also by division.

Pests and diseases These ferns are only subject to disease if they are kept too warm or too dry. Aphids, scale insects, mealy bug, thrips, and occasionally eelworms may be troublesome.

Cyrtomium caryotideum

● ⊜ ⓦ ⓥ ⊛ ⊛ ▢

Syn. *Aspidium caryotideum; Cyrtomium falcatum caryotideum.* Graceful pinnate foliage, gently curving at the tip, and a fresh green colour – not as dark as the other species. The leaflets are lobed at the base, toothed nearer the tip.

Cyrtomium falcatum

Syn. *Aspidium falcatum; Polystichum falcatum.* In its natural environment the leaves may grow to 60 cm (2 ft) long and 25 cm (10 in) across. In cultivation they remain considerably smaller. Each stalk bears 11 to 25 leathery, coarsely toothed pinnae, usually dark green and glossy, smooth edged at the tip. The leaf stalks are covered in brown scales, especially near the base. 'Rochefordianum' is even finer and more robust than the species. It has sharply pointed pinnate leaves, of a beautiful glossy green. The name *falcatus*, or sickle shaped, refers to the fairly deep irregular incisions in the foliage.

Cyrtomium fortunei

This has slightly wider leaves than *Cyrtomium falcatum* and 15 to 45 somewhat smaller pinnae, dull green and serrated at the top. In many cases they are sickle shaped. The entire leaf stalk is covered in brown scales. This, too is an excellent plant for greenhouse or living-room, but it is rarely available.

Cytisus
Leguminosae
Broom

Name The Greek *kytisos* referred to a shrub belonging to the family of *Leguminosae*.
Origin The genus includes more than 60 species, natives of the Mediterranean area and of Central Europe, as well as of the Canary Islands.
Description You probably know the hardy species growing wild or in gardens. The non-hardy species makes an excellent indoor plant, although it dislikes warm, dry air. A large number may be sold just before Mother's Day. Its cheerful yellow butterfly flowers make a welcome addition to your home.
Position If you have bought or been given a flowering plant, put it in a well-lit position out of the midday sun. It is important that it should have a cool environment. By spraying very often you might try to keep it in the warm living-room, but usually both leaves and flowers will soon drop in such an atmosphere. In summer the pots may be buried in a sunny spot in the garden.
Care In the flowering season the temperature should preferably be kept at 12 to 18°C (53 to 64°F). After flowering the plant may be cut back a little to improve the shape, and it could be repotted at the same time. In mid-September brooms that have been moved to the garden should be brought indoors to overwinter at 4 to 8°C (39 to 46°F).

Cytisus × *racemosus*, the indoor broom

Watering Water generously in the flowering season. In winter the water supply depends on the temperature – water very sparingly if the plant is kept cool. A degree of humidity between 50 and 60 per cent is sufficient.
Feeding In the growing and flowering season feed every fortnight at standard concentration.
Propagation Increase from half-ripe cuttings taken in spring or summer and rooted under glass at 17°C (62°F).
Pests and diseases Aphids and red spider mite are potential enemies.

Cytisus × *racemosus*
◐ ⊖ ⓥ ⊛ ▣
Syn. *Cytisus* × *spachianus; C. fragrans; Genista fragrans; G. racemosa.* Evergreen shrub with small, three-lobed leaves and yellow flowers in terminal clusters, up to 10 cm (4 in) long. 'Everestianus' is a darker yellow and flowers more profusely.

Darlingtonia
Sarraceniaceae

Name Named after a Dr W. Darlington, an American botanist.
Origin The genus occurs mainly in damp pastures in the mountains of northern California and southern Oregon.
Description With a little imagination you will realise why the popular name for this carnivore is Cobra Plant: the two small flaps hanging from the curving tip of the tubular leaves immediately remind one of a snake's head. The inside of the tubes is covered in hairs pointing downwards, which prevent insects from escaping.
Position The best place is a humid, shady spot in a cool greenhouse, preferably kept at a constant temperature. Indoors it can only be kept in an enclosed flower window.
Watering Mature plants should be kept even more humid than young specimens.
Repotting Repot every second year, when the plants are least active; this is usually in July. Use a mixture of peat and sphagnum moss, sharp sand and charcoal.
Propagation Increase from seed or from cuttings in a bed of sphagnum moss, under glass.

Darlingtonia californica
● ⊖ ⓥ ⊛ ▢
Carnivorous bog plant with 30- to 50-cm (12- to 20-in) tubular, emerald-green leaves, curving at the tip so that the opening of the tube points downwards. This is to prevent rainwater, which would dilute the digestive juices, entering the tubes. A two-lobed flap in the colours green, dark brown and purple hangs near the opening. Every year a new rosette of leaves develops at the end of a short rootstock. The flowers are yellow-green to brownish red.

The carnivorous *Darlingtonia californica*

Dasylirion acrotrichum, a large tub plant with spined foliage

Dasylirion
Agavaceae

Name Derived from the Greek *dasys*, rough, and *leirion*, lily. The 'rough' refers to the spined foliage which makes it almost impossible to take hold of the plant.
Origin Fifteen different species occur in southern states of the U.S.A., Arizona and Texas, as well as in Mexico.
Description Mature plants, in particular, are unapproachable because of their radiating stiff, sharply spined leaves, which together form a complete or a half sphere. The dasylirion is somewhat reminiscent of the yucca, but the leaves are much narrower and less sharply pointed.
Position On the Riviera these plants grow out of doors, and in our climate it is clearly a tub plant rather than a house plant. Like the yucca, the plant must be kept cool in winter to prevent infestation by insects in subsequent seasons.
The dasylirion is also suitable for unheated stairwells and entrance halls, especially where it is used to prevent visitors walking into a glass wall. Once you have accidentally come into contact with the plant you will never do so again!
Care From the end of May or early June onwards place the plant on a sunny terrace or balcony, possibly in a tub, or bury the pot so that the plant cannot dry out while you are on holiday. It must be brought indoors before the first night frost occurs, probably by mid-September, to overwinter in an airy and cool environment. The temperature may fall to practically zero, for this is a strong and vigorous plant.
The tips of the leaves end in a small, fibrous plume, which is better left alone. In any case it is quite decorative. When the plant is dirty or stained, it is best hosed down, for it is impossible to sponge it. In transporting it, the spreading leaves have to be turned up and tied, or it would be impossible to handle.
Watering In summer the compost must be kept continuously, but moderately, moist, preferably with rainwater. Spraying is not really necessary, but if you want to do so, use lime-free water to avoid ugly stains. Water very moderately in winter, not at all in very cold weather.
Feeding Once the plant has started into growth it may be given a measure of fertiliser or organic manure once every three weeks. Stop feeding in August.
Repotting The compost should be fairly heavy. Use $\frac{1}{3}$ clay or loam, $\frac{1}{3}$ rotted leaf-mould, $\frac{1}{6}$ rotted cow manure and $\frac{1}{6}$ sharp sand or perlite. Mature plants need not be repotted every year – it is in any case quite a job with those spines. The plant will show to best advantage in a well-drained ornamental tub.
Propagation The plants can only be increased from seed, under glass, and in a bottom temperature of 20 to 25°C (68 to 77°F), but the seeds are not easily available.

Dasylirion acrotrichum
◯ ⊜ ⓥ ⊛ ▢
Syn. *Dasylirion gracile*. A plant with a short, thick stem and a very large number of linear leaves, 1 m (3 ft) long and 1 cm ($\frac{1}{2}$ in) wide, green to grey-green. The edges are covered in fine teeth and slightly curved pale yellow, brown-tipped spines. The leaf ends in a graceful plume. In temperate climates the 2- to 4-m (6- to 13-ft) tall flower spike does not appear.

Datura

Solanaceae

Thorn Apple

Name Goes back through Hindi to the ancient Indian word *dhatura*, which referred to a plant with thorny fruits. It is not known whether this was the plant now called *Datura*.
Origin The genus includes about 25 species found in warm regions all over the earth. The shrubs and tree-shaped species are natives of South and Central America, the herbaceous species originate in the temperate zones of Europe and Asia.
Description There is a great variety of growth forms within the genus. Most species have large leaves and enormous, trumpet-shaped flowers, frequently with a strong, sweet scent, and thorny fruits. In the case of shrubs and trees the flowers are pendulous, in herbaceous plants they are erect growing. All parts of these plants are very poisonous – a fact which will be familiar to anyone who has read Carlos Castaneda's 'The Teachings of Don Juan'. In medicine these poisons are used in remedies against nervous diseases. It is hardly necessary to stress that the plant must be kept out of reach of children.
Position Growth is at its most vigorous if daturas are planted out in the greenhouse, but as a rule they are grown as tub plants. In summer they should be placed in a sunny, sheltered spot out of doors. In autumn they should be brought into the greenhouse, together with other tub plants, to spend the winter in a cool environment.
Care They must be overwintered in a cool greenhouse at 7°C (44°F). After flowering the plants should be drastically pruned.
Watering Water generously during the growing and flowering seasons. A level of humidity of about 50 to 60 per cent is adequate. Water very sparingly in winter.
Feeding Feed weekly while the plant is in growth, using the concentration recommended on the label.
Repotting Daturas like nutritious, porous compost. Add extra loam, rotted cow manure and sand to a proprietary potting mixture.
Propagation The finest plants are obtained by rooting cuttings in spring, in bottom heat. The young plants may flower the following September or October.
Pests and diseases Red spider mite and virus disease are apt to appear.

A young plant of *Datura candida* 'Plena'

Datura candida
○ ⊜ ◎ ⊛ ▢
A tree bearing magnificent white flowers, up to 20 cm (8 in) long. 'Plena', a white-flowering form, is sometimes sold as a house plant.
Datura sanguinea
A densely leaved, tree-like shrub, producing a large number of orange-yellow flowers, 20 cm (8 in) long, mainly in winter.
Datura suaveolens
An erect-growing shrub, up to 5 m (16 ft) in height. The leaves are oblong to oval, 15 to 30 cm (6 to 12 in) long, faintly hairy on the underside. It has pendulous white flowers, up to 25 cm (10 cm) long, which are fragrant. The calyx has five short sepals. 'Plena' is a double form.

A large specimen of *Datura sanguinea* growing on the island of Mainau

Dendrobium superbiens

Dendrobium phalaenopsis schroederianum

Dendrobium

Orchidaceae

Name Derived from the Greek words *dendron*, tree, and *bios*, life. The name is meant to indicate that the plant is an epiphyte.
Origin An enormous genus represented by at least 1000 species and innumerable hybrids. Their native habitat is in tropical regions of Asia and as far off as New Zealand.
Description The genus embraces a great variety of sizes and shapes. The smallest are only a few inches in height and have pseudobulbs from which one or two flowers appear. The larger forms may grow as high as 2 m (6 ft) and have thick stalks with hundreds of flowers. The pseudobulbs are actually storage organs in the shape of elongated stems. The leaves are usually oblong to oval. The flowers are similar in structure; the sepals are equal in length and the two side sepals are joined to the base of the style. The petals have the same length as the sepals, but are often somewhat broader. The lip varies in shape, but is usually keeled.

When cultivating these plants their natural habitat should be taken into account. Species from tropical highlands are grown in a cool greenhouse, lowland species in a hothouse and natives of regions in between these extremes will thrive in a temperate greenhouse.
Position They need plenty of light, but will not tolerate direct sunlight. Robust species such as *Dendrobium nobile* and *Dendrobium thyrsiflorum* may temporarily be kept in the living-room.
Care Deciduous species require a dormant season, during which they are not watered. Evergreen species should be watered sparingly in winter. In summer water moderately; give plenty of water only when the temperature is very high and the air is dry.
Feeding Vigorous species should be given a dose of orchid fertiliser at recommended concentration once a fortnight. Less vigorous species should be given half the concentration indicated on the label.
Repotting Repot into relatively small pots, or small species also on to blocks of fern. Make a very porous mixture of chopped fern or beech roots and sphagnum moss in the proportion 2 : 1.
Propagation Increase by division, which can best be done soon after flowering.
Pests and diseases Guard against aphids.

Dendrobium aggregatum
◐ ⊜ ◎ ⊛ ⊛ ▢
This bears clusters of five to fifteen golden yellow flowers, up to 3 cm (1 in) across, each with a hairy white lip and orange throat. It flowers from March to May.
Dendrobium chrysanthum
Syn. *Dendrobium paxtonii*. Golden-yellow flowers in late summer. There are two red patches on the lip.
Dendrobium chrysotoxum
◐ ⊜ ◎ ⊛ ⊛ ▢
Golden-yellow flowers with a brown patch on the lip appear in March–April.
Dendrobium fimbriatum
◐ ⊜ ◎ ⊛ ⊛ ▢
Eight to fifteen flowers hang in pendulous clusters in spring. They are clear orange-yellow, 5 to 6 cm (2 to $2\frac{1}{4}$ in) across. There is a frilly lip, pale yellow with orange yellow.
Dendrobium nobile
◐ ⊜ ⊖ ◎ ⊛ ⊛ ▢
This species flowers in winter and early spring. The flowers are pink to purple, slightly paler at the base, with a white and purple lip edged in whitish yellow and with an amethyst-coloured tip. It grows in a moderately heated greenhouse, but should spend its dormant season in a cool greenhouse.
Dendrobium phalaenopsis
A hothouse species with rose-pink to cherry-red flowers, 8 cm (3 in) across, growing in groups of four to twelve in loose clusters. The lip is veined with dark purple and has a dark throat.
Dendrobium superbiens
◐ ⊜ ◎ ⊛ ▢
Up to 70 cm (28 in) tall; the purplish-pink to red flowers appear from March to May. The lip is somewhat darker, with white scales.
Dendrobium thyrsiflorum
◐ ⊜ ◎ ⊛ ⊛ ▢
Flowers profusely from March to May, displaying multiflowered pendulous clusters of white flowers with orange-yellow lips, 2 to 5 cm ($\frac{3}{4}$ to 2 in) across.
Dendrobium wardianum
Flowers from January to March. The flowers grow on leafless stalks, usually in pairs. They are 8 to 10 cm (3 to 4 in) across, white and purple. They have a white lip with purple tip and an ochre-yellow throat with two purple patches.

Dichorisandra
Commelinaceae

Name Derived from *dis*, twice, *chorizo*, to divide, and *aner*, male. The anthers are two celled.
Origin There are approximately 30 species, originating in tropical zones of America.
Description Herbaceous perennial plant, often bearing clusters of attractive little flowers, but also grown for its multicoloured foliage. The stems are erect growing or pendulous, frequently branching. The flowers consist of three green or coloured sepals, usually equal in size, and three contrasting petals. They grow fairly rapidly.
Position The dichorisandra prefers a position in half shade in a hothouse with a high degree of humidity and is therefore a problem child in the living-room.
Care Make sure that the plant is never subjected to a low temperature. Variegated forms need more light than the green species.
Watering Water normally in summer. In winter the plant needs far less water.
Feeding From May to September feed

Dichorisandra reginae

every fortnight, using 1 teaspoonful of fertiliser to 3 litres (5 pints) of water.
Repotting Repot in a mixture of equal parts of peat, loam and leafmould and add some sharp sand.
Propagation Increase by division, from cuttings or from seed.

Dichorisandra reginae
◐ ⊜ ⓜ ⊛ ▢
With its erect-growing stalks, lanceolate dark green leaves with two silvery lengthwise stripes and a violet mid-rib, this is a most attractive variegated species with lavender-coloured flowers. This plant grows fairly slowly. It is easily increased from cuttings.
Dichorisandra thyrsiflora
This is the best-known green-leaved species. It is cultivated chiefly for its fine dark blue flowers which appear in late summer. In winter give the plant a rest by keeping it completely dry at a temperature of 15 to 18°C (59 to 64°F). Repot every three to four years when it starts into growth.

Didymochlaena truncatula

Didymochlaena
Aspidiaceae

Name From the Greek *didymos*, meaning double, and *chlaina*, cloak.
Origin This fern (the genus is represented by only one species) is found in tropical regions all over the world.
Description A particularly fine fern with doubly pinnate foliage, dark green or sometimes brownish, glossy and leathery.
Position Since the fern requires a high degree of humidity it is advisable not to grow it as a specimen plant, but to place it among other ferns in a mixed container. These plants thrive even in very shady spots. They prefer a moderate temperature.
Care The dormant season occurs between October and February. During this time the plant should be kept a little cooler, perhaps between 12 and 14°C (53 and 57°F). If it sheds part of its foliage in summer it means that the compost has not been kept sufficiently moist.
Watering During the growing season the fern should be watered generously. Use demineralised water or rainwater, preferably tepid, and keep the compost constantly moist. In the dormant season keep the plant a little drier and do not spray. At all other times it requires a high degree of humidity. When the new fronds uncurl it is particularly important to mist-spray several times a day, using tepid water.
Feeding In the growing season give a strongly diluted solution, possibly one third of the recommended concentration, once every fortnight.
Repotting When the plant is pruned at the end of the winter, repot in a mixture of standard potting compost and leafmould.
Propagation Increase from spores, which ripen indoors. They should be sown in a temperature of 24 to 26°F (75 to 78°F). It can also be increased by division.

Didymochlaena truncatula
● ⊜ ⓜ ⊛ ▢
Large, bipinnate leaves, glossy green and leathery. The blunt leaflets grow close together, and five to six oval spore clusters appear along the outer edge of the pinnae.

Dieffenbachia
Araceae
Dumb Cane

Name Named after someone called Dieffenbach, but it is not certain whether this was Joseph Dieffenbach, head gardener of the Botanical Garden in Vienna, who lived in the 19th century, or the 19th century Prof. J.F. Dieffenbach from Berlin, or Prof. E. Dieffenbach, who was an explorer.
Origin The genus includes about 30 species, originating in tropical regions of Central and South America.
Description They are evergreen perennial plants, grown for their magnificent foliage. Usually the leaves grow on firm stalks on a straight stem. They are large and irregularly flecked and streaked in green and creamy white. The flowers show clearly that the dieffenbachia belongs to the arum family. The plant is poisonous in all its parts. It causes skin irritation and also easily affects mucous membranes. The sap contains enzymes which act on albumen, needle-shaped calcium oxalate crystals and other poisonous matter causing pain. According to the Dutch Journal of Medicine, 121, No. 50, 1977, it is also possible that a proteolytic enzyme present in the plant may act like trypsin, which is said to release histamine. However, there is no cause for alarm, for of the 206 cases of dieffenbachia poisoning known in the Netherlands up to January 1977, not a single patient was lost, although two cats died after eating the leaves.

It is advisable to keep the plants out of reach of children and domestic pets and out of sight of mentally disturbed people. Children who have bitten into a leaf of the plant should be taken straight to hospital. Fortunately it has proved to be untrue that the dieffenbachia contains strychnine, as had been thought in the past.
Position In their natural habitat these plants are used to a humid atmosphere, warmth and filtered light. If you are able to reproduce these conditions indoors, the plants will give you a great deal of pleasure. Place them in a half-shady spot, where bright sunshine cannot reach. In poor light the marking of the foliage will suffer.
Care Even in winter the temperature must not drop below 15 to 18°C (59 to 64°F). Never put the plant in a draught, for this will make it more prone to pest infestation. The dormant season occurs

Dieffenbachia maculata

Dieffenbachia bowmannii 'Arvida'

Dieffenbachia × bausei

Dieffenbachia amoena 'Tropic Snow'

from September to March and during this time make sure that the development of new leaves is restricted to a minimum by watering moderately and not feeding.
Watering Give plenty of water during the growing period, using tepid, demineralised water, preferably rainwater. During the rest period, water moderately. The compost must never entirely dry out – this would result in brown edges to the foliage. It is advisable to use the deep-plate method to improve the atmosphere, for dieffenbachias need a high level of humidity throughout the year. Spray or mist-spray frequently and clean the plant regularly using warm water and, if it is difficult to remove the lime deposits, possibly some leaf gloss.
Feeding From March to August give a lime-free fertiliser solution every fortnight, following the instructions on the label.
Repotting Repot every year in spring, each time into a slightly larger pot. Make a friable and nutritious mixture, for instance comprising leafmould, clay and rotted cow manure in the proportions 3:1:1, plus a small quantity of peat. A few pieces of charcoal are also appreciated.
Propagation Old plants which have grown bare at the base may be improved if you cut them back to 10 to 15cm (4 to 6in) from the soil. Healthy plants will put forth new shoots in the course of time. The bare stems which you have removed may be cut into 8-cm (3-in) sections and tip cuttings can be taken from the leafy part. The cuttings are then rooted under glass in a temperature of 24 to 26°C (75 to 78°F). In the case of tip cuttings you can reduce evaporation by rolling the leaves, so minimising the surface, or alternatively removing half the leaf. Root the cuttings in peat, which may be mixed with sphagnum moss to ensure good drainage.

Air-layering is another good way of rejuvenating your dieffenbachia stock.
Pests and diseases Aphids, scale insects, mealy bugs and root mealy bug, red spider mite, thrips and root rot are all possibilities. However, if the plants are correctly cultivated they will rarely be subject to infestation.

Dieffenbachia amoena
◐ ⊜ ◎ ◎ ◎ ◎
This species develops very large leaves on a thick stem which may grow to over 1m (3ft) in height. The oblong leaves, 60cm (2ft) long, appear successively on stalks which at a later stage take on the appearance of stems. The foliage is dark green with white or cream marbling along the side veins. There are various strains: 'Tropic Snow' has more white spots.
Dieffenbachia × bausei
The 20-cm (8-in) long marbled stalks on dark green stems bear yellow-green leaves up to 30cm (1ft) long which are marked with a number of dark green and white patches. The margins are dark green as well.
Dieffenbachia bowmannii
Syn. *Dieffenbachia reginae*. This is the largest species; the leaves may grow as long as 75cm (30in). It has pale green stems, green stalks and dull green leaves with numerous dark green, and a few white, patches. 'Arvida' also has dull green leaves, but they are irregularly, though densely, flecked on the upper surface.
Dieffenbachia humilis
An all-green species which will thrive even in deepest shade.
Dieffenbachia imperialis
A vigorous grower, with three to four thick stems up to 60cm (2ft) long; the leaf stalks are 1cm (½in) across. The leaves grow to 60cm (2ft) in length and 30cm (1ft) wide. They are thick and leathery, dark green with irregular yellow-green marking.
Dieffenbachia leopoldii
Bright green, lilac-flecked leaf stalks grow from a short stem. The leaves are up to 25cm (10in) long and 6cm (2¼in) across and are dark green with a white stripe along the central vein.
Dieffenbachia maculata
Syn. *Dieffenbachia picta*. This has a vigorous stem, which may grow to 1m (3ft) in height. The leaves are heart shaped at the base, 40 to 60cm (16 to 24in) long and 20cm (8in) wide. There are a large number of strains, variously marked with spots and streaks. 'Jenmannii' has white bands between the lateral veins; 'Memoria' whitish streaks and spots, as well as grey-green patches, along the lateral veins.
Dieffenbachia seguine
This develops a strong green stem. The leaf stalks are largely sheath shaped, green, with white patches or streaks. It has oval to oblong leaves, variegated in a number of ways. 'Lineata' is white streaked; 'Liturata' has a white central vein, and 'Nobilis' is green flecked.

Dionaea
Droseraceae
Venus Fly Trap

Name Dionaea was one of the names of the Greek goddess Aphrodite.
Origin The original habitat of these carnivores was in the marshy regions near the coast of Carolina, U.S.A. The species is at present threatened, because tradesmen remove them from their natural environment without regard for the ecology, and distribute them all over the world in plastic pots. In our heated living-room they have little chance of survival and will die in one to two years. I would suggest that you do not buy these plants unless you can provide the conditions specified below.
Description The sessile leaves grow in rosettes; the blade is divided into two sections and is sensitive to the touch. The edges are covered in stiff hairs. As soon as the plant feels anything, the two halves of the leaf fold along the midrib and the marginal hairs interlink. If anything edible is caught in between, the leaf will not unfold until the prey has been digested. Otherwise they will separate after about half an hour.
Position Keep the plant in maximum light; sun is tolerated. Screen them around midday only on the hottest days. In winter they still require plenty of light; give them, if you can, 10 to 12 hours of light a day by artificial methods.
Care The plant should be kept as cool as possible. Although it will grow in a warm environment, it will not survive for long. Keep it at 3 to 10°C (37 to 50°F) in winter. It is best cultivated all the year round in an unheated greenhouse.
Watering Give it plenty of water, especially in summer. The compost must

This dionaea has caught a spider

never dry out. An atmospheric humidity of 80 per cent is essential. Indoors this can be achieved only by using the deep-plate method, and filling the space between the pot and its cover with damp sphagnum moss, then covering both plant and pot with a plastic bag. In a greenhouse it is much easier to provide the correct degree of humidity.
Feeding Do not feed the Venus Fly Trap.
Repotting Repot in March–April in a mixture of peat, moorland soil and sphagnum moss, which must first be thoroughly washed to get rid of the mineral salts. Cover the surface of the

Dionaea muscipula, the Venus Fly Trap

compost in more sphagnum, which should be kept thoroughly damp.
Propagation Increase by division, from leaf cuttings or from seed.

Dionaea muscipula
● ⊜ ◎ ◎ ◎
Rosette-forming carnivores with inverted heart-shaped leaves, bearing three hairs on either leaf section and large hairs along the edges. The flowers are white.

Dipladenia
Apocynaceae

Name Derived from the Greek words *diploos*, double and *aden*, gland.
Origin About 40 species are known, all natives of tropical regions of America.
Description Semi-shrubs and shrubs which frequently become climbers at a later stage. The leaves are opposite and the plants have large trumpet-shaped flowers in white, pink or purple.
Position They require a well-lit position in a temperate or warm greenhouse, but many people are able to grow magnificent plants indoors. Full sun is not tolerated.
Care When growth slows down in autumn, the plant enters its dormant season, which lasts until March. During this time the temperature should be kept at 13°C (55°F), and the plant watered only if it threatens to droop. In March begin by raising the temperature to 16°C (60°F) for a time and gradually increase it as the plant starts into growth. In the growing season plenty of fresh air must be provided. Since these plants flower on the current year's shoots, it is best pruned in the autumn. Often only 5cm (2in) of the young growth may be left to develop.

Dipladenia atropurpurea

Watering Water moderately during the rest period in winter. From March onwards gradually increase the water supply and give it plenty of water in summer, when it is warm. For this plant, too, the atmospheric humidity in the living-room presents a problem. Try to provide the highest possible degree with the aid of a humidifier or a plant spray. The fact that it can be done is proved by the multiflowered plants found in some private homes. Use lukewarm water both for watering and spraying. After it has flowered, decrease the water supply until the dormant season sets in.
Feeding From April to August the plant must be fed every week, using the fertiliser concentration recommended on the label. If you continue to feed for too long, the wood will not ripen properly and this will have a negative effect on flower production in the following season.
Repotting Repot every year in March, each time in a slightly larger pot. Make up a porous, nutritious compost and provide a drainage layer in the bottom of the pot. The mixture may consist of 2 parts leafmould, 2 parts well-rotted cow manure, 1 part clay, 1 part peat as well as a small amount of sharp sand.
Propagation In March–April take cuttings of young shoots with a heel attached. In June–July new plants may be grown from cuttings from mature stems, each with two leaves. The sections should be 7 to 8cm (2¾ to 3in) long and rooted at a minimum temperature of 25°C (77°F) in a mixture of fine leafmould and sharp sand. They should first be dipped in rooting powder.
The young plants must be brought into growth in a hothouse. In the living-room both the temperature and the atmospheric humidity will be too low.
Pests and diseases Leaf curl is the result of excessively dry air and too much light. Other troubles may be scale insects, red spider mite and mealy bug.

Dipladenia sanderi 'Rosea', the best known commercial strain

Dipladenia atropurpurea
◐ ⊜ ⓞ ⊛ ▢
A climber with smooth stems and pointed-oval green leaves up to 5cm (2in) long. The axillary inflorescence consists of two flowers, and the flower stalks are slightly longer than the leaves. The flowers are dark purple with a 5-cm (2-in) corolla tube, but unfortunately in cultivation it usually only flowers at a late age.
Dipladenia boliviensis
Syn. *Mandevilla boliviensis*. Another summer-flowering climber, with smooth stems. The shiny green leaves grow to 5 to 9cm (2 to 3½in) in length and there are trumpet-shaped, fragrant white flowers, 5cm (2in) across, with a yellow throat. They frequently appear in spring and early autumn as well as in summer.
Dipladenia eximia
A climber with reddish, smooth stems and short-stalked, 3- to 4-cm (1- to 1½-in) long, round-oval to elliptical leaves. Flowers of a bright rose-red colour, 6 to 8cm (2¼ to 3in) across, with a 5-cm (2-in) long, cream-coloured tube. The flowers grow in clusters of six to eight.
***Dipladenia* hybrids**
In the course of time a large number of hybrids have been developed. To mention only a few there are 'Amoena', with bright pink flowers, slightly darker in the centre and with a yellow throat; 'Rosacea', soft pink petals with a darker margin and a yellow throat; and 'Rubiniana', with a deep pink corolla, 8cm (3in) across, and somewhat bulging leaves.
Dipladenia sanderi
Syn. *Mandevilla sanderi*. Closely resembling *D. eximia*, this species has thicker leaves with a longer point.
The flowers may be as much as 7cm (2¾in) across, pink with a yellow throat. The latest and most vigorous hybrid is 'Rosea', with large, trumpet-shaped salmon-pink flowers with a yellow throat.
Dipladenia splendens
Syn. *Mandevilla splendens*. Like the previous species, this is a summer-flowering plant. It has smooth stems with almost sessile, pointed, elliptical leaves, 10 to 12cm (4 to 4¾in) long, heart shaped at the base and hairy on the reverse with conspicuous veins. Axillary flower clusters extend beyond the leaves; they consist of four to six rose-coloured flowers, 10cm (4in) across. The throat is deep pink and the outside white. *D. s. profusa* has even larger flowers, bright pink with a yellow-streaked throat.

Dipteracanthus
Acanthaceae

Name Derived from Greek words meaning double-winged. This refers to the two large bracts at the base of the calyx.
Origin Tropical South America, especially Brazil.
Description Small, herbaceous, tropical foliage plants with velvety, beautifully coloured leaves. Although they are chiefly cultivated for their foliage, the flowers are attractive as well.
Position In their native habitat in the tropical jungle they grow as ground cover, and they are used for the same purpose in greenhouses and plant containers. If they are kept in separate pots in the living-room they often have to contend with dry air and they are therefore much better planted in mixed containers, where the degree of humidity is always a little higher. They are also very suitable for bottle gardens and tanks. They prefer a semi-shady position.
Care These plants must be kept warm throughout the year. When your plant becomes unsightly make sure of its succession by taking cuttings.
Watering During the growing season water regularly, keeping the compost constantly moist. Water slightly less during the rest of the year, but the compost must never completely dry out. A high degree of humidity is essential. Do not spray directly on the foliage or it will become stained.
Feeding During the growing season give a dose of standard fertiliser solution once a fortnight.
Propagation Increase from cuttings, which will root readily under glass and with some bottom warmth; also from seed.
Pests and diseases Whitefly may appear.

Dipteracanthus devosianus
◐ ⊜ ⓞ ⊛ ▣
Syn. *Ruellia devosiana*. Dark green leaves 6cm (2¼in) long, with a cream-coloured central vein, are borne on more or less recumbent stems. The underside is purple. The flowers have a white corolla with lilac streaks.
Dipteracanthus makoyana
Syn. *Ruellia makoyana*. Soft stalks carry olive-green, often purplish, leaves with a fairly wide, branching, cream-coloured central streak; they are up to 7cm (2¾in) long. There are deep pink flowers.

Dipteracanthus makoyana

Dizygotheca
Araliaceae
Finger Aralia, False Aralia

Name From the Greek *dizyx* or *dizygos*, double-yoked, and *theke*, anther.
Origin This genus includes nearly 20 small shrubs and trees, which have their natural habitat in Australia and in some of the islands in the Pacific.
Description Evergreen trees and shrubs with finger-shaped leaves. The flowers have five sepals and five petals. They are cultivated for their vigour and their unusual foliage.
Position Give them as much light as possible throughout the year, but out of direct sunlight, except in the morning and evening. They make magnificent specimen plants, but are also very useful in plant combinations.
Care In the dormant season, lasting from October to February, the mercury must not drop below 15°C (59°F). The bottom temperature must be kept as constant as possible, at 18 to 20°C (64 to 68°F). Cold and wet feet are frequently fatal, especially to young plants which have not yet adapted to their environment. Lanky plants may be cut back to 10cm (4in), when they will develop fresh foliage. The prunings should be discarded; they cannot be used as cuttings.
Watering Water moderately in the growing season, preferably using tepid, demineralised water. In the dormant season water sparingly, but do not let the compost dry out. Maintain the highest possible level of humidity with the aid of a humidifier, by frequent spraying and by using the deep-plate method.

Dizygotheca veitchii 'Gracillima'

Young foliage in particular should frequently be sprayed. If the plant is kept in a cooler situation in the dormant season it should be sprayed less often.
Feeding During the growing season, from April to mid-August, give fertiliser solution at normal concentration once every three weeks.
Repotting Repot young plants every year, mature specimens every second or third year. Pot them each time in a slightly larger pot, in a proprietary compost or in conifer needle compost.
Propagation For an amateur it is not easy to increase these plants. Sowing in extra bottom heat may yield good results, but will only succeed if the seeds are very fresh.

Another method of propagation is to graft the plant on *Meryta denhamii* stock, but this is certainly a job for a specialist.

Dizygotheca veitchii, the common broad-leaved form

Dizygotheca veitchii 'Castor'

Cuttings hardly ever strike successfully.
Pests and diseases Direct sunlight and insufficient humidity frequently lead to infestation by red spider mite and scale insects. Lack of humidity also often causes the lower leaves to fall.

Dizygotheca elegantissima
Syn. *Aralia elegantissima*. Palmate leaves with seven to eleven narrow fingers, 11cm ($4\frac{1}{2}$in) long and 1cm ($\frac{1}{2}$in) wide, slightly pendulous, dark brownish green with a white to red midrib and a toothed to lobed margin. The leaf stalk has conspicuous white marking. It is probable that this species is the original form of the species *D. veitchii* mentioned below. There appear to be forms with narrower and with broader leaves. As the plant matures, the width of the foliage increases, and since the length does not increase in proportion the shape of the leaves eventually becomes quite different.
Dizygotheca kerchovei
Syn. *Aralia kerchovei; Dizygotheca kerchoveana*. An evergreen shrub with nine- to eleven-lobed finger-shaped leaves. The leaflets are oval to lanceolate, up to 8cm (3in) long and 2 to 3cm ($\frac{3}{4}$ to $1\frac{1}{4}$in) wide; bright green with a pale central vein, roughly and irregularly dentate. The leaf stalk is practically unmarked. The reverse of the leaves is reddish.
Dizygotheca veitchii
An evergreen shrub with an erect-growing pale brown stem. The 10- to 15-cm (4- to 6-in) leaf stalks bear nine to eleven spreading leaflets, up to 15cm (6in) long and 5cm (2in) wide, touching; bright green on the upper surface, reddish or green with fine brown veining on the underside. The margin is smooth and wavy. The central vein is pale in colour. There are spreading bracts at the base of the leaf stalks.

It is probable that the cultivar 'Castor' belongs to this species. This is a very small plant with compact habit and dentate leaves. Another cultivar is 'Gracillima', which bears extremely narrow leaves and resembles an immature *Dizygotheca elegantissima*. Unfortunately the nomenclature is still very confused and therefore the above may well be incorrect.

Dolichothele longimamma seedlings in a pot

Dolichothele
Cactaceae

Name From the Greek *dolichos*, long, and *thele*, nipple. If you look at the photograph you will realise that the name is apposite.
Origin The genus includes six species, originating in Mexico and Texas.
Description The plant readily produces offsets. It has a soft fleshy body and the flowers, usually yellow, have an elongated tube.
Position Give them a position in the best possible light throughout the year. Direct sunlight is tolerated well and is in fact essential to their development. Their attractive appearance makes them very suitable in a mixed cactus arrangement, where they help to give contrast, but they are also effective grown singly.
Care After being kept in a moderately warm environment throughout the spring and summer, they need a rest in a temperature of 5 to 10°C (41 to 50°F) in a cool greenhouse. Give them plenty of fresh air all the year round.
Watering Water sparingly throughout the year, but be particularly careful in the dormant season in winter, for these delicate plants rot easily. It is advisable to give only just enough water to prevent the plants from shrivelling up. In warm summer weather they may occasionally be mist-sprayed, but it is not essential.
Feeding The plant requires very little nourishment. During the growing season give a measure of special cactus fertiliser at the recommended concentration once or twice a month.
Repotting Repot preferably every year in spring, in a mixture of potting compost, sharp sand and clay or loam. A proprietary cactus mixture is also available.
Propagation Increase from seed.

Dolichothele camptotricha
A clump-forming, flattened spherical cactus with twisted thorns and conical tubercles. The white flowers are approximately 1.5cm ($\frac{1}{2}$in) across.
Dolichothele longimamma
Syn. *Mammilaria longimamma*. An unusual cactus with a flattened spherical body, up to 10cm (4in) tall, consisting of cylindrical tubercles, green with yellowish thorns. It produces large canary-yellow flowers.

Doryopteris palmata

Doryopteris

Sinopteridaceae

Spear Fern

Name Derived from the Greek words *dory*, spear, and *pteris*, fern.
Origin The genus includes about 35 species found in all tropical countries.
Description Ferns with small, undivided foliage, usually incised or forked, smooth and leathery. The spore clusters often occur in an uninterrupted band along the very edge of the leaves. It makes an attractive plant for mixed plant containers.
Position Place these ferns in a shady spot in a moderate to warm room. Since they require a high degree of humidity they are best used in combination with other plants, where the atmosphere is always somewhat more humid.
Care In winter it is advisable to keep these plants at a temperature of 12°C (53°F), but provided you spray frequently they may come to no harm in the warm living-room.
Watering In summer water generously when it is warm, less when the temperature is moderate. Make sure that the compost is always slightly moist to the touch. The plants require an atmospheric humidity of over 60 per cent. You will therefore have to spray frequently, use the deep-plate method or install a humidifier. Keep moderately moist in winter.
Feeding In the growing period feed once every 10 to 14 days, using a solution at normal concentration.
Repotting Use an acid mixture, for instance a proprietary compost to which some peat and leafmould has been added. These ferns are best grown in plastic pots to minimise evaporation.
Propagation Increase from spores.

Doryopteris palmata
Syn. *Doryopteris pedata palmata*. A compact species with fairly thick, leathery foliage. Fertile and sterile leaves are easily distinguished. Plantlets are developed on the leaves.
Doryopteris pedata
A small fern with thin, leathery, bright green foliage, palmate in shape. The pinnae are incised in their turn, creating a graceful appearance. As in the previous species, the leaves are borne on thin black stalks.

Dracaena reflexa 'Song of India'

Dracaena

Agavaceae

Dragon Tree

Name From the Greek word *drakaina*, a female dragon or snake.
Origin The 40 species of this genus are natives of the Canary Islands, tropical and subtropical Africa, Asia and in the archipelago between Asia and Australia.
Description A genus of vigorous, undemanding house plants, practically immune to pests and graceful in appearance. They are evergreen shrub-like plants or trees, which may grow to a great height in their natural habitat. Many of them resemble palms. They do not develop offsets. The leaves are lanceolate and, depending on the species, erect growing or trailing. There are green-leaved species as well as magnificent multicoloured species and strains, streaked or speckled. Most dracaena plants develop an inflorescence only in maturity. This consists of loose umbels or clusters of greenish-white or cream-coloured flowers, sometimes delightfully scented. The flower stalk appears just beside the growing point and the plant does not die down after flowering.

The plant is frequently confused with the cordyline, but the two genera are really quite distinct. The Dragon Tree has yellow to orange rootstock and does not produce offsets, whereas cordylines have white roots and *do* have offsets. In addition dracaenas have one seed in each anther cell, and cordylines have three.

The 'dead' wooden stems from which leaf sections appear are called 'Ti-plants'.

The dracaena was originally a hothouse plant, but present-day strains will thrive in both the greenhouse or in the living-room and offices.
Position Put them in a well-lit spot – about 3 m (10 ft) from the window is fine. They dislike direct sunlight at midday, especially between March and September, although morning and evening sun is tolerated. Variegated species, in particular, require plenty of light to maintain their colouring. Apart from these points the plants are tough enough not to languish in the shade.
Care Although most species may be kept in the same spot for years on end, it is best to give them an annual resting period in winter. The minimum winter temperature varies from one species to another: Both *Dracaena deremensis* and *Dracaena fragrans* require 13°C (55°F); *Dracaena godseffiana* and *Dracaena sanderiana* 10°C (50°F) and *Dracaena draco* 7°C (44°F). Brown leaf tips are the result of draughts, too little or irregular watering or overfeeding.
Watering Carefully balance the water supply, for too wet is as bad as too dry. Excess water in the bottom of the pot will soon cause root rot, so make sure there is a good drainage layer. The variegated *Dracaena* species especially suffer if the compost is too dry. From May to September water freely. During the cool resting period, from November to March, the Dragon Tree should be kept on the dry side, and in the intervening periods water sparingly. A moderate degree of humidity is enough for hardened plants, but when the plant first comes from the nursery or garden shop it is accustomed to a humid atmosphere. On arriving in your warm and dry living-room it is almost certain to lose some of its foliage and your pleasure may turn into annoyance. You can minimise the chances of such a tragedy by always buying a dracaena in spring, never in the autumn. As the days lengthen and the heating is gradually turned down, the growing conditions will constantly improve, whereas in autumn the opposite happens. You can increase the humidity by frequent spraying, preferably with rainwater. It is also very helpful occasionally to put the plant out in the rain in summer. By covering the compost with plastic or tinfoil you can prevent the soil ball becomine drenched. The deep-plate method is an excellent way of creating a moist atmosphere and an electric humidifier

Dracaena deremensis 'Warneckii'

Dracaena marginata

Dracaena fragrans 'Massangeana' in the form of a Ti-plant

Dracaena godseffiana

Dracaena sanderiana

will also give good results. Once a month wipe the leaves with damp cottonwool or a sponge. If the dirt is difficult to remove you can use a little leaf gloss, but do not use too much, as this would give an unnatural shine.

Feeding Once the plants are well into growth they may be fed every fortnight from April to August, using a solution at the concentration recommended on the label. Older plants may be fed every week.

Stop feeding in good time, to allow the plants to prepare for the dormant season.

Repotting April is the best time for this operation. Young plants should be repotted every year, older specimens only when the roots grow through the pot hole. Use a nutritious mixture such as leafmould, rotted cow manure and peat fibre in the proportions 2:1:1, plus a little sharp sand.

Propagation Increase from cuttings or from seed. Either tip cuttings or sections of bare stem with two to three eyes may be rooted in a mixture of equal parts peat and sand at a temperature of 21 to 24°C (70 to 75°F). Be patient when you are growing variegated species from cuttings. At first only green foliage will appear, as the coloured leaves only develop after a few months. *Dracaena draco* can also be grown from seed. The time it takes for the seed to germinate will vary.

Pests and diseases If the plant does not like the conditions in which it is grown it becomes fairly prone to red spider mite, thrips, scale insects and mealy bug. If it is properly cared for it will rarely suffer.

Dracaena cantleyi

At first sight this species resembles a sansevieria: the lanceolate leathery leaves are fresh green in colour and are marked with yellowish patches. They are stalkless and stemless, curled up in the early stages. It is a pity that this beautiful species is so seldom available.

Dracaena deremensis

This species can grow to a height of 5 m (16 ft). The leaves are up to 50 cm (20 in) long and 5 cm (2 in) wide. They are stalkless (that is, sessile), developing from a straight stem, sword shaped and dark green. 'Bausei' has a lengthwise white stripe on otherwise green leaves and 'Warneckii' has a green and white striped central band and narrow white lines along the margin.

Dracaena draco

This very robust species forms a tree-like stem bearing rosettes of sessile, sword-shaped dark green leaves. The lower leaves stand out horizontally or are slightly curved.

Dracaena fragrans

Resembling *Dracaena deremensis*, the leaves of this species are longer and broader. It is trunk forming and has fairly limp curving leaves. 'Lindenii' has foliage with creamy lengthwise stripes and wide yellow-green margins. 'Massangeana' has yellow-green streaks down the centre of the leaf. 'Victoria', with bright yellow stripes, is one of the finest. Mature plants sometimes produce delightfully scented flowers.

Dracaena godseffiana

Entirely different in appearance from the previous species. It forms shrubby growth with thin stems and pointed-oval, glossy green foliage with undefined cream marking. It flowers at an early age, producing greenish-yellow fragrant flowers, followed by red berries.

Draceana goldieana

A species only really suitable for the hothouse. It has a straight, slender stem bearing its leaves at regular intervals. These are stalked to 20 cm (8 in) long and 12 cm (4½ in) wide, green and shiny, with clear white crossbanding and spots.

Dracaena hookeriana

Forms a strong trunk bearing narrow green leaves, 80 cm (32 in) long. 'Latifolia' and 'Variegata' are variegated.

Dracaena marginata

A very robust species. It has narrow, red-edged leaves, to 40 cm (16 in) long. In 'Tricolor', syn. *D. concinna*, the foliage is striped in green, cream and red.

Dracaena reflexa

Readily develops more than one stem or branches and is therefore very decorative. The white variegated strain 'Song of India' is a splendid plant to possess.

Dracaena sanderiana

This has oval to lanceolate pointed leaves, green with pure white, yellowish and silvery lengthwise stripes.

Dracaena thalioides

A little-known species, conspicuous because of the long leaf stalks bearing the oblong, sharply pointed, furrowed leaves.

Dracaena umbraculifera

A hothouse plant, forming a trunk 1.75 m (almost 6 ft) in height and bearing a rosette of 100 to 200 sword-shaped leaves, 1 m (3 ft) long and up to 6 cm (2¼ in) wide at the midline.

A typical inflorescence of a dracaena

Dracaena fragrans 'Victoria'

Dracaena draco

Duchesnea indica, Indian Strawberry

Duchesnea
Rosaceae
Indian Strawberry

Name The genus was named after the French botanist A. N. Duchesne, 1747–1827.
Origin Only one species belongs to this genus, which originates in Indonesia and Japan.
Description It closely resembles the edible strawberry, *Fragraria × ananassa*, but the house plant has yellow instead of white flowers. As it makes such a large number of runners it is very popular as a hanging plant or as ground cover, and is also useful as a balcony plant. With its attractive red fruits it makes an irresistible house plant.
Position The Indian Strawberry requires a particularly well-lit position, since otherwise it will not flower. On the other hand direct sunlight turns the foliage yellow and the plant must therefore be screened during the hottest part of the day.

It prefers a moderately warm environment. In summer it may be moved to the garden or to a balcony.

It is almost hardy and, covered with a light blanket of straw or leaves the duchesnea can occasionally survive the winter out of doors.
Care Keep at 10 to 12°C (50 to 53°F) in winter. As a rule older plants die, but this is not a disaster, since so many new plantlets are developed.
Watering In summer water generously; always keep the compost moist, and ensure a moderate to high degree of humidity.
Feeding During the growing season give a dose of fertiliser solution at normal concentration once a fortnight.
Propagation Increase from seed by removing the seeds from the pseudo-fruits and sowing them in mid-April in some warmth. They germinate within a month. You can also pot up the offset plantlets.
Pests and diseases Red discoloration of the foliage indicates lack of moisture or nourishment.

Duchesnea indica

Indian Strawberry. A runner-forming plant with three-lobed green leaves and red pseudo-fruits.

Echeveria
Crassulaceae

Name Named after Atanasio Echeverria, a 19th-century Mexican botanical illustrator.
Origin The genus includes about 150 species, which occur mainly in an area stretching from northern California through Mexico to Peru.
Description These easily cultivated succulents are grown chiefly for the colouring of their foliage rosettes. In some species the vividly coloured flowers also play their part. The fleshy, spiralled rosettes are common to all species. Some species develop runners at the base. The leaves are usually not true green, but bloomed or hairy. There are stemless perennials as well as stemmed semi-shrubs and shrubs, branching or non-branching. The flower stalks usually do not develop from the centre, and the bell-shaped or urn-shaped flowers are borne on spikes, in clusters or racemes. They come in white, yellow, pink, orange or red or a combination of these colours. As a rule the plants flower in winter or in spring.
Position See that they are in the best possible light throughout the year, in summer in full sun. From May until the end of September the pots may be buried in a sunny, sheltered position in the garden. The finest colouring is developed in plenty of sun, and this also encourages flowering.
Care Echeverias need a resting period to be able to thrive. Non-winter-flowering species should be overwintered at 5 to 10°C (41 to 50°F). In winter they are prone to lose their leaves. If the plants become too bare, the tips may be used as cuttings. The old stem may also be used – see Propagation.
Watering In their growing season echeveria plants appreciate a fair amount of water, but it will do no harm if they are occasionally overlooked. The foliage contains sufficient moisture reserves and the roots are able to absorb more oxygen if the compost is not kept constantly moist. If the plants are kept cool in winter, give just enough water to prevent the rosettes drying out. Do not water directly on to the leaves; this may damage the waxy layer and stagnant water in the rosettes may lead to rotting. Root rot will occur if the compost is kept constantly moist. The dry atmosphere of a living-room is tolerated.
Feeding From March until August give a dose of cactus fertiliser once a month.
Repotting Repot in spring, young plants every year, older specimens every second or third year. Use a porous compost, adding extra sand to a proprietary mixture.
Propagation When a plant has grown bare, the top is often still in good condition and can be used as a cutting. Allow it to dry out for two days and then insert it in damp, sandy compost. The old stems may put out new shoots at the points where the leaves used to grow. When the shoots are large enough, remove them carefully, dry and pot them up. The species may also be grown from seed and if the plants develop runners, the offset rosettes can be separated off. Finally, new plants can also be grown from leaf cuttings. Choose thick, healthy leaves and cut them off without damaging the base, from which the new shoots will appear. After allowing them to dry out, root them in a sandy medium at a minimum temperature of 16°C (60°F).

Echeveria affinis

Dense rosettes consisting of 5-cm (2-in) long, 2-cm (¾-in) wide, brown to greenish leaves, convex below, flat on the upper surface. It has a composite inflo-

Echeveria flowers are usually borne on long stalks. This is the species *Echeveria harmsii*

Echeveria setosa

Echeveria agavoides

Echeveria secunda 'Pumila'

Echeveria agavoides 'Cristata'

rescence; the corolla is red in colour.

Echeveria agavoides
Agave-like rosettes up to 20 cm (8 in) across with grey-green leaves, up to 6 cm (2¼ in) long, the tip ending in a sharp brown point. Multiflowered plumes of red and yellow flowers appear in May–June.

Echeveria carnicolor
Grey-green rosettes, 8 cm (3 in) across, often with a blue or red tinge. It develops so many runners that it may also be used as a hanging plant. Numerous orange-red flowers are borne on long stalks.

Echeveria derenbergii
These form compact rosettes, 7 cm (2¾ in) in diameter. The grey-bloomed leaves curve inward in a draught, giving the rosette a spherical shape. They have red margins and a sharp red point at the tip, and the flowers are orange.

Echeveria elegans
Syn. *Echeveria perelegans.* Rosettes of up to 15 cm (6 in) across, consisting of thick, bluish-white leaves, sometimes with a violet tinge. The bloomed pink stalk bears pink and yellow flowers from March to July.

Echeveria gibbiflora
Large rosettes are formed at the top of up to 50-cm (20-in) stems. Thick grey-green leaves are bloomed with a blue or red haze and bright red flowers appear in autumn. Only cultivars are in cultivation, such as 'Metallica', with wider foliage, pale lilac pink in colour and with a fine bloom; 'Pearl of Nürnberg', very regularly shaped rosettes, lilac pink.

Echeveria harmsii
Up to 7-cm (2¾-in) wide rosettes are borne on branching stems. The green leaves, reddish in colour near the tip, are covered in short hairs. Large – up to 3-cm (1¼-in) – red and yellow flowers appear in groups of only one to three in May–July.

Echeveria peacockii
Rosettes up to 10 cm (4 in) across, with a bluish-white bloom. The margin of the leaves is often slightly reddish. Red, bloomed flowers are borne in a two-row raceme from April to July.

Echeveria pulvinata
Probably similar to *Echeveria leucotricha.* They form fairly loose rosettes, 15 cm (6 in) across, with reverse oval leaves, 4 cm (1½ in) wide at the tip, blunt or pointed, pale green, densely covered in white hairs and reddish along the margin. The flowers are red.

Echeveria purpusorum
Rosettes up to 10 cm (4 in) across, leaves to 4 cm (1½ in) long and 3 cm (1¼ in) wide, grey-green tinged with red, and about six red and yellow flowers on long stalks.

Echeveria secunda
This makes rosettes up to 15 cm (6 in) wide, with a heavy bloom and bluish-white leaves with a fairly sharp point. A profusely flowering species, with up to 20 red and yellow flowers to a stalk in April–May. A popular variety is *E. s. glauca*, known as Blue Hen and Chickens.

Echeveria setosa
Dense, sessile or short-stalked rosettes, 10 cm (4 in) across. Both sides of the leaf are coated in recurved white hairs, and there are red, yellow-tipped flowers from April to July.

Echinocactus grusonii, the Golden Barrel Cactus, is a very popular species

Echinocactus
Cactaceae
Hedgehog Cactus

Name The Greek word *echinos* means hedgehog. Because of their spreading thorns these cacti resemble to some extent a rolled-up hedgehog.
Origin After comprehensive reclassification within the cactus family, the genus *Echinocactus* now includes only seven species, all natives of Mexico.
Description It has a spherical to cylindrical habit, very slow growing. In their natural habitat these cacti can reach a diameter of nearly 1 m (3 ft). They are cultivated for the sake of their magnificent thorns. In the wild, flowers appear from the woolly and felty crown; as a rule they are yellow, scaled on the outside and encased in woolly hairs. In cultivation the plants rarely flower.
Position These cacti require as much light and sun as possible practically all the year round. They should be screened from full sunshine only in spring, when the plants start into growth. Give them plenty of ventilation in summer.
Care It is essential to give these cacti a rest from October to March, when they should be kept dry in a frost-free, well-lit environment at 5 to 10°C (41 to 50°F).
Watering During the growth period water moderately. Excess water must never be left in the saucer. From mid-August onwards decrease the water supply and if kept cool in winter keep them practically dry. Too much moisture causes rotting. The dry atmosphere of the living-room suits them very well.
Feeding In the active season give them a measure of cactus fertiliser at normal concentration once every ten days.
Repotting In order to develop their beautiful thorns they require heavy, nutritious compost, which must at the same time be porous. Use a cactus mixture or commercial potting compost with some extra sand and clay. But be careful: the roots break easily.
Propagation Sow in April in a temperature of 21°C (70°F) and cover the seeds with a thin layer of soil. The medium may consist of cactus compost or of a mixture of equal parts of sand, peat fibre and leafmould. The problems occur when the seedlings are pricked out: see Repotting.
Pests and diseases The most prevalent pests are mealy bug and root mealy bugs.

Echinocactus grusonii
Golden Barrel Cactus. A spherical, later slightly more cylindrical cactus which may grow very old and may then be nearly 1 m (3 ft) in diameter. The cactus body is dark green and multi-ribbed: 20 to 37 sharp ribs are no exception. It is covered in sharp, golden-yellow thorns and has a woolly crown. The areoles bear four central thorns and eight to ten radial thorns. In its native habitat the plant produces tubular yellow flowers, up to 5 cm (2 in) long, in spring. They grow in a circle at the top of the individual 'barrels'.

Echinocactus horizonthalonius
This species has the best chance of flowering in the living-room. It has a flattened spherical body, bluish green, with eight to thirteen ribs, covered in greyish-white bloom and up to 30 cm (1 ft) across. It has 4-cm (1½-in) long, magnificently coloured yellow thorns, straight or slightly curved, and tubular rose-red flowers up to 5 cm (2 in) long.

Echinocactus ingens
Syn. *Echinocactus grandis; Echinocactus palmeri.* A grey-blue cactus which may grow to enormous size. It is barrel shaped with numerous ribs and a woolly crown. The areoles bear eight straight radial thorns, 2 to 3 cm (¾ to 1¼ in) long, and one central thorn. Young plants are frequently crossbanded in red. The flowers are yellow. There are a number of varieties, which some people consider to be independent species, for example the varieties *ingens* and *palmeri.*

Echinocereus procumbens, not a very attractive cactus but it has a beautiful flower

Echinocereus

Cactaceae

Name From the Greek *echinos*, hedgehog, and the generic name *cereus*.
Origin The 60 species originate in the south-western part of the United States and in central and northern Mexico.
Description Columnar cacti, solitary or branched at the base, with fleshy, erect-growing or recumbent stems. There are green, practically bare species, but also densely thorned or haired species, which require different treatment. They have funnel-shaped flowers, often brightly coloured, with green stigmata, open during the day. This genus has spectacularly flowering species.
Position All species require plenty of light and sun for 365 days in the year. Green species may be moved to a sheltered, warm garden position in full sun in summer, provided you water them regularly when it does not rain.

The densely thorned and hairy species should remain indoors all through the year. Keep them in a warm, sunny and well-ventilated spot.
Care Hairy species must be kept warm in summer, but green species can be put in the garden. All of them enter upon a dormant season in October, when green species should be kept in a temperature of 5 to 10°C (41 to 50°F), and the others at 10 to 12°C (50 to 53°F).
Watering All species must be kept cool in winter and in that period should receive practically no water. In summer the green species require more water than the hairy and thorned plants. Spray regularly to prevent an attack by red spider mite. In general they require a moderate degree of humidity.
Feeding In the growth period give a dose of cactus fertiliser once a month.
Repotting Branching species need heavier compost than the others and should be potted in a cactus mixture with extra clay.
Propagation Species which put forth shoots are increased by cutting off the shoots and, after they have been allowed to dry out, inserting them in a mixture of sand and peat in the proportion 2:1. Other species can be grown from seed sown in April in a mixture of sharp sand and leafmould, at a temperature of 21°C (70°F).
Pests and diseases Keep a look out for red spider mite and rotting.

Echinocereus berlandieri

A clump-forming cactus with five- to six-ribbed stems, 1 to 2cm (½ to ¾in) across, six to eight bristly radial spines and one yellow-brown central thorn. It has purple-red flowers with a paler centre.

Echinocereus knippelianus
This has a very dark green, glossy body, 5cm (2in) in diameter, five ribbed with groups of one to three thin thorns, and carmine-pink flowers, 4cm (1½in) long.

Echinocereus pectinatus
An almost spherical blue-green species with 12 to 13 ribs and thorns in groups of three or four, yellow at first, later turning grey. It bears a profusion of white to rose-red flowers. Several forms are classified under this species, such as f. *frigidissimus*, the Rainbow Cactus. The thorns grow close together and are in zones of yellow, red, brown and white.

Echinocereus procumbens
Syn. *Echinocereus pentalophus*. This species branches profusely and has protruding tubercles and woolly areoles. Its thorns are horizontal and dark brown; the central thorn is 2cm (¾in) in length. There are purple flowers.

Echinocereus purpureus
Syn. *Echinocereus reichenbachii*. A columnar, branching species with brown-tipped white thorns and purple flowers.

Echinocereus salm-dyckianus
Dark green, branching at the base, this has a spreading habit and yellowish thorns with red tips. It produces a profusion of orange flowers.

Echinocereus scheerii
The stems are more slender and longer than those of the previous species and they are also a little more densely thorned. It bears long-lasting, deep pink flowers.

Echinopsis

Cactaceae

Name *Echinos* is Greek for hedgehog and *opsis* means 'like'.
Origin About 40 species occur in South America, chiefly in Argentina and Uruguay.
Description A spherical cactus, sometimes slightly columnar and at a later stage frequently profusely branching. It has continuous or notched ribs with many-thorned areoles. The funnel-shaped flowers are often enormous in proportion to the cactus body. They appear to one side of the crown and open wide; usually they are white and fragrant.
Position It appreciates plenty of light. In summer it may be kept in a well-ventilated position indoors or in the garden. In spring and summer it should be screened from the brightest sunlight. Turn the cactus as little as possible; as a rule the flowers develop on the shady side. After flowering it may be turned.
Care Let it spend the dormant season in a temperature of 5 to 10°C (41 to 50°F). Poor flowering is the result of excessive watering, too much nitrogen, or lack of phosphorus.
Watering Keep practically dry during its winter rest and water moderately in summer.
Feeding In the growth period give a dose of cactus fertiliser every ten days.
Repotting Repot into nutritious cactus compost.
Propagation Increase from cuttings or from seed.

Echinopsis eyriesii

Spherical at first, later more columnar in shape. It has 11 to 18 sharp ribs with short, dark brown spines and greenish-white, scented flowers, 20 by 12cm (8 by 4½in).

Echinopsis mamillosa
A spherical, yellowish-green body 25 to 30cm (10 to 12in) tall, with 21 notched ribs and yellow thorns, 1cm (½in) long. There are pure white flowers, up to 18cm (7in) in length.

Echinopsis obrepanda
A dark green globe with 16 to 25 ribs, dark brown thorns, paler at the base, and white flowers, red on the outside.

Echinopsis tubiflora
A more or less columnar body with 12 to 13 ribs, dark green, and pale brown thorns. The flowers are up to 24cm (9½in) long and 10cm (4in) across, greenish brown on the outside and white inside.

Echinopsis mamillosa

Elettaria

Zingiberaceae

Cardamom

Name Adopted from the name given to the plant on the island of Malabar.
Origin The genus is represented by two species, which originated in Sri Lanka (Ceylon), India and Indonesia. It is also grown on a large scale in Latin America.
Description A perennial plant with a thick rootstock. Its habit shows clearly that it belongs to the ginger family. The leaf-bearing stems are sterile. By rubbing the foliage a spicy aroma is released. The flower stalks do not bear leaves, only small scales and a plume-shaped inflorescence with a small stigma. The dried fruits and seeds are eaten in curry dishes, and they are also chewed after meals. This is supposed to stimulate digestion and it freshens the mouth. Cardamom is also used in the preparation of certain kinds of sausage and in medicinal preparations, in the manufacture of perfumes and of incense.
Position The plants must be placed in the best possible light throughout the year, but in spring and summer they

Elettaria cardamomum

should be screened against bright sunlight. They will thrive in a hothouse or in the living-room.
Care During the short winter days a temperature of 14 to 16°C (57 to 60°F) should be maintained.
Watering Keep the compost moderately moist, and water regularly. If the compost is too dry, the tips of the leaves often die off. The foliage is somewhat leathery and the dry living-room atmosphere is tolerated fairly well.
Feeding In the active season give a dose of fertiliser solution at normal concentration every ten days.
Propagation Increase from seed or from tip cuttings.

Elettaria cardamomum

A fleshy, horizontal rhizome with densely leaved stems which may grow to 3m (10ft) in height. It has a short-stalked leaf, smooth on the upper surface and slightly hairy underneath, and bears white flowers with a blue and white striped, yellow-edged lip.

Elisena longipetala

Elisena
Amaryllidaceae

Name Named after Napoleon's sister, Princess Elise.
Origin Three species, which closely resemble each other, occur in the Andes Mountains in Peru.
Description The plant is related to the genus *Hymenocallis* (q.v.), but in the genus *Elisena* the flower tube is shorter.
Position The bulbs grow in summer and can therefore be kept in the living-room.
Care The bulbs, which are available from specialist firms, are potted in February or March. Cultivation is similar to that of the hippeastrum (Amaryllis), the difference being that the foliage need not entirely die down in winter. However, it needs a fairly strict resting period starting in October and lasting until early spring when the minimum temperature should be 15°C (59°F).
Watering Always keep the compost moderately moist in summer and in winter water very sparingly, so that part of the foliage turns yellow. It is advisable to use rainwater.
Feeding In summer give some fertiliser solution every fortnight, especially if the plant has not been repotted in spring.
Repotting This need not be done every year, but the topsoil must be replaced every spring. Always use a mixture of standard potting compost and pulverised clay or loam, in proportions of $\frac{1}{3}$ loam, $\frac{1}{3}$ leafmould, $\frac{1}{6}$ sharp sand and $\frac{1}{6}$ rotted cow manure. Make sure there is a good drainage layer in the bottom of the pot.
Propagation In the course of time offset bulbs will develop. These should be removed when the plant is repotted, since they would otherwise exhaust the parent bulb, and they can then be grown in separate pots until they flower, which will take several years.

Elisena longipetala
In appearance this is practically identical to the hymenocallis. It has a flattened flower stalk up to 1m (3ft) long, ending in six white flowers, each one up to 7cm ($2\frac{3}{4}$in) across, with recurved, undulate petals.

Epidendrum
Orchidaceae

Name From the Greek words *epi*, upon, and *dendron*, tree, to indicate that they are epiphytes.
Origin The genus includes between 500 and 1000 species, all natives of tropical and subtropical regions in America.
Description There is considerable variation in the size and shape of the plants and the colour and size of the flowers. Some species have pseudobulbs with a number of leathery leaves while others have rush-like stems, often densely covered in foliage. They either have a terminal inflorescence, erect growing or curved, with individual flowers, or several flowers in racemes or spikes. The lip is usually larger than the sepals or petals. The majority flower between February and November.
Position Many epidendrum species require plenty of light (some even need sun) to be able to flower, and they also like plenty of fresh air. Apart from this the following general rule may be applied: species with oblong pseudobulbs require a cool to temperate environment while species with round to oval pseudobulbs belong in a mod-

Epidendrum Rainbow hybrid

Epidendrum radicans 'Cross of Christ'

erately heated greenhouse or in the living-room, and epidendrum species with leafy stems need plenty of room and a moderate to high temperature. All species are easy to grow in the greenhouse or in flower windows, and with some care they can be kept in the living-room.
Care In addition to the rule which divides the species according to their temperature requirements, it may be said that species with strong, hard pseudobulbs require a dormant season from November to March. In this period they should be watered as little as possible. Hothouse species are kept at 18°C (64°F); those belonging in the temperate greenhouse at 12°C (53°F). Species with softer pseudobulbs and thick stems should be kept slightly moist throughout the year.

Epidendrum ciliare

Watering In general little water should be given: water plants grown in clay pots twice a week, those in plastic pots once a week. In sunny weather during the growing season they may be given more. In the dormant season they should have just enough water to prevent the pseudobulbs drying out. In winter 50 per cent atmospheric humidity is enough, but in summer it must be over 60 per cent. Mist-spray in sunny weather, and preferably use demineralised water both for watering and spraying.
Repotting These orchids may be cultivated on tree bark, in orchid baskets or in pots. They like osmunda fibre, sphagnum moss and beech leaves in the proportions 4:2:1.
Propagation Increase from seed and by division, and the thick-stemmed species can be grown from cuttings.
Pests and diseases Scale insects may be troublesome.

Epidendrum ciliare
Spindle-shaped pseudobulbs up to 25cm (10in), with two leaves. The loose racemes of four to eight flowers appear in winter. The bracts are often sticky to the touch. The narrow petals are greenish yellow and the lip is white, with fringed side lobes.
Epidendrum cochleatum
Oblong pseudobulbs, 12cm ($4\frac{1}{2}$in) long, with two pointed leaves. It flowers from November to February. The racemes of five to eight fragrant flowers protrude beyond the leaves. They have very pale green petals and a dark violet lip with yellow marking.
Epidendrum × obrienianum
A cross between *Epidendrum evectum* and *E. ibaguense*, this has firm, long, climbing stems bearing numerous leaves. The compact, umbel-shaped inflorescence consists of a considerable number of carmine-red flowers, 3cm ($1\frac{1}{4}$in) across. The Rainbow hybrids, with flowers ranging between white and dark purple, belong to this group.
Epidendrum radiatum
The pseudobulbs are up to 10cm (4in)

Epidendrum cochleatum

long and have two to three leaves. It flowers from May to July, bearing erect-growing or pendulous multiflowered racemes of white-petalled flowers with a purple-veined lip.
Epidendrum radicans
A thick, leafy stem, which grows to at least 1m (3ft), bears fleshy, oblong, pale green leaves. The long-stalked, dense inflorescence consists of numerous orange-red flowers with yellow marking on the fringed lip. The main flowering season is February–May.
Epidendrum stamfordianum
This has hard, spindle-shaped pseudobulbs with two to four leaves. It flowers in March and April, bearing axillary racemes of numerous fragrant yellow flowers, 4cm ($1\frac{1}{2}$in) across, with purple-brown blotches; the lip is yellow to white.
Epidendrum vitellinum
Oval pseudobulbs, up to 9cm ($3\frac{1}{2}$in) long, with two leaves, it flowers from October to December, producing terminal racemes of orange-red flowers with a yellow lip. In 'Majus' the clusters are denser and the flowers are larger and more brightly coloured.

Epiphyllum

Cactaceae

Orchid Cactus

Epiphyllum hybrid 'Pride of Bell'

Name From the Greek words *epi* and *phyllon*, respectively meaning upon, and leaf. This refers to the fact that the flowers are borne on the foliage.
Origin Their natural habitat is in Central and South America, especially in Mexico. They grow together with other epiphytes on the trees in tropical rain forests and they therefore require a more humid environment and less sun than most other cacti.
Description The stems of these shrub-like epiphytic cacti are round at the base, but otherwise the long notched stems are leaf shaped. The foliage has been reduced to small bristles growing from the notches. The magnificent flowers appear only on stems at least two years old. In spite of their spectacular inflorescence and the ease with which they may be cultivated, they are not all that easy to obtain. The reason may be that flowering plants do not like being moved and in their non-flowering state they are anything but attractive. In recent years the choice has been enriched with a large number of hybrids in all sorts of colours, varying from white and salmon pink to carmine red. Bicoloured species especially are popularly referred to as 'Orchid Cacti'.
Position These cacti require plenty of light, but dislike sunlight. In good weather they may be given a warm and sheltered position in the garden. If they are kept in the living-room in summer you should see that they are well ventilated. In early autumn the plants should be brought inside and they then enter their resting season. Once an epiphyllum has been given its own position it should be turned as little as possible, for any buds it may bear would certainly drop. In strong sunlight or bright light the foliage may turn red.
Care In winter the plant prefers a temperature of 8 to 10°C (46 to 50°F), but lower temperatures are tolerated. The dormant season lasts from November till February. It is advisable also to give the plant a short rest each time just after it has flowered. You will encourage flowering by stopping the longest stems, as well as by giving the plant a rest. Lanky and old stems should be removed in spring, and long stems must be staked. Severe temperature fluctuations between night and day will cause the buds to drop.
Watering The roots like to be kept in a slightly moist medium. Water freely in the growth period, using tepid, demineralised water or rainwater. In the dormant season water sparingly, depending on the temperature, then gradually increase the water supply in spring and reduce it in autumn. Provide a fairly high degree of humidity in the active season. Often the plant will indicate that the humidity is correct by developing aerial roots, but in the dormant season it will accept a low degree of humidity. In summer too little water and too dry an atmosphere will lead to reddening of the foliage.
Feeding In spring and summer feed generously, using a cactus solution at normal concentration. Too high a concentration will cause reddening of the stems; underfeeding causes bud fall.

Epiphyllum crenatum

Germinated seeds inside a ripe fruit

Repotting This should be done as rarely as possible, since it has an adverse effect on flowering. Use a light mixture, nutritious and rich in humus, perhaps a standard potting compost mixed with extra clay, sand, sphagnum moss and peat.
Propagation Increase from seed or from cuttings consisting of 10-cm (4-in) stem sections. Make an oblique cut at the base, just below the areoles. Leave the cuttings to dry for a week before inserting them to a depth of 1 to 2 cm (½ to ¾ in) in sand and peat. Water sparingly and do not provide bottom heat.
Pests and diseases Red spider mite and mealy bug may appear if the air is too dry in summer. Excess moisture in winter causes root rot.

Epiphyllum crenatum

Syn. *Phyllocactus crenatus*. A shrub up to 60 cm (2 ft) tall with stiff, flattened, fleshy and deeply notched joints. At the base the joints narrow to a thin stem. The structure can be seen if you hold a stem against the light or cut it across. The actual stem is in the centre and develops lateral shoots at regular intervals; these end in the areoles which can be seen on the surface. The whole construction is encased in the fleshy leaf tissue. The very large, funnel-shaped flowers with their long thin tube appear from the areoles. All the flowers are up to 22 cm (8¾ in) in length and are greenish yellow on the outside and creamy white inside. A large number of hybrids in all possible colours are available.

Epiphyllum hybrids

These are the results of crossing *Epiphyllum* species with species of *Nopalxochia*, *Heliocereus* or *Selenicereus*. In most cases the stems are erect, sometimes triangular, sometimes winged, flattened, or with a crenate or wavy edge. The large flowers have a long tube and frequently a trumpet-shaped margin.

There are literally hundreds of hybrids, many of them individually named, in shades of lilac, red, orange and, of course, white.

Episcia
Gesneriaceae
Carpet Plant

Name The Greek word *episkos* means shady. Plants belonging to this genus prefer shady spots.
Origin There are about 40 species, belonging mainly in tropical areas of South and Central America, where they grow in the shade of the trees in damp and warm rain forests.
Description Hairy, occasionally bare, herbaceous perennials or shrubs with a short, thick centre stem. They readily produce large numbers of runners. The leaves are opposite and they have axillary flowers, growing singly or in small groups, white, bluish or red. Sometimes the petals are smooth edged, in other species they are fringed. The plants are grown both for their fine foliage and for their sometimes vividly coloured flowers.
Position They prefer a well-lit situation, without direct sunlight, to fairly deep shade. Because of their need for warmth and humidity they are particularly suitable for cultivation in the hothouse, in flower windows and in mixed plant containers, where they may be grown either as ground cover or as hanging plants.
Care In winter the temperature must not fall below 16°C (60°F). Keep the plant warm throughout the year. Remove dead flowers.
Watering Water regularly, always keeping the compost slightly moist. High humidity is particularly necessary when the temperature is high.
Feeding In the period of active growth feed every fortnight. Use a solution at the concentration recommended on the label.
Repotting Repot preferably in porous forest soil, such as conifer needle compost with a little rotted cow manure, but they can also be grown in standard potting compost with the addition of a little extra peat.
Propagation They are easily increased from leaf cuttings or stem cuttings or by cutting and potting the plantlets appearing on the nodes of the runners. The temperature must be at least 20°C (68°F).

Episcia reptans

Episcia cupreata 'Silver Queen'

Episcia lilacina

Episcia cupreata
Creeping Plant or Flame Violet. It has long branching stems with round to oval, or slightly elliptical leaves with rough hairs on the upper surface, brownish dark green to coppery, whitish along the centre vein. The reverse is reticulate, reddish. There are scarlet flowers in summer. Forms which deviate from the species in size and leaf marking are 'Emerald Queen', 'Silver Queen', 'Acajou', 'Frosty' and 'Metallica'.
Episcia dianthiflora
Lace Flower Vine. A low-growing plant with long runners and oval dentate leaves 3 to 4 cm (1 to 1½ in) in length, it bears white flowers with fringed margins in summer. These sometimes hardly emerge from the foliage.
Episcia punctata
Syn. *Drymonia punctata*. A semi-shrub with succulent, erect-growing stems and diamond-shaped to oval-pointed leaves, roughly toothed and of a succulent green. The flowers grow singly on long axillary stalks; they are creamy yellow with violet patches, hairy and fringed.
Episcia reptans
Syn. *Episcia fulgida*. Long, branching runners with elliptical dark green or brownish, fluted leaves, up to 8 cm (3 in) and a long silvery-green centre vein. In the lateral veins this colour fades towards the margin. The reverse is reddish. It bears bright red flowers in summer.

Erica gracilis will flower out of doors from September to December

Erica
Ericaceae
Heather

Name Ancient Greek writers always referred to the heather as *ereike*.
Origin About 500 to 600 species are known and the majority are natives of South Africa. A few species are found in the high mountains elsewhere in Africa and in Mediterranean countries. Sixteen species belong in Europe and most of these are hardy.
Description Evergreen shrubs and semi-shrubs, some of which are used in heath gardens, others as indoor plants. The needle-like leaves grow in whorls round the stems. Bell-shaped, tubular or globe-shaped flowers are borne in terminal racemes; they are white, pink, purple or bicoloured. The four-sepalled calyx is usually much shorter than the corolla.
Position Put them in a well-lit place, but out of the sun. In summer they are best taken outside. Since they like to be kept cool, they are suitable for use on a balcony or a terrace. *Erica gracilis* is particularly suited for this purpose; it may provide colour even after a frost. The general rule is the cooler they are kept, the longer they will last.
Care Keep erica plants at 6 to 8°C (43 to 46°F) in winter. After flowering remove the flower clusters and slightly cut back the stems, but never remove more than a third. With the species *Erica gracilis* you would do better not to try to overwinter these plants: they are extremely sensitive to mildew. The other species mentioned may also disappoint you in this respect.
Watering Water moderately with demineralised water or rainwater. If this is not available, then repot every year to remove excess minerals.

In winter, when the plant is kept cool, water sparingly. In summer spray frequently.
Feeding Not necessary, but it will do no harm to give a dose of fertiliser solution every two weeks from May to September, using half the recommended concentration.
Repotting They detest lime, so use a lime-free compost or conifer needle compost, possibly mixed with peat and lime-free sand.
Propagation Take cuttings in July–August or January–March. These can be rooted under glass in a mixture of sand and peat, at a temperature of 16°C (60°F).

Erica x willmorei

Pests and diseases They may suffer from mildew.

Erica gracilis
Urn-shaped white or rose-red flowers are borne in winter, up to 50 cm (20 in) in height.
Erica hyemalis
White, salmon-pink or rose-red flowers appear from February onwards, tubular in shape, widening at the top.
Erica ventricosa
This has white or lilac flowers in summer.
Erica × willmorei
Clusters of tubular red flowers appear in spring.

Erythrina crista-galli, the Coral Tree, may be put out of doors in summer

Erythrina

Leguminosae

Coral Tree

Name From the Greek word *erythros*, red.
Origin The genus includes more than 100 species, which occur in tropical and subtropical areas throughout the world.
Description Non-hardy, perennial trees, shrubs and semi-shrubs, often with thick, thorny branches, and with three-lobed to pinnate deciduous leaves. They bear magnificent red flowers growing in groups or pairs, together forming dense clusters. In contrast to several other members of the family, the flag hangs downward in the erythrina, the wings are practically lacking and the keel curves towards the flag. The flowers are pollinated by birds: the American species by colibris and the African by honey birds.
Position The Coral Tree is best grown as a tub plant. In the warm summer months it can be put out of doors in the garden, on the terrace or on a draught-free balcony. From October to April the plants undergo a strict dormant season and should be kept in a cool greenhouse, conservatory or garage. Put them in the brightest possible light – sun is tolerated well.

Well cared-for Coral Trees may grow to a considerable age, and the plants frequently form part of the legacy of elderly plant lovers. A manageable size can be maintained by annual pruning in spring.
Care The plant develops underground tubers which may be planted out in the garden and lifted early in autumn, to overwinter in a cool greenhouse. A more practical method is to cultivate them in plastic-covered wire baskets, which make it easier to lift the plants without damaging the roots. I always keep my own Coral Tree in an enormous earthenware pot and this works very well. In winter it is kept among other tub plants at a temperature of 4 to 7°C (39 to 44°F). In spring the shoots are cut back to 15cm (6in) from the base and in April we rouse the plant from its rest by increasing the temperature, giving a little water and possibly providing some bottom heat.

From the end of May onwards, when the plants have hardened, they can be put outside. New shoots develop with incredible rapidity. In September, before the first night frost, plants should be brought indoors.
Watering Do not give a single drop of water in the dormant season. Start watering in April and at the same time gradually increase the temperature. Give plenty of water in the growing and flowering seasons, then gradually reduce the water supply when flowering is over, and stop watering from October onwards. If the plant is kept in the greenhouse in summer, it should be sprayed from time to time and you should provide plenty of fresh air. Screen on particularly warm days.
Feeding In the period of active growth they can take quite a lot of nourishment. Give them a weekly dose of fertiliser solution at the recommended strength. Stop feeding from early August on.
Repotting Use a nutritious, sandy mixture, for instance a proprietary compost with an extra measure of clay and sand.
Propagation Increase from seed. The seeds germinate fairly easily, but it will take three to five years before the plants will flower. The plants may also be increased by division, or by taking heeled cuttings from young shoots, which are rooted in equal parts of sand and peat in 20 to 25°C (68 to 77°F).
Pests and diseases Red spider mite is the chief pest to look out for.

Erythrina crista-galli
A semi-shrub which in our climate may reach a height of about 1.5m (5ft). The branches die down in autumn. In spring the woody rootstock develops new stems, bearing hooked thorns. The three-lobed, pale green leaves grow horizontally on the stems and coral-red flowers are borne in loose racemes. 'Compacta' is compact in habit.

Espostoa

Cactaceae

Name Named after N. E. Esposto, a 20th-century Peruvian botanist.
Origin Three or four species originate in a region between northern Peru and southern Ecuador.
Description A cactus which, like the well-known Old Man Cactus, is surrounded by fine hairs. Espostoa is columnar in shape, sometimes reaching 4m (13ft) in height, or branching at the base, giving the plant a candelabrum-like appearance. The body is multi-ribbed and densely haired. The flowers are bell shaped to funnel shaped and appear from the side of a shoot.
Position Always provide it with plenty of warmth and sun. Nature gave the plant its fine hairs to protect it from bright sunlight, so it will tolerate quite a lot.
Care In winter these cacti like to be kept slightly warmer than most other cactus plants – the minimum temperature is 15°C (59°F). If it is found that they are not thriving on their own root system, they can be grafted on to *Trichocereus spachianus* stock.
Watering Water moderately during the growing period, sparingly in the winter months. A low level of humidity is sufficient, but indoors it is advisable to mist-spray occasionally when the temperature is high.
Repotting Repot into nutritious, porous compost. Cactus compost is satisfactory.
Propagation Increase from seed.

Espostoa guentheri
Syn. *Cephalocereus guentheri*. The body is covered in yellow to red thorns and branched at the base. At a later stage a woolly mass of hairs twists round the body and bristly, brownish-red thorns, 6cm (2$\frac{1}{4}$in) long, develop.
Espostoa lanata
Syn. *Pilocereus lanata*. In cultivation this species is unbranched and grows to 1m (3ft). It is so densely and closely covered in hairs that the thorns can hardly be felt.
Espostoa melanostele
Syn. *Cephalocereus melanostele; Pseudoespostoa melanostele*. Shrub-like habit; the plant branches at the base. Felty and white at first, it is later covered in brown-black hairs.

Espostoa lanata

Eucharis

Amaryllidaceae

Amazon Lily

Name The Greek word *eucharis* means agreeable. This refers to the graceful white flowers.
Origin The 10 species are natives of Colombia, where they grow mainly in the Andes range.
Description In addition to their bulb all species have a corona in common, consisting of broadened filaments. Most species have scented flowers, which to some extent resemble a narcissus. In the second half of the last century the eucharis was sometimes grown for cutting, but today it is sporadically available as a pot plant. At weddings it may make its appearance as a buttonhole, replacing the ubiquitous carnation. The flowers are also sometimes used in bridal bouquets.
Position The plants should be placed in a well-lit position where they can be screened from sunlight.
Care Planted out with bottom heat on the staging of a hothouse, they will flower three times a year. If they are cultivated in pots they grow less rapidly.

Eucharis grandiflora

Watering Plant out in March or in August, and at first water very sparingly. Give more water when the plant has started into growth and feed weekly. Keep the humidity high by frequent spraying. At night the temperature should be between 15 and 18°C (59 and 64°F); in the daytime 20°C (68°F), slightly cooler when the plant is in flower. After flowering the plant should be given a month's rest, during which it is watered sparingly. When it starts into growth once more, increase the temperature before giving it more water.
Repotting Repot once every three years. Plant the bulb 4 to 5cm (1$\frac{1}{2}$ to 2in) below the surface, preferably in a mixture of leafmould, rotted turves, sharp sand and rotted cow manure in the proportions 3:2:1:1.
Propagation Usually a large number of offsets are produced. These can be removed and potted up separately. They may flower after being cultivated in bottom heat for a few years.

Eucharis grandiflora
Syn. *Eucharis amazonica*. A perennial which may grow to 50cm (20in). The spherical brown-skinned bulbs develop fresh green, slightly undulate, pointed leaves, 12 to 16cm (4$\frac{1}{2}$ to 6$\frac{1}{2}$in) wide and at least 30cm (1ft) long. They may flower three times a year, in winter, spring and summer. The flowers have pure white petals and a greenish-white corona.

Eucomis bicolor, a summer-flowering bulb

Eucomis
Liliaceae
Pineapple Flower

Name From the Greek *eu*, beautiful, and *kome*, tuft, crest.
Origin About 10 species are known, all natives of South Africa.
Description These are bulbous plants and the bulbs are usually fairly large. They have sessile strap-shaped leaves and greenish flowers in dense clusters. The inflorescence bears a tuft of green bracts, more or less like the pineapple.
Position Stand the plants in a sunny spot on the terrace or balcony or in the garden.
Care Pot in February and bring into growth with the aid of some bottom heat. Then keep them in a cool, well-ventilated position at a temperature of 8 to 10°C (46 to 50°F) until the end of May. They may now be placed outside, and remember that they will grow more rapidly if planted out than if kept in their pots.
Watering Water generously in summer. After flowering gradually decrease the water supply. In winter they should be kept entirely dry in an unheated greenhouse.
Feeding During the growing and flowering seasons feed once every 10 days, using a solution at normal concentration.
Repotting Use a mixture of pulverised loam, leafmould and rotted cow manure.
Propagation Increase from offset bulbs or from seed which will take two to three years to produce flowering plants.

Eucomis bicolor
This forms rosettes of five to six strap-shaped leaves with a wavy margin, 60cm (2ft) long and 10cm (4in) wide. The 50-cm (20-in) long flower stalk bears a spiked inflorescence consisting of pale green florets with purple-edged bracts, topped by a tuft of green bracts.

Eugenia
Myrtaceae
Fruiting Myrtle

Name Named after Prince Eugenius of Savoy, 1663–1736.
Origin Nearly 1000 species are found in tropical and subtropical regions throughout the world.
Description Evergreen trees and shrubs with opposite or, less frequently, alternate leathery leaves, exuding an aromatic scent when rubbed or bruised. The flowers grow in the axils of the leaves, either singly or in small groups. They are four or five petalled, white or cream coloured. In many species the fruit consists of a berry or stone fruit.
Position Keep in winter in a cool greenhouse and in summer in a sunny, sheltered position in the garden – out of the wind, to which they are very sensitive. They also look very attractive on a terrace or on the balcony. Hothouse species must naturally be kept in a heated greenhouse in winter, and can stay there in summer or be brought indoors.
Care Cold greenhouse species are grown as tub plants and should be left to overwinter at 5°C (41°F) in a cool greenhouse, conservatory or orangery. This promotes flower formation. If they grow very vigorously it is advisable to tie up some of the heavy branches. Cut the plants back a little after flowering. Hothouse species must be kept warm throughout the year, in winter at a minimum temperature of 14°C (57°F).
Watering Always use demineralised water. Species for the cool greenhouse must not be left to dry out entirely in winter, since this would cause too much foliage to fall. Both the hothouse species and the cold greenhouse species must be watered freely in summer. They require a moderate degree of humidity. Sponge the leaves regularly.
Feeding Feed generously in the growing and flowering seasons, once every ten days until approximately mid-August, using the recommended concentration.
Repotting Repot in a mixture made up of rotted turves rich in humus, leafmould, sand and some moorland soil and manure. Young plants must be repotted every year, older specimens every second year.
Propagation In the case of cold greenhouse species half-woody cuttings can be taken in spring, and rooted at a temperature of 12 to 16°C (53 to 60°F). It is also possible to take cuttings in autumn, but these rarely survive the winter without problems. It takes a long time to root cuttings of hothouse species. This should be done in March in a medium consisting of equal parts of sand and peat with a bottom temperature of 25 to 35°C (77 to 95°F).
Pests and diseases Eugenias may be plagued by scale insects, mealy bug, thrips and whitefly.

Eugenia myriophylla
A small, slow-growing, densely branched shrub. The small linear leaves are scattered in groups of three or are opposite and are dark green, short stalked, and up to 4cm (1½in) long and 3cm (1in) wide. Young twigs are initially covered in downy hairs.

Eugenia paniculata
Syn. *Syzygium paniculatum*. A tall shrub or tree, which may grow to more than 10m (33ft) in height. The colour of young leaves and twigs is a beautiful red. Mature leaves are up to 7cm (2¾in) long, dark green and glossy, oblong to lanceolate, and short stalked. In spring white flowers, 2cm (¾in) across, emerge from the foliage, followed by egg-shaped rose-red fruits. The variety *australis* remains smaller and is the form most often cultivated.

Eugenia uniflora
A shrub or small tree with 5- to 10-cm (2- to 4-in) long, oval or slightly lanceolate, practically sessile leaves, round at the base, pointed at the tip. The flowers grow singly on long stalks; they are white and faintly scented and are followed by 1- to 2-cm (½- to ¾-in) long edible fruits. This is a rare plant.

Eugenia paniculata

Euonymus
Celastraceae
Spindle Tree

Name Adopted from the Greek plant name *euonymus*.
Origin The 170 species originate mainly in Asia, Europe, North and Central America and Malagasy. The house plant *Euonymus japonicus* is a native of Japan.
Description This genus includes many trees and shrubs which are grown in the garden for their fine foliage, their magnificent autumn colouring, and their attractive fruits. The house plant is grown chiefly for its beautiful glossy foliage, although so long as they appear in large enough numbers, the small flowers are also not to be despised.
Position They tolerate both sun and half shade. They should in any case be given plenty of light, since otherwise their foliage marking will fade. In addition they are best grown in a cool environment, or their leaves will fall.
Care Give the plant a resting period at a temperature of 4 to 6°C (39 to 43°F) from October to February. Afterwards it may be kept slightly warmer. Since it will survive a light night frost, it may go out of doors from April onwards. Prune drastically in spring.

Euonymus japonicus 'Argenteo-variegatus'

Watering Water regularly, keeping the compost moderately, but constantly, moist. Give a little more water in early summer. Slightly decrease the water supply from August onwards, but be careful not to let the plant dry out and lose its leaves. Ensure a moderate degree of humidity and wipe the foliage.
Feeding Every fortnight from April to August give it a fertiliser solution.
Propagation Increase from tip cuttings.
Pests and diseases Mildew and scale insects may be a problem, especially if the plants are kept too warm in winter.

Euonymus japonicus
An erect-growing shrub with angular branches. The leaves are reverse oval in shape, 3 to 7cm (1 to 2¾in) long, roughly toothed. The upper surface is green and glossy, the reverse paler. 'Argenteo-variegatus' has white marking; 'Albo-marginatus' has white leaf edges; 'Aureo-variegatus' has dark green foliage with a golden-yellow centre, and in 'Microphyllus' the leaves are 2cm (¾in) long.

Euphorbia pseudocactus

Euphorbia trigona

Euphorbia grandicornis

Euphorbia meloformis

Euphorbia
Euphorbiaceae
Spurge, Milkwort

Name The origin of this name is not yet entirely clear. According to Backer the plant was named after Euphorbos, personal physician to King Juba II of Numidia, who discovered the medicinal properties of *Euphorbia resinifera.*

Origin The genus includes about 2000 species, which have their natural habitat in the temperate, subtropical and tropical zones of Europe, Africa, Asia and America. The Crown of Thorns (*Euphorbia milii*) is a native of Malagasy, the Poinsettia (*Euphorbia pulcherrima*) originates in the humid mountain regions of Central America and Mexico. Many of the cactus-like succulents come from Africa.

Description The various species differ considerably in habit. There are herbaceous plants, shrubs and trees, as well as more than 400 succulent species. They are annual, biennial or perennial, deciduous or evergreen, water plants, climbers, clump-forming plants or tall trees. Of course they have a number of characteristics in common, such as the milky sap (latex) and the very unusual inflorescence. All species contain a milky white juice, and in some species this is extremely poisonous and causes skin irritations or blisters.

The flowers are very insignificant, but the bracts are all the more conspicuous. In *Euphorbia fulgens*, grown for its cut flowers, two brightly coloured bracts have coalesced, and the same pattern is encountered in the Crown of Thorns. The male and female flowers are extremely simple in structure; monoecious or dioecious, according to the species.

Position As a general rule euphorbias require a sunny position, certainly in good light. A flowering Poinsettia is the only one which does not tolerate direct sun. In summer they may be placed in a sheltered, warm spot outside, with the exception of the succulents, which must be kept fairly warm throughout the year. In climates with a heavy rainfall they are best kept indoors. If there are children in the house the spined species must be kept in a safe spot. Try to move the Crown of Thorns as little as possible, since this frequently causes the leaves to fall.

Care The bracts of the Poinsettia retain their colour for a very long time, but eventually they will turn green and take on the function of leaves, or drop off. After flowering the shoots may be cut back to half their length. Dust the cuts with ash or charcoal powder. The plant should then be kept a little cooler at 12 to 15°C (53 to 59°F); it will soon start into growth once more. If you think it necessary you can prune it again after two or three months. Repot after pruning to avoid yellowing of the leaves.

If the plant is put out of doors, it must be brought inside again in early September and kept at a temperature of 17°C (62°F). To flower once more it requires only ten hours of light a day, for it is a short-day plant. For the remaining 14 hours the Poinsettia must be kept in complete darkness. After about three weeks of this treatment the plants should flower and the bracts will colour. To keep them in good condition the temperature should not exceed 18 to 20°C (64 to 68°F). *Euphorbia fulgens* is another short-day plant, and so is the Crown of Thorns, but in the case of the latter the temperature must be kept at 20°C (68°F) or above. The fact that it frequently flowers in summer too proves that it reacts to other stimuli as well. The plant may be given a resting period in winter, but it is not strictly necessary.

In the case of succulents their place of origin must be taken into account. Species originating in warm, tropical regions should be given a minimum temperature of 12 to 14°C (53 to 57°F); the others at 8 to 10°C (46 to 50°F), although many of them will tolerate as little as 5°C (41°F). The cooler they are kept, the less water and the more light they require. When moving or repotting them remember the poisonous juice, and wear gloves to avoid any risk.

Watering In the flowering period the Poinsettia should be watered regularly with tepid water. When flowering has ceased, reduce the water supply and put the plant in a cooler environment. This plant requires a moderate amount of humidity. In a heated room it should be sprayed with tepid water from time to time. Succulent species can be given little water and tolerate low humidity. During their resting period in winter they should be kept almost dry or watered sparingly, according to the species. The Crown of Thorns does not need a dormant season and may be kept in the living-room throughout the year. In the growing season keep it moderately moist but during the rest of the year water it sparingly, only just enough to prevent the compost drying out. Overwatering causes leaf drop. The low

Imported specimen of *Euphorbia tirucalli*

Euphorbia pulcherrima 'Annette Hegg', one of the many Poinsettia cultivars

Euphorbia milii, better known as Crown of Thorns

humidity in your living-room is ideal.

Feeding The Poinsettia requires a great deal of nourishment during its period of active growth. Give it a weekly dose of fertiliser at normal concentration from April to September. The Crown of Thorns should be given a fortnightly dose of cactus fertiliser at normal strength from April to September and succulent species should be given the same feeds, but only from May to mid-August.

Repotting Young Crown of Thorns plants should be repotted every year or two, older specimens every three or four years in a sandy mixture. Succulent species can be repotted in cactus compost or in a proprietary potting compost with a little extra sand added.

Propagation The Poinsettia can be increased from tip cuttings in spring or summer. Dip the cuttings in charcoal or rooting powder, to stop the latex flow, and insert them in a mixture of peat and sand at a temperature of 18 to 21°C (64 to 70°F). The Crown of Thorns can be increased from cuttings taken in spring. Take mature shoots, which do not rot quite so readily, and allow the cuttings to dry for a day before inserting them in a mixture of peat and sand. Once they have started into growth the tips should be pinched out to encourage branching.

The plants may also be grown from seed; succulents are easily grown this way. This frequently occurs spontaneously: the ripe seed erupts from the capsule and may germinate in the compost of other house plants. You won't mistake the seedlings for weeds: it is obvious that they are euphorbia plants. In many cases it is difficult to grow succulent species from cuttings. Leave them to dry for a week and insert them in a mixture of 2 parts sand and 1 part peat. They rot easily and do not readily strike.

Pests and diseases In too dry an atmosphere the Poinsettia may suffer from infestations by mealy bug and scale insects, and sometimes red spider mites. Also grey mould, thrips, aphids, leaf deformation and seedling or root rot may cause problems. The Crown of Thorns is sometimes prone to mealy bug, foliage drop as a result of temperature and humidity fluctuations, and root rot, and succulent species are vulnerable to scale insects.

Euphorbia abyssinica

A native of Ethiopia and Eritrea, it may grow there into a tree several feet in height. The succulent octagonal stems are olive green with paler and darker markings. The ribs are sharp, wavy and incised and are closely covered in corky tubercles and pairs of pale brown thorns, pointing downwards.

Euphorbia canariensis

This species occurs mainly on the southern side (the driest side) of the Canary Islands, where it grows into a large shrub with numerous erect-growing columnar stems, usually unbranched, four, five or six sided. The small flowers are brownish red.

Euphorbia caput-medusae

Medusa's Head. Very unusually branched, this species has a short stem and almost horizontal branches, dipping near the stem and bending up towards the tip which is surrounded with tiny leaves. It has a green inflorescence.

Euphorbia coerulescens

Of broad habit with entangled branching, it is an unusual blue-grey colour. The branches are five sided with flat surfaces, and it has a small, yellow inflorescence.

Euphorbia fulgens

A shrub 1.25m (4ft) tall, with gracefully curving branches bearing elliptical to lanceolate dark green leaves. From autumn until spring bright orange or white flowers appear, all facing upwards. This is a difficult plant to grow, but it makes fine cut flowers. Plunge the cut surfaces in boiling water for a few seconds to stop the juice flowing.

Euphorbia globosa

A native of the Cape Province, this is an easily cultivated small species. It has spherical joints at the base, from which

The Poinsettia, *Euphorbia pulcherrima*

longer, reverse oval joints develop, giving the plant the appearance of a pile of 'bulbs' and 'eggs' in various shapes. At first the colour is dark green, then later grey to greyish white. The inflorescence, up to 10cm (4in) long, appears at the tips of the joints and consists of frilly green flowers. It flowers practically throughout the summer.

Euphorbia grandicornis

From tropical Africa, this is a fairly rapidly growing small shrub with a twisting, triangular stem, branching at different levels. The vigorous ribs end in thin broad wings, deeply notched and irregularly jointed, and there are up to 7-cm ($2\frac{3}{4}$-in) long thorns, at first pale yellow, later turning grey. The branches are initially blue-green, later lead coloured.

Euphorbia lophogona

Syn. *Euphorbia fournieri*. A remarkable species with four- to five-sided stems, turning woody at a later stage and bearing a tuft of fresh green, spatula-shaped leaves at the top; the leaves drop fairly soon and leave a halfmoon-shaped mark. It has small pseudo-flowers. They produce seed which is ejected.

Euphorbia meloformis

A low-growing, spherical plant with eight to ten ribs and a concave growing point. The plant is leafless and looks like a cactus, reaching the size of a large apple. The colour is green to grey-green, in plenty of sun sometimes slightly reddish, and there are small yellow-green flowers.

Euphorbia milii

Crown of Thorns. A succulent shrub with obvious leaves, it grows to over 1m (3ft). The circular woody stems are somewhat grooved and are covered in horizontally projecting thorns. It has reverse oval- to spatula-shaped leaves, blunt and green, and the inflorescence has a sticky stalk and bright red bracts. A very strong plant, but when the leaves fall give it a month's rest.

Euphorbia obesa

A South African species. Young plants are flat to spherical; at a later stage they are reverse oval in shape. They have eight flat ribs; the pale green ridges are densely covered in brown speckles, which divide the body from top to bottom into regular sections. Green inflorescences develop on the crown, and they are dioecious.

Euphorbia pseudocactus

A shrub, branching from the base, with square branches with yellowish-green marking and slightly wavy ribs. The edge is horny with grey spines.

Euphorbia pulcherrima

Poinsettia. A vigorous, erect-growing shrub with oval, 10-cm (4-in) long leaves, sometimes narrowing at the mid-point; they grow on fairly long leaf stalks. The large bracts under the small flowers are bright red, white or salmon pink.

Euphorbia tirucalli

Pencil Tree, Milkbush. Originates in Asia, where it grows up to 10m (33ft). It has circular branches and pencil-shaped, glossy green twigs with narrow leaves, and it is deciduous.

Euphorbia trigona

A candelabrum-shaped succulent with triangular to three-winged stems. It has crenate ridges, pale green marking and deciduous oval leaves.

Exacum

Gentianaceae

Name Probably a Roman plant name.
Origin There are about 40 species, originating in tropical and subtropical regions in Asia, in Malagasy and in tropical Africa. *Exacum affine* was discovered on the island of Socotra at the beginning of this century.
Description Annuals, biennial or perennial plants or semi-shrubs with square stems. The leaves grow opposite and are smooth edged, three to five veined. The flowers appear in compound racemes and are followed by numerous small seeds. The only species grown on a large scale is *Exacum affine*, originally biennial, but cultivated as an annual. A cheerful, rewarding little plant, easily cared for.
Position This Blue Busy Lizzie, or Persian Violet, should be given a well-lit, but not too warm situation. Avoid strong sunlight and ensure that it has plenty of fresh air. In a good, warm and fairly dry summer these plants will also do well in plenty of light in a sheltered, warm spot in the garden or on the balcony. They dislike draughts.
Care In general the temperature should be between 15 and 23°C (59 and 73°F). Remove the dead flowers regularly, as they take nourishment from the plant. After flowering it is best to discard the plants and buy or grow new ones from seed the following year. They are not easy to keep and are rarely attractive in the second year.
Watering In the period of active growth they should be kept constantly moist. If the compost dries out too much the flowers will fade. Preferably use softened water or rainwater. The normal living-room atmosphere is sufficiently humid and the plants therefore need not be sprayed.
Feeding If they have been planted in a nutritious compost in the spring, they will need no extra feeding, otherwise they should be given a fertiliser solution at the recommended strength every 10 or 14 days.
Repotting If you buy the plant in a small pot entirely filled with roots, it is best to repot it, using a proprietary compost mixed with a little extra sand and peat.
Propagation The fine seed is sown in February or March on the surface of fine soil and will germinate under glass in a temperature of 18°C (64°F). The seedlings should be pricked out twice and finally potted in a proprietary potting compost or in a mixture of equal parts of leafmould, clay and rotted cow manure. Stop them a few times and plant several seedlings in a pot to obtain fine bushy plants. They will flower about six months after sowing. They can also be sown in August. The seed should be taken from plants with the finest colouring.

Exacum affine

A biennial plant with bare, erect-growing stems, freely branching. The oval leaves are 2 to 4 cm ($\frac{3}{4}$ to $1\frac{1}{2}$ in) long, three to five veined, fresh green and opposite. The star-shaped, fragrant lilac-blue flowers, over 1 cm ($\frac{1}{2}$ in) across, have yellow stamens and resemble the flowers of potato plants, though the plant belongs to the gentian family. 'Atrocoeruleum' has dark lilac flowers and is more beautiful than the species.

Exacum affine

× *Fatshedera lizei*

× *Fatshedera lizei* 'Variegata'

× Fatshedera

Araliaceae

Name The genus × *Fatshedera* is the result of crossing *Fatsia japonica* 'Moseri', the Japanese Aralia, with an ivy, *Hedera helix* 'Hibernica'.
Origin The plant was created in 1912 by the French tree growers Lizé-Frères in Nantes.
Description A beautiful, fast-growing evergreen foliage plant which, provided it is given some support, may reach a height of 5 m (16 ft). Mature plants may flower if they have been kept cool in winter.
Position It likes a cool environment at a minimum night temperature of 16°C (60°F), otherwise the lower leaves will soon drop. The variegated form requires a little more warmth and light than the green plant, which will thrive even in bad light. In summer it can be put in a shady spot in the garden.
Care The plants tend to grow straight up to the ceiling, without branching. If you don't like this, you can encourage bushy growth by stopping. Keep it in a good light at a temperature of about 9°C (48°F) in winter.
Watering Water moderately, but take care that the compost does not dry out, or the young leaves will be damaged. On the other hand too much water is equally bad: a footbath immediately causes the lower leaves to fall. If the plant is kept in the living-room in winter it must be regularly sprayed to avoid damage caused by dry air.
Feeding During the growing season feed once a fortnight, using a foliar feed or standard fertiliser.
Repotting Regular repotting in a mixture of a conifer needle compost and rotted cow manure is the best way of encouraging growth.
Propagation Take ripe, approximately 10-cm (4-in) long tip cuttings or sideshoots in August. Remove the lower leaves and halve the remaining leaf surface to minimise evaporation. Root the cuttings under glass or plastic in a mixture of leafmould or peat and sharp sand. They will most readily strike in bottom heat of about 18 to 20°C (64 to 68°F), but will also root in water. The variegated form should be kept a little warmer. × *Fatshedera lizei* may also be grown from seed sown in late March in bottom heat.
Pests and diseases These are really only a threat if the plant is kept too warm, when thrips or red spider mite may attack.

× *Fatshedera lizei*

An evergreen semi-climber with three- or five-lobed leaves on limp, scaly stems. Initially the shoots grow upwards; they later become recumbent. It occasionally flowers around October, producing greenish plumes consisting of numerous round umbels. The white- to yellow-marked form 'Variegata' grows more slowly than the species.

Fatsia

Araliaceae

Japanese Aralia

Name The name *Fatsia* is thought to have been derived from the Japanese word *hachi*, eight; this is also the Japanese name for the plant.
Origin South East Asia.
Description An excellent foliage plant with seven- to nine-lobed leaves, brown and felty when they first appear, later turning smooth and leathery. *Fatsia* species have enormous powers of resistance and you will therefore be able to enjoy them for a long time. Mature plants occasionally produce inconspicuous green to cream flowers in spring; after pollination they develop into dark berries.
Position The plant should be kept throughout the year in a cool position out of the sun, for instance near a

Fatsia japonica

north-facing window. It is an ideal plant for corridors, entrance halls, unheated conservatories and other cool areas. In summer it may be moved to a shady spot out of doors. Provided it is wrapped up warmly, it may even spend the winter there, although it is not completely hardy.

Care The fatsia appreciates having its foliage sponged once every four weeks. If the leaves turn yellow it means that the plant is asking for a cooler position – in winter the ideal temperature for variegated strains is between 14 and 16°C (57 and 60°F), for green forms to 12°C (53°F) – less light, a higher degree of humidity or a more balanced water supply. It is sensitive to natural gas.

Watering Be sure to give enough water when new leaves are developing (as a rule five to six leaves appear at a time). From August onwards water more sparingly and during the dormant season adapt the water supply to the temperature of the environment. Never let the compost dry out, but do not leave it standing in a footbath either.

Feeding From April to the end of August feed every week.

Repotting Use a loamy and light mixture, rich in humus, perhaps 2 parts leafmould, 2 parts rotted cow manure and 1 part sharp sand. A standard potting compost is also satisfactory.

Propagation Both the green and the variegated forms may be grown from cuttings, and when the stems have become woody they can be air-layered. The green species can also be grown from seed.

Pests and diseases Many infestations, and especially foliage diseases, are the result of incorrect placing. Insect enemies are red spider mites, scale insects and thrips.

Fatsia japonica

Syn. *Aralia japonica, A. sieboldii*. A vigorous evergreen shrub, developing few branches. The leaves are 20 to 40cm (8 to 16in) across, dark green and long stalked. Compound flower umbels appear in October. 'Moseri' is a more compact strain with larger leaves. Variegated strains are *Fatsia japonica* 'Variegata', 'Albomarginata' and 'Reticulata', all somewhat slower growing than the species. They are slightly more sensitive than the green strains and require a little more warmth.

Fatsia japonica 'Variegata'

Faucaria

Aizoaceae

Name From the Latin *fauces*, which means throat. From a distance the opposite leaves remind us of a throat.

Origin More than 35 species have their natural habitat in South Africa, especially in the eastern part of the Cape Province.

Description Small, clump-forming succulents with fleshy leaves growing in crosswise pairs and joined at the base. In many cases the leaves are toothed and have an uneven surface. The radial flowers, usually yellow, appear from the end of August onwards.

Position Keep it on a sunny windowsill. In summer it may also go outside.

Care When the leaves start to shrivel up in autumn, the plant should be given a rest in a temperature of 5°C (41°F), and the atmosphere must be kept dry, otherwise the tissue will rot.

Watering In summer, while in growth, the plant requires a generous water supply. Keep dry in the dormant season, and resume watering in May.

Repotting Repot every three years in April in a light mixture, which may con-

Faucaria tigrina, Tiger's Chaps

sist of 2 parts standard potting compost and 1 part sharp sand or grit.

Propagation In spring, increase from seed at 21°C (70°F). Cuttings may be taken from June to August. Leave them to dry for two days to prevent rotting.

Pests and diseases Mealy bug and root mealy bug are possible threats.

Faucaria bosscheana

This has glossy green leaves with white, slightly toothed, upcurving margins and yellow flowers.

Faucaria felina

Grey-green foliage with white stipples. It has yellow to orange flowers.

Faucaria tigrina

Tiger's Chaps. The best known species, it has green, white-speckled leaves and long, thin spines and grows to 5cm (2in). There are golden-yellow flowers.

Faucaria tuberculosa

With dark foliage covered in white tubercles and up to 7.5cm (3in) in height, this species bears yellow flowers.

Ferocactus recurvus. The broad, curved thorns are characteristic of the species

Ferocactus

Cactaceae

Barrel Cactus, Fishhook Cactus

Name The prefix *fero* is based on the Latin *ferus*, which means fierce. The cactus owes its characteristic appearance to the numerous firm, hard thorns.

Origin The 35 species originate in the south-western desert regions of the United States and Mexico, where their enormous columns are raised against a background of blue sky.

Description Young, barrel-shaped specimens with sharp ribs are the plants most frequently seen cultivated. The colourful spines are usually curved. The flowers appear in spring or in summer, depending on the species.

Position In summer they should be put in the sun to improve the colouring of the thorns, in a warm spot in the garden or on a south-facing window-sill. In winter they must be kept in a well-lit, cool environment.

Care Rest them in a temperature of 5°C (41°F) in winter; this is essential for flower formation.

Ferocactus latispinus

Watering Keep dry from late October until early March. After repotting, resume normal watering with softened water or rainwater. Allow the compost to dry out between watering. Spray in very warm weather.

Repotting Repot in March using a special cactus mixture. For good thorn development it is important that the compost should be rich in minerals. Plants that have not been grafted should not be repotted every year.

Propagation Increase from seed, in April, in a temperature of 21°C (70°F). Keep the seedlings slightly moist during the first winter. They may also be propagated from offsets.

Pests and diseases Rotting occurs if too much water is given in winter. If the cactus is kept too dry in summer it becomes susceptible to red spider mite and mealy bug.

Ferocactus acanthodes

Syn. *Echinocactus acanthodes*. The Devil's Pincushion. Densely covered in pink or red thorns. The centre thorns grow to 12cm (4½in) in length; they are flattened and tortuous. The flowers are reddish yellow.

Ferocactus latispinus

Syn. *Echinocactus corniger; E. latispinus*. Devil's Tongue. The popular name refers to the scarlet, hooked central thorns. The cactus body is blue-green and has about 20 ribs. In temperate climates the red flowers rarely appear.

Ferocactus melocactiformis

Syn. *Echinocactus electracanthus*. In cultivation it retains its spherical shape, blue-green, with a maximum number of 25 ribs. In the wild this cactus branches. It has strongly curved, amber-coloured thorns and pale yellow flowers in June and July.

Ferocactus recurvus

A fresh green spherical cactus with about 13 ribs and yellowish thorns with hooked, red central thorns. The carmine-red flowers rarely appear.

Ferocactus stainesii

Syn. *Echinocactus stainesii*. A spherical cactus, becoming columnar at a later

Ficus elastica 'Schryveriana'

Ficus rubiginosa

stage, with 15 to 20 ribs. The four to six central thorns are initially red, but later fade to yellow-grey. Soft white hairs are developed from the areoles. Unlike *Ferocactus latispinus*, the species flowers fairly readily; the flowers are orange.

Ficus

Moraceae

Fig

Name *Ficus* is the Latin name for fig.
Origin Most species of this extensive genus (it includes more than 1000) originate in Asia and Africa, but many of them occur also in Central and South America and Australia. The Fig Tree has been known in southern Europe for a very long time. Most of the species now cultivated as house plants have their natural habitat in South East Asia. Some specific names are an indication of the natural habitat: *Ficus australis* (now called *Ficus rubiginosa*) and *Ficus benghalensis*.
Description More species have come on to the market in recent years than of any other genera. One or more *Ficus* species are found in most living-rooms and offices. They vary considerably in appearance: in addition to erect-growing tropical trees and shrubs there are trailing epiphytes and climbers. Most species have undivided foliage, but in the case of the Fig the leaves are lobed.

In spite of the great variety there are, of course, also similarities, such as the inflorescence, the shape of the fruits and the milky sap they contain. The main source of the latex from which rubber used to be made was the *Ficus elastica*. Since the Brazilian rubber tree (hevea) has come into use as a source of latex, the economic importance of this ficus has been restricted to its use as a house plant. The manner in which flowering, pollination and fruit formation are brought about in the Fig Tree is unique in the world of plants (only in the yucca do we find something similar). The greatly thickened, fleshy receptacle develops into a pocket-shaped socket containing the monoecious flowers: the male flowers at the top, the female ones below. A minuscule opening allows insects to enter to pollinate the plants. *Ficus deltoidea* and *Ficus cyathistipula* are two of the few species which will develop fruits in the living-room; they do so at quite an early age.

Position The ficus is often used as a specimen plant, but it is also frequently seen in mixed plant containers, flower windows and office landscapes. It is very suitable for hydroculture. Some people use *Ficus pumila* as living wallpaper. The ficus dislikes being moved and you should therefore take care to choose a well-lit, but not too sunny position where it can be left year after year. If it grows too much in one direction, it may be turned, but preferably a little at a time. It is important to keep it at a fairly constant temperature and out of draughts. *Ficus deltoidea*, *F. pumila* and *F. radicans* tolerate a fair amount of shade.
Care In addition to temperature fluctuations, the ficus is also sensitive to excessively wet or cold feet, such as a bottom temperature below 12 to 15°C (53 to 59°F), and too warm or too cold conditions in winter. In the dormant season 12 to 15°C (53 to 59°F) is a satisfactory temperature for most green species, but a healthy plant will accept higher temperatures and may therefore be kept in the living-room. If the plant is kept at below 12°C (53°F) for long periods, and especially if it is overwatered at the same time, damage will occur. *Ficus macrophylla* and *Ficus rubiginosa* are exceptions to the rule: they prefer to be kept at a temperature of 10°C (50°F). *Ficus pumila* is less demanding and may be kept cool at 5°C (41°F) as well as warm – 18°C (64°F) – in winter. If kept warm it should however be sprayed regularly, since otherwise the leaves will curl. Species which require at least 18°C (64°F) in winter are *Ficus aspera* and *Ficus dryepondtiana*. Variegated species require a slightly higher temperature than green plants. They are more sensitive and also demand higher humidity and more light. *Ficus religiosa* is a green ficus requiring plenty of light.
Watering Give very little water in the dormant season from October to February and use tepid water. The amount of water given should depend on the temperature. Increase the water supply when the ficus starts into growth. Large specimens sometimes drink more than you think. Throughout the year never water when the surface of the compost is still moist and never allow it to dry out completely. The degree of acidity of the water should be about pH 6. Some species, such as *Ficus lyrata* and *Ficus pumila*, require a higher degree of humidity than others. In general their leathery foliage allows them to accept a fairly dry environment, but all species will do better if regularly sprayed with tepid water. In summer an occasional rain shower is very good for them. The cause of ficus diseases may frequently be found in incorrect cultivation and you should therefore keep a careful eye on the water supply and the drainage, as well as on the temperature. Ficus species with large leaves should regularly be sponged clean either with water or with leaf gloss.
Feeding From the time new leaves appear until mid-August give a dose of fertiliser solution at normal concentration once every ten days.
Repotting Large plants need only be repotted every second or third year, and often it is sufficient to replace the top layer of compost. When repotting, which is usually done in February, choose a pot only one, or at most two, sizes larger than the old one, even if it appears a little small in proportion to the plant. Guarantee good drainage by covering the hole in the pot with a crock, convex side upwards. A proprietary potting compost may be used, but it is better to mix your own: loamy garden soil or rotted turves, mixed with ⅓ volume of leafmould and possibly some sand or peat. At the same time branching species can be pruned a little, for instance *Ficus deltoidea*, *F. pumila* and *F. radicans*. Pruning encourages branching and allows you to keep the plant in better shape.
Propagation Increase from cuttings, by air-layering or from seed. Although the latter is possible, it is rarely done because the seeds, imported from Australia or Indonesia, do not readily germinate. If you decide to try, sow immediately on arrival of the seed, preferably in June or July, and keep in good

Ficus pumila

Ficus aspera 'Parcelli', one of the few species which will bear fruit

Ficus lyrata, an unusual, long-lasting plant for a constantly heated, large room

Ficus deltoidea bearing fruits

light at a temperature of 25°C (77°F).

Air-layering is the method used if cuttings of a certain species do not readily strike and if the stems of the plant have become woody, the plants have become bare at the base, or if you want to shorten a plant which refuses to branch and shoots straight up towards the ceiling. May to August is the best time. The method is chiefly used in the case of *Ficus elastica* and *Ficus lyrata*. See also the information section page 76.

Cuttings should be taken in spring. You can use tip or sideshoots with a maximum of three to four leaves removed in pruning. Try to prevent sap flow by dipping the cutting in water or charcoal powder. The cut on the parent plant must be sprinkled with white sand or charcoal powder. It is by no means always possible to root cuttings in water, and you run the risk that the transfer from water to compost will not suit the cuttings. The best results are obtained by owners of an indoor propagator, where bottom heat of 25 to 35°C (77 to 95°F) can be maintained. Eye cuttings can also be rooted in such propagators. These are obtained by cutting the stem 1cm ($\frac{1}{2}$in) above and below a leaf. This gives you a cutting with a node (that is, an eye), a leaf stalk and a leaf. If the leaf is very large, as with *Ficus elastica*, you can lessen evaporation by rolling the leaf up and securing it with a rubber band. Sometimes rooting powder will speed up the process; it also checks the sap flow. The cuttings medium may consist of equal parts of sand and peat and should be thoroughly moistened and put in good light, but out of the sun. Cuttings will also strike in pure perlite. The process will take four to five weeks.

The plantlet must now be hardened by slightly opening the propagator during the day. When the first new leaf appears the old leaf and leafstalk may be carefully removed. The plantlet must now be able to obtain its own nourishment and should therefore be moved to a more nutritious mixture, such as equal parts of leafmould and sharp sand. Keep it under glass or plastic for the next few weeks and spray regularly to ensure adequate humidity. Screen against sunlight and give a little fertiliser every fortnight.

Pests and diseases Too much sunlight or draughts often lead to attacks by red spider mites or thrips and if your ficus is kept in a warm, enclosed space in too dry an atmosphere, you run the risk of mealy bug or scale insects. The plant is also prone to infestation by eelworm, mites, root mealy bug and root rot. Leaf spot (*Glomerella cingulata*) is usually the result of severe temperature fluctuations or overwatering in the dormant season. Depressed yellow-brown blotches occur on the foliage and these bear spores. Affected leaves should immediately be removed and the remainder must be sprayed with an organic mould preventative. Cold or wet feet may cause yellow-brown patches along the margins of the leaves. Drooping foliage indicates either too warm a position in winter or incorrect watering. If the drainage is poor, or if the plant has been overwatered, the roots cannot absorb sufficient air and die. Sap pressure decreases and the leaves drop. If the plant is quickly repotted in a pot of the same size and the rotted roots removed, it may sometimes be saved.

Ficus aspera

A small shrub with large, hairy, white and green marbled leaves and cherry-like, red- and white-veined figs at a fairly early age. 'Parcelli' is the best-known cultivar.

Ficus benghalensis

Syn. *Ficus indica*. Banyan Tree. It resembles *Ficus elastica*, but young leaves are covered in brownish hairs on the reverse. Adult leaves are up to 20cm (8in) long, hairy on both sides, oblong, leathery and dark green. In the wild the tree often begins its life as an epiphyte on other trees; it anchors itself in the soil by means of its aerial roots until a complete circle of large and small trunks encircles the host tree. In the course of centuries they develop rampant growth in all directions, finally covering a large area. In India and Indonesia, markets (or banyans) are frequently held in the shade of these immense trees, which is why they are sometimes called Banyan Trees. There is a legend that the form 'Krishnae' folded its leaves in such a way that dew was retained to quench the Hindu god's thirst. Greyish branches bear leathery, dark green leaves, shaped like irregular cups, with slightly protruding ivory-coloured veins.

Ficus benjamina

Syn. *Ficus nitida*. Weeping Fig. In India this makes a very tall tree with a broad crown and arching branches. In cultivation its graceful appearance is retained because of its pendulous twigs and leaves, but as a rule it does not grow beyond 2.5 m (8 ft). It grows fairly fast and branches readily. The leaves do not grow beyond 12 cm (4½ in) and are leathery and glossy dark green in colour, pointed at the base. The surface is frequently wavy. Young leaves are soft green in colour. Like *Ficus religiosa*, *Ficus benjamina* is a strangler; it germinates on other trees and puts down long aerial roots which form a network round the host plant. When the strangler becomes strong and dense the host plant dies and the ficus will eventually lead an independent existence.

Ficus buxifolia
Leathery, wedge-shaped leaves, 6 cm (2¼ in) long on curving twigs.

Ficus cannonii
○ ◐ ⊜ (″) ⊛ ▣
This forms a shrub which may grow to 3 m (10 ft) in height, with short-stalked, 10- to 25-cm (4- to 10-in) long leaves, very thin and varying in shape. They may be heart shaped, three lobed or sometimes deeply incised. The foliage is always brownish purple on the upper surface and wine red on the underside. The centre vein and the leaf stalk are red.

Ficus cyathistipula

Ficus rubiginosa 'Variegata'

Ficus carica
○ ⊜ (″) ⊛ ▣
The Common Fig. A broad, evergreen tree, which in Mediterranean regions may grow to 10 m (33 ft). The thick, leathery leaves are palmately incised; the upper surface is rough. In temperate climates it is sometimes grown out of doors, but in that case it must be completely wrapped up in winter unless in a very sheltered spot. The fruits appear within a few years.

Ficus cyathistipula
◐ ⊜ (″) ⊛ ▣ ▢
A strongly branching, shrubby plant with dark green, reverse-oval and sharply pointed foliage. The leaves are up to 25 cm (10 in) long, with dark green stipules at the base. The plant bears fruit at an early age; even in cultivation it may produce spherical pseudo-fruits, 3 to 4 cm (1 to 1½ in) across.

Ficus deltoidea
Syn. *Ficus diversifolia*. Because it grows as an epiphyte on trees it is called the Mistletoe Fig. In cultivation it is a branching shrub, up to 80 cm (32 in) tall. It has leathery leaves, 7 cm (2¾ in) long, with a blunt tip and tapering towards the base. The foliage is dark green above, sometimes with brownish patches, and pale green underneath. The yellowish-green pseudo-fruits are the size of a pea and may appear throughout the year, even on young plants. It's a slow-growing plant.

Ficus dryepondtiana
Undulate leaves with a sharp point, to 30 cm (1 ft) long. The upper surface is a deep olive green, the reverse is red.

Ficus edulis
◐ ⊜ (″) ⊛ ▣
A small plant which does not branch easily. Leaves are rather thin and egg shaped and are a pale red colour as they unfold. Clusters of small figs, the size of peas, appear at the lower end of the trunk. These are edible.

Ficus benghalensis

Ficus elastica 'Decora'

Ficus elastica
◐ ⊜ (″) ⊛ ▣ ▢
The familiar Rubber Plant. The species does not branch readily. The leaves are up to 30 cm (1 ft) long, oval, leathery, dark green and glossy. Young leaves are sheathed in red stipules, which soon drop. Plants available at the garden shop are chiefly cultivars. Green-leaved forms are 'Decora', with very shiny, fairly broad leaves; 'La France', with smaller leaves and a twisted tip; 'Robusta', with very broad leaves and leaf nodes growing closer together, giving the plant a compact appearance. Variegated cultivars are 'Doescheri', with clearly marked foliage with white margins; the centre vein and leaf stalk are reddish. 'Schryveriana' has narrower leaves, finely marbled in dark and pale green and yellowish white. The palest zones have stippled markings. 'Tricolor' has irregular cream, pale and dark green patches.

Ficus lyrata
Syn. *Ficus pandurata*. Fiddle Leaf Fig. The popular name refers to the enormous, upside down violin-shaped waxy leaves, 50 cm (20 in) long, dark green with slightly paler, sunken veins. The margin is wavy. The small dark stipules at the base of the leaves remain on the plant for a long time. It is a tall and erect-growing plant, which rarely branches spontaneously.

Ficus macrophylla
◐ ⊜ (″) ⊛ ▣ ▢
Moreton Bay Fig. Oblong, leathery leaves, blunt at the tip, up to 25 cm (10 in) long. They are heart shaped at the base, green and shiny, with ivory-coloured veins.

Ficus montana
◐ ⊜ (″) ⊛ ▣ ▢
Syn. *Ficus quercifolia*. A creeper or erect-growing small shrub with arching shoots. The leaves are up to 12 cm (4½ in) long and bear a faint resemblance to oak leaves. The figs are small and inconspicuous.

Ficus nekbudu
Syn. *Ficus utilis*. Oval, up to 30-cm (1-ft) long fresh green leaves, rounded at the tip and with whitish veins. The leaves are thick and spread horizontally.

Ficus pumila
◐ ⊜ ⊖ ⊝ (″) ⊛ ▣ ▢
Syn. *Ficus repens*. Creeping Fig. Limp, creeping stems, which climb with the aid of clinging roots. They may also be grown as hanging or creeping plants. The plants encountered in cultivation are usually young specimens, with heart-shaped small leaves, up to 3 cm (1 in) long and 2 cm (¾ in) across, growing horizontally in two rows on sterile stems. The adult form looks entirely different. It has thicker leaves, longer – 10 cm (4 in) – and narrower at the base on fertile stems, often standing away from the young stems. The cultivar 'Minima' has thin leaves, only up to 1.5 cm (½ in) long. In 'Serpyllifolia' the leaves are even smaller and oblong in shape. 'Variegata' has white marbled foliage, which readily reverts to green. Not a vigorous grower.

Ficus buxifolia

Ficus radicans
◐ ⊜ (″) ⊛ ▣ ▢
The limp stems root on the nodes, hence the name (radix = root). It has broad lanceolate leaves with a sharp point, up to 10 cm (4 in) long. 'Variegata' has narrower, white-marked foliage. It can be used as ground cover, as a climber or a hanging plant.

Ficus religiosa
The Bo-tree. Buddhists believe that it was under this tree that Buddha found enlightenment. The dull green leaves end in a long slender tip.

Ficus rubiginosa
◐ ⊖ ⊝ (″) ⊛ ▣ ▢
Syn. *Ficus australis*. Rusty Fig. A recumbent, branching shrub; the stems root where they touch the soil. It has oblong, dark green leaves, at least 10 cm (4 in) long. Young leaves are covered in brown hairs on the underside, at a later stage only the veins are hairy. The cultivar 'Variegata', with yellow and white oval leaves, is the one most often grown.

Ficus sycomorus
This has oblong, 7- to 9-cm (2¾- to 3½-in) long leaves, heart shaped at the base and blunt at the tip and a fresh to deep olive green. The ancient Egyptians used the wood for making sarcophagi.

Ficus triangularis
◐ ⊜ (″) ⊛ ▣ ▢
This produces 6- to 10-cm (2¼- to 4-in) long dark green leaves in the shape of an equilateral triangle, with the leaf stalk at the top. The lower corners are rounded.

Fittonia

Acanthaceae

Name Named after Elizabeth and Sarah Mary Fitton, who wrote 'Conversations on Botany'.
Origin The tropical rain forests of Peru.
Description These low-growing herbaceous plants are grown for their beautifully marked foliage. They are erect or creeping in habit. The small yellowish flowers usually appear spring; they are very inconspicuous and have no ornamental value. Typical hothouse plants, they are often grown under larger plants in containers.
Position Ideal for use as ground cover in a flower window. You may be able to grow it in the living-room if you

Fittonia verschaffeltii 'Argyroneura'

choose a well-lit (but not sunny) or shady spot and provide a high degree of humidity. Grown in a pot in the living-room the foliage will always remain somewhat smaller than when it is given its head planted out.
Care The best temperature for growing a fittonia is 20°C (68°F). In winter the strain *Fittonia verschaffeltii* 'Argyroneura' will not tolerate a temperature below 16°C (60°F); for other species the minimum temperature is 13°C (55°F).
Watering From spring until autumn keep the compost moist. In cloudy and cold weather, as well as in winter, keep it a little drier. Use tepid, demineralised water with a pH of 4 to 4.5 and keep the humidity high throughout the year by regular spraying. It is very difficult to maintain a fittonia in good condition in winter. A satisfactory micro-climate may be created if you put the plant in a plastic bag or apply the deep-plate method.
Feeding Apart from the twelve darkest weeks of the year feed every fortnight, using a weak, lime-free fertiliser solution.
Repotting Fittonia species have a creeping, shallow root system and are therefore best grown in wide and shallow dishes, in a light, nutritious mixture of peat, sharp sand and pulverised clay or rotted cow manure. Put a layer of crocks in the bottom of the dish to provide drainage.
Propagation Increase from cuttings rooted in spring in a bottom temperature of 20°C (68°F). Rooted runners may also be used. Stopping the young plants will encourage bushy growth. Cuttings can be rooted in a mixture of 4 parts standard potting compost, 1 part sharp sand and 1 part peat.
Pests and diseases Fittonia plants are the favourite food of slugs.

Fittonia gigantea

An erect-growing plant up to 60 cm (2 ft) with green foliage with red veining. It has violet-red stems with four rows of white hairs.

Fittonia verschaffeltii

Creeping stems with oval, 7- to 10-cm ($2\frac{3}{4}$- to 4-in) long, matt green leaves with carmine marking and small yellow flowers in erect-growing spikes, with fairly large bracts. The strain 'Argyroneura' has glossy green foliage with silvery veining. In 'Pearcei' the marking is an even deeper red than in the species.

A standard fuchsia, 'Temptation'

Fittonia verschaffeltii 'Pearcei'

Fuchsia

Onagraceae

Lady's Eardrops

Name Named after Leonhard Fuchs, who lived from 1501 to 1566. He was a botanist and physician and was the author of one of the earliest books on herbs.
Origin There are about 100 species, whose native habitat is in Central and South America, the Falkland Islands, Tahiti and New Zealand. The majority are found in mountain forests near the equator, sometimes at heights of up to 3000 m (9800 ft). A French explorer called Charles Plumier discovered the fuchsia in Central America in about 1700. Little more than a century later it was cultivated on a large scale in Europe.
Description Because of the great variety within the genus, the fuchsia can be used in many ways. The hardy species make graceful garden plants; the non-hardy forms may be used to decorate your greenhouse, living-room, conservatory or balcony. Erect-growing species can be grown as a shrub, but may also be cultivated as standards, and other species make rewarding hanging or creeping plants. All these fuchsia plants are grown for the sake of their magnificent single or double bell-shaped flowers, consisting of a tube ending in four spreading sepals and four overlapping petals which form a bell shape and frequently differ in colour from the sepals. The main flowering season is August–September, often extending into October, and the flowers are followed by berry-like fruits. The thousands of strains in cultivation make popular subjects for collections, as they are easy to grow from cuttings, flower profusely and are appreciative of personal care. For these reasons associations of fuchsia lovers have been founded in many countries.
Position If you remember that the genus originates in cool and humid mountain forests, you will realise that fuchsias demand a cool situation out of the sun in the living-room. They should be kept in very light, but cool, conditions in winter. From mid-May onwards they may be placed outside, preferably in a sheltered spot, although they will flower even against a north-facing wall.
Care During the dark winter months the fuchsia should be given a rest in good light, at a temperature of 6 to 10°C (43 to 50°F), after having first been cut back

a little. If you want to take cuttings in the spring, the plants should be pruned drastically at the beginning of January, then kept at a temperature of 20°C (68°F) and be given a little more water. If you don't intend to take cuttings, delay the pruning and shaping of plants which have developed too vigorously until the end of February, when they should be cut back to 8 to 10cm (3 to 4in) from the main stem. If you lack space indoors they can be left to overwinter outside. Dig a pit about 50cm (20in) deep, put in a layer of dead leaves, put the plants in their pots on top and cover them with straw and more leaves, and finally with a layer of soil. In spring dig them up carefully and gradually introduce them to higher temperatures.

Watering When fuchsia plants are kept out of doors, the water supply must naturally depend on the weather. Make sure that the compost is kept moist. For this reason it is better to use plastic pots for plants kept outside, since less water evaporates. In winter the plants may be kept a little drier, but the compost must never completely dry out. Fairly high relative humidity is required – between 50 and 60 per cent is enough – otherwise the fuchsia will drop its buds. This frequently happens when a fuchsia enters your dry home straight from a humid greenhouse in the nursery. If the transition is too abrupt, flowers, buds and foliage will fall within a few days.

Feeding From early May until the end of August feed every ten days. Fuchsia plants kept outside welcome a dose of liquid organic manure for a change.

Repotting After pruning, repot into standard potting compost or a mixture of leafmould, rotted cow manure, loam and some dried blood. The new pots should be only slightly larger.

Propagation Increase from seed only if you wish to cultivate new forms, for the seedlings of cultivars will differ from the parent plants in habit and colour. Seed should be sown immediately after being harvested, possibly at the beginning of August, under glass and in a mixture of leafmould with peat and sand. Once the seedlings have started into growth, stop them a number of times to obtain bushy plants. They should not be given a dormant season in winter, but be grown on in a temperature of 10 to 13°C (50 to 55°F). The new plant will flower the next year, so you won't have long to wait for the outcome of your experiment.

Cuttings can be taken at any time of the year, but usually it is done between May and September, to produce flowering plants the following spring, or in February–March for summer-flowering specimens; in the latter case the plants will remain a little smaller. Parent plants which have been kept in cool and light conditions throughout the winter should be moved to a warmer place early in February and given more water. The herbaceous shoots which then appear can be used as cuttings, about 8cm (3in) long. Carefully remove the two lower pairs of leaves and with a sharp knife cut the stem just below the bottom node. The cuttings will root in water or in a mixture of equal parts of peat and sharp sand; the bottom temperature should be 15 to 20°C (59 to 68°F). Rooting in soil will be speeded up by about ten days if the cuttings are dipped in rooting powder first and this often promotes a better root system. Once the cuttings have struck they should be moved to a mixture of leafmould, peat and sand and kept in a cool and humid atmosphere. Screen against sunlight. Pinch out the tip a number of times to induce bushy growth. Normally the plant will flower in early June. By continuing to nip out the growing points, flowering may be delayed to a later time. Trailing fuchsia plants should be stopped infrequently or not at all, since they are required to develop long shoots. It is better to group three plantlets in a pot for a bushy effect. In May and June most of the shoots will also bear buds. Use shoots with 5 to 6 pairs of leaves as cuttings, removing the buds, otherwise treat as above. By means of stopping, training and bending all sorts of shapes can be cultivated.

Standard fuchsias deserve special attention. Cuttings are taken in September; when they have rooted a vigorous shoot is trained vertically. Lateral shoots are stopped after the first pair of leaves. The plants are usually repotted in December and February, but never when the compost is dry. If you want to cultivate a 1-m (3-ft) plant, insert a 1-m (3-ft) stake in the pot. When the main stem has reached the top of the stake the growing point should be pinched out; this will be approximately in April or May. You must now encourage the plant to develop a crown. Remove all leaves except the top six pairs. Allow the shoots which will now appear to produce five to six pairs of leaves each, before removing the growing points. Repeat the operation as required. Once the plant is shaped to your liking the shoots can be left to develop flower buds. You will have a flowering standard within a year.

Pests and diseases Watch out for aphids, grey mould, red spider mite and whitefly. In the case of rust, *Pucciniastrum epilobii*, clusters of brown spores will develop on the foliage and affected leaves will drop. Destroy the affected parts and spray the plant with a solution of zineb at the recommended rate. Do not use soil containing conifer needles.

Fuchsia 'El Camino'

Fuchsia 'La Campanella'

Fuchsia 'Water Nymph'

Fuchsia 'Cover Girl'

Fuchsia hybrids

The origin of the forms now cultivated is usually obscure and they are therefore generally referred to as fuchsia hybrids. Original species are rarely encountered outside botanical collections.

The selection at present available may be classified as follows:

1. Single-flowered fuchsia plants. 'Tolling Bell' has a carmine-red calyx and white corolla; 'Winston Churchill', a large red calyx and purple-blue corolla.
2. Double-flowered fuchsia plants. 'Dollar Princess' is among the best-known forms: it has a red calyx and the corolla is red and blue.
3. Hanging fuchsia plants. 'Mrs Rundle' sports a long pink calyx and vivid orange corolla. 'Pink Galore', which has entirely deep soft pink flowers, is one of the finest.
4. *Triphylla* hybrids, the results of crossing with *Fuchsia triphylla*, which was initiated by the German grower Bonstedt. 'Gartenmeister Bonstedt' was called after him; it has a slender, salmon-orange calyx and dark, reddish foliage. The olive-green foliage and bright red calixes of 'Leverkusen' also form a magnificent combination.

Gardenia

Rubiaceae

Cape Jasmine

Name Named after Alexander Garden, an American physician and naturalist, who lived from 1730 to 1791.

Origin The genus includes about 60 species, originating in the tropical and

Fuchsia 'Gartenmeister Bonstedt'

Fuchsia 'Pink Galore'

subtropical zones of Asia and Africa, many of them in China.
Description Non-hardy, partly or entirely evergreen flowering shrubs or small trees. *Gardenia jasminoides*, the only species in general cultivation in the West, used to be grown on a large scale for its delightfully scented flowers, which were used in table arrangements or as buttonholes. The main flowering season occurs in summer.
Position They require plenty of light and even some sun throughout the year, but must be screened against the brightest sunlight in summer. In fine summers they can be put outside from the beginning of July onwards, but they must be brought indoors again early in September.
Care Summer-flowering plants should be rested in winter at a temperature of 12 to 15°C (53 to 59°F). Winter-flowering forms should be kept at 16 to 18°C (60 to 64°F) at that time. The temperature must be kept as steady as possible. In summer a daytime temperature of 20 to 22°C (68 to 71°F) is desirable, and at night the temperature should be a minimum of 16°C (60°F). The buds are probably formed at a temperature of more than 17°C (62°F), but to ensure their further development the night temperature should be below 17°C (62°F). In addition the plant dislikes cold feet. A steady bottom temperature of 18 to 20°C (64 to 68°F) is best during the growing season. Mature specimens can be drastically pruned in the spring. They are then repotted and gradually given warmer conditions. Young plants flower most profusely so it is best to renew your stock from year to year.
Watering During the growing and flowering seasons keep the compost slightly moist, using tepid, demineralised water. If the compost is too damp or too cold, the leaves will turn yellow. Atmospheric humidity should be fairly high. The sunnier and warmer the conditions, the more often you should mist-spray.
Feeding In the growing and flowering season give a fortnightly dose of lime-free fertiliser at the recommended concentration.
Repotting Repot in spring, in lime-free compost; this might consist of a mixture of leafmould, rotted turves and sharp sand. Mature plants are only repotted every third or fourth year. Be careful when handling the root system.
Propagation Towards the end of the winter non-flowering tip cuttings can be taken, 7 to 8cm (2¾ to 3in) long, preferably with a heel. These are rooted under glass at a temperature of 24 to 26°C (75 to 78°F). The plants should be stopped a number of times to produce bushy growth. They can also be grown from seed, but this is much more difficult.
Pests and diseases Red spider mite, thrips, mealy bug, bud fall and chlorosis are possible problems.

Gardenia jasminoides
Syn. *Gardenia florida*. A bare, evergreen shrub, 1.5m (5ft) tall. Leaves are up to 10cm (4in) long, dark green and glossy and there are singly growing, double flowers, fragrant and waxy white in summer. 'Fortunei' has larger leaves and flowers, and 'Veitchii' flowers in winter.

Gardenia jasminoides

Gasteria
Liliaceae

Name From the Greek *gaster*, stomach. This refers to the belly-shaped base of the corolla tube.
Origin All 75 species are natives of South West Africa and the Cape Province.
Description Succulents, stemless or with a very short stalk; in many cases the leaves are arranged in two rows. They often grow in small groups. The foliage is flat or triangular, thick, sword shaped or dagger shaped and may be pale or dark green to grey, covered in pearly warts or grey spots. Graceful little flowers appear in slender racemes on long stalks. The plants are more robust than the haworthia and their untoothed leaves distinguish them from the aloe. They make very easy house plants, mainly grown for their fine foliage.
Position They tolerate sun as well as light shade. In summer they can be kept in a warm and sheltered spot outside. Indoors they will thrive both in warm rooms and in moderately heated to cool areas. The typical two-row foliage structure makes them suitable for the narrow window-sills which modern architecture has imposed upon us.
Care A resting period encourages flower formation. From October to March the plants should be kept fairly dry at a temperature of 6 to 12°C (43 to 53°F); the minimum is 5°C (41°F). But do not allow them to shrivel up.
Watering They do not require much water, but in the growing season you need not be mean. In cold periods and in the dormant season generous watering is fatal and will rapidly cause their death from rotting. If the plants are kept in a fairly warm room indoors in summer, be careful not to allow the air to become too dry, for this would make them susceptible to all kinds of insect pests.
Feeding In the period of active growth the plants should be given a solution of cactus fertiliser every fortnight, at a third of the concentration indicated on the label.
Repotting Repot into a heavy but porous mixture of clay, leafmould and sharp sand.
Propagation In principle they may be grown from seed, but few species grow true to type. Species with offsets can be increased by division, and the others may be propagated from leaf cuttings. Leave them to dry for a few days before inserting the base in pure sand.
Pests and diseases If gasteria plants are incorrectly cultivated they may become prone to infestation by aphids, scale insects, mealy bug, root mealy bug, red spider mite and thrips. If they are kept outside be on the lookout for woodlice and slugs.

Gasteria angulata
These have fleshy leaves in two rows, 25cm (10in) long and 5cm (2in) wide, green, with crosswise bands of small, sunken white spots, especially on the lower surface, and orange-red flowers.

Gasteria maculata

Gasteria armstrongii
A slow-growing low plant with rough, tongue-shaped, dark green leaves up to 5cm (2in) long and 3cm (1in) wide. The tips of the oldest leaves curve downward. Initially they grow in two rows but at a later stage they form rosettes.

Gasteria caespitosa

Gasteria caespitosa
Vigorously growing species with 10- to 14-cm (4- to 5½-in) long leaves, 2cm (¾in) wide, slightly convex on both surfaces. They are 7mm (¼in) thick, dark green with numerous white spots appearing in irregular crosswise bands. The flowers are reddish or rose red.
Gasteria liliputana
The smallest species, it has green foliage with white patches. Leaves are 5cm (2in) long and keeled underneath, growing in spirals on a short stalk, and there are clusters of small rose-red flowers in spring.
Gasteria maculata
This species has tongue-shaped, irregularly triangular green leaves with white patches and a horny edge growing more or less in two rows, and red flowers.
Gasteria pulchra
A densely leaved plant up to 25cm (10in) in height. The leaves grow almost in two rows. They are sword shaped, irregularly triangular, long and sharply pointed, dark green and smooth, with white spots, and there are bright red, green-striped flowers.
Gasteria trigona
Leaves up to 20cm (8in) long are arranged in spirals and are green with white spots. The flowers are orange-red with a green tube.
Gasteria verrucosa
The leaves are in two rows, 15cm (6in) long and 2cm (¾in) wide. The upper surface is concave, the reverse convex, with numerous white warts, and there are long clusters of red flowers with green tips.

Gerbera

Compositae

Transvaal Daisy

Name Named after Traugott Gerber, an 18th-century German botanist.
Origin The genus includes about 45 species, originating in southern Africa and in Asia.
Description Herbaceous, non-hardy perennials with lanceolate, hairy leaves, conspicuously deeply incised and arranged in rosettes. The daisy-like flowers occur in the most wonderful colours, from cream and yellow to scarlet and purple, and are very suitable for cutting, since they last well in water.
Position Gerbera species are best planted out in a moderately heated greenhouse. It is possible to grow them in pots, but they will flower less profusely.
Care If you want to attempt to grow the plant in a pot, you are advised to get hold of the original species *Gerbera jamesonii*, with single, or better still double, flowers; it does not develop impractically long stalks. Put the plants in 20-cm (8-in) pots and place these in full sun in the greenhouse or on the window-sill. In summer the air temperature must drop below 16°C (60°F), but slightly warmer compost – between 22 and 25°C (71 and 77°F) – is appreciated. The easiest way to provide this temperature is to use an electric heating cable, specially made for soil heating. With a thermostat connected to a soil thermometer you can maintain the exact degree of warmth.

The plants should be sprayed daily with rainwater. They flower from June until autumn. In winter the gerbera must be kept slightly cooler, preferably in a moderately heated greenhouse with minimum temperature of 12°C (53°F). Older plants produce fewer flowers and should therefore be replaced after a few years.
Watering In summer they may be watered freely, but in any case it is important that the compost should be kept constantly moist. In winter the plants can be kept a little drier.
Feeding Mix a little fertiliser with the water every fortnight in the period of active growth.
Repotting In greenhouses gerbera plants are best grown in sandy clay. For pot cultivation a mixture may be made of equal parts of clay or loam, leafmould and rotted cow manure, though some people maintain that the plants can be grown satisfactorily in standard potting compost. You should in any case use plastic pots to reduce evaporation with consequent cooling of the compost, and provide good drainage. If young plants are put in 20-cm (8-in) pots in spring, they need not be repotted for two years. After this the plants are usually renewed, so that repotting is actually superfluous.
Propagation There are various ways of increasing gerberas. Amateurs will probably find it easiest to grow them from seed. This should be sown in February, in a soil temperature of 15 to 20°C (59 to 68°F) under glass. Older plants may be divided. It is also possible to grow them from cuttings, taken from two-year-old plants which are drastically cut back. The young shoots which will then appear will root in bottom heat if mist-sprayed.

Gerbera jamesonii

A perennial with a taproot. The leaves are 15 to 25 cm (6 to 10 in) long, 5 to 7 cm (2 to 2¾ in) wide, more or less incised and roughly toothed and the lower surface is covered in woolly hairs. The leaf stalk is 15 to 20 cm (6 to 8 in) long. About 30 radial flowers in a variety of colours grow on straight stalks, 25 to 45 cm (10 to 18 in) in length. 'Florepleno' is a double-flowered strain. For cutting, growers cultivate single-flowered forms, which keep better, but the double-flowered strain is much more beautiful.

A double-flowered form of the original species, *Gerbera jamesonii*

Glechoma hederacea

Glechoma

Labiatae

Ground Ivy

Name Adopted from an ancient Greek plant name, *glechon*.
Origin There are about six species, indigenous to the northern hemisphere.
Description Perennials with long, creeping stems which readily root on the nodes and circular to kidney-shaped leaves with a crenate edge. The variegated form of *Glechoma hederacea* is cultivated as a house plant. It is a very strong hanging plant which can give others as well as ourselves a great deal of pleasure, for it is easily grown from cuttings.
Position Put it in a well-lit spot, but out of direct midday sun. If it is kept too dark the fine foliage marking will deteriorate.
Care It is advisable to grow new plants every year, or to cut them back very drastically in spring. Overwinter them at a temperature of 6 to 10°C (43 to 50°F) in a cool greenhouse.
Watering In summer make sure that the compost is kept moist. If the plant is kept cool in winter water sparingly, and keep the level of humidity between 50 and 60 per cent.
Feeding In the growing season feed it every ten days with a fertiliser solution at normal concentration.
Propagation If you allow the plant to creep it will develop roots on the nodes. By cutting the stem on either side you will obtain new plants. Unrooted stems may be divided into sections with two nodes each. Remove the lower pair of leaves and insert the node in a mixture of sand and peat.
Diseases Whitefly can be a nuisance.

Glechoma hederacea

Syn. *Nepeta hederacea*. A creeper or hanging plant with hairy, kidney-shaped, fresh green leaves with a white margin, and pale blue flowers. The leaves are fragrant to the touch.

Gloriosa

Liliaceae

Glory Lily

Name From the Latin word *gloriosus*, famous.
Origin A native of tropical regions of Africa and Asia.
Description Non-hardy perennial climbers, growing on tubers. The initially single stems branch at a later

Flower of *Gloriosa rothschildiana*

stage and may grow to up to 2 m (6 ft). The leaves end in tendrils with which the plants attach themselves to other plants in their native forests. They are cultivated for the sake of their magnificent, vividly coloured flowers which grow on long stalks from the axils of the upper leaves. The corolla consists of six recurved petals, wavy or frilly at the edge. In previous decades the plant was grown chiefly for cutting, but in recent years it has come on the market as a house plant as well.
Position When you obtain a flowering plant it should be placed in the best

Gloriosa rothschildiana

light available. It need not be screened against the sun. In winter the tuber should be kept in the greenhouse or in a cupboard.
Care Dead flowers must be removed. In autumn the foliage will turn yellow, indicating that the plant is dying off. From then onwards it must be kept dry and placed, pot and all, in a temperate greenhouse or in a cupboard, at a temperature of 10 to 12°C (50 to 53°F).
Watering Keep the compost thoroughly moist during the growth and flowering periods. Use tepid water, preferably rainwater. Reduce the water supply when flowering has ceased, and keep the plant completely dry in the dormant season. In the living-room the low atmospheric humidity often presents a problem and you will have to mist-spray frequently.
Feeding Feed weekly from March to August, giving it at half the concentration indicated on the label.
Repotting In spring remove the old compost and repot the tubers in wide, shallow pots in a mixture of loam, leafmould and sharp sand. Handle them gently, for the growing point is very delicate. A tuber develops one to three stems each season and wastes away entirely after producing two new tubers. In order not

to discourage this development, keep the nose of the tuber as far away from the side of the pot as possible. After potting up the young tubers give them bottom heat of at least 20°C (68°F), and make sure that the tendrils have something to attach themselves to.
Propagation Increase from seed or from offsets. It will be a long time before the plants flower. Division of the tubers is a risky operation.
Pests and diseases Draughts and too low a temperature lead to aphid infestation.

Gloriosa rothschildiana
These have deep pink flowers with wavy yellow margins in summer. There are numerous fine cultivars.
Gloriosa superba
Similar to the previous species, but the margins of the petals are more frilly and the flowers are initially yellow-green, then orange and finally scarlet.

Graptopetalum
Crassulaceae

Name The generic name is derived from the Greek and means 'with painted petals'.
Origin The 12 known species all originate in Arizona and Mexico.
Description A small, but nevertheless varied, genus which includes low-growing rosettes, shrubby climbers or hanging plants. They are cultivated for their decorative foliage, their attractive little flowers and perhaps also because they are so easy to grow indoors. The flowers are arranged in compound umbels with one to ten axes and erect-growing florets. The florets are fairly small; the petals are fused to half their length and bear horizontally spreading slips.
Position They need plenty of light throughout the year. Full sun is ideal: the colouring will be improved and the plant will be encouraged to develop more flower stalks. In summer they may be moved to a sheltered spot in the garden.
Care From October to March give them a rest in a temperature of 5 to 10°C (41 to 50°F).
Watering These succulents need little water. Be particularly sparing in the dormant season.
Feeding In the growing period give a doubly diluted fertiliser solution once every three weeks.
Repotting Repot in spring, in well-draining compost, for instance a proprietary mixture with extra sand.
Propagation Increase from tip or leaf cuttings, occasionally also from seed.

Graptopetalum amethystinum

Pests and diseases They are susceptible to aphids, blackleg, root rot and mildew.

Graptopetalum amethystinum
Syn. *Pachyphytum amethystinum*. The leaf rosettes occur at the end of recumbent or hanging stems. The leaves are thick, bloomed, reverse oval and amethyst coloured to grey. The flowers are red, but fairly inconspicuous.
Graptopetalum paraguayense
Syn. *Sedum weinbergii*. Mother of Pearl plant. The opal-coloured leaves are arranged in small rosettes at the tips of branching, recumbent or hanging stems. The flowers have cream-coloured petals with red to purple speckles.

Grevillea
Proteaceae
Silk Bark Oak

Name Named after C. F. Greville, one of the founders of the Royal Horticultural Society, 1749–1809.
Origin The genus includes 190 species, most of them natives of Australia, though some have their natural habitat in Tasmania, New Caledonia and other Melanesian islands.
Description Evergreen trees and shrubs with alternating leaves. In cultivation it is known only as a foliage plant, since it never reaches the age where it will produce its magnificent flowers. These flowers occur in pairs in axillary or terminal racemes. The style usually protrudes far beyond the corolla; it is this fact which gives the flowers their unusual appearance. You may have seen them as cut flowers at the florist's, together with other species of the genus. In their natural environment the trees may reach a height of up to 50m (160ft).
Position If it is stopped from time to time the grevillea will develop into a shrub, otherwise it will retain a tree-like appearance. As it is such a graceful ornamental plant, it is much better on its own, displayed as a solitary specimen rather than in a mixed group. Put it in good light, in a spot out of the spring and summer sun. A well-lit hall or conservatory, where the temperature never exceeds 20°C (68°F), would be a good spot. The lower the temperature, the finer its shape and appearance. In summer it may be put outside.
Care In winter it prefers a rest in a temperature of 6 to 10°C (43 to 50°F). It grows rapidly, and when it has nearly reached the ceiling it can be cut back.
Watering In warm summer weather you will have to mist-spray frequently to

Foliage detail of a grevillea

Grevillea robusta shows to better advantage if several specimens are grouped together

keep the plant in good condition. In moderate temperatures a degree of humidity of 50 to 60 per cent is sufficient. Water freely in the growing period, making sure that the compost is kept constantly moist. If it is kept cool in winter it must be watered very sparingly.
Feeding This is quite unnecessary – the plant grows rapidly enough.
Repotting Young plants should be repotted every year, mature specimens only when the roots emerge from the pot. Mix a proprietary potting compost with sand and clay, or make a mixture of equal parts leafmould and clay, with the possible addition of some rotted cow manure.
Propagation They are fairly difficult to grow from cuttings, but you might try. Half-ripe cuttings, up to 8cm (3in) long and with a heel, should be taken in spring and rooted under glass in a bottom temperature of 18 to 20°C (64 to 68°F); the process may take several months. It is easier to grow them from seed sown in January–February in a temperature of 18 to 20°C (64 to 68°F).
Pests and diseases Aphids will occur if the plant is kept too warm in winter. Whitefly can also be a nuisance.

Grevillea robusta
A graceful tree, which in cultivation is usually grown as a shrub. The leaves are bipinnate or tripinnate. Young leaves are covered in silky hairs, giving them a silvery glow. Older leaves are fairly dark green and may reach a length of 45cm (18in). In cultivation flowers practically never appear.

Guzmania
Bromeliaceae

Name This bromeliad has been named after A. Guzman, an 18th-century Spanish apothecary and botanist.
Origin The 120 species of this genus originate in Central and South America, but chiefly in the tropical rain forests of South America.
Description The genus includes epiphytes as well as terrestrial-growing species. They have smooth-edged leaves, usually arranged in rosettes in which water can be stored. The bracts are brilliantly coloured and as a rule provide the greatest attraction. The white or yellow flowers are fused in a

Guzmania minor 'Orange Variegata'

tube and have three bracts. They appear either in the leaf rosette or on stalks and usually soon disappear, while the vivid bracts may retain their colour for several months.

The plants usually flower from November to January.

Position Because they demand high humidity they are more suited to cultivation in a flower window and in the hothouse than in the living-room. Place them in light shade in summer and in plenty of light in winter.

Care In spring and summer they must be kept warm and in winter the mercury must not drop below 16 to 18°C (60 to 64°F). After flowering the rosettes die, but new plants may be grown from the offsets which have meanwhile appeared and which must not be separated until the parent plant is starting to fade.

The use of a growth regulator has made it possible to market flowering guzmania plants throughout the whole of the year.

Watering In a normally heated room it will be necessary to spray very frequently. In addition use the deep-plate method or best of all, invest in a humidifier. Always use tepid, demineralised water or rainwater. Water freely in the period of active growth, but keep the plant a little drier in winter. Water may be poured into the 'funnel' only in summer, unless the plant is kept near a radiator in winter. Watch carefully to see that the funnel does not rot and do not pour water into it when the inflorescence appears there. Spray frequently in the growing season, especially when the new leaves appear, but don't spray in winter.

Feeding In the growing period feed once a fortnight, using a solution at half the concentration indicated on the label. The fertiliser may be poured into the funnel and foliage feeding is also possible.

Repotting When potting new plants a light and acid mixture is best, consisting of chopped fern roots, sphagnum moss, rotted beech leaves and a little sharp sand. Use plastic pots and provide good drainage.

Propagation Detach rooted shoots from the parent plant and pot them separately. They can also be grown from seed. A minimum temperature of 15°C (59°F) is essential for germination.

Guzmania angustifolia

A clump-forming plant with 8- to 12-cm (3- to 4½-in) long and more than 1-cm (½-in) wide leaves, green with red shading. The vivid yellow flowers have short stalks and bright red bracts with a dark tip.

***Guzmania* hybrids**

This group includes the well-known hybrids 'Intermedia' and 'Magnifica'. The magnificent scarlet bracts of the latter maintain their beauty for as long as six months. They have white flowers and soft green leaves with red marking.

Guzmania lindenii

A stalkless plant which develops a large funnel-shaped rosette. The inflorescence may reach a height of up to 2m (6ft), and each leaf may grow up to 70cm (28in) in length and is 5 to 7cm (2 to 2¾in) wide, pointed and yellowish green with brown-green streaks in crosswise bands.

Guzmania lingulata

This forms rosettes 80cm (32in) across and 30cm (1ft) tall. The leaves are bright green and glossy, narrow and ribbed, with wine-red lines at the base. The flower stalk, up to 30cm (1ft) tall, bears bright red bracts, each up to 6.5cm (2½in) in length, triangular and spreading, with a cluster of yellow-white flowers in the centre. The form 'Splendens' has more red marking on the leaves.

Guzmania lingulata

Guzmania minor

Syn. *Guzmania lingulata* var. *minor*. Small, dense rosettes which do not grow beyond 20cm (8in) in height. The leaves are up to 12cm (4½in) wide, often with red shading. The inflorescence rarely extends beyond the foliage and is surrounded by bright red bracts. It carries small white flowers.

Guzmania monostachya

Syn. *Guzmania tricolor*. Growing to 40cm (16in) tall, the narrow green leaves are slightly curved and are arranged in a rosette which sometimes has a diameter of 75cm (30in). The flower stalk extends beyond the leaves and is encased in broad-oval pointed bracts, greenish brown or almost black at the base. The white flowers hardly emerge from the bracts. The form 'Variegata', which has white vertical striping, is the one most frequently cultivated.

Guzmania zahnii

This makes loose rosettes of tongue-shaped, pointed leaves, yellowish to reddish in colour, with lengthwise red striping. The flower stalk grows to 40cm (16in) and is entirely encased in red leaves. Bracts and flowers are yellow.

Gymnocalycium

Cactaceae

Name The botanical name is composed of the words *gymnos* and *kalix*, 'bare calyx'. This refers to the hairless flower tube, which is covered in broad, white-edged scales.

Origin The genus includes more than 50 species, all originating in South America. Many have their native habitat in Argentina.

Description Solitary or clump-forming cacti, usually in the shape of a flattened sphere, occasionally more columnar. The ribs are notched to a greater or lesser extent. They are hairless, but frequently bear magnificent, conspicuous thorns, which often appear to curve inwards towards the cactus body. The funnel-shaped flowers appear near the crown. These are white, yellow, greenish or red and have a short or long tube with scaling in the shape of a half moon on the outside. Most species are capable of flowering at an early age. The genus has only become generally known after the introduction of the unusual cultivars of *Gymnocalycium mihanovichii friedrichii*, which suddenly flooded the market when they were imported from Japan. They are bought in large numbers from supermarkets, to be used as presents or discardable plants. We know them as 'Yellow Cap', 'Orange Cap', 'Red Cap', 'Black Cap' and 'Oprima Rubra'. The caps lack chlorophyll and to survive they must be grafted on to green cacti. They may, however, produce flowers.

Guzmania zahnii

Position You can keep them in the living-room or in the greenhouse, in plenty of light, but out of direct sunlight in spring and summer.

Care From October to March they should be rested at 6 to 10°C (43 to 50°F).

Watering Water moderately in summer, very sparingly in the cool resting period – just enough, in fact, to prevent the cactus bodies shrivelling up. Dry living-room air presents no problem, but in hot summer weather it will do no harm to mist-spray from time to time.

Feeding Not absolutely essential, but they may be given some cactus fertiliser once a fortnight.

Repotting Repot into a nutritious, porous compost – cactus compost is excellent.

Propagation Most species develop a large number of offsets. These can be carefully removed from the parent plant and used as cuttings. Coloured shoots must be grafted. When grafting, both the shoot and the stock should be cut straight across; they are then pressed together and temporarily secured. *Trichocereus spachianus* and *Eriocereus jusbertii* provide good stock.

Gymnocalycium andreae

Syn. *Echinocactus andreae*. A compact species, shaped like a flattened globe, dark blue-green in colour, up to 4.5cm (1¾in) across. It has about eight broad, slightly notched ribs and short, brown-black thorns which appear to be pressed against the cactus body. The flowers are up to 4.5cm (1¾in) long, greenish yellow on the outside, sulphur yellow inside.

Gymnocalycium baldianum

Syn. *Echinocactus baldianus*. Unlike the previous species this does not develop offsets. It makes a flattened sphere, blue-green, up to 7cm (2¾in) in diameter, with nine to twelve, slightly lumpy ribs and five yellowish, incurving thorns, and produces purple-red flowers at an early age.

Gymnocalycium denudatum

Various forms of gymnocalycium. Coloured bodies must always be grafted

Gymnocalycium quehlianum, an extremely lumpy cactus

Gymnocalycium bruchii
Syn. *Gymnocalycium lafaldense.* A vigorous clump-forming species, up to 2cm (¾in) in diameter, with eight to twelve notched ribs and curved white thorns. The flowers are delicate pink with a dark streak in the centre.
Gymnocalycium denudatum
Spider Cactus. Up to 20cm (8in) in height, it forms a glossy dark green sphere with five broad, flat ribs. The areoles bear curved yellow thorns, pressed towards the body. The white or pink flowers are 5 to 7cm (2 to 2¾in) long. There are various hybrids.
Gymnocalycium gibbosum
Syn. *Echinocactus gibbosus.* A blue-green species, 20cm (8in) tall, with nine to twelve very lumpy ribs and seven to ten pale brown thorns. It bears pink-white flowers.
Gymnocalycium mihanovichii
Syn. *Echinocactus mihanovichii.* This has a grey-green body, 3 to 5cm (1 to 2in) in diameter, with red shading and marked with crosswise bands. There are small curved thorns and yellow-green flowers. The variety *friedrichii* has pink flowers. In cultivation both forms only thrive if grafted on stock.
Gymnocalycium multiflorum
Syn. *Echinocactus multiflorus.* The body is broad spherical, blue-green, with 10 to 15 nobbly ribs and up to 15cm (6in) across. It has yellow thorns, 3cm (1in) long and spreading, often red at the base, and white-pink flowers.
Gymnocalycium quehlianum
Syn. *Echinocactus quehlianus.* A flattened sphere, grey-green, turning brown in the sun, it has eight to thirteen nobbly ribs and five curved thorns. The flowers are whitish, up to 7cm (2¾in) long with a carmine-red throat.

Gynura
Compositae

Name From the Greek *gyne*, woman, and *oura*, tail.
Origin There are about 25 species, originating in tropical regions of Asia.
Description A herbaceous or shrubby plant with opposite-growing foliage. The flowers are yellow, orange, blue or purple, and the calyx is tubular to bell shaped. Only those species in which the foliage is shaded purple because of the velvety purple hairs covering the green leaves are usually cultivated. They are very rewarding hanging or erect-growing plants, easily grown from cuttings. Their unusual colouring makes them very suitable for adding a bright note to plant combinations.
Position Give them the best possible light throughout the year, but in spring and summer see that the brightest sunrays cannot reach the plant, for too much sun frequently scorches the foliage, though plenty of light ensures that the purple hairs maintain their fine colouring. If gynura plants are kept too dark they frequently become infested by aphids, the leaves revert to green and few flowers are produced. They also do not tolerate draughts. In summer these plants may also be kept in the garden.
Care In winter the gynura usually becomes unsightly as a result of too little light. Actually only young plants are beautiful and it is advisable to take cuttings at frequent intervals. If you wish to overwinter them, they must be kept at 15 to 18°C (59 to 64°F) in the daytime, and at night the temperature must not fall below 12°C (53°F). Give enough water to prevent the stems becoming limp.

Gynura aurantiaca

Watering During the growing season the plant should be watered freely, for the gynura requires plenty of moisture. Never pour water on the foliage or spray it directly, for this will cause staining. Water moderately in winter. A degree of atmospheric humidity of 50 to 60 per cent is high enough.
Feeding In the growing season the plants should be fed once every three weeks, using half the concentration recommended on the label, for if the plants grow too rapidly much of their purple shading will be lost.
Repotting Young plants are best potted in leafmould and clay, mixed with a little rotted cow manure.

Gynura flowers have an unpleasant smell

Propagation In spring and autumn increase from cuttings up to 10cm (4in) long which readily root in water or in a mixture of peat and sand, with some bottom heat.
Pests and diseases Aphids may appear.

Gynura aurantiaca
A plant with purple-velvet leaves and erect-growing stems, reaching a height between 50 and 100cm (20 and 40in). All parts are covered in purple hairs. It has triangular to oval dark green and purple leaves, up to 15cm (6in) long, and usually lightly incised, with clusters of orange-coloured flower heads.
Gynura procumbens
Syn. *Gynura sarmentosa.* Purple Passion Vine. This resembles the previous species, but has creeping or trailing stems and more deeply incised foliage. The orange-yellow flowers have a disagreeable smell for the first few days. They later form silver-haired bells.

Inflorescence of *Haemanthus multiflorus*

Haemanthus

Amaryllidaceae

Blood Lily, Red Cape Tulip

Name Derived from the Greek *haima*, blood, and *anthos*, flower. The best-known species has blood-red flowers.
Origin About 50 species, varying greatly in appearance, are found in Africa, from Ethiopia to Cape Town.
Description Bulbous plants, occurring in many forms. Among the best-known species one has broad, thick, clivia-like leaves and white flowers; the other develops thinner leaves and a large red flower.
Position All species can be cultivated in a light spot in the living-room.
Care *Haemanthus albiflos* is a vigorous, perennial house plant whose foliage must never entirely die down. It tolerates full sun but is also satisfied with less light. In winter it must be kept cooler, at between 12 and 15°C (53 and 59°F). This clivia-like plant has unfortunately become very rare. The foliage of *Haemanthus katharinae* must also never entirely die down. The other species may be given so little water in autumn that all the leaves die. The bulb is then kept in the pot at a minimum temperature of 12°C (53°F). In spring it is repotted and forced into flower like the hippeastrum.
Watering The compost must never be more than moderately moist, while in winter deciduous species should be kept dry and the others very slightly moist. In spring start watering very sparingly, gradually increasing the supply.
Feeding In summer all species may be fed every fortnight until the end of July.
Repotting The most satisfactory mixture consists of equal parts of leafmould, clay or loam, and rotted cow manure. The plants do not stand up well to repotting and for that reason usually only the top layer of compost is renewed annually. However, if the soil ball is kept intact when the plant is repotted, no damage will be done. Make sure the drainage is good and leave the neck of the bulb visible.
Propagation *Haemanthus albiflos* can be increased by division, but it is advisable to delay this operation until the plant has really become too large. Leaves cut from the plant and left in a dry room often develop little plantlets on the cut surface, and these may be potted up separately. The other species produce offset bulbs, which are removed when the plants are repotted, to be cultivated separately. Propagation from seed is also possible.

Haemanthus albiflos
Elephant's Ear; African Blood Lily. The bulb is up to 7cm ($2\frac{3}{4}$in) in diameter. It is stalkless, with two to six fairly thick leaves, 15 to 20cm (6 to 8in) long and 4 to 8cm ($1\frac{1}{2}$ to 3in) wide, arranged in two rows, and dark green. The flower heads, up to 5cm (2in) across, are puff shaped, with green-veined white bracts and white flowers. The variety *pubescens* has hairy foliage.
Haemanthus × hybridus
A cross between *H. katharinae* and *H. puniceus*. It has five to ten oval leaves, 30cm (1ft) long and 15cm (6in) wide, green, with an erect-growing long stalk and a sheath densely covered in purple patches. The flower stalks are longer than the leaves and bear a multiflowered pseudo-umbel up to 25cm (10in) across. The inflorescence is surrounded by six green and spreading bracts. The flowers have a red tube and slips. In cultivation this plant is usually referred to as 'Prince Albert'.
Haemanthus katharinae
This resembles the following species, but the leaves appear when the plant is in flower and the petal slips are equal in length to the tube.
Haemanthus multiflorus
Between three and five leaves are grouped on a short pseudo-stalk; they are oval in shape, up to 25cm (10in) long and appear after flowering has ceased. The sheath is often slightly flecked. The flowers appear in spherical pseudo-umbels, 20cm (8in) in diameter, and there are four pale green, purple-flecked bracts. The flowers are red, and the slips are twice the length of the tube. The cultivar 'Superbus' bears slightly larger, deep red flowers.

Inflorescence of *Haemanthus albiflos*

Hamatocactus setispinus, Strawberry Cactus

Hamatocactus

Cactaceae

Name From the Latin *hamatus*, hooked.
Origin Three species occur in Mexico.
Description Spherical or slightly columnar cacti with large, hooked central thorns. The plants readily produce a profusion of enormous flowers.
Position Preferably keep it in a cool greenhouse, where, together with other succulents, the plants will receive plenty of sun and warmth in summer, while in winter the thermostat is turned so low that they all nearly freeze. These are the ideal conditions for prolific flowering.
Care If you prefer, the plants may spend the summer on a sunny window-sill instead, but in that case take them out of the cramped little pots in which they are sold. In a reasonably sized plastic pot the compost will not dry out so quickly and a reserve of moisture will keep the roots alive. Towards winter the collection will have to be moved to a cool environment, where the temperature can be kept at a minimum of 5°C (41°F). Here they should stay until spring, slightly screened against spring sunshine in order to get them gradually accustomed to the increasing light and the new growing season setting in.
Watering In summer always keep moderately moist, but in winter keep constantly dry if possible.
Feeding Feed with a nitrogen-free fertiliser, in summer only.
Repotting Use the standard cactus mixture, consisting of 50 per cent ordinary potting compost and 50 per cent perlite, which has the correct pH, drains well and always retains a little moisture. Young plants should be repotted every spring, later every two or three years.
Propagation Sow in spring, under glass, in sterilised compost. It may take some time before all the seeds have germinated. They are then pricked out and grown separately. During the first few months it is essential to keep them out of bright sunlight.

Hamatocactus hamatacanthus
These form globular bodies which may grow to 30cm (1ft) across. They have about 13 ribs bearing white thorns. The central thorns, one to four in number, are reddish, to 12cm ($4\frac{1}{2}$in) long, and curved. The flowers are up to 7cm ($2\frac{3}{4}$in) long, and pale yellow with red throat. This species is sometimes classified under *Ferocactus*.
Hamatocactus setispinus
Strawberry Cactus. A globe shape to 10cm (4in) in diameter, later increasing in height to 15cm (6in). It has 12 to 15 ribs, white or brownish thorns, and one to three hooked, brown, central thorns. The flowers are up to 7cm ($2\frac{3}{4}$in) across, yellow, and red at the base.
Hamatocactus uncinatus
Syn. *Ancistrocactus uncinatus*. Forms a short column, to about 20cm (8in) tall, dark blue-green in colour. There are nine to thirteen nobbly ribs with hooked, initially red, thorns. The flowers are reddish brown.

Harpephyllum

Anacardiaceae

Name Derived from the Greek *harpe*, sickle, and *phyllon*, leaf. The pinnae are actually sickle shaped.
Origin As far as is known two species grow in South Africa.
Description A fairly unfamiliar house plant – at a later stage in fact an indoor tree – which has lately become more popular. The leaves are pinnate and are grouped at the end of the twigs. The plants develop edible stone fruits resembling olives. As far as I know they are not produced in cultivation.
Position Another of those tub plants, which therefore requires to be kept cool in winter, but which are nevertheless marketed as house plants. Perhaps we should not blame the growers – it has been done before and, what is more, sometimes with success. Just think of the hibiscus.

Care In botanical gardens this plant is by no means a rarity, but it is too early to say how it will behave as a house plant. The standard method of cultivation is that from late May onwards the plants should be placed out of doors, where they may spend the summer in a sunny, or at any rate well-lit and sheltered spot. Towards autumn, in any case before the first night frosts occur, they should be moved to the cool greenhouse, where they are given plenty of fresh air in good weather and kept at 5°C (41°F) when it is freezing outside. In spring the temperature should be kept as low as possible by ventilation in sunny weather; this is to prevent the plants starting into growth too early. When there is no more danger of night frosts the plants may be taken outside again.

If you want to try to grow a harpephyllum in the living-room the problems will clearly arise in winter rather than in summer. Place the plant as close to the window as possible, at most screening it from the sun between 11 a.m. and 4 p.m. Keep it in a cool environment in winter, perhaps in a well-lit, frost-free spot, and spray the foliage frequently.
Watering In summer always keep it moderately moist but in winter keep the plant fairly dry if the temperature is low. The foliage must not drop. Ordinary tap water is satisfactory.
Feeding In summer feed every fortnight.
Repotting The mixture should contain loam or clay, or you might try standard potting compost. The pots or tubs (which might be of plastic) must always be well drained.
Propagation Harpephyllums are increased from imported seed, which germinates in bottom heat. For the first two years the plant must be cultivated in a hothouse; it can then be hardened off for cooler conditions.

Harpephyllum caffrum
In its native country this is a tree of more than 10m (33ft). It has evergreen foliage, leathery, glossy, pinnate, with 11 to 15 lanceolate, slightly sickle-shaped leaves with a covered central vein.

Hatiora cylindrica, the Coral Cactus

Harpephyllum caffrum looks good in a modern interior

Hatiora
Cactaceae
Coral Cactus

Name An anagram of the name of Thomas Hariot, a 16th-century English botanist.
Origin About four species are found in south-eastern Brazil.
Description Very curious, readily branching plants with cylindrical joints. They resemble some species of the genus *Rhipsalis*, but the joints are more cylindrical and club shaped.
Position In summer the plants may be cultivated out of doors or in the greenhouse, in winter in the greenhouse or the living-room.
Care Very similar to that of the Christmas Cactus or zygocactus, that is to say they should be kept in a shady position out of doors. Hanging pots could be tied to the lower branches of a tree. A cool and dry resting period before flowering is essential. This is preferably given in September–October, when the plants are kept dry, but frost-free, for six to eight weeks. Give a little water only when the flower buds become visible, then gradually increase the supply. They should then be given another rest in a cool environment and at the end of May move them to the garden once more.
Watering Always keep them moderately moist in the growing season, preferably by means of plunging. In the first resting period give no water at all, in the second keep the plants almost dry. Always use rainwater.
Feeding In summer feed every two weeks.
Repotting Repot preferably in a mixture of leafmould and sphagnum moss with a little rotted cow manure. If possible use hanging baskets.
Propagation Increase from joints taken off the plant and left to dry, also from seed.

Hatiora cylindrica
An epiphytic, readily branching cactus with pale green, red-blotched joints, 2 to 3cm ($\frac{3}{4}$ to 1in) long, and cylindrical, with red and orange flowers.
Hatiora salicornioides
Syn. *Rhipsalis salicornioides*. Club-shaped joints, 3cm (1in) long, arranged in whorls of three to five, narrowing towards the base. Flowers initially yellow, later more rose red; 1cm ($\frac{1}{2}$in) in diameter.

Haworthia
Liliaceae
Wart Plant

Name Named after the English botanist Adrian Hardy Haworth, 1767–1833.
Origin There are approximately 160 different species, mainly occurring in the Cape Province.
Description Succulent plants with leaves arranged in rosettes; they resemble the aloe and the gasteria. In some species 'windows' occur on the leaves. In their natural habitat the plants are sometimes entirely buried in the soil, with only the 'windows' in the tips of the leaves showing to catch the light.
Position Species with non-translucent leaves are easily grown house plants, which must be kept just out of bright sunlight. 'Window' species must be grown in a moderate greenhouse and are essentially collectors' plants.
Care Species with non-translucent leaves, often covered in pearly warts, are frequently available and will thrive in the living-room, provided they do not receive too much sunlight. Their dormant season occurs in winter, so from October onwards the temperature must fall to 10 to 12°C (50 to 53°F) if possible. Indoors the plants should be kept in a cool room at that time, where they should be placed close to the (single glazed) window and, of course, given less water.

'Window' species have their resting season in our summer and usually start into growth in October. These plants must therefore be kept slightly warmer in winter, at about 16°C (60°F), and the compost must be kept slightly moist. Provided the rest and growth periods are strictly observed, 'window' species may also be grown in the living-room, as the temperature tallies reasonably well. However, they are seldom encountered there. Usually they are only available from growers specialising in succulents; the non-translucent species, on the other hand, may be bought from practically any garden shop.
Watering None of the species should ever be entirely dry, although the 'window' forms need extremely little water in summer, while the others are so tough that they will survive even if kept cooler and drier than has been indicated. I have sometimes kept them completely dry at practically zero degrees, and most of them were alive in the spring.
Feeding In the growing season (that is, either in summer or in winter) very little cactus fertiliser need be given.
Repotting Non-translucent species do well in a standard cactus mixture, that is, equal parts of potting compost and perlite. 'Window' species prefer slightly heavier compost, with a little loam or clay added. Repot in spring in plastic pots with good drainage.
Propagation Nearly all species develop offsets from the lower leaves. These may be removed and, after having been left to dry for a few days, can be rooted in sandy soil. They may also be grown from seed.

Haworthia attenuata
◐ ⊜ ◯ ⊛ ⊡
Slender rosettes of narrow fleshy leaves, covered in small white warts which form a central line on the upper surface; on the reverse they are arranged in crosswise bands. Small white flowers appear on pendulous stalks.
Haworthia cuspidata
◯ ⊜ ◯ ⊛ ⊡
These form dense rosettes of fleshy leaves, up to 2.5 cm (1 in) long, obliquely shaped and ending in an abrupt point. The colour is grey-green; at the tip the tissue is translucent with some green marking.
Haworthia fasciata
◐ ⊜ ◯ ⊛ ⊡
Thick, slightly incurving leaves are arranged in a rosette. They are glossy green with white pearly warts on the lower surface only; these form crosswise bands. This is the best-known species.
Haworthia margaritifera
This resembles the previous and the first-mentioned species, but the rosettes are broader and the warts are not arranged in bands.

Haworthia attenuata with a small flower

Haworthia obtusa
◯ ⊜ ◯ ⊛ ⊡
Small, thick leaves form rosettes. The upper part is clear and translucent and bears a kind of bristle.
Haworthia reinwardtii
◐ ⊜ ◯ ⊛ ⊡
The fleshy, triangular leaves are densely covered in white pearly warts, arranged in bands. The rosette is arranged in a dense spiral around a central axis, so that the plant forms a column of up to 20 cm (8 in) in height and 8 cm (3 in) across.
Haworthia tessellata
◯ ⊜ ◯ ⊛ ⊡
A rosette of triangular, fleshy and recurving leaves, with reticulate marking.
Haworthia truncata
The leaves grow in two opposite rows, 2 to 3 cm ($\frac{3}{4}$ to 1 in) long and 1.5 to 3 cm ($\frac{1}{2}$ to 1 in) wide; at the tips, which are blunt as if they had been cut across, clear windows allow the light to reach the assimilating tissue inside. This is a typical collector's item. In the wild it grows almost entirely underground.

Hebe speciosa

Hebe
Scrophulariaceae

Name Hebe was the beautiful daughter of Zeus and Hera and was cup-bearer to the gods. The plants are frequently called *Veronica*, but this is a genus of herbaceous plants, whereas *Hebe* is a genus of shrubby growths.
Origin More than 100 species occur in Australia, New Zealand and Tasmania.
Description Small, evergreen shrubs with leathery foliage and white, purple or red flowers arranged in spikes.
Position These plants are not sufficiently hardy to be kept outside in temperate climates, nor do they tolerate warmth sufficiently well to be kept indoors. They should therefore be placed on a terrace or balcony in autumn, and kept cool in winter.
Care They are not exactly ideal for living-room cultivation; but they are usually available because they flower so attractively in autumn. If the plants are put in the warm living-room, both foliage and flowers will soon fall, although the process may be delayed a little by spraying. However, it is better to keep the plants in a really cool spot, for instance in an unheated entrance hall, a porch, or on a sheltered balcony. Hebes tolerate full sun. After flowering keep your plant as cool as possible so that the foliage is retained and in mid-May you can move it out to the garden.
Watering The compost must be kept moderately moist throughout the year. Always use rainwater, for hebes are lime haters.
Feeding In summer feed every two weeks.
Repotting Use an acid compost rich in humus, for instance a conifer needle compost mixed with peat and rotted cow manure. Repot every spring.
Propagation Tip cuttings can be rooted at almost any time of the year, provided they are kept under plastic and in a temperature of 20 to 25°C (68 to 77°F).

***Hebe andersonii* hybrids**
◯ ⊖ ◯ ⊛ ◐
A cross between *Hebe salicifolia* and *Hebe speciosa*. The leaves are opposite, reverse oval, 5 to 10 cm (2 to 4 in) long, green and glossy. Flowers are borne in spikes, violet-red in 'Albertine', violet-blue in 'Imperial Blue' and white in 'Snowflake'. 'Variegata' has white-edged foliage.

Haworthia fasciata in its resting season, when the plant acquires a spherical shape

Haworthia rugosa with flower stalk

Hedera helix makes an attractive house plant

Hedera helix 'Garland'

Hedera

Araliaceae

Ivy

Name Derived from an ancient Latin plant name; the basic meaning is probably 'to grip'. The plant attaches itself to walls by means of clinging roots.

Origin About seven species are distributed over Europe and Asia.

Description The species and strains grown as house plants are all climbers with usually variegated evergreen foliage.

Position All forms of *Hedera helix* like a low temperature, especially in winter. Only the variegated form of *Hedera canariensis* will survive a position in a warm room throughout the year. All variegated forms require a fair amount of light, but they do not tolerate bright sunlight. Green strains and species need far less light.

Care The most popular variegated ivy, *Hedera canariensis* 'Variegata', better known as 'Gloire de Marengo', must be cultivated in fairly good light at temperatures above 10°C (50°F). In winter the mercury should preferably not rise above 18°C (64°F), for this would make the plant susceptible to aphids in spring or summer. It is very helpful to spray the variegated foliage at frequent intervals – evaporation will cool it.

The numerous green and variegated strains of *Hedera helix* must be given slightly cooler conditions. Many of them will even tolerate a few degrees of frost and may therefore be kept on the balcony practically all through the winter. They will in any case stand this a great deal better than the conditions in a warm room, for if they are kept too warm in winter they will inevitably suffer all kinds of pest infestations.

Hedera helix cultivars are particularly suitable for brightening cool stairwells and entrance halls. The plants will thrive in temperatures varying between 3 and 15°C (37 and 59°F).

Hedera plants can sometimes cling to rough brickwork or wood, but usually some form of support, such as wire, stakes or trellis must be provided.

Watering The compost must never be allowed to dry out. In summer water moderately, in low winter temperatures naturally a little less. If possible use lime-free water.

Feeding In the growing season feed every fortnight.

Repotting It is advisable to replace the compost every year. Use plastic pots with efficient drainage. The most suitable potting mixture consists of 2 parts leafmould and 1 part rotted cow manure, or conifer needle compost can be used instead of leafmould. The plants also do well in standard potting compost.

Propagation Increase from cuttings only. Tip cuttings will strike readily at any time of the year, but best of all in autumn. The cutting medium may be cool, in which case the roots will not develop until spring. If you take cuttings from mature, well-grown shoots you will obtain spreading plants, not readily climbing. If, on the other hand, you use cuttings from young shoots with smaller leaves, its youthful form will often be maintained and you will acquire a small-leaved, vigorously climbing plant.

Pests and diseases Red spider mite, thrips, scale insects: those are the chief enemies of ivy plants which have been kept too warm in winter.

Hedera canariensis

A climbing plant with dull red stems and leaf stalks. The leaves are slightly lobed; in the form 'Variegata' (often referred to as 'Gloire de Marengo') the margins are white.

Hedera helix

A climber with three-to-five lobed leaves. The common species is a hardy garden plant, but the house strains are more or less tender. 'Garland' is a non-climbing strain with deeply incised foliage. 'Gavotte' has single-lobed, narrow and pointed green leaves. 'Goldheart', also known as 'Jubilee', has small leaves with a golden yellow patch in the centre. 'Glacier' develops silvery to grey-green foliage with white margins. 'Green Ripple' has wedge-shaped, glossy green leaves with pale green veining. 'Hahn's Variegated', also known as 'Hanny', has five-lobed leaves with a great deal of pale green and white marking. 'Harald' (also called 'Herald' or 'Herold') has fairly large leaves in various shades of green and white. 'Pittsburgh' has small leaves, pale green all over, and 'Shamrock' is all green with crisped edges.

Hedera canariensis 'Variegata'

Hedera helix 'Glacier'

Heliconia

Musaceae

Name After Helicon, the mountain retreat of the Greek muses.
Origin About 150 species occur in tropical regions of America.
Description Here we are concerned with the species with fine variegated foliage, but the cultivated or imported cut flowers, reminiscent of strelitzias, are better known.
Position A plant for the hothouse and possibly for a warm room, where it must be placed in full light.
Care As yet we have had little experience with this house plant. Try to grow it on a sunny window-sill, where there is a little shade only at the hottest time of the day. In winter the day-time temperature must not fall below 20°C (68°F) and for this the heated living-room is ideal. Spray the foliage at least twice a day with tepid rainwater. The pot should preferably stand on a warm window-sill, where the bottom heat is about 20°C (68°F).
Watering Pure rainwater is best. The compost must always be moderately moist both in summer and in winter. Make sure the water is at the right temperature.

Heliconia indica 'Aureostriata'

Feeding Feed every two weeks in the growing season.
Repotting The most favourable potting mixture consists of leafmould or conifer needle soil, rotted cow manure and sharp sand. Use roomy plastic pots and provide good drainage.
Propagation The species described below can be increased only by division of mature plants. Keep the divided plants in the hothouse for some time.

Heliconia indica

Syn. *Heliconia illustris-rubricaulis.* Just as in the banana plant, the rolled leaf-sheaths form a pseudo-trunk. The leaves are oval to oblong, with a sunken mid-rib, the surface is pink along the veins and the leaf stalks are red. In the form 'Aureostriata' the leaves are streaked with golden yellow along the veins and the leaf stalks are striped in green and yellow. Some people consider this plant to be a form of *Heliconia bihai.*

Helleborus niger, the only true Christmas Rose, now extremely rare in the wild

Helleborus

Ranunculaceae

Hellebore

Name Derived from the Greek words *helein*, to kill, and *bora*, food. The Christmas Rose contains a deadly poison, especially in the roots.
Origin About 20 species occur in the Mediterranean area, in Central Europe and in eastern Asia.
Description An evergreen perennial plant, suitable for use in the garden. Up to the late 1960s one species, *Helleborus niger*, used to be forced into flower fairly early and was then marketed as a house plant. Unfortunately these charming Christmas Roses are now seldom available. They have had to make way for the stridently coloured Poinsettia (see Euphorbia).
Position They are really garden plants which may temporarily be brought indoors at Christmas, when they flower.
Care You can force them into flower by digging the plants up early in November, potting them up and putting them in a cold frame or greenhouse. The pots are then plunged into the soil. The plants must now be thoroughly rinsed, and for the time being the old foliage should be retained. Towards mid-November the temperature should be raised to 4 to 7°C (39 to 44°F). Two or three weeks after the pots have been buried (that is, around mid-November), the old leaves are removed and at the same time all light is excluded from the cold frame or greenhouse. The first flowers will appear about 10th December. If they are numerous, the greenhouse should be kept dark; if few, give them a few hours of light every day.

In the living-room the plants must, of course, be kept as cool as possible. Spray them frequently. After flowering put them in a cool environment and plant them out in the garden again in April.

It is not advisable to force these plants into flower a second time, for the forcing process will have weakened them to such an extent that they will need to recover in the garden for several years. Professional growers always raise these plants from seed; they can then be forced two or three years later. However, any good nursery will be able to provide you with plants in spring and these can be forced into flower the following November. They'll make an original Christmas present!
Watering The Christmas Rose likes permanently moist compost. It therefore needs a shady, sheltered spot even in the garden and should be sprayed if necessary, preferably with rainwater.
Feeding In summer give a dose of organic or artificial fertiliser every fortnight.
Repotting In the garden they are planted in a hole filled with plenty of peat and the same kind of soil should be used in pots.
Propagation The seed should be sown immediately after it has been harvested, in seed compost. The trays are then covered with glass and placed out of doors; the compost must freeze. They could also be put in the refrigerator for a fortnight. When the seed has germinated, the plants should be raised out of doors. Division of mature plants is also a possibility.

Helleborus niger

Christmas Rose. An evergreen perennial with sessile compound pedate foliage; the leaflets are oval to wedge shaped. It has white, later slightly purple, flowers, with yellow stamens. Special strains with larger flowers are often used for indoor cultivation.

Hemigraphis

Acanthaceae

Red Ivy

Name From the Greek *hemi*, half, and *graphis*, paintbrush.
Origin About 20 species occur in south-eastern and eastern Asia, where they grow in damp, shady spots.
Description Fairly inconspicuous, recumbent herbaceous plants with green or brownish leaves and small flowers.
Position In view of their humidity requirements, these are plants for the greenhouse, flower cases or flower windows. They must never stand in full sun.
Care If you are determined to try them out in the living-room, keep your plant spray always at the ready, or grow the plants over a large bowl of water. They probably look more attractive in a bottle garden or in a small glass aquarium. Plenty of light is essential to maintain the fine colour of the foliage, but it must never be unscreened sunlight.

A dormant season in winter is not advisable and the plants should therefore be grown throughout the year in

Hemigraphis alternata

Hibiscus rosa-sinensis 'Cooperi', the only variegated form, with small red flowers

Hibiscus rosa-sinensis: salmon-orange strain

Hibiscus rosa-sinensis, with double flowers

Single orange-yellow *Hibiscus rosa-sinensis*

temperatures of at least 20°C (68°F). Naturally the night temperature may be a few degrees lower.

This plant makes excellent ground cover in the greenhouse, and is best planted out underneath the staging.

Watering The compost must be constantly moist and regular watering is therefore essential, but make sure that excess water can readily drain away. Use completely soft water, perhaps pure rainwater, and always at room temperature. Also spray regularly with lime-free water.

Feeding In the period when the new leaves appear, the plant must be given a dose of a commercial fertiliser every fortnight, at the concentration recommended on the label.

Repotting These plants are best cultivated in a mixture of equal parts of pulverised loam, rotted leafmould and coarse peat. Use shallow but wide pots or bowls with good drainage. Repot the plants at least once a year.

Propagation Tip cuttings can be rooted in bottom heat throughout the year.

Hemigraphis alternata

Syn. *Hemigraphis colorata.* Recumbent, sparsely haired stems with oval to ovate leaves up to 8 cm (3 in) long. The upper surface is silver grey and quilted, the reverse is purple. It bears white flowers, in spikes.

Hemigraphis repanda

Syn. *Ruellia repanda.* The leaves are more lanceolate, fairly deeply toothed. The upper surface is green and the reverse reddish.

Hibiscus
Malvaceae
Rose Mallow

Name *Hibiscus* is an ancient Greek plant name, later assigned to the entire genus.

Origin There are about 200 species, distributed over tropical countries throughout the world. In subtropical regions the Rose Mallow has become a well-known garden plant.

Description A shrub with ovate, toothed leaves and originally single, rose-pink, funnel-shaped flowers. It is now seldom encountered in this form. The strains now marketed are nearly all double flowered, with very large, rather limp flowers in shades of yellow, salmon pink and red – a pity, for these forms are much less strong. Formerly the hibiscus, kept from year to year, was often a shrub of more than 1 m (6 ft) in height; a veritable showpiece which could be placed outside on the terrace in summer. To obtain such a plant now you would have to buy the common garden form.

Position Not only has the hibiscus been spoiled by its present floppy flowers, it has also been deprived of its dormant season. In winter it should be kept at a low temperature, about 12 to 15°C (53 to 59°F), possibly even cooler.

Care Nowadays most people regard the necessity of a dormant season as nonsense. After all, the hibiscus continues to flower if it is kept warm; it will even produce flowers in December. True, but if this is kept up for one or two seasons, the plant will become completely exhausted. If it is left in a warm environment in winter, the foliage will moreover become so susceptible to infestations that it will soon be covered in pests. This is one of the reasons why so few large specimens are now seen.

In spring (or possibly in autumn) the plants should be cut back a little; they can then be repotted and given warmer conditions. Full sun is desirable, but make sure that the plants are kept out of a draught. Dead flowers must immediately be removed. When the plants are in bud it is not advisable to turn them, for the buds will soon fall as a result of the different angle of the light. This also often happens when a new plant has been purchased. Mark its position facing the light, for instance with a matchstick, and leave the plant alone.

Contrary to what is sometimes said cultivars with large double flowers should be kept indoors in summer. These strains are appreciably more tender than the species and out of doors it is too cold and too damp for them. Near the window indoors it may be desirable to screen them a little against the brightest summer sun. The old-fashioned single-flowered red hibiscus is much stronger. It can successfully be kept on a sheltered balcony or on the terrace, in which case the pot should be made of wood or of plastic, to prevent the compost drying out too readily. Clay pots are better plunged into the soil, but should not be overlooked when you are watering your plants. The warmer and sunnier the summer and the more sheltered the position, the more profusely the plant will flower. In early September it must be brought indoors.

Watering The hibiscus can be watered with ordinary tap water. When the new shoots appear, and also in summer, it is a good idea to spray the foliage. In addition the pot should occasionally be plunged to replace the air among the roots. In winter water sparingly, but make sure that the shrub does not dry out entirely.

Feeding The hibiscus appreciates some nourishment in summer, starting about the middle of June, when the nutrients in the old compost have been exhausted. A solution of dried cow dung, or even better still, well-rotted cow manure, is ideal, but artificial fertilisers are also satisfactory. Feed every two weeks, but stop in early August to allow the wood to ripen before the winter.

Repotting The hibiscus will of course grow in standard potting compost, but you could also make a special mixture for the plant. Take pulverised clay or loam, leafmould and rotted cow manure in equal proportions and use pots with good drainage. Repot every spring.

Propagation Tip cuttings may be taken between April and August. They will root under glass or plastic with slight soil heat. During the first year the young plants must not be put outside and must be screened against bright light. In the course of the season they should be repotted once or twice.

If you are able to obtain seed of the botanical species *Hibiscus rosa-sinensis* you could sow in spring in heated soil.

Pests and diseases Buds may fall if the plant is turned, if the compost is too dry or as a result of excessive fluctuations in temperature or humidity. Aphids and mealy bug may also occur; occasionally also red spider mite.

Hibiscus rosa-sinensis

An erect-growing shrub with spreading branches and pointed oval leaves, smooth, green and glossy, entire towards the base and roughly toothed nearer the tip. Axillary flowers, up to 12 cm ($4\frac{1}{2}$ in) across, grow singly on long stalks. The petals are smooth edged and uncurved; the anthers are all situated near the top of the staminal tube.

A large number of strains with single, semi-double or double flowers are cultivated in red, yellow and orange-red. The strains are seldom named. One well-known form is called 'Anita Buis'. The cultivar 'Cooperi' has smaller foliage with fine white and pink marking and with a pink-tinged margin. In 'Albovariegata' the leaves are marked in white and green only, without pink.

Hippeastrum

Amaryllidaceae

Amaryllis

Hippeastrum hybrid 'Fire Dance'

Name From the Greek *hippeus*, a knight, and *astron*, star. The plant is always called Amaryllis, but this is somewhat confusing, since there is a genus called *Amaryllis*, of which the species *bella-donna* flowers in summer.
Origin About 70 species occur in tropical and subtropical regions of America, where they inhabit the savannas or wooded areas with periods of complete drought. At that time the foliage dies down.
Description A well-known bulbous plant which in winter may be forced into flower in the home. Bulbs in a variety of sizes with named colours are available in autumn at supermarkets, by mail order, from garden centres and flower shops. However, the named strains marketed at low prices by a number of specialists are much more beautiful.
Position The Amaryllis is easily forced into flower in the living-room. It does not require a period in the dark like tulips or hyacinths.
Care The bulb should be potted up some time between November and February (see below). Only buy bulbs with a good root system. Bulbs without any or with only short roots are inferior. Carefully distribute the compost between the roots and leave the neck of the bulb above the surface. Moisten the compost a little, and place the pot in a warm spot, if necessary on top of the radiator if it is not too hot. The flower stalk will appear after a short time. The only thing that may go wrong at this stage is if the compost is left to dry or the bulb is overwatered, when it will rot. As soon as the flower stalk is 15 to 20 cm (6 to 8 in) tall, the pot must be placed near a well-lit window, if it has not been there from the start. The soil heat may now be decreased a little and, as the stalk grows, the water supply should be increased.

In due course the plant will flower, sometimes with one or frequently with more than one flower stalk, depending on the size of the bulb. There are bulbs of a diameter of 15 cm (6 in) which are capable of producing six or seven flower stalks. The leaves develop after the flowers. It will do no harm to spray the foliage from time to time as it appears. There is now a greater degree of evaporation and this must be taken into account when the plant is watered.

If flowering plants are kept cool, the flowers will last much longer. After flowering cut the stalk (unless you want to gather the seed) and continue to care for the plant. After mid-May the Amaryllis may be kept in the greenhouse or even outside if necessary.

At the beginning of September stop watering and allow all the foliage to die down. The bulb should be kept in the pot at a minimum temperature of 16°C (60°F). If you want the plant to flower particularly early, stop watering in August, lift the bulb in September and keep it at 17°C (62°F) for four to five weeks. Then raise the temperature to 23°C (73°F) for four weeks, pot the bulb and provide soil heat of 20°C (68°F). Some bulbs may flower before Christmas.
Watering See above. It is preferable to use rainwater if possible.
Feeding When the foliage is developing feed every fortnight.
Repotting Every second year the compost should be replaced by ordinary potting compost. In the intervening years only replace the top layer. It is best to use plastic pots, with a layer of crocks in the bottom.
Propagation Offsets which have developed their own roots can be removed and grown separately, preferably in a greenhouse. Don't forget the resting periods! They will flower after three years.

By artificially pollinating your plants you can obtain seeds. The pollen of other strains may also be used. The seeds should be left to ripen and then immediately sown in soil heated to 22°C (71°F).
Pests and diseases Red spider mite, thrips, aphids, mealy bug and fire disease are troubles which seldom occur if the plant is cultivated correctly.

Hippeastrum hybrids

Syn. *Amaryllis* hybrids; *Hippeastrum* × *hortorum*. A bulbous plant with strap-shaped, green, up to 50-cm (20-in) long leaves and two to four large, funnel-shaped flowers spreading horizontally at the tip of a long, hollow flower stalk. They have protruding stamens with yellow anthers.

Numerous hybrids in one or two colours are available. The 'Picotee' strains, whose flowers are edged in a different colour, are particularly striking.

Hippeastrum 'Picotee' strain

A collection of modern hippeastrum hybrids in a hothouse

Homalocladium platycladum

Homalocladium

Polygonaceae

Name Derived from the Greek: *homalos* is similar and *klados* is shoot.
Origin The genus consists of a single species, a native of the Solomon Islands.
Description A remarkable plant with flattened stems which have partially taken over the functions of leaves. They are not phylloclades, as in the genus *Phyllanthus* (q.v.), but platyclades. Ordinary, lanceolate leaves appear on the flattened main shoots. The plants are fairly rare, but may occasionally be encountered.
Position An easy plant to grow, which in summer may also be put outside.
Care A homalocladium requires plenty of light and will tolerate full sun. From the end of May onwards it may be given a warm and sheltered position out of doors.

The small leaves growing on the flattened stems tend to drop easily, as if they are not really needed. This should therefore be regarded as a normal feature. In winter the plant should preferably not be kept too warm; a maximum temperature of 16°C (60°F) is recommended, and during this period the minimum temperature should be 8°C (46°F).
Watering Always keep the compost moderately moist and a little drier in winter.
Feeding In the period of active growth the plant may be fed once a month.
Repotting Normal potting compost can be mixed with a little pulverised clay or loam. Make sure it is well drained.
Propagation Increase from cuttings. The flattened stems should be cut just below a node (where a leaf appears), then rooted with some bottom heat. They may also be grown from seed.

Homalocladium platycladum

Syn. *Muehlenbeckia platyclados*. An erect-growing shrub with flat, 1·5-cm (½-in) wide, jointed green stems and lanceolate leaves, 1·5 cm (½ in) long, dropping readily. It bears small white flowers in sessile clusters and small pink fruits, later turning purplish red.

Howeia

Palmae

Kentia Palm

Name Named after the Lord Howe Islands, to the east of Australia. Kentia is the capital of the largest island. *Howea*, that is, without the *i*, is another spelling.
Origin The Lord Howe Islands. There are two species.
Description Well-known palms with decorative, broad fronds, composed of a large number of gracefully curving pinnae.
Position Very suitable for a position in the living-room where the sun does not reach.
Care It seems remarkable that palms are always said to be intolerant of sunlight, for in their natural habitat they grow in full sun all day long. This apparent contradiction may be explained by the fact that young plants originally grow among taller trees in the jungle, where they will certainly receive little sunlight. And since a palm small enough to be grown in the living-room must inevitably be a young plant, it should most definitely not be placed in the sun. On the other hand it is not advisable to put them too far from the window – they will not thrive there and will eventually languish. In summer it is a good idea to spray the foliage regularly with rainwater. Best of all put the palm in a shower outside, covering the pot with plastic or foil to prevent the compost getting drenched. Alternatively if you haven't a garden or balcony put it under the shower indoors. In winter the howeia should be grown in a temperature between 14 and 18°C (57 and 64°F). This last used to be a normal living-room temperature, but today many people keep their thermostat at 22°C (71°F), which is not very favourable for many plants, including this palm. In any case spray daily.
Watering Palms do not give off a great deal of moisture, but it is still helpful to plunge them occasionally in summer. Preferably use well-draining pots. Water a little less in winter and if possible always use rainwater, which must not be too cold.
Repotting Palms like to grow in deep pots. The modern plant cylinders are very suitable, but since they lack drainage excess water may collect at the bottom. It is therefore advisable to use plastic containers with holes in the base and in addition to provide a layer of crocks.

The most favourable potting mixture consists of leafmould (or conifer needle compost) with rotted cow manure and some sharp sand. The plants need not be repotted every spring, but the top layer of compost should be replaced to get rid of excess minerals.
Propagation This palm can only be grown from fresh seed, sown in March in a temperature of 25 to 30°C (77 to 86°F). The seed will probably take several months to germinate. Young plants should be tended in the greenhouse and eventually potted in groups.
Pests and diseases Scale insects occur fairly frequently; sometimes also red spider mites, thrips and mealy bug.

Howeia belmoreana

Syn. *Kentia belmoreana*. Curly Palm. This has a tall, thin green stem with short reddish leaf stalks and pinnate, arching foliage consisting of numerous erect pinnae. The edges are densely covered in woolly hairs, and the reverse is unscaled. The opposite leaves form an angle of 90 degrees. It is the less vigorous of the two species.

Howeia forsteriana

Syn. *Kentia forsteriana*. Less arching fronds, the pinnae are broader, horizontal or slightly drooping. The underside is covered in fine scaly patches and the opposite leaves grow practically in line with each other.

A number of young plants of *Howeia forsteriana* grouped in a container

Hoya carnosa, the Wax Flower

Hoya

Asclepiadaceae

Wax Flower

Name Named after Thomas Hoy, gardener to the Duke of Northumberland in the late 18th and early 19th century.
Origin There are about 200 species, distributed over southern China, the Indian archipelago and Australia. Only three are known as house plants.
Description Evergreen climbers with thick, somewhat succulent leaves and waxy flowers in pendulous clusters.
Position *Hoya carnosa* and *Hoya australis* make good house plants, although they must be kept cool in winter. *Hoya bella*, the Miniature Wax Plant, is a hothouse plant.
Care The first two species, both sometimes called Wax Flower, like plenty of light; only the brightest sunlight must be avoided. The more light, the more profusely they will flower in summer. In the living-room the long tendrils are best tied round a wire hoop and in the greenhouse they can be trained along the framework. When the buds are developing the plant must not be turned. The flowers will always face the window.

From October onwards the Wax Flower must be kept cool and dry in a temperature between 10 and 14°C (50 and 57°F). In a warm living-room this presents a problem and you should therefore try to find a cool, but well-lit, place where the plant can spend the winter.

Hoya bella must be cultivated at a higher temperature; it requires less light, but a higher degree of humidity. The minimum winter temperature is 18°C (64°F). The plant will flower more profusely if grafted on *Hoya carnosa*. Plants grown from cuttings will produce fewer flowers.
Watering In summer the compost must never be allowed to dry out and in winter it should be watered as little as possible.
Feeding Since too much feeding affects the flowering, great care needs to be taken. Feed only when the plant is actually in flower, approximately every three weeks.
Repotting For all species the best compost mixture consists of ⅓ loam or clay, ⅓ leafmould, ⅙ rotted cow manure and ⅙ sharp sand or perlite, but *H. carnosa* and *H. australis* will also grow in standard potting compost. The Miniature Wax Plant prefers a lighter mixture containing some sphagnum moss. Large plants need not be repotted every year: it is sufficient to replace the top layer of compost.
Propagation Increase in summer from

half-woody shoots, that is, tip cuttings, and also from eye cuttings, with a soil heat of 20 to 25°C (68 to 77°F). *Hoya bella* can also be increased by grafting it on to *Hoya carnosa*.
Pests and diseases Mealy bug, scale insects and red spider mites will appear if the plant is kept too warm in winter. The Miniature Wax Plant is susceptible to root rot, so good drainage is therefore essential.

Hoya australis
○ ◐ ⊜ ⓥ ⊛ ◼ ▢
Wax Flower. A climber with virtually circular, fleshy dark green leaves, up to 7 cm (2$\frac{3}{4}$in) across. It bears fragrant white flowers in pendulous clusters.

Hoya bella
◐ ⊜ ⓥ ⊛ ▢
Miniature Wax Plant. This species has trailing, subsequently recumbent stems, fleshy leaves, oval to lanceolate, only 2.5 cm (1 in) long, and clusters of eight to twelve pure white flowers with a purple centre (the corona). The clusters are so pendulous that the interior of the flower can only be seen from below.

Hoya carnosa
○ ◐ ⊜ ⓥ ⊛ ◼ ▢
Syn. *Asclepias carnosa*. Wax Flower. Similar to the first-named species, but the leaves are oval to oblong, up to 8 cm (3 in) long. The flowers are slightly larger, creamy white to soft pink. 'Variegata' has creamy-edged foliage.

Hoya bella, the Miniature Wax Plant

Hyacinthus orientalis 'Amethyst', grown in gravel

Hyacinthus
Liliaceae
Hyacinth

Name Named after *Hyakinthos*, a beautiful boy loved and accidentally killed by Apollo.
Origin About 30 species occur in the countries round the Mediterranean and in Asia Minor.
Description Everyone knows this bulbous plant. Although it is a garden plant it is quite possible to force it into flower in the living-room. The scent is heavenly.
Position Keep it in the living-room when it is in flower, but preferably as cool as possible.
Care For early or normal flowering the bulbs should be potted at the beginning of October, and the pots then buried in the garden. They can also be kept in a dark box on the balcony, but the temperature must never exceed 12°C (53°F), otherwise no roots will develop. If the bulbs are to flower late, they can be buried up to the beginning of December. They may be brought into the light when the flower bud can clearly be felt. Do not put them in too warm an environment and cover them with a plastic bag for a few days to restrict evaporation.

The bulbs can also be forced in a dark, absolutely cool, cupboard or cellar. Cover them with black plastic bags to keep out the light. If the bulbs are cultivated in special hyacinth glasses the method is the same; the water must reach to 2 mm ($\frac{1}{10}$in) below the bulb.

Prepared bulbs sold for early flowering have already undergone treatment at a special temperature.
Watering Potted bulbs should always be kept moderately moist.
Feeding This is unnecessary since they are generally discarded after flowering.
Repotting Use a sandy mixture if the bulbs are grown in pots. Garden soil is satisfactory, but a mixture of equal parts of peat and sharp sand is probably easier to handle. Provide good drainage, so that the bulbs are never left standing in water.
Propagation The hyacinth can be increased by removing offsets, but when treated as a house plant it is not necessary to consider this method. Buy new bulbs every year.
Pests and diseases If the flower bud stops growing it means that the bulb has been brought into the light too soon. It could be kept wrapped in black plastic or covered with a box during its first week in the living-room.

Hyacinthus orientalis
◐ ⊜ ⓥ ⊛ ▢
A bulb with a pale to bluish membrane. The leaves are 4 to 7 cm (1$\frac{1}{2}$ to 2$\frac{3}{4}$in) long, narrow and gutter shaped. It carries a stalked, erect-growing raceme of flowers. There are a great number of named cultivars in a variety of colours. The so-called 'Multiflora' hyacinths produce several small flower stalks to each bulb, an attractive sight.

Hydrangea
Saxifragaceae
Hortensia

Name Derived from the Greek words *hydor*, water and *aggeion*, a vessel. When the fruit bursts it assumes the shape of a water vessel.
Origin At least 90 different species grow in China and South East Asia as well as in North and South America.
Description These house plants with their immense flower clusters in shades of blue and red have been known of old.
Position Now that the temperature in our modern, centrally heated rooms with windows at either end is so much higher than it used to be, the sale of hydrangeas has decreased. They do not like too much warmth and prefer a cool corridor or a moderately heated room out of the sun. In summer these plants belong in the garden.
Care Flowering plants are usually bought in spring. At home they must be placed out of the sun in the coolest position available. Spray them several times a day, especially on the foliage. After flowering keep them cool and do not let them dry out; at the end of May they may go outside where they can be planted out in a shady spot.

Since the plants flower on the previous year's wood, they must be pruned before the end of June. Earlier or later pruning will involve the loss of flower buds. On a branch that has flowered you will notice a dark and a paler section. The correct place to prune is two pairs of eyes above the dark wood. The plants should now be kept a little drier for a time until they start into growth again, then the water supply should be increased and feeding begun. In late August both the water and the nutrient supply should be reduced once more until in October all the foliage falls. Now the plants must be kept very cool, but frost-free, until February, with a minimum temperature of 4 to 6°C (39 to 43°F). Of course this is easiest in a cool greenhouse, which should be thoroughly ventilated on mild days in autumn or winter. In the absence of a greenhouse keep the plants outside as long as possible, but wrap them up well in cold winter weather. The entire plant may in fact be buried. Not all winter strains are equally hardy; although the branches will survive, the buds may freeze. The plants may flower after a mild winter, but not after severe winter weather. In February the hydrangea can be brought into a warmer environment, up to about 18°C (64°F). Place it in good light near a window and start to spray the foliage as soon as it appears.
Watering Hydrangeas are sensitive to lime and must therefore only be given rainwater. In a warm room a great deal of moisture may evaporate and the foliage may suddenly droop. At such times the plant can only be saved by plunging the pot immediately in a large bowl of water to soak the compost thoroughly.
Feeding Hydrangeas adore food and must be fed from the moment they start into growth in spring. After they are pruned they should have a short rest, but as soon as they put out new shoots again in June or July they must be fed again.
Repotting The correct time to repot is after pruning in summer. These plants

Hyacinthus orientalis 'Carnegie'

Hydrangea macrophylla, with a blue tinge

are acid lovers and the mixture must therefore contain plenty of peat fibre or peat moss, as well as rotted cow manure. Conifer needle compost is also excellent.

Iron or aluminium in the soil, combined with a low pH, will make the flowers turn blue. Blue-flowered plants must therefore be kept particuarly acid. The iron content of the soil can be increased by burying rusty nails in it, but the addition of alum (obtainable from the chemist) is a more professional method. On three occasions in August and September the plants should be given ⅓ tablespoonful per pot. Cultivars with rose-red flowers are most suitable for this treatment. The treatment must be repeated every year after repotting. If hydrangeas are planted out in the garden, a large hole should first be filled with acid soil (peaty soil, peat fibre, peat moss).

Propagation Summer prunings may be used as cuttings. The tip cuttings must be neither too soft nor too woody; the correct term is 'half ripe'. The cuttings will readily root, even in water; no bottom heat is required. As soon as new growth appears they should be stopped once or twice. After having tended the plants for another season you will in the third year have fine new specimens which may successfully be brought into flower.

Pests and diseases Aphids may occur if the plants are kept in a draught, and red spider mite is another possibility. Malformed or green flowers are the result of a virus disease for which there is no cure. Yellowing leaves may indicate chlorosis due to too much lime in the compost or to watering with calciferous tap water. The iron ions are retained by the lime so that the plant cannot utilise them, which causes the leaves to turn yellow.

Hydrangea macrophylla

A shrub with thick branches. The leaves are broad oval in shape, coarsely toothed, up to 15 cm (6 in) long, green and glossy. It bears a spherical inflorescence with large, sterile flowers and white or pink petals which may turn blue after soil treatment. Forms grown indoors belong to the subspecies *H. m. macrophylla* f. *otaksa*.

Hymenocallis speciosa

Hydrangea macrophylla ssp. *macrophylla* f. *otaksa*, red and white cultivars

Hymenocallis

Amaryllidaceae

Name From the Greek *hymen*, membrane, and *kallos*, beautiful. The stamens of these truly magnificent flowers are linked at the base by a membrane.

Origin There are about 40 species, many of them beach dwellers, in tropical and Central America.

Description A bulbous plant, usually with fragrant white flowers consisting of a corolla with long slips and a corona similar to the trumpet in the daffodil.

Position The bulbs start into growth in summer and may therefore be kept in the living-room.

Care Bulbs are available from mail-order firms or other specialist growers and must be potted in February–March. Cultivation is similar to that of the hippeastrum (Amaryllis), except that the foliage does not die down in winter in all species. The plants should, however, be given a rest at that time at a minimum temperature of 15°C (59°F).

Watering In summer always keep the compost moderately moist, and in winter fairly dry (in the case of plants which retain their foliage), to completely dry.

Feeding In the period of active growth feed every fortnight.

Repotting Use a proprietary potting compost mixed with a little pulverised clay. Repot every second year, and in the intervening years replace the top layer of compost.

Propagation Offsets can be removed and potted up separately.

Hymenocallis × festalis

Syn. *Ismene × festalis*. This is actually a hybrid, the result of crossing *Hymenocallis narcissiflora* and *Elisena longipetala*, and is a well-known form with very large white flowers with recurving petals. The foliage dies down.

Hymenocallis narcissiflora

Syn. *Hymenocallis calathina; Ismene calathina; Pancratium narcissiflorum*. Leaves grow in groups of five to eight, up to 50 by 6 cm (20 by 2¼ in), encasing each other at the base. The flowers are in groups of three to six, pendulous, white and fragrant; the corona is funnel shaped and fringed, and the petals are lanceolate. It dies down in autumn.

Hymenocallis speciosa

Syn. *Pancratium speciosum*. This has numerous leaves up to 50 cm (20 in) long and 12 cm (4½ in) wide. The flowers are in groups of six to twelve. The recurving petals are up to 12 cm (4½ in) long, the corona 3 to 5 cm (1 to 2 in) long, all white. The foliage is retained in winter.

Hypocyrta

Gesneriaceae

Name From the Greek *hypo*, beneath, and *kryptos*, curved. This refers to the shape of the corolla.

Origin Nearly all the nine species have their native habitat in Brazil.

Description The only species valued as a house plant has glossy, leathery leaves and unusually shaped, bulging orange flowers.

Position The plant can be kept in the living-room throughout the year, but a cool resting period is essential to bud formation.

Care The hypocyrta requires a well-lit place on the window-sill and will even tolerate sunlight, provided it is filtered a little in the middle of summer. From the end of May onwards the plant may be put in a warm spot outside. If you want it to flower another year it must be cut back a little after flowering and otherwise tended normally in summer, but must be rested from December to February at a temperature of 10 to 14°C (50 to 57°F), in plenty of light (sunny if possible).

It also looks good as a trailing plant grown in a hanging basket.

Watering Keep moderately moist in summer but leave it fairly dry in winter.

Feeding Feed every fortnight in summer.

Repotting The most satisfactory compost mixture consists of leafmould, sphagnum moss and charcoal. Repot every year either after flowering or after the dormant season, using particularly well-draining pots or hanging baskets.

Propagation Tip cuttings will strike without problems throughout the summer. Group a few together to obtain bushy plants. Older plants may also be divided. They may even be grown from seed.

Hypocyrta glabra

A plant with erect-growing to arching stems. The leaves are leathery and fleshy, dark green and glossy; they are elliptical in shape, up to 4 cm (1½ in) long. It bears axillary orange, waxy flowers of which the tube is curiously bulged at the base.

Hypoestes

Acanthaceae

Name From the Greek *hypo*, beneath, and *estia*, house.

Origin The approximately 150 known species occur in Malagasy and in South Africa.

Description Attractive plants with red-patched or red-veined leaves and an erect habit.

Position In view of its need for damp air it is really only suitable for the hothouse.

Care If, however, you want to make an attempt to grow the plant indoors, it must be sprayed very frequently with tepid water. The small leaves require plenty of light to retain their fine marking, but bright summer sun must be avoided.

A resting period in winter is not required, but because of lack of light that plant will not grow very much at that time. It should therefore be kept somewhat drier and cut back a little at the end of the dark season.

Hypocyrta glabra

Hypoestes phyllostachya

Watering Keep the compost moderately moist at all times; it must certainly not be allowed to dry out in winter.

Feeding Give a dose of fertiliser solution every three weeks in the growing period.

Repotting Standard potting compost can be used, but some people advise a mixture of pulverised loam or clay, leafmould and rotted cow manure. Pot into shallow pots with good drainage.

Propagation Plants grown in the hothouse frequently develop seed which will germinate anywhere. Otherwise propagate from tip cuttings rooted under glass in heated cuttings compost.

Hypoestes phyllostachya

Syn. *Hypoestes sanguinolenta; Hypoestes taeniata*. A small plant with erect-growing, branching stems and sharply pointed oval leaves, 7 cm (2¾ in) long, green with pale red patches. It has axillary flowers; the corolla is rose pink with a white throat. This is the best-known species.

Hypoestes sanguinolenta

Syn. *Eranthemum sanguinolentum*. Distinguished from the previous species because of its scarlet veins. It has no patches on the foliage.

Illicium

Illiciaceae

Aniseed Tree

Name Derived from the Latin *illicere*, allure, attract. The foliage exudes an alluring scent.

Origin About 40 species are known. They occur in South East Asia as well as North America and the Caribbean.

Description Fairly rare, almost hardy shrubs with evergreen foliage and multipetalled flowers with conspicuous stamens.

Position These are shrubs for the cool greenhouse. They can be put outside in summer.

Care Keep them in the greenhouse in winter at a minimum temperature of 5°C (41°F).

Watering The compost must always be kept moderately moist, even in winter.

Feeding In the growing season, up to mid-August, feed every fortnight.

Repotting The plants dislike lime and you should therefore use a lime-free compost such as a mixture of conifer needle soil and rotted cow manure.

Illicium verum

Propagation Tip cuttings will root in heated cuttings compost in the spring or in late summer. They can also be grown from seed.

Illicium verum

Aniseed Plant. The leaves smell of aniseed when rubbed. It bears spherical flowers, fragrant, with 10 petals and an equal number of stamens.

Impatiens

Balsaminaceae

Busy Lizzie

Name From the Latin *impatiens*, impatient. Ripe seed pods burst open at a touch and eject the seeds.

Origin Most of the 400 species known are distributed over tropical and subtropical Asia, tropical Africa and the islands to the east of Africa. Only eight species occur in the temperate zones of Asia, Europe and America.

Description The Busy Lizzie is a well-known house plant with succulent stems and single or double flowers in a range of colours.

Position To flower profusely the plants need plenty of light. In summer they may be grown outside.

Care As long as it receives plenty of light and even sunshine, this little plant rarely disappoints. The newest garden and balcony strains, on the other hand, are suitable for shady spots, but this does not mean that they should be relegated to the back of the room.

The Busy Lizzie can be overwintered in the living-room. After a few years it will have become lank and unsightly and it is therefore sensible to grow new plants from cuttings every spring.

Watering In summer a plant placed in a sunny spot uses up a great deal of water. In winter it needs far less. It's best to use rainwater.

Feeding In the growing season it is very important to feed every week. This will lengthen the flowering season.

Repotting Standard potting compost is satisfactory. Use plastic pots with added drainage.

Propagation Tip cuttings will root without problems at any time of the year, even in a bottle of water. It is advisable to grow new plants from cuttings at least once a year. They are also easily grown from seed which will germinate in a temperature of 18 to 20°C (64 to 68°F).

Impatiens walleriana with single flowers and a double-flowered pink *Impatiens balsamina*

Impatiens hybrid 'Confetti'

Pests and diseases Aphids, whitefly and red spider mite will occur as a result of inadequate feeding and dry air. Spraying on the flowers will cause staining.

Impatiens balsamina

○⊜ⓜ⊛◙

Syn. *Balsamina hortensis*. A garden annual with fleshy stems, often tinged with red, and lanceolate leaves. It has double flowers in the colours rose red, lilac and white. The low, compact-growing forms are frequently sold as house plants.

Impatiens marianae

A small perennial with creeping stems and broad oval leaves, finely toothed along the edge and with white markings along the veins. It rarely flowers.

Impatiens walleriana

Syn. *Impatiens holstii; Impatiens sultani*. Busy Lizzie. An erect-growing perennial with fleshy stems and elliptical pale green leaves, alternate at the base of the stems, in whorls at the top. The flowers consist of a flat disc, 3 to 5cm (1 to 2in) across, a narrow tube and a long thin spur, in a wide range of colours. The form 'Petersiana' is strongly tinged with red on all its parts.

Iresine herbstii

Iresine

Amaranthaceae

Name From the Greek *eiros, eirion*, wound with wool. This refers to the hairy surface of the flowers in some species.

Origin About 70 species are found in North and South America, in the Antilles, in Australia and in the Galapagos Islands.

Description Small, watery plants with conspicuously marked foliage and insignificant flowers.

Position Full sun is essential to maintain the colouring. In southerly regions it makes a good bedding plant.

Care The hottest south-facing window, without any screening, is not too hot for the iresine. Even then the leaves stretch towards the light and show to best advantage. The plant is not hardy, but from the end of May until the beginning of September it can be put outside on the terrace or on a balcony.

During the winter months the little plant can remain on the same window-sill. It would now be an advantage if the temperature could be lowered a little, say to 15°C (59°F), but it appears that the iresine will even survive in a warm room, though it will have lost most of its beauty by spring and the stems will have become lanky and limp. No matter; the plant is very easily renewed. Quickly root a few cuttings and start again.

Watering A large amount of moisture evaporates through the foliage, and in summer the plant must therefore be plentifully watered. In winter it may be kept a little drier.

Feeding In the growing season give a dose of standard fertiliser once a fortnight.

Repotting Iresines have proved to do well in standard potting compost. Use plastic pots to reduce evaporation in summer.

Propagation Tip cuttings root very readily in a mixture of peat and sharp sand, or even in a bottle of water. Once roots have developed, the cuttings should be stopped a few times, to make bushier plants. The pinched-out parts may in their turn be used as cuttings. Finally the plants should be potted with possibly several to a pot to ensure a bushy effect.

Pests and diseases Occasionally aphids occur.

Iresine herbstii 'Aureo-reticulata'

Iresine herbstii

○⊜ⓜ⊛◙

Syn. *Achyranthes verschaffeltii*. This species has erect-growing, angular, slightly transparent red stems. The leaves are usually spatula shaped and arched, incised at the tip and sometimes pointed. The surface is uneven, dark brown-red in colour, carmine red along the main lateral veins, and there are plumes of greenish flowers. In 'Aureo-reticulata' the leaves are blotched and streaked with golden yellow; 'Brilliantissimum' has hollow, more chestnut-brown foliage with pale red veining and 'Wallisii' develops small round to kidney-shaped leaves with a recurving tip and upcurved margins, often tinged with purple.

Iresine lindenii

Syn. *Achyranthes lindenii*. This plant is reddish all over; the leaves are oblong to lanceolate, to 6cm (2¼in) long, with a sharp point; they are blood red in colour, with a red band along the main vein. 'Formosa' develops bright yellow, green-speckled and red-veined leaves.

Ixora hybrid

Ixora

Rubiaceae

Name Derived from a Sanskrit word meaning god. It is the name of a god in Sri Lanka.

Origin No fewer than 400 species are known, distributed over tropical regions throughout the world.

Description Only hybrids created by crossing original species are used as house plants. The very conspicuous orange flowers grow in dense clusters.

Position They are hothouse plants which have a difficult time in the living-room, hence they are rarely marketed. In the sixties these plants were seen fairly often.

Care The flowers may appear from May to September. Place the plant in good light but out of full sun, and frequently spray the foliage with tepid rainwater. Prune after flowering and overwinter the plant in a hothouse at a minimum temperature of 18°C (64°F). When the plant first enters your home the flowers will usually drop because the angle of the light has changed. The pots should therefore never be moved.

Watering Always use pure rainwater or demineralised water. In summer keep the compost moderately moist and in winter give less water, to allow the plant to rest.

Feeding Feed every fortnight in the growing period.

Repotting The most favourable potting mixture consists of conifer needle compost and rotted manure. Use plastic pots with particularly good drainage and replace the compost every spring.

Propagation Young tip shoots can be rooted in spring in heated soil at a temperature of 25 to 30°C (77 to 86°F). The process will take three to four weeks.

Pests and diseases The plants are very susceptible to scale insects, which must be combated in good time.

***Ixora* hybrids**

◐⊜ⓜ⊛▢

An erect-growing shrub with elongated oval green leaves, firm and leathery. Flowers occur in terminal dense clusters; the corolla is 1cm (½in) across, with a thin tube, to 3cm (1in) long. The colours range from yellow through orange to orange-red.

Jacaranda mimosifolia, foliage detail

Jacaranda
Bignoniaceae

Name Jacaranda is the popular Brazilian name for this tree.
Origin About 50 different species occur in South America. Only one of them has become known as a house or tub plant.
Description At first sight this shrub, which in Brazil grows into the large tree which supplies palisander wood, reminds us of a fern. The foliage also resembles that of *Mimosa pudica*.
Position Young plants must be cultivated in a warm environment and can be kept in fairly good condition in the living-room. Older specimens should be treated as tub plants.
Care Although young plants must not be placed in full sun, they still require plenty of light to grow. It is advisable to spray the fine foliage at least once a day, for the plant requires a high degree of humidity. If you do not succeed in keeping the foliage in good condition indoors, the plant should be moved to the greenhouse. In the first four years the winter temperature must not drop below 12°C (53°F). Older plants can be grown in tubs and placed outside in summer. In winter they should be kept in a cool greenhouse or orangery.
Watering In summer keep the compost moderately damp. Water slightly less in winter, and use rainwater.
Feeding Feed every fortnight in summer.
Repotting The compost must be lime free. A conifer needle compost is ideal with the addition of a little rotted cow manure. Repot every spring.
Propagation This tree is always grown from fresh seed. The seed needs a temperature of about 25°C (77°F) to germinate.

Jacaranda mimosifolia

Syn. *Jacaranda ovalifolia*. A tree with opposite-growing leaves which drop in spring; they are doubly pinnate as in ferns. There are numerous small pinnae, trapezium shaped to oblong, with downy hairs and plumes of violet-blue flowers; these do not appear in cultivation.

Jacaranda mimosifolia strongly resembles a fern, but it is a shrub

Jacobinia pauciflora

Jacobinia
Acanthaceae

Name Probably named after Jacobina, a place to the north-west of Bahia in South America.
Origin About 40 different species occur in warm zones in America.
Description Two species, rather different in appearance, are occasionally marketed as house plants. One resembles the Cigar Flower (see *Cuphea*), the other has pseudo-spikes with strikingly coloured tubular flowers.
Position These are plants for a temperate greenhouse. In summer they may be put out of doors.
Care *Jacobinia pauciflora* is the stronger of the two species. From June onwards it may be grown in a very sheltered and sunny position outside. At the beginning of September it should be moved to a well-lit, cool spot, preferably a temperate greenhouse, or even a cool greenhouse. It will flower in December–February. *Jacobinia carnea* can stay in the greenhouse, or possibly in the living-room, throughout the summer. Screen it against bright sunlight. It usually flowers in August or September. The plants are then pruned and given a rest in a temperate greenhouse or in a cool room with a minimum temperature of 12°C (53°F).
Watering The plants must always be watered moderately to plentifully. *Jacobinia pauciflora*, in particular, reacts quickly to dry compost: the foliage immediately falls. In winter, when the temperature is lower, the plant should naturally be given less water, but the soil ball must always remain sufficiently moist.

Jacobinia carnea

Feeding Both these species may be fed weekly in their period of active growth.
Repotting *Jacobinia pauciflora* must be repotted in not too large a pot after flowering, that is, in spring. The most favourable mixture consists of rotted turves and rotted leaves, to which a little rotted cow manure has been added. If necessary you can use a proprietary compost. Always use plastic pots; the compost will not dry out so quickly.
Jacobinia carnea may also be repotted in spring. The same mixture, or standard potting compost, may be used. Choose roomy pots, for this species develops more roots, and if necessary repot again in summer. Provide good drainage and preferably use plastic pots.
Propagation *Jacobinia pauciflora* can be

increased in January or February, when it is still in flower, from tip cuttings taken from non-flowering shoots. These will root readily if kept under glass and given some bottom heat. It is best to keep young plants in the greenhouse for a few months. They can then be hardened off and moved out of doors. It is advisable to pinch out the growing point once or twice.

Jacobinia carnea is grown from tip shoots from February onwards; they root fairly rapidly in bottom heat. They will flower in June. If cuttings are taken in March–April, the flowers will appear in September–October. Every time the plant is potbound it must be repotted. If the plant is stopped two or three times, it will develop more flower spikes. Instead of stopping them, try combining a few plants in one pot.

Jacobinia carnea

Syn. *Justicia carnea; Cyrtanthera magnifica; Cyrtanthera carnea.* Brazilian Plume. The erect-growing stems carry oval leaves up to 15cm (6in) long and somewhat rough to the touch; they narrow towards the 8-cm (3-in) long leafstalk. Flowers occur in dense pseudo-spikes. The bracts are often tinged with purple; the narrow, two-lipped corolla is 6cm (2⅜in) long, and lilac pink in colour.

Jacobinia pauciflora

Syn. *Libonia floribunda; Justicia rizzinii.* This has strongly branching, short-haired stems and opposite oval leaves, unequal in size. The numerous flowers grow singly; the corolla is 2 to 3cm (¾in to 1in) long, red tinged with yellow.

Jasminum officinale 'Grandiflorum', a beautiful greenhouse jasmine

Jasminum

Oleaceae

Jasmine

Name Derived from an Arabian plant name.

Origin About 200 species occur in tropical regions of Africa, Asia and Australia; one grows in America.

Description Trailing plants with small white or rose-red flowers. It is related to the well-known garden plant *Jasminum nudiflorum*, or Winter Jasmine, which produces yellow flowers in December. *Jasminum officinale*, with its delightfully scented white flowers, produces the valuable jasmine oil which in the south of France is used as a base in the perfume industry.

Position These are plants for a cool or temperate greenhouse, and in summer they may be kept either in the garden or in the living-room.

Care All species must be placed in full sun in summer. From the end of May onwards they may be put in a sheltered spot outside. The plants grow best if planted out in a cool greenhouse, where the long shoots can be trained along the roof. If pots are used, they must on no account be too small and there must be a wood or wire frame along which the shoots can be wound.

If the plant is to flower in the following year, it is essential to keep it cool in winter. It seems that they enjoy a temperature of 2 to 8°C (35 to 46°F). New growth appears early in spring and sufficient ventilation must be provided to prevent the plant growing too fast, for this would result in elongated, weak shoots which would later be susceptible to aphids. The plants should not be put outside until the end of May or beginning of June. The growing points must be nipped out from time to time to encourage flowering in the following year.

Watering In the growing season a fair amount of water is needed, but in winter the plant needs to be given only just enough to prevent it dying. It is a good idea always to use lime-free water, possibly rainwater, for both watering and spraying.

Feeding In the period of active growth the long shoots require plenty of nourishment. If the plant has been repotted in spring, it need not be fed for the first six weeks, but after that a little liquid fertiliser should be added every time it is watered. This should be continued until September.

Repotting Since the plants start into growth very early, they must be repotted early in spring. The flowers appear on last year's wood and the plants must therefore not be pruned too drastically when they are repotted, or flower buds would be lost.

A satisfactory compost mixture consists of ⅓ pulverised clay or loam, ⅓ rotted beech leaves, ⅙ crumbly rotted cow manure and ⅙ sharp sand or perlite.

Standard potting compost can also be used.

Propagation Half-ripe shoots can be rooted in some degree of bottom heat from the spring until late summer. Cover the trays with glass or plastic. When the plantlets have started into growth they should be stopped from time to time to promote bushy plants. It is also possible to grow new plants from runners. In winter the plants also develop numerous ground shoots where they touch the soil, and in spring these may be used as cuttings.

Pests and diseases Damage by aphids may occur if the plants have been kept too warm in winter or have grown too rapidly in spring. It can also happen that shoots growing very close to the window may become frozen. If the greenhouse is equipped with matting covers, these should be lowered in a sharp frost, or the greenhouse may be protected with quilted plastic.

Jasminum mesnyi

Syn. *Jasminum primulinum.* An evergreen shrub with square twigs and leaves divided into three; the leaflets are lanceolate, 3 to 7cm (1 to 2¾in) long. The bright yellow flowers, 3 to 5cm (1 to 2in) across, grow singly and have six or more petals.

Jasminum officinale

A deciduous shrub, having composite leaves consisting of five to nine leaflets, each 1 to 3cm (½ to 1in) long; the terminal leaflet is much longer. There are sparsely flowered clusters with white flowers 2.5cm (1in) in diameter. The petals are equal in length to the tube. The form 'Grandiflorum' is the one most frequently cultivated; its white flowers are larger, up to 4cm (1½in) across.

Jasminum polyanthum

This resembles the previous species, but the flowers grow in plumes. The corolla is up to 4cm (1½in) across, white inside, tinged with rose red on the outside. The petals are half the length of the tube.

Jasminum sambac

Arabian Jasmine. An evergreen shrub, occasionally with climbing shoots. The apparently simple-compound leaves are broad elliptical in shape, dark green, up to 7cm (2¾in) long and 5cm (2in) wide. The leaf stalk is short and slightly upcurved. The strongly scented white flowers are usually double and grow in sparse clusters.

Jatropha

Euphorbiaceae

Name From the Greek *iatros*, physician, and *trophe*, food. The 'Physician's Food' is meant to be a medicine, but both the milky sap and the seeds are simply poisonous.

Origin About 160 different species occur in tropical zones of Africa and America.

Description A plant with a thick, bottle-shaped body which from time to time puts forth a few long-stalked leaves and bright red flowers.

Position At last, a succulent which can be kept in the warm living-room throughout the winter.

Care It is remarkable that such an unusual plant is so easy to grow. It requires no cool dormant season, but may be kept at room temperature all the year round. The only thing that will happen is that the leaves will gradually turn yellow in autumn and will then drop. Afterwards watering should practically cease, since otherwise the attractive plant would inevitably rot. It does not start into growth again until March, when it may be given very little water.

Watering Little water is needed at any time and in winter give the plant hardly any at all.

Feeding Unnecessary – this plant thrives on starvation.

Repotting The most satisfactory potting compost consists of clay and leafmould. Exceptionally good drainage must be provided. The compost need not be replaced every year.

Propagation Seed may develop if the flowers are artificially pollinated with a small paint brush. When the capsules ripen they burst and the seed flies in all directions. The trick is to tie a small linen bag round the capsules to catch the seed, which should be sown immediately.

Jatropha podagrica

Jatropha podagrica

A succulent shrub, up to 60cm (2ft) tall. The stem is thickened in the shape of a tuber. Shield-shaped, three to five-lobed leaves grow on long stalks and it bears bright red flower umbels, also on long stalks. The flowers appear early in spring, before the leaves.

Kalanchoe

Crassulaceae

Name This appears to be the Latin version of a popular Chinese plant name.
Origin More than 200 species have been described, many of them natives of Malagasy.
Description The best-known species is *Kalanchoe blossfeldiana*, of which numerous brightly coloured hybrids are marketed in their hundreds of thousands. But in addition there are unusual, very succulent species. The viviparous – those which produce plantlets or offsets – plants formerly known as *Bryophyllum* species, have now also been classified under the *Kalanchoe* genus.
Position In principle all species mentioned should be overwintered in an unheated greenhouse, but many of them, especially those producing offsets, are so strong that they can stay in the warm living-room throughout the winter.
Care *Kalanchoe blossfeldiana* has fleshy leaves, but is less succulent than some of the other species. However, it must be treated like a succulent if it is to flower in the following year. This means that the plant must be kept in very good light in spring and summer; only the brightest midday sun must be filtered. It is quite easy to check: if the foliage turns red then the plant has had too much sun. All spent flowers should be removed, and towards the winter the plant must be kept a little cooler, although not as cool as the other species. The minimum temperature should be about 16°C (60°F). In the living-room it helps to keep the plant close to the window.

The kalanchoe is a short-day plant, which means that it only develops flower buds if the day lasts for less than 12 hours. If this fact is ignored, the buds will not start to develop until November and no flowers can be expected until the following spring. Growers therefore create artificial short-day conditions by keeping the plants in the dark at certain times. You might like to try this yourself. Take well-developed plants and start the treatment towards the end of August. The shortest day is eight to nine hours and the plants must therefore be kept in total darkness between, for instance, 5 p.m. and 8 a.m. This may be achieved by putting them in a dark lavatory, or by covering them with a black plastic bag or a bucket. The treatment must be continued for three or four weeks. As soon as the first few flower buds are large enough they should be removed by hand and this will promote more profuse flowering. You may expect the plants to be in full flower within 12 to 15 weeks from the beginning of the treatment.

Viviparous plants require different treatment. Their flowers are insignificant and they are therefore grown for their foliage and for the attractive plantlets which develop in large numbers along the margins of the leaves. These drop spontaneously and shortly afterwards the pot, as well as the pots of other nearby plants, are crowded with hundreds of plantlets.

These plants must be placed in a sunny position and, according to the rules, they should be kept cool in winter, preferably in a cool greenhouse at a minimum temperature of 5°C (41°F). This is possible only if the plants are kept entirely dry; they will then retain a fine compact shape. In practice it has been found that these plants will not be harmed if kept in the warm living-room throughout the winter. They will then grow very lanky, sometimes up to 1 m (3 ft) in height, but this does not matter, since new plantlets are cultivated in spring and the old one can be discarded as soon as it is replaced.

The remaining kalanchoe species, including a number of very succulent plants, do not tolerate such high temperatures in winter. New plants are not grown every year and the plants must therefore be kept cool in winter to retain their characteristic appearance. The flowers are insignificant, but the foliage is often very fine. They are best overwintered in a temperate greenhouse at a minimum temperature of 12°C (53°F). In summer they must be kept in a sunny spot, but make sure that the temperature does not become too high.
Watering All species are succulent and therefore do not need a large amount of water; it is logical that species with the largest leaf surface require the most. The flowering species *Kalanchoe blossfeldiana* should therefore be given most water. In summer keep the compost constantly, but moderately, moist, and in winter water a little more sparingly.

Species producing offsets and other forms may be kept moderately moist to fairly dry in summer. In winter the lower the temperature, the less water they should be given and at 5°C (41°F) they should be kept completely dry. It is advisable always to use rainwater or demineralised water.
Feeding *Kalanchoe blossfeldiana* likes a little liquid fertiliser in its growing season – once every three weeks is enough. If viviparous species are given a lot of nourishment they will grow into enormous specimens: try it if you like such large plants. Without fertiliser they will remain compact in habit.

Other species may in summer be given some cactus fertiliser from time to time. Too much nitrogen would destroy their character.
Repotting *Kalanchoe blossfeldiana* grows best in potting compost to which $\frac{1}{3}$ loam or clay has been added. Offset-producing plants can be grown in standard potting compost. The other succulents grow best in standard potting compost to which a little extra sand or perlite has been added.

Kalanchoe manginii

Kalanchoe blossfeldiana 'Kuiper's Orange'

Kalanchoe laxiflora 'Fedschenko'

Kalanchoe tomentosa, also called the Panda Plant

Kalanchoe blossfeldiana

Kalanchoe daigremontiana with its offsets

Propagation Professionals usually raise *K. blossfeldiana* forms from seed, but the amateur is advised to take shoots which root fairly readily in a temperature of 20 to 25°C (68 to 77°F). Do not let the cutting medium become too moist.

Offset-producing plants present no propagation problems: they fall into your lap, as it were. Remove the plantlets and pot them, however small they are. The other succulents can be increased from tip cuttings or from leaf cuttings. Fleshy leaves should be left to dry for a few days first.

Flowering species

Kalanchoe blossfeldiana

A small shrub with round stems and oval, roughly serrate leaves, the surface of which is glossy or dull green. Flowers are in fairly short-stalked clusters; the corolla is red to orange-red, narrowed at the base. Only hybrids are cultivated, in flower colours of red, yellow, orange and lilac.

Kalanchoe longiflora

Like the above, but larger and with square stems and yellow flowers in long-stalked clusters; the corolla broadens at the base. One cultivar is the form 'Coccinea', with concave leaves.

Kalanchoe manginii

A small plant with initially erect-growing, later arching stems. The leaves are lanceolate to spatula shaped, 2 to 4cm ($\frac{3}{4}$ to $1\frac{1}{2}$in) long and 5 to 1.5cm ($\frac{1}{4}$ to $\frac{1}{2}$in) wide. It has pendulous red flowers, growing singly or in small groups, 2cm ($\frac{3}{4}$in) long.

Viviparous plants

Kalanchoe daigremontiana

Syn. *Bryophyllum daigremontianum*. An erect-growing plant with elongated triangular leaves, green, with purple patches on the reverse. The bases of the lobes curve upwards, and the margin is covered in numerous tiny purple plantlets.

Kalanchoe laxiflora

Syn. *Bryophyllum crenatum; Kalanchoe crenata*. Similar to the above, but all its parts are blue bloomed. The leaves are oval, with crenate margins, frequently covered in tiny plantlets. A cultivar with smaller leaves is known as 'Fedschenko', and there is also a white-edged form called 'Marginata'.

Kalanchoe tubiflora

Syn. *Bryophyllum tubiflorum*. A small, erect-growing plant with cylinder-shaped leaves, pale green with darker marking and slightly tinged with red;

Kalanchoe tubiflora also produces offsets

the upper surface is furrowed. Only the tips of the leaves are toothed and it is there that the plantlets develop, dropping spontaneously.

Other species

Kalanchoe marmorata

Syn. *Kalanchoe grandiflora; Kalanchoe macrantha*. An erect-growing plant with reversed-oval leaves, narrowing at the base, green with blue bloom, and irregular brown spots on both surfaces.

Kalanchoe tomentosa

Panda Plant. This species has erect-growing, branching stems and thick, spoon-shaped leaves arranged in loose rosettes, densely covered with woolly hairs. The tips are brown and slightly crenate.

Kohleria

Gesneriaceae

Name Named after Michael Kohler, a 19th-century teacher of science at the Zurich Academy of Teacher Training.

Origin There are about 65 species, distributed over mountain regions in Mexico and the northern part of South America.

Description The plants remind one of the better-known genera *Smithiantha* or *Rechsteineria*, but the flowers have more striking marking.

Position These are greenhouse plants, requiring a humid atmosphere and cool winter conditions.

Care Cultivation usually begins with the purchase of a number of the scaly rhizomes, which in a humid and warm environment (under glass) put forth shoots fairly readily. The plant should preferably be cultivated in a well-lit hothouse. In autumn gradually reduce the water supply, but do not let the foliage die down entirely, as in the case of achimenes. Minimum temperatures in winter should be 10 to 12°C (50 to 53°F).

Watering Keep moderately moist in summer and in winter give only just enough water to prevent the foliage dying. Never spray directly on to the leaves.

Feeding In the growth period the plant may be fed every fortnight.

Repotting The compost should consist of rotted leafmould, rotted cow manure and some sharp sand or perlite. Repot every spring.

Propagation In spring the rhizomes may be divided. In autumn tip cuttings can be rooted in bottom heat. Plants can also be grown from seed.

Kohleria hybrids

Syn. *Isoloma* hybrids; *Tydaea* hybrids. Erect-growing or recumbent plant with oval to oblong, hairy leaves, velvety green, brownish or with contrasting tints along the veins. The flowers are tubular and occur in shades of orange, red, yellow-orange and orange-red, with a spotted interior. This is a general description of the *Kohleria amabilis* hybrids, *Kohleria bogotensis* hybrids, *Kohleria eriantha* hybrids and *Kohleria sciadotydaea* hybrids, which differ in a number of details.

Kohleria eriantha hybrid

Lachenalia
Liliaceae

Name Named after Werner von Lachenal, 1736–1800, Professor of Botany in Basle.
Origin About 50 species occur in South Africa, where the bulbs undergo a strict dormant season in summer.
Description A bulbous plant which has been unable to adapt its rhythm to the northern hemisphere. It has fleshy leaves and tubular yellow or orange flowers in racemes.
Position Put it out of doors in summer and in winter keep it in a well-lit, cool environment.
Care Cultivation usually starts in September with the potting of new bulbs ordered by mail. Group several in one pot. Initially give a little water and keep in a temperate greenhouse or cool room in a temperature between 10 and 14°C (50 and 57°F).

Alternatively, the bulbs can stay in a cold frame until the end of October, when they are placed in a cool greenhouse at the temperatures of between 5 and 10°C (41 and 50°F) usually found there. The bulbs flower from February until late March and must then be kept at the same temperature for a time, until the foliage dies down. From May to September the bulbs should stay in the pot, in full sun in a dry spot.
Watering It has low water requirements, but keep it moderately moist in the growth period. After May stop watering.
Feeding Feed weekly during the last few weeks before, during, and some weeks after flowering.
Repotting Repot every year in September in standard potting compost to which a little pulverised clay may be added.
Propagation Offset bulbs can be removed and grown separately. They may flower after two years.

Lachenalia aloides

Syn. *Phormium aloides*. The bulbs are 4 cm (1½ in) in diameter with two to three fleshy leaves, 30 cm (1 ft) long and 5 cm (2 in) wide, arching, and usually blotched. The flower stalk is green or purplish brown; the flowers appear in racemes and are pale yellow, usually green at the tip. The outer petals are orange-yellow, the centre ones slightly reddish and twice as long. The plants in cultivation are mainly hybrid forms, with yellow, orange or reddish flowers.

Lachenalia bulbifera

Lachenalia bulbifera
Syn. *Lachenalia pendula*. Like the previous species, but the leaves grow erect and are usually not blotched. The flower stalk is purple-brown. The flowers grow in racemes, at first erect and slanting, later pendulous, and are orange-red. The inner petals are not much longer than the outer ones.

Lachenalia aloides hybrid, with practically white flowers. This is an ideal winter-flowering plant for the cool greenhouse

Laelia pumila will occasionally grow indoors

Laelia
Orchidaceae

Name It has been said that the genus has been named after the Roman orator and philosopher Gaius Laelius (±140 B.C.), but Lindley who named the genus may equally well have been inspired by the Roman girl's name Laelia.
Origin About 35 species occur from Mexico to Brazil.
Description Epiphytic orchids with oblong pseudobulbs bearing one or two fleshy leaves. The erect inflorescence arises from the top of the pseudobulbs. The flowers are large.
Position Species whose native habitat is in Mexico, southern Brazil and the coast of the Atlantic should be cultivated at a minimum winter temperature of 10 to 12°C (50 to 53°F). The others can be kept a little warmer with a minimum night temperature in winter of 12 to 15°C (53 to 59°F).
Care These orchids, which are somewhat easier to grow than the related cattleyas, must be cultivated throughout the summer in plenty of light, but protected from bright sunlight. In warm weather the greenhouse must be thoroughly ventilated, at night as well as during the day, while at the same time you should attempt to maintain a fairly high degree of relative humidity. You can do this by keeping the greenhouse floor wet and by spraying the plants themselves.

In winter all those species which flower at other times have a dormant season. They should be given very little water and the temperature lowered as indicated above. At this time they must not be screened.
Watering Use only rainwater or demineralised water; a fair amount in summer, in winter give only just enough water to prevent the pseudobulbs shrivelling up.
Feeding In the growing season feed once a month.
Repotting The standard mixture consists of equal parts of sphagnum moss and osmunda fibre. These orchids can also be grown in 4 parts peat, 1 part perlite and 3 parts tree fern, to which a pinch of Dolomite limestone powder has been added. The rhizomes must be placed on the surface of the compost. The pots or baskets should not be too large for the size of the plant.
Propagation The plants may be divided when they are repotted every second year, in spring.

× *Laeliocattleya* 'Hugo de Groot', a large-flowered cultivar

Species for 10 to 12°C (50 to 53°F) winter minimum

Laelia anceps

Oval, compressed pseudobulbs with flowers in December–January up to 12 cm ($4\frac{1}{2}$ in) across, usually violet-pink with purple-red and yellow lip.

Laelia gouldiana

These have oblong/oval pseudobulbs and fragrant flowers 10 cm (4 in) across, purple with yellow crests on the lip, in December–January.

Laelia pumila

Cylindrical pseudobulbs up to 7 cm ($2\frac{3}{4}$ in) long, and small leaves. The flowers appear in September–October and usually grow singly. They are pale violet-pink with a red patch on the lip. The many varieties may occasionally be grown in an east-facing window.

Species for 12 to 15°C (53 to 59°F) winter minimum

Laelia cinnabarina

Slender, cylindrical pseudobulbs bearing one leaf. Flowers appear in February–May in clusters of five to fifteen, with a dentate lip, orange-red with yellow.

Laelia purpurata

Very large pseudobulbs, up to 60 cm (2 ft) long, bearing one blunt, thick, leathery leaf. The flower stalk carries three to five flowers, each 20 cm (8 in) across, white, flushed with pink. The funnel-shaped lip is purple-red with dark veining and a yellow throat. It flowers in May–June.

× *Laeliocattleya*

The result of crossing *Cattleya* and *Laelia*. There are numerous large-flowered strains which require a less-strict dormant season at a minimum 15°C (59°F).

Lagerstroemia

Lythraceae

Name Named after Magnus von Lagerstroem, 1691–1759, Director of the Swedish East India Company, who collected many plants for Linnaeus.

Origin There are about 30 species in Australia and southern and eastern Asia.

Description In the tropics it is well known as an ornamental shrub with dark red, rose-red or white flowers. In temperate climates it is a rare house plant or greenhouse plant.

Position A plant for a cool greenhouse, it can also be used as a tub plant.

Care From the end of May onwards the lagerstroemia may be put in a sunny spot out of doors. The flowers appear from August onwards, until the onset of frost. The plant must then be brought indoors, preferably into a cool greenhouse, or else a well-lit unheated room where a minimum temperature of 2 to 5°C (35 to 41°F) can be guaranteed. A shed or an unused room might serve the purpose. Check that the temperature does not rise too rapidly in spring, for this would cause the plant to put out shoots too early. In April it may start into growth, but it is advisable to prune drastically before this, especially in the case of older plants. The flowers appear on the new growth.

Watering In summer it must always be kept moderately moist. In winter, when the temperature is kept low, give little water.

Feeding During the period of growth feed every fortnight.

Repotting Young plants should be repotted every year, older specimens every two years, in standard potting compost. The addition of a little extra loam is helpful.

Propagation Seed – if, indeed, it is available – germinates very slowly. In August–September ripe tip shoots may be used as cuttings, with some warmth.

Lagerstroemia indica, a rare house plant

Lagerstroemia indica

A deciduous tree or shrub with square branches and sessile or very short-stalked leaves, elliptical or oval, 2 to 7 cm ($\frac{3}{4}$ to $2\frac{3}{4}$ in) long and 1 to 3 cm ($\frac{1}{2}$ to 1 in) wide. It has multiflowered terminal plumes and the flowers are about 4 cm ($1\frac{1}{2}$ in) across with six long-pointed petals and a broad, wrinkled and fringed disc, white to dark red.

Lampranthus blandus needs a sunny position

Lampranthus

Aizoaceae

Name From the Greek *lampros*, brilliant, magnificent, and *anthos*, flower.

Origin At least 100 species are known, most of them originating in South Africa.

Description Small plants with creeping stems and fleshy, almost cylindrical leaves. The glossy, silky radial flowers open in the sun.

Position These are suitable plants for a sunny window-sill. In warm summers they may go outside.

Care It is strange that these easy plants are so rarely available. They immediately feel happy on any sunny, south-facing window-sill. They need not be screened since because of their succulent character they do not easily dry out. In a really warm summer try planting one out in a trough on the terrace or on the balcony. You will be amazed at the hundreds of magnificent flowers produced for months on end. In cloudy weather the buds remain closed.

Watering Water moderately in summer. If the plant is kept cool in winter it can be given little or no water. Be careful not to overwater.

Feeding In the growing season the plant should be fed once a fortnight.

Repotting Standard potting compost will be made a little less rich by the addition of sharp sand or perlite. Repot and cut back in spring.

Propagation Tip cuttings root most readily in the late summer or autumn. Propagation from seed is also possible; this should be done early in spring.

Lampranthus blandus

A small shrub with recumbent stems and fleshy green leaves, 5 to 7 cm (2 to $2\frac{3}{4}$ in) long and 3 to 5 mm ($\frac{1}{8}$ to $\frac{1}{4}$ in) wide, cylindrical, flattened and concave above. It bears purple-red or white flowers.

Lampranthus brownii

Distinguished from the above by its small leaves, only 5 to 15 mm ($\frac{1}{4}$ to $\frac{1}{2}$ in) long and 1 mm across and entirely covered in grey bloom. The flowers grow singly and are a maximum of 2.5 cm (1 in) in diameter in orange to red.

One of the rarer species of *Lapeirousia*, with white flowers. This is an unusual spring-flowering plant

Laurus nobilis, with an unusually shaped trunk

Lapeirousia
Iridaceae

Name Named after Jean François Galoup de la Peyrouse, 1741–1788, a French naval officer and world traveller.
Origin About 50 species occur in tropical areas of Africa and in southern Africa.
Description A bulbous plant with sword-shaped leaves. It bears small, funnel-shaped or almost saucer-shaped flowers with long stamens; they are mostly red.
Position Plants for the cool greenhouse, but they can also be successfully cultivated in a cool room.
Care The bulbs should be ordered in August, possibly from a mail-order firm, and potted in groups of eight to twelve in September. The compost should be thoroughly moistened, but no more water given until shoots appear. Place the pots near a window in plenty of light. The temperature need not be high; approximately 12°C (53°F) is adequate, but in a warm room the plant can be forced into flower if they are kept near a window. They normally flower in spring.

After flowering the water supply should gradually be decreased until the foliage has entirely died down. A minimum temperature of 5°C (41°F) is sufficient for keeping the bulbs. In September the compost should be renewed.
Watering Do not water until the leaves appear. In the resting season the bulbs should be kept perfectly dry.
Feeding When the foliage is developing the plant may be given a dose of artificial fertiliser every fortnight.
Repotting Replace the compost every year in September. Ordinary potting compost is acceptable.
Propagation Increase by removing the offset bulbs or by sowing seed in heated compost in March.

Lapeirousia laxa

Syn. *Gladiolus laxus; Anomatheca cruenta*. Long, sword-shaped pointed leaves with a conspicuous centre vein, 15 to 20 cm (6 to 8 in) long and 6 to 10 mm (¼ to ¾ in) across. The thin flower stalks are longer than the leaves and the flowers are arranged in a one-sided ear. They have a 3-cm (1-in) long tube and spreading petals, and are bright orange-red with a red margin. Other species are also cultivated.

Laurus
Lauraceae
Bay Tree

Name This is the original Roman name for the Bay Tree.
Origin Only two species are known, both growing wild in the Mediterranean region.
Description In our climate it is a well-known tub plant, often trimmed in the shape of a pyramid, column or standard tree. The aromatic leaves are used in cookery.
Position From the end of May onwards the Bay Tree may be grown in a sunny and somewhat sheltered position out of doors. It is essential that it is kept cool in winter, since otherwise the plant is very prone to disease.
Care The Bay Tree is a strong shrub, not really a house plant but rather a tub plant, which in summer is best kept outside. Indoors the temperature is easily too high and there is not enough fresh air.

Difficulties may be encountered in winter. From September, when the first frosts occur, until the end of May it is absolutely necessary to keep the plant cool. An unheated greenhouse is not really suitable, since it may become far too warm if the sun is shining in February–March, inducing the Bay Tree to start into growth too soon. One solution might be to use an unheated room with northern aspect, where the window is always left open in frost-free weather. The minimum temperature should be 2°C (35°F). Another possibility is to take the tubs outside whenever there is no frost, but this can be quite a job. The Bay Tree does not like cold feet. On a stone floor always put some wood blocks under the tub.

If required to be trained the trees should be trimmed in August. The unusual trunk shown in the photograph is achieved by training the shoots of very young plants, joining them if necessary by grafting. At a much later stage it will start to function like a real trunk. All side branches should be constantly removed.
Watering Water fairly plentifully in summer, and in winter only just enough to prevent the foliage dropping. If possible use rainwater, which in winter must first be warmed.
Feeding In summer the plant may be regularly fed, perhaps every three weeks, with artificial fertiliser or a dried blood product.
Repotting An ideal compost consists of ⅓ clay or loam (pulverised lumps or soil collected from fresh molehills), ⅓ rotted leafmould or conifer needle compost, ⅙ rotted cow manure (keep it an extra year before using it) and ⅙ sharp sand. Large plants should be repotted every second year.
Propagation Tip cuttings should be taken in September and inserted in sharp sand in a frost-free place such as a cold frame. They will root in spring.
Pests and diseases Scale insects, mealy bug and red spider mites will occur if the Bay Tree has been kept too warm in winter.

Laurus nobilis

An evergreen tree with oval to lanceolate, leathery dark green leaves, exuding a strong aromatic scent when crushed. The margin is usually undulate. It bears inconspicuous greenish flowers.

Lily varieties that have been forced

Lilium
Liliaceae
Lily

Name This is the original Roman name for the plant.
Origin At least 100 species are indigenous in temperate zones in the northern hemisphere.
Description A well-known bulbous plant, generally classified as a garden plant. What is less well known is that some species may be forced into flower in the living-room.
Position After having flowered indoors the plants may be put in the garden at the end of May.
Care Lily bulbs suitable for indoor cultivation can be ordered from a mail-order firm or another specialist. They will reach you in winter and may be potted from January onwards. Small bulbs should be potted in groups of three to five, larger specimens singly. Since most lily species develop roots on the upper side of the bulb as well as below, the bulbs should be planted about 10cm (4in) below the surface. In addition there must be at least 5cm (2in) of soil below the bulb, plus a 3-cm (1-in) drainage layer of crocks. This adds up to 18cm (7in), so taking into account the depth of the bulbs you will be able to calculate how deep the pot should be (usually 25cm, 10in). Carefully place the bulbs in the compost and firmly press down, then add sufficient water to make it moderately moist to the touch.

The pots must now be placed in a cool environment, possibly a cold frame. A dark cellar is also suitable. The bulb is buried in the soil, out of the light, but when the shoot develops it should also be allowed to grow in the dark for a time. Little water is needed in this period; the compost should just be kept very moderately moist.

When the developing flower buds become visible at the top of the shoots, the lilies may be kept a little warmer, perhaps at 10 to 12°C (50 to 53°F). This probably occurs in February or March. The plants may now be placed in full light. On no account forget to water, for because of the developing growth and the higher temperature evaporation will increase appreciably. After about two weeks the temperature may rise to a maximum of about 16 to 18°C (60 to 64°F); a higher degree is not tolerated. The flowers will appear in April–May.

When the temperature is approximately equal inside and outside, the lilies may be stood out in the garden or on the balcony, where they should be in partial shade and not in full sun.

Towards autumn the bulbs die down. Stop watering and when all the foliage has turned yellow keep the bulbs in their pots until the time for forcing has come again. This will succeed a second time only if the lilies have had the best possible care in summer. If you are unsure it is better to take new bulbs and leave the old ones in the garden to recuperate. Specially treated lily bulbs, possibly kept in cold storage to flower in the autumn, cannot be forced a second time.
Watering The compost should be kept moderately moist only in the growing period. If possible use rainwater.
Feeding Feed every fortnight in the growing season.
Repotting The most satisfactory potting compost for lilies consists of 1 part loam or clay taken from molehills, 1 part completely rotted stable manure and 1 part washed river sand or perlite. A few pieces of charcoal may also be added.

The bottom of the 25-cm (10-in) deep plastic pot should first be covered with a 3-cm (1-in) layer of crocks, followed by a tuft of sphagnum moss to keep in the compost. The bulb is then planted as described above.

If the bulbs are forced every year in January, it is advisable to make a fresh mixture each time. If, on the other hand, they are to be forced only once, then discarded or put in the garden afterwards, a proprietary potting compost may if necessary be used. To increase the level of acidity add one third to half the volume of pure peat.
Propagation Lilies can be increased from offset bulbs, but it is not easy to get them to flower in the living-room.

Lilium speciosum is sometimes sold as a cut flower

Lilium Mid-Century hybrids

This group is particularly suitable for pot cultivation. To mention a few there is 'Destiny', yellow with brown spots; 'Enchantment', cherry red, and 'Joan Evans', bright yellow. Other species and hybrids suitable for greenhouse or indoor cultivation are *Lilium auratum*, *L. longiflorum*, *L. regale*, *L. speciosum* and the American hybrid 'Golden Splendor'.

'Fire King', a cultivar suitable for pot cultivation

Liriope
Liliaceae

Name Derived from the Greek *leilion*, lily, and *opsis*, resembling. One might therefore think that the flower resembles a lily, but nothing is further from the truth. The species described and illustrated is more reminiscent of the Grape Hyacinth.
Origin Three or four species are known, natives of Japan and China.
Description When in flower the plant closely resembles a Grape Hyacinth with yellow-striped foliage. It is even more easily confused with its relative, *Ophiopogon* (q.v.). It is strange that both these plants are so seldom available. In some countries they are very popular, because they rarely present problems in cultivation.

Liriope muscari

Position A plant for a warm room, although in winter it likes to be kept a little cooler.
Care The all-green species does not require as much light as the more beautiful striped form, which must have plenty of light to maintain its colouring. However, do not put it in the sun. High atmospheric humidity is unnecessary and even undesirable. After flowering cut off the flower stalks, unless you want to wait for the black berries. In winter the temperature may drop to 5°C (41°F), but as much as 18°C (64°F) is tolerated, though in the latter case it should be put close to the window.
Watering Always keep moderately moist in winter and summer, but when the mercury falls very low the plant must be kept much drier.
Feeding Feed every two weeks in the period of active growth.
Repotting Standard potting compost offers a reasonable alternative to a clay or loam mixture.
Propagation The plant does not develop offsets and can therefore only be increased by division or from seed.

Liriope muscari

Syn. *Ophiopogon muscari*. Big Blue Lily-turf. Evergreen stalkless plant with strap-shaped, erect-growing leaves, 30cm (1ft) long and 12mm (½in) wide, with conspicuous veining. Flowers grow in dense racemes, which are of approximately equal length to the leaves; the colour is purple to violet and they are followed by black berries. In the cultivar 'Variegata' the leaves are striped lengthwise with yellow.

Lithops ruschiorum, a Living Stone

Lithops
Aizoaceae
Living Stone

Name From the Greek *lithos*, stone, and *opsis*, resembling. The plants undoubtedly resemble stones.
Origin At least 50 species are known, all originating in South Africa.
Description Remarkable succulents, difficult to find in the wild because they blend into their environment. This mimicry serves to protect the plants from their natural enemies. Except for a very narrow split the two very thick leaves are fused. From this split two new leaves are produced, which in winter absorb the sap from the old pair. Some species grow partially underground and receive light by means of a small 'window'.
Position These plants belong in the succulent collection in the greenhouse, where they will receive plenty of sun and where in winter the temperature does not fall below 8 to 10°C (46 to 50°F).
Care It is fun to plant them out in a mini-landscape in which a few real stones are incorporated. Visitors will be unable to see the difference between the real and the living stones. They never need screening or spraying.
Watering To prevent the sensitive plants rotting, the little water required is best supplied at the base. From October until the spring, when the new leaves break out, not a drop of water is needed. No water must ever lodge between the two thick leaves.
Feeding Only if the plants are kept year after year in the same compost might they be given a little nitrogen-free cactus fertiliser once a year, but it should remain an exception.
Repotting The best mixture consists of pulverised loam or clay, rotted leafmould and perlite, in equal parts. A little slug powder may be added. Use very well-drained flat bowls, which can draw in water from the bottom when partially plunged. The larger part of the small plant can remain above ground. To prevent rotting the surface may be sprinkled with some very fine gravel.
Propagation It is possible to glean seed from flowering plants. Most species do not flower until autumn and they are all self-sterile, which means that a second plant of the same species is required to pollinate the first. This can be done with a small paintbrush. It is easy to cross several species. The ripe seed may be sown in autumn. Pricking out is a fiddly job: the young plantlets have the tendency to withdraw into the soil and sometimes have to be pulled up several times.

Lithops bella
This species has leaves with a greyish-yellow tinge and slightly sunken darker marking. The flowers are brilliant white.
Lithops optica
Leaves are of a loamy grey colour. The upper side is convex and is furnished with a large clear window, and there are white flowers tinged with a little pink.
Lithops pseudotruncatella
A changeable species with grey, pink, brown, yellowish or blue-green leaves and yellow flowers from July onwards.
Lithops ruschiorum
The two leaves are unusually wide apart, and the colour varies from greyish to yellow with red. This species is sometimes called the 'primeval' lithops.
Lithops turbiniformis
A species with deeply incised dark marking on the grey leaves.

Littonia
Liliaceae

Name Named after Dr Samuel Litton, a professor of botany in Dublin; period unknown.
Origin Seven species occur in tropical Africa and in South Africa. Only one of them is cultivated.
Description A rare greenhouse climber with a tuberous rootstock and very unusual bell-shaped flowers.
Position Preferably in a greenhouse, but it should also be possible to cultivate it on a sunny window-sill.
Care The tuberous rhizomes can be obtained from a mail-order firm and are potted in March. The compost should be moistened slightly and the pots given a warm environment, possibly on a not-too-hot radiator. When the shoots appear they must be carefully tied along the window frame or the greenhouse roof, and the flowers will appear in the course of the summer. It should, in fact, be possible to put the plant in a very warm spot out of doors from the end of May onwards, preferably planted out.
In September the foliage begins to die down and the littonia should no longer be watered. The tuber remains in the completely dry compost throughout the winter, at a temperature of 12°C (53°F).
Watering When the plant has truly started into growth, watering can be started again. It is best to use rainwater.
Feeding In the growing period give a dose of fertiliser at normal concentration every two weeks.
Repotting The compost should contain finely pulverised loam or clay, leafmould and rotted cow manure. Pots must be very well drained and the plants should be potted on every year.
Propagation If the rootstock spreads, a section may be removed after the plant has started into growth. The plant may also be grown from seed.

Littonia modesta
A climber with elongated oval leaves ending in tendrils. The flowers are angled on up to 5-cm (2-in) long stalks. They are 2 to 3 cm (¾ to 1 in) in diameter and orange in colour. Together the petals form a kind of bell shape. The form most frequently cultivated is 'Keitii', which branches more profusely and has larger flowers than the species.

Littonia modesta 'Keitii'

Lobivia
Cactaceae

Name Lobivia is an anagram of Bolivia, the country where most species originate.
Origin About 70 different species occur in the tablelands of the Andes mountains, not only in Bolivia, but also in northern Argentina and Peru.
Description Spherical or more or less columnar cacti with warty ribs and beautiful thorns and hairs. The plants flower at an early age. They are easy to grow and therefore very suitable for a beginner.
Position A cool greenhouse is the best place. Cool conditions in winter are essential to healthy growth.
Care In summer the plants require full sun, but at the same time plenty of fresh air. The more sun, the finer the thorns will be. The cactus flowers in early summer. The flowers do not last very long, but quite a few blooms will appear in succession.
From October onwards the lobivia must be kept practically dry at a temperature between 5 and 8°C (41 to 46°F). In sunny, frost-free weather the greenhouse should be properly ventilated. If you do not have a greenhouse find another well-lit area where the ideal temperature can be maintained.
Watering The lobivia needs slightly more water than most other cacti; in warm sunny weather it will do no harm to water it all over, but at the end of October you should stop being generous, for the plants need a rest. The water should be relatively lime free; it is best to use rainwater.
Feeding In summer give a dose of cactus fertiliser once a month.
Repotting In spring the cacti should be repotted in reasonably sized plastic pots filled with a mixture of 70 per cent standard potting compost and 30 per cent perlite. In the case of large plants the compost need not be renewed every year.
Propagation Various species develop offsets and some of these actually have roots. When the plant is repotted these offsets can be removed. Unrooted offsets can be used as cuttings. If an incision is made in the top of the plant, several

A cultivar of *Lobivia famatimensis* with enormous flowers

offsets will develop on the cut surface and these, too, may be used as cuttings. The cacti may also be grown from seed sown in March in a soil temperature of 20 to 25°C (68 to 77°F).

Pests and diseases Mealy bug and root aphids are the most likely pests, but if the plants are kept too warm in winter red spider mite may also occur.

Lobivia boliviensis

A clump-forming, grey-green cactus with 12 to 20 ribs, 10 to 12 brown radial thorns and one central thorn, up to 8 cm (3 in) long and curved at the tip. It produces fairly small flowers in orange-red through a prolonged flowering season.

Lobivia densispina

Syn. *Echinopsis densispina*. A short cylindrical, densely thorned cactus, single or slightly branching. It has 18 to 24 ribs, usually straight, and bristly whitish thorns to 1·5 mm (½ in) long. There are wide funnel-shaped yellow, red or orange flowers, to 6 cm (2¼ in) across.

Lobivia famatimensis

Syn. *Lobivia pectinifera*. A cylinder-shaped, red-brown cactus with 20 ribs. The yellowish thorns are arranged in the form of a comb and there is no central thorn. The flowers are yellow with a green throat, and there are cultivars in a variety of other colours.

Lobivia hertrichiana

Cob Cactus. A spherical, fresh green cactus with 11 notched ribs, covered in short, outward-curving yellow thorns and large, bright red flowers.

Lobivia pentlandii

Globular dark green cactus with 12 to 15 notched ribs. The thorns are brownish in colour and the central thorn is up to 4 cm (1½ in) long. They have orange-red flowers, and several cultivars have white or yellowish flowers.

Lobivia hertrichiana

Lycaste lasioglossa

Lycaste virginalis

Lycaste

Orchidaceae

Name From a Greek girl's name, Lycaste.

Origin It occurs in the Andes ranges and in the mountain ranges of the West Indies.

Description An easily cultivated epiphytic (growing on trees or rocks) orchid with thin leaves and oval pseudobulbs.

Position Orchids for a cool or temperate greenhouse; they can sometimes be successfully grown in the living-room.

Care From April onwards the plant must be screened if grown in the greenhouse. In the living-room an east- or west-facing window is best. The plants must on no account be kept too dark. In October they need no longer be screened, but the temperature must drop to a minimum of 12°C (53°F) in the temperate greenhouse, and to 5°C (41°F) for cool greenhouse species. The strongest species will tolerate more warmth, but in the living-room they should be placed close to a single-glazed window, where it is pleasantly cool.

Watering Always use rainwater. In summer make sure that the leaves are dry in the evening, in order to avoid rotting. In the dormant season give only just sufficient water to prevent the pseudobulbs shrivelling up.

Feeding In the growing period they may be fed every fortnight.

Repotting A mixture of chopped fern roots, peat moss, leafmould, rotted turves and perlite is satisfactory, but other mixtures can also be used. Repot in spring, after the resting period.

Propagation Divide the plants when they are repotted.

Lycaste aromatica

Leaves are about 25 cm (10 in) long, and folding. There are small, golden-yellow flowers with a red-blotched lip in March–April; they have a cinnamon scent. Each pseudobulb may produce up to 20 flowers.

Lycaste candida

Syn. *Lycaste brevispatha*. This has folded leaves, up to 30 cm (1 ft) long. The flowers are up to 5 cm (2 in) across, with white and green sepals, white petals with pale pink tips, and the lip is blotched with purple-red. The flowering season is December–March.

Lycaste cruenta

This resembles the first-named species; the flowers are up to 5 cm (2 in) in diameter, orange-yellow or green-yellow, with a yellow lip blotched with bright red, and appear from March–May. It may also be grown in the living-room.

Lycaste virginalis

Syn. *Lycaste skinneri*. The leaves are up to 60 cm (2 ft) long and the flowers to 15 cm (6 in) in diameter, with white to rose-red sepals and rose-red petals. There is a fleshy lip, white, with red tips, and the flowering period is between November and March. A strong species, suitable for indoor cultivation.

Malvastrum
Malvaceae

Name From the Greek *malva*, the generic name, and *astrum*, star. The plant looks like *Malva*.
Origin At least 75 species occur in South Africa and America.
Description An old-fashioned, fairly rare house plant, profusely branched and bearing numerous small dark red flowers.
Position It may be put outside in summer. In winter the temperature should be similar to that in a temperate greenhouse.
Care The greatest problem is to find the plant in the first place. Fortunately it is fairly easily grown from cuttings. In summer it should be cultivated in plenty of light near a window, or placed on a sheltered terrace or balcony towards the end of May. The flowers appear in large numbers and in Germany it is sometimes called a 'Busy Lizzie'. However, the plant should not be confused with the impatiens, the 'official' Busy Lizzie. The plant is not hardy and must be brought indoors before the first night frosts occur. It will be satisfied with a temperature of 8°C (46°F). A cool greenhouse is the ideal place in winter, but an unused, moderately heated room indoors is also satisfactory. At one time the plant could be kept in the conservatory in winter.
Watering Keep moderately moist throughout the summer, a little drier in winter.
Feeding Feed every fortnight in the period of active growth.

Malvastrum capense, a rare house plant

Repotting A proprietary compost is satisfactory; a little loam or clay may be added.
Propagation Tip cuttings will readily root at almost any time of the year, if necessary even in a bottle of water. The plants are also fairly easily grown from seed.

Malvastrum capense

Syn. *Anisdontea capensis*. An erect-growing, vigorously branching, hairy and slightly sticky plant, with 2- to 5-cm ($\frac{3}{4}$- to 2-in) long and 1- to 3-cm ($\frac{1}{2}$- to 1-in) wide leaves, which vary in shape, becoming smaller towards the top of the plant. The axillary flowers grow singly or in pairs. They are long stalked and 2cm ($\frac{3}{4}$in) in diameter, rose red.

Mammillaria sheldonii

Mammillaria zeilmanniana

Mammillaria denmosa 'Erytrocephala'

Mammillaria
Cactaceae
Nipple Cactus

Name From the Latin word *mamilla*, nipple.
Origin Most of the more than 200 species known occur in Mexico, the others in the West Indies and in the southern part of the United States.
Description Spherical or columnar cacti, often with many branches and forming clumps, frequently covered with nipple-shaped tubercles arranged in spirals. In many cases the flowers appear in a ring around the top of the body, and are usually quite small.
Position All species belong in the unheated or cool greenhouse. The sole exception is *Mammillaria plumosa*, a winter-flowering cactus which prefers to be kept a little warmer.
Care Practically all the species may be kept in full sun throughout the summer. They need only be lightly screened in the spring. Pale green species with delicate tissue need light screening in summer as well. Older, somewhat columnar plants tend to grow towards the light; this can be prevented if you turn the plant from time to time. Like some other cacti, the plants have a tendency towards cristate formation. As a result of as yet unknown causes, the growing point may widen into a band, creating the most bizarre shapes, as you can see on page 197. These characteristics may be maintained by grafting or by growing new plants from cuttings. The phenomenon, also called 'fasciation', occurs in several *Mammillaria* species.
Watering Because of the shape of the cactus body there is a danger of stagnant water lodging in parts of the body and this might damage the plant. White-haired species are particularly sensitive to a shower. It is therefore advisable to water the entire collection from the bottom, not difficult to do if all the pots are assembled in a large flat dish or bowl with a layer of water in the bottom. After about an hour the excess water should be poured away. The same method may be used to feed the cacti. My own small cactus collection stands in an aluminium gutter placed just below the glass of a greenhouse. Once a week, or in cloudy weather once a fortnight, the gutter is filled with water, and is easily emptied by turning on a tap. In this way rotting and cork formation on the cactus bodies are avoided.
Always use demineralised water or rainwater to prevent damage caused by excess lime. From October onwards stop watering unless the temperature in the greenhouse becomes so high that the cacti might dry out. But this does not happen very easily.
Feeding In the growing season the plants may be given a dose of special, nitrogen-free cactus fertiliser.
Repotting All species will thrive in the cactus mixture described on page 70. It will do no harm if a little pulverised clay or loam is added; it will provide extra nourishment. If your cacti are growing in miniature pots you should transfer them immediately to reasonably sized plastic pots. If you have a lot of plants square pots will make the maximum use of available space.
Propagation Cluster-forming species can be propagated from cuttings or by grafting. The latter method is not often used in the case of mammillaria plants. Cuttings must be left to dry for a few days first. The plants are frequently grown from seed, which germinates in a temperature of 20 to 25°C (68 to 77°F).
Pests and diseases Damage may be caused by mealy bug and root aphids.

Mammillaria bocasana

Spherical to cylindrical in shape and clump forming, it is densely covered all over in white hairs. The thorns are hooked. It has a profusion of reddish flowers, white inside, streaked with red.

Mammillaria gracilis

This has a short body, columnar or club shaped; they are clump-forming, with green and white thorns. The tubercles are widely spaced; there are 12 to 16

A group of established mammillaria plants, some of them densely covered in fruits

thorns, straight or slightly curved, and funnel-shaped pale yellow flowers, 1cm (½in) long.

Mammillaria hahniana
Old Lady Cactus. A globular clump-forming cactus, densely covered in white thorns and with long hairs. Rose-red funnel-shaped flowers form a ring around the top.

Mammillaria magnimamma
A globular species, flattened at the top, with a clump-forming habit, grey to blue-green in colour. It has white woolly hairs in the axils and three to five brownish to pale yellow thorns with a dark tip; the lower one is the longest, up to 1cm (½in). Flowers are up to 2.5cm (1in) across, red or white with a pink central stripe.

Mammillaria plumosa
A vigorously clustering cactus with delicate tissue. It has up to 40 soft thorns, white or yellowish in colour, entirely covering the plant. There are inconspicuous yellowish to green-white flowers in winter, which means that this species, unlike the others, must be kept a little warmer in winter.

Mammillaria prolifera
Globular to short cylindrical in shape, a dark grey-green with long hairs in the axils, there are 30 to 50 radial thorns 5mm (¼in) long, and 6 to 12 centrals, reddish-yellow, to 8mm (⅜in) long. It has funnel-shaped flowers, greenish with pink and yellow. The variety *multiceps* is sometimes described as *Mammillaria multiceps*.

Mammillaria rhodantha
Usually globular and growing singly, it is densely covered in yellow, brown or reddish-brown thorns, with white woolly hairs and bristles in the axils.

Mammillaria guelzowiana

Mammillaria rhodantha

The 16 to 20 radial thorns are thin, up to 1cm (½in) long; the four to seven centrals are usually yellow and up to 3cm (1in) long. The deep pink flowers have three to four red stigmata.

Mammillaria spinossissima
Distinguished from the previous species only by its invariably straight central thorns and the seven to eight green stigmata of the flowers.

Mammillaria vaupelii 'Cristata', a well-known cristate form

Mammillaria vaupelii
A small, isolated globe, closely covered in tubercles and equipped with yellowish radial thorns and long, transparent centrals. The flowers are yellow. The form 'Cristata' consists of a large number of thorny, sausage-shaped bodies, together forming a dense sphere. Often grafted on stock, although it is perfectly capable of assimilation.

Mammillaria verhaertiana
Of spherical habit, to 5cm (2in) in diameter, it has widely spaced tubercles, bearing fine yellow-white thorns radially arranged and three to four dark centrals. The flowers are white, 2cm (¾in) long.

Mammillaria wildii
Clump forming and branching, a columnar cactus with soft tubercles and long, loose hairs. There are eight to ten straight, white radial thorns arranged in a star shape; they are 8mm (⅜in) in length. The centrals are three to four in number, pale yellow, later turning brownish, and hairy; the lower one is hooked, the others straight.

Mammillaria zeilmanniana
Rose Pincushion. A clustering short-cylindrical cactus, densely covered in white thorns. The tubercles are soft, the thorns hairy. The 15 to 18 radial thorns are thin, straight and white; they are arranged in a star shape and get entangled with neighbouring thorns. The three to four centrals are reddish-brown, and the lower one is hooked. It has bell-shaped violet or white flowers.

Maranta
Marantaceae
Prayer Plant

Name Named after Bartolomeo Maranta, an Italian physician and botanist who died in 1574.
Origin Twenty five species have been found in tropical regions of America.
Description Herbaceous plants with tuber-shaped roots and beautifully marked foliage.
Position These are really hothouse plants, but they may also be grown in a flower window, a glass case, a bottle garden or, possibly, in a mixed container.
Care These plants will not tolerate sunlight, but in poor light the beautiful foliage marking will be lost. Give them the maximum degree of humidity; this is the chief problem when the plant is grown indoors. As they are quite small, the plants can be grown in flat dishes or above a bowl of water. In the growing period they require a temperature of 18 to 22°C (64 to 71°F); in winter it may fall to 14°C (57°F) at night. Warm compost is an advantage.
Watering Always use rainwater at room temperature, and spray the foliage frequently.
Feeding In summer feed every fortnight.
Repotting Standard potting compost is acceptable, but conifer needle compost mixed with rotted cow manure is even better. If possible do not grow your maranta in a pot – it will flourish better in wide containers or planted out on the greenhouse staging.
Propagation The best method of propagation is by division in spring.

Maranta leuconeura 'Kerchoveana'

Maranta bicolor
Syn. *Calathea bicolor.* A tuberless species; the leaves are round to oval, up to 15cm (6in) long, and the upper surface is blue-green, pale green along the main vein, with six to eight brown patches on either side between the main vein and the margin. The lower surface is purple. Small white flowers are borne in a narrow spike.

Maranta leuconeura
This species has tubers. The leaves are slightly smaller, with white streaks along the veins. Only cultivars are marketed, for example 'Fascinator' with red lateral veins; 'Kerchoveana', also known as the Prayer Plant, with four to five dark purple or dark green patches between the vein and the margin though the leaf itself is bright green and pale blue-green on the reverse; 'Massangeana', with darker green foliage and conspicuously white veins and vein axils; the underside of the leaves is pale purple.

Maranta leuconeura 'Fascinator'

Maranta bicolor

Medinilla magnifica, a large hothouse shrub

Medinilla
Melastomataceae

Name Named after José de Medinilla y Pineda, who around 1820 was governor of the Marianas, then a Spanish colony.
Origin At least 125 species grow on the islands in the Indian Ocean and in the surrounding countries.
Description The only species sometimes cultivated as a hothouse plant has angular branches, large, folding leaves and long, drooping flower plumes with large pink bracts.
Position Occasional attempts to grow this plant in the living-room have rarely succeeded. In the hothouse, on the other hand, the plant presents no problems.
Care In summer the medinilla demands a warm situation, 18 to 22°C (64 to 71°F) and even more when the sun shines. However, screening is essential. A period of rest follows between November and February, during which time a minimum night temperature of 15°C (59°F) must be maintained. Without this resting period the plant would continue to grow and no flower buds would be developed. As soon as the buds are visible the water supply and the temperature should be increased a little.

If the plant is grown indoors the foliage must be constantly moistened, and these temperatures should be strictly adhered to.
Watering In summer the compost must be kept moderately moist at all times. Occasionally the plant should be plunged. In winter keep it just dry enough to prevent the foliage suffering. If possible always use rainwater at room temperature.
Feeding In summer feed every fortnight, preferably with organic manure. Stop feeding in September.
Repotting The most favourable compost consists of $\frac{1}{3}$ clay (nice and loose, like molehills, or dried and pulverised), $\frac{1}{3}$ rotted leafmould, $\frac{1}{6}$ rotted cow manure and $\frac{1}{6}$ washed sharp sand. Repot in spring, older plants every second year. Use roomy pots, plastic containers or

Medinilla flower

tubs and cover the drainage holes with a deep layer of crocks.
Propagation When the plants have grown tall it is advisable to cut them back a little when they are repotted. The shoots which are removed in the process can serve as cuttings. The lower leaves should be removed from the tip cuttings, the stem cut just below and the cut surface dipped in rooting powder. Bottom heat should be 30 to 35°C (86 to 95°F) and the tray should be covered with glass. With luck the cuttings will root in about five weeks.

Medinilla magnifica
◐ ⊜ ⊘ ⊛ ⊙

An erect-growing shrub with winged branches and bristly hairs on the nodes. Leaves are opposite, sessile, oval and leathery, with sunken veins; they fold lengthwise and are up to 30 cm (1 ft) long. Flowers grow in drooping plumes, up to 40 cm (16 in) long, and are rose red in all their parts, with striking bracts and violet-coloured stamens.

Melocactus
Cactaceae
Melon Cactus

Name Derived from the Latin *melo*, melon, and *cactus*, cactus. Older plants become melon shaped.
Origin About 30 species are known from Mexico to Brazil and in the Antilles.
Description Flowering specimens of this cactus are distinguished by a woolly and bristly body at the top of the plant, the so-called cephalium. This is actually a terminal flower stalk developed from crossing spirals. This is where the thornless areoles which bear the flowers are clustered.
Position These are plants for a temperate or cool greenhouse; the minimum temperature is actually 10°C (50°F), but most species will survive at 5°C (41°F) provided they are kept dry.
Care At one time rootless specimens were often taken from the Antilles, among other places. I understand that the export is now restricted by law; a good thing, for the imported plants practically always died. On the other hand species grown from seed do very well. So don't just be tempted by a mature specimen with a beautiful cephalium. This 'cap' will appear spontaneously after about seven years, certainly when young plants are grafted, and in the course of time it may grow taller than the cactus itself.
Watering In summer you can water plentifully, if possible with rainwater. In winter, that is, from October to early April, little or no water should be given.
Feeding During the period of growth the plants may be given a dose of special cactus fertiliser every fortnight. This is of particular importance when it is thought unwise to repot older specimens. Stop feeding in August.
Repotting In their natural environment the plants develop a large root system, which penetrates into rock crevices. In the greenhouse the plants do best if planted out on the staging, but this is unfortunately not always possible. You should in any case use plastic pots which are wide rather than deep. Few roots will develop once the cephalium has appeared and repotting older specimens is therefore not without risk. For that reason attempts are often made to overcome the lack of nutrients by feeding. However, the plants are even more endangered by the mineral deposits caused by harmful water.

The best compost mixture consists of 1 part beech leafmould, 1 part rotted cow manure and 1 part perlite.
Propagation Imported seed should be sown in March, in warm conditions and under glass. The seedlings may be grafted on to stock.

Melocactus bahiensis
○ ⊜ ⊘ ⊛ ⊛ ⊙

Forms a flattened globe with nine to eleven ribs, dark green in colour, and eight to nine reddish thorns turning grey at a later stage.

Melocactus intortus
Turk's Cap. This is a barrel-shaped cactus with 14 to 20 ribs and yellow or brown thorns. Mature specimens have a large, woolly cephalium. With its red bristles it looks like a Turkish cap.

Melocactus maxonii
A species with 12 sturdy ribs covered in firm reddish to yellow thorns in groups of nine. In this species the cephalium is brownish in colour.

Melocactus peruvianus
A spherical cactus with 12 to 14 ribs. The radial thorns occur in groups of ten, each 1 to 3 cm ($\frac{1}{2}$ to 1 in) long. Usually there is one, slightly longer, central thorn. All thorns are red-brown in colour. The cephalium is covered in red hairs.

All species develop inconspicuous flowers and oblong red fruits in maturity.

A group of *Melocactus bahiensis* showing their characteristic cephalium

Microcoelum
Palmae
Dwarf Coconut Palm

Name From the Greek *mikros*, small, and *koilon*, hollow.
Origin Only two species occur in the Brazilian jungle.
Description A small palm (even in its native environment), with gracefully arching pinnate leaves.
Position Unlike most other palms, this plant must be kept warm throughout the year in a fairly high degree of humidity. A hothouse is therefore ideal, but for some reason it will survive for a year or two in the living-room as well.
Care At all times of the year the minimum temperature is 18°C (64°F). In the living-room the microcoelum is best cultivated among other plants in a container, where it must, however, be kept in a separate pot since it is a particularly thirsty plant. The damper atmosphere created by the surrounding plants will benefit the Dwarf Coconut Palm. It is also advisable to spray the foliage several times a day but not, of course, with tap water, which would cause ugly spotting. In winter the plant should be placed close to the window, where it is usually somewhat cooler. Keep it away from the hot air rising from the central heating radiators, otherwise the tips of the leaves would soon turn brown.
Watering Although it is not shown in the picture, in order to survive for any length of time this palm should always be kept in a saucer of water. Always use rainwater if you can, for the microcoelum detests lime.
Feeding In summer feed every fortnight, possibly by plunging. Ordinary artificial fertiliser is satisfactory, but a solution of cow manure is greatly recommended.
Repotting The pot in the photograph looks attractive, but is really not very suitable. A tall, narrow plastic pot with good drainage and a deep plastic saucer would be better. Use a mixture of conifer needle compost and rotted cow manure and make sure that no roots break off when the plant is repotted, or this would stop growth. Put some large crocks over the drainage hole of the pot to prevent the roots growing through.
Propagation The microcoelum can only be increased from seed, which is imported. First soak the seed in warm water for two days before sowing it at a soil temperature of 25 to 30°C (77 to 86°F). The seedlings must be cultivated in a hothouse and potted on several times, but the pots should not be too large.

Microcoelum weddellianum
Syn. *Cocos weddelliana; Syagrus weddelliana; Microcoelum martianum.* Dwarf Coconut Palm. Trunk 1.5 m (5 ft) tall and 3 cm (1 in) in diameter, covered all over in brown fibres. Fronds up to 1 m (3 ft) long, curving, pinnate, with up to 50 narrow linear pinnae on either side of the central rib, threadlike and covered in brown scales towards the tip. The pinnae are dark green on the upper surface and greyish underneath.

Microcoelum weddellianum, better known as the Dwarf Coconut Palm

Microlepia
Dennstaedtiaceae

Name From the Greek *micros*, small, and *lepis*, scale.
Origin About 45 species occur in tropical zones of Asia and Africa.
Description Ferns with feathery, soft, bright green foliage growing from a creeping rootstock. This plant is rarely found in cultivation, probably because it will not survive for long in the living-room.
Position The thin foliage indicates that this fern dislikes dry air, and a greenhouse, a flower window or a glass case is therefore the obvious place for it.
Care The plant will survive in the living-room for a short time, especially in summer, when the relative atmospheric humidity is higher than in winter. The situation can be fairly dark and the microlepia may therefore successfully be grown in a mixed container. You must, however, bear in mind that it will not last for very long – this need not matter if you take it into account in advance. Spray as often as possible with rainwater, and in winter give the plant a rest at a minimum temperature of 15°C (59°F).
Watering In summer water plentifully. Pots with a self-watering system are ideal. In winter keep it a little less moist.
Feeding Feed every fortnight in the growing season, preferably by plunging the pot.
Repotting Use deep plastic pots and repot every year (if the plant has survived, that is!) in a very nutritious mixture, such as 3 parts leafmould, 2 parts rotted cow manure and 1 part sharp sand.
Propagation Large plants can be divided when they are repotted. Spores may be sown in March, under glass and in a soil temperature of 20°C (68°F).

Microlepia speluncae

Microlepia speluncae
The leaf stalks are 30 to 50 cm (12 to 20 in) long; the fronds are triangular, three or four pinnate. The midrib is hairy and the leaflets are incised, soft and pale green. In the cultivar 'Cristata' the pinnae are widened towards the tip, as is the case with some other ferns.

Mikania
Compositae

Name Named after Joseph Gottfried Mikan, 1743–1814, a professor in Prague. He compiled a list of all plants known at that time.
Origin Most of the 200 species known are natives of Brazil, but the species described below grows wild as far as Florida.
Description A jungle weed with bronze-coloured leaves and climbing stems.
Position In summer these plants may be kept out of doors, but in winter they really belong in a temperate greenhouse, though they can be grown in a cool room as well.
Care These plants are bought chiefly for their unusual colouring, possibly to provide a contrast in a mixed container. It is doubtful whether they will survive for long in such conditions. Full sun is tolerated, provided the plant is gradually introduced to the light in spring.

These little plants enjoy damp air, but it is not advisable to provide this by spraying the foliage, which is hairy and would therefore stain.

Mikania ternata

The winter rest is best spent in a temperate greenhouse at a minimum temperature of 12°C (53°F), but if the plant is properly cared for it may be kept in the living-room.
Watering Always keep the compost moderately moist both in summer and in winter.
Feeding Feed every fortnight during the summer.
Repotting The recommended potting mixture consists of loam, rotted cow manure, leafmould and sand. Replenish with new plants at frequent intervals, for older plants quickly become unsightly.
Propagation Increase by division, from seed or from cuttings. The latter can be taken in spring and rooted in warm cuttings compost. Young plants will grow only if they are kept under glass.

Mikania ternata
A hairy plant with creeping, trailing, or slightly climbing stems, red to purple in colour. The leaves are palmate, grey-green in colour, with violet-purple lustre and violet veining. The species is sometimes marketed as *Mikania apiifolia*.

One of the many *Miltonia* hybrids. It can be seen why this plant is called the Pansy Orchid

Miltonia
Orchidaceae
Pansy Orchid

Name Named after the statesman Viscount Milton, later Earl Fitzwilliam, 1786–1857, owner of a magnificent orchid collection.
Origin The approximately 20 species known occur mainly in Brazil and Colombia.
Description The flowers of these fine orchids look a little like pansies. The plants have pseudobulbs, but do not require a pronounced dormant season.
Position In summer miltonia plants require a cool position and at that time they may be grown in the living-room. In winter they must be kept in a cool or moderate greenhouse. A room with the central heating turned low might be possible, except that the air is rather too dry there.
Care Cultivation is not unlike that for odontoglossums, but the miltonia likes a little more warmth and light. Until April the temperature should be warm compared to the outside air, but from May onwards the plants must be kept as cool as possible. In June the growing season is practically at an end, and the plants must then be kept particularly cool in a shady position. Flowering usually ceases in August–September. Give them less water, but continue to keep the plants cool. They also need less shade, and from the end of October onwards stop screening and provide a little warmth. The minimum temperature should be between 6 and 10°C (43 and 50°F).
Watering From May onwards water generously and spray the foliage every day. In September keep a little drier, but the compost must remain moist. Use rainwater.
Feeding From May to June give an occasional feed at half strength.
Repotting These orchids are best grown in plastic pots with a deep layer of crocks in the bottom, or in hanging baskets. The potting medium may consist of 4 parts peat, 1 part perlite and 3 parts tree fern, plus a pinch of Dolomite limestone powder, or of 2 parts osmunda fibre, 1 part sphagnum moss and some perlite. Repot after flowering.
Propagation Occasionally the plants may be divided when they are repotted, but a better harvest is obtained from seed. Unfortunately only specialists can use this method.

Miltonia hybrid

Pests and diseases Thrips are the miltonia's greatest enemy. The best cure is to spray frequently, keeping the plants constantly damp.

Miltonia candida
This has narrow oval pseudobulbs, each bearing two strap-shaped leaves, 30 cm (1 ft) long. The flowers are 9 cm (3½ in) across, yellow with chestnut brown patches, with a white lip, wavy along the margin, and appear from August–November.
Miltonia phalaenopsis
Oval psuedobulbs, each with one strap-shaped, pale green leaf. The flower stalk is 15 cm (6 in) tall, with two to four white flowers; the lower half of the lip is dark purple. It flowers from August–November.
Miltonia spectabilis
This has pseudobulbs up to 7 cm (2¾ in) long, compressed, each with two yellow-green tongue-shaped leaves. It bears erect-growing single flowers, 10 cm (4 in) across, white, with a lilac-red lip, darker in the centre and with three dark, yellow-edged crests at the base.

Many hybrids of the various species are in cultivation; many have also been crossed with other genera.

Mimosa
Leguminosae
Sensitive Plant

Name From the Greek *mimos*, mimic. When touched these plants imitate wilting. They should not be confused with *Acacia dealbata* (q.v.), popularly called Mimosa.
Origin About 500 species occur in the tropical and subtropical regions of America.
Description The only species grown as a house plant has feathery leaves which fold soon after being touched. This happens only if the temperature is above 18°C (64°F). After a time the leaves unfold again. The same phenomenon may be observed when it becomes dark.
Position The plant feels happiest in a hothouse. In the living-room it should preferably be grown in a glass case or under a glass bell.
Care It is possible to carry the mimosa over from one year to another by putting it in a temperate greenhouse in winter, but by the end of the summer the plant

Flowering *Mimosa pudica*

will have greatly deteriorated and it is therefore better to grow new plants from seed every year. The plants enjoy humid air and must be kept out of bright sunlight. They may be put in a very sheltered, warm spot out of doors.
Watering In summer keep the compost moderately moist, using rainwater if possible.
Feeding In the growing season feed every fortnight.
Repotting The potting mixture should consist of leafmould, pulverised clay, rotted cow manure and a little sand. Plants that have been overwintered should be repotted in spring.
Propagation Sow in March–April under glass, with a soil temperature of 20 to 25°C (68 to 77°F). The young plants must be cultivated in warm conditions. In autumn they often produce more seed, which may be kept until the following season. It is also possible to buy seed.

Mimosa pudica
◐ ⊜ ⓥ ⊛ ▢
A semi-shrub, usually grown as an annual, with spiny stems and bipinnate foliage. Four feathery leaves are borne at the tip of the leaf stalk; the pinnae retract to the touch. They bear globular lilac-pink flower heads.

Monstera
Araceae
Swiss Cheese Plant

Name Probably derived from the Latin word *monstrum*, monstrosity. This is supposed to refer to the incised leaves.
Origin Twenty-seven species occur in tropical regions of America. The majority grow as epiphytes.
Description A very well-known, vigorous house plant with deeply incised, sometimes perforated, leaves, and long aerial roots.
Position The plant is reasonably at home in a heated living-room, but if you have ever seen it growing in a greenhouse you will realise that exceptionally large leaves are the reward of a high degree of humidity.
Care These plants are so strong that they are frequently put in too dark a position and they will then practically stop growing at a certain stage. As a rule, however, the long stems will cheerfully surround the entire window-frame or arch. Properly looked after the Swiss Cheese Plant may last a lifetime.
The more light, the larger the leaves and the more holes develop. The long, trailing aerial roots can be inserted in the pot, where they will promptly turn into ground roots and start to absorb nutrients. They may also be guided into other compost-filled pots or tied to a moss-covered stake, but if they are removed the plant will still survive. In indoor cultivation the aerial roots do not anchor themselves and the plant will need to be securely supported and tied.

Monstera deliciosa 'Variegata'

Monstera obliqua 'Leichtlinii'

Monstera deliciosa in a setting worthy of its sculptured structure

A mature plant may produce a large, yellowish flower, shaped like that of the Arum Lily. With a bit of luck it may be followed by hexagonal, violet-coloured berries with a pineapple scent. Although they are supposed to be edible I cannot recommend the taste, for they burn the mouth. The minimum winter temperature is about 12°C (53°F).
Watering Care should be taken to keep the compost moderately moist. The water should be warm and not contain too much lime. The plant will not immediately die if watered with poor-quality water, but will certainly not appreciate it. You should therefore try to obtain rainwater or to demineralise the water. Frequent spraying and sponging, especially in winter, is very helpful. If the plant is kept a little cooler in winter (though this is not essential), the water supply should be slightly reduced.
Feeding The foliage of a monstera may remain small if the plant is insufficiently nourished. It is important to allow the aerial roots to play a part, especially in the case of large plants. It is also essential to give a dose of a suitable fertiliser or organic manure every fortnight from June onwards. If the plant grows in a pot with drainage holes it is a good idea to plunge it once a month in a large bucket or bath filled with tepid rainwater. In this way the air in the compost is replaced by fresh air when the water drains away, bringing oxygen to the roots. Some fertiliser may be added to the water.
Repotting If you want to make your Swiss Cheese Plant really happy, give it a mixture of equal parts leafmould, completely rotted cow manure and sharp sand. However, it will also do well in standard potting compost. Use roomy pots, well drained, and if possible repot it annually.
Propagation Older plants that have grown bare at the base can successfully be air-layered. New plants may also be grown from tip cuttings. If you want to acquire a large number of new plants the method is different: take eye cuttings, which will readily root in a soil temperature of 25 to 30°C (77 to 86°F). The leaves may be rolled up and secured. Always root the cuttings under glass or plastic. Propagation from seed is another possibility, but the seed must be very fresh. It will germinate (in warm conditions) within two to four weeks.

Monstera deliciosa
◐ ● ⊜ ⓥ ⊛ ⊛⊛ ■ ▢
Syn. *Philodendron pertusum*. A climbing

Murraya paniculata with flowers and fruits

Young specimen of *Musa* × *paradisiaca*

shrub with thick stems and numerous aerial roots. Initially the leaves are heart-shaped and entire, later they may grow to 60 cm (2 ft) across, and become incised as well as perforated along the centre vein. A form frequently cultivated is 'Borsigiana', smaller in all its parts, with leaves to 30 cm (1 ft) across. The cultivar 'Variegata' has irregular cream-coloured marking.

***Monstera obliqua* 'Leichtlinii'**
A youthful form with perforated leaves; the margins are intact. It is a weak grower.

Murraya
Rutaceae

Name Named after J. A. Murray, 1740–1791, Professor of Botany at Göttingen.
Origin Ten different species occur in the Malaysian area.
Description This is a relation of the more familiar orange tree. It has glossy foliage and delightfully scented white flowers.
Position The best spot is in a temperate greenhouse, where the air is humid, but the plant is sometimes grown out of doors in summer.
Care The species occasionally cultivated originates in the islands of the Pacific, among other places. As everyone knows, the temperature always remains agreeably high in those regions, and so is the humidity. If the plant is grown in the living-room you should therefore attempt to keep the air as moist as possible by frequent spraying. The plant must be partially screened from full sun, but it is a mistake to put it too far from the window. Where there is a very sheltered terrace you might try to grow it outside from the end of May onwards.

In winter the plant should be kept at a temperature of around 12°C (53°F). A cool room in the house might be suitable.
Watering In summer keep moderately moist; in winter a little less so.
Feeding In the period of growth feed every fortnight.
Repotting The most favourable potting mixture consists of equal parts of conifer needle compost, rotted cow manure and sharp sand or perlite. Renew the compost every spring, use plastic tubs and provide good drainage.
Propagation Fresh seed will germinate in a temperature of 30°C (86°F) and tip cuttings will root at the same temperature, under glass.

Murraya paniculata
A strongly branching evergreen shrub with compound foliage, having five to nine short-stalked leaves, 3 to 5 cm (1 to 2 in) long and 2 to 3 cm (¾ to 1 in) wide, green and glossy. It bears multiflowered terminal clusters. The flowers are bell shaped, 1·5 cm (½ in) long, white and fragrant, and there are globular red fruits with glands.

Musa
Musaceae
Banana

Name Named after Antonius Musa, 63–14B.C., personal physician to the Emperor Augustus.
Origin There are 70 to 80 species, distributed over tropical zones of the eastern hemisphere. Cultivated forms are grown on plantations throughout the world.
Description Large herbaceous plants; the leaf sheaths form a so-called pseudo-trunk. Initially the leaves are entire, but after they uncurl wind and weather tear the edges along the lateral veins.
Position The plants grown from seed for indoor use become very large, really too large for the living-room. They can only develop fully in the greenhouse of a botanical garden.
Care The banana requires plenty of light, even in the winter months. It frequently fails because our winters are so dark, but artificial lighting (see page 47) may be useful. Our summers are usually too cool, which means that the banana must be kept behind glass throughout the year. The minimum winter temperature is 12°C (53°F), but it will do no harm if the plant continues to grow all through the winter, possibly in the heated living-room, provided the degree of relative humidity never drops below 50 per cent.
Watering A great deal of moisture is evaporated and if the foliage turns brown the cause may nearly always be found to be a shortage of water. Roomy pots with self-watering systems are recommended.
Feeding Since the banana continues to grow in winter, it must be fed once a week or every fortnight.
Repotting This is a vigorous plant and a young specimen must therefore be repotted several times until it ends up in a large plastic container. The best potting medium consists of ⅓ clay or loam, ⅓ leafmould or conifer needle compost and ⅓ rotted cow manure. The pots or tubs must have good drainage.
Propagation Banana plants which can be grown from seed (usually *Musa ensete*) are really far too large for the living-room. The smaller cultivars are much more suitable, but these do not produce fertile seed and can be propagated only by removing the suckers which appear at the base after the old plant has died. Such shoots are not easy to obtain.

Musa acuminata
Syn. *Musa cavendishii; Musa nana*. Dwarf Banana. Height about 2 m (6 ft). The leaves are elliptical, 60 to 90 cm (2 to 3 ft) long and 30 cm (1 ft) wide. It bears flowers with leathery purple-red bracts and subsequently 'hands' with edible fruit. A special cultivar is known as 'Dwarf Cavendish', and is closely related to the consumer banana.

Musa ensete
A species without suckers, up to 10 m (33 ft) tall. Leaves are up to 5 m (16 ft) long and 1 m (3 ft) wide, with a red centre vein, and it has dry fruits with black seeds. This is the species which is sown; quite unsuitable for indoor cultivation, although it is often used for this purpose.

Musa* × *paradisiaca
A group of crossed forms used on plantations. The height is 2 to 6 m (6 to 20 ft), with leaves up to 3 m (10 ft), and large, edible, seedless fruits. These are the bananas you usually see growing when you are on holiday. *Musa acuminata*, mentioned above, is probably one of its numerous cultivars. Ornamental strains with variegated foliage also exist, but they are rarely grown as house plants.

Myrtillocactus
Cactaceae

Name The plant owes its name to the bilberry, *Vaccinium myrtillus*, because in its native habitat small bilberry-like fruits appear at the base of the myrtillocactus.
Origin Three or four species occur in Mexico and South America.
Description In their natural habitat these cacti form large, strongly branching columns up to 4 m (13 ft) tall. In cultivation only young specimens are known, which rarely branch.
Position The most familiar species, *Myrtillocactus geometrizans*, grows best in a temperate greenhouse. The other species may also be cultivated in a cool greenhouse. However, since they cannot be expected to flower in our climate, the cool winter period may be ignored and the plants may be kept in the living-room throughout the winter.
Care Unlike other cacti, the fine blue columnar plant illustrated may be kept fairly warm in winter. It therefore makes an ideal cactus for living-room cultivation, as it need be given only a slight rest in winter. A minimum temperature of 12°C (53°F) should be maintained and the plant must be put close to the window, for it will retain its fine colouring only if the light is good. In summer it will tolerate full sun.

Watering This cactus can always be kept moderately moist, for it is quite a thirsty plant. In winter, too, the compost must never be allowed to dry out entirely. Use rainwater, which in winter must first be brought to room temperature.
Feeding In the growing season give a little cactus fertiliser once a month.
Repotting The compost should be nutritious and the most favourable mixture consists of 1 part pulverised clay or loam, 1 part rotted leaves and 1 part perlite. A little dried blood or bonemeal may be added. Use plastic pots, not too small, with good drainage and repot every year in spring. The finest development will be achieved if the cacti are planted out on the greenhouse staging.
Propagation As the myrtillocactus does not flower here it is necessary to import fresh seed, which should be sown in spring in a soil temperature of 20°C (68°F). It is also possible, of course, to take cuttings from older specimens which have branched. The cuttings must be left to dry for a few days first.

Myrtillocactus cochal
A branching columnar cactus with club-shaped joints of a pronounced bluish colour. It develops six to eight ribs bearing black areoles, each with a firm grey thorn. This is the species in which red, berry-like edible fruits follow the small purple flowers, but not in indoor cultivation.
Myrtillocactus geometrizans
This has beautifully blue-bloomed ribs, five to six in number, with vague V-shaped marking; the thorns are inconspicuous. This is the best-known species.
Myrtillocactus schenckii
A dark green columnar cactus with seven to eight ribs. The areoles bear tufts of short, thin thorns.

Myrtillocactus geometrizans

Flowers of *Myrtus communis*, the Myrtle

Myrtus
Myrtaceae
Myrtle

Name The ancient Greek name for the myrtle was *myrtos*; the Romans knew it as *myrtus*.
Origin There are about 100 species, most of which have their natural habitat in tropical and subtropical regions of America; eight occur in Australia, four in New Zealand, and one, the species described below, in the Mediterranean area.
Description An evergreen shrub with glossy, leathery leaves and fragrant white flowers: the protruding stamens are their most striking feature.
Position The plant must have a very sunny situation, if possible out of doors in summer. In winter it must be cool.
Care This tub plant is not often grown. Its main attractions are the flowers and the fragrance. It can be cultivated either as a shrub or as a standard. Indoors the ideal position is a south-facing window. The plant should occasionally be turned to avoid one-sided growth. Put the myrtle outside from the end of May onwards if you have a sunny and sheltered terrace or balcony. After flowering the plant may be cut back a little and in mid-September it should be moved to its winter quarters, where it should be kept in very good light at a temperature of between 4 and 12°C (39 and 53°F). In warm weather give it good ventilation during the daytime.
Watering Always use lime-free water, such as rainwater. It is essential to keep the compost always moist.
Feeding Feed every fortnight during the period of growth.
Repotting The plant is a lime hater and grows best in a mixture of conifer needle compost and rotted cow manure. Repot every year in spring.
Propagation In summer increase from tip cuttings with a heel, taken from non-flowering shoots, which may be rooted under glass in a temperature of 15 to 20°C (59 to 68°F). The plants may also be grown from seed, but this is a lengthy process.

Myrtus communis
An erect-growing evergreen shrub with oval to lanceolate leaves up to 5 cm (2 in) long. The fragrant white flowers grow singly and are 2cm ($\frac{3}{4}$in) in diameter, with numerous long stamens. Occasionally it bears black-purple fruits.

Narcissus
Amaryllidaceae

Name From the Greek *narkao*, I am intoxicated. This naturally refers to the delightful scent. The plant may also have been named after Narcissus, the beautiful demigod who fell in love with his own reflection.
Origin About 30 species occur in Mediterranean countries and in Central Europe. Only hybrids are cultivated indoors.
Description Everyone knows the narcissus with its delightfully scented flowers. The bulbs can be forced into early flowering and this quality is exploited in indoor cultivation.
Position Forcing means providing extra warmth and the narcissus tolerates warmth fairly well. But a really hot room is too much of a good thing. While the bulb is being forced the temperature must be kept at 15 to 20°C (59 to 68°F).
Care A good catalogue (perhaps one from a mail-order firm) will indicate which bulbs are suitable for forcing. The easiest forms for this purpose are 'Grand Soleil d'Or' and 'Paperwhite' which need not be kept in the dark to begin with. They can be brought straight into a moderately heated room, often in bowls filled with gravel, but they can also be planted in potting compost. This should be done between September and February.

Other narcissi first have to be rooted in a cool – 8 to 10°C (46 to 50°F) – and dark spot. They are not brought into the light until it is clear that the flower bud has left the bulb. The easiest way of guaranteeing a sufficiently low temperature and high enough humidity is by digging a pit. Pot the bulbs in October and place them in the pit, covering it in such a way that the pots can be reached even in frosty weather. Towards the end of January dig the pots up to see whether the bulbs are sufficiently far advanced to bring indoors.

In the absence of a garden a dark, frost-free box can be constructed on the balcony, or the bulbs can be rooted in a dark cellar.

Narcissus 'Grand Soleil d'Or'

Watering When bulbs are grown in gravel, in particular, there is a risk that the water level will be too high. The water should never touch the bulb. When the plants are first brought into the living-room the young shoots should be frequently sprayed.
Feeding This is unnecessary, since the bulbs are nearly always discarded after flowering.
Repotting The bulbs may be grown in gravel or in a light compost consisting of equal parts of standard potting compost and sharp sand.
Propagation Not applicable indoors.

***Narcissus* hybrids**
Practically all groups of narcissi produce a number of strains which may be forced into early flowering. Only the Poeticus strains are less successful. Follow the instructions given in any good catalogue.

Narcissus 'Paperwhite' does not have to be started off in the dark

Nautilocalyx lynchii, a striking plant with reddish, almost black foliage

Nautilocalyx

Gesneriaceae

Name Derived from the Greek *nautilos*, naval, and *kalyx*, calyx.
Origin About 11 species occur in the northern part of South America.
Description These little plants are closely related to the episcia, which they resemble. The foliage is beautifully coloured or marked; the stems are fairly thick.
Position This is a foliage plant for the hothouse, or for a glass case, flower window or bottle garden.
Care The plants must always be kept out of full sun, and the temperature must never drop below 16°C (60°F), so they don't need a resting period. If you want to try growing the nautilocalyx in the living-room you will have to ensure a high degree of atmospheric humidity. Perhaps it could be placed above a bowl of water, or near a humidifier. Otherwise at least spray the foliage several times a day. The plants will survive for a few months or half a year in a mixed plant container, where the micro-climate is locally favourable.
Watering The compost must always be kept moderately moist. It is advisable to use only tepid rainwater or demineralised water, for the plant is intolerant of lime.
Feeding In the period of active growth, between May and October, the plant may be given a dose of fertiliser solution every fortnight.
Repotting Use a friable mixture, rich in humus, for instance rotted leafmould or lumps of peat with old, rotted cow manure and some sharp sand or perlite to provide drainage. Replant every spring in wide, shallow dishes or bowls.
Propagation Tip cuttings will root fairly readily with a soil temperature of 20 to 25°C (68 to 77°F), provided they are kept under glass. Take cuttings at frequent intervals, for older plants are usually less beautiful. The plants can also be grown from seed.

Nautilocalyx bullatus

Syn. *Centrosolenia bullata; Episcia tessellata*. This is a plant with fleshy, hairy stems and oval to lanceolate leaves, at most 20cm (8in) long and 8cm (3in) across. The upper surface is quilted and hairy, dark olive green with a bronze sheen; and the reverse is wine red. The flowers grow in axillary clusters; the tubular corolla has a short spur and is 5cm (2in) long, yellow with five short lobes.

Nautilocalyx forgetii

This has glossy pale green foliage, with dark brown or reddish marking along the veins; the reverse is also red along the veins, and there is an undulate margin.

Nautilocalyx lynchii

Syn. *Alloplectus lynchii*. The smooth, elliptical leaves, to 15cm (6in) long, narrowing towards the stalk, are a glossy dark green with a red sheen and hairy veins. The short-stalked flowers are yellow-white with a pale red throat.

Neoporteria

Cactaceae

Name From the Greek *neo*, new and from C. E. Porter, a 20th-century Chilean entomologist.
Origin About 30 to 35 species occur in Chile and northern Argentina. At one time they were classified under other genera.
Description Spherical, later slightly columnar, small cacti, which may produce more than one flower from a single areole. The thorns are their most striking feature. The neoporteria is not always easy to cultivate.
Position These are typical plants for a well-tended amateur collection, that is to say, suitable for a temperate or cool greenhouse.
Care Cacti whose native habitat is in Chile start into growth early in our winter and the dormant season must therefore begin as early as possible (September), while the temperature should be increased a little in January. In the intervening months a temperature of 5°C (41°F) may be maintained; this is the usual winter temperature for a cool greenhouse. After mid-January provide a minimum temperature of 12 to 14°C (53 to 57°F). In spring the plants must gradually become accustomed to the sun, but once they are it is essential to keep them in very good light. These

Neoporteria is a densely thorned globular cactus, not always easy to cultivate cacti are frequently grafted (usually on *Eriocereus jusbertii* stock). This method is recommended if the plants are to be grown in the living-room.

Watering When the temperature rises in spring, a very small amount of water must be given. Slowly increase the supply until the normal, usually weekly, allowance has been reached. In autumn the plant should be kept cool and dry earlier than other cacti. Always use rainwater.

Feeding It is helpful to give a dose of special cactus fertiliser once every three weeks in summer, especially if the plants are not repotted annually.

Repotting In spring the plants may be repotted (young specimens every year) in a mixture of ⅓ pulverised clay or loam, ⅓ rotted leafmould and ⅓ perlite.

Propagation The neoporteria can be grown from seed sown in March, under glass. They may also be grafted, which results in better growth.

Neoporteria napina

○⊜◯⊛▢

Syn. *Malacocarpus napinus; Neochilenia napina.* A grey-green or more blackish-red cactus with 14 ribs divided in round tubercles which bear 3-mm (⅛-in) long black thorns. The flowers are pale yellow with a little red.

Neoporteria paucicostata

Neoporteria nidus

Syn. *Echinocactus nidus.* Bird's Nest Cactus. With age this cactus becomes cylinder shaped. It is entirely hidden in the long yellowish or grey thorns. It bears reddish flowers.

Neoporteria nigrihorrida

Syn. *Chilenia nigrihorrida.* A flattened sphere with 16 to 18 ribs, dark grey-green in colour. It has long grey thorns which turn black when they are wet.

Neoporteria senilis

Syn. *Echinocactus senilis; Neoporteria nidus* f. *senilis.* This resembles the *N. nidus* species, but the thorns are thread-like, long, twisted and very numerous, so that the entire cactus looks like a grey beard.

Neoporteria villosa

Syn. *Echinocactus villosus.* In time this cactus becomes cylindrical, with a dark violet to black body and 13 to 15 ribs. The 2- to 3-cm (¾- to 1-in) long thorns are pale brown or grey, and it has pale pink or white flowers.

The small blue flowers of the neoregelia remain almost hidden in the tube

Neoregelia carolinae

Neoregelia
Bromeliaceae

Name From the Greek *neo*, new, and after A. von Regel, 1815–1892, Curator of the Botanical Garden in what was then St Petersburg.

Origin Thirty three species grow in Brazil and one in Guyana. In their natural environment the plants grow on the branches of jungle trees. In many species the foliage becomes beautifully coloured when the plant flowers.

Position The plants must be cultivated in a hothouse, but may then be kept in the living-room for quite some time.

Care It is the old story: as soon as a bromeliad flowers it is already in the process of dying. The plant is usually bought in flower or when it is about to flower, so it does not matter all that much how it is tended. A fairly cool position, up to 12°C (53°F), will delay the dying process to some extent. The plant does not require a great deal of light, for the marking has already developed and little further assimilation will take place. Flowering occurs deep in the rosette and the flowers are insignificant – don't expect them to emerge.

After three to six months the plant loses much of its beauty and should then be discarded, for each rosette flowers only once. Meanwhile one or more offsets will have developed at the base and these require entirely different treatment.

For vigorous growth these bromeliads require plenty of light, but no direct sun. Between March and August the temperature should be between 22 and 25°C (71 and 77°F). In winter 15 to 18°C (59 to 64°F) is enough. In summer the neoregelia needs fairly high humidity, but in winter it will put up with a little less. Clearly these conditions are most easily met in a greenhouse. Conditions in the living-room are much less favourable. Think, for instance, of the temperature: who keeps the central heating on at 25°C (77°F) in May? In a glass case the light is usually not good enough. A flower window might be a possibility if the angle of the light is right.

If everything goes to plan, plants grown from young offsets may flower after two or three years. The fine red colouring or marking does not develop until just before the plant flowers.

Watering If at all possible the plant should only be watered with rainwater at room temperature. The compost must always be moderately moist and the rosette cup must always be filled with water. Even the flowers may open under water. The foliage should be sprayed as often as possible.

Feeding In the growing season the plant may be fed every fortnight. The fertiliser solution can be poured on the compost or into the cup. The cup should, however, be emptied and rinsed from time to time to prevent a deposit forming of non-absorbed nutrients.

Repotting Although these plants are usually grown in pots, they can be cultivated equally well, or even better, in hanging baskets or on a tree trunk. Since they are epiphytes by nature, they are happiest in a mixture of rotted leaves, some rotted cow manure and sphagnum moss. Avoid all calcareous ingredients. If they are grown in pots good drainage is essential.

Propagation The plants are increased from offsets, but do not remove them too soon – not, in fact, until the parent plant is deteriorating. By then the young plantlets will have developed some roots and will more easily establish themselves. If necessary use a sharp knife to remove the offsets.

The neoregelia can also be grown from seed, but this will result in all-green forms only. Multicoloured forms can only be propagated from offsets.

Pests and diseases Scale insects and thrips may attack if the plant is weakened by errors in cultivation. Too much or too cold water may cause the plant to rot.

Neoregelia carolinae

◐⊜◯⊛⊛▢

Syn. *Aregelia carolinae; Nidularium meyendorffii.* The leaves are arranged in a flat, broad rosette widening slightly at the base and are up to 40 cm (16 in) long, 5 cm (2 in) wide, finely toothed along the margin. Both the surfaces are green and glossy. When the plant is in flower the part of the foliage surrounding the inflorescence turns a beautiful shade of red. Plants in cultivation are always cultivars, such as 'Meyendorffii' with 4-cm (1½-in) wide olive-green leaves in funnel-shaped rosettes, and 'Tricolor' with narrow leaves with lengthwise yellowish streaks.

Neoregelia concentrica

Syn. *Aregelia concentrica; Nidularium acanthocrater.* This forms large, broad rosettes. The leaves are up to 30 cm (1 ft) long and 12 cm (4½ in) wide with short brown spines along the margins. The upper surface of the leaves is green with irregular patches; the inner leaves are shorter and violet coloured. There are several cultivars.

Neoregelia carolinae 'Tricolor'

Nepenthes hybrid

Detail of the pitcher

Nepenthes
Nepenthaceae
Pitcher Plant

Name From the Greek *ne*, not, and *penthos*, grief. The liquid from closed pitchers is drinkable and according to Homer has a cheering effect.
Origin About 70 species occur in tropical Asia, in the Seychelles, Malagasy, Australia and the Indian archipelago.
Description A genus of mostly epiphytic plants. At the tip of the leaves is a tendril which may develop into a liquid-filled beaker, which is initially closed with a lid. At a later stage the lid opens and insects are attracted by the scent, only to fall into the liquid, where they are digested.
Position This is a typical plant for the hothouse, where the atmosphere is humid. However, some species may successfully be grown in the living-room, provided that the temperature can be lowered a few degrees in winter.
Care In the hothouse the temperature must be at least 18°C (64°F) throughout the year, preferably even higher. In these conditions no problems will arise. In the living-room the plants must often be sprayed. In winter they should be moved closer to the window and humid air created around them. Bright sunshine must be avoided at all times of the year.
Watering In the period of active growth a great deal of water is required, which is easily provided by plunging the plant. Always use lime-free water.
Feeding Put a few insects into the beaker occasionally during the growing season; they will be digested and absorbed as food.
Repotting The extremely delicate root system of the Pitcher Plant must be repotted every spring with exceptional care into a mixture of fern roots, leaf-mould, sphagnum moss and rotted cow manure. Preferably use hanging baskets or very well-draining hanging pots.
Propagation In winter or in spring leaf cuttings can be taken. Insert them in an upside-down flower pot with the bottom removed. Hold the cutting in place with sphagnum moss and place the pot on a layer of damp sphagnum moss. The cut surface must be open to the air, and the bottom temperature should be 35°C (95°F). Root formation may take eight weeks. Spray the leaf regularly to prevent wilting.

***Nepenthes* hybrids**
Epiphytes with foliage consisting of three parts: a leaf sheath broadened like a leaf, usually lanceolate, a longer or shorter stalk and a beaker-like organ which represents the leaf blade. The pendulous beakers are usually green with fine red marking. There are numerous strains.

Nephrolepis
Oleandraceae
Ladder Fern

Name From the Greek *nephros*, kidney, and *lepis*, scale.
Origin About 30 natural species are known, distributed over tropical regions in all parts of the world. They are terrestrial or epiphytic plants. There are an incredible number of cultivars.
Description *Nephrolepis exaltata* is a particularly well-known and vigorous indoor fern, possibly the most beautiful of them all. The long, feathery fronds curve gracefully and each plant easily reaches a diameter of 50 to 60 cm (20 to 24 in). It is advisable to find a grower who is able to supply fine, well-developed plants, for the cheap little specimens sometimes sold have little ornamental value. Have a good look at the photographs in this book. However, these plants have recently become much more widely available, and you should be able to find a well-grown specimen of good value.
Position In essence these ferns are of course plants for a hothouse or a temperate greenhouse, where the high relative humidity induces tremendous growth. However, it has repeatedly been proved that a nephrolepis will survive for a year or more even in a centrally heated room. It may not grow much larger but it will still remain in good condition.
Care From this you may deduce that the nephrolepis should be regarded as a disposable plant, but at any rate it is a particularly fine one which will resist decline for a long time. If you count on three or four months your expectations can only be exceeded. Naturally it makes a difference as to whether you buy the plant just before the winter, when the light is getting worse and the heating is turned up, or in April, when the heating is turned down, the days grow longer and the relative humidity increases daily. It also makes an enormous difference whether or not you are generous with spraying and whether the plant is kept at 18°C (64°F) rather than at 23°C (73°F) as happens in some households. The difference in relative humidity will be at least 10 per cent. If you have a humidifier put it close to the plant.

The nephrolepis does not need a great deal of light. Certainly no direct sunlight, but if the plant is put in a very

Nephrolepis exaltata 'Rooseveltii' needs little light

Nephrolepis exaltata 'Teddy Junior'

Nephrolepis exaltata is especially happy in the bathroom with its humid atmosphere

dark spot the foliage will begin to drop after a few weeks. Sometimes an electric light placed nearby can make a difference. The length of the day is also important when deciding how much light a plant is receiving.

If the plant loses some of its beauty, usually because the pinnae fall or turn yellow, an old trick sometimes helps. Keep it about 5°C (9°F) cooler and slightly drier. Remove the old foliage and leave it for a month or two. Now repot the fern and try to bring it into growth again, preferably in a greenhouse to start with. In many cases you will have a magnificent fern again in a few months.

Watering With a nephrolepis it is very difficult to maintain an even degree of moisture, because the plant reacts immediately both to too wet and too dry a compost. Pots with a self-watering system are therefore ideal – they cannot go wrong. If the reservoir is always kept topped up the plant will remain in good condition, even in a heated room. Such a pot soon pays for itself. It is advisable to use rainwater, and the same applies to spraying so that chalk marks may be avoided.

Feeding Ferns require a great deal of nourishment but cannot take it in concentrated form. You should therefore add a little fertiliser every time you water the plant, using half or even a quarter of the recommended strength. But when the plant is not growing, that is in winter, do not feed it. Also refrain from feeding in possible intermediate resting periods.

Repotting The potting medium must be lime free and should therefore consist of 1 part leafmould or conifer needle compost, 1 part rotted cow manure and 1 part perlite or sharp sand. Repot every spring.

Propagation These ferns develop runners on which young plantlets appear, and these can be removed in the course of the summer. Only original species can be grown from spores.

Pests and diseases Incorrect cultivation and draughts will lead to infestation by aphids, scale insects and thrips.

Nephrolepis cordifolia

Syn. *Nephrolepis tuberosa*. A species with runners and 2- to 5-cm (¾- to 2-in) thick tubers, pinnate leaves, 30 to 60 cm (1 to 2 ft) long and 5 to 6 cm (2 to 2¼ in) wide, with a dark scaly stem, 5 to 8 cm (2 to 3 in) long. The pinnae grow close together and are 3 cm (1 in) long and 1.5 cm (½ in) wide. In the form 'Plumosa' the tips of the leaves are bipinnate.

Nephrolepis exaltata

A tuberless species with pinnate leaves up to 70 cm (28 in) long and 10 cm (4 in) wide with an unscaled leaf stalk, green in colour.

Among the strains with single-pinnate foliage are 'Maassii', of compact habit and with undulate pinnae; 'Rooseveltii' and 'Teddy Junior', crimped and undulate pinnae. Strains with bipinnate leaves are 'Rooseveltii Plumosa', in which the tips of the pinnae are deeply incised or feathery, and 'Whitmanii', with a broad habit and leaves to 40 cm (16 in) long and curving, all the leaflets deeply incised or pinnate or bipinnate. 'Bornstedt', finally, has even more finely divided foliage, and the pinnae are rounded at the tip.

Nerine

Amaryllidaceae

Guernsey Lily

Name Probably named after the Nereids, in Greek mythology the 50 beautiful daughters of Zeus with the appearance of sea nymphs.

Origin About 50 different species occur in South Africa.

Description A bulbous plant with long, strap-shaped leaves and beautiful flower umbels, fairly well known as cut flowers.

Position The bulbs grow in winter and are dormant in our summer. This makes their cultivation rather difficult.

Care If you want to grow the nerine as a pot plant, the best species to choose is *Nerine sarniensis*, the Guernsey Lily. In September three or five bulbs are potted and put outside. The flowers appear first, the leaves almost immediately after. They are not hardy, so the nerine must therefore be moved to a cool or temperate greenhouse in good time. Here the foliage must be left to develop, for otherwise the plant will not flower in the following year. Some extra light is an advantage. In spring the leaves die down and the pots should be laid on their sides to stop water getting in. The bulb can be kept in the pot.

Nerine sarniensis 'Corusca Major'

Watering Because of the low temperature little water is needed, otherwise the bulbs will rot.

Feeding Since the bulbs are not often repotted the plants must be fed every fortnight in winter.

Repotting The bulbs react unfavourably to repotting and this should therefore not be done too often. Only replace the top layer of compost every year. A little loam may be added to a proprietary potting compost.

Propagation When the bulbs are repotted a number of offsets may be removed and potted up separately. Ripe seed may be sown in spring.

Nerine sarniensis

Guernsey Lily. The 30- by 1.5-cm (12- by ½-in) leaves appear after the flowers. These form umbels of eight to twelve flowers, red, fragrant, with petals 4 to 10 mm (¼ to ½ in) wide, recurving and slightly curly; they are shorter than the stamens. 'Corusca Major' is the form usually in cultivation. It has larger, bright orange-red flowers.

Nephrolepis cordifolia 'Plumosa'

Nephrolepis exaltata 'Maassii'

Nerium

Apocynaceae

Oleander

Name Dioskorides used the name *Nerium indicum;* at a later date *Nerium* began to be applied to the entire genus.
Origin Two species are known, occurring mainly in the countries round the Mediterranean and in Asia.
Description A well-known and well-loved plant with leathery leaves like those of the willow. It is frequently encountered in the resorts of southern Europe. In summer it bears single or double flowers, white, rose red, violet-pink or striped.
Position In the time when few houses had central heating but many had a conservatory, the oleander was grown on a large scale. From this you will gather than the plant requires a cool winter environment to be able to flower the following year and to prevent pest infestation.
Care The oleander can be grown near a sunny window, but if a sheltered terrace or balcony is available it is better moved outside from the end of May onwards. It will benefit from the fresh air. Always put it in full sun. So far there are no difficulties, but in September the plant must be moved to cool, well-lit winter quarters: a really cool room with a minimum temperature down to 5°C (41°F) and a maximum of 10°C (50°F), or into a cool greenhouse. In warm weather the place should be ventilated throughout the day, so that the temperature cannot rise. In this period it is unnecessary to spray the foliage. In spring the plant may go outside quite early if necessary: a little night frost will do less harm than premature growth.

Remember that the oleander is extremely poisonous in all its parts, so don't let it near your mouth and keep it well away from the baby.

Nerium oleander, single white

Nerium oleander, double-flowered form

Watering The oleander is an exceptionally thirsty plant. It will do no harm if a little water remains in the saucer on sunny days. Many people keep the plant too dry, resulting in poor development and flowering. Rainwater is preferred.

In winter restrict the water supply, but never let the compost dry out completely. The plant likes to be warm at the base in winter; at one time it was occasionally put on a foot-warmer. You should in any case pour hot water into the saucer and discard the surplus after a few hours.

Feeding In summer feed every fortnight, preferably using an organic fertiliser. Stop feeding in August; the wood will then ripen better.
Repotting In view of the plant's moisture requirement it should never be grown in clay pots through which water evaporates too easily. Use a plastic container or treat yourself to a teak tub – it may even become an heirloom. It is essential that the pots should have good drainage. The oleander likes to absorb water from the bottom, so ideally there should be a 2-cm ($\frac{3}{4}$-in) layer of crocks at the bottom, followed by a mixture of leafmould, clay or loam and rotted cow manure, enriched with 50 g (2 oz) of dried blood, hoof and horn and bonemeal for every 10 litres ($2\frac{1}{4}$ gal) of the medium. The plant is put on top and the container is then filled with the normal potting mixture. Large specimens do not have to be repotted every year.
Propagation In June and July tip cuttings will root easily, even in a bottle of water. This is the only way to perpetuate cultivars such as double-flowered forms true to type. Propagation from seed is also possible, but in many cases the plants will revert to the original species.
Pests and diseases Scale insects and mealy bug may appear if the plant has been kept too warm in winter.

Nerium oleander

An evergreen shrub with lanceolate, leathery leaves arranged in threes. Flowers grow in terminal clusters, originally rose red, now also white and lilac, single or double forms. In the cultivar 'Variegatum' the leaves are edged with white or cream. The Common Oleander, with single, rose-red flowers, is the most vigorous. It is advisable to take this into account if you wish to grow the plant indoors.

Unfortunately the commercially available forms are usually strains difficult to cultivate. However, you may be able to get a cutting of the common species or grow it from seed.

Nertera

Rubiaceae

Bead Plant

Name From the Greek *nerteros*, lowest. It is a particularly low-growing plant.
Origin About eight species occur in various mountain regions in the southern hemisphere. Only one is cultivated as a house plant.
Description A clump-forming plant with red berries.
Position The plants must be grown in cool conditions. One reader wrote to say that he had successfully left his Bead Plant outside all winter; it grew on the edge of a small pond. Usually a minimum temperature of 10°C (50°F) is recommended.
Care The plant is usually bought when it is covered in berries. Give it a very well-lit situation, just out of the brightest sun, with plenty of fresh air. Grow outside when possible. Towards October put it in a cool, frost-free room (or try it outside) and give it a rest. A cold frame makes good winter quarters. Flowering starts in late April. You should then ensure that there are no drops of water on the plant, for this would inhibit fruit formation. In the period before and after flowering the temperature must not be too high – this, too, will affect fruit formation, although a lot of foliage is developed. The most favourable maximum temperature is 13°C (55°F). When the berries colour the nertera may be brought into the living-room for a time.
Watering Always water from the bottom to avoid rotting, and use rainwater. In summer keep the compost constantly moist, but in winter it can be kept a little drier.
Feeding In the period of growth a little fertiliser may be added to the water.
Repotting Some clay mixed with the compost is beneficial; otherwise add leafmould and rotted manure. Repot in spring.
Propagation Seed may be sown under glass in February–March, with some degree of soil heat, but it is more usual to increase by division in August. The sections are immediately potted up. Cultivate in the best possible light.
Pests and diseases Aphids will occur if the plant is kept in a draught. Grey mould is caused by watering or spraying the foliage.

Nertera granadensis

Syn. *Nertera depressa*. Bead Plant. A clump-forming perennial with creeping, densely leaved stems. The leaves are broad-oval, 4 to 8 mm ($\frac{1}{8}$ to $\frac{1}{4}$ in) across, pale green and somewhat fleshy. It bears insignificant green flowers followed by bright orange-red berries, 8 mm ($\frac{1}{4}$ in) in diameter.

Nertera granadensis, the Bead Plant

Notocactus purpureus

Notocactus
Cactaceae

Name From the Greek: *noton*, back, and *cactus*, cactus.
Origin About 15 different species are found in southern Brazil, northern Argentina, Paraguay and Uruguay, many on rocky slopes.
Description Fine globular cacti which not only flower early and profusely, but also have strikingly beautiful thorn formation. The ribs are divided into tubercles on which the areoles occur.
Position A temperate greenhouse is the best place for these plants, for unlike most other cacti they need not be kept particularly cool in winter; the best minimum temperature is 10°C (50°F). Because of this the notocactus is fairly easily grown indoors.
Care There is another exception to the rule applying to cacti: the notocactus tolerates some shade. In early spring bright sunlight is, in fact, harmful to the small globes. In summer partial shade is enough to bring the plants into flower.

If this cactus is to be cultivated in the living-room, for which it is quite suitable, a window with south-eastern or south-western aspect is the best position. If the window is a little draughty the temperature close to the glass may hardly rise above 10°C (50°F), just right for this cactus. Otherwise move the plant to a cool bedroom or spare room.

If the growing conditions are not ideal it will benefit the plant to be grafted, for instance on *Eriocereus jusbertii* stock, which will certainly promote flowering.
Watering The water requirements of these cacti are also somewhat unusual. In summer it is advisable to keep the compost constantly moist, that is, slightly damper than is usual in the case of cacti. In winter the compost must not be completely dry, although an occasional drop of water poured down the rim of the pot is sufficient; it should depend to some extent on the temperature. Tap water is acceptable, but rainwater or demineralised water is better.
Feeding While the plant is growing, that is from May to August, a dose of nitrogen-free fertiliser, so-called cactus fertiliser, is recommended.
Repotting The standard cactus mixture, consisting of 50 per cent proprietary compost and 50 per cent perlite, is very suitable. Some people recommend a medium consisting of pulverised clay, leafmould and sharp sand in equal parts.

Notocactus horstii

Notocactus mammulosus

Plastic pots are to be preferred and these should be well drained. Young plants should be repotted every spring, but at the third year it is sufficient to repot in alternate years.
Propagation As a rule these plants are raised from seed. Sow in March in some degree of soil heat, under glass, and prick out as soon as the seedlings can be handled. Species producing offsets can also be increased from cuttings, which must be left to dry for a week to prevent rotting. Grafting is often a good way of reviving weakly specimens.
Pests and diseases Damage may be caused by mealy bugs and root aphids.

Notocactus apricus
Syn. *Malacocarpus apricus.* A small species with 15 to 20 notched ribs, 18 to 20 bristly radial thorns and four slightly longer centrals, 2 to 3 cm ($\frac{3}{4}$ to 1 in) long. It has yellow flowers to 8 cm (3 in) long.
Notocactus concinnus
Syn. *Malacocarpus concinnus.* A broad and spherical cactus, green and glossy, with a lumpy sunken and thornless crown; the areoles bear bristly yellow or reddish thorns. There are 18 ribs. Flowers are 7 cm (2$\frac{3}{4}$ in) long, yellow, with a silky sheen; the exterior is red.
Notocactus graessneri
Syn. *Malacocarpus graessneri; Brasilicactus graessneri.* A pale green, spherical cactus, flattened at the top, with 50 to 60 ribs. The areoles are covered in yellow wool and thorns and the flowers are pale green.
Notocactus haselbergii
Syn. *Malacocarpus haselbergii; Brasilicactus haselbergii.* Spherical or slightly columnar cactus with a sunken crown, densely covered in white thorns, with 30 ribs. The flowers are orange-red to red.
Notocactus leninghausii
Syn. *Malacocarpus leninghausii; Eriocactus leninghausii.* Golden Ball Cactus. A cluster-forming columnar cactus with 20 to 30 ribs; the areoles are arranged close together and bear fine yellow thorns. It has yellow flowers with a silky sheen, 5 to 6 cm (2 to 2$\frac{1}{4}$ in) across.
Notocactus mammulosus
Syn. *Malacocarpus mammulosus.* A spherical or somewhat columnar dark green cactus with 18 to 20 ribs divided into chin-shaped tubercles. The crown is covered in white woolly hairs. There are yellow-brown thorns, with centrals brown at the tip and up to 2 cm ($\frac{3}{4}$ in) long, and sulphur-yellow flowers, reddish on the outside, 3 to 5 cm (1 to 2 in) long.
Notocactus scopa
Syn. *Malacocarpus scopa.* Spherical cactus, later becoming columnar, with 30 to 40 ribs; the areoles are arranged close together. It has bristly white radial thorns, brownish centrals, to 1 cm ($\frac{1}{2}$ in) long and yellow flowers up to 6 cm (2$\frac{1}{4}$ in) across.

Odontoglossum pulchellum

Odontoglossum grande, the easiest species

Odontoglossum
Orchidaceae

Name From the Greek *odoon*, tooth, and *glossa*, tongue.
Origin About 80 to 90 species occur in mountain forests at high altitudes in tropical zones of America, where they grow on the trees.
Description Orchids with pseudobulbs, palmate foliage and small to very large flowers with a kind of tooth at the base of the lip.
Position Species originating in Central America can often be grown successfully in the living-room, especially *Odontoglossum grande*. The other species must be grown in very cool conditions and need a cool or temperate greenhouse.

Odontoglossum bictoniense

Care The indoor species are least sensitive to warmth. They have firm, hard pseudobulbs and after flowering must be kept dry and cool for a time, just dry enough to prevent the pseudobulbs from shrivelling up. After about a month the plants may be allowed to start into growth once more. Bright sunlight must be avoided, but a little morning sun will do no harm. A really well-lit east-facing window is very suitable. If necessary the plants can stay there all the year round.

Greenhouse species have soft pseudobulbs and hardly need a dormant season. In this case the problem is that the greenhouse soon becomes too warm in summer, while outside the air is too dry. They are usually cultivated in greenhouses with some kind of cooling system – a ventilator, for instance. By frequent ventilation and screening growers try to keep the temperature as low as possible. Even in winter the greenhouse is sometimes ventilated, except, of course, when it is freezing outside. It is not advisable to try to grow these plants indoors.
Watering To start with the plants must be given lime-free water if at all possible. Clean rainwater, which must be brought to room temperature, is best. The plants are easily overwatered, which causes the roots to rot. In the dormant season they need practically no water at all.
Feeding During the period of active growth they can be given a fertiliser solution at half the recommended concentration once a month.
Repotting The recommended potting medium consists of peat moss and chopped tree fern, but every amateur has his own pet recipe. Perlite and lumps of peat are sometimes used. The plants should be repotted after flowering and the pots half filled with potsherds or perlite.
Propagation The plants may be divided when they are repotted. They can also be raised from seed, but it is a very complicated process.

Species for indoor cultivation
Odontoglossum bictoniense
Pseudobulbs up to 10 cm (4 in) tall with racemes of about 12 flowers on up to 1-m (3-ft) long, usually unbranched, stalks. The flowers are 3 to 4 cm (1 to 1½ in) in diameter, reddish brown and violet in colour.
Odontoglossum grande
This species has flowers to 15 cm (6 in) across, yellow with brown and white. This is the strongest and best-known species for the living-room. There are a number of varieties.
Odontoglossum pulchellum
The fragrant white flowers are arranged in racemes. The lip is fiddle shaped with a yellow, red-tipped crest.
Odontoglossum schlieperianum
Resembles *Odontoglossum grande*, but the flower is no more than 9 cm (3½ in) in diameter, paler yellow with brown patches.

Species for a cool or temperate greenhouse
Odontoglossum cervantesii
A dwarf species with oval pseudobulbs and a pendulous flower stalk to 20 cm (8 in) long. It bears small, fragrant, white and yellow flowers.
Odontoglossum cordatum
Oval pseudobulbs; the flower stalk is 30 to 40 cm (12 to 16 in) long and bears five to six flowers in a loose raceme. They are up to 8 cm (3 in) across, with small petals, yellow with brown patches; the lip is heart shaped, white with a few brown patches.
Odontoglossum crispum
Oval pseudobulbs up to 6 cm (2¼ in) long with flowers in arching racemes, up to 20 on one stalk. They are 10 cm (4 in) in diameter, white with pink and brown patches, very variable. There are a large number of varieties.
Odontoglossum maculatum
Closely resembles *Odontoglossum cordatum*. It has flowers with brown sepals and pale yellow petals with brown patches.
Odontoglossum oerstedtii
A dwarf species with oval pseudobulbs and pure white flowers, yellow only at the base of the lip.
Odontoglossum rossii
Oval, 3-cm (1-in) long pseudobulbs and clusters of up to three fragrant flowers, each to 6 cm (2¼ in) across, white with brown and pink patches and a rounded lip with yellow crest.

Olea europeae, the olive, a strong house plant

Olea
Oleaceae
Olive

Name The Greek word for olive is *elaia*; in Latin it is *olea*.
Origin There are about 40 species, which occur in Africa, tropical Asia and countries round the Mediterranean.
Description A readily branching, erect-growing or spreading shrub with grey-green leaves; in our climate it is not hardy. The plant is gradually becoming better known as a house plant, especially since the selections carried out by Mr Jurriaanse, Principal of the School of Horticulture in Frederiksoord, Holland.
Position Jurriaanse discovered that this plant tolerates a living-room atmosphere very well. Actually the plant should be overwintered at a slightly lower temperature, but up to 20°C (68°F) is accepted.
Care Ideally the olive should be kept in good light at a temperature of 5 to 10°C (41 to 50°F) in winter, but it has been proved to survive in the living-room as well. In summer the plants may stand in full sun outside on a terrace or balcony, but it will do no harm if they are kept indoors all the year round.

One disadvantage is that the olive may grow quite large in the course of time, but this can be overcome by occasional pruning. Fragrant white flowers appear in summer. The fruits do not ripen until the winter.
Watering In summer the olive accepts fairly dry conditions, but it is better to keep the compost moderately moist at all times, even in winter. If it is kept too dry the foliage will drop.
Feeding In the growing season the plant may be fed every fortnight.
Repotting It helps if the potting mixture contains some clay or loam, but the plant will also do well in standard potting compost. Repot every spring.
Propagation It is not easy to increase the plant from cuttings. Half-ripe tip cuttings are used, taken in summer. Cut the stem just below an eye, remove the lower leaves and dust the cut with a little rooting powder. Root the cuttings under glass or plastic in a soil temperature of 30 to 35°C (86 to 95°F); the medium must be kept moist. If you are able to obtain seed, plants may be propagated by this method as well.
Pests and diseases Unfortunately it is rather sensitive to scale insects, especially if kept too warm in winter.

Olea europaea
An evergreen shrub. In Mediterranean countries it is a small tree with short-stalked lanceolate grey-green leaves, 4 to 7 cm (1½ to 2¾ in) long and 7 to 12 mm (¼ to ½ in) wide. The lower surface is covered in white or rust-coloured hairs, and it bears yellow-white flowers in axillary clusters.

Oncidium kramerianum

Oncidium
Orchidaceae

Name From the Greek *onkidion*, tubercle. The upper surface of the lip is slightly pimpled or swollen.
Origin No fewer than 530 species are known, distributed over large areas of Central and South America, where they grow as epiphytes on the trees.
Description Most species have obvious pseudobulbs bearing one or two large leaves, but other forms appear as well. The flowers also vary; often they are arranged in extremely long racemes.
Position Considering the large area of distribution it is not surprising that treatment also varies considerably. There are, for instance, species – as well as numerous hybrids – for the hothouse, for the temperate greenhouse and for the cool greenhouse. Only a few species can be successfully cultivated in the living-room.
Care Species raised in a cool greenhouse should be kept as cool as possible in summer. This may be done by frequent ventilation, by spraying the roof and by screening. To maintain the humidity the floor should be watered copiously. The plants themselves must also be kept moderately moist at all times and for this reason they are preferably grown in pots and not on blocks of fern or in hanging baskets. A strict dormant season is unnecessary in the cool greenhouse. Minimum temperature in winter should be 5°C (41°F).

In summer plants kept in a temperate greenhouse may be watered generously, but in winter, after flowering has ceased – usually between November and March – only just enough water should be given to keep the pseudobulbs from shrivelling. In this case, too, the plants must be screened from sunlight and the atmosphere must be kept very humid.

Hothouse species should receive the same treatment as those in the temperate greenhouse, except that the minimum temperature in winter should be 18°C (64°F). Give them plenty of light, especially in winter.

Species which can be cultivated indoors should be kept near a fairly cool, east-facing window. After flowering they should be given a rest by turning the thermostat back even further and reducing the water supply.

A few species, such as *Oncidium kramerianum*, flower for years on end on the same stem, so of course this stem should not be removed after flowering. Other species, especially those originating in Brazil, develop such a tremendous flower stalk that it must be shortened to prevent the orchid flowering to death.
Watering All species must be watered with lime-free water. In summer the pots or fern blocks can occasionally be plunged, but in the dormant season the compost should almost dry out, though the pseudobulb must not be allowed to shrivel. Do not spray the foliage too often.
Feeding Growing plants may be given a small feed once a month.
Repotting For many species a mixture of 2 parts fern roots (osmunda fibre) and 1 part sphagnum moss is recommended. Sometimes peat is used. A few species are cultivated on blocks of tree fern. Pots must be given a very good drainage layer of crocks.
Propagation Increase by division when the plants are repotted in spring. Propagation from seed is a job for the expert.
Pests and diseases The plant may be attacked by red spider mite and scale insects.

Species for the living-room
Oncidium ornithorhynchum
This bears multiflowered arching plumes with flowers up to 4cm (1½in) long, fragrant, lilac pink with a yellow pimple on the lip. It flowers in October–November.
Oncidium varicosum
This species produces a profusion of flowers arranged in slightly arching plumes; they are yellow with brown patches and a large yellow lip. The form most frequently cultivated is *Oncidium varicosum rogersii*, which has larger flowers in a more beautiful shade of yellow. It flowers between October and January.

Species for the cool greenhouse
Oncidium crispum
The flowers are 5 to 7cm (2 to 2¾in), pale chestnut brown with yellow patches and the lip is brown and yellow. It flowers in September–December.
Oncidium marshallianum
Flowers are up to 7cm (2¾in), golden yellow with crosswise dark blotches in the centre. The lip is yellow with red tips. It flowers in May–June.

Species for the temperate greenhouse
Oncidium cavendishianum
This carries a branching flower stalk with numerous fragrant flowers, 3 to 4cm (1 to 1½in) across, yellow with red-brown blotches; the lip is golden yellow. It flowers in April–May.
Oncidium wentworthianum
The flower stalk is up to 2m (6ft) with innumerable yellow flowers, blotched with brown. It flowers in June–August.

Hothouse species
Oncidium altissimum
This has a pendulous flower stalk up to 1.5m (5ft) long. The flowers are bright yellow with brown marking and there is a yellow lip with brown centre. It flowers in April–June.
Oncidium kramerianum
The upper petals are shaped like feelers, the lateral petals are brown with yellow marking.

Ophiopogon jaburan in flower

Ophiopogon
Liliaceae
Snake's Beard

Name From Greek *ophis*, snake, and *pogon*, beard. Nobody knows what a snake's beard is and why this plant is supposed to resemble it.
Origin To date eight species are known, distributed between Japan and the Himalayas.
Description A plant with grass-like foliage, closely resembling the *Liriope* (q.v.), with which it is often confused. The liriope has a superior ovary and oblique growing flowers, often purple, while in *Ophiopogon* the ovary is semi-inferior and the flowers are white and pendulous. In the absence of flowers there is hardly any difference between the two plants.
Position The ophiopogon may be kept in a heated living-room, out of the sun, but it should preferably be kept a little cooler in winter.
Care The plants tolerate a moderate degree of humidity. In a greenhouse problems may in fact arise when the relative humidity is too high, in which case the stems will rot. They do not need a great deal of light, although striped forms must be well lit to prevent them reverting to green.

Flowering occurs in summer and is followed by the development of green berries which later change to a fine dark blue shade. In winter the temperature may fall to 5°C (41°F). If the plants stay in the warm living-room the foliage must be sprayed from time to time.
Watering In summer the compost can be kept moderately moist at all times. Tap water of reasonable quality is perfectly acceptable. In winter the plants should be kept drier at lower temperatures, but in a warm environment you may continue to water as in summer.
Feeding In the period of active growth feed every fortnight with a standard preparation.
Repotting Correctly treated plants will practically burst out of their pots and annual repotting is therefore advisable. Standard potting compost may be used, with possibly the addition of a little pulverised clay or loam to give even better results.
Propagation The plants will develop numerous runners, especially if they are planted out, for instance on the greenhouse staging. This only applies to the species *Ophiopogon japonicus*. The off-

Ophiopogon jaburan 'Vittatus'

sets may be removed in spring and used for propagation. Old clumps can also be divided when they are repotted. Ripe berries can be sown, but the variegated form will revert to green.

Ophiopogon jaburan
◐ ● ⊜ ⊘ ⊛ ◙
White Lily-turf. A sessile evergreen plant without runners. The leaves are 30 to 60cm (1 to 2ft) long and 1 to 1.5cm (½in) wide, strap shaped and erect growing. The flower stalk is flattened, about the same length as the leaves. The flower clusters are up to 10cm (4in) long, the individual white flowers are 1cm (½in) in diameter and are followed by violet-coloured berries.

In the cultivar 'Vittatus' the leaves are striped lengthwise in white, and this is the finest form.

Ophiopogon japonicus
This species does develop runners. The leaves grow close together and are 10 to 20cm (4 to 8in) long and only 2 to 3mm (⅛in) wide, arching and dark green in colour. The flower spikes are much shorter than the leaves; the flowers are 5mm (¼in) across, pendent, white or tinged with purple. The berries are initially green, later blue.

It appears that there is a white-striped form called 'Variegatus', but it is rarely available.

Oplismenus
Gramineae

Name From the Greek *oplismenos*, the armed one. This refers to the fact that the lower beards of the flower spike are prickly.
Origin There are about 12 species which occur in nearly every country.
Description A plant with long runners trailing over the rim of the pot. The surface of the stalkless leaves is undulate.
Position Attractive hanging plants for a room which should preferably be kept a little cooler in winter – a conservatory, for instance. They also make good ground cover in a greenhouse.
Care In summer the plant must be kept out of full sunlight, but the variegated form, in particular, still needs plenty of light to retain its fine colouring. In the dark winter months it must be kept close to the window. As they age the plants lose some of their beauty; you should therefore grow new plants from cuttings taken at frequent intervals.

In winter the best temperature is between 10 and 20°C (50 and 68°F); better on the cool side, but room temperature if necessary. However, as it is unlikely you will want to keep them for another season it matters little where the plants are overwintered so long as they are kept alive. In spring you can then take cuttings to grow fine, well-shaped and beautifully coloured new specimens.

Plants which suffer from dry air should be sprayed daily.
Watering At high temperatures the plant requires a great deal of water. Be careful not to let the compost dry out; this will result in foliage drop. If it is used as a trailing plant the danger of drying out is particularly great. Take down and plunge the pots every two days.
Feeding Give an occasional small feed in the summer months. Too much feeding will affect the plant's beauty, especially in the case of variegated forms.
Repotting In spring the plants can be repotted in standard potting compost. Young plants grown from cuttings must be potted on. Use plastic pots to reduce evaporation of the compost.
Propagation The long runners frequently root spontaneously, and the simplest method of propagation is to remove the plantlets and pot them separately. In addition young tip shoots may be cut in spring and rooted under glass in a soil temperature of 20°C (68°F). The cuttings will also root readily in a bottle of water, but this method is recommended only if you intend to grow the plants on in hydroculture.

Oplismenus hirtellus
◐ ⊜ ⊘ ⊛ ◙
A plant with creeping, often trailing stems bearing lanceolate leaves, 5 to 15cm (2 to 6in) long and 1 to 2cm (½ to ¾in) wide, with a sharply pointed tip and undulate surface; they are yellowish-green in colour. The cultivar 'Variegatus' (syn. *Panicum variegatum*), or Ribbon Grass, has tricoloured foliage: white, rose red and green. This is the finest form.

Oplismenus hirtellus, an attractive hanging plant

Opuntia phaeacantha may be cultivated on a terrace or balcony

Opuntia
Cactaceae
Prickly Pear

Name *Opuntia* is an ancient Latin name, used by Pliny and later applied to this genus.
Origin The more than 200 wild species originate in North and South America.
Description The genus is divided into a number of groups. *Opuntia* species are the well-known pad cacti; *Cylindropuntia* species have cylindrical branches and *Tephrocactus* species develop short, oval or spherical joints. Elsewhere the group names are used as generic names, but not in this book.

In addition to the normal, prickly thorns, most opuntia species have tufts of so-called glochids on their areoles. These dangerous spines are found even on the fruits. They break at a touch and lodge in the skin. Since they are so small and are moreover barbed, they are very difficult to remove. Never handle an opuntia without wearing gloves.
Position All species must be kept in a warm and sunny environment in summer and cool and dry in winter. Some of them are hardy and will survive frost and ice in the garden, provided the soil is exceptionally well drained.
Care In summer the plants must be kept in full sun. This may be in a cold frame, on the balcony or on the terrace. However, the plant feels happiest behind an unscreened south-facing window. Because of the low intensity of light at our latitudes not all species will produce flowers.

Towards winter the plants should be moved to a cool, well-lit area, such as an unheated or cool greenhouse, a conservatory, or an unused bedroom. Moisture is stored in the flattened joints, but not as much as in spherical cacti. For this reason, opuntia species can never be left entirely dry; they must occasionally be given a few drops of water. The plant's condition will be evident from the extent of shrivelling of the joints. People who keep these cacti in the warm living-room in winter must certainly continue to give reasonable amounts of water. Because the plant is very strong they sometimes survive this treatment, although they will probably grow lanky.
Watering Little moisture is evaporated by these cacti and consequently they need little water. In summer it is advisable to keep the compost between dry and moderately moist; in winter the plants only need an occasional drop of water if they are kept cool. Ordinary tap water will not harm this strong genus.

Opuntia clavarioides

Feeding Feed occasionally, but only in summer, using special nitrogen-free cactus fertiliser.
Repotting This must be done in spring. Standard potting compost is satisfactory for the stronger species with flattened pads. The other groups prefer a cactus mixture. Pots must be well drained.
Propagation Pads or joints may be removed and used for propagation. In spring take joints which have developed in the previous year, in summer half-ripe joints of the current season. Allow them to dry out for a few days before inserting them in a fairly dry medium, and do not water them at first. Seeds sometimes germinate very slowly; it may take as much as a year. Soak the seed in water for a day first. It is fun to bring a packet of mixed opuntia seed into growth.

Opuntia tunicata

Opuntia microdasys 'Albispina'

Pests and diseases The plant may be subject to an infestation of mealy bug, especially round the areoles. Cork formation on the older joints is almost inevitable and does not indicate serious disease.

Opuntia basilaris
This has flattened joints, fairly narrow, reverse oval to spatula shaped. They are strikingly blue-green in colour, often with reddish margins, finely wrinkled across the pads, and have numerous areoles without thorns but with brown glochids. There are carmine-red flowers.
Opuntia bergeriana
Narrow oval flattened joints, to 15cm (6in) long, are a dull pale green, sometimes a little bluish. There are two to three thorns, 4cm (1½in) long and yellow glochids. The flowers are red.
Opuntia clavarioides
Syn. *Austrocylindropuntia*. The species has cylindrical to club-shaped joints, brownish in colour. It must be grafted on stock.
Opuntia cylindrica
Syn. *Austrocylindropuntia*. Cylindrical joints up to 7cm (2¾in) thick, green, with fairly flat tubercles and hexagonal wrinkles, and leaves 15cm (6in) long which soon drop. There is usually one thorn on each areole up to 3cm (1in) long, and the flowers are pink.
Opuntia diademata
Syn. *Tephrocactus*. This features short round joints, to 5cm (2in) long, and soft white to brownish thorns, with pale yellow flowers.
Opuntia exaltata
Syn. *Austrocylindropuntia*. The cylindrical joints, up to 5cm (2in) diameter, have elongated tubercles; leaves are up to 3cm (1in) long and soon drop. There is one thorn per areole, to 3cm (1in) long, yellow-grey. The flowers are pink.
Opuntia ficus-indica
Fig Cactus. The pads are oblong to spatula shaped, up to 50cm (20in) long. There are yellow glochids; the thorns are sometimes lacking. The flowers are yellow with red. It makes suitable stock for grafting.
Opuntia leucotricha
The flat joints, to 20cm (8in), oval to oblong, are green in colour. They are covered in velvety hairs, but this can only be seen under a magnifying glass. The areoles are arranged quite close together and bear one to three fairly soft thorns and a few long, twisted hairs. It has yellow flowers.
Opuntia microdasys
Rabbit's Ears. Flat, round, pale green joints are fairly closely covered in areoles, which only bear brown glochids, and it has yellow flowers. There are a number of cultivars.
Opuntia phaeacantha
Of recumbent habit, this has oval to round joints up to 15cm (6in) long. The areoles are widely spaced and bear brown-yellow glochids and slightly flattened thorns. The species has yellow flowers with an orange heart, and is hardy.
Opuntia scheerii
With flat, oval blue-green joints to 30cm (1ft) long, the numerous areoles are covered in brownish felt and glochids, in addition to 12 yellow thorns and numerous yellow and white hairs. There is a pale yellow flower.
Opuntia subulata
Syn. *Austrocylindropuntia*. The joints here are cylindrical, to 5cm (2in) in diameter, with long oval tubercles. The leaves, 3 to 10cm (1 to 4in) long, remain on the plant for a long time. Each areole bears one thorn, yellow-grey, to 3cm (1in) long. The flowers are pink. There is a well-known monstrose form.
Opuntia tunicata
Syn. *Cylindropuntia*. Cylindrical joints, up to 5cm (2in) in diameter and 30cm (1ft) long, carry small green leaves which readily drop. There are six to seven thorns 4cm (1½in) long, white to whitish-brown, and yellow-green flowers.

Oreocereus celsianus

Oreocereus
Cactaceae

Name From the Greek *oros* or *oreos*, mountain, and the generic name *Cereus*.
Origin About eight species are known. Their native habitat is in the Andes range of South America, at an altitude of 4000m (12,825ft).
Description Large, columnar cacti, usually white haired and densely covered in thorns.
Position Not very suitable for the living-room, for in their native habitat there is a considerable difference between the day and the night temperature. These plants can, however, be successfully grown in a cold frame.
Care In summer the glass should be removed from the cactus frame (preferably a fairly tall cold frame with a removable glass top), so that the plants can be kept warm during the day and cool off at night. Some spraying at night is beneficial. The temperature may drop to zero at night, provided it rises to 12 to 15°C (53 to 59°F) during the day, otherwise the frame must be covered and the water supply stopped. Ventilation should be resumed as soon as the weather gets warmer.
Watering In summer the plants should be kept moderately moist; in winter they need be given practically no water if the temperature is low.
Feeding Be sparing with nourishment, to prevent the plants from growing lanky.
Repotting The plants grow most vigorously if they are planted out on the staging. The compost should not be too nutritious; standard potting compost mixed with 50 per cent sharp sand is quite good, or use a cactus mixture, that is 50 per cent standard compost and 50 per cent perlite.
Propagation Increase from cuttings or from seed.

Oreocereus celsianus
A columnar cactus, 10 to 15cm (4 to 6in) in diameter with 10 to 20 ribs and a woolly crown. It has yellow thorns, turning darker at a later stage, and coarse white hairs, and the flowers are pink. *Oreocereus celsianus trollii* (syn. *Oreocereus trollii*) is smaller; it branches at the base and is more woolly and more densely covered in hairs, and the thorns are thinner. *O. c. fossulatus* (syn. *Oreocereus fossulatus*) is a fairly strongly branching columnar cactus, to 8cm (3in) across, with eight to ten undulate ribs and yellow thorns interspersed with white hairs. The flowers are brownish pink, up to 10cm (4in) across and coarsely haired.

Oreopanax capitatus

Oreopanax
Araliaceae

Name Derived from the Greek *oros* or *oreos*, mountain, and the generic name *Panax*.
Origin About 120 species are known, all originating in the tropical mountain forests of South America.
Description Fairly rare plants; the foliage is somewhat similar to that of the ivy.
Position In recent times they have proved to be suitable house plants, though as yet little is known about them. In summer they will thrive out of doors.
Care It is pleasant to note that these

plants tolerate fairly high temperatures in winter, something hardly to be expected of plants which can grow outside in summer. If the plants are to be regularly put out of doors and brought in again, it is essential that they should be introduced very gradually to the sun and to the lower temperatures outside in spring, the reverse process applying in the autumn, for if the plant is not acclimatised slowly, scorching may occur in spring, and foliage drop in autumn. Perhaps it is best of all to keep the plant in good light in a not-too-warm room throughout the year. In winter the foliage must frequently be sprayed.

The plant produces attractive flowers and puts out enormous shoots from which several leaves develop simultaneously.

Watering Keep moderately moist both in summer and in winter.

Feeding The plant may be fed when it is in growth, but do not give too much, for it grows fast enough in any case.

Repotting All kinds of mixtures are recommended, but I have found that the plant will do very well in standard potting compost.

Propagation Tip cuttings, dipped in rooting powder, will root in a soil temperature of 30 to 35°C (86 to 95°F), under plastic.

Oreopanax capitatus

○⊜⦾⊛◙

Syn. *Oreopanax nymphaefolius*. A small evergreen tree with glossy, oblong, dark green leaves, strikingly veined, slightly gutter shaped and long stalked. The white inflorescence resembles that of the ivy.

Oxalis purpurata bowei

Oxalis deppei

Oxalis
Oxalidaceae
Wood Sorrel

Name Probably derived from the Greek *oxys* meaning acid and *hals, halos*, salt.

Origin There are more than 800 species, most of them natives of South Africa and South and Central America. A few are indigenous to Europe.

Description The clover-like plants described below have four or more leaves.

Position In a warm room or greenhouse these plants soon collapse. They belong in a cool or unheated greenhouse; some species are in fact hardy.

Care The little plants are often available towards Christmas. Place them in a cool room or in a corridor and keep them alive until they can be moved to the garden or the balcony in May. *Oxalis deppei* (Lucky Clover) can remain there, but neither *O. carnosa* nor *O. vulcanicola* are hardy.

You can also grow your own Lucky Clover for Christmas. Buy the bulbs in September and pot them in small groups, 5 cm (2 in) below the surface of the compost. Initially the temperature should be kept at 6 to 8°C (43 to 46°F), but once the bulbs have rooted it may be raised to a maximum of 12 to 14°C (53 to 57°F).

Watering Plants raised from bulbs should be watered sparingly, a little more generously if the environment is too warm.

Feeding Feed once a week in the growing season.

Repotting Repot preferably in light, loamy soil.

Propagation Increase from offsets.

Oxalis carnosa

○⊜⦾⊛◙

A creeping plant with thick stems and fleshy, fresh green leaves, coated in bloom on the reverse, and small yellow flowers. Suitable for use indoors.

Pachycereus pringlei

Oxalis deppei

○⊖⦾⊛◙

Lucky Clover. This bears four bright green leaves with pink cross-banding, and the flowers are rose red with a yellow heart. It can be grown outside.

Oxalis purpurata bowei

○⊜⦾⊛◙

It has long-stalked tripartite leaves, and large rose-pink flowers appear in July. Suitable for pot cultivation (in cool conditions).

Oxalis vulcanicola

This species has three-fold leaves, red stems and golden-yellow flowers. It's a greenhouse plant.

Oxalis vulcanicola, a beautiful species for the greenhouse where it will feel at home among other plants

Pachycereus
Cactaceae

Name From the Greek *pachys*, thick, and the generic name *Cereus*.

Origin About 10 species occur in Mexico.

Description Columnar cacti which in their native country may reach immense heights. Young specimens are very fine and are therefore sold as house plants.

Position This cactus, too, is best kept in a cool greenhouse, thoroughly ventilated in summer and kept at 5°C (41°F) in winter. In the living-room it should be placed close to a sunny window.

Care In the course of a few years the plants grow far too large for the living-room or even the greenhouse. They only produce flowers at an advanced age and there is therefore nothing to look at except the cactus body. Because they grow so fast and look so attractive when young they are very popular and growers gladly meet the demand. Keep the plant in a sunny position in summer, but definitely cool in winter when it must not be allowed to grow, otherwise it would soon become lank and limp. Keep it in good light.

Watering In summer always keep the compost moderately moist, but in winter, when the temperature is low, give hardly any water. Ordinary tap water is satisfactory.

Feeding It is not advisable to encourage this fast-growing plant by feeding it.

Repotting Standard potting compost mixed with 50 per cent of sharp sand is satisfactory, but if available pre-packed or home-mixed cactus compost may be used.

Propagation Pachycereus is usually grown from seed.

Pachycereus hollianus
○⊜◎⊛◎
In this species there are seven to fourteen ribs. One of the central thorns is very long, to 4cm (1½in), and the areoles are not linked by felty bands.
Pachycereus pringlei
A columnar dark green cactus, to 10cm (4in) in diameter, with 11 to 13 ribs. As the plants age the felty grey areoles become linked by felty bands. The one to three central thorns are white with a dark tip, the ten to fourteen radials are white to bright grey.

Pachyphytum
Crassulaceae

Name From the Greek *pachys*, thick, and *phyton*, plant.
Origin In Mexico eight species grow wild. The plants have on many occasions been crossed with *Echeveria*; the resulting forms are discussed overleaf under the name × *Pachyveria*.
Description These plants have fleshy to very thick leaves, arranged in a loose rosette. Botanically they are characterised by the fact that the stamens, placed in front of the petals, bear a filmy scale on either side; this is not the case with echeverias.
Position Easily grown succulents with few demands. Organically they belong in a cool greenhouse, where they can be kept dry and cool in winter. This encourages profuse flowering and fine colouring of the foliage. However, unless they are kept in too dark a spot or are drowned in water they will survive in the living-room.
Care Always keep these plants in the sun; indoors, this means a south-facing window-sill. After mid-May they may be put in the garden or on the balcony. The pots must be heavy, so that they cannot be blown over by the wind.

In autumn, before the first night frosts occur, the pachyphytum must be moved indoors, preferably to cool, well-lit quarters. If such conditions cannot be provided the plant must in any case be kept as cool as possible, perhaps by placing it very close to a window. The minimum winter temperature is about 5°C (41°F). At such a temperature the compost must be perfectly dry.
Watering In summer the plants can be watered sparingly to moderately with either tap water or rainwater. Never pour water on the foliage. A good method is to plunge the pots from time to time, enabling the compost to become drenched. In sunny weather the plants can then be left alone for at least a fortnight. In winter they should be watered only if kept in too warm an environment. If they are kept cool watering is superfluous.
Feeding A pachyphytum need not be fed, for if it grows too fast it will lose its character.
Repotting All species grow best in a cactus mixture, such as described in the section on page 70 on the care of cacti. The compost must be very porous, but must still be capable of retaining some moisture. The plant should be repotted after its resting season in winter, but for older plants once every two or three years is sufficient.
Propagation The easiest method is to take one or more leaf cuttings. Leave them in a dry place, but out of the sun. Wait until the first stages of roots can be seen before inserting the cuttings in fairly dry compost. The plants can also be increased from tip cuttings or from seed. The seed of a large number of species may be obtained from specialist cactus growers.
Pests and diseases The plants may be infested by root knot eelworm as well as by mealy bug and root aphids. When the plants are repotted you may notice tubercles on the roots; this is where the eelworms live. The simplest way to combat the pests is to take cuttings from the old plant and root them in fresh compost; infested roots should be discarded immediately.

Pachyphytum compactum

Pachyphytum bracteosum
○⊜◎⊛◎
The leaves are arranged along stems which may grow to 50cm (20in); they are 5 to 8cm (2 to 3in) long and 1.5 to 3cm (½ to 1in) wide; the thickness is a little less. They are reverse oval to spatula shaped, blunt, very fleshy and coated with violet-coloured bloom. The inflorescence is fairly long, and initially angled. The flowers all face one way and have large bracts covered in bloom. The sepals are bloomed as well and are longer than the dark red to orange-red petals.
Pachyphytum brevifolium
A plant with sticky, arching stems and scattered thick leaves, coated in bluish bloom with a red sheen. The bell-shaped flowers are red.
Pachyhytum compactum
Stems are up to 20cm (8in) long, the leaves grow close together and are 2 to 3cm (¾ to 1in) long, 1 to 2cm (½ to ¾in) thick and wide. As a result of the pressure of the neighbouring leaves they become angular. The colour is grey-green with a little bloom. The inflorescence has small bracts, and the sepals are shorter than the petals, which are red at the base and green towards the tip.
Pachyphytum hookeri
Stems reach a maximum of 60cm (2ft), 1 to 2cm (½ to ¾in) thick and are not readily branching. In young plants the leaves are arranged close together, at a later stage they are more scattered. They are practically spherical, slightly flattened at the top, with a short point, and the colour is pale grey-green. The leaves are 2 to 4cm (¾ to 1½in) long and 1.5 to 2cm (½ to ¾in) wide. The flowers are bright red with yellow tips.
Pachyphytum oviferum
This has short, branching stems, and the entire plant is coated with white bloom. Leaves are up to 4cm (1½in) long and 2 to 2.5cm (¾ to 1in) wide, very thick, and egg shaped. Where they touch they become slightly flattened. There are red flowers; the sepals are unequal in length, blue-bloomed. This is one of the finest species.

A young plant of *Pachypodium lameri*

Pachypodium
Apocynaceae

Name From the Greek *pachys*, thick, and *podion*, foot.
Origin About 20 species occur in arid regions in Angola, South West Africa and Malagasy.
Description This plant looks like a cross between a foliage plant and a cactus. The columnar, cactus-like body is crowned with a tuft of green leaves.
Position In its own habitat the foliage develops in the rainy season and drops in the dry period.
Care We must try to imitate these conditions at home. It appears that the plants are capable of reversing the seasons, for in the southern hemisphere they would of course be dry when it is winter in our part of the world. At our latitudes the plant may therefore be kept in a sunny and warm spot in summer, when it is watered reasonably freely. A window with southern aspect is very suitable; screening is unnecessary. The leaves will now appear and develop. Towards autumn gradually reduce the water supply, so that the foliage turns yellow and dies and only the bare cactus trunk remains. The plants may be left where they are and need not be moved to an unheated greenhouse. The minimum temperature is 13°C (55°F). New leaves will appear in spring; only then can a little more water be given.
Watering As described above. If you continue watering after the leaves turn yellow this will inevitably result in rotting. If the leaves should turn yellow at any other time of the year than autumn, stop watering immediately and allow the plant to rest until it spontaneously starts into growth once more. If this should happen the plant may be considered to be 'confused'; it was probably imported and is mixing up the seasons. In winter little or no water is needed.
Feeding It is unnecessary to feed.
Repotting Repot in spring using a potting mixture containing leafmould and clay.
Propagation Increase from imported seed. The plants must be raised at a high temperature.

Pachypodium brevicaule
○⊜◎⊛◎
This lumpy plant looks like a stone. The leaves are arranged in a rosette and are 2 to 3cm (¾ to 1in) long, about 1cm (½in) wide, and interspersed with a few thorns.
Pachypodium geayi
Young plants are unbranched. The stem

Pachystachys lutea

is greyish in colour and covered in tubercles and hairy brown thorns, with linear leaves to 20cm (8in) long and 6mm (¼in) wide, brown-green and hairy.

Pachypodium lameri
In this species the thorns are hairless and the leaves are wider, up to 11cm (4½ in); they are up to 40cm (16in) long. The colour is bright green.

Pachypodium succulentum
A species with a short, thick trunk and linear leaves, hairy on the upper surface, smooth underneath, with two thorns at the base.

Other species or cultivars may occasionally be available.

Pachystachys

Acanthaceae

Name From the Greek *pachys*, thick, and *stachus*, stalk.
Origin The species described below is a native of Mexico and Peru. It is a so-called 'new' plant, but in actual fact it was already cultivated in the late 19th century and is mentioned in old books.
Description The pachystachys is reminiscent of a yellow beloperone with an erect-growing inflorescence, or of an aphelandra. It is related to both these genera.
Position The plants must be cultivated in a high temperature and in high humidity. In winter they may be kept a little cooler. In other words, they are greenhouse plants which will survive for a short time in the living-room – apparently not very well however, for after their successful re-introduction in the early seventies interest in these plants is now rapidly on the wane.
Care The plant develops yellow bracts which enclose the white flowers. The latter do not last long, but fortunately the yellow bracts, which are the plant's most decorative feature, keep much longer. It is a pity that when a plant is moved (in other words after being purchased) the entire inflorescence is often lost, flowers, bracts and all. However, if the plant is correctly tended, new shoots will appear in the course of time and these will develop inflorescences at the tip, with bracts and flowers.

If the plant is kept indoors the foliage must be sprayed regularly at this time. The plant needs plenty of light and tolerates even the brightest midday sun. The more light, the more compact and vigorous the plant.

In winter this plant should be kept a few degrees cooler. In spring it should be cut back a little and if all goes well it will start into growth once again.
Watering In the period of growth the compost must remain moderately moist. Tap water is acceptable. In winter it can be kept a little drier, but make sure that the foliage does not wilt.
Feeding When the new growth appears the plant may be given a fortnightly dose of a standard preparation.
Repotting The plant has proved to grow very well in standard potting compost. It should be repotted in spring, preferably in plastic pots with a drainage layer of crocks.
Propagation Non-flowering shoots will readily strike under glass or plastic with some degree of soil heat. After they have rooted they should be grouped in threes in 12-cm (5-in) pots. To prevent them becoming too tall and lanky the young plants should be stopped once or twice to encourage branching. The more terminal shoots there are, the more profuse the flowering.

Pachystachys lutea
A small shrub with angular green branches and pointed oval leaves, bright green with conspicuous veining. The inflorescence consists of erect-growing bright yellow bracts enclosing the white flowers.

× Pachyveria

Crassulaceae

Name A combination of the generic names *Echeveria* and *Pachyphytum*. The × indicates the results of intergeneric crossing.
Origin The work of cross-fertilisation started more than a century ago.
Description As far as their characteristics are concerned, these plants come halfway between both parents. They do not have the thin, spatula-shaped leaves of the echeveria, nor the sometimes cylindrical or egg-shaped leaves of a pachyphytum. Instead they still have very thick, spatula-shaped leaves, arranged in a recognisable rosette.
Position Like both parents, these are plants for the cool greenhouse but they will tolerate a position on the window-sill in a warm room.
Care In summer, that is, from the end of May onwards, these plants may be moved outside, provided they are given a very sunny and sheltered position. Indoors they must be found a south-facing window.

In winter these succulents may be kept very cool and dry. This will have a positive effect on flowering and on the fine colouring and bloom of the foliage. The lowest admissable temperature is about 5°C (41°F).
Watering These succulents do not require a great deal of water. In summer water moderately to sparingly, depending on the temperature and amount of sun, and in winter give little or no water. However, the leaves must not be allowed to shrivel; if that happens give them a little more water, at room temperature.
Feeding Feeding is not recommended; the plants would lose their character and might easily rot.
Repotting This is best done in spring, after the dormant season. Special cactus mixture, commercially available or mixed at home (see page 70), is very suitable. It must be porous but must nevertheless retain some moisture.
Propagation The easiest method is to remove some leaves, leave them to dry for a few days and root them in a mixture of sand and peat which is initially kept almost completely dry. Tip cuttings will also strike and seed is available too.

× ***Pachyveria*** **'Clavata'**
A cross between an unknown *Echeveria* species and *Pachyphytum bracteosum*, achieved in France in 1874. It has spatula-shaped leaves, blue-green, with little bloom; the colouring is hardly affected by the sun. There are small flowers with an orange-red corolla.

× *Pachyveria* 'Glauca'; the plant in the foreground is a *Sedum stahlii*

× ***Pachyveria*** **'Clavifolia'**
The same parents. The foliage is in an elongated rosette; the leaves are 5cm (2in) long, 1.5cm (½in) wide and 5mm (¼in) thick, widest above the mid-line. Both surfaces are rounded, blue-green with reddish margins. The flowers are powdery white outside, red inside.

× ***Pachyveria*** **'Glauca'**
Probably *Echeveria glauca* × *Pachyveria compactum*. A sessile rosette of 6cm (2¼in) long, 1.5-cm (½-in) wide and 1-cm (½-in) thick leaves, level on the upper surface and rounded on the reverse. They are pointed, grey-green and coated with bloom. It bears red flowers which are yellow inside.

Pandanus

Pandanaceae

Screw Pine

Name From *pandang*, a popular Malay name. The plant owes the name Screw Pine to the fact that the leaves are arranged in a spiral round the stem.
Origin No fewer than 600 species occur in Madagascar, the Indian archipelago, and islands in the Pacific. Only a few are grown as greenhouse or house plants.
Description Stately plants, especially when they grow older, with very long arching leaves, sharply spined along the edges.
Position The pandanus enjoys very humid air and not too low a temperature. It is therefore a greenhouse plant, but properly looked after it will thrive in the living-room as well.
Care The first essential is a well-lit position, but not in full sun. Give the plant plenty of room, for it may grow very large, as you will see in the photograph on page 34.

The temperature must not fall below 18°C (64°F). It is therefore not a plant which may occasionally be moved outside. Too low a temperature at any time may cause it to die several months later.

In winter the pandanus may be kept in the warm living-room. The dry atmosphere will create difficulties and it is therefore advisable to spray the foliage with lime-free water (to avoid staining) or to purchase a humidifier.
Watering Preferably use lime-free water and never pour water among the leaves. In summer water sparingly. From September onwards keep the compost a little drier. The water must always be at room temperature, especiallly in winter.
Feeding In the period of active growth the pandanus likes plenty of nourishment, and a fortnightly dose of fertiliser is recommended.
Repotting Young plants may have to be repotted several times a year. As they age, once a year in spring is sufficient. A proprietary potting compost is satisfactory, but the addition of some clay and rotted beach leaves is even better. Make sure that excess water can drain away easily, and avoid the fashionable cylinder pots without drainage holes, unless you have an efficient moisture meter.
Propagation Older plants develop suckers at the base. These can be removed and rooted under glass at a temperature of 20 to 25°C (68 to 77°F).

Young specimen of *Pandanus veitchii*. A much larger plant is illustrated on page 34

Pandanus baptistii
◐⊜⊘⊛▣
A species without spines along the leaves, which are sunken along the midrib. It has lengthwise yellow stripes.
Pandanus sanderi
This has long leaves, the lower ones arching, with very fine spines along the margins and lengthwise yellow striping.
Pandanus veitchii
Very similar to the previous species. The leaf edges are slightly more coarsely spined, but the main difference lies in the pure white lengthwise striping in the leaves. Mature plants develop beautiful stilt-like aerial roots; the same applies to the other species. This is the best-known species.
Pandanus utilis
A species with blue-green, unstriped leaves and red-brown spines along the margins. It may be kept a little cooler, down to 16°C (60°F).

Paphiopedilum
Orchidaceae
Venus's Slipper

Name *Paphia* was another name for Venus; *pedilum* means slipper. It is sometimes called *Cypripedium*.
Origin About 50 botanical species are distributed over the entire Indian archipelago, where they grow terrestrially.
Description Plants without pseudobulbs. The flowers have a very striking sepal, usually called the flag, and the 'slipper' which is the lip of the flower.
Position There are hothouse species and species for the temperate greenhouse. *Paphiopedilum callosum* and *Paphiopedilum sukhakulii* occasionally succeed in the living-room, preferably near a north- or east-facing window.
Care All species require plenty of light in winter, but filtered light between February and October. The relative humidity must be high, but in summer good ventilation must be provided, especially at night. A dormant season is rarely required, but if the temperature drops in winter the water supply must naturally be decreased to some extent.

It is easy to see which species belong in the hothouse and which in the temperate greenhouse. Species with evergreen foliage must be cultivated in temperate conditions, which means a minimum winter temperature of 14°C (57°F). There is one exception, namely *Paphiopedilum insigne*, for which the temperature may drop to 10°C (50°F). This species must be kept as cool as possible, particularly in summer.

Species with marked foliage should be grown in a hothouse at a minimum winter temperature of 18°C (64°F).
Watering Always use rainwater or demineralised water. On sunny days the plants may be sprayed in the morning, but usually it is sufficient to water them properly once a week.

Paphiopedilum callosum should be kept completely dry for a few weeks after being repotted.
Feeding When they are in growth the plants may be given small doses of lime-free fertiliser.
Repotting An old-fashioned potting mixture consists of 95 per cent chopped sphagnum moss and 5 per cent finely chopped tree fern. A more modern medium is made up of 20 per cent granular peat and 80 per cent perlite. If the latter mixture is used the plant must be fed a little more often in summer. Green-leaved species should be repotted in February, the others in June. Provide a good layer of crocks for drainage.
Propagation Increase by division when the plants are repotted.

Paphiopedilum callosum
●⊜⊘⊛▢
Leaves up to 25cm (10in) long, pale blue-green. The flower is 10cm (4in) across, with a striped white flag and a purple-brown slipper. It flowers in March–July.
Paphiopedilum fairieanum
This has linear leaves, to 15cm (6in), and flowers to 6cm (2¼in) across. The flag is greenish-white with violet streaks; the petals are yellowish with violet streaks. There is a brownish-green lip with purple-red veining. Flowers appear in July–September.

Paphiopedilum sukhakulii

Paphiopedilum hybrid 'Memoria F. M. Ogilvie'

Paphiopedilum insigne

This species has pale green foliage and flowers up to 13 cm (5 in) across, yellowish green on long, hairy, purple stalks, and a flag with red-brown streaks and blotches, white at the tip. The petals curve forward and are veined with brown; the lip is marked with brown. There are numerous strains, among others 'Sanderae' with yellow flowers, flag whiter towards the tip, finely speckled at the base. It flowers October–January.

Paphiopedilum niveum

The dark green foliage with grey marking is purple on the reverse. Flowers are up to 8 cm (3 in) across, white with a few scattered red speckles; the flag is practically circular, the lip small and oval. Flowering season is April–August.

Paphiopedilum spicerianum

The green leaves are up to 25 cm (10 in) long and the flowers are 6 cm (2¼ in) across. The snowy-white flag, slightly greenish at the base, has a lengthwise purple central stripe. The petals are green with fine brown speckles, and the slipper brownish with violet spots. It flowers November–January.

Paphiopedilum sukhakulii

The dark green leaves with pale green marking are 25 cm (10 in) long. Flowers are 14 cm (5½ in) across, the pale green flag has dark lengthwise striping and the sharply pointed petals are pale green with violet speckles; the slipper is pale green with red-brown marking. It flowers October–November.

From left to right *Paphiopedilum venustum, P. spicerianum* and *P. fairieanum*

Paphiopedilum venustum

This has grey-marbled leaves, pale brownish purple on the reverse. The flag is whitish with green stripes. There are spreading petals, reddish or greenish at the base; the point is brown with small black warts. The slipper is yellow-green with green veining. Flowering season is November–January. Although it has marked foliage, this particular species must be cultivated in cool conditions.

Paphiopedilum villosum

With glossy green foliage and flowers to 12 cm (4½ in) across, the flag is olive brown, brown-purple from the base to the centre, with a narrow white margin. The petals are broad, yellow-brown, darker above, with a dark purple-brown central stripe and the slipper is yellow-brown with pale veining. Flowering season is December–April.

Parodia

Cactaceae

Name Named after Domingo Parodi, a Paraguayan botanist.

Origin About 40 species occur in Argentina, Bolivia, Brazil and Paraguay.

Description Spherical cacti, some becoming cylindrical as they age, with fine thorn formation and large flowers even early in life. The plants are frequently grafted, although not all species need this.

Position In summer the plants must be kept in full sun, either on the window-sill or in the greenhouse, but if they are not kept very cool in winter parodias will not flower in the following year.

Care These are ideal cacti for the amateur, especially where there is little space available. The plants grow fairly slowly and produce clusters of flowers at an early age.

The best winter temperature is 9 to 12°C (48 to 53°F), but provided they are kept very dry the plants may be placed with other cacti in a cool greenhouse, where a minimum temperature of 5°C (41°F) is usually maintained in this season.

Watering In summer the plants must be kept moderately moist, in winter dry. Use rainwater at room temperature. The neck of the root is soon affected by water and it is therefore better to plunge the plants.

Feeding In summer the cacti may be given a measure of special nitrogen-free cactus fertiliser once every three weeks.

Repotting In spring the plants may be repotted in the well-known cactus mixture consisting of potting compost and perlite. Other mixtures are sometimes used as well. Plastic pots are very suitable.

Propagation Most species do not produce offsets and so it is difficult to obtain cuttings. We are therefore dependent on seed. Germination is fairly easy, but the seedlings grow very slowly at first. It is quite difficult to keep the seedtray free of algae. First sterilise the seed compost and keep the operation as sterile as possible. After about four months the seedlings can be grafted on to suitable stock. In the first year they must be protected from the brightest sunlight.

Pests and diseases Rotting at the base is the result of incorrect watering. Water carefully, preferably from the bottom.

Parodia suprema

Parodia mutabilis

Parodia aureispina

A spherical cactus, up to 12 cm (4½ in) in diameter. Every areole bears about 40 fine radial thorns and four firm, golden-yellow centrals, one of which is hooked. It bears golden-yellow flowers, 3 cm (1 in) across.

Parodia chrysacanthion

A flattened spherical yellow-thorned cactus, 12 cm (4½ in) across. The areoles are arranged in spirals. There are 20 to 40 pale yellow radial thorns, and four straight centrals; yellow flowers, felty and white on the outside.

Parodia maassii

This forms a bright green sphere with woolly hairs on the crown and firm brown thorns, one of them curved. The flowers are coppery red in colour.

Parodia microsperma

A spherical cactus, to 10 cm (4 in) in diameter, it has transparent radial thorns and red-brown central thorns; one of them is hooked. The flowers are orange-red or yellow.

Parodia mutabilis

A spherical cactus up to 8 cm (3 in) in diameter. Dense thorn formation consists of about 50 hair-fine white radial thorns and four yellow or red-brown hooked centrals. The flowers are yellow.

Parodia nivosa

A cylindrical cactus 15 cm (6 in) tall and 8 cm (3 in) in diameter. The crown bears woolly hairs. There are numerous fine white radial thorns and four large white centrals, and pale red flowers.

Parodia ritteri

Cylindrical as it ages, and up to 10 cm (4 in) in diameter, the body is densely covered in thorns; 10 to 14 straight, spreading radials and one to four slightly curved central thorns. The thorns are initially rose red in colour, later becoming pink and white spotted. The flowers are blood red to brown-red.

Parodia suprema

The blue-green cactus body is divided into 15 to 25 ribs. The colour of the thorns varies between whitish through yellow-brown to black, and it has scarlet flowers. This plant is sometimes regarded as a variety of *P. maassii*.

Parthenocissus henryana

Parthenocissus
Vitaceae
Virginia Creeper

Name From the Greek *parthenos*, virgin, and *kissos*, ivy.
Origin The species described here is a native of China and is one of the few which are not entirely hardy. Other ivy-type species are often grown in the garden.
Description A deciduous climber with palmate, fairly thick leaves with some white along the veins.
Position The species described is almost hardy and can therefore be kept very cool. An ideal climber for the unheated greenhouse, it is also suitable for practically unheated stairwells or corridors.
Care The plant is capable of attaching itself, but if the wall is very smooth it will need some support. It is seldom grown in the living-room, although it is quite suitable for the purpose so long as the environment is not too warm in winter. In fact, this is not so important, for in autumn the foliage will drop in any case and the bare stems will not be greatly affected by warmth. The only problem is that in such temperatures the parthenocissus may start into growth too early, and in the dark season the light will be insufficient for the young foliage.
Watering In summer keep the plant reasonably moist; in winter, when the foliage has dropped, the compost should be kept barely moist. Ordinary tap water is acceptable.
Feeding Apply a solution of fertiliser every fortnight in the growing season.
Repotting Repot in spring using standard potting compost, or add a little loam or clay.
Propagation In summer, half-ripe tip cuttings may be successfully rooted under glass with some degree of soil heat. The cuttings will strike quickly. The growing tip should be pinched out from time to time.

Parthenocissus henryana
A clinging climber with angular stems and palmate foliage. The leaves are 3 to 5 cm (1 to 2 in) long, smooth, somewhat thickened, and dark green with white marking along the veins, tinged with pink. In autumn the colour of the foliage may become a beautiful red, but it is doubtful whether this will happen indoors, where it is too warm. The small green flowers are arranged in plumes.

Passiflora
Passifloraceae
Passion Flower

Name From the Latin *passio*, suffering, and *flos*, flower. The inflorescence of *Passiflora caerulea* is said to be symbolic of aspects of the Passion of Christ. The ten petals were seen as the ten good apostles (excluding Peter and Judas), or, according to other views, the ten commandments. The five upper petals were linked to the five main events (birth, suffering, death, interment and hell). The three-coloured corona: the purple cloak in which Christ appeared before Herod. The centre of the corona is white: the cloak in which Christ was sent back to Pontius Pilate by Herod. The brown interior: the seamless linen cloak. The stigma: the sponge. Below the stigma five points: the five wounds. The cross on the stigmata: the three nails with which Christ was nailed to the cross, and the stalked ovary: the Lord's goblet. Other examples might be given.
Origin Most of the 400 species occur in tropical zones of America, some in subtropical areas and a few in Australia, Polynesia and tropical Asia.
Description These are climbers with very striking flowers and beautiful, sometimes edible, fruits. Only a few of the species are cultivated as house or greenhouse plants.
Position No problems arise if the plants are grown in a greenhouse. In coastal areas and occasionally inland *Passiflora caerulea* can be grown outside in a sheltered spot against a south-facing wall. A few species will for a time remain in good condition in the living-room.
Care The strongest and fairly generally available species is *Passiflora caerulea*. In summer this plant may be kept in a sunny spot in the living-room, with the tendrils trained round and round a wire hoop. However, in winter it must be kept very cool: 5 to 10°C (41 to 50°F) is the ideal temperature. It appears that the plant will tolerate slightly greater extremes of warmth and for that reason it is frequently planted out in a good-sized hole made in a sunny, sheltered terrace, or a reasonably sized container on the balcony will also serve. During the first few years the foot of the plant should be protected. In such a position the Passion Flower can grow very large and produce thousands of flowers every year. These are followed by orange fruits. This method of cultivation is certainly preferable.

Passiflora caerulea

The Passion Flower symbolises the Passion of Christ

The other species, which require more warmth, are better grown in a cool greenhouse (minimum temperature in winter 5°C (41°F). They will do best if planted out in the soil. The tendrils may be trained along the framework of the greenhouse, and initially it will be necessary to tie them here and there. They must be screened from bright sun.
Watering In summer the plants require a great deal of water, but little is needed in winter. The foliage may turn yellow, but must not drop.
Feeding In summer Passion Flowers will take plenty of nourishment, especially if they are growing out of doors.
Repotting If they are not planted out in the garden or the greenhouse, young plants must be repotted every year. Use loamy potting compost or a standard mixture. The plants should be severely cut back when they are repotted, and must be kept out of full sun for some time afterwards.
Propagation The easiest method is to remove the runners. In addition half-ripe tip cuttings may be rooted under glass in warm conditions. Ripe fruits may yield seed capable of germinating, but plants grown by this method do not usually flower well. Imported seed is sometimes available.

Passiflora violacea

Pests and diseases If they have been kept too warm in winter the plants will be susceptible to mealy bug, and excessively dry air in summer may lead to an attack by red spider mite.

Passiflora caerulea
A climbing shrub with deeply incised foliage. The five to seven lobes are lanceolate in shape. The flowers grow singly, and are up to 10 cm (4 in) in diameter, slightly fragrant, greenish white. The petals are blue at the tip, white in the middle and purple at the base. The cultivar 'Constance Elliott' has white flowers with a little blue.

Passiflora quadrangularis
A vigorous climber, too large for a small greenhouse. It has winged stems and oval leaves, and very large fragrant flowers, white, red and purple, followed by edible fruits, yellow-green with a little purple; they are occasionally sold at the greengrocer's. This species requires a minimum temperature of 14°C (57°F) in winter.

Passiflora racemosa
Climber with alternate leaves, deeply incised into three lobes; occasionally the leaves are not incised. The leaf stalk is 5 cm (2 in) long, usually with four glands. It bears pendulous clusters of up to 20 unscented flowers, each to 12 cm (4½ in) across, red with conspicuous tube.

Passiflora violacea
The leaves are divided into three lobes, sometimes partly fused; the upper surface is green, the reverse grey-green. The flowers are at most 10 cm (4 in) in diameter, fragrant, and grow on long stalks. The colour is purple-pink with violet and some white.

In addition to the species described above there are innumerable hybrids which are occasionally to be found.

Pavonia

Malvaceae

Name Named after the Spanish explorer José Pavon, who died in 1844.
Origin Nearly 200 species are known, distributed over tropical regions of America, as well as in Africa, Asia and Australia.
Description Small shrubs with striking red sepals and a purplish corona.
Position This is a plant for the temperate greenhouse, where it benefits from the high degree of humidity. Lately it has sometimes become available for indoor cultivation.
Care When the plant is cultivated in the living-room, there is the problem of dry air to contend with. The 40 per cent level of relative humidity often encountered in centrally heated rooms is far too low for most plants, and certainly for the pavonia. Try to move it to a cooler room in winter; the minimum temperature should be 12°C (53°F). The degree of relative humidity will automatically be higher in such an environment.

In summer it must be placed in good light, but kept out of full sun, and the foliage should be sprayed every day. Buds will appear when no more leaves are developed.
Watering In summer the plant must always be kept moderately moist. In winter give a little less water, but do not let the compost dry out. Ordinary tap water may be used.
Feeding Give some fertiliser every fortnight in the growing season.
Repotting Repot in spring in an acid, humusy mixture, such as rotted leafmould and conifer needle compost, mixed with rotted cow manure. Cut back the stems to half their length.
Propagation In spring or autumn tip cuttings can be taken, dipped in rooting powder and rooted in a soil temperature of 30 to 35°C (86 to 95°F), but it is not an easy matter. The new plants must be raised in warm and humid conditions.

Pavonia multiflora
◐ ⊜ ⓥ ⊛ ▢
This species is a shrub covered in radial hairs. The oblong leaves are 15 to 20 cm (6 to 8 in) long, 4 to 5 cm (1½ to 2 in) wide. Erect-growing flowers are borne in terminal racemes; there are numerous red bracts, linear and hairy, and longer than the red sepals. The petals are dull purple in colour and remain closed. The blue-grey stamens protrude long before flowering.

Pavonia multiflora

Pedilanthus tithymaloides 'Variegatus'

Pedilanthus

Euphorbiaceae

Name From the Greek *pedilon*, shoe, and *lanthanos*, concealed.
Origin About 15 species are known; they occur mainly in Central America.
Description The plant looks as if it is diseased: it has zigzag branches and curled foliage. The milky sap is extremely poisonous.
Position A hothouse plant, striking because of its unusual habit. It is occasionally grown indoors, with reasonable success.
Care Practically the only form cultivated is *Pedilanthus tithymaloides* 'Variegatus', with variegated foliage, which requires plenty of light to retain its colouring. Only the brightest sunlight, between 10 a.m. and 5 p.m., must be screened. The plant does not need a high degree of humidity; on the contrary, this would cause mildew. It would therefore be quite a suitable plant for the living-room, but it is rarely seen.

In winter the plant can stay in the warm living-room. A few leaves will probably fall, when it may do better in a lower temperature.
Watering In summer the compost must always be kept moderately moist, and in winter a little drier. Ordinary tap water is acceptable.
Feeding In summer a normal measure of fertiliser should be given once a fortnight.
Repotting In spring, after the dormant season, the plant should be repotted in a proprietary standard potting compost.
Propagation Tip cuttings can be taken in the spring; they are dipped in hot water to make the sap coagulate and left to dry for a day before being rooted in a soil temperature of 25°C (77°F). When the plants are established pinch out the growing point from time to time to encourage branching.
Pests and diseases Too high a degree of humidity will lead to mildew. Aphids may also occur.

Pedilanthus tithymaloides
◐ ⊜ ⓥ ⊛ ▣
Jacob's Ladder. A shrub with zigzagging green stems, somewhat fleshy, and 5- to 8-cm (2- to 3-in) long, oval to lanceolate leaves, slightly rounded and pale green. It bears small flowers with bright red bracts. The form most generally cultivated is 'Variegatus', in which the leaves have a white margin, lightly tinged with pink.

Pelargonium

Geraniaceae

Geranium

Name From the Greek *Pelargos*, stork. Amateurs always call this plant by the name Geranium, but the plant should be distinguished from the garden plant of that botanical name.
Origin There are about 250 wild species, mainly occurring in South Africa.
Description In addition to the generally known house and garden geraniums which are grouped in the categories *Pelargonium zonale, P. peltatum*, and *P. grandiflorum* (see below), there are succulent species which lose all their foliage in winter, and scented gernaiums, which are grown for the fragrance of their leaves. There are also a number of natural species which come somewhere in between, but these are rarely grown by amateurs.
Position The so-called balcony geraniums, which include hybrids of *P. zonale* and *P. peltatum*, may be grown out of doors from the end of May onwards. They require full sun. The French Geranium, that is, the *P. grandiflorum* type, is more sensitive to cold

Pelargonium zonale hybrid 'Friesdorf'

Pelargonium zonale hybrid 'Dawn'

Pelargonium zonale hybrid with white-edged leaves

Pelargonium zonale hybrids with tricoloured foliage, such as this cultivar 'Mrs Pollock', are surprisingly little known

Pelargonium × citrosum 'Variegatum'

Pelargonium graveolens 'Variegatum'

and is usually cultivated indoors. It makes an excellent house plant. The special variegated forms of *Pelargonium zonale* are best grown under glass, lightly screened. The scented geraniums make strong house plants.

Care In general geraniums require sun to be able to flourish. Even the 'common' geraniums have slightly succulent stems, which means that they need little water. In winter all species must be kept cool, since otherwise they continue to grow and become limp and discoloured because of insufficient light. The strong garden geraniums, that is the *P. zonale* and *P. peltatum* groups, tolerate minimum temperatures to nearly 0°C (32°F). *P. grandiflorum* types should be kept at a minimum of 8 to 10°C (46 to 50°F), and so should the other botanical species and scented geraniums. Very succulent species should be kept at a minimum temperature of 10 to 12°C (50 to 53°F) in winter, that is, in the conditions prevailing in a temperate greenhouse.

Garden geraniums as well as the French or *P. grandiflorum* types are usually carried over from one year to another only if particularly large or long plants are required; if not, cuttings should be taken in August and the old plants discarded. Standard geraniums, such as are sometimes seen in public parks and gardens, are cultivated by training one shoot vertically upwards, removing all other shoots and keeping the plant in this state for one or two winters. It is then left to grow naturally. Needless to say strains which grow tall of their own accord are used for this purpose.

It is incorrect to keep geraniums in a dark cellar in winter, as is sometimes done. The temperature need only be a few degrees too high for the plants to start into growth. They will then develop long, pale shoots which will exhaust the plants. Burying them in the garden, although rather a drastic measure, is preferable.

Scented geraniums are sometimes kept in the warm living-room in winter, since the flowers are in any case not their main feature. Provided the plants are shaped a little in spring this is perfectly reasonable.

Watering The pelargonium is satisfied with little water. However, on a sunny day the French Geranium, in particular, with its large, soft leaves evaporates a good deal. But you should never overwater, for if there is one way of killing the plants it is by drowning them. In winter plants which are kept cool may remain practically dry. The others should be given only just enough water to prevent them collapsing.

Feeding Rapidly growing geraniums, that is, the garden plants, benefit especially from an occasional dose of fertiliser in summer. Succulent species should not be fed and strains with variegated foliage should be fed sparingly, since otherwise they may lose their fine marking.

Repotting Most species will thrive in standard potting compost. Good drainage must be provided, for the plants dislike excess water. Succulent species are best grown in cactus compost: that is, a very porous mixture.

Propagation The geranium owes its popularity mainly to the fact that it is so easily grown from cuttings. A tip is removed, left to dry a little, and inserted in a sandy mixture – success is guaranteed. The best time is mid-August; you will then have rooted plants before the winter which are strong and take up little space. The old plants are usually discarded because they will have lost some of their beauty. Geranium flowers are at their best in the first and second year.

It is now possible to obtain seed of some of the garden forms. This should be sown in January, in warm conditions, to provide flowering plants in May. Unfortunately these strains are not among the most beautiful and this method of cultivation is chiefly intended to propagate an enormous number of bedding plants in a short time. Succulent species are also best grown from seed. They can be grown from cuttings, but the plant is mutilated

Pelargonium grandiflorum 'Maréchal Foch'

Pelargonium grandiflorum hybrid

Pelargonium zonale hybrid, several years old

Pelargonium zonale hybrid 'Horace Read'

to some extent if the tips are removed.
Pests and diseases Aphids and whitefly may eat into the foliage. Virus diseases and other problems fortunately only occur in mass cultivation; amateurs rarely face these difficulties. Grey mould will result from stagnant water.

Pelargonium carnosum
○⊜◎⊛▢
A very succulent species with a short stem, 4 to 5cm (1½ to 2in) in diameter, to 15cm (6in) tall. It has deeply incised leaves and pink flowers.
Pelargonium* × *citrosum
○◐⊜◎⊛▣
Syn. *Pelargonium crispum*. Lemon-scented Geranium. A cross-breed with short-stalked, frizzy, toothed leaves, 1 to 2cm (½ to ¾in) across, and lemon scented. It bears clusters of pink flowers with darker veining on 5-cm (2-in) flower stalks. In 'Variegatum' the foliage is blotched with white.
***Pelargonium grandiflorum* hybrids**
French or Odier Geraniums. These are the results of crossing *Pelargonium grandiflorum*, *Pelargonium cordatum* and others. They have fairly thin stems and green leaves 4 to 10cm (1½ to 4in) across with an undulate margin. The flowers grow in umbels to 6cm (2¼in) across in a variety of colours, always with a darker patch. These strains flower under the influence of a short day when the length of day is less than 12 hours, and also a long day provided the temperature remains below 10°C (50°F). Both conditions can be produced by artificial means, most easily in summer when the plants do not usually flower, but cooling down in summer is not very practical. Normally they are short-day plants.

Pelargonium graveolens
Rose-scented Geranium. A spreading plant with palmately divided, deeply incised fragrant leaves, blue-green in colour. It has rose-red flowers with a deep violet patch on the two upper petals. 'Variegatum' has white-edged foliage.
***Pelargonium peltatum* hybrids**
○⊜◎⊛▣
Ivy-leaved or Trailing Geraniums. These have straggling, soft stems and shield-shaped pentagonal green leaves, 5 to 8cm (2 to 3in) across, fleshy and glossy. The leaf stalk is attached just inside the margin. The plant bears lilac, rose-red, and white flowers, and is really suitable only for the balcony or hanging basket.
Pelargonium radens
○◐⊜◎⊛▣
Lemon-scented Geranium (there are at least four lemon-scented species). It has scented palmate leaves, 5 to 8cm (2 to 3in) across, with narrow pinnate lobes like crow's feet. Short-stalked flowers are arranged in umbels; they are pink with darker veining.
***Pelargonium zonale* hybrids**
Syn. *Pelargonium* × *hortorum*. A very important group of hybrids, characterised by their thick, erect-growing, fleshy and hairy stems. The shield-shaped leaves have a darker ring, and are typically scented when bruised. Flowers appear in a variety of colours. The best-known garden and balcony geraniums belong to this group. There are also dwarf strains, such as 'Friesdorf', with fairly deeply incised foliage and narrow petals. The most unusual forms are those with foliage in the colours yellow, red and green in combination, such as 'Mrs Pollock'.

Pellaea
Sinopteridaceae

Name From the Greek *pellos*, black. This refers to the colour of the leaf stalks.
Origin About 80 species are known, growing mainly in dry areas of South America, South Africa and New Zealand.
Description Most species are xerophytes, which means that they grow in dry conditions, such as on rocks. They are well-known ferns with dark green leaves and a spreading habit.
Position The fact that these ferns have their native habitat in dry regions is useful in the warm living-room. Little moisture evaporates through the leathery foliage, but bright sunlight is harmful.
Care The plants are satisfied with little light and if necessary may be kept in a warm room throughout the year. However, it is better if the temperature can be lowered slightly in winter, perhaps to 12 to 15°C (53 to 59°F). Often a north-facing window is sufficient. The plant grows particularly well in a hanging basket.

Although the plant tolerates dry air, this does not mean that it would be wrong to spray the foliage from time to time: on the contrary, this will definitely promote growth.
Watering In their natural environment these plants grow on rocks, which means that they get little water, but are never entirely dry. The rocks in question retain water in narrow splits and a humus layer develops below the roots, protected from drying out by the plants themselves. The conclusion is that the compost should never completely dry out. Ordinary tap water is satisfactory.
Feeding In summer the plant may be fed every fortnight.
Repotting These plants have a very shallow root system, and wide shallow pots or bowls or hanging baskets should therefore be used. Give them particularly good drainage in the shape of a thick layer of crocks and do not forget

Pellaea falcata

the drainage holes. The potting mixture should consist of rotted beech leaves, rotted cow manure and peat, in equal quantities. Standard potting compost is sometimes successfully used. The plants enjoy a little lime.
Propagation It is possible to grow new plants from spores. These are found underneath the leaves of mature plants and should be sown under glass in a temperature of 18°C (64°F). They must be screened. A simpler method of propagation is to divide the plants when they are repotted.
Pests and diseases Few if any pests trouble this plant, but occasionally scale insects occur on the stems between the leaves.

Pellaea rotundifolia
●⊜◎⊛⊛▢
A fern with creeping rootstock. The fronds are 20 to 30cm (8 to 12in) long and 4cm (1½in) wide, pinnate; there are 10 to 20 pairs of pinnae, round to oval in shape, dark green and leathery.
Pellaea viridis
This has larger fronds, bipinnate; the leaves are paler green and triangular.

Pellaea rotundifolia

Pellionia pulchra

Pellionia repens

Pellionia
Urticaceae

Name Named after Alphonse Pellion, an 18th-century French officer who was a member of the Freycinet expedition. For a long time the genus was called *Elatostema*.
Origin In tropical and eastern Asia and in the islands of the Pacific 15 to 20 species occur.
Description Low-growing creeping plants, a kind of ground cover, with attractively marked foliage. The plants are related to the better known pilea (q.v.).
Position Because of their need for humid air they must in the first place be regarded as greenhouse plants. However, the degree of humidity in bottle gardens, glass cases, flower windows and even among other plants in mixed containers is sufficient and the plants will feel at home there.
Care If the pellionia is to be cultivated in a warm room it is essential to spray the foliage at frequent intervals. Another good method is to grow them above a bowl of water. This condition is particularly important in winter when the heating has been turned on. Bright sunlight is very undesirable, but the plants must be kept in good light if they are to keep their fine colouring. In winter the temperature may fall to 12°C (53°F), but it is not essential.
Watering It is best to use rainwater only. The compost must be kept moderately moist. In winter it may be a fraction drier if the temperature is lowered.
Feeding In summer the plants may be fed normally, that is, once a fortnight.
Repotting This may be done in spring, preferably in a mixture of rotted leafmould, rotted cow manure and peat. Use shallow plastic pots with a good layer of crocks to provide drainage. If the plants are used as ground cover they will be satisfied with the available compost, but they do not like too much lime.
Propagation Tip cuttings strike fairly readily under glass in compost heated to about 25°C (77°F). The cuttings should be rooted in groups in a pot in order to produce fine bushy plants. Young plants should initially be cultivated in warm and humid conditions, say 24°C (75°F).
Pests and diseases If the air is too dry, or if the plants are kept in a draught, red spider mite and aphids may occur.

Pellionia pulchra
Syn. *Elatostema pulchrum*. A creeping plant with somewhat fleshy stems; the leaves are oblique and oblong, 4 to 8 cm ($1\frac{1}{2}$ to 3 in) long and 2.4 cm (1 in) wide, very dark along the veins and olive green in between; the reverse is purple. The male flowers occur in stalked racemes, up to 10 cm (4 in) long, the female flowers in small, sessile clusters.
Pellionia repens
Syn. *Elatostema repens*; *Pellionia daveauana*. The upper surface of the leaves is olive green, tinged with brown and with a broad paler band in the centre.

Pentas
Rubiaceae

Name From the Greek *pente*, five.
Origin About 30 species occur in the Middle East, Malagasy and tropical Africa. In most tropical countries all over the world it is a well-known garden shrub.
Description A shrubby plant with carmine-red flowers arranged in racemes, it resembles the bouvardia.
Position It is a plant for a temperate greenhouse, where the air is not too dry.
Care In summer these plants are not difficult to grow. They must be kept in good light, but certainly not in full sun. It is advisable to pinch out the tips from time to time to encourage branching. Flower buds which may appear before September are better removed. The first flowers will then appear in September and the pentas can be brought into the living-room if the temperature can be kept on the low side. The foliage should be sprayed frequently.
Watering Overwatering will cause the leaves to turn yellow. Water with great care; never allow the compost to be more than moderately moist. After flowering the plants should be kept a little drier.
Feeding In summer feed every fortnight with one of the well-known preparations.
Repotting The best potting mixture consists of rotted leafmould with soil from molehills found on clay soil, but the plant will also do reasonably well in standard potting compost. Add a little perlite to assist drainage and put a few crocks in the bottom of the pot.
Propagation Young shoots may strike under glass with some bottom heat in March or April. When the plantlets are established they should be stopped once or twice. The plants can also be grown from seed, but the colour of the flowers will not be true to type.

Pentas lanceolata
Egyptian Star Cluster. A hairy, erect-growing shrub with pale green oval leaves 5 to 12 cm (2 to $4\frac{1}{2}$ in) long and 2.5 cm (1 in) across. Flowers grow in terminal clusters, white to carmine red. The corona has a narrow, 2-cm ($\frac{3}{4}$-in) long tube, widening slightly at the top, and ending in a five-lobed 'star'.

Pentas lanceolata

Peperomia
Piperaceae

Name The derivation is uncertain; possibly from the Greek *peperi*, pepper, and *omos*, resembling.
Origin At least 1000 species are known, most of them growing in tropical and subtropical regions of America, partly as epiphytes (growing on trees), partly growing terrestrially in tropical rain forests.
Description Most species are low-growing plants with a creeping or trailing habit, thick stems and fleshy foliage. They are semi-succulent; both the stem and the leaves may have the capacity to retain water. If one of the thick leaves is cut across, the water-retaining layer is clearly visible below the epidermis. The flowers usually consist of thin white spikes.
Position Since little water evaporates through the fairly hard, leathery leaves with their special water reservoir just below the epidermis, the plants usually tolerate the dry atmosphere in the living-room fairly well. They will also grow well in the more humid atmosphere of a temperate greenhouse.
Care Green-leaved species do not require much light and may thrive near a north-facing window. Bright sunshine is in any case fatal.

Variegated species need more light because they contain less chlorophyll. If these plants are kept too dark they will start to produce more chlorophyll to survive, with the result that they lose their fine marking.

In winter the temperature may fall to a minimum of 12°C (53°F) in the coldest nights; in other words, the temperature prevailing in a temperate greenhouse. Indoors the plants will do well if the mercury falls to about 16°C (60°F). During the day, when it is light, all species will tolerate living-room temperatures.

The glossy foliage may be sprayed from time to time with warm water, which must be lime free to avoid ugly staining.

Properly cared for, the plants will occasionally flower – quite an attractive sight. Do not remove the flowers until they have become unsightly.
Watering Too much cold water in winter may easily cause the stems to rot. Keeping the peperomia too dry will do far less harm than giving it too much water. When the plant starts to wilt you may still be able to save it by increasing the water supply a little, but once the

Peperomia serpens

Peperomia griseoargentea, showing the grey-green foliage with dark veining

Peperomia clusiifolia in flower

stems begin to rot it will be too late. In that case you will have to take cuttings.

Rainwater at room temperature is to be preferred to tap water with its harmful minerals and other pollution.

Feeding The plants need not grow very rapidly, but once they have started they may be given some fertiliser once a month. Use one of the established commercial preparations.

Repotting Since most species grow as epiphytes, they have a small root system, one which is, moreover, adapted to acid, humusy soil. After all, practically no lime is present on tree trunks or in the upper layers of jungle soil. The best potting mixture is therefore one you make yourself, consisting of rotted leaf-mould, some peat, rotted cow manure and a little sharp sand. It is quite possible to grow the plants on an epiphyte tree or in lattice baskets. Some sphagnum moss should be inserted between the roots and the tree.

If the plant is grown indoors use wide, shallow pots or bowls with good drainage.

Propagation Species which develop long shoots are best grown from tip cuttings or eye cuttings. These should preferably be taken in spring, inserted under glass and in warm compost. Species with rosettes of fleshy leaves are more easily grown from leaf cuttings. A leaf is cut with a piece of the stem attached; it is allowed to dry for a day before being inserted in a fairly dry, sandy mixture. Some bottom heat is advisable. The system in which a plastic bag is placed over the cutting is rather risky, for the cuttings rot easily. Cuttings should be rooted at regular intervals, for older plants do not always retain their beautiful appearance.

Occasionally it is possible to obtain seed, but unfortunately this is exceptional.

Pests and diseases The foliage will become drab coloured if the level of atmospheric humidity is too high or if the peperomia is kept too damp. Root rot is caused by poor drainage, too wet a compost, or water that is too cold. Scale insects may nibble the stems and the leaves. Slugs occasionally cause damage in greenhouses.

Peperomia argyreia

Syn. *Peperomia arifolia argyreia; Peperomia sandersii.* Shield-shaped leaves are borne on long red stalks; they have beautiful, half-moon-shaped silvery marking. The rest of the leaf is dark green.

Peperomia arifolia

An erect-growing plant with the same leaf shape as the previous species, but the surface is dark green and glossy.

Peperomia blanda

This species is densely haired all over. The leaves are arranged in groups of three or four; they are 3 to 6 cm (1 to 2¼ in) long and 1 to 2 cm (½ to ¾ in) wide, an elongated ellipse in shape and red on the underside.

Peperomia caperata

The leaf is approximately oval, 3.5 cm (1⅓ in) long and 2 to 3 cm (¾ to 1 in) wide. The unusual feature of this species is that the surface of the white and green blotched leaf is deeply corrugated and grooved between the veins. The white flower spikes protrude far above the plant. There are a number of varieties with different leaf shapes.

Peperomia clusiifolia

Syn. *Peperomia obtusifolia clusiifolia.* Closely resembles the species *P. obtusifolia* (see below), but the leaf stalk is lacking and the slightly curved leaf margin is red. The leaves are large and leathery.

Peperomia fraseri

Syn. *Peperomia resediflora.* This has erect-growing fleshy stems and circular to heart-shaped dark green leaves, usually arranged in whorls along the leaf stalk. There are fragrant white flower spikes.

Peperomia glabella

A vigorous species with trailing stems and heart-shaped, yellow, white and green-marked foliage, suitable as a hanging plant.

Peperomia griseoargentea

Syn. *Peperomia hederifolia.* Ivy Peperomia. The practically circular leaves are borne on long white, red-streaked stems. They are 6 cm (2¼ in) long, green with darker coloured veining. Between the veins the surface is deeply corrugated. The margin is lightly undulate and the lower surface of the leaf is pale green.

Peperomia incana

All parts are felty white; the leaves are oval to round.

Peperomia metallica

Slender, unbranched, erect-growing stems and lanceolate leaves, 2 cm (¾ in) long, on very short red leaf stalks. It has a metallic brown-green surface with grey and a bright green stripe in the centre. The reverse of the leaf is red veined.

Peperomia obtusifolia

Syn. *Peperomia magnoliifolia.* The thick, firm leaves on short stalks vary in shape

Peperomia blanda

Peperomia obtusifolia

Peperomia argyreia

Flower spike of *Peperomia fraseri*

Peperomia polybotrya with shield-shaped leaves and numerous flower spikes

Peperomia puteolata

but are usually 5 to 12 cm (2 to 4½ in) long and 3 to 5 cm (1 to 2 in) wide, glossy, with yellow-green patches. The strain 'Greengold' has more pronounced leaf marking.

Peperomia puteolata
A trailing plant with angular stems and slender, lanceolate, leathery leaves up to 10 cm (4 in) long, dark green, with five contrasting luminous yellow grooves in the surface.

Peperomia rotundifolia
Syn. *Peperomia nummulariifolia; Peperomia prostrata.* This species develops very thin creeping stems. A trailing plant; the circular leaves are only 1 cm (½ in) in diameter and the upper surface is usually marbled in brown and dark green.

Peperomia serpens
Syn. *Peperomia scandens.* Initially creeping stems, later they grow slightly erect. It has small leaves, broad oval or kidney shaped, fresh green with a waxy surface.

Peperomia velutina
This has hairy reddish stems and leaves 7 cm (2¾ in) long, 4 cm (1½ in) wide, dark green, slightly haired along the edges and at the tip. There are silvery stripes along the veins.

Peperomia verticillata
A plant covered in white hairs, with erect-growing red stems and small leaves in groups of four to six. They are 1 to 2 cm (½ to ¾ in) long, reverse oval in shape and blunt at the tip; green with paler veining.

Pereskia
Cactaceae
Barbados Gooseberry

Name Named after Fabrice de Peirese, 1582–1637, French botanist.
Origin About 20 species are known to grow in tropical areas of America and in the West Indies.
Description It is thought that this plant is a transitional form between ordinary foliage plants and cacti. The stems bear felty areoles with strong thorns. In our climate the plant hardly ever flowers.
Position In summer it may be kept in the living-room, but in winter it should preferably be kept at a lower temperature.
Care The pereskia should always be kept in full sun; this brings out the beauty of the olive-coloured foliage. The leaves seldom need to be sprayed. Towards autumn the leaves become greener and some or all of them will fall. The plants should then be kept drier and the temperature may drop to 10°C (50°F).
Watering Unlike other cacti these plants require a fair amount of water in summer. Ordinary tap water is satisfactory.

Pereskia aculeata

In winter, when the leaves have fallen, the plants may be kept practically dry.
Feeding In the growing season give a measure of fertiliser solution once a fortnight.
Repotting Repot in spring in standard potting compost. Provide good drainage by means of crocks or perlite.
Propagation In summer half-ripe tip cuttings can be rooted under glass in a sandy mixture. Give them some bottom heat and remove some of the foliage. The plant can also be propagated from seed sown in spring, in which case the soil temperature should be 22°C (71°F).

Pereskia aculeata
Syn. *Peireskia.* A climbing shrub with long stems. The pale green leaves are 5 to 7 cm (2 to 2¾ in) long, oval to oblong, with a short point. Short thorns are arranged in pairs and usually curved. Flowers are borne in small groups, 3 to 4 cm (1 to 1½ in) across; they are yellow-pink with a disagreeable scent. The form most commonly cultivated is 'Godseffiana' with olive-green leaves, tinged with a little red.

Perilepta
Acanthaceae

Name From the Greek *peri*, around, and *leptos*, thin. The plant is often called by its former name *Strobilanthes.*
Origin About eight different species occur in tropical forests in Asia.
Description Herbaceous plants with particularly beautiful foliage with metallic marking.
Position A plant for a humid hothouse. It may temporarily be kept indoors or even in the garden.
Care Only young plants present the characteristic foliage marking. As the shoots age, or if the plant is kept too cool (in principle they may be kept out of doors), the fine colouring will be lost.
Bright sunshine must be avoided, for this too affects the development of the beautiful colours. The perilepta likes to be kept in good light, but the very brightest light must be filtered.
In winter it can stay in the hothouse. Mature plants will have done their duty if they survive long enough to provide cuttings.
Watering The compost must always be kept moderately moist. Ordinary tap water may be used, but rainwater is better.
Feeding Since new plants are constantly being raised from cuttings and grown in fresh compost, they need not be fed.
Repotting The plants will thrive in standard potting compost, but a home-made mixture of leafmould, rotted cow manure and rotted turves is of course better.
Propagation Increasing stock is important, because only young plants possess the fine colouring. You should therefore frequently take cuttings. Tip cuttings will strike readily in a heated tray, under glass. If the growing tips are pinched out the plants will branch, but the leaves will be smaller.

Perilepta dyeriana
Syn. *Strobilanthes dyerianus.* A roughly haired shrub with square twigs and long oval leaves sheathing the stalks. The upper surface is bright green, violet between the veins, later turning grey or violet all over. The under-surface is purple. Pale violet flowers are arranged in spikes.

Perilepta dyeriana

Persea
Lauraceae
Avocado Pear

Name The ancient Greek name for an Egyptian tree which bore fruits on its trunk. The name was later transferred to the Avocado Pear.
Origin About 135 species occur in North and South America, a few in South East Asia and one in the Canary Islands.
Description A strong house plant with beautiful pale green leaves. In cultivation it does not produce fruit.
Position It can stay in the warm living-room throughout the year, but it is better to keep the persea a little cooler in winter.
Care The persea requires fairly high relative humidity and must therefore be sprayed frequently with tepid rainwater. In winter it becomes a little difficult to keep the plant in good condition and it helps to give it a rest at a temperature of 10 to 12°C (50 to 53°F). A temperate greenhouse or even a fairly cool bedroom are suitable places. In spring the persea can be brought into growth again, possibly after having first been pruned a little.
Watering In summer water generously, in winter, if the plant is kept at a low temperature, give only just enough to prevent it from losing all its leaves.
Feeding Feed every fortnight when the plant is in growth.
Repotting The Avocado Pear grows best in a mixture of leafmould, pulverised clay and rotted cow manure. In standard prepacked potting compost the foliage often turns rather yellow.

A germinated avocado stone

The resulting plant: Persea americana

Propagation This plant is nearly always acquired by the germination at home of an avocado stone. This is not difficult if some soil heat is provided. It can even be done above a jar of water: just stick a few matches into the stone to keep it just above the surface of the water. After a time the stone will split into two and the germ becomes visible in the centre.

Persea americana
Syn. *Persea gratissima*. An evergreen tree with alternate leaves oval to oblong, 10 to 15 cm (4 to 6 in) long and 5 to 10 cm (2 to 4 in) wide. The lower surface is blue-green and a little hairy and the leaf stalk is 2 to 3 cm (¾ to 1 in) long. It rarely flowers in cultivation.

Phalaenopsis
Orchidaceae
Moth Orchid

Name From the Greek *phalaina*, moth, and *opsis*, like.
Origin About 40 species occur in humid jungles in Asia and as far as Australia. They are epiphytes, in other words they grow on trees.
Description These are without pseudobulbs, but with a short rhizome bearing oblong to oval, thick and fleshy leaves. The flowers are often butterfly shaped and arranged in a loose cluster.
Position The phalaenopsis belongs in the hothouse.
Care From March onwards the plants must have a shady position in relative humidity of 70 to 80 per cent. In winter, from the end of October onwards, the screening must be removed, since otherwise there wouldn't be enough light. A period spent at a low temperature, to about 12°C (53°F), promotes flowering, especially in hybrids. In this period, which should last 3 to 4 weeks, the plant should not be watered.
Watering Always use pure rainwater. The plant should be kept moderately moist in summer but in winter, after flowering has ceased, it must be kept drier. Never spray the foliage with cold water: this would cause ugly staining.
Feeding In summer the plant may be given some fertiliser every fortnight – preferably special orchid fertiliser.
Repotting At one time these orchids were frequently grown in osmunda fibre (fern roots), mixed with a little sphagnum moss. Granulated peat mixed with 20 per cent perlite is now preferred. The compost should be put in plastic pots without a drainage layer, but the drainage holes must be large. Sometimes the phalaenopsis is tied to blocks of tree fern. It need be repotted only once every two years, and this is best done in May.
Propagation This is mainly done from seed, a professional job. Many plants are imported from abroad as this has proved cheaper than growing them from seed. Specialist orchid growers will be able to supply numerous species and especially hybrids.
Pests and diseases Sometimes aphids occur and if the plant is kept too dry, red spider mite. Slugs like to eat the roots and woodlice also appreciate them.

Phalaenopsis amabilis
Syn. *Phalaenopsis grandiflora*. Flowers are up to 10 cm (4 in) across, white with some yellowish and red streaks on the lips. Flowering season is October–January. There are a large number of varieties.

A modern *Phalaenopsis* hybrid

A variety of Phalaenopsis amabilis

Phalaenopsis esmeralda
Syn. *Phalaenopsis buissoniana*. This has an unbranched flower stalk bearing 10 to 15 flowers, each up to 4 cm (1½ in) in diameter. The colours vary from lilac to white, the lip being darker. It flowers in August–November, and will tolerate more light.
Phalaenopsis lueddemanniana
The flower stalk carries three to four flowers, each 4 cm (1½ in) across, white with rose-red markings. The lip is violet coloured with paler marking. The flowers, May–June, keep a long time.
Phalaenopsis schilleriana
The leaves have grey-green marking. A pendulous, branched flower stalk bears numerous flowers, each 9 to 10 cm (3½ to 4 in) across, like *P. amabilis* in shape, but rose red in colour. The lip is blotched with red at the base and has yellow and red marking. It flowers in January–March.
Phalaenopsis stuartiana
Resembles the previous species. It has white petals, slightly blotched with red-brown and a yellow lip with red-brown patches. Flowers in January–March.
Phalaenopsis violacea
A short flower stalk bears two to five flowers, each 6 to 8 cm (2¼ to 3 in) across. The colour is greenish white, violet at the base with a violet and yellow lip. It flowers May–July.

Philodendron

Araceae

Name From the Greek *philein*, to love, and *dendron*, tree. The plant likes to climb up trees.
Origin About 275 species occur in the rain forests of Central and South America.
Description These are popular house plants, many of them with large, glossy leaves, incised or entire, climbing stems and long aerial roots.
Position In a greenhouse, where they can enjoy a high degree of humidity, these plants may grow enormously tall. In the living-room several species will thrive in a shady position.
Care The following notes are mainly confined to indoor cultivation, for in the greenhouse these plants grow like weeds. The temperature should never fall below 14°C (57°F) and should preferably be 20°C (68°F) or more throughout the year. The philodendron can therefore never be put outside to be hosed down! Instead rinse it indoors with tepid water – this is most beneficial.

The plant should not be put too far from a window, as it needs a fair amount of light to be able to grow. In its natural habitat it lives quite high in the trees, where it is not really dark. The variegated strains, in particular, require more light.

In winter the use of an electric humidifier will be much appreciated, preferably placed close to the plant. Water containers hung on the radiators do not help a great deal. If no humidifier is available, at least moisten the foliage with rainwater a couple of times a day (rainwater does not stain), or lower the temperature a little. This will raise the degree of relative humidity, for cold air can contain more water vapour than warm air and the foliage will therefore not dry out so quickly.

Many species are now sold grown against a moss-covered pole. It looks very attractive, but it is quite a job to keep the moss constantly moist, and that, after all, is its purpose. See page 64 on how to make a perforated moss pole, which must be enclosed at the bottom. Water is then poured in from the top, and runs out of the small holes to moisten the moss.

When the shoots of your plant become too long for the moss pole they may be trained along the wall or up the stairs. Aerial roots can be trained into the pot. It is helpful to place the plant in such a way that it can be sprayed without any visible damage to the wallpaper.

A fine *Philodendron domesticum* in a plastic cylinder, with plectranthus as ground cover

Leaf stalk of *Philodendron squamiferum*

Philodendron micans

Some species fairly readily produce flowers with white, arum lily-like spathes and a white spadix. Sometimes flowering indicates that the plant is dying, but it can also mean that it enjoys its treatment. The flower should not be removed until the fruit sets. It is unlikely that the seed will ripen and in any case it is much easier to grow the plant from cuttings.
Watering It is advisable always to water your philodendron with pure rainwater or demineralised water. The minerals and other harmful elements contained in present-day tap water are not appreciated by the roots, which are accustomed to an acid, humusy medium such as is found in the axils of trees. Always warm the water, for the plant particularly dislikes having cold feet.
Feeding A nitrogen-free fertiliser solution may be given every fortnight when the plant is in growth.
Repotting Ordinary potting compost is not ideal for the philodendron as it is often too solid and contains too much lime. Although it will grow in a standard peat-based compost, it feels happier in a mixture of conifer needle compost, rotted cow manure and possibly some granular peat. Rotted beech leaves, fern roots and perlite also make an excellent mixture. The pots must be extremely well drained. Repot every spring to get rid of the waste matter in the old compost. Small species can successfully be grown in hanging baskets. Philodendron plants also thrive in hydroculture.
Propagation Tip cuttings will root fairly readily if they are cut just below a node and cultivated in bottom heat under

Philodendron melanochrysum 'Andreanum'

Philodendron panduriforme

Philodendron radiatum

Philodendron scandens

glass or plastic. If you require a large number of plants it is better to use eye cuttings. Air-layering is another possibility: this is chiefly done with plants which have become bare at the base. Sometimes imported seed is available, and it will germinate readily provided it is fresh. The result remains to be seen. If the plant develops aerial roots the sections bearing the roots may be cut off. The root is then rolled up and potted and the plant will continue to grow.

Pests and diseases In general it is not susceptible to disease, though incorrectly tended plants may be attacked by scale insects. Yellowing leaves indicate too much – or sometimes too little – water.

Philodendron bipinnatifidum

A non-climbing species with a straight, densely leaved stem. The leaf stalks are 40 to 50 cm (16 to 20 in) long. The leaf is heart shaped, 40 to 60 cm (16 to 24 in) long. The margin is deeply incised to one third from the centre vein.

Philodendron cordatum

Species with large, heart-shaped leaves resembling those of the monstera, but without incisions and perforations.

Philodendron domesticum

Syn. *Philodendron hastatum.* This has dark green foliage resembling that of *P. erubescens*, but is more arrow shaped.

Philodendron elegans

A vigorous climber with 60-cm (24-in) long circular leaf stalks, often lightly blotched. The heart shape of the 40- to 70-cm (16- to 28-in) long leaf can hardly be recognised because it is incised to the centre nerve, which thus separates it into numerous narrow strips.

Philodendron erubescens

A species with greenish-red stem which later turns grey. The young leaves are surrounded by 7- to 14-cm ($2\frac{3}{4}$- to $5\frac{1}{2}$-in) rose-red sheaths, which soon drop. The glossy dark green leaves are an elongated heart shape or arrow shape, 20 cm (8 in) long, not incised (except at the base) and have a purple sheen. A number of strains exist of this frequently cultivated species, among others 'Red Emerald', 'Green Emerald' and 'Bourgogne'. In these strains the foliage is either a little redder or a little greener than in the species.

Philodendron gloriosum

This has a creeping dark green stem with little distance between the nodes. The young leaves are surrounded by pink sheaths; they remain on the plant. The leaf stalk is 30 to 50 cm (12 to 20 in) long; the leaf is heart shaped and up to 40 cm (16 in) long and 30 cm (1 ft) wide. The margin is not incised. The surface is a velvety dark green with a creamy centre vein and white lateral veins.

Philodendron ilsemannii

Possibly a youthful form of *Philodendron sagittifolium*, in which case it should be called *P. sagittifolium* 'Ilsemannii'. It has arrow-shaped leaves, up to 40 cm (16 in) long and deeply incised at the base. The surface is blotched in green, rose-red and cream. It requires plenty of light and is slow growing.

Philodendron imbe

A plant with a green or purple stem and 25- to 35-cm (10- to 14-in) long leaf stalks. It has papery, arrow-shaped leaves 20 cm (8 in) long and deeply incised only at the base.

Philodendron laciniatum

Syn. *Philodendron laciniosum; P. amazonicum; P. pedatum.* The leaf stalks are 40 to 50 cm (16 to 20 in) long and the leaves are thin, divided into three by incisions. The two lateral slips and the centre part are also incised; not infrequently the centre lobe in turn consists of a point and two wings.

Philodendron martianum

Syn. *Philodendron cannifolium.* A non-climbing species with a short, thick stem and swollen, 40-cm (16-in) long leaf stalks. The leaves are oblong, dark green, up to 50 cm (20 in) long, with a thick centre vein.

Philodendron melanochrysum

Syn. *Philodendron andreanum.* A climber with pendulous leaves, velvety green, always with white veining. 'Melanochrysum' is the youthful form, with small, short heart-shaped leaves, and 'Andreanum' is the mature form, in which the leaves are an elongated heart shape. Both may occur on the plant at the same time.

Philodendron micans

This is like the previous species, but smaller in all its parts. The foliage is pale brown, the veins are finely speckled with green and the reverse is purple.

Philodendron panduriforme

The leaf stalks are 25 to 35 cm (10 to 14 in) long and the leaf, 20 to 25 cm (8 to 10 in), with a very thick centre vein, is an elongated arrow shape, narrowing at the tip. This is sometimes called 'fiddle shaped'.

Philodendron radiatum

Syn. *Philodendron dubium.* This has broad, deep green leaves, deeply incised.

Philodendron scandens

Syn. *Philodendron cordatum; P. cuspidatum.* A thin-stemmed climber with small, heart-shaped leaves, 8 to 14 cm (3 to $5\frac{1}{2}$ in) long, green and leathery. This is one of the most popular species.

Philodendron selloum

A non-climbing species with a stem of up to 150 cm (5 ft). The leaf may grow to 50 to 90 cm (20 to 35 in) and is heart shaped. The margins of the leaves are incised all round and are somewhat undulate. The leaf surface presents several transparent patches.

Philodendron squamiferum

Climber with deeply incised five-lobed leaves to 30 cm (1 ft) long. The leaf stalk is also up to 30 cm (1 ft) long and is densely covered in thick, curly hairs, and there is a pale yellow and red sheath.

Philodendron verrucosum

Syn. *Philodendron daguense; P. triumphans.* The leaf stalks are up to 50 cm (20 in) and densely covered with a kind of wart. Heart-shaped leaves, to 20 cm (8 in) long, are a velvety green with bronze; the reverse is red.

Philodendron laciniatum

Philodendron selloum

Philodendron ilsemannii, possibly a cultivar of *Philodendron sagittifolium*

Phlebodium

Polypodiaceae

Name Generally known as *Polypodium*, which is derived from the Greek *poly*, many, and *podos*, foot. I do not know the derivation of the new name.
Origin The genus includes only one species, a native of South America.
Description A fern with unusual incised blue leaves and a golden-brown creeping rhizome.
Position This plant is particularly suitable for the warm living-room, where it can remain throughout the year.
Care It might be thought that all ferns invariably need humid air, but this is not always the case. It certainly does not apply to the phlebodium which has proved to tolerate dry air exceptionally well. Few people know this and that is why the plant is so seldom cultivated. It is, however, advisable to spray the foliage from time to time. A position near a north-, east- or west-facing window is very suitable – a window with a southern aspect would be too light for the fern. In winter the temperature may fall to 16°C (60°F), a convenient factor at night, when the thermostat is lower.

Phlebodium aureum 'Mandaianum'

The handsome rhizome is normally hidden under the compost, but when you repot the plant you might leave a small part visible – it's an attractive sight.
Watering Always use rainwater or at any rate soft water and keep the compost moderately, but constantly, moist. It is a very suitable plant for hydroculture or for an automatic watering system.
Feeding In the growing season feed every fortnight.
Repotting Use plastic pots filled with a mixture of leafmould, rotted manure and sharp sand, and repot every spring.
Propagation Increase by division of the rhizome or from spores.

Phlebodium aureum

Syn. *Polypodium aureum*. A fern with blue-tinted leaves and a long, creeping rhizome covered in pale brown scales. Leaves are 30 by 50cm (12 by 20in), deeply incised, and attached to a long, yellowish stem. The form 'Mandaianum' has undulating leaf slips, irregularly crinkled and serrated.

Phoenix

Palmae

Date Palm

Name A Greek word which has three meanings: date palm, Phoenician and purple-red.
Origin There are about 10 species which occur in Africa and Asia.
Description The true Date Palm and the Canary Date Palm are stiff, prickly palms; the species *Phoenix roebelenii* resembles the Dwarf Coconut Palm *Microcoelum weddellianum*.
Position Suitable for a warm room but some species should preferably be kept a little cooler in winter.
Care *Phoenix roebelenii* requires a warm position all the year round with a minimum temperature of 16°C (60°F). Spray frequently to provide the highest possible degree of humidity and put the plant in a shady spot.

Phoenix dactylifera, the true Date Palm, and *Phoenix canariensis* may be kept in full sun and in summer may even be moved out of doors. They must be kept a little cooler in winter, the Date Palm at a minimum of 8°C (46°F) and the Canary Date Palm at a minimum of 4°C (39°F). The latter is therefore a plant for the unheated greenhouse, and is kept with cacti and other succulents in winter.
Watering In summer the plant may be watered generously, so that the compost never dries out. Occasional plunging to replace the air in the compost is also recommended. Hard water may cause the tips of the fronds to turn brown; this will also happen if the plants are overwatered in winter, especially if the water is very cold. Finally the leaf tips may turn brown if the compost should dry out entirely in summer.
Feeding Palms appreciate some nourishment and in the months between April and September may be fed every week.
Repotting Palms like to grow in deep, narrow pots. Good drainage is advisable, but, provided they are watered sensibly, they may also be grown in a modern cylinder. The palm roots tend to grow through the drainage hole, which can become clogged. For this reason a generous layer of crocks should always be placed over the hole. Plastic pots are to be preferred.
Propagation Even the stones of preserved dates may germinate. They should first be soaked in water for a time. Seed of the other species can be obtained, and *P. roebelenii* can be propagated by division.
Pests and diseases Scale insects may occur particularly if the plants have been kept too warm in winter. Poor light causes small yellow spots to appear.

Phoenix canariensis

This has a fairly thick stem and feathery fronds, initially stiffly erect, later arching. The pinnae are in pairs, 1cm (½in) wide, with a sharp point; the lower pinnae turn into yellow thorns.

Phoenix dactylifera

The Common Date Palm. Like the previous species, but it has leaf sheaths covered in long brown hairs.

Phoenix canariensis

Phyllanthus angustifolius

Phoenix roebelenii

With gracefully arching pinnate fronds, the pinnae are 15 by 1cm (6 by ½in), dark green, and the margin is entire.

Phyllanthus

Euphorbiaceae

Name From the Greek *phyllon*, leaf, and *anthos*, flower. In some species the flowers appear on the leaf-shaped twigs.
Origin About 480 species are found distributed over numerous tropical and subtropical regions. The species described below originates in Jamaica.
Description A rarely seen but interesting plant, and a valuable acquisition for a private greenhouse. The twigs have broadened into leaves; they are called phylloclades. The purpose of this metamorphosis is to restrict the evaporating surface of the leaves. The phylloclades also serve to store moisture. The flowers appear along the edge.
Position The plant belongs in a hothouse, where it will grow in light shade.
Care Considering its somewhat succulent character and the limited evaporating surface, the phyllanthus might be thought suitable for living-room cultivation and occasionally this is successfully attempted. The plant must always be kept warm and requires a well-lit but shady position, for instance near an east-facing window. The foliage, however, should occasionally be sprayed.
Watering Because of its succulent form the plant should be watered sparingly; even less in winter.
Feeding In the period of active growth it may be fed every fortnight.
Repotting Use a mixture of leafmould and rotted cow manure.
Propagation Cuttings will root under glass in a bottom temperature of 30°C (86°F). Fresh seed may also be sown.

Phyllanthus angustifolius

Similar to the next species; the difference lies in the narrower phylloclades, 6 to 8mm (½in) wide, less obviously narrowed at the base.

Phyllanthus speciosus

A shrub with flattened, leaf-like twigs, 5 to 10cm (2 to 4in) long and 1 to 2cm (½ to ¾in) wide, arranged in two rows; they are green and abruptly narrowed at the base. Inconspicuous whitish flowers appear in the upper axillae of the shallow incisions.

Phyllitis scolopendrium 'Undulatum'

Phyllitis
Aspleniaceae
Hart's Tongue Fern

Name From the Greek *phyllon*, leaf. The popular name is Hart's Tongue Fern.
Origin A terrestrial-growing fern occurring in Europe and North America.
Description This is really a hardy garden plant. It has undivided, leathery, green and glossy leaves in the shape of a tongue.
Position The plant may be kept indoors, but must then be given the coolest possible environment. It is therefore very suitable for fairly dark situations in cool stairwells, corridors or entrance halls.
Care It should preferably be cultivated near a north-facing window but must at any rate be kept out of the sun. Spray as often as possible, preferably with lime-free water to avoid those ugly white stains.

In summer the plant can be kept anywhere in the house, but in winter it must be given a cooler position, otherwise problems will occur. It is always possible to move the fern to the garden if it does not thrive indoors. A damp and shady spot is essential.
Watering In summer water freely; in winter keep a little drier if the temperature is low. The foliage must be retained.
Feeding In summer this fern must be fed every fortnight. The faster it grows the more beautiful it will become.
Repotting Use humusy soil, containing leafmould, or standard potting compost. In their natural habitat these ferns grow in woodland soil with a calciferous substratum, such as limestone rocks, so it is not a lime hater. Repot in spring in well-drained plastic pots.
Propagation Only the common species can be grown from spores. These are sown in March, under glass. Cultivars are propagated by division, but it is also possible to take cuttings from the lower sections of the leaf stalks with a piece of the rhizome and to root these in warm soil. Initially small globules will appear, followed by roots. This operation can be begun in October; the plantlets will start into growth in February.
Pests and diseases If a phyllitis is kept in a warm and dry environment in winter, thrips will soon make their appearance. In addition small beetles may nibble the leaf edges.

Phyllitis scolopendrium
● ⊖ ⊛ ⊛ ⊡
A fern with short leaf stalks, closely arranged. The undivided leaves may grow to 40 cm (16 in) in length and 6 cm (2¼ in) in width and are tongue shaped. The spores occur in dark crosswise bands on the underside of the erect leaves, parallel to the lateral veins. There are a number of cultivars, of which 'Undulatum' with its beautifully wavy leaf margins is probably the best known.

Phyllitis scolopendrium

Pilea
Urticaceae
Artillery Plant

Name From the Greek *pilos*, cap. The popular name refers to the sudden contraction of the filaments in a flowering plant, which causes the pollen to be forcefully expelled. The phenomenon occurs if the flowers are suddenly moistened on a sunny day.
Origin About 200 species are distributed in all tropical countries, except Australia.
Description Low-growing foliage plants with particularly fine marking.
Position The plants require a well-lit situation, or the foliage will deteriorate. In winter the temperature may fall a little. A temperate greenhouse is ideal for them, a well-lit window-sill acceptable.
Care The plants require a fairly high degree of humidity and this is the reason why they so often fail in the living-room. Fortunately the temperature may be allowed to fall to 15°C (59°F), or if necessary even to 12°C (53°F) in winter, and the atmosphere will automatically become more humid.

Sometimes the plants are grown out of doors from the end of May onwards. This will do no harm especially in the case of the species *Pilea microphylla*.
Watering Frequent spraying of the foliage is inadvisable – it may cause black stains, especially in the species *Pilea involucrata* with its quilted foliage. In summer the compost must always be kept moderately moist. In winter, when

Pilea microphylla

Pilea spruceana 'Norfolk'

Pilea cadierei

the temperature is lower, the plants should be watered a great deal less.
Feeding In the period of growth the pilea may be given a measure of fertiliser every fortnight.
Repotting A very good potting mixture is one consisting of 2 parts leafmould, 1 part rotted turves, 1 part rotted cow manure and 1 part sharp sand or perlite. Repot at least once a year in spring, in wide, shallow bowls with good drainage. If necessary the plants can be cut back a little.
Propagation Young tip cuttings can be taken in May, when they will root readily. It is necessary to take cuttings at frequent intervals, since older plants usually become less attractive.

Pilea cadeirei
A foliage plant, 15 to 40 cm (6 to 16 in) tall, with elliptical to oval leaves, up to 10 cm (4 in) long and 5 cm (2 in) wide and sharply pointed. The leaves are beautifully marked with three lengthwise dark green sunken stripes, the outer ones slightly curved; they are linked by smaller crosswise lines. Between the lines the surface is silvery white.
Pilea involucrata
Syn. *Pilea pubescens*. This has oval, slightly fleshy leaves, very deeply quilted. They are dark green with a coppery sheen and pale green along the margins.
Pilea microphylla
Syn. *Pilea muscosa*. Artillery Plant. A low, densely leaved plant; the pale green leaves are 2 to 6 mm ($\frac{1}{10}$ to $\frac{1}{4}$ in) long and 1 mm wide, opposite; of each pair one leaf is smaller and shorter stalked than the other.
Pilea nummulariifolia
A plant with succulent, creeping and hairy stems, and round leaves 1 to 2 cm ($\frac{1}{2}$ to $\frac{3}{4}$ in) in diameter, brownish green and glossy, purplish on the reverse. Both surfaces are covered in flattened bristly hairs.
Pilea serpyllacea
Syn. *Pilea globosa*. This closely resembles the species *P. microphylla*, but is larger in all its parts. Leaves are up to 1 cm ($\frac{1}{3}$ in) long, and it has very thick succulent stems.
Pilea serpyllifolia
Resembles the previous species, but the leaves are slightly larger. Of each pair one is smaller than the other.
Pilea spruceana
A species with oval, wrinkled leaves, up to 8 cm (3 in) long, quilted between the wrinkles. There are two strains: 'Silver Tree', with a silvery central stripe and white spots along the bronze-coloured margin, and 'Norfolk', with two white bands closer to the margin.

Piper crocatum

Piper
Piperaceae
Pepper

Name The Latin word *piper* means pepper.
Origin This is one of the largest genera in the vegetable kingdom. There are at least 700 species, distributed over all tropical regions. Several species are grown commercially for the condiment pepper.
Description Usually climbing plants with frequently heart-shaped, sometimes beautifully marked foliage.
Position It should really be grown in a hothouse, but will sometimes survive in the living-room. The plants require plenty of warmth; the temperature must never drop below 12°C (53°F). *Piper nigrum*, the least interesting in appearance, is the strongest: it puts up with light or full shade and tolerates dry air fairly well. The beautifully marked variegated species need plenty of light and also demand high humidity. Full sun, on the other hand, is too much of a good thing. The tendrils must be trained along supports; alternatively the pepper may be grown as a hanging plant.
Watering The compost must always be kept moderately moist. In winter the foliage can be sprayed to keep it damper, preferably with rainwater.
Feeding From March to August pepper species may be fed once a fortnight.
Repotting A potting mixture consisting of leafmould, rotted cow manure and sharp sand is best, but if necessary use a proprietary compost. Repot every spring, when the plants may be cut back.
Propagation Tip cuttings as well as eye cuttings root fairly readily in a tray or pot kept at a temperature of more than 20°C (68°F) and covered with glass or plastic.
Pests and diseases Curling leaves indicate too low a degree of relative humidity. Damage may be caused by aphids.

Piper crocatum
A climber with thin, thread-like stems and leaf stalks. The sharply pointed, elongated oval leaves are dark olive green with clear white marking along the sunken vein areas and rose-red patches among the white and green. The reverse is purplish. This species is frequently confused with *Piper ornatum*.
Piper nigrum
Pepper Plant (black and white pepper). A trailing plant with leaf stalks less than 5 cm (2 in) in length and leathery oval leaves to 15 cm (6 in) long, pointed and dark green all over. In cultivation the plant rarely bears flowers, but these may be succeeded by bunches of green berries, which later turn red and finally black. After being dried these are sold as peppercorns.
Piper ornatum
A climber with thin, reddish stems and leaf stalks and broad heart-shaped leaves with a sharp point, up to 12 cm ($4\frac{1}{2}$ in) long. They are waxy, dark green, marked with pink, and later white, dots. The underside is pale green.

Pisonia
Nyctaginaceae

Name Named after William Piso, 1611–1648, a physician from Leyden, who later moved to Amsterdam. He was the founder of tropical medicine.
Origin About 30 species occur in Australia, New Zealand, Hawaii and other Pacific islands.
Description The plant resembles the ficus to such an extent that it is difficult to distinguish between the two. And yet it belongs to an entirely different family, which also includes the bougainvillea.
Position Because of its need for a high degree of humidity, the pisonia really belongs in the hothouse, but properly cared for it can be grown in the living-room.
Care It is strange that only the variegated form is cultivated. There is, of course, an all-green species, which must undoubtedly be stronger. The variegated form requires a fair amount of light and indoors the foliage cannot be sprayed sufficiently often. This should be done with rainwater to prevent the surface being marred by innumerable chalky spots. Sponging the leaves is also very beneficial.
The temperature can be kept high in winter, as with the ficus, but strong midday sun must always be avoided.
Watering The compost must be kept moderately moist all the year round. It is preferable, but not essential, to use rainwater.
Feeding In summer the plants may be fed every fortnight with a standard commercial preparation.
Repotting A particularly good potting mixture consists of equal parts of leafmould, pulverised clay or loam and rotted cow manure, but the plant will also grow in standard potting compost.
Propagation Both tip cuttings and eye cuttings will strike without too much difficulty provided the soil temperature is maintained at about 25°C (77°F). Cover with glass or plastic.

Pisonia umbellifera
Syn. *Heimerliodendron umbellifera; H. brunonianum; Pisonia brunoniana*. A shrub with 30-cm (1-ft) long oval, thin leathery leaves, arranged almost in whorls round the stalk. The plant cultivated is nearly always the form 'Variegata', with irregularly white-blotched leaves. The form 'Aureovariegata' has yellowish blotches.

Pisonia umbellifera 'Aureovariegata'

Pisonia umbellifera 'Variegata'

Pittosporum undulatum. All species described are best placed outside in summer

Pittosporum

Pittosperaceae

Name From the Greek *pitta*, tar, and *sporos*, seed. The seeds are covered with a tar-like pulp.
Origin About 160 species are known, distributed over the whole of Asia and parts of Africa.
Description Sizable shrubs with small leathery leaves and fragrant cream-coloured flowers which appear in spring.
Position They look like house plants, but since they must be kept cool in winter they are in fact what may be called tub plants. They are particularly suitable for a cool, frost-free position indoors.
Care Grown in tubs the plants become fairly large and this occasionally presents problems when winter quarters have to be found. Unless you possess a large unheated greenhouse, a cool room, hall or corridor, you are advised to avoid the pittosporum. They are in any case not particularly unusual, although they are attractive evergreens.

From the end of May onwards the plants may go out of doors in our climate – in full sun according to the text books, but personally I have had better results by placing them in light shade. Usually the plant will have stopped flowering by that time, for most species flower between February and April. When the plants have been pollinated you might expect fruits. At the end of September, before the onset of night frosts, the shrubs must be moved to their winter quarters, where they can be kept at a minimum temperature of 5°C (41°F).
Watering In summer the pittosporum uses up quite a lot of water and since most of the foliage is retained in winter it must not be forgotten at that time either. Preferably use rainwater.
Feeding In summer the plants can do with some nourishment; once a fortnight in the growing season is sufficient. On no account feed at other times.
Repotting Some clay or loam in the potting mixture is very beneficial, for instance $\frac{2}{3}$ clay and $\frac{1}{3}$ leafmould. Young plants should be repotted every spring; large, mature specimens every second or third year. Use well-drained plastic containers. Real teak tubs are, of course, the most attractive, and they will last for a century.
Propagation Half-ripe tip cuttings may be rooted in August in heated soil, under glass. The plants may also be propagated from fresh seed.
Pests and diseases If the plants are kept too warm in winter they will fall prey to scale insects in the next season.

Pittosporum crassifolium
A shrub with reverse oval leaves, up to 8cm (3in) long, narrowing at the base into a short, thick leaf stalk. The surface is leathery, dark green on the upper side, felty pale brown underneath. It bears purple-red flowers.
Pittosporum eugenioides
An evergreen shrub with alternate leaves; the leaves are grouped at the tips of the shoots and are oval to lanceolate, 5 to 10cm (2 to 4in) long and 1.5 to 3cm ($\frac{1}{2}$ to 1in) wide, undulate, and green. Flowers appear in very dense clusters, yellowish white and fragrant. In 'Variegatum' the margin of the leaf is white.
Pittosporum tobira
This has reverse-oval to spatula-shaped leaves, blunt at the tip, with the edges often rolled back; they are thick, leathery and dark green. The form 'Variegatum', which has white-blotched leaves, is fairly well known.
Pittosporum revolutum
When it starts into growth all parts of this shrub are covered in red-brown hairs. It has narrow oval leaves, to 10cm (4in) long, dark green and glossy on the upper side and covered in rust-coloured felt underneath, and bears fragrant yellow flowers.
Pittosporum undulatum
The oblong leaves are 7 to 15cm ($2\frac{3}{4}$ to 6in) long and 2 to 5cm ($\frac{3}{4}$ to 2in) wide, and very wavy. It has creamy flower clusters.

Pittosporum eugenioides

Pittosporum flowers

Pittosporum tobira 'Variegatum'

Supporting leaves of Stag's Horn Fern

Platycerium

Polypodiaceae

Stag's Horn Fern

Name From the Greek *platys*, broad, and *keras*, horn.
Origin There are 18 species, distributed over the tropical jungle regions of Asia, Australia, Africa and South America. They grow on trees, up to 30m (100ft) from the ground.
Description These unusually shaped ferns have two kinds of fronds: the sterile supporting fronds which grow in the shape of a nest at the base of the plant, and fertile fronds forked like a stag's antlers, which may grow to more than 1m (6ft) in length.
Position The waxy layer which prevents excessive evaporation protects the plant from dry air. It is therefore very suitable for a centrally heated room.
Care The Stag's Horn Fern was extremely popular for quite a long time, but today it is not seen very often. Obviously it has become unfashionable. It is not the first time this has happened – fashions in plants come and go. Those who love the plant know that it is a true friend, which may grow to enormous size even in the darkest corner. It is quite wrong to remove the 'dust' from the plant when you are in a cleaning mood; this is a protective layer of scales which prevents the plant from drying out. Nor should the plant be sprayed. The temperature can stay at 20°C (68°F) throughout the year, but it is better if it drops appreciably in winter, which would make the atmosphere relatively more humid. It is known that most species tolerate temperatures of a few degrees below zero in their natural habitat, but conditions are then very dry.
Watering The easiest method is to plunge the plants, preferably in rainwater. Afterwards they may be left for a week.
Feeding Some fertiliser may be mixed with the water in which the plant is plunged, but only in the growing period.
Repotting The Stag's Horn Fern must be cultivated as a hanging plant and prefers to grow in a basket suspended from the ceiling. The best compost mixture consists of leafmould or conifer needle compost, osmunda fibre and sphagnum moss, mixed with rotted cow manure.
Propagation With the exception of *Platycerium grande*, all species develop offsets which may be removed and potted separately. They will quickly root under

Platycerium bifurcatum

glass. In addition all species can be grown from seed, which should be sown in sterile compost, under glass, at a temperature of 25°C (77°F). It is not an easy matter to raise the young plants.

Pests and diseases Scale insects will occur if the plant is kept too warm in winter. Move the Stag's Horn Fern to a cooler room.

Platycerium bifurcatum

◐ ● ⊜ ⊖ ⓥ ⊛ ▢

Syn. *Platycerium alcicorne*. The sterile fronds are barely incised; they are up to 30cm (1ft) in diameter, rounded, green at first, soon turning brown.

The fertile fronds are bifurcated or trifurcated, pale grey-green with arching lobes and bearing spores at the tips.

Platycerium grande

The sterile fronds are nest shaped, with upturned forked lobes. The fertile fronds droop, and are strongly forked like antlers, initially hairy. The lobes are broad lanceolate in shape, and spores occur in the first fork.

Platycerium hillii

This resembles the previous species, but the fertile fronds are longer and more erect, broader at the base with numerous more pointed lobes, less grey, more green.

Platycerium willinckii

Like *P. grande*, but smaller in all its parts, with white felty fertile fronds. The spores occur at the tips of the bifurcations.

Varieties exist of all these species. Because of their deviating shapes they are difficult to classify.

Plectranthus oertendahlii

Plectranthus fruticosus

Plectranthus

Labiatae

Name From the Greek *plectron*, spur, and *anthos*, flower. In some species the flowers are spurred.

Origin About 120 species are distributed over tropical and subtropical zones of Africa, Asia and Australia and into Polynesia.

Description Simple little plants, reminiscent of the coleus, but the foliage is less beautiful. The scent of the species *Plectranthus fruticosus* is supposed to keep away moths and to cure rheumatism at the same time. You never can tell.

Position These are easy plants which can stay in the living-room all the year round, even though the temperature is really far too high there in winter.

Care *Plectranthus fruticosus* will tolerate full sun but is also satisfied with less light. In winter the temperature may drop to 12°C (53°F). The plants become less attractive as they age and should therefore be renewed from cuttings every year.

Plectranthus oertendahlii requires a higher degree of atmospheric humidity and must be screened from full sun in summer. *Plectranthus parviflorus* tolerates the most shade.

Watering In summer *Plectranthus fruticosus* needs a great deal of water. In winter less water should be given with the lower temperatures.

Feeding The plants usually grow fast enough of their own accord but a little nourishment in summer can do no harm.

Repotting Repot every spring. If you want to grow very large plants repot again early in summer. Standard potting compost is satisfactory.

Propagation All species are extremely easily propagated from cuttings: tip cuttings will invariably root either in water or in compost. It is advisable to propagate new plants at frequent intervals, for young plants are the finest.

Plectranthus oertendahlii often produces seed from which new plants can be grown.

Plectranthus fruticosus

○ ◐ ⊜ ⊖ ⓥ ⊛ ◼

An erect-growing semi-shrub, covered in soft hairs; it is fragrant in all its parts. The oval to heart-shaped leaves are up to 15cm (6in) long, pale green on both sides. Lilac flowers are borne in large branched racemes; the corolla is fairly small.

Plectranthus oertendahlii

◐ ⊜ ⊖ ⓥ ⊛ ◼

A creeping plant with oval to round leaves to 4cm ($1\frac{1}{2}$in) long, pale green with white-marked veining; the reverse is rose red. The small flowers are borne in fairly short racemes; the corolla is white or very pale lilac.

Plectranthus parviflorus

○ ◐ ⊜ ⊖ ⓥ ⊛ ◼

Syn. *Plectranthus australis*. Closely resembles the previous species, but the leaves are thicker, glossy and green all over. A similar plant is sometimes called *Plectranthus strigosus*, of which a white-edged plant called 'Elegance' is supposed to be a cultivar.

Large Stag's Horn Ferns bear enormous patches of spores. Note the difference between the sterile and the incised fertile fronds

Pleione
Orchidaceae

Name Named after the nymph Pleione, mother of the Pleiades, the seven virgins pursued by Orion. Zeus changed them into doves and later into stars (the Pleiades).
Origin There are 15 species, distributed over the Himalayas and China.
Description Beautiful small orchids with pseudobulbs and violet-pink flowers, sold for both indoor and garden cultivation.
Position The plants will grow in a shady but fairly well-lit position on the window-sill or in a sheltered spot in the garden.
Care The plants are usually purchased (perhaps from a mail-order firm) and potted in spring. Initially they must be kept indoors until the leaves appear and must be well ventilated and occasionally sprayed. Towards autumn the foliage may die down and the pleione should then be kept cool and dry until the following spring. The minimum temperature is 5°C (41°F)
Watering Give a little water when the first shoots appear, water generously in the growing season and in the autumn keep drier until the foliage falls. Afterwards the plant should be kept completely dry in its pot. Always use rainwater.

Pleione bulbocodioides

Feeding While the plant is in growth it may be given a light feed every fortnight.
Repotting The pleione must be repotted every spring in a mixture of tree fern, chopped sphagnum moss, some perlite and a little dried cow manure. It is best if several plants are grouped together in shallow, very well-draining pots or bowls.
Propagation When the plants are repotted the young pseudobulbs may be removed and potted separately.

Pleione bulbocodioides
Syn. *Pleione limprichtii; Pleione formosana; Pleione henryii.* Pseudobulbs to 3cm (1in) in diameter, short oval, bearing one lanceolate leaf. They carry singly growing flowers, violet-pink, up to 10cm (4in) across with a fringed lip marked with yellow and white. There are a number of cultivars in a variety of shades.

Plumbago auriculata

Plumbago indica

Plumbago
Plumbaginaceae
Leadwort

Name From the Latin *plumbum*, lead. The juice of *Plumbago europaea* turns the skin a leaden grey colour.
Origin Twenty species are distributed over all warm countries of the world.
Description A fairly well-known trailing plant with clusters of sky-blue or red flowers.
Position The blue species can be kept out of doors in summer and must be kept cool in winter. The red-flowering species is a greenhouse plant.
Care The plants are at their most beautiful if they are planted out in the greenhouse. From May onwards *Plumbago auriculata* may be put in a very sheltered position outside, preferably not in full sun all day, but lightly shaded between 11 a.m. and 3 p.m. In autumn this species must be brought indoors once more, where it is kept cool at 13 to 16°C (55 to 60°F) until December, afterwards at a minimum of 7°C (44°F). *Plumbago indica* belongs in a temperate greenhouse. If no greenhouse is available, the plant may be grown indoors, where the minimum temperature should be 13°C (55°F) in winter. The plants must not be allowed to start into growth too early in spring and should therefore be kept particularly cool at that time.
Watering In summer the compost must always be kept moderately moist. In winter care must be taken not to let the plant dry out entirely, but that is all.
Feeding From May until August the plant may be fed every fortnight.
Repotting A mixture containing clay or loam is best, for instance $\frac{1}{3}$ clay, $\frac{1}{3}$ leaf-mould or potting compost and $\frac{1}{3}$ rotted cow manure. The plants will also grow in a proprietary potting compost. They should be repotted in spring and at the same time cut back drastically. Use plastic tubs with good drainage.
Propagation *Plumbago auriculata* can be grown from tip cuttings rooted in July. In the case of *P. indica* young shoots should be removed as early as April–May. In both cases a soil temperature of 20°C (68°F) should be maintained. If seed is available it may be sown in spring in warm compost.
Pests and diseases Occasionally root knot eelworm is found in the compost; lumpy galls will develop on the roots. Take cuttings and discard the old plant. Too high a temperature or inadequate light in winter will lead to limp shoots susceptible to aphids.

Plumbago auriculata
Syn. *Plumbago capensis.* Cape Leadwort. A shrub with initially erect-growing, later winding stems. It has short-stalked alternate leaves, 5 to 10cm (2 to 4in) long and 3 to 5cm (1 to 2in) wide with the under surface covered in white scales (as is the stem), no 'ears' at the base and large kidney-shaped stipules. Pale blue flowers are borne in short, hairy clusters. In 'Alba' the flowers are white.
Plumbago indica
Syn. *Plumbago rosea; Plumbago coccinea.* Like the previous species, but the leaves are eared and the stipules are lacking. It bears red flowers in hairless clusters.

Podocarpus
Podocarpaceae

Name From the Greek *podos*, foot, and *karpos*, fruit.
Origin About 65 species occur in subtropical regions in the southern hemisphere.
Description Evergreen shrubs belonging to the conifer division of the gymnosperm group.
Position In southern Germany these shrubs can remain outside in winter, which means that in a cooler climate they must be overwintered in a very cool environment. In other words, they are tub plants.
Care In the summer months the podocarpus may be kept indoors, where it must be put near a very well-lit window. Some sunshine will certainly do no harm. If you have a balcony the plant may be kept there from the end of May onwards. In Japan the podocarpus is frequently grown in pots, with great success. Finally the plant may be cultivated successfully on a sheltered terrace during the summer months.
In winter this conifer must be moved to an unheated greenhouse; a very cool but well-lit position such as a frost-free stairwell or a similar environment is also satisfactory. Provided the plant is not too moist a few degrees of frost will not harm it.
Watering Water moderately in summer; at low temperatures in winter a great deal less.
Feeding In summer the plant may be fed once a fortnight.
Repotting Use a potting mixture containing some clay or loam, as well as leafmould, peat and some dried cow manure.
Propagation Tip cuttings can be rooted under glass.

Podocarpus macrophyllus
As it ages the plant grows into a tree with arching branches and leaves arranged in two rows. The leaves are 7 to 10cm ($2\frac{3}{4}$ to 4in) long and 1cm ($\frac{1}{2}$in) wide, lanceolate, green and glossy, paler on the underside.
The cultivar 'Maki' has erect-growing branches; the leaves grow closer together and are smaller, up to 7cm ($2\frac{3}{4}$in) long and 7mm ($\frac{1}{4}$in) wide. The edges are slightly curled.

A young plant of *Podocarpus macrophyllus*

Polyscias
Araliaceae

Name From the Greek *polys*, many, and *skias*, shade. This probably indicates that it is a very shady tree.
Origin More than 70 species are known, occurring in Malagasy, tropical East Asia and in the Pacific islands.
Description From the way in which the leaf stalk is attached to the stem it can be seen that this is a member of the aralia family, along with *Hedera*, *Fatsia* and *Trevisia*. The leaves are always compound and the top leaflet is stalked. Occasionally the leaflets are incised. Sometimes the surface is green and in certain strains it is marked with yellow, white or grey.
Position All species described require a high degree of relative humidity and therefore feel happier in a greenhouse than in a heated room. However, the strongest species will occasionally survive in the living-room for a considerable time.
Care The minimum temperature is approximately halfway between that of a hothouse at 18°C (64°F) and of a temperate greenhouse, 12°C (53°F), in other words around 15°C (59°F). If you are able to provide these conditions indoors, perhaps in an unused bedroom, the overwintering of these fine plants will present few problems. The foliage must be retained, so you should continue to moisten the compost in winter. If the plants are kept at a higher temperature you run the risk of the foliage drying out, unless a reasonably high level of humidity can be provided (as in a hothouse).

Very frequent spraying is a good way of preventing the foliage from dropping; it should be done several times a day. Always use rainwater for the purpose. As is the case with the dracaena, large numbers of stems are now imported. These are rooted under glass in a high temperature and then hardened off before being marketed. These 'Ti-plants' possess neither advantages nor disadvantages, but some people consider them attractive.
Watering In summer the compost must always be kept moderately, or even extremely, moist. If possible water the plant with rainwater, for it dislikes too much lime. In winter the compost may be allowed to become a little drier.
Feeding When the plant is in growth it may be given a fortnightly fertiliser solution, but do not feed after mid-August, or the wood will not ripen satisfactorily.
Repotting Two potting mixtures are recommended: an absolutely lime-free mixture consisting of conifer needle compost with a little rotted cow manure, or a mixture containing some clay (and therefore some lime), consisting of $\frac{1}{3}$ pulverised loam or clay, $\frac{1}{3}$ leafmould (perhaps beech leaves), $\frac{1}{6}$ sharp sand or perlite and $\frac{1}{6}$ rotted cow manure. Both mixtures yield good results: the choice is yours.
Propagation Cuttings may be taken in spring; these may consist of the prunings, but a section of the stem must be attached. One compound leaf will not root on its own. The cuttings should be rooted under glass in a temperature of 25 to 30°C (77 to 86°F). Young plants should be stopped a few times.
Pests and diseases If the plants are kept too warm in winter they will prove to be very susceptible to scale insects in spring.

Polyscias balfouriana 'Pennockii'

Polyscias guilfoylei

Polyscias balfouriana

Syn. *Aralia balfouriana*. A shrub with grey-speckled branches; the compound leaves, usually consisting of three leaflets, are borne on 15-cm (6-in) long leaf stalks. Each leaflet is almost circular, 7 to 10 cm ($2\frac{3}{4}$ to 4 in) in diameter, heart shaped at the base, green and glossy with grey or yellow-green marking and a narrow white margin. The cultivar 'Pennockii' has somewhat larger leaves with white veins.

Polyscias filicifolia

The leaf stalks bear 9 to 13 leaflets, pale green in colour; in young plants they are fairly deeply incised.

Polyscias guilfoylei

Syn. *Nothopanax guilfoylei*. This has five to seven pale green leaflets with a white margin on each leaf stalk. In the strain 'Victoriae' the leaflets are deeply and irregularly incised.

Polyscias paniculata

There are seven leaflets on each leaf stalk; usually the leaflet at the tip is the largest. The edge is finely toothed. 'Variegata' has yellow-blotched foliage.

Spore clusters on the underside of the frond

Polystichum tsus-simense

A mixed planting of *Primula obconica* in a variety of colours

Polystichum
Aspidiaceae

Name From the Greek *polys*, many, and *stichos*, row. The spores are arranged in rows. The garden species are popularly known as Shield Fern or Iron Fern.
Origin There are approximately 225 species, distributed over all parts of the world.
Description Beautiful ferns with divided fronds. Some of the species are suitable for indoor cultivation.
Position Thanks to their leathery surface these ferns tolerate a dry atmosphere fairly well. With a little care they can be grown in the living-room.
Care The plant must be grown in plenty of light, but of course not in full sun. The more often the foliage is sprayed, the better. The fern is at its finest if grown among other plants in a large container. The evaporation of moisture from the surrounding plants keeps the atmosphere more humid.

In winter the plant may be kept a little cooler; temperatures down to a minimum of 10°C (50°F) are well tolerated. In this period it must be sprayed, unless it is placed in a temperate greenhouse, where it will happily spend the winter under the staging.
Watering In summer it may be watered freely, preferably with lime-free water – rainwater or demineralised water is appreciated. Even in winter the compost must be kept moderately moist.
Feeding Ferns are at their finest when they are growing vigorously and therefore need plenty of nourishment, although in weak concentration. In the growing period they should be fed weekly with a fertiliser at half the normal strength.
Repotting A very good potting mixture consists of leafmould, rotted cow manure and a little sharp sand. If necessary a proprietary potting compost may be used.
Propagation The plants can be divided in spring. They may also be propagated from the spores, which are sown under glass in a temperature of 18 to 20°C (64 to 68°F). The compost should be sterilised to prevent algae formation. It is not an easy matter to raise the plantlets.

Polystichum auriculatum

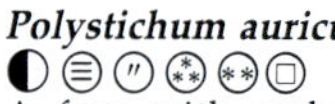

A fern with scaly rhizomes and leaf stalks. It has lanceolate, leathery fronds up to 30 cm (1 ft) long. The leaflets are practically sessile, oval to diamond shaped and curved; the edge is coarsely toothed.

Polystichum tsus-simense

A species with dark leaf stalks and arrow shaped, 20 cm (8 in) long, with bipinnate dark green leaves. This is the most popular species.

Primula
Primulaceae

Name From the Latin *primus*, first; *primula* is a diminutive of the word. It refers to the early flowering of some species.
Origin The approximately 550 known species occur mainly in the mountain regions of Europe, temperate zones of Asia and North America. Only a few species are used as house plants: most of them flower in the garden.
Position Primulas will give you most pleasure if they are kept in a cool spot. The window-sill of a heated room is certainly not the right place.
Description Most species must unfortunately be regarded as throw-away plants, for it is impossible, or at any rate difficult, to carry them over to another season. It is therefore important to try and keep them in flower for as long as possible, since after flowering they are not an attractive sight. This is achieved by cool conditions. When you buy primula plants you should put them in the corridor, in a bedroom, near a window set ajar; in short, in the coolest spots in the house. If possible, keep the windows open towards summer. Naturally the plants should not be in a draught: it is merely a question of ensuring the lowest possible temperature. Of course they must be kept in good light, too, but not in the sun.

An exception to the rule is *Primula obconica*, the species which for some people causes a rash. This species can be carried over to the following year but this is best done in the garden. Towards autumn it should really be moved to an unheated greenhouse or a cold frame, if it is to flower again in winter. This species tolerates most warmth. The rash is caused by a poisonous substance called primine, which is present in all parts of the plant, but mainly in the calyx and the flower stalks. The hairs on the foliage can also transmit primine to the skin when touched. Strangely, sensitivity to primine varies between 0 and 100 per cent. By means of selection growers have succeeded in cultivating primine-free strains, but stupidly there is never an indication on the pot whether it is primine free.

Primula malacoides can also be put in the garden, but it is doubtful if it will flower again. *Primula vulgaris*, still frequently sold as a house plant, is better planted in the garden straight away, that

Primula vulgaris is really a garden plant

Primula praenitens, the Chinese Primula

is, if you like the bright colours. It is not a house plant at all. The same applies to *Primula elatior*. There is also the Chinese Primula, which tolerates warm air fairly well. This plant may be kept at a minimum temperature of 5°C (41°F) in winter. If it is then brought into a slightly warmer environment in January the chances are that it will flower again. But remember, only people with really green fingers are able to keep their primulas through the winter. Ninety per cent of the plants are discarded after flowering.

Watering All species require plenty of moisture when they are in flower, especially *Primula vulgaris*, which may be kept in a bowl of water at all times. At the same time excess water can be harmful, especially in the case of the Chinese Primula and *Primula obconica*. The plants are sensitive to mineral damage and pure rainwater is therefore best for them. It is not advisable to spray or pour water on to the foliage.

Feeding Occasional feeding during the flowering season will help to prolong it. Always use fertiliser at half the recommended concentration.

Repotting In recent times the plant is grown more and more in peat compost. A proprietary soil-based potting compost is also satisfactory. If you want to keep the plants they should be repotted immediately after flowering. Remove all flower stalks and unsightly leaves, and use plastic pots with good drainage.

Propagation The plants are grown from seed, which is fairly easily obtainable. All growers use it. The best temperature for germination is 16°C (60°F); the seed should only just be covered with soil or not at all. The best time to sow is in June–July, sometimes a little earlier, for flowering in the next spring. The earlier you sow, the larger the plants will be. The young plants are pricked out twice and may then be grown in the garden until mid-September, when they should be transferred to a cold frame or unheated greenhouse, where they will continue to grow in a very moderate temperature until flowering begins in spring.

Pests and diseases Yellowing leaves are usually the result of iron deficiency, caused by too high a pH. The correct degree of acidity is 6.0 to 6.5.

Primula malacoides 'Pink Panther'

Primula × kewensis

A hybrid, the result of crossing *Primula floribunda* and *Primula verticillata*. It has spatula-shaped leaves, pale green, often coated with a white powder, and large yellow flowers in whorls one above the other.

Primula malacoides

This flowers in rosettes. The leaf stalk is 8cm (3in) long and the flower stalks protrude far above them. The flowers are arranged in two to six tiers around the stalk; they have a yellow eye and the colours vary between white through rose red to lilac pink.

Primula obconica

A small number of people are sensitive to this species. It has pale green leaves, oval and hairy. The flowers are arranged in long-stalked dense umbels forming a semi-sphere; they are large and occur in a variety of shades.

Primula praenitens

Long-stalked, fairly deeply lobed leaves are arranged in rosettes; the lobes are toothed. The flowers grow in long-stalked loose umbels, sometimes with a further tier of flowers under the umbel, and come in colours of red, orange or white. Strains with incised petals are classified under the 'Fimbriata' group.

Primula vulgaris

Syn. *Primula acaulis*. The Primrose. A clump-forming plant with oblong leaves and sessile flower umbels, usually with a yellow eye.

Pseuderanthemun atropurpureum 'Tricolor'

Pseuderanthemum

Acanthaceae

Name From the Greek *pseudos*, spurious, and *Eranthemum*, a generic name. The plant closely resembles an eranthemum, but among other differences has yellow-veined or brown leaves, while the eranthemum is green.

Origin About 70 species are distributed over many tropical countries.

Description Very modest little foliage plants. The best known is red-brown all over.

Position Hardly suitable for the living-room, these are only for bottle gardens, glass cases, flower windows and greenhouses. They must be kept out of the sun.

Care In view of their high humidity requirements these plants must always be grown under glass. They may be kept warm throughout the summer, but towards winter a moderate resting period may be provided. At that time the temperature should not, however, drop below 16°C (60°F).

The foliage may be sprayed, preferably with lime-free water to prevent staining.

Watering In summer the compost must always be moderately moist, in winter fractionally drier. Always use rainwater, for the plants dislike lime.

Feeding In summer feed every fortnight, using half the recommended concentration.

Repotting Use a mixture rich in humus, consisting of leafmould, rotted cow manure and sharp sand, and shallow, wide pots which must have good drainage.

Propagation Tip cuttings will root readily in some degree of soil heat. Take cuttings at frequent intervals, for young plants are the finest.

Pseuderanthemum atropurpureum

The plant is red-brown in all its parts. It has erect-growing stems and oval leaves, up to 15cm (6in) long and 8cm (3in) wide, usually much smaller. The flowers are arranged in spikes; they have a reddish calyx and a white, pink-blotched corolla with narrow petals. The form 'Tricolor' has rose-red and white marking on the foliage.

Pseuderanthemum reticulatum

Narrower leaves, not brownish, but dark green, the youngest with striking yellow veining. It bears white flowers with a purple throat, in plumes.

Pteris quadriaurita

Pteris quadriaurita 'Argyreia'

Pteris

Pteridaceae

Ribbon Fern, Table Fern

Name From the Greek *pteron*, wing. The fronds are sometimes wing shaped.
Origin There are about 280 species, distributed over tropical and subtropical zones in all parts of the world; some also occur in temperate zones. They are terrestrial plants growing in humid forests.
Description These ferns develop a short, scaly rhizome, producing fronds, usually singly pinnate, on long stalks. Many species are extremely variable in appearance.
Position The green-leaved species and strains may be grown in fairly cool conditions but variegated forms must be kept warmer. No sunlight, and a high degree of humidity – in other words they are more suitable for the greenhouse than for the warm living-room.
Care If the plants are cultivated in a greenhouse or other glass-enclosed space (flower window, glass case, or bottle garden), few problems occur. The green forms put up with little light, the variegated strains must be placed closer to the window but won't tolerate sunlight. In winter the temperature may drop to 12°C (53°F) for the green-leaved species; the variegated forms must be kept at a minimum temperature of 16 to 18°C (60 to 64°F).

For successful indoor cultivation it is advisable to try to raise the level of relative humidity. The pteris may, for instance, be grown among other plants in a large container. You should take care to find a spot where it does not suffer from the hot air rising from a radiator, and you should be generous with spraying. In winter matters become even more difficult, because the relative humidity in the living-room frequently drops to 40 per cent at that time, which does not agree with this fern (most plants dislike it in any case). Try to find a cool place, possibly an unused bedroom, where conditions will be better.

I have little faith in just placing a saucer of water under these plants. The intention is good, but you will realise that in the case of a large fern most rising damp air bypasses the leaves. To be effective with such large, tall plants a veritable pond would have to be created underneath.
Watering In summer the compost must never, repeat never, dry out, but must always remain moderately moist. The best pH for the water lies between 4.5 and 5.5, which means that most tap water is far too hard. You should therefore use rainwater, unpolluted by oil or other impurities which occur in industrial regions. In winter the water supply should be reduced with the temperature.
Feeding Ferns enjoy nourishment, but are sensitive to excessive mineral concentration in the compost. The fertiliser should therefore always be used at half the recommended concentration, but it should be given weekly, at least when the plant is in growth.
Repotting The compost must not contain too much lime. The ferns will grow in standard potting mixture, but you might prefer to make a special mixture of equal parts of leafmould (preferably beech leaves), completely rotted cow manure and sharp sand or perlite. This humusy combination resembles the woodland soil in which the ferns grow in their natural habitat.

Preferably use plastic pots, in which the compost does not dry out quite so abruptly as in red clay pots. Always provide good drainage. Wide bowls, plant containers, automatic watering systems and hydropots are all suitable.
Propagation If only a few new plants are required, this fern can be propagated by division. This should be done when the plant is repotted, that is, in spring. If you want to grow a larger number of plants it is better to sow the spores. These can be supplied by specialist seedsmen, but it is also possible to collect ripe spores from mature plants. The seed compost must first be sterilised; the spores will then germinate in a temperature of about 25°C (77°F). Care and patience are needed to raise the plantlets, which should remain under glass for the first few months.
Pests and diseases Leaf-blotch eelworm may create large black patches between veining. Affected plants are best discarded. Occasionally scale insects will attack.

Pteris cretica

The yellow or pale brown leaf stalks grow fairly erect and may reach up to 30cm (1ft). The leathery foliage may attain 30cm (1ft) in length and 20cm (8in) in width; it is pale green and divided in two to six pinnae on either side of the midrib. These pinnae may be crenate or incised in numerous fantastic variations. Sometimes they bear a central white stripe as well. The most important strains are 'Albo-lineata', which has broader pinnae with a clear white lengthwise central stripe; 'Alexandrae', also variegated, but the tips of the pinnae are incised and crisp; 'Gauthierii' with broad, irregularly shaped, deeply incised, pointed pinnae, and 'Major', which resembles the species, but is more vigorous and has broader pinnae fused at the base. 'Parkeri' has

Back row *Pteris cretica* 'Alexandrae'; *P.c.* 'Major'; *P.c.* 'Parkeri'; **Front row** *P.c.* 'Albo-lineata'; *Doryopteris palmata*; *Pteris ensiformis* 'Victoriae'

Pteris cretica 'Nobilis' in a pot with automatic watering system

very wide, non-crisp pinnae which are rough to the touch. 'Rivertoniana' closely resembles 'Gauthierii', but the foliage is somewhat finer and denser and the pinnae are broader and sometimes lobed at the tip; 'Roeweri' is a much-branched form with 'stalked' pinnae, lobed and crisp at the tip. 'Wimsettii', a vigorous and popular cultivar, also resembles 'Gauthierii', but the tips of the irregularly divided pinnae are crisped.

Pteris ensiformis
Syn. *Pteris crenata*. This has thin, straw-coloured leaf stalks, to 15 cm (6 in) long. The fertile (spore-bearing) fronds have long terminal pinnae and two to four pairs of smaller, smooth-edged lateral pinnae. The sterile fronds have shorter, blunt pinnae, deeply crenated along the edges. A number of cultivars are the most popular, such as 'Evergemiensis, with broad white lengthwise bands on the pinnae, and 'Victoriae', with similar but less pronounced marking and more green; the fertile pinnae are narrower. These two forms are occasionally mixed up.

Pteris multifida
Syn. *Pteris serrulata*. Brown leaf stalks, fronds to 50 cm (20 in) long, divided into very small, widely spaced pinnae; the colour is dark green. In the form 'Cristata' the pinnae are branched and curly at the tip; it is a fairly weak grower.

Pteris quadriaurita
Straw-coloured leaf stalks, with fronds up to 50 cm (20 in) long, bipinnate and triangular in shape. The smallest pinnae are sessile (unstalked). In the cultivar 'Argyreia' they bear a greenish-white stripe down the centre.

Pteris tremula
Australian Brake. This has brown leaf stalks up to 30 cm (1 ft) long, with fronds to 100 cm (39 in); all blades are two to three pinnate. Towards the tips of the fronds the pinnae are more widely spaced; at the base the foliage is much denser and the pinnae are longer – up to 30 cm (1 ft), resembling a carrot plant.

Pteris umbrosa
Red-brown leaf stalks, to 50 cm (20 in) long, have fronds to 60 cm (2 ft) long and 30 cm (1 ft) wide, with one terminal pinna and six to nine lateral pinnae, all dark green in colour. The upper pinnae are finely toothed; the lower are branched or bipinnate. It resembles *Pteris cretica* 'Major' with which it is often confused.

Pteris vittata
Syn. *Pteris longifolia*. A species with yellow-green leaf stalks, 20 cm (8 in) long, lightly scaled. It has elongated oval fronds up to 70 cm (28 in) long and 10 cm (4 in) wide, singly pinnate; 20 to 30 pinnae occur on either side of the centre vein. It is less often available.

Punica
Punicaceae
Pomegranate

Name From the Latin *punicum*, of Phoenecia; in Roman times the best pomegranates came from the Phoenician province Carthage.
Origin The pomegranate has been cultivated since time immemorial. It originated in the regions around Iran and north-east India, where the apple was the symbol of fertility. Not only was the pulp pressed to make a drink, the skin, too, proved to be useful as a cure for sore throats. A kind of tea was made from the leaves and the roots supplied a remedy against tapeworms.

The pomegranate was probably one of the first tub plants.
Description In Mediterranean countries it is a deciduous, thorny shrub with small leaves which at a later stage produces the well-known pomegranates, the flesh of which is edible. The fruits are even more often used for pressing and the concentrated juice is known as grenadine. In our climate the ornamental form 'Nana' is practically the only one cultivated, since the fruits do not ripen here. They start to develop, but soon drop.
Position From the end of May onwards the pomegranate prefers to grow in a sunny, warm and sheltered spot outside. If necessary the little shrub may be kept on a sunny window-sill.
Care Towards autumn the punica must be transferred to cool, well-lit winter quarters, perhaps a cool greenhouse. If space is lacking the longest shoots may be shortened a little. The minimum temperature is 5°C (41°F).
Watering In the period of active growth the compost must always be moderately moist. From August onwards the water supply should be reduced to promote ripening of the twigs. In winter it should be kept practically dry.
Feeding Bird manure appears to give very good results. Feed every fortnight in the growing season.
Repotting A little clay or loam in the mixture is appreciated. Repot in spring.
Propagation Half-ripe cuttings may be rooted in bottom heat. It is also possible to sow seed in February.

Punica granatum
A deciduous, thorny shrub. The leaves are oblong, 3 to 8 cm (1 to 3 in) long and 2 to 5 cm (¾ to 2 in) wide, alternate or in short-stalked whorls. The flowers are arranged in groups of two to five at the tip of the twigs; the fleshy calyx is retained, and the corolla is orange-red. The juicy fruits are spherical in shape and have two cores, one above the other. 'Nana' is the cultivar chiefly grown as house plant or tub plant; it is smaller in all its parts. The flowers are up to 2 cm (¾ in) across. Some less well-known cultivars are 'Pleniflora' with large double flowers; 'Albescens', with double white flowers and 'Multiplex', also with double white flowers.

Pyrrhocactus
Cactaceae

Name From the Greek *pyrrhos*, fire, and the Latin *cactus*, cactus. The flowers are very vividly coloured.
Origin About eight species occur from Argentina to central Chile.
Description Spherical to somewhat columnar cacti with deeply incised ribs and strong thorns. The exterior of the flowers is hairy.
Position It requires full sun and a cool position in winter.
Care These cacti are best kept in a cool greenhouse where they will be warm, receiving all available sun in summer, and cool, to a minimum of 5°C (41°F), and dry in winter. Only cool overwintering will ensure the much desired flower formation, while the cactus body remains firm in this dormant season, and will not rot. Indoors the cactus can be kept on a sunny window-sill in summer; that's no problem, but giving it cool winter quarters is a more difficult matter.
Watering In summer the plants may occasionally be sprayed at the top, but the compost must never become drenched. In winter the plants should be kept perfectly dry at temperatures of a few degrees above zero.
Feeding In the growing season they may be fed once a month with a special (nitrogen-free) cactus fertiliser.
Repotting Use the usual home-made cactus mixture (see page 70) or a proprietary cactus compost. These have the correct degree of acidity and are porous. Use plastic pots with good drainage.
Propagation Sow in spring, under glass, at a temperature of 20°C (68°F). Prick out the seedlings and allow them to harden off. Keep them out of the sun for the first few months.

Pyrrhocactus strausianus
Syn. *Echinocactus strausianus; Malacocarpus strausianus*. A grey-green spherical cactus with 12 to 18 thorns divided into tubercles. The thorns are red-brown, grey, grey-brown to black, 3 cm (1 in) long, usually lightly curved. The flowers are brownish and hairy on the outside, deep salmon coloured inside.

Punica granatum 'Nana'

Rebutia
Cactaceae
Crown Cactus

Name Named after the cactus grower P. Rebut, who lived in Paris in the second half of the 19th century.
Origin There are about 50 natural species, all originating in northern Argentina and the adjoining regions of Bolivia, where they grow at high altitudes. The genera *Aylostera* and *Mediolobivia* which are sometimes treated separately, are here classified under *Rebutia*.
Description The majority of these flattened spherical cacti are very small. The ribs are divided into tubercles arranged in spirals. Shoots appear at the base of the cactus body, as do the flowers. These cacti may flower profusely at an early age; hence their popularity among cac-

Pyrrhocactus scoparius

tus collectors. Usually the flowers are red, but species with yellow, orange or violet-colourerd flowers also occur.

Position The rebutia is best kept in an unscreened greenhouse with a reasonable degree of atmospheric humidity, but they will also thrive on a sunny window-sill, provided they are kept cool in winter. The strongest species will tolerate a little shade, but in that case the colouring of the thorns will be less beautiful.

Care They like it warm and sunny in summer, but definitely cool and dry in the winter season with a minimum temperature of 5°C (41°F), when water should preferably be withheld.

Watering In spring, when the buds become visible, carefully give the plants a little water, then gradually increase the supply until summer, when they can be normally watered from the top. This will at the same time increase the atmospheric humidity. In autumn gradually reduce the water supply until the plants are kept entirely dry from November onwards.

Feeding In summer a little cactus fertiliser (nitrogen free) may be mixed with the water from time to time.

Repotting The plants grow best in the standard cactus mixture described on page 70, but they will also do reasonably well in poor-quality compost. Repot in spring, not necessarily every year, using reasonable-sized pots.

Propagation This is very simple: the plants frequently develop offshoots at the base. Remove these, leave them to dry for a few days and root them in sandy compost. The plants also readily produce seed, which will germinate very easily. Rebutia seed is also commercially available. The seeds should be covered extremely thinly. Grafting is another method of propagation, but it is rarely applied in the case of rebutia species, since they grow so well on their own root system.

Pests and diseases Red spider mite and mealy bug will occur if the plants are kept too dry in summer.

Rebutia aureiflora

The huge flowers of *Rebutia gracilis*

Rebutia senilis; the flowers appear at the base

An attractive rebutia collection, showing an impressive number of plants in flower

Rebutia aureiflora

Syn. *Mediolobivia aureiflora*. A flattened sphere with 15 to 20 thorns which are soft, brushy, brown or yellow, and up to 5mm (¼in) long. The two to three centre thorns are slightly longer, up to 3cm (1in), and upright. It bears orange, yellow or red flowers, 4cm (1½in) across, in spring and summer.

Rebutia deminuta

Syn. *Aylostera deminuta*. Slightly taller than wide, it has eight to twelve brushy, yellowish-white thorns, 4 to 5mm (¼in) long; the centrals are similar to the radials. There are red to orange-red flowers, 3cm (1in) long and wide, in spring and summer. The variety *pseudominuscula* is more globular; the central thorns vary more from the radials and the flowers are lilac red in colour.

Rebutia fiebrigii

Syn. *Aylostera fiebrigii*; *Echinocactus fiebrigii*. A flattened sphere with 30 to 40 brushy white thorns 1cm (½in) long; the two to five central thorns are clearly longer, brown, white at the base and white tipped at a later stage. There are flowers, 2cm (¾in) in diameter, in spring and summer.

Rebutia marsoneri

A broad, flattened sphere, slightly dented at the top, with 30 to 35 thorns, the lower ones white, the upper ones red-brown. Golden-yellow flowers, 4cm (1½in) in diameter, appear in spring.

Rebutia minuscula

Flattened sphere with thorns in groups of 20 to 30, brushy, white or yellowish and 2 to 3cm (¾ to 1in) long. Red flowers, up to 4cm (1½in) in diameter and in length, appear in spring and summer.

The variety *grandiflora* produces larger flowers. There is also a variety *minuscula* of which various forms are available: f. *knuthiana*, also known as *Rebutia knuthiana*, and the better known f. *violaciflora*, usually called *Rebutia violaciflora*. The latter has lilac-pink flowers, 4cm (1½in) across, which appear in June.

Rebutia pseudodeminuta

Syn. *Aylostera pseudodeminuta*. A fairly large flattened sphere, freely producing offsets at the base. The nine to seventeen radial thorns are up to 7mm (¼in) long and glassy. The two to three centrals are longer, white with a brown tip. Orange-red flowers up to 3cm (1in) are borne in spring and summer.

Rebutia pygmaea

Syn. *Echinopsis pygmaea*; *Lobivia pygmaea*. Slightly oval in shape, this species is initially very small, but it may grow to 10cm (4in) in height. There are nine to twelve thorns per aerole, white at first, later grey. It bears purple flowers, 2.5cm (1in) in diameter, in May–June.

Rebutia ritteri

Syn. *Mediolobivia ritteri*. A small globular cactus, producing offsets at the base, and covered in small white thorns with longer, gold-coloured central thorns. It has carmine-red flowers up to 5cm (2in) in diameter in early summer.

Rebutia senilis

A flattened sphere, to about 8cm (3in) in height, densely covered in white thorns, 2cm (¾in) long, in groups of 20 to 30. There are bright red flowers, up to 4cm (1½in) long and 2cm (¾in) across, in spring and summer.

There are several varieties of this variable species; they have yellow, lilac or orange flowers.

Rebutia spinosissima

Syn. *Aylostera spinosissima*. This has a somewhat elongated cactus body, slightly dented at the top. The aeroles are arranged close together and carry numerous white thorns and five to six thicker, yellow centrals. The rose-red flowers, to 4cm (1½in) across, are produced in summer.

Rebutia xanthocarpa

One of the smallest species in the entire genus, only 3 to 4cm (1 to 1½in) tall. It has thin white thorns, 15 to 20 in number and only 3 to 7mm (¼in) long, and carmine-red flowers, 2cm (¾in) in diameter, in summer.

Rechsteineria

Gesneriaceae

Name Named after the 19th-century Swiss clergyman Rechsteiner.
Origin About 75 species occur in humid tropical forests in South America.
Description These are plants with tuberous rhizomes and often beautifully marked leaves, covered in velvety hairs and growing opposite or in whorls around the stem. The vividly coloured flowers are pipe shaped and are arranged in umbels or racemes.
Position All species are hothouse plants, thriving in a high degree of humidity.
Care The rhizomes should be potted in early spring, about February–March; the eyes should remain above the surface. Cover the pots with glass or plastic and keep the compost at a temperature of between 20 and 25°C (68 and 77°F) until the rhizomes start into growth. Take care that they do not rot. Always screen against bright sunlight, but keep them in good light. After about a month start to harden the plants off and transfer them to slightly larger pots. When they are flowering the plants may be kept temporarily in the living-room.

Rechsteineria leucotricha, a rare species

In September the water supply should be gradually restricted, until by the end of the month the plant can be kept completely dry and all the foliage will then die down. The rhizome can be left in the pot or kept in dry peat at a minimum temperature of 12°C (53°F).
Watering Water sparingly when the tuber starts into growth, but gradually increase the supply. Young plants may have water poured over their foliage, but this does not agree with mature plants. In summer the plant must never be allowed to dry out. Preferably use rainwater.
Feeding From June onwards until flowering is over a measure of fertiliser solution should be given every fortnight.
Repotting Renew the compost every spring. Ideally it should consist of a special mixture of coarse peat lumps, beech leafmould and rotted cow manure. Use wide, shallow plastic pots or bowls with very good drainage.
Propagation Both tip cuttings and shoots will readily root if the soil temperature is sufficiently high and evaporation is restricted. The plants may also be grown from seed either in spring or at other times of the year. In winter the seedtrays should be artificially lit. It is also possible to divide the rhizomes when they have just started into growth and the eyes are visible.
Pests and diseases These are unusual.

Rechsteineria cardinalis

Syn. *Gesneria cardinalis; G. macrantha; Corytholoma cardinale.* This has oval leaves up to 15cm (6in) long, bright green and covered in white hairs. The bright red flowers spread approximately horizontally; the corolla is 7cm ($2\frac{3}{4}$in) long, and the upper lip is much longer than the lower. The flowering season depends on the period when the plants were sown, but usually occurs in summer. 'Compacta' does not grow beyond 30cm (1ft).

Rechsteineria leucotricha

The reverse-oval leaves, to 15cm (6in) long, are silvery grey with grey hairs, and the flowers are salmon pink.

Rechsteineria cardinalis, the best-known species

Rhaphidophora aurea (better known as *Scindapsus aureus*) 'Marble Queen'

Rhaphidophora

Araceae

Name From the Greek *rhaphis*, needle, and *phorein*, to bear. Commercially the plant is still called a *Scindapsus*.
Origin More than 100 species occur in the Indian archipelago.
Description A climber with aerial roots and heart-shaped, leathery leaves. The common species grows fairly rapidly, but the variegated form is not very vigorous.
Position The common species is satisfied with little light. It is often the only plant to survive in a mixed plant container placed too far from a window. The variegated form, however, must be placed in much better light, although it will not tolerate full sun.

As it is a climber the plant may be trained up a wall, but it can also be grown as a hanging plant. Usually some support is required.
Care This strong plant feels happiest in a normally heated room. A resting season is not essential, but it will do no harm if in the winter the temperature should drop to about 15°C (59°F). The absolute minimum appears to be 12°C (53°F); this applies only to the common species. Rhaphidophora is by no means demanding; it is one of the easiest plants to grow in the living room, almost an indoor weed very hard to kill.
Watering In summer the plant must always be kept moderately moist. If the temperature is lowered in winter the water supply should also be reduced. It will tolerate too dry or too damp compost temporarily, but prefers lime-free water.
Feeding The common species, which is fairly vigorous, must be fed every fortnight. Do not feed when the plant is not growing.
Repotting A light, acid mixture is preferred – this could consist of conifer needle compost with peat lumps and rotted cow manure, but this strong plant will also grow in a proprietary potting compost or other soil which contains a

Rhaphidophora aurea

little lime. It is advisable to provide good drainage.
Pests and diseases These seldom occur.

Rhaphidophora aurea

Syn. *Epipremnum aureum; Scindapsus aureus.* A climber attaching itself by means of aerial roots. The leaves are usually heart shaped, oblique at the tip, and the surface is marked with yellow streaks and blotches. Mature leaves are frequently incised.

The variegated strain 'Marble Queen' is very beautiful, but grows very slowly for lack of chlorophyll. If the plant is kept in poor light the fine white colour fades to dirty grey.

Rhipsalidopsis gaertneri, the well-known Easter Cactus

Rhipsalidopsis rosea, a rarer species

Rhipsalidopsis

Cactaceae

Easter Cactus

Name The name of the plant *Rhipsalis*, not described in this book, is derived from Greek *rhips*, reed; *opsis* means 'resembling'. In other words, a plant resembling the *Rhipsalis*.
Origin This is epiphyte growing in the tropical forests of southern Brazil. There are only two true species.
Description Epiphytic jointed cacti growing on trees or rocks. The arching shoots have the functions of leaves. They are flat to five sided and the margins are lightly incised. A few scattered areoles bear the rudiments of thorns.
Position The finest flowering is achieved in a warm, shady greenhouse, but cactus collectors also arrive at excellent results when growing the plants in the living-room. The resting season is important; without it the cacti will not flower. This means that they must be kept in a cool greenhouse in winter.
Care Unlike the Christmas Cactus (*Zygocactus truncatus*, q.v.), the Easter Cactus flowers in spring. Bud development is dependent on the temperature and on the length of the day. This means that the plants must be kept cool in winter; the most favourable temperature lies between 10 and 15°C (50 and 59°F). At a temperature between 17 and 20°C (62 and 68°F) the length of day must not exceed 12 hours.

After flowering the plants may be repotted and are then often placed in a sheltered, shady position in the garden. However, they can be cultivated indoors as well with reasonable success, though a greenhouse is the best place of all. In autumn, before the first night frosts occur, the cacti must be moved to their cool winter quarters.
Watering Water generously when the plants are in growth, but in winter only just sufficiently to prevent the joints shrivelling.
Feeding In summer these cacti may be given a little nourishment until August.
Repotting Repot into an acid, humusy compost, making sure it is extremely well drained. The plants grow best in cane or lattice baskets.
Propagation Tip segments of joints can be removed in May and after having been left to dry for a day or so are rooted in a temperature of 20 to 25°C (68 to 77°F). *Rhipsalidopsis gaertneri* can also be grown from seed.
Pests and diseases If the pot is turned the buds will drop. In the garden the plants may be attacked by slugs. Occasionally red spider mite or mealy bug occur.

Rhipsalidopsis gaertneri

Syn. *Epiphyllum gaertneri; Schlumbergera gaertneri.* A strongly branching cactus with arching stems. The upper joints are flat, the lower are triangular to hexagonal. Each joint is lightly incised in about five places; the margin is purple, the rest dull green. It has terminal scarlet flowers, growing singly or in groups of two or three; the petals curve lightly outwards and are sharply pointed, and there are red stamens and white styles. It flowers in April.

Rhipsalidopsis × graeseri

A hybrid between the previous and the following species. The flowers are slightly smaller, orange-red to lilac in colour; the petals have short points. It is often grafted on *Eriocereus jusbertii* stock.

Rhipsalidopsis rosea

Syn. *Rhipsalis rosea.* More erect growing in habit, the joints are between 2 and 5cm ($\frac{3}{4}$ and 2in) long and it has fragrant rose-red flowers. This species, too, is usually grafted in order to encourage it to grow more vigorously.

Rhododendron

Ericaceae

Azalea

Name The Greek word *rhodos* means rose and *dendron* means tree. In other words, the rose tree. All azaleas cultivated indoors as well as the garden species have been classified under the genus *Rhododendron* for some time.
Origin The species cultivated in the living-room originate in eastern Asia, that is China, and in Japan.
Description For indoor cultivation two species are distinguished. Firstly the Indian Azalea, botanical name *Rhododendron simsii*, a non-hardy shrub with large double flowers, easily forced into early flowering. Secondly the Japanese Azalea, *Rhododendron obtusum*, a small shrub which can also be grown in the garden.
Position Considering their natural habitat it may be concluded that these shrubs enjoy fresh, and especially humid, air and a shady position. They are therefore certainly not suitable for a dry, heated living-room, but they will just about tolerate being kept there while flowering.

In summer azaleas can be put in the garden, provided they are given a sheltered, shady position out of the wind. In the transitional period, both in autumn, before they flower, and in spring after flowering, when it is too cold outside, these azaleas must be kept in a cool, well-lit, frost-free place, for instance a cold frame or a greenhouse, a conservatory or a garden room. In our modern homes it is sometimes difficult to provide such an environment and this is one of the reasons for the decline in popularity of these beautiful plants.
Care An indoor azalea is usually bought when it is about to flower. Remember that the flowers will develop more slowly in proportionally lower temperatures. A cool hall or porch is therefore a better place than the warm living-room. Direct sunlight must be avoided, but in winter or spring, the time when the plants flower, this need not be a problem. Spraying the foliage is very beneficial, but the flowers may become stained by water. In this respect the Japanese Azaleas are the stronger.

After flowering the faded blooms must be removed carefully, together with the stalks. The plant can now be moved at once to a cooler environment, preferably at a temperature of 6 to 10°C (43 to 50°F). Probably a few shoots will appear as a result of the high temperature prevailing while the plant was in flower. These should be removed. Only shoots appearing after mid-April should be left on the plants. Towards the end of May the azalea may be moved to the garden or to a sheltered balcony. Use a

Rhododendron obtusum, better known as the Japanese Azalea

Single-flowered Indian Azalea

Double-flowered white Indian Azalea

clay pot and bury it up to the rim. If a plastic pot is preferred it should be buried a little deeper, so that the garden soil is in thorough contact with the pot compost. The plant will grow in summer and start to develop buds which will flower in the following spring. In September the Indian Azaleas are the first to be brought indoors. The Japanese forms tolerate a somewhat lower temperature. Be sure to put your plant in a cool, humid and well-lit environment. If the air is too dry buds and foliage will drop. The temperature should be gradually increased only when the buds begin to swell. The plant must now be frequently sprayed until it flowers.

New shoots will appear as the plant flowers

Watering It is very important that the azalea should always be given lime-free water. Use pure rainwater or buy a demineraliser or water softener. Hard tap water will inevitably kill the plant. Make sure that the compost never dries out; plastic pots are better than clay at retaining moisture.

Feeding In summer the plant may occasionally be given a lime-free fertiliser.

Repotting The best time to repot is about a month after flowering has ceased, when the plants start into growth once more. A special lime-free proprietary potting compost is acceptable – standard composts contain too much lime and should therefore never be used. Conifer needle compost is best, or coarse peat lumps may also be used with the addition of completely rotted cow manure. The pot must be well drained.

Propagation Vigorous young shoots can be rooted in spring or in August–September in a soil temperature of 20 to 25°C (68 to 77°F). Keep the cuttings under plastic or use mist watering apparatus. The tips of the plantlets should be pinched out for the first time soon after they have rooted. It is also possible to graft the plants on stock of *Rhododendron concinnum*.

Pests and diseases Yellowing foliage indicates chlorosis. Azalea moths will cause leaf curl. Remove them or spray with a derris preparation. Tortrix caterpillars, which spin a web to draw the leaves together, are combated in the same way. Red spider mite occurs if the atmosphere is too dry, and incorrect cultivation may lead to various moulds.

Rhododendron obtusum

◐ ⊜ ⊖ ⓡ ⊛ ◐

The result of crossing *Rhododendron kaempferi* and *Rhododendrom kiusianum*. A partially evergreen shrub with 4-cm (1½-in) long, spatula-shaped leaves. The flowers grow in groups of two to five, single or double, in a variety of colours. It may also be used as a garden plant.

Rhododendrom simsii

Syn. *Azalea indica*. This species is the progenitor of the so-called Indian Azaleas. An evergreen shrub, its leaves are up to 5 cm (2 in), and densely covered in rough hairs underneath. The flowers are 5 cm (2 in) across, single or double, in numerous shades and there are early (from October onwards), intermediary (from January) and late-flowering (from February onwards) strains.

Rhododendron simsii, the Indian Azalea, a bicoloured double form

Rhoeo

Commelinaceae

Moses-in-the-cradle

Name Derivation unknown.

Origin There is only one species, occurring in Central America.

Description The sword-shaped leaves are arranged in rosettes and it bears white flowers in shell-shaped bracts.

Position A well-lit place in the living-room all the year round will suit it well.

Care Avoid the strongest sunlight. From spring onwards give normal care and from October onwards keep it slightly drier and cooler, but not below 15°C (59°F). In other words it has no actual dormant season. Spray the foliage as often as possible.

Watering Always keep the compost moderately moist in summer, using water at room temperature. Ordinary tap water is acceptable, but rainwater is better.

Feeding When the plant has started into growth it may be fed every fortnight. Stop feeding at the beginning of autumn.

Repotting The plant will grow well in standard potting compost. Repot every

Rhoeo spathacea (syn. *Rhoeo discolor*) 'Vittata'

year; plastic pots are satisfactory but must have good drainage. The plants may be cut back when they are repotted.

Propagation Shoots and tip cuttings will readily shoot. If there are not enough tip cuttings they may be promoted by removing the top of the plant. Spring is the best time for taking cuttings, but it may also be done later in the year. Sometimes offsets are produced at the base of the parent plant, and these can be removed and potted separately.

In addition the plants produce seed which will usually germinate if scattered in a sandy mixture kept at a temperature of about 20°C (68°F) under glass.

Pests and diseases The plants will rot if they are kept too wet in winter. Occasionally red spider mite or thrips will occur.

Rhoeo spathacea

◐ ⊜ ⓡ ⊛ ◼

Syn. *Rhoeo discolor*. A practically stalkless plant with 15- to 30-cm (6- to 12-in) long and 3- to 6-cm (1- to 2¼-in) wide leaves arranged in rosettes; they are dark green and purple on the reverse. It has a compound inflorescence consisting of white florets in shell-shaped bracts. The strain 'Vittata' has lengthwise yellow stripes on the foliage.

Rhoicissus capensis

Rhoicissus
Vitaceae

Name From the Greek *rhus*, the name of the sumach tree, and *kissos*, ivy.
Origin The only species still treated as belonging to this genus, *Rhoicissus capensis* is, as the name indicates, a native of the Cape Province. The popular species *rhomboidea* is included in the section on the genus *Cissus*, under which it is now classified as *Cissus rhombifolia*.
Description A decorative climber with large, emerald green leaves. It does not flower.
Position This plant should really be grown in a rather cool environment and a high degree of humidity is beneficial. However, in many cases it has survived in a constant living-room temperature of 20°C (68°F), but the best results will be achieved if the rhoicissus is cultivated in a fairly cool, reasonably lit corridor, hall or stairwell.
Care The young shoots should be tied, for they will not spontaneously attach themselves to the wall. They will, however, support themselves if a trellis is provided. In winter the temperature may drop to 7°C (44°F); if the temperature is higher the plant must be frequently sprayed. The foliage should occasionally be sponged.
Watering In summer the plant may be watered generously, but if it is kept cooler in winter the compost must also be somewhat drier. Usually ordinary tap water is acceptable.
Feeding In summer the plant may be given a fertiliser solution every fortnight.
Repotting This is best done in spring. In addition to the ordinary roots you will find a kind of tuber in the pot, and these need a fair amount of room. There is no reason why you should not use standard potting compost; the plant belongs to the vine family and a certain amount of lime will therefore do no harm. Either plastic or clay pots may be used and make sure they are well drained by the addition of a layer of crocks.
Propagation The plant is quite easily grown from cuttings, preferably eye cuttings. The stem should be cut just above and just below the spot where the leaf stalk joins it. The dormant eye will be found in the axil and must be induced to develop. To restrict evaporation the leaf can be rolled up or halved. A compost temperature of 18°C (64°F) is sufficient. Cover the cuttings with glass or plastic. The rhoicissus can also be propagated from tip cuttings. When the plantlets are potted they are generally grouped in threes.
Pests and disease Brown leaves, leaf fall or stains on the foliage may indicate too little as well as too much water. Take the plant out of the pot and inspect the roots.

Rhoicissus capensis
A climbing shrub covered in brown hairs with practically heart-shaped leaves, long stalked and up to 15 cm (6 in) across. The upper surface is emerald green, initially hairy, later becoming smooth. The underside of the leaves is rust brown and felty.

Rivina
Phytolaccaceae

Name The plant was named after the Leipzig botanist August Quirinus Rivinus, 1652–1723.
Origin It occurs in the southern part of the United States and Mexico. It also grows wild in many tropical countries.
Description Its decorative value depends mainly on the fine red berries. The plant is seldom found at the florist's or garden shop.
Position On the whole it is a hothouse plant, but it will temporarily survive in the living-room. As usual the high level of atmospheric humidity required is the problem.
Care The plants must be kept fairly warm, but screened against the brightest sunlight. Be generous with water, especially in summer, but do not spray the plants, for this would prevent the seed from ripening. Older plants become rather lanky and it is therefore advisable to grow new plants from cuttings every year. In winter the temperature may fall to 12°C (53°F); the berries will retain their beauty all the longer.
Watering Ordinary tap water may be used if it is not too polluted. In winter keep the plant a little drier.
Feeding In summer the plant may be fed every fortnight.
Repotting New plantlets can be grown from cuttings in spring and planted in standard potting compost. Plastic pots are excellent, but make sure they are well drained.
Propagation In May the ripe fruits may be sown in sandy compost. Give them some degree of bottom heat and cover the seedtrays with glass or plastic. The seedlings should be pricked out once and then potted in groups of three in 12-cm ($4\frac{1}{2}$-in) pots.

Another method is to take tip cuttings in spring and root them in a temperature of 20 to 25°C (68 to 77°F).

Rivina humilis
A semi-shrub, about 60 cm (2 ft) tall, with oval pale leaves, pointed at either end, fairly thick and lightly haired. The white or pink flowers occur in long racemes from January to October, but they have little ornamental value. The pea-sized red or orange-coloured berries which may decorate the plant for several months on end are much more striking.

Flowers and fruits of *Rivina humilis*

Rochea
Crassulaceae

Name Named after François de la Roche, a French botanist who died in 1813.
Origin Four species occur; all have their native habitat in South Africa.
Description The genus is closely related to the *Crassula*. It has fleshy leaves arranged in four rows along the stiff stems.
Position In summer the rochea must be cultivated in a well-lit, but not too warm environment, in other words, a cool window-sill, a cold frame or a greenhouse.
Care The plant is usually purchased when it is in flower, that is, in spring. After flowering cut the stems back a little, and if necessary repot the plant and keep as cool as possible, perhaps in a very sheltered position in the garden or on the balcony, but avoid strong sunlight. In autumn the rochea must be moved to frost-free quarters; a temperature of 5°C (41°F) is all right and a cool greenhouse is therefore ideal. In practice it is not all that easy to bring the plant into flower again, but if these conditions can be met it is worth the trouble.
Watering In summer the plant must be watered moderately to sparingly and in winter, when the plant is kept cool, it should hardly be watered at all. A little water may be given only if the leaves are shrivelling badly.
Feeding If the plant is repotted in spring it need not be fed.
Repotting The plant grows best in a mixture of equal parts of clay, rotted beech leaves and washed sharp sand. The pot (clay or plastic) must be very well drained.
Propagation If the rochea is cut back after flowering, the prunings should be left to dry for a few days before being rooted in a sandy mixture at a soil temperature of 15 to 20°C (59 to 68°F).

Rochea coccinea
Syn. *Crassula coccinea*. A stiffly erect-growing little shrub, branching at the base, with reverse-oval to oblong leaves, 3 to 5 cm (1 to 2 in) long and 1 to 2 cm ($\frac{1}{2}$ to $\frac{3}{4}$ in) wide, regularly arranged in rows along the stems and multiflowered umbel-shaped clusters of red flowers. There is also a white-flowered form called 'Alba'.

Rochea coccinea

Rodriguezia secunda, a very profusely flowering orchid

Rodriguezia
Orchidaceae

Name Named after the Spanish botanist J. D. Rodriguez, 1780–1846. At one time this plant was known by the name *Burlingtonia*.
Origin Most of the approximately 35 species occur in Brazil. They are also found in Central America and the Antilles.
Description Epiphytic orchids with pseudobulbs, exceptionally rich flowering.
Position These plants can only be cultivated in a temperate, humid orchid house.
Care They should be grown throughout the year at a minimum temperature of 18°C (64°F), as close to the glass as possible, since the plants require a great deal of light. However, they must be screened against bright sunlight. The relative atmospheric humidity needs to be at least 70 per cent. In winter the water supply should be slightly reduced, but an actual dormant season is not required.
Watering Only use absolutely lime-free water, in other words, warmed rainwater or filtered tap water if necessary. In summer water generously from time to time, but in winter give only just enough water to prevent the plants from shrivelling.
Feeding In the period of active growth some fish emulsion or other orchid fertiliser may occasionally be mixed with the water.
Repotting The plants are frequently grown on blocks of tree fern. If pots or lattice baskets are used they should be filled with a mixture of tree fern and osmunda fibre, with a deep layer of crocks at the bottom.
Propagation The plants may be grown from seed, but that is an expert's job. Most plants are imported. Propagation by division is not recommended, because large plants are much more beautiful.

Rodriguezia decora

A plant with very elongated rhizomes. The compressed pseudobulbs occur at 10-cm (4-in) intervals. These are 3cm (1in) long and each carries one slender, 6- to 9-cm (2¼- to 3½-in) long pointed leaf. The inflorescence, which may be as much as 30cm (1ft) in length, consists of ten to fifteen white flowers with red-brown patches, each flower being up to 5cm (2in) in diameter. The flowering season is November–May.
Rodriguezia secunda
The pseudobulbs are compressed, up to 4cm (1½in) long, each of them usually carrying one leathery leaf. The racemes of at least ten flowers, all facing one way, bear flowers up to 2cm (¾in) across, lilac pink, which appear in autumn.
Rodriguezia venusta
The pseudobulbs are no more than 2cm (¾in) long. White flowers are borne in summer, not more than ten in each cluster.

Rosa
Rosaceae
Rose

Name The name *Rosa* was already used in Roman times.
Origin About 200 species of wild roses are known, distributed over all countries of the northern hemisphere. Roses for indoor cultivation are usually restricted to descendants of *Rosa chinensis* 'Minima', probably originating in Japan and known since the beginning of the last century. Another plant to play an important part in crossing the species was *Rosa roulettii*, discovered growing as a house plant in Switzerland in 1918.
Description The plants which now belong to the group of dwarf or miniature roses are all hybrids. The tiny shrubs are perfect miniatures, sometimes no more than 15cm (6in) tall, with genuine single or double rose flowers. Some are even fragrant.
Position Most miniature roses are hardy and are therefore really garden plants. Growers sometimes have spares which they sell off as indoor plants. They will do very well on the window-sill, but even better on the balcony.
Care Give them plenty of light (no screening is necessary) and ventilation, and remove all faded parts. When the days shorten and autumn approaches the miniature roses must be given a cooler environment, similar to conditions out of doors. The best thing is to put the plants, still in the pot, into the ground in the garden. They may also be kept on the balcony, but when it freezes they will have to be wrapped up to prevent them turning into lumps of ice. In most cases you will find that the miniature rose has started into growth again in March. This is the time to prune it. Just as with a large shrub rose, it is sufficient if three to five firm branches are left, each with about three eyes. The branches will therefore be about 5 to 7cm (2 to 2¾in) long. Do not give them too much warmth at first; the buds should not start into active growth until the middle of April. In May the miniature rose may be returned to the window-sill, but it can also be planted out in a sunny spot in the garden.
Watering In spring and summer the compost must always be kept reasonably moist. Roses tolerate lime and will not be harmed by fairly hard tap water.
Feeding In the growing season give them a dose of fertiliser solution every fortnight until mid-August.
Repotting Roses are usually repotted in autumn, but it can also be done in spring. Use standard potting compost and well-drained plastic pots.
Propagation In August–September miniature roses can be propagated from cuttings rooted out of doors in frost-free conditions. Professional growers usually propagate them by grafting.
Pests and diseases They can be affected by mildew, aphids, or red spider mite.

Rosa chinensis 'Minima'

Syn. *Rosa lawrenceana; Rosa roulettii.* A small shrub, 10 to 30cm (4 to 12in) tall, with compound leaves consisting of three to five leaflets. The flowers usually grow singly; the hips are brown. Only hybrids in a large variety of shades and shapes are in cultivation.

A standard miniature rose

African Violets, both single and double, are available in many colours

Saintpaulia
Gesneriaceae
African Violet

Name This little plant is named after a District Officer called Walter von Saint Paul-Illaire, 1860–1910, who discovered it in the course of his service in the former German colony in East Africa.
Origin The native habitat of the African Violet is in the Usambara mountains in East Africa, where there are tropical forests. There are about 20 natural species.
Description All species are practically sessile, compact perennials with long-stalked leaves frequently arranged in rosettes.
Position Whereas the African Violet was originally regarded as a fairly delicate greenhouse plant which would only thrive in a very high degree of humidity, this idea has now been proved to be a myth. Probably the plant has become more tolerant of dry air as a result of hybridisation, for it certainly thrives and flowers untiringly on thousands of window-sills all over the world. An east-facing window is undoubtedly the best, since the saintpaulia does not like too much sun. In winter, when the plants in any case hardly flower, they are best kept in a warm greenhouse.

The saintpaulia can also be cultivated with great success in flower windows or glass cases. A minimum illumination value of 5000 lux is essential for profuse flowering.
Care African Violets are usually bought in spring when they are in flower. Put them in good light but out of the sun. If they are kept on a window-sill, make sure that no warm air can rise through the foliage – the plants dislike this intensely. If the air proves to be too dry it may be a good idea to grow the plants above a bowl of water. The pot should be placed on an 'island' to avoid water being absorbed from the bottom. Spraying is not a good idea: the foliage is hairy and drops of water collecting among the hairs cause ugly brown or pale yellow stains. The same applies should the leaves become wet when the plant is watered.

The development of flower buds depends on the intensity of the light (the minimum should be 5000 lux, as mentioned above), but also on the length of day. It is therefore not surprising that most of the flowers appear in the summer. If a little extra light is provided in autumn (an ordinary lamp will do) the flowering will continue over a longer period. If the saintpaulia is cultivated under a special plant lamp, so that both the length of the day and the intensity of the light are increased, it will not stop flowering at all. However, it is advisable to allow the plants a rest for at least one month in the year. At this time the temperature may drop to 16°C (60°F) and the water supply may be reduced. After the resting period the compost should be renewed and the cycle will start again.

Sometimes the African Violet produces a great deal of foliage but few flowers. This means that the compost or the fertiliser contains too much nitrogen. The easiest way to solve the problem is to remove the largest leaves until the excess nitrogen has been used up. More flower buds will automatically appear.
Watering If you are living in a hard-water area, it is advisable not to use tap water for your African Violet, for the plants dislike lime. Demineralised water or rainwater at room temperature or just above is best. The compost should never become wet; it is better to keep it on the dry side. As soon as the leaves become limp you can give a little water.
Feeding In the period of growth the little plants must be fed once a month. If too much foliage is developed you would do better to use a nitrogen-free fertiliser, as used for cacti. Otherwise give them a standard fertiliser.
Repotting You are strongly advised to repot the saintpaulia every spring. A large amount of minerals from the water are deposited in the compost and they act like poison. Use lime-free compost and wide, shallow pots with good drainage. If you only have a standard soil-based potting compost, mix in a fair amount of peat.
Propagation The African Violet is very easily grown from cuttings. Each leaf with a 2- to 5-cm ($\frac{3}{4}$- to 2-in) stalk is capable of producing several new plants. Insert the leaves upright in cutting compost under glass, at a temperature of 20 to 22°C (68 to 71°F). Roots will also develop on the stem in a bottle of water. Carefully remove the young plants and pot them separately, initially still under glass or in an indoor propagator. They can then be hardened off and cultivated separately. It is advisable to take cuttings from older plants at frequent intervals.
Pests and diseases These hardly occur if the rules of cultivation are adhered to and if the plant is regularly renewed.

Saintpaulia ionantha

A sessile, roughly haired perennial; the leaves are round to oval, the hairs are vertical and are all approximately equal in length. The axillary flowers appear in two- to eight-flowered clusters; they are 2 to 3cm ($\frac{3}{4}$ to 1in) in diameter and deep violet in colour.

Crossing with *Saintpaulia confusa* and others has resulted in the well-known indoor strains with larger flowers in a wide range of colours, single as well as double, and in strains with quilted foliage.

An old washbasin planted with African Violets

Sandersonia aurantiaca

Sandersonia
Liliaceae

Name Named after John Sanderson, a South African botanist, who was probably born in 1820 and died in 1881.
Origin There is only one species, a native of Natal.
Description A tuberous plant with approximately 60-cm (2-ft) long limp stems bearing sessile leaves. Urn-shaped axillary flowers appear in summer.
Position This is a greenhouse plant; cultivation is similar to that of the better-known gloriosa. You might try to grow it on the window-sill, but it is doubtful if the plant will last for more than a year.
Care Tubers may be obtained from a few mail-order firms or from a well-stocked seedsman. They are potted in February–March; the eyes should be 3 to 5cm (1 to 2in) below the surface. Keep the pots in a fairly warm environment and until the first shoots appear on no account give them too much water. Once the plants have started into growth they will tolerate a little more moisture until summer, when they may be watered freely. As the shoots are fairly limp they must be tied to stakes or to the wall of the greenhouse.

After flowering the water supply should be gradually reduced until finally all the foliage dies down. The tubers may be left in the pot and kept in a dry corner of the greenhouse, perhaps under the staging. In spring the cycle is started again.
Watering It is advisable to use rain-water. Water generously in summer.
Feeding In the period of active growth give them a measure of fertiliser solution every fortnight.
Repotting The most satisfactory potting mixture consists of equal parts of peat, rotted beech leaves and pulverised loam. Use plastic pots with good drainage.
Propagation Increase by division of the tubers.

Sandersonia aurantiaca

A tuberous climber with 7-cm ($2\frac{3}{4}$-in) long lanceolate, stalkless leaves often ending in a tendril. Bulbous, urn-shaped angled flowers, orange-yellow in colour and 2.5cm (1in) long, appear in summer.

Sansevieria

Agavaceae

Mother-in-law's Tongue

Name These indestructible plants have been named after Raimondo de Sangro, prince of Sanseviero in Naples 1710–1771. The unkind common name refers to the sharp leaves. Other names are Devil's Tongue and Bowstring Hemp.
Origin About 12 species grow wild in Ethiopia among other places. They are desert plants which can put up with poor conditions; they are, for instance, incredibly tolerant of drought. A number of species are grown for a fibre which is used in rope making, but the importance of this industry is rapidly waning.
Description These plants have thick creeping rhizomes bearing stalkless, fleshy, bayonet-shaped leaves. A certain amount of moisture is stored in the leaves, useful in times of drought. The plants are closely related to the cordyline and the dracaena.
Position Since they are desert plants, sansevierias naturally require plenty of sun, but they have proved to be indestructible even in a shady spot, although in that case the foliage marking will become less beautiful. They are therefore obviously ideal plants for an unscreened south-facing window.
Care A great deal might be said about treatment, but practice has shown that one would have to be abysmally bad at looking after plants to kill a sansevieria. Overwatering is the only thing that might occasionally harm the plant. In addition the temperature should not drop below 14°C (57°F) for long stretches of time; this usually causes rotting at the base.

For those who want to go by the book, here are a few rules. Give the plant plenty of light, be particularly sparing with water, except in summer when new growth appears. Even then the compost should never be actually moist. In winter the plants can be kept a little cooler and drier.
Watering The plants are often grown in ornamental pots in which excess water can slowly collect and this is extremely harmful. In plastic cylinders, too, it is difficult to determine whether there is too much moisture. Always remember that these plants come from the desert and are satisfied with very little. Whether hard or soft water is used is not very important.
Feeding Once the plant has started into active growth in summer it may be given a small feed once a fortnight or once a month. Some people recommend a nitrogen-free fertiliser, such as special cactus fertiliser. The foliage will then grow less rapidly and become more striking. It is also said to stimulate the development of the flowers, which are not unattractive.
Repotting Sansevieria plants are so vigorous that they sometimes burst out of their pots. If they are given extra large containers there is no stopping them at all. If possible therefore they should not be repotted more than once every two years. Spring is the best time, and red clay pots are the most suitable. Plastic pots must be provided with particularly good drainage. Standard potting compost will do for the Mother-in-law's Tongue.
Propagation The best results are achieved by dividing the plants. The common green species can also be grown from leaf cuttings. Cut a leaf into 7-cm ($2\frac{3}{4}$-in) sections, allow these to dry for a few days and insert them in a sandy mixture with a soil temperature of 25°C (77°F), but make sure the sections are planted the right way up or no roots will develop.

Sansevieria trifasciata 'Laurentii'

A sansevieria in flower

Sansevieria trifasciata 'Golden Hahnii'

Sansevieria trifasciata 'Hahnii'

Pests and diseases Brown blotches on the leaves, or occasionally corky patches, are caused by too much moisture or excessive temperature fluctuations.

Sansevieria trifasciata

The leaves, growing from rhizomes, are up to 1.5 m (5 ft) long and 7 cm ($2\frac{3}{4}$ in) wide, and are slightly gutter shaped, dull green with pale green cross-banding. Fragrant greenish-white flowers are borne in narrow racemes which are half the length of the leaves.

The frequently cultivated form 'Laurentii' has yellow leaf margins. 'Gigante' is a cultivar with broader, grey-green foliage. 'Hahnii' develops a short, funnel-shaped rosette. 'Golden Hahnii' is similar to the previous form, but has grey-green leaves with yellow bands along the margins. 'Silver Hahnii' has silvery foliage with delicate whitish marking.

Stems and foliage of *Sauromatum venosum*

Sauromatum

Araceae

Name From the Greek *sauros*, lizard, and *matos*, search. The spotted bracts are somewhat reminiscent of the reptile.
Origin Six species are known; they occur in tropical Africa, India and in Sumatra.
Description It is questionable whether this should be called a house plant. The sauromatum is sold as a so-called dry-flowering plant, that is, a bulb which without any soil or water produces an elongated, arum lily-like inflorescence. It is not very attractive, for the flower rarely opens and it has a very disagreeable scent, but it is sometimes grown as a curiosity.
Position While the flower is developing the plant may be kept on the windowsill, that is, if you can bear the carrion smell.
Care Initially there is little to be done. After flowering the plant is usually discarded, but it may also be planted in the garden and then becomes really interesting. A beautifully spotted stem develops in spring, bearing deeply incised foliage of enormous size. As the bulbs are not completely hardy, it is advisable to choose a very sheltered position. In autumn the leaves will die and the bulb may be brought indoors to flower once more.
Watering Out of doors rainfall is sufficient. If you want to grow the plant in a pot it must be watered moderately.
Feeding A small amount of fertiliser should be given in the growing season.
Repotting Potted bulbs can be grown in standard compost.
Propagation In the garden the bulb will develop offsets which may be cultivated separately. They may flower after three years.

Sauromatum venosum

Syn. *Sauromatun guttatum*; *Arum guttatum*; *A. venosum*. A bulbous plant with a foot-shaped compound leaf blade, up to 50 cm (20 in) across, on an erect-growing stem. The dry bulb develops a detailed bract, greenish purple on the outside, green with purple patches inside. The inflorescence smells of carrion.

Saxifraga

Saxifragaceae

Saxifrage, Rockfoil

Name From the Latin *saxum*, rock, and *frangere*, to break.
Origin Most species are hardy garden plants, whose native habitat is in the high mountains where they do, in fact, cause stone to break. The 'Mother of Thousands' (*Saxifraga stolonifera*), with which we are mainly concerned here is one of the few non-hardy species. It grows wild in China and Japan.
Description The Mother of Thousands plant develops trailing stems from which young plantlets develop. It should not be confused with the tolmiea, which is also sometimes called Mother of Thousands.
Position The common green Mother of Thousands species is almost hardy and may therefore be grown in a very cool and well-ventilated environment, especially in winter. It likes plenty of light, but full sun should be avoided. The variegated form 'Tricolor' requires a much warmer position, at least 16°C (60°F). The plants are best grown in hanging pots.
Care Always make sure they have plenty of fresh air, especially the green species. In summer the plant must be protected from strong sunlight and should always be kept moderately moist. In winter it may have a light rest, but the variegated form must not be too cold. As soon as the plants flower their end is near, so make sure that young plants have been rooted in good time.

A few words about the rosette-forming species, *Saxifrage cotyledon*. This plant should be kept in the living-room only when it is in flower. Afterwards it is advisable to move it out to the garden as soon as possible, as this species is hardy. Each rosette flowers only after two to four years.
Watering The water need not be softened, unless it is extremely hard. Do not be too generous with water, but on the other hand do not let the compost dry out either. Plants which are given a winter rest in a cool environment naturally need very little moisture.
Feeding In summer the Mother of Thousands should be fed with a fertiliser solution every fortnight.
Repotting Spring is the best time to repot. Standard potting compost is satisfactory, but you might prefer to mix your own from beech leaves, peat, rotted cow manure and rotted turves. Plastic pots must be especially well drained.
Propagation It is as simple as it looks. Often the young plantlets which nearly always develop already have a few roots. Remove them, pot them separately, putting a few together in one pot, and keep them under glass or plastic until they are well established. The plants may also be grown from seed.
Pests and disease If the plants are kept too warm they become very susceptible to aphids. If the temperature is too high and the air too dry in winter red spider mite may appear. Both can be avoided by correct cultivation.

Saxifraga cotyledon

Syn. *Saxifraga pyramidalis*. A perennial from the Pyrenees with large, loose rosettes of spatula-shaped leathery leaves, 4 to 8cm (1½ to 3in) long. In May or June (a little earlier if the plant is forced) it produces an enormous cluster of white flowers, up to 50cm (20in) tall.

Saxifraga stolonifera

Syn. *Saxifraga sarmentosa*. Mother of Thousands. This is a hanging plant with long, soft runners or stolons, on which young plantlets develop. It has alternate leaves, 4 to 6cm (1½ to 2¼in) across, broadly toothed; the upper surface is dull green with white veining, the underside is red, and there is a long leaf stalk. The white flowers appear in loose, hairy plumes. The strain 'Tricolor', which is the one most frequently cultivated, has smaller leaves, more deeply incised, with a broad white margin and scattered red and white spots.

A cluster of *Saxifraga cotyledon* flowers

Saxifraga stolonifera with runners

Saxifraga stolonifera 'Tricolor', Mother of Thousands

Schefflera actinophylla, a strong foliage plant for a cool environment

Schefflera

Araliaceae

Name Named after an 18th-century Danzig botanist called J. C. Scheffler. He was a friend of Linnaeus.
Origin The best-known species has its natural habitat in Australia. The other 150 species are distributed over nearly all tropical countries of the world.
Description In their natural environment these are small trees or shrubs with large, palmately divided leaves. In cultivation they rarely flower.
Position Although these plants originate in the tropics, they grow at high altitudes and this explains their need for fresh air. The living-room is not a good place: it is too warm. A stairwell, cool vestibule, in summer a spot out of doors, all these are more appreciated. It is sometimes grown as a tub plant.
Care Keep it out of the strongest sunlight and give it a sheltered position if the plant is grown out of doors. In winter the temperature may drop to about 12°C (53°F). Lower temperatures will be tolerated, but will cause leaf fall; new foliage will then appear in spring.
Watering Water moderately in summer and a little less when the plant is kept at a lower temperature in winter. The water need not be soft.
Feeding When the plant is in growth in summer a monthly feed is sufficient. Use a standard house plant fertiliser.
Repotting The plants grow fairly vigorously and you may have to repot it twice in the first year. Afterwards repot once a year in spring, using standard potting compost and large plastic con-

Probably *Schefflera venulosa*

Probably *Schefflera octophyllum*

tainers which are very well drained.
Propagation The plant cannot be grown from cuttings. Imported fresh seed will germinate under glass at a temperature of 20 to 25°C (68 to 77°F). The seedlings are then pricked out and hardened off.
Pests and diseaes Scale insects may occur especially if the plant is kept at too high a temperature.

Schefflera actinophylla
Syn. *Brassaia actinophylla*. This is the best-known species. In its natural environment it is a tree, up to 30m (100ft) tall; here it may grow to 2 to 3m (6 to 10ft). It has palmately divided leaves, five to ten oval to oblong leaflets, each 10 to 20cm (4 to 8in) long and 4 to 6cm (1½ to 2¼in) wide; they are leathery and glossy green. The leaf stalks are up to 4cm (1½in) long.

Schefflera digitata
A smaller species with five to ten leaflets, like parchment. They are sharply pointed, pale green, and finely toothed in mature plants.

Schefflera octophyllum
Here too the foliage is palmately divided into eight or nine leaflets, but the leaflets point slightly upwards; they are about 7cm (2¾in) long and 3cm (1in) wide, bright green with conspicuous veining.

Schefflera venulosa
Syn. *Heptapleurum venulosum*. There are seven to eight leaflets in each compound leaf, initially lanceolate, later oval, and 15cm (6in) long, dark green with a dull sheen.

It is not always easy to distinguish the various species and their nomenclature is rather confused. The only species on which everybody agrees is *Schefflera actinophylla*.

Scilla
Liliaceae

Name *Skilla* is an ancient Greek plant name.
Origin Most species originate in the temperate zones of Europe, Asia and Africa. The species described below have their native habitat in South Africa.
Description The scilla is a well-known bulbous plant for the garden. If they are forced in very cool conditions they may also be kept in the living-room for a time. Their decorative value lies in the beautiful foliage.
Position The plant will grow well at temperatures between 10 and 20°C (50 and 68°F). Sometimes a greenhouse is recommended, but a sunny window-sill will be satisfactory.
Care Contrary to what might be expected, this bulbous-rooted plant retains its foliage throughout the year. It therefore has no distinct dormant season in winter, when all the foliage dies. In summer it must have plenty of light, possibly outside; too high a temperature is harmful. After flowering the plant should be kept a little drier and cooler, but nothing too extreme. Keep it in a not-too-warm environment in winter and spray the foliage.
Watering The plant must be kept fairly dry, even in summer. Ordinary tap water will do little harm.
Feeding When the scilla is putting out new leaves it may be fed occasionally. About once a month is probably enough.
Repotting This may be done either in spring or autumn. Standard potting compost is satisfactory, or you could make a mixture of rotted beech leaves, pulverised loam and rotted cow manure. The pots must have good drainage.
Propagation A large number of offsets develop on the bulb, and these can be potted separately in spring.

Scilla paucifolia
Like *Scilla violacea*, but the foliage is pale green with darker patches and is not purple-red on the reverse.

Scilla violacea
Half the vigorously sprouting bulb grows above the surface. The upper surface of the leaves is olive green with silver streaks; the underside is wine-red and glossy. It bears greenish flowers with violet-coloured stamens on long stalks.

Scilla violacea, a fairly rare bulbous plant

Scindapsus
Araceae
Devil's Ivy

Name The Greek name for an ivy-like plant.
Origin There are about 20 species of evergreen climbers, related to the philodendron and other plants. They occur in South East Asia and Indonesia.
Description Since the nomenclature of the genus was changed only one species is regularly available as a houseplant. The other and much better known species, *Scindapsus aureus*, is now called *Rhaphidophora aurea* (q.v.). The plant discussed here has soft stems and heart-shaped leaves with lively marking.
Position In view of the plant's need for a high level of humidity it is more suitable for a hothouse than for the living-room. It is sometimes used in mixed containers, where the slightly damper microclimate ensures that it will remain in good condition for a time. The plant feels very much at home in a terrarium, bottle garden or flower window, and it grows well on an epiphyte tree.
Care The scindapsus may be cultivated throughout the year in a hothouse or a similar environment. It is advisable to train the soft shoots on moss-covered poles. The moss should always be kept thoroughly moist, but this is sometimes difficult to maintain.
Watering Preferably use demineralised water or rainwater. In summer water moderately; in winter the plant can often be kept a little drier.
Feeding In the active growth period a little fertiliser may be given once a fortnight.
Repotting The potting mixture should be light and acid. Peat, rotted beech leaves, sphagnum moss and rotted manure are all excellent ingredients. It is important to ensure good drainage.
Propagation Shoots and eye cuttings will root early in summer at a temperature of 20 to 25°C (68 to 77°F), under glass. Shoots will even root in a bottle of water.

Scindapus pictus 'Argyraeus'

Scindapsus pictus
A climber with warty stems, this plant has thick leaves which are heart shaped with a sharp point and emerald green on the upper surface, with blue-green and white speckles. The cultivar 'Argyraeus', which is the form most frequently available, has smaller foliage with clearer marking and a paler margin.

Scirpus
Cyperaceae
Club Rush

Name From the Latin word for rush, *scirpus*.
Origin About 250 *Scirpus* species may be found in all parts of the world; some are natives of this country. The only species cultivated in the living-room occurs in Mediterranean countries and elsewhere.
Description The plant resembles a large wig of hanging hair, a beautiful fresh green in colour.

Scirpus cernuus or Club Rush

Position Plenty of light is an essential condition, but bright sunlight is undesirable. An east-facing window-sill is therefore a good spot, and so is a greenhouse or a terrarium. The best temperature is between 16 and 20°C (60 and 68°F). It can also be grown as a hanging plant.
Care The plant may stay in the living-room or the greenhouse all the year round. If it is warm enough in winter it will continue to grow. After a time the centre becomes unsightly and the plant should therefore be divided at least once a year and the outer, fresher parts used to provide new plants. In view of its need for high humidity the plant should not be placed in a hot air stream and should often be sprayed, especially in winter.
Watering This is one of those plants which must be kept standing in a water-filled saucer throughout the year, but if the entire soil ball is immersed in the water the scirpus will die. It is a very suitable subject for hydroculture and automatic watering systems.
Feeding In the growing period – that is, practically all the year round – feed every fortnight.
Repotting When the plant is divided the compost should be renewed at the same time. Standard potting compost is satisfactory.
Propagation Division is the simplest method. Only use the youngest, outer sections of the clump. The scirpus may also be grown from seed.
Pests and diseases Growth will be retarded if it is subjected to poor light or dry air.

Scirpus cernuus
Syn. *Isolepis gracilis*. A dense, clump-forming grassy perennial, pale green, with thread-like arching stems bearing brush-shaped leaves with a brownish ear at the tip, and up to 20 cm (8 in) tall.

Sedum pachyphyllum, for which the apt German name Schnapsnase means 'Red Nose'

Sedum
Crassulaceae
Stonecrop

Name It appears that the name is derived from the Latin *sedare*, to hold. The Romans grew these plants on the roofs of houses, like the *Sempervivum*; the roots held the plants in place.
Origin There are about 500 species, distributed over temperate zones throughout the world. The plants used for indoor cultivation are often those occurring in Mexico.
Description The species described below are succulents; they store moisture in their fleshy leaves, which are often beautifully coloured. The genus includes fine hanging plants and species with practically cylindrical leaves.
Position A few species are very easy to grow and may be kept in the living-room all the year round. Full sun is essential, but if the plants are kept very warm in winter also, they will lose much of their characteristic colouring. The best position is therefore a cool greenhouse or a frost-free cold frame which can be left open in summer.
Care The plants grow in summer, but if kept at a temperature of 5°C (41°F) in winter they require practically no water. So much reserve moisture is stored in the fleshy leaves that in a low temperature it will last for several months. Only when the leaves are seen to shrivel need a little tepid water be poured down the inside edge of the pot. If the plants are kept warm in winter, which is incorrect, they will naturally need a little more moisture.
Watering Even in summer these plants need little water. Tap water may be used, but it should always be warmed.
Feeding If the plants are repotted regularly feeding is unnecessary.
Repotting This should be done in spring. Use a very porous compost, rich in humus, but containing little lime. Cactus compost is very satisfactory, or make your own mixture from leafmould, pulverised clay, rotted cow manure and sharp sand or perlite. Very good drainage is essential.

Sedum griseum

Sedum rubrotinctum

Propagation Some species drop leaves which root spontaneously. Otherwise you can remove some of the leaves and allow them to dry for a few weeks before rooting them. Tip cuttings can also be used, or the plants may be grown from seed.
Pests and diseases These seldom occur. Rotting is the result of too much moisture at a low temperature, and occasionally there may be an attack of mealy bug.

Sedum bellum
A compact little plant with leaves which are initially folded like buds. They spread in the second year and are then thick and spatula shaped. It bears five-petalled star-like white flowers.
Sedum dasyphyllum A very compact plant, not more than 5 cm (2 in) in height, with creeping stems and 3-mm (1/8-in) long fleshy leaves in four to six tiers. They are blue-green in colour and covered in short hairs. White flowers are borne in sparse clusters.
Sedum griseum
Compact little shrub with erect-growing stems bearing cylindrical grey-green leaves coated with white powder, and white flowers.
Sedum morganianum
Donkey's Tail. A hanging plant with stems which resemble tails. The cylindrical, slightly curved and pointed pale grey leaves overlap like roof tiles. It's a striking plant, with pink flowers.
Sedum pachyphyllum
A well-known, remarkable looking species with erect-growing branches. The stems bear spreading, cylindrical leaves, 3 to 4 cm (1 to 1½ in) long and 8 to 10 mm (¼ to ½ in) wide, slightly curving upwards. The colour is bluish-green, but they are red-brown at the tip; hence the German name 'Schnapsnase' (Red Nose). The flowers are yellow.
Sedum platyphyllum
A species with thick, erect-growing stems and yellow-green spoon-shaped leaves, coated in bloom; they are grouped at the end of the stems. The greenish-white flowers have red speckles.
Sedum praealtum
A vigorous shrub with thick, spatula-shaped, glossy green leaves, slightly curving upwards. The yellow inflorescence may grow to 10 cm (4 in) in length. The best-known form is 'Cristatum' in which the leaves have broadened into a strap shape; a remarkable sight.
Sedum rubrotinctum
Syn. *Sedum guatemalense*. Christmas

Sedum stahlii

Cheer. This succulent is seen fairly frequently. It has thin, erect-growing stems bearing cylindrical leaves, 1 to 2 cm ($\frac{1}{2}$ to $\frac{3}{4}$ in) long and 4 to 8 mm ($\frac{1}{8}$ to $\frac{1}{4}$ in) in diameter, glossy green to red-brown in colour which, as is the case in most of the species, is positively affected by drought and sunshine. The flowers are yellow. A frequently cultivated form is 'Aurora' with pink to salmon-coloured leaves.

Sedum sieboldii
This plant is slightly atypical since it is also sold as a bedding plant for gardens and window-boxes. It must in fact be grown in very cool conditions. It has flexible stems with blue-green, white-edged, slightly reddish leaves in groups of three at intervals of 3 cm (1 in). The pink flowers appear in October. In the form 'Mediovariegatum' the leaves are blotched with white in the centre.

Sedum stahlii
This has thin, spreading stems with 1- to 1.5-cm ($\frac{1}{2}$-in) long and 5- to 7-mm ($\frac{1}{4}$-in) wide cylindrical leaves which resemble coffee beans. They are green in colour, usually tinged with brownish shade (depending on the amount of sun) and readily fall. The flowers are yellow.

Selaginella
Selaginellaceae

Origin There are about 700 species. Their habitat is in tropical rain forests.
Description Low-growing, moss-like plants, most of which are pale green.
Position If possible place them under glass, for instance in a bottle garden or a glass case. They will not survive for long in a warm living-room.
Care Selaginellas should be grown throughout the year at a minimum temperature of 15°C (59°F), in good light but out of the sun, and require an exceptionally high degree of humidity.
Watering Never allow them to dry out.
Feeding In summer give an occasional foliar feed.
Repotting Use flat bowls with very good drainage and a compost containing plenty of sphagnum moss.
Propagation Increase by division.
Pests and diseases Beware of slugs.

Selaginella apoda
A very low-growing species with clump-forming habit and pale green, finely toothed leaves.

Selaginella kraussiana
Spreading Club Moss. This has creeping stems up to 30 cm (1 ft) long, with pinnately divided green side stems and fresh green foliage. 'Aurea' is yellow-green, 'Brownii' is very compact, and in 'Variegata' the stem tips are white.

Selaginella lepidophylla
The short stems with pinnate side stems curl up in a drought and open again when moistened. It closely resembles the Rose of Jericho (see *Anastatica*).

Selaginella martensii
Initially the stems of this species are erect, later more recumbent; they bear aerial roots. The foliage is pale green. The best-known form is 'Watsoniana' in which the tips of the stems are silvery white and slightly arching. There is also a very compact form called 'Compacta', and 'Variegata', in which the tips of the stems and the lateral leaves are white or white striped.

Selenicereus
Cactaceae
Night Cactus

Name *Selene* is Greek for moon and *Cereus* is a cactus genus.
Origin About 25 species are known, growing mainly in Central and South America.
Description These are cacti with a shrubby habit, producing 1-m (3-ft) long climbing shoots, often bearing aerial roots. The flowers may be of enormous size, but open only for a short time.
Position In view of its immense size this cactus is more suitable for a greenhouse, but there are people who put their entire window at the plant's disposal and in that case cultivation may succeed. The need for fairly high humidity is a problem. Plenty of light is required too, but the strongest sunlight must be filtered.
Care Planted out in a warm greenhouse the shoots may reach lengths of at least 3 m (10 ft). Cultivation presents few problems in such conditions: in summer the plant must be watered moderately and in winter it should be kept as dry as possible and the temperature may drop to about 10°C (50°F) This is important and makes cultivation in the living-room practically impossible, but as with other cacti, cool and dry conditions in winter encourage bud development. The plant itself may survive being kept warm, but it will not flower and since otherwise its appearance is very uninteresting it should certainly be induced to flower.

The long shoots must be tied. Make sure that the supporting ties are strong enough for in time the entire plant will depend on them.

When the moment of flowering comes the buds will start to swell in the afternoon. By ten o'clock in the evening they will be fully open and remain in that way until dawn, when they will collapse like a pricked balloon. While the flower is open a delightful fragrance is noticed. A good-sized plant may produce quite a few flowers in the course of the summer, so it is not a very rare phenomenon. However, young plants take a long time to flower.
Watering It is best to use rainwater in summer, for the Night Cactus dislikes lime. In winter give it practically no water.
Feeding In view of the plant's vigour some nourishment is not out of place. If the cactus is planted out its roots will find sufficient nutriment, but plants grown in pots or tubs should be given a measure of cactus fertiliser once a month.
Repotting It is not an easy matter to repot this 1-m (3-ft) long prickly mass. Try wrapping the whole thing in an old blanket to make it less unwieldy and less apt to be damaged. A mixture of peat, leafmould, rotted manure and sharp sand or perlite is a very suitable potting mixture. If necessary a peat-based compost for acid-loving plants may be used.
Propagation Increase by leaving 10-cm (4-in) long stem sections to dry for a week, then root them in sandy compost. The plant can also be grown from seed.

Selenicereus grandiflorus
Syn. *Cereus grandiflorus*. Queen of the Night. This is the largest-flowered species. It has stems with five to eight ribs, 2 to 3 cm ($\frac{3}{4}$ to 1 in) across, thorns in groups of seven to eleven, 4 to 6 cm ($1\frac{1}{2}$ to $2\frac{1}{4}$ in) long and intermingled with numerous whitish hairs. The flowers are up to 30 cm (1 ft) in diameter with inner petals white and outer petals yellow with a little red, and they are vanilla scented.

Selenicereus pteranthus
Princess of the Night. The 4-cm ($1\frac{1}{2}$-in) thick stems have four to six inconspicuous ribs. The thorns are more cone shaped than in the previous species and are intermingled with hairs only in younger plants. They have smaller flowers.

From left to right *Selaginella martensii* 'Watsoniana', *S. martensii* and *S. apoda*

The enormous flowers of *Selenicereus grandiflorus*, the Queen of the Night

Sempervivum
Crassulaceae
Houseleek

Name From the Latin *semper*, always, and *vivum*, alive. It is practically impossible to kill these plants.
Origin They are found in mountain regions in the northern hemisphere; there are about 20 to 30 species.
Description These are rosette-forming plants which may spread over large areas. They grow in the most impossible places, such as on corrugated iron roofs.
Position All species are suitable for the rock garden and are therefore completely hardy. However, they are often sold as house plants. They will grow very well near a sunny window, but it is better to keep them in a very cool environment in winter. If you plant them in the garden or in a shallow, well-drained bowl placed on the balcony, you will have no problems at all.
Care The various houseleek species thrive on starvation; you can hardly please them more than by neglecting them.

Too much water, manure or warmth causes the plants to grow limp and lose their character.
Watering Hardly any is required. Naturally they need an occasional drop, but most people overwater them.
Feeding The plant is accustomed to finding its own nourishment, if necessary from the sides of the pot, and will not appreciate feeding. Do not spoil it!
Repotting This is hardly necessary; the nutrients contained in fresh compost will not benefit the plants. They should therefore be repotted as seldom as possible. The quality of the compost is immaterial. All they need is extremely good drainage.
Propagation Rooted rosettes are easily detached. The plants may also be grown from seed.

Sempervivum arachnoideum
○ ⊖ ◐ ⊛ ■
Cobweb Houseleek. This develops small rosettes covered as if with cobweb. It has bright red flowers on 15-cm (6-in) stalks in June–July.

Sempervivum tectorum
Common Houseleek. A very variable species; usually the rosettes are fairly large. It has leathery leaves, bright green in colour with a chestnut-brown tip and pink flowers. There are innumerable hybrids.

A trough containing various species of sempervivum, very suitable for a balcony

Senecio
Compositae
Groundsel

Name From the Latin *senex*, old man, or *senecta*, grey-haired.
Origin This is an extremely large genus, for it includes about 1300 species distributed over all parts of the world. The species we are dealing with are the cineraria, a native of the Canary Islands, a number of succulents mainly originating in South Africa and two foliage plants with the same native habitat.
Description The cineraria is *Senecio cruentus*, a well-known plant sold in large quantities for Mother's Day. Some of the succulent species consist of a row of pea-shaped bulbous leaves strung on stems. The foliage plants, which are also somewhat succulent, bear some resemblance to a variegated ivy.
Position The cineraria likes to live in a cool, well-lit environment out of the sun and out of a draught, otherwise it will be infested by aphids.

The succulents should be grown in full sun and if possible kept cool in winter. The foliage plant *Senecio mikanioides* tolerates shade and may be grown in fairly cool conditions. *Senecio macroglossus*, on the other hand, is cultivated like the succulents.
Care To start with the cineraria, *Senecio cruentus*, it is usually bought in spring, when it is in flower. Put the plant in the coolest possible position, spray it from time to time and provide plenty of (filtered) light. Discard after flowering.

Senecio citriformis in flower

Senecio cruentus, the cineraria

Senecio macroglossus 'Variegatum'

The succulent species and the foliage plant *Senecio macroglossus* require a great deal of sun and warmth in summer, but if possible should be kept in cool and dry conditions in winter. Fortunately they are strong plants and often survive in the living-room. Try to place them as close to the window as possible: it is a little cooler there.

The thin-leaved *Senecio mikanioides* must be kept fairly cool; it is not suitable for a warm and dry room. It makes a good climbing or hanging plant, satisfied with a little less light than the other species.
Watering A good deal of water is evaporated through the large leaves of the cineraria and it may be necessary to plunge the plant regularly in water at room temperature.

Species with fleshy leaves, that is the succulents, need little water in summer and practically none if they are kept at about 10°C (50°F) in winter. *Senecio mikanioides*, the variegated foliage plant, must always be kept moderately moist. All species accept ordinary tapwater, provided it is not too hard.
Feeding It may be necessary to give the cineraria some extra nourishment – not too concentrated – to prolong your pleasure by a few weeks.

If the succulent species are repotted every year they need little nourishment. *Senecio mikanioides* must be fed every fortnight in summer.
Repotting *Senecio cruentus* need never be repotted, for it is a disposable plant. Plants grown from seed should be potted in standard compost.

The succulent species enjoy a very porous mixture, such as cactus compost.

Senecio mikanioides, again, can be potted in standard compost; it must be repotted every spring.

Propagation It is not easy to grow *Senecio cruentus* from seed. The watchword is cool, cool and again cool. The grower should sow in July–August and place the seedlings in a cold frame or greenhouse, where the temperature is kept at a minimum of 5°C (41°F) in winter. The plants will then flower in spring.

The easiest method of growing the succulent species is from cuttings. The cut surfaces must be left to dry for a few days. The foliage plant *Senecio mikanioides* is also easily grown from tip cuttings, even in a bottle of water.

Pests and diseases As soon as the cineraria is subjected to a few degrees of excessive warmth or to a draught, it becomes prey to the well-known voracious greenfly. Too high a degree of atmospheric humidity may lead to mildew. In addition these plants are very sensitive to mineral concentration in the compost which will cause the leaves to turn yellow and make them curl up at the edges like saucers. You should therefore beware of overfeeding or watering with the wrong kind of water.

The succulent species may be attacked by mealy bug or root mealy bug and will rot if they are kept too damp at low temperatures.

Senecio articulatus

Syn. *Kleinia articulata*. A small shrub with thick, cylindrical joints bearing deeply incised leaves on long stalks. These fall in the dormant season. The entire plant is coated in white bloom; the colour of the foliage is blue-green. It bears yellow flowers with a disagreeable scent.

Senecio citriformis

A small plant with short, recumbent stems; the leaves are lemon shaped, up to 2cm (¾in), and covered in bluish bloom with transparent lines. It has small white flowers.

Senecio rowleyanus and Senecio herreianus

***Senecio cruentus* hybrids**

Syn. *Cineraria* hybrids. Cineraria. A shrub-like hairy plant; the leaves are large and irregularly incised, faintly lobed. The inflorescence consists of broad, dense, terminal clusters, up to 8cm (3in) across, in all colours except yellow. A variety of types have been cultivated.

Senecio haworthii

Syn. *Kleinia tomentosa*. Woolly white shrub-like plant with cylindrical pointed leaves, up to 3cm (1in) long.

Senecio herreianus

Syn. *Kleinia gomphophylla*. A small plant with trailing stems bearing almost spherical grey-green leaves with a short point, sometimes with red marking. This is often confused with *Senecio rowleyanus*.

Senecio macroglossus

Wax Vine. A trailing plant with small, clearly succulent leaves resembling those of the ivy. The finest form is 'Variegatum' with white leaf margins. It is not to be confused with the following species.

Senecio mikanioides

Syn. *Mikania scandens*. German Ivy. A climbing plant with 5- to 10-cm (2- to 4-in) wide ivy-like lobed leaves, pale green, thin and long stalked. No variegated form exists of this species.

Senecio rowleyanus

This is a trailing plant with stems bearing small leaves in the shape of a pea. The flowers are white with lilac.

Setcreasea

Commelinaceae

Name Derivation unknown. The plant is frequently, but incorrectly, referred to as a tradescantia.

Origin The few species known have their natural habitat in Mexico. They have been used as house plants since 1955.

Description The most striking feature of this plant is its all-over purple colour, something which rarely occurs in the world of house plants. The decorative value depends chiefly on the foliage.

Position To retain its fine colouring the plant must be cultivated in a sunny, or at least a very well-lit spot. Whether the environment is very warm or cool is of little importance. In a mild winter the setcreasea may even spend this season out of doors, perhaps against a south-facing wall.

Care Provided it receives enough light this is certainly not a difficult plant to grow. It will benefit from being kept a little cooler and drier in winter, but even this is not essential. When the setcreasea has lost its beauty new plants can be quickly grown from cuttings. It is advisable to do this every year.

Watering Try not to spill water on the foliage to avoid staining. In summer the compost should always be moderately moist; in winter a little drier if the temperature is kept lower. Tap water will be acceptable.

Feeding When the plant is growing well it may be given a measure of fertiliser solution every fortnight, but it is not essential. Too much nourishment will cause the plant to become limp.

Setcreasea purpurea

Repotting Repot preferably every year in spring. Standard potting compost is satisfactory.

Propagation The setcreasea is easily increased from 7- to 10-cm (2¾- to 4-in) long tip cuttings, preferably in spring, but it may also be done at other times of the year. Leave the cuttings to dry for a day or so; it is slightly succulent.

Setcreasea purpurea

An entirely purple perennial. The leaves are gutter shaped, 15cm (6in) long and 5cm (2in) wide, with numerous dark veins and the edges are fringed with long hairs. It has erect-growing flower stalks, shell-shaped bracts and a violet-coloured corolla.

Siderasis

Commelinaceae

Name It appears to be derived from the Greek *sideros*, rust-coloured fur. This obviously refers to the brown hairs which cover the plant.

Origin There is only one species, which originates in Brazil.

Description The brown hairs contribute a great deal to the plant's striking appearance. The blue, sometimes reddish little flowers form an attractive contrast.

Position The plant is really more suitable for a humid hothouse, for it enjoys humid air. However, some people succeed in growing it on the window-sill. It is a matter of experiment. Bright sunshine is undesirable.

Care The plant does not require an actual resting season and may therefore be kept in a warm environment all the year round. The minimum temperature is about 16°C (60°F).

In a warm room the plant should be sprayed frequently; even better, put a large bowl of water or a humidifier nearby, for drops of water on the foliage easily cause ugly stains.

Watering Although the degree of relative humidity must be high, the compost does not require very much water; it should in fact be kept fairly dry. Ordinary tap water is acceptable.

Feeding In summer the plant may occasionally be given a light feed. Too much nourishment will cause it to lose its characteristic appearance.

Repotting It is advisable to repot every year. Use plastic pots with a deep layer of crocks for drainage. Standard potting compost is very satisfactory.

Propagation It is not easy to grow this plant from cuttings or from seed. It is usually increased by division.

Siderasis fuscata

A small plant with thick oval leaves arranged in rosettes; they are 7 to 10cm (2¾ to 4in) long and 3 to 5cm (1 to 2in) wide. The surface is green and covered in long brown hairs. A white stripe runs along the centre vein, and the underside is reddish. Short-stalked bluish or purple flowers grow singly.

Siderasis fuscata

Sinningia speciosa, the well-known old-fashioned gloxinia

Sinningia

Gesneriaceae

Gloxinia

Name Named after Wilhelm Sinning, 1794–1874, Curator of the Botanical Gardens in Bonn. Benjamin Peter Gloxin was a physician from Colmar.
Origin About 20 natural species occur in the tropical rain forests of Brazil. The forms now available are the results of crossing natural varieties of *Sinningia speciosa*.
Description Sessile plants with large leaves and tubers up to 3cm (1in) in length. The large funnel-shaped flowers occur in striking colours.
Position In view of the plant's need for warmth and humidity a hothouse is the best position. There are enthusiasts, however, who succeed in cultivating the gloxinia in the living-room, though their number is decreasing. Bright sunshine must be avoided.
Care Find a warm, well-lit position out of the sun and ensure the highest possible degree of humidity. The temperature must not drop below 18°C (64°F).

After flowering the plant may be allowed to grow a little more, but towards the end of the summer the water supply must gradually be decreased until finally all the foliage turns yellow and dies. The tuber can now be left in the dry compost and kept in a dry environment at a minimum temperature of 15°C (59°F). At the end of February the old compost is removed and the tuber repotted and brought into growth at a temperature of about 20°C (68°F). Leave only two shoots on each tuber. The plant should preferably be cultivated in a hothouse.
Watering The gloxinia needs a great deal of water and is very sensitive to mineral salts. You should therefore always use unpolluted rainwater or demineralised water. If the leaves collapse the plant must immediately be plunged. The water should always be tepid.
Feeding The gloxinia is a real glutton. It likes a little fertiliser every time it is watered, but give it at half the recommended concentration or even less.
Repotting If the plant is sold in a very small pot it may benefit from being repotted immediately. Use lime-free potting compost. The best medium is a mixture of equal parts leafmould, peat and rotted cow manure.
Propagation The simplest method of increasing the plant is to take leaf cuttings or offsets. In the nursery the plant is grown from seed sown in autumn under glass, with special plant illumination. The temperature should be between 20 and 22°C (68 and 71°F). After three weeks the seedlings are pricked out; this operation is repeated a month later. Usually the plant is sold in a 12-cm (5-in) pot. The earliest strains may flower in April.
Pests and diseases Leaf curl indicates that either the air or the compost is too dry. Cold water causes basal rot. Dark brown circles on the leaves indicate a virus disease which is incurable. Occasionally begonia mites or cyclamen mites occur on the leaves.

Sinningia speciosa
◐ ⊜ ⓜ ⊛ ◐

Syn. *Gloxinia speciosa*. The oval to oblong leaves rise directly from the tuber; they are up to 25cm (10in) long, covered in velvety hairs, and the underside is often red. The flowers grow singly or in small groups and are long stalked and usually erect growing. The corolla is bell shaped, to 5cm (2in) long. Hybrids are available in a variety of colours.

Skimmia japonica covered in berries

Skimmia

Rutaceae

Name *Skimmi* is the Japanese name for this plant.
Origin About 12 species are known in China, Japan and the Himalayas.
Description The skimmia is best known as a garden plant. In coastal regions with reasonably mild winters some species are grown with particular success. They are small evergreen shrubs with conspicuously large red berries. A few specimens of *Skimmia japonica* are occasionally marketed as house plants.
Position You will have realised that this is not a plant for a warm living-room, but is more suitable for a cool corridor or an unheated holiday house. It will readily tolerate a few degrees of frost. It is also a useful plant for a sheltered balcony or for the garden. Do not put it in full sun.
Care Indoors the foliage must frequently be sprayed. Be sure to remove the plant from the living-room before the heating is turned on. It is useful to know that it is a dioecious plant; male and female flowers do not therefore appear on the same shrub. If you want to see the berries appear on your female plant for a second time you will need a male plant plus either some bees or, in an emergency, a little brush. It is clear that in practice they are not plants to enjoy year after year.
Watering Preferably use rainwater when watering.
Feeding In summer a measure of fertiliser solution may be given once a fortnight.
Repotting This plant needs an acid compost, rich in humus. Conifer needle compost is very suitable.
Propagation Ripe berries will produce viable seed which can be sown in autumn; no heat is required. In addition 10-cm (4-in) long tip cuttings may be rooted in August; again no heat is needed. In both cases the temperature need be only a few degrees above zero.

Skimmia japonica
◐ ● ⊖ ⓜ ⊛ ◐

A shrub up to 1m (3ft) in height with elliptical leathery leaves 7 to 10cm (2¾ to 4in) long and whitish flowers followed by bright red berries.

An orange-yellow *Smithiantha* hybrid

Smithiantha
Gesneriaceae
Temple Bells

Name Matilda Smith was a botanical artist attached to Kew Gardens. *Anthos* means flower.
Origin In Mexico and Guatemala four or five species are known, growing in humid mountain forests.
Description Plants with rhizomes and delicate, often heart-shaped deciduous leaves.
Position They should be grown in a hothouse, a glass case or a flower window. With great care it might be possible to keep them on the window-sill for a short time, but usually the air is too dry.
Care You will not often find a smithiantha at the garden shop, but the rhizomes may be obtained from a number of mail-order firms. The adventure will start with the receipt of a packet of sawdust in which sections of root are packed.

Plant the rhizomes in humusy compost, peat or damp sphagnum moss, and leave them in a temperature of 20 to 25°C (68 to 77°F) until they put out shoots. Keep them under glass for the time being, but look out for excessive moisture which will cause rotting.

When the shoots are clearly visible the rhizomes may be potted in groups of three or five in a 12-cm (4- or 5-in) pot. If you have enough rhizomes it is better not to start them all at once. Plant a few at a time; you will as a result have a longer flowering period.

It is advisable to keep the potted plantlets under glass for a while, otherwise you will find that they will abruptly stop growing. Make sure that both air and compost temperature are maintained at 20 to 22°C (68 to 71°F). After a few weeks you may carefully start to harden off the plants; it will soon become obvious how much dry air they tolerate. If at all possible they should remain in an inexpensive indoor propagator or in some other form of glass case. When the plants stop flowering, probably towards the end of summer, the water supply must be gradually reduced until the foliage dies. The rhizomes can spend the winter in dry soil at a minimum temperature of 12°C (53°F).
Watering In summer the compost must always be kept moderately moist; in winter no water is of course given at all. It is advisable to use tepid rainwater only.
Feeding When the plants are growing well they may be given a light feed every fortnight.
Repotting This happens automatically when the rhizomes are potted up again. The compost must be very light and humusy, and a mixture of peat, leafmould and rotted cow manure will therefore be ideal. Use very little lime.
Propagation After the rhizomes have developed shoots they may be divided, but make sure that each section bears at least one shoot. Leaf cuttings may be taken in summer. The leaf stalk should be shortened a little; the temperature of the cuttings compost should be 20 to 25°C (68 to 77°F).

Smithiantha cinnabarina
Syn. *Gesneria cinnabarina; Naegelia cinnabarina*. A hairy little plant with round to heart-shaped green leaves, up to 10 cm (4 in) across, lightly quilted; the hairs are red. It has red and white flowers.
***Smithiantha* hybrids**
The results of crossing the following species. These are the plants most frequently available.
Smithiantha multiflora
This has a cream-coloured flower with a little yellow.
Smithiantha zebrina
The green leaves with velvety hairs are brown along the veins, and the red flowers have a speckled throat.

Solanum
Solanaceae
Nightshade

Name A plant name from Roman times; its derivation is obscure. Possibly from *solamen*, consolation, comfort.
Origin In all about 1500 species are distributed over all parts of the world. Many are extremely poisonous.
Description These are small shrubby plants laden with spherical berries. They are usually marketed in autumn.
Position It is of great importance that the plants should not be kept too warm in winter. A temperature of 10°C (50°F) is quite enough. In summer the plants are best grown in the garden or on the balcony.
Care If the plants are brought straight into the heated living-room in October they will soon die. They should in any case be sprayed frequently. When the fruits have become unsightly the plant should be cut back drastically and moved to a cool environment.

In the spring the solanum will put out new shoots. After being repotted the plant must be kept in a cool place for the time being, but from the end of May onwards it can be moved out of doors. The plant will flower in summer and provided there are enough insects about to pollinate them, the flowers will be succeeded by plenty of berries. In autumn the plant must be brought indoors once more, for it is very sensitive to night frosts.
Watering In summer the solanum must be watered generously. Early in winter it continues to lose a great deal of moisture and care should be taken that the plant does not dry out in warm air. The foliage will provide a warning. Ordinary tap water is satisfactory.
Feeding Give a little nourishment every fortnight in summer, but avoid too much nitrogen.
Repotting Standard potting compost is satisfactory.
Propagation The plants are usually grown from seed sown in December–January in a soil temperature of 20°C (68°F). The seedlings should be pricked out and stopped several times, since otherwise the plants will become lanky. The temperature may now fall to 15°C (59°F). Around mid-May the plants can be moved to a sunny spot outside.

It is also possible to take tip cuttings in the winter. From now onwards the plantlets should be cultivated as above. Some extra light in the dark winter months may do wonders both for seedlings and for cuttings.
Pests and diseases Too warm a situation may lead to an infestation by aphids. Thrips and whitefly are other possible pests.

Solanum pseudocapsicum
Syn. *Capsicum capsicastrum*. Jerusalem Cherry. A small shrub with undulate, lance-shaped leaves, 5 cm (2 in) long, fresh green in colour. It bears clusters of greenish-white flowers, of which only one is fertile, and spherical berries, orange coloured and glossy.

The best-known cultivars are 'New Patterson', very compact; the fruits are initially green, later orange-red. In 'New Patterson Goldball' the fruits are white at first, later yellow. 'Christmas Cherry Jubilee' berries are at first white, later cherry coloured, and 'Red Giant' has extra large red fruits and is a vigorous grower.

Smithiantha hybrids have beautifully shaded foliage

Solanum pseudocapsicum, Jerusalem Cherry

Soleirolia
Urticaceae

Name This plant is generally known as the *Helxine*, which is derived from the Greek *helkein*, to draw, to pull. It was given its new name in honour of Captain Soleirol, who collected plants in Corsica in the 19th cenury.
Origin Corsica is the native habitat of this little plant. Only one species is known.
Description A low-growing, creeping plant, pale green in colour; it makes good ground cover.
Position Ideal as a ground-cover plant in greenhouses. It does not grow so well on the window-sill.
Care The plant does not need a great deal of warmth – 15°C (59°F) is enough – and in the living-room the atmosphere is usually too dry. Frequent spraying helps a little. However, rather than being grown in a pot, the soleirolia feels happier as ground cover in a large mixed container, where a certain amount of moist air rises from the compost.

Bright sunlight is undesirable, but plenty of light is appreciated. If the light is poor the stems will stretch badly. In winter the temperature may fall to 10°C (50°F).
Watering Always keep the compost moderately moist. Tap water may be used.
Repotting The plant has the characteristic tendency to grow outside the pot. Repotting therefore means providing an appropriately sized pot and this must be done every year. Use standard potting compost and wide bowls.
Propagation Very easily increased by division at any time of the year. In the beginning the new plants should be protected from evaporation by being put under glass.

Soleirolia soleirolii

Soleirolia soleirolii
Syn. *Helxine soleirolii*. A creeping plant with rooting stems, growing upwards to a height of 5 cm (2 in). The leaves are round and asymmetrical, 4 mm ($\frac{1}{4}$ in) across and pale green. 'Argentea' has silvery foliage and 'Aurea' is golden yellow.

Sonerila margaritacea

Sonerila
Melastomataceae

Name It appears to be derived from a Javanese name, Soothi-Soneri-ila.
Origin Java. About 70 species are known, distributed over the Indian archipelago and South China.
Description Small foliage plants with exceptionally fine marking on the leaves and beautifully contrasting flowers.
Position The plant requires a high degree of relative humidity and is therefore most at home in a hothouse, a flower window, a glass case or even in a bottle garden. During the summer months it may be kept on the window-sill, on condition that exceptional humidity can be maintained.
Care The temperature should always be above 20°C (68°F), except at night, when it may fall to 16°C (60°F) and in winter, when 18°C (64°F) is acceptable. In the living-room the plant must be cultivated above a bowl of water. Another way of giving it a high level of humidity is to plant it out in a wide and shallow container. Spraying the foliage does not agree with the plants.

Plenty of light is needed to maintain the beautiful foliage marking, but bright sunlight must be avoided.
Watering It is advisable to use demineralised water or rainwater, for the plants dislike lime. Always keep the compost moderately moist.
Feeding In summer give a measure of fertiliser solution every fortnight.
Repotting The sonerila likes an acid, porous compost. Conifer needle compost to which some rotted manure has been added is best. Wide, shallow bowls are most suitable, but they must be very well drained.
Propagation In early summer tip cuttings will readily root under glass, in a soil temperature of 20 to 25°C (68 to 77°F).

Sonerila margaritacea
A small plant with recumbent red stems and broad elliptical leaves to 7 cm ($2\frac{3}{4}$ in) long. The upper surface is green, with white patches which fuse into lines, and the underside is reddish. It has small lilac-pink flowers. 'Hendersonii' is the form most frequently cultivated. The foliage is more olive green with a red centre vein.

Sparmannia
Tiliaceae
African Hemp

Name Named after Andreas Sparmann, 1748–1820, a Swedish botanist.
Origin Seven original species are known; they grow in Africa and in Malagasy. The species described below occurs in South Africa.
Description A tree-like shrub with large, very delicate pale green leaves. The white flowers have beautiful yellow and red-brown stamens, which slowly spread outwards when touched by insects.
Position The African Hemp is a suitable plant for indoor cultivation, even in a centrally heated room, but it would appear to be rapidly losing its popularity. If it can be kept in a cool environment in winter it will present no problems.
Care Correctly tended, the sparmannia will flower between January and April. Afterwards it is advisable to give the plant a resting period by placing it in a cool environment and giving less water. Towards the end of May the plant is best laid on its side in the garden or on the balcony to avoid too much rainwater collecting in the pot, but it must be kept out of the sun. The plant may now be neglected for about a month and should then be vigorouly pruned to a height of 20 to 30 cm (8 to 12 in), repotted, and again put outside in a sheltered and shady position. It will subsequently develop into an immense shrub and by September it may be as much as 2 m (6 ft) tall. Before the first night frosts

Sparmannia africana, the African Hemp, has delicate hairy foliage

occur the plant must be moved indoors, and this may present some problems, for it will gradually have to become accustomed to the drier atmosphere. It is best, of course, to keep it as cool as possible, at a minimum temperature of 5°C (41°F). If the temperature is higher the plant must be sprayed frequently.
Watering In May the plant should be given a rest, during which period it is kept fairly dry, nor should it be given too much water after being pruned. Once it starts into full growth again it may be watered freely. In winter the water supply should depend on the temperature which will affect the rate of evaporation. Reasonably hard tap water will do no harm.
Feeding In the growing season the plant may be fed almost weekly. Stop feeding in August.
Repotting If you want to have a large plant within a short time it is advisable to repot every second month, until the plant ends up in a roomy plastic container. Standard potting compost is satisfactory, but if you prefer to mix your own the African Hemp will greatly appreciate a recipe consisting of equal parts of rotted beech leaves, pulverised clay or loam and rotted cow manure.
Propagation In spring cuttings can be

Flowers of *Sparmannia africana*

taken from the lateral shoots of flower stalks. Experience has shown that such cuttings produce better flowering plants than cuttings from non-flowering shoots. Warm cuttings compost is essential and the cuttings must be kept under glass until they have rooted. The young plants are stopped several times to encourage branching. In summer the plantlets may already be moved to the garden or the balcony.
Pests and diseases The foliage is very sensitive to carbon monoxide, gas and smoke. Yellow leaves may be caused by too much, too little or too cold water and also by lack of nourishment. Repotting usually helps. The plant may be infested by aphids, thrips and whitefly.

Sparmannia africana

A large shrub with heart-shaped pale green leaves up to 25 cm (10 in) across and covered in vertical hairs. The flowers appear in dense, long-stalked umbels with pendent buds. Each white flower is 3 to 4 cm in diameter; the sterile stamens are yellow with purple tips, the fertile ones are purple with yellow anthers. The plant flowers in spring.

Spathiphyllum wallisii resembles a white Flamingo Plant

Spathiphyllum
Araceae
Peace Lily

Name From the Greek *spathe*, blade, and *phyllon*, leaf. The name refers to the shape of the flower spathe and the spadix.
Origin Most species originate in tropical regions of America; only two have their native habitat in the Indian archipelago.
Description The plants resemble a white anthurium, but on closer inspection the leaves and the shape of the flower spathe are different. Cultivation follows fairly similar lines.
Position Undoubtedly the best spot is a hothouse with its high level of humidity, but many enthusiasts manage to keep their spathiphyllum in the living-room throughout the year.
Care The fairly thin leaves allow quite a lot of evaporation and this presents the greatest problems. Grow the plant above a basin of water – good advice, but think how large such a basin must be! An electric humidifier placed near the plant and surrounding the foliage with its mild steam will promise a more rosy future.

One advantage is that the plants have a dormant season in winter and at that time tolerate dry air a little better. During this period the temperature must not fall below 16°C (60°F).
Watering The water must always be tepid. Water generously in summer, but keep only moderately moist in winter.
Feeding Feed only in summer, approximately every fortnight.
Repotting In spring the plant may be repotted in standard potting compost. Plastic pots are suitable.
Propagation The easiest method is to divide the plants when they are being repotted. It is not difficult to raise new plants from seed, but the seed is not readily available.
Pests and diseases Brown leaf tips may indicate over-feeding or harmful minerals. Repot at once.

Spathiphyllum floribundum

The elongated oval leaf blade is dark green in colour, 10 to 20 cm (4 to 8 in) long and 5 to 9 cm (2 to $3\frac{1}{2}$ in) wide. The angle between the lateral and the centre veins is about 70 degrees. The flower stalk is longer than the leaves; the bract (that is, the spathe) is 7 by 3 cm ($2\frac{3}{4}$ by 1 in), white in colour, curving backward. This is the species most often cultivated.

Spathiphyllum patinii

The leaves of this species are a little darker and glossier and the angle between lateral and centre veins is about 45 degrees. The flower is practically the same as in the previous species.

Spathiphyllum wallisii

This plant again resembles the previous species; the angle between the veins is 45 degrees in this case also. It varies from the above species in that the flower spathe curves inwards instead of outwards and is somewhat larger.

Sprekelia
Amaryllidaceae
Jacobean Lily

Name Named after J. H. von Sprekelsen, a Hamburg town clerk who died in 1764. The colour and shape of the flower are connected with the red cross of the Knights of St Jacob of Calatrava.
Origin There is only one species, a native of Central America.
Description A bulbous plant somewhat reminiscent of the better-known hippeastrum or Amaryllis. The flower has a very unusual shape.
Position The bulbs may be forced on the window-sill, but they will also grow in the garden or on the balcony. Flowering will be extended if the plants are kept at a fairly low temperature.
Care The bulbs are usually ordered from a specialist grower or mail-order firm and delivered in spring. They should be potted with the neck showing above the compost. At first little water should be given and the pots kept in a warm environment to encourage the bulbs to start into growth. They may even be put on the radiator, but take care not to let the compost dry out. As soon as the bulbs are making some headway they must be moved to a cooler position, since otherwise the flowering season would be very short. After flowering the foliage must be retained to allow the bulb to feed for a time. The plants should therefore be placed in good light and given a feed from time to time. Do not stop watering until early July; the foliage will then die down. The bulbs may be kept in their pots at a minimum of 15°C (59°F) and repotted in November.
Watering Keep moderately moist only while the foliage is growing.
Feeding Again, feed only while the foliage is growing.
Repotting This is done at the end of the dormant season. Proprietary potting compost is quite satisfactory. Provide good drainage and use plastic pots.
Propagation Offset bulbs can be detached and potted separately; they may flower after three or four years. Fresh seed can also be sown.

Sprekelia formosissima

Syn. *Amaryllis formosissima*. Jacobean Lily. A bulbous plant with sword-shaped leaves, up to 40 cm (16 in) long. The long-stalked flowers grow singly; they are symmetrical, dark red and shiny, with golden yellow stamens.

Sprekelia formosissima, the Jacobean Lily

Stapelia variegata, the Carrion Flower

Stenandrium lindenii

Stapelia
Asclepiadaceae
Carrion Flower

Name Named after Johannes Bodaeus van Stapel, a Dutch physician who died in 1636.
Origin There are about 100 species, most of them occurring in South and South West Africa.
Description Plants with succulent stems and very conspicuous star-shaped flowers smelling of decaying flesh.
Position They are best in a temperate greenhouse, but it is pssible to grow this plant on a sunny window-sill in summer.
Care The plants are happiest in lattice baskets hung in the greenhouse, for the most important condition is perfect drainage. The fleshy stems rot only too easily, especially when too much water is given when the temperature is low. It is possible to overwinter the plants at 5°C (41°F) among other succulents in a cool greenhouse, but in that case the compost must be kept perfectly dry, otherwise they will inevitably rot. If the plants are kept too warm in winter, they will survive but will not flower.
Watering In summer they must be watered with great care; on cold and rainy days do not water them at all or the stems may rot. The plant will not easily die from lack of water. It is advisable always to use rainwater.
Feeding If the plant is repotted every year it need not be fed.
Repotting The best potting mixture consists of leafmould, some loam, rotted cow manure and sand. The pots must have exceptionally good drainage.
Propagation Break off stems and allow them to dry for about a week before inserting them in a fairly dry medium. Propagation from seed is also possible.

Stapelia variegata
Starfish Flower; Toad Flower. The quadrangular grey-green stems are tinged with red and the flowers are vividly marked. This is the strongest species for indoor cultivation. About 20 varieties exist. Enthusiasts grow numerous other species not described here; cultivation is similar.

Stenandrium
Acanthaceae

Name From the Greek *stenos*, narrow, lean, and *andros*, man.
Origin About 30 different species occur in tropical and subtropical regions of America. Only one is cultivated.
Description A creeping plant with beautifully marked foliage and spikes of yellow flowers.
Position This plant requires a high degree of humidity and is therefore not suitable for a heated living-room. However, it will flourish in a flower window, a bottle garden or an enclosed glass case.
Care The plant may be cultivated in a warm environment throughout the year; a minimum temperature of 20°C (68°F) is essential. In winter the mercury may fall to 13°C (55°F). If it is grown in the living-room the highest possible degree of humidity must be maintained, perhaps by frequent spraying. In summer these plants must be kept out of full sun, but in winter plenty of light is required to maintain the foliage marking. Some form of artificial lighting may be useful.
Watering In summer the compost must always remain moderately moist. If the temperature falls in winter the water supply must naturally be reduced. It is advisable to use warmed rainwater.
Feeding When the plant is putting out new shoots it may be fed a little every fortnight.
Repotting The potting mixture must be porous and contain plenty of humus and little lime. Coarse peat lumps, rotted cow manure, conifer needle soil: these are the best ingredients. Use shallow bowls with good drainage.
Propagation The plants may be increased by division or from tip cuttings. In both cases the new plants must be kept under glass at a temperature of 30°C (86°F) for the time being.

Stenandrium lindenii
Small plants with short, creeping stems and reverse-oval leaves, to 10 cm (4 in) long. The upper surface is velvety green with yellow veining; the underside is reddish. Flowers have a yellow corolla in narrow spikes, to 7 cm (2¾ in) long.

Stenocarpus
Proteaceae

Name From the Greek *stenos*, narrow, and *karpos*, fruit.
Origin About 30 species occur, distributed over New Caledonia, Australia, New Guinea and the southern Moluccas.
Description A fairly rare house plant; occasionally some of the species are available. It is reminiscent of a codiaeum which has reverted to green. The leaves are very irregularly incised.
Position Contrary to many people's opinion this is a plant for a cool greenhouse or for other places which are kept fairly cool in winter. The plant will deteriorate if it is kept in the warm living-room throughout the year.
Care Cultivation varies little from that of the grevillea, another of those Australian trees which in its native habitat may grow to enormous size. This rarely happens in our climate, unfortunately, for large specimens may produce magnificent clusters of red and orange-yellow flowers in summer. If the plant is grown in a very large greenhouse, where it may reach 4 to 6 m (13 to 20 ft) in height, flowers may appear, but smaller plants will not flower.

In summer the plants may be grown outside, provided they are given a sheltered position out of very bright sunshine. In other words it makes an attractive tub plant. In September the stenocarpus should be moved to its winter quarters, where a minimum temperature of 4 to 10°C (39 to 50°F) can be maintained.
Watering In summer it is advisable to give the plant plenty of water from time to time and to plunge it occasionally, but when the temperature falls in winter the plant needs less water. Ordinary tap water will not be catastrophic.
Feeding In favourable conditions the plants are very vigorous and it is therefore useful to feed them once a fortnight in summer.
Repotting The plants should preferably be repotted every spring, if only to get rid of harmful minerals in the compost. Standard potting compost yields good results.
Propagation In August tip cuttings may be taken; these should be kept under glass at a temperature of 5 to 10°C (41 to 50°F) throughout the winter. If no roots have developed by the spring some additional soil heat will be helpful. In the first year the young plants must be cultivated in the greenhouse. Propagation from seed presents few difficulties. The seed is sown in January–February, at a temperature of 20°C (68°F).

Stenocarpus salignus
In its natural habitat this is a tree. In cultivation it forms a shrub with red-brown twigs and lanceolate leathery, practically sessile leaves. It bears fragrant creamy-white flowers.
Stenocarpus sinuatus
A robust shrub with very irregularly shaped, incised leaves, green and glossy, with very conspicuous veining. The flowers grow in axillary and terminal clusters; they are scarlet in colour with yellow stamens and yellow bracts.

Stenocarpus sinuatus, a plant for a cool environment

Stenotaphrum secundatum 'Variegatum'

Stenotaphrum

Gramineae

St Augustine's Grass

Name From the Greek *stenos*, narrow, and *taphros*, trench.
Origin About eight species occur in many coastal areas in the tropics.
Description A broad-leaved creeping grass. In the tropics its common green form is used as lawn grass.
Position No harm will be done if the plants are placed in full sun, in summer out of doors.
Care It is a strong plant which will survive in all sorts of conditions. In winter it prefers to be kept a little cooler; at this time a little less water should be given. In summer really good light is necessary to maintain the foliage marking.

The plant shows to best advantage if grown in a hanging pot.
Watering Any kind of water is satisfactory. If the plant is placed in full sun in summer it must be watered freely to keep it from drying out.
Feeding Generous feeding will encourage the plant to spread rapidly, but too much nitrogen will make variegated forms revert to green.
Repotting The stenotaphrum accepts standard potting compost, but will grow better if a little loam or clay is added to the mixture. It is a good idea to divide the plant every year in spring and to pot up the best parts.
Propagation In many cases plantlets complete with roots develop on the long shoots, and these can be detached. Division is another easy method of propagation and also the plant can be increased from tip cuttings.

Stenotaphrum secundatum
○⊜⊘⊛◙
Syn. *Stenotaphrum americanum; Stenotaphrum glabrum*. This is a plant with flattened creeping stems. The leaves are 15 by 1 cm (6 by ½ in), blunt tipped and broadly sheathed at the base. The flexible flower spikes break up into pieces.

The form usually cultivated is the cultivar 'Variegatum' (Buffalo Grass) in which the leaves have a creamy lengthwise streak.

Stephanotis

Asclepiadaceae

Wax Flower

Name From the Greek *stephanos*, crown, and *ous, otos*, ear.
Origin There is only one species: in Malagasy, its natural habitat, it is a climbing shrub growing in mountain forests.
Description In cultivation the long shoots are usually trained around a wire hoop to make the plant easier to transport. The fragrant white flowers are the pride of any plant enthusiast – and of many a traditional bride as well.
Position This is a true house plant, although this does not alter the fact that it flourishes even more in the greenhouse, where it will be easier to provide the desired low temperature in winter.
Care Many people encounter problems with this attractive plant. Either it refuses to flower, or the buds fall, or it is infested by pests. All these symptoms may be ascribed to incorrect cultivation. The right treatment is therefore described here in detail.

If you have purchased a flowering plant in spring, you are advised to put it in a well-lit position, out of the midday sun. As is so often the case, an east-facing window-sill is ideal. The foliage may occasionally be lightly sprayed. All new tendrils are carefully trained round the wire hoop, for the plant must remain transportable. At first some of the buds may drop as a result of the change in the angle of the light. Mark the pot and always keep the plant facing in one direction. Maintain a temperature of 18 to 20°C (64 to 68°F), which may fall to 15°C (59°F) at night.

As autumn approaches the water supply should be slightly reduced and it is essential to move the plant to a cooler environment with a temperature of 12 to 14°C (53 to 57°F). A very well-lit unused bedroom is very suitable. If the plant is kept in a warmer spot you will have nothing but trouble in the following year.

Bud formation starts towards the end of the winter, when the days are beginning to lengthen. Flowering can be advanced by means of artificial illumination, lengthening the amount of light to 12 hours; an ordinary lamp will do.

In a heated greenhouse the Wax Flower is best planted out in the compost with the long shoots trained along the framework. Screening must be provided in summer. The necessary winter temperature can easily be achieved by turning down the thermostat by a few degrees, but even without this measure the atmosphere near the glass, where most of the shoots are growing, is appreciably cooler.
Watering The water must not be too hard and rainwater is therefore best. In summer the compost must always be kept moderately moist; allowing it to dry out may have an adverse effect on the plant. In winter the compost may feel a little drier to the touch without harm. At that time use tepid water.
Feeding During the months of active growth the plant may be given a light feed every fortnight. If in your opinion the plants are growing rapidly enough they need not be fed. The pot compost contains sufficient nutrients for a whole year.

Stephanotis floribunda. The tendrils have been trained on wires

Repotting Annual repotting in spring is advisable; a great deal of waste matter is disposed of with the old compost. The best potting mixture consists of rotted turves, rotted cow manure, leafmould and sharp sand. As this mixture is not always easy to obtain, standard potting compost is often used with great success. Always insert a layer of crocks for drainage. Young plants must be provided with a wire hoop along which the tendrils can be trained.
Propagation The best method of increase is to take cuttings from the previous year's wood; this is done in spring. Do not take tip cuttings from the fresh growth – in other words, use eye cuttings or stem cuttings. Rooting may be encouraged by the use of a little rooting powder. The soil temperature should be 20 to 25°C (68 to 77°F) and it is essential to cover the cuttings with glass or plastic. Rooting may take as long as two years.

Sometimes the plant, to our great surprise, suddenly produces a large plum-like fruit. It takes at least a year to ripen. It then bursts and flat brown seeds with silvery fluff appear.

Sown in heated seed compost these seeds will germinate readily. It is of course great fun to increase your plant collection in this manner, but unfortunately experience has shown that plants grown by this method flower either very late or not at all, and propagation from cuttings is therefore a much better and more rewarding method.

Flowers of *Stephanotis floribunda*

Pests and diseases The stephanotis is rather susceptible to red spider mite, mealy bug and scale insects. Control is possible, but bearing in mind that these pests are nearly always the result of too high a temperature in winter it is obviously better to correct errors in cultivation.

Stephanotis floribunda
◐⊜⊘⊛◙▢
Wax Flower. An evergreen shrub with oval, glossy green leaves, to 9 cm (3½ in) long and 5 cm (2 in) wide. It bears axillary clusters of fragrant white flowers; the corolla is trumpet shaped with spreading petals.

Strelitzia reginae, Bird of Paradise Flower

'Constant Nymph', a very popular *Streptocarpus* hybrid

Strelitzia

Musaceae

Bird of Paradise Flower

Name The plant was named after Charlotte von Mecklenburg-Strelitz, 1744–1818, who married King George III. The flower looks like the head of a bird of paradise.
Origin Five different species occur in South Africa, but only one is cultivated as a house plant.
Description These are plants with very large leaves, reminiscent of those of the banana plant, and unusual, long-stalked flowers.
Position The plants are happiest in a temperate greenhouse, where they may grow to considerable size, but they can also be treated as tub plants. In the living-room it is rather too warm for them in winter.
Care Both indoors and outside the plant can grow in full sun. In winter it prefers a temperature of between 8 and 14°C (46 and 57°F). If you do not have a temperate greenhouse try to find another well-lit position. The very striking flowers appear in December–January.
Watering In summer the plants can take plenty of water, but in winter they should be kept appreciably drier, although the foliage must not be allowed to wilt. The water should be tepid.
Feeding Feed every fortnight in the growing season.
Repotting The plants have fleshy roots which easily rot if damaged. They must therefore be repotted as carefully and as seldom as possible. In the case of mature plants once every three years is sufficient, although the top layer of compost must be renewed every spring. This is where the greatest pollution occurs. If in spite of your care the roots become damaged, they should be trimmed with a sharp knife and dusted with charcoal powder.

The most favourable potting mixture consists of equal parts of clay or loam, rotted beech leaves and rotted cow manure. After the ingredients have been thoroughly mixed a little charcoal and a handful of bonemeal should be added.
Propagation Large plants may be divided when they are repotted. Propagation from seed is another possibility, but the seed must be very fresh. The plants will flower after four years. I am sometimes asked whether cut flowers can be rooted, but of course this is not possible.

Strelitzia reginae

The long-stalked leaves rise from the roots. The leaf blade is up to 80 by 25 cm (32 by 10 in) in size; it is gutter shaped with a wavy margin, leathery and blue-green in colour. The flowers possess a boat-shaped bract; the buds are submerged in water. When they emerge the orange and blue flowers develop.

Streptocarpus

Gesneriaceae

Cape Primrose

Name Derived from the Greek *streptos*, twisted, and *karpos*, fruit. The seed pods are indeed twisted.
Origin About 90 species are known, all originating in wooded areas of South Africa and Malagasy.
Description The large leaves are the conspicuous feature of these plants, and they are even larger in the original species. Hybrid cultivation has mainly been aimed at creating smaller foliage. The violet-coloured, rose-red or white flowers are long stalked.

Occasionally the leaf sap may cause an itchy rash.
Position Grown in a greenhouse the plants present no problems, but fortunately they will also thrive in the living-room. An east- or west-facing window is best.
Care Treated as long-day plants they flower in the summer months and this is fortunate for in that season the degree of relative humidity in the living-room is higher than in winter and these forest plants require a reasonable degree of humidity. Bright sunlight is undesirable, especially between the hours of 11 a.m. and 5 p.m.

A red strain of streptocarpus

One of the original species

When the plant is in flower some of the older leaves may be removed from time to time; they will soon be succeeded by young foliage. Faded flowers should be cut out at the base of the stalk. Properly cared for, these plants will flower profusely from May to October, and the flowering season may be prolonged if the plants are situated below an electric light which artificially lengthens the day. Cut flowers will last in winter for nearly a week.

In winter it is advisable to allow the streptocarpus a dormant season in a cooler environment; 12°C (53°F) is enough. An unused bedroom, a spot below the greenhouse staging or a similar position are suitable. If there isn't enough space the largest leaves can be removed.

After being repotted in April the plants are brought into growth once more; they will soon get into their stride.
Watering In summer the compost must always be kept moderately moist. Slightly wilting leaves will soon recover if the plant is watered immediately. Preferably use rainwater. In winter the plant should be kept drier.
Feeding In the growing period the plants may be fed every fortnight.
Repotting The best time to repot is after the dormant season and it is advisable to repeat the operation every spring. Fairly roomy plastic pots with good drainage are best. Put them in plastic saucers to catch the excess water. Standard potting compost is quite acceptable. The plants can be divided when they are being repotted; only the young growth is used. The plants are at their most beautiful when they are two years old. Older specimens should be discarded.
Propagation There is a very original method of propagating these plants from leaf cuttings. In early summer a leaf is cut along the centre vein and both halves are inserted vertically into the cuttings medium, which is kept warm and under glass. In time a row of plantlets will develop along the cut edges, and these may be potted up separately. It is advisable to keep them under glass for a time.

Seed may be sown at any time of the year at a temperature of about 18°C (64°F). The seedlings are pricked out once, still under glass, and are then hardened.

Named hybrids will not grow true to type from seed; you may have all sorts of surprises.
Pests and diseases Aphids and thrips are the chief threats.

***Streptocarpus* hybrids**
The foliage of the different hybrids varies in shape, but the leaves are always long, sometimes smooth and occasionally wrinkled. They are arranged in rosettes or grow singly, all depending on the various characteristics of their progenitors. Among the well-known strains are 'Constant Nymph', with lilac purple dark-veined flowers, and the 'Wiesmoor' hybrids which occur in a range of shades including rose red, white and blue.
Streptocarpus wendlandii
This is an original single-leaved species; the leaf may grow to a length of 50 cm (20 in) and is quilted. The underside is reddish. Small but numerous blue flowers are borne in very long plumes.

Stromanthe
Marantaceae

Name From the Greek *stroma*, blanket, and *anthos*, flower.
Origin Thirteen species occur in tropical regions of South America.
Description These fairly rare plants are easily confused with the *Ctenanthe* and the *Calathea* genera. The foliage is conspicuously marked.
Position They are hothouse plants. In the living-room the air is too dry, especially in winter when the central heating is turned on.
Care These plants must be grown at temperatures of between 18 and 22°C (64 and 71°F) at all times of the year. A dormant season is barely perceptible. Between 9 a.m. and 5 p.m. bright sunlight must be avoided. The plants are sometimes sold to be grown in mixed plant containers, but indoors they will nearly always give disappointing results. On the other hand they will flourish in an enclosed space such as a glass case or a flower window.
Watering It is advisable to use unpolluted rainwater.
Feeding In the period of active growth they may be fed normally, that is, given a fortnightly allowance of fertiliser solution.
Repotting The stromanthe prefers wide, shallow pots or bowls with good drainage and also likes being planted out on the greenhouse staging, where its root system has room to develop. Perlite must be added to standard potting compost to make it more porous.
Propagation Division is the best means of increase.

Stromanthe amabilis
An erect-growing plant with firm oval leaves with a short point. The surface is pale green with grey cross-banding, and the reverse is grey-green.
Stromanthe sanguinea
A stiffly erect-growing plant with fleshy, lanceolate leaves, to 40 cm (16 in) long, dark green and glossy, with a pale centre vein. The underside is blood red.

Syngonium
Araceae

Name From the Greek *syn*, common, joint, and *goeia*, procreation.
Origin About 20 species occur in the tropical rain forests of Central and South America.
Description The plants closely resemble the philodendron; only the smaller variegated species are visibly different. They are cultivated in the same way.
Position The strongest species will grow well in a warm living-room. The others prefer a hothouse. The plants do not require a great deal of light.
Care These climbers must be tied, for instance to a moss-covered pole. The temperature should be kept at 15°C (59°F) throughout the year, preferably even a few degrees higher, but bright sunlight must be avoided. Daily spraying and a monthly sponge-down are much appreciated. Aerial roots may be trained towards the compost.
Watering The plant likes fairly acid conditions and it would be a pity to spoil this by watering with calcareous water. Rainwater is therefore preferable, and it must be warmed. The compost must be kept moderately moist at all times of the year.
Feeding When new growth is developing the plant may be given a measure of fertiliser solution once a fortnight.
Repotting It is advisable to repot these fast-growing plants every year, for they quickly exhaust the compost. The best potting mixture consists of rotted leaf-mould, coarse peat lumps and rotted manure. Conifer needle compost is also very suitable. The plants will grow reasonably well in standard compost, preferably peat based as a soil-based medium is often not really sufficiently friable.
Propagation Increase from tip cuttings or from eye cuttings, whichever you prefer. Bottom heat is essential and the cuttings must be covered with glass or plastic. Plants that have grown too tall may be air-layered.
Pests and diseases Sometimes mealy bug or scale insects occur, especially if the plant has been kept in a draught.

Syngonium auritum
This has thick, glossy green leaves, three lobed or five lobed. With a little imagination you might compare the leaves of mature plants to the five fingers of a hand, with a very small thumb and little finger.
Syngonium podophyllum
Arrowhead Vine. Foot-shaped compound leaves with five to eleven lobes. There are many forms with attractive marking, including 'Albolineatum'.
Syngonium vellozianum
This is the species which most closely resembles the philodendron, but it is distinguished among other things by the very variable leaves. At an early age they are arrow shaped, they then become three lobed, later still five lobed, usually with two small ear-shaped appendages.
All species may produce Arum Lily-like flowers, but this rarely happens.

Syngonium podophyllum 'Albolineatum'

Syngonium podophyllum

Stromanthe amabilis

Tetraclinis articulata

Tetraclinis
Cupressaceae

Name Derived from the Greek *tetraclinos*, which means 'four beds'. This refers to the leaves which are arranged in four tidy rows and bear a slight resemblance to small beds.
Origin This is a monotypic genus; in other words it consists of only one species. It occurs in Algeria, Morocco and also in Malta.
Description The plants found at the garden shop have usually either been imported or greenhouse grown from seed. They resemble small cypresses and have a characteristic blue-green colour.

The wood of these trees is hard and fine grained. It appears that it was greatly valued by the Romans, who paid high prices for it. It was, and still is, used in the manufacture of furniture. In addition the trees produce a fragrant resin, used at one time in high-quality varnish.
Position These conifers can be kept in the living-room in summer, but may equally well be grown out of doors. The winter must be spent in frost-free quarters.
Care It is doubtful whether the tetraclinis should be regarded as a house plant, but because of its unusual appearance (hardly any other indoor conifers exist) it is occasionally bought for this purpose. Grown indoors it will remain in good condition for a longer time if the foliage is sprayed very often. Choose a spot in good light but out of the sun. In Africa large trees will tolerate sun, but a young plant cannot take it very well. Towards the winter move the plant to a cool greenhouse or orangery, where it should be kept at a minimum temperature of 5°C (41°F).
Watering Keep moderately moist in summer and drier in winter.
Feeding When the plant is in growth give it a measure of fertiliser solution every fortnight.
Repotting A little clay in the potting compost is recommended.
Propagation Increase from imported seeds, which germinate under glass.

Tetraclinis articulata

Syn. *Callitris quadrivalvis; Thuja articulata.* A small tree with round, spreading branches. The needle-like little new leaves become scale shaped in maturity, and the plant bears bullet-shaped to oval cones.

Tetrastigma
Vitaceae
Chestnut Vine

Name From the Greek *tetra*, four, and *stigma*, stigma. The stigmata in fact consist of four parts, in contrast to those of all the other genera of the vine family.
Origin Nearly 100 species occur in tropical Asia, as far as New Guinea and one species is found in Australia.
Description This is a climber with five-lobed foliage, an obvious member of the vine family.
Position This climber feels extremely happy in a greenhouse, where it will rapidly grow into a troublesome creeper, obstructing the exit.
Care The plant may or may not thrive in the living-room. If it does grow there it will do so in spurts, producing fragile shoots several feet long. The shoots, especially the young ones, bear small, transparent 'pustules', which appear to indicate some disease, but they are, in fact, part of the plant and disappear at a later stage.

It is advisable to keep this plant in not too warm an environment: warm air is a little too dry. It will grow best in surroundings kept at a temperature of between 12 and 18°C (53 and 64°F); in winter the mercury may fall to 10°C (50°F). When the plant becomes too large it should be pruned vigorously and the tendrils securely tied.
Watering Always keep the compost moderately moist.
Feeding When the plant is in growth it may be fed every fortnight.
Repotting The plant will grow well in standard potting compost. Use roomy pots with good drainage.
Propagation It is best increased from eye cuttings; the stem is cut just above and just below an eye. The leaf stalk and the leaf are retained, but the leaf may be reduced in size. A compost temperature of 25°C (77°F) is essential for rooting.

Tetrastigma voinierianum

Syn. *Vitis voinieriana*. An evergreen climber with palmately divided leaves consisting of five leaflets, each 15cm (6in) long and 6cm (2¼in) wide. The upper surface is green and glossy, the underside is covered in brownish hairs. The plant rarely flowers.

Tetrastigma voinierianum

Thunbergia
Acanthaceae
Black-eyed Susan

Name Named after Carl Peter Thunberg, 1743–1822, a Swedish botanist who was a friend of Linnaeus. He later became Professor of Botany at Uppsala.
Origin About 100 species occur in East Africa, Malagasy and tropical Asia. Only one is regularly marketed as a house plant.
Description A small climber with thin stems and numerous yellow-orange flowers with a black centre.
Position It will flourish on a sunny window-sill, but after the end of May it may successfully be kept in the garden or on a balcony.

Thunbergia alata

Care As a rule these plants are grown as annuals. They must be kept out of a draught, but otherwise present no problems. They may be carried through the winter in a cold greenhouse and after they have been cut back and repotted in early spring they might again flower profusely. There are other species suitable for cultivation in a hothouse or a temperate greenhouse, but they are rarely available.
Watering In summer they need a fair amount of water; ordinary tap water will do. In winter the plants should receive only just enough water to survive.
Feeding The flowering season will be prolonged if the Black-eyed Susan is given some nourishment at normal concentration every fortnight in summer.
Repotting This is only necessary if the plants are kept through the winter. In that case use standard potting compost.
Propagation Anyone can grow these plants from seed. It is easily obtainable from some mail-order firms or from a seedsman. From February onwards sow four to six seeds directly in the pot, which should be kept under glass at a temperature of 20°C (68°F). After germination keep the plants under glass or plastic at first. The tendrils must be carefully tied.

Thunbergia alata

A hairy annual climber with thin, heart-shaped to arrow-shaped leaves, coarsely toothed and with winged stalks. The axillary flowers grow singly; the corolla is up to 4cm (1½in) across, yellow to orange with a very dark ring in the centre. There are strains with white, pale yellow and pure orange flowers.

Thunbergia grandiflora

A hairless climber with oval to lanceolate leaves, sometimes lobed. They are up to 15cm (6in) long; the leaf stalk is not winged. The flowers are borne in dense, pendent clusters; the corolla is blue and may reach a diameter of 7cm (2¾in). This species is only suitable for large hothouses.

Tillandsia

Bromeliaceae

Name Named after Elias Tillands, 1640–1693, a Swedish professor of biology.
Origin There are more than 400 species, distributed over the southern states of North America and over the whole of South America.
Description The funnel shape, so characteristic of bromeliads, is not always very obvious. Some species have very small leaves.
Position Species with scaly leaves require plenty of light and warmth, combined with fresh air. The degree of humidity needed may be variable. Non-scaly species are satisfied with less light, but demand a higher and more constant level of humidity.
Care All species must be protected from bright sunshine. Since most of them prefer to grow on trees they may be used successfully in flower windows, glass cases and greenhouses, where they can be cultivated on bromeliad trees. As is the case with all bromeliads, each rosette flowers only once.

Species with scaly leaves may be kept a great deal cooler in winter. A temperate greenhouse is what they like best with a minimum temperature in winter 12°C (53°C). The other species belong in a hothouse where the minimum temperature is 18 to 20°C (64 to 68°F).
Watering Tillandsia plants are very sensitive to lime and it is therefore essential to use only unpolluted rainwater or demineralised water. It is not always easy to pour the water in the correct spot, for instance the axil of a stem, and in that case it is better to water by spraying. Species which are kept cooler in winter should be given less water at that time, or even none at all.
Feeding The nutrients are also best supplied by means of spraying. Special foliar fertilisers are available, which are very suitable for the purpose. Feed only when the plant is in growth.
Repotting Epiphytic species with scaleless foliage may also be grown in pots in a mixture of perlite, rotted beech leaves and chopped osmunda roots. They are repotted every year. Scaly species must carefully be tied to tree branches, together with some sphagnum moss, tree-fern or osmunda fibre; copper wire may be used for the purpose.
Propagation Young offsets with a section of root can be detached from the parent plant. They should be kept under glass for a time.

Tillandsia flabellata

Tillandsia lindenii

Tillandsia usneoides, Spanish Moss

Tillandsia leiboldiana

Non-scaly species

Tillandsia cyanea

Syn. *Tillandsia morreniana*. This plant is about 30cm (1ft) in diameter. The narrow leaves, arranged in rosettes, are reddish brown at the base and are striped lengthwise with brown. A firm flower stalk bears a 5-cm (2-in) wide and 8-cm (3-in) tall inflorescence consisting of overlapping green bracts, from which a few small, dark blue flowers without a white eye protrude.

Tillandsia flabellata

This plant is 20 to 50cm (8 to 20in) in height; the leaves are 4cm (1½in) wide and up to 40cm (16in) long, green or reddish. It has a very short flower stalk with red bracts in an elongated spike and blue flowers with protruding yellow stamens.

Tillandsia leiboldiana

This plant is 30 to 60cm (1 to 2ft) tall. The soft green leaves are 30cm (1ft) long and 5cm (2in) wide. It has a long flower stalk with spreading, curled-up bracts surrounding tubular blue flowers.

Tillandsia lindenii

A plant 40cm (16in) tall, the green leaves are 25 to 35cm (10 to 14in) long and 1 to 2cm (½ to ¾in) wide. Long flower stalks carry a large inflorescence, and the bracts are violet pink, the flowers dark blue with a white eye.

Species with scaly foliage

Tillandsia argentea

The leaf sheaths form a complete sphere. The leaves are rolled up and bodkin shaped, covered all over in silvery scales, 1mm thick at the base and 2 to 3cm (¾ to 1in) long. There are spreading red or green bracts and blue or red flowers.

Tillandsia usneoides

Spanish Moss. This plant grows suspended from tree branches; it lacks roots and is covered all over in grey scales. The cylindrical leaves are 5cm (2in) long and it has inconspicuous yellow-green flowers.

Tolmiea menziesii, the Pick-a-back Plant

Tolmiea

Saxifragaceae

Pick-a-back Plant

Name Named after Dr W. F. Tolmie, died 1886, an American physician and plant collector.
Origin There is only one species; it occurs on the west coast of North America.
Description A simple plant with green leaves bearing plantlets in the centre.
Position They are strong house plants and will flourish anywhere as long as they are kept out of full sun. In summer the plants may be moved to the garden.
Care Anyone can grow this plant and it is surprising that it is not sold in greater numbers. It will continue to grow even in a fairly dark environment. Never mind if the temperature falls to 10°C (50°F) in winter. At the same time the tolmiea will also thrive in a heated room, where the temperature may sometimes be as much as 22°C (71°F). Spraying is appreciated, but is not absolutely essential. When the plants become too large or mishapen they can be cut back drastically.

If they are grown out of doors they quite often produce flowers.
Watering Large plants require a fair amount of water. If the foliage should collapse the plant will recover immediately as soon as it is plunged.
Feeding In summer a measure of fertiliser solution may be given every fortnight.
Repotting Repot in spring in standard compost, using plastic pots.
Propagation The method is very simple. Detach a 'parent leaf', cut off the leaf blade surrounding the plantlet and bury it just below the compost so that the plantlet remains just visible. Mature plants are also easily increased by division.

Tolmiea menziesii

The long-stalked leaves are arranged in rosettes. The leaf is heart shaped, three to five lobed, bi-dentate, green and hairy. Young plantlets appear at the base. It bears green to brownish flowers in up to 25-cm (10-in) long clusters.

Torenia fournieri, an annual plant

Torenia
Scrophulariaceae

Name Named after Olaf Toren, 1718–1753, a Swedish clergyman who discovered the plant.
Origin More than 40 species occur in tropical and subtropical zones of Asia and Africa.
Description Attractive annuals, but not very often available at the garden shop. They bear small purple flowers with a little yellow.
Position In summer the plants may be grown in good light on the window-sill, but will also do well on a sheltered balcony or terrace.
Care The plants are usually sold in flower early in the summer. Keeping them in flower until the autumn is not difficult. There is no point in trying to keep the plant, for once it has flowered, as an annual it will die anyway.
Watering In summer the compost must always be kept moderately moist. The torenia loses a fair amount of moisture in evaporation, especially if it is kept in a sunny spot. Ordinary tap water will do no harm.
Feeding The plant is usually grown in a small pot and by the time it starts to flower its nutrient supply will have been exhausted. It will then be helpful to give it some fertiliser every fortnight.
Repotting This is normally unnecessary. Home-grown plants can be planted in standard potting compost.
Propagation Seed may be obtained from mail-order firms and is sown in February, under glass, at a temperature of about 18°C (64°F). Seedlings are pricked out in groups of five to ten in their permanent pots, which should have a diameter of 12cm (4$\frac{1}{2}$in). They should then be slowly hardened off and the growing point pinched out a number of times to encourage branching. Keep them out of bright sunlight.

Torenia fournieri
An annual plant with at first recumbent, then erect-growing stems. It has oval leaves, 3 to 5cm (1 to 2in) long and 1 to 2cm ($\frac{1}{2}$ to $\frac{3}{4}$in) wide, the base narrowing towards the fairly long leaf stalk. The flowers grow in terminal clusters; the calyx has spreading wings, the corolla is pale violet in colour. Three of the four lobes bear a large deep violet patch, and the throat is yellow at the bottom. In the form 'Alba' the corolla is white with purple patches. 'Grandiflora' produces extra large flowers.

Tradescantia
Commelinaceae
Spiderwort

Name Named after John Tradescant. John the father, who died in 1638, was gardener to Charles I; his son John, died 1662, was a botanist and explorer.
Origin More than 30 species grow in North and South America. The indoor species were discovered long after the garden plants.
Description Usually recumbent, stem-rooting plants with interesting colouring and marking. They are used mostly as hanging plants.
Position Species with white marking on the foliage require a fairly well-lit position, since otherwise the leaves will turn dull green. A warm living-room is a good spot, but most species can be grown outside in summer. In greenhouses the plants are frequently used as ground cover under the staging.
Care In winter these plants often suffer from excessively dry air and it is therefore advisable to keep them a little cooler at that time, but temperatures below 10°C (50°F) should be avoided.

Apart from this point they are undemanding plants which present few problems. When the foliage colouring deteriorates new plants are quickly grown from cuttings.
Watering The plants have slightly succulent stems, which means that they do not need a great deal of water in summer. If they are kept in a cooler environment in winter the compost may be allowed to dry out completely from time to time. A little tepid water should be given only if the plants become really limp.
Feeding They are vigorous plants and may therefore be fed every fortnight in summer. Stop feeding in winter.
Repotting The plants frequently present an untidy appearance and it is therefore advisable to shape them or renew them from cuttings at frequent intervals. These should be potted in fresh compost. Standard compost is satisfactory; the plants have no particular requirements. Use plastic pots or special hanging pots with good drainage. If they are provided with a saucer you will not be bothered by drips.
Propagation The runners spontaneously develop roots when they touch the soil, so you can imagine how easily these plants are grown from cuttings. A few tip cuttings placed in a bottle of water or in compost will invariably root. Summer is the best time.
Pests and diseases The parent plant is rarely subject to pests though greenfly may appear if the plant is often in a draught. They will disappear if this condition is improved; in any case they may be disposed of by harmless domestic remedies.

Tradescantia blossfeldiana 'Variegata'

Tradescantia albiflora 'Rochford Silver'

Tradescantia albiflora
A hairless plant with creeping or trailing stems and short-stalked green leaves, up to 1.5cm ($\frac{1}{2}$in) wide, 4.5 to 6cm (1$\frac{3}{4}$ to 2$\frac{1}{4}$in) long, and white flowers. The form most often cultivated is 'Albo-vittata' with cream-coloured lengthwise stripes on the foliage. The newer strain 'Rochford Silver' has more pronounced clear white marking. 'Tricolor' has white and pale purple striping.
Tradescantia blossfeldiana
A hairy plant with creeping stems and slightly fleshy leaves, 4 to 8cm (1$\frac{1}{2}$ to 3in) long and 2 to 4cm ($\frac{3}{4}$ to 1$\frac{1}{2}$in) wide, growing fairly close together in two distinct rows. The upper surface is dull green and hairless, the underside violet coloured and hairy. It bears pink flowers, white at the base. Of this species there is also a white-striped form, 'Variegata'.
Tradescantia fluminensis
Resembles *T. albiflora* to some extent, but it is easily distinguished by its sap, which is violet coloured in this species and colourless in *T. albiflora*. In addition the leaves are a little more compact, only two to three times longer than they are wide. There is again a form 'Variegata', with lengthwise white striping.
Tradescantia sillamontana
The entire plant is covered in long white hairs. The stems are creeping, the leaves fairly small and the flowers pink. This species has a strict dormant season in winter when the surface growth dies down.

Trevesia sanderi

Trevesia
Araliaceae

Name Named after the Italian family Treves di Bonfiglio, who stimulated botanical research.
Origin About eight species are known, distributed over tropical Asia and the islands of the Pacific.
Description These are large green foliage plants with unusually incised leaves. The flowers are not very interesting.
Position At one time these plants were only grown in tropical greenhouses, but they are now occasionally sold as house plants. They are really more suitable grown as tub plants rather than in the warm living-room.
Care In a greenhouse the plants may grow several feet tall, but indoors they will grow less rapidly. A certain amount of shade is tolerated reasonably well, but the foliage must be sprayed frequently.

If you decide to cultivate this plant as a tub plant it should be moved outside early in June. Choose a very sheltered position out of the brightest sunlight. Towards winter both the tub plants and those which have been grown in the living-room must be transferred to a somewhat cooler environment; the temperature should be about 14 to 16°C (57 to 60°F). You might try to treat the trevesia like a ficus in a warm room. As yet little is known about this method of cultivation.
Watering Keep it moderately moist in summer, a little drier in winter.
Feeding When the plant is growing it may be fed every fortnight.
Repotting Repot every year in a proprietary potting compost.
Propagation Shoots will only root in a soil temperature of 30 to 35°C (86 to 95°F). Air-layering is occasionally successful. The simplest method of growing new plants is from fresh seed, if available.

Trevesia sanderi
A small tree; the leaves are grouped at the end of the branches and are 30 to 40cm (12 to 16in) wide, divided into five to nine lobes which are initially incised in their turn but later grow into the shape of a goose foot. Young foliage is covered in small grey-white scales which later disappear. The plant is often referred to as *Trevesia palmata*, but in this plant the foliage has its mature shape from the start.

Trichocereus

Cactaceae

Name From the Greek *trichos*, hair, and the generic name *Cereus*.
Origin About 30 species occur in South America, decorating the landscape with their columnar or candelabra shapes.
Description Vigorous, ribbed, columnar cacti with strong thorns. The flowers open at night.
Position These plants are strong enough to be put outside in summer, obviously in full sun. In winter they should be stored in good light in a very cool and dry environment; a cool greenhouse is ideal. The minimum temperature should be 5°C (41°F).
Care Cactus collectors grow some of the species in their original shape. They are very beautiful and develop flowers at an early age.

However, this cactus is best known as stock on which more delicate species can be grafted. A long column is cut into sections of about 7 cm (2¾ in) to produce stock for several plants. The sections are left to dry and are then used as cuttings; new growth will develop at the top. These shoots can again be used as cuttings in their turn, but do leave a small piece of this new growth behind. The actual method of grafting is described on page 76.
Watering In summer the plants may be watered generously, preferably with rainwater. In winter they should be kept completely dry.
Feeding Give them a nitrogen-free cactus fertiliser in summer.
Repotting Use special cactus compost or standard potting compost if necessary.
Propagation Increase from cuttings, as described above, and also from seed at a temperature of 20°C (68°F).

Trichocereus spachianus and *T. pasacana*

Trichocereus schickendantzii
A clump-forming plant with stems up to 25 cm (10 in) tall, with 14 to 18 ribs and 10 to 12 yellowish thorns. The flowers are white.
Trichocereus spachianus
This columnar cactus does not readily branch. It has 10 to 15 ribs and eight to ten needle-shaped thorns up to 1 cm (½ in) long and yellow-brown in colour, and produces white flowers. This is the species best known as stock for grafting.

A collection of forced tulips. **From left to right** 'Golden Melody', 'Sunlight', 'Angelique' and 'Apeldoorn'

Tulipa

Liliaceae

Tulip

Name From the Persian word *toliban*, which in its turn is derived from *dolbend*, turban.
Origin About 150 wild tulip species occur in eastern and central Asia, Europe and North Africa.
Description Everyone knows the hybridised tulips which are planted in gardens in their millions. An actual house plant tulip does not really exist; all that is done is that suitable forms are forced into early flowering. Sometimes the bulbs have undergone treatment at a special temperature for the purpose (prepared bulbs).
Position To be successful, forced tulips should not be kept in too warm an environment. A cool hall, conservatory or corridor is the best place for them. In a warm, dry atmosphere the plants will soon cease to flower and will wilt.
Care Not all tulips are suitable for forcing. They must be able to tolerate a certain degree of warmth, otherwise they might as well stay in the garden. A good catalogue will always indicate which strains will be able to put up with a slightly higher temperature, and this information is usually reliable.

The best results are still achieved by burying the bulbs in their pots. For this purpose choose a fairly dry spot in the garden, and dig a pit to a depth of about 40 cm (16 in). The bulbs are potted with their necks just below the compost and the pots are then arranged in rows in the pit. Each pot may be marked with a stake protruding from the surface, or only the corners of the pit need be indicated in this manner. The pit should now be filled in and in freezing weather covered with a layer of bracken, straw or leaves.

Mid-October is the best time to bury the bulbs. Towards the end of January the pots should be dug up to check the growth. When the noses have grown to about 7 cm (2¾ in) and especially when the flower bud can be felt in the shoot, the pots may be taken from the pit. Strains which are less advanced must remain buried for a time; they should in any case not be brought into the light.

It is advisable not to bring the pots straight into a warm room. At first a temperature of 15°C (59°F) is sufficient. To avoid the shoots drying out the pots are sometimes covered with a plastic bag. As soon as the buds show colour the plants may be brought into a slightly warmer environment and you will then be able to enjoy the flowers for several days or even several weeks, depending on the temperature. Forcing exhausts the bulbs and they are therefore usually discarded after flowering.

In the absence of a garden the pots can be put in a dark place at a temperature which must not exceed 12°C (53°F). They must be kept in complete darkness; if necessary cover them with black plastic bags. If the temperature is too high the bulbs will not root – 9°C (48°F) is ideal for the purpose.

In modern houses such a dark spot is difficult to find and burying the pots in the garden is much better. Flat dwellers might construct a frost-free box on the balcony in which to stand the pots, covered with a layer of peat. This method is preferable to keeping the bulbs in a shed.

Tulipa 'Prince Carnaval'

Watering While the roots are developing the compost must be kept moderately moist. If the pots are kept in a dark cupboard they must be given a drop of water from time to time.
Feeding This is superfluous.
Repotting The bulbs should be potted in a mixture of equal parts of sharp sand and standard potting compost.
Propagation Not applicable.
Assortment available Consult a good catalogue.

Vallota speciosa

Vanda coerulea

Vallota
Amaryllidaceae
Scarborough Lily

Name Named after Pierre Vallot, 1594–1671, a French physician who among other things wrote a description of Louis XIII's garden.
Origin Only one species grows wild, and that is in South Africa.
Description The plant is somewhat reminiscent of the hippeastrum, but the flowers, which appear in summer, are much smaller.
Position It is possible to put the pots out of doors in summer, but the plants will grow better on a well-lit window-sill, especially in a rainy summer.
Care Bulbs may be ordered from a mail-order firm or a well-stocked garden centre. They are potted in March–April and do not have to be kept in the dark. Gradually increase the water supply as the foliage appears. The plant flowers in summer; afterwards it should be given less water. The foliage need not necessarily die off; it may be retained if that suits you better. However, the plant must be rested in a well-lit environment, possibly a cool greenhouse, at a temperature between 5 and 10°C (41 and 50°F). Give very little water. The bulb may be left in the pot even if the foliage is allowed to wither. In early spring (February) the old leaves should be cut back and the pot returned to a warm environment.
Watering Water freely only in summer.
Feeding In the growing season it is advisable to give the plant a weekly feed.
Repotting It is unnecessary to repot the bulb every year, though the top layer of compost should be renewed. A proprietary potting compost is satisfactory, but preferably a soil-based mixture containing clay.
Propagation Offset bulbs can be detached and cultivated separately. The plants may also be grown from ripe seed in a soil temperature of 18°C (64°F).

Vallota speciosa
A bulbous plant with green leaves arranged in two rows; they are 30 to 50 cm (12 to 20 in) long and 2 to 3 cm (¾ to 1 in) wide. The orange-red flowers are up to 8 cm (3 in) in diameter and occur in groups of three to ten in terminal umbels on oblique stalks. 'Major' has larger flowers, more red in colour, and 'Alba' is white.

Vanda
Orchidaceae

Name The name appears to come from the Sanskrit.
Origin About 60 species are known, originating in all warm regions of Asia.
Description All species are monopodial, which means that they grow only at the top. The leathery leaves are arranged in two rows along the firm central stalk. Many species are in cultivation and in addition there are numerous cultivars and strains resulting from intergeneric crossing, among others with *Aerides*, *Arachnis* and *Phalaenopsis*.
Position All species require a high degree of atmospheric humidity. Orchid collectors grow them in a hothouse or in a temperate greenhouse, or occasionally in a glass case or a flower window.
Care The plants need a great deal of light and are therefore grown close to the glass. Many growers provide screening only in the middle of the day. During the day the temperature may be quite high, but on warm summer nights it is advisable to open a roof vent. The minimum night temperature is 12°C (53°F).
The vanda does not develop pseudobulbs or pseudotubers and a strict dormant season is therefore undesirable. The plants should be watered throughout the year, although in winter, at minimum temperatures of 18°C (64°F), transpiration is restricted to some extent.
Watering Needless to say these orchids must only be given unpolluted rain-water or completely demineralised water which must not be too cold.
Feeding The idea that orchids should not be fed has been proved to be wrong. An occasional feed in the growing period is perfectly acceptable, but at only half the recommended concentration. Orchid collectors swear by algae manure and fish emulsion.
The urine of a pregnant cow is considered to be a special treat – that is, for the plants!
Repotting The plants are sometimes grown in pots, but also in lattice baskets. Good drainage is essential in either case. Suitable ingredients for the potting mixture are perlite, osmunda roots, sphagnum moss and coarse peat. The proportions vary: every grower has his own pet recipe, so it is really a question of experiment. Sometimes the vanda is cultivated on nothing but tree bark, or on blocks of tree fern. The choice is wide.
Propagation Sideshoots can be detached if they have true roots. The plants are also grown from seed, but this is a job for the professional.

Species for the temperate greenhouse
Vanda amesiana, *V. bensonii*, *V. coerulea*, *V. coerulescens* and sometimes *tricolor*.

Hothouse species
Vanda hookeriana, *V. kimballiana*, *V. lamellata*, *V. luzonica*, *V. merrillii*, *V. sanderiana* (now called *Euanthe sanderiana*), *V. teres*, *V. tesselata* and sometimes *V. tricolor*.

One example
Vanda coerulea
This species has a central stalk up to 60 cm (2 ft) long and furrowed leaves to 20 cm (8 in), with 20 blue flowers to an umbel. Each is up to 12 cm (4½ in) in diameter. The petals are reverse-oval; the lip has spreading lateral lobes and a darker coloured centre lobe.

Veltheimia
Liliaceae

Name Named after August Ferdinand Veltheim, 1741–1801, a German botanist.
Origin All the five known species have their natural habitat in South Africa. The plant resembles the kniphofia, a garden plant popularly called Red Hot Poker.
Description A bulbous plant which in winter produces clusters of pipe-shaped salmon-coloured flowers at the tip of long stalks.
Position In winter the plant must be kept at a maximum temperature of about 12°C (53°F). In a warmer environment the attractive flowers will fall.
Care The bulbs are potted in autumn and brought straight into the light. Initially they should be given little water; in the first week the temperature should be kept at 20°C (68°F), but lower it as soon as the foliage appears. A temperate, or even a cool greenhouse is the best spot. The flowers appear between January and April. When it is not freezing the plant can be moved outside; it will flower all the longer.
When the plant has stopped flowering, that is around May or June, the water supply must gradually be reduced until the leaves have faded; this will take about a fortnight. This dormant season may be spent out of doors under cover. It lasts until September, when the first green shoots will often appear again.
Watering At first give little water, then more when the foliage appears, but none in the dormant season.
Feeding Feed once a fortnight when the plant has started into growth.
Repotting The best mixture consists of leafmould, pulverised clay and rotted manure. The compost should be renewed every year in September. Combine three bulbs in one pot.
Propagation The best method of increase is to detach offset bulbs. These will develop most readily if the base of the parent bulb is hollowed out. The offsets are potted separately and may flower after two years. Plants grown from seed will take four years before coming into flower.

Veltheimia capensis
Oval bulbs with 10 to 12 leaves, 20 to 30 cm (8 to 12 in) long and 6 to 8 cm (2¼ to 3 in) wide; they are green and glossy with a slightly undulating margin. The tubular flowers are obliquely pendent and arranged in dense clusters. The flower stalks are 5 to 8 mm (¼ to ½ in) long, the flowers are 3 to 4 cm (1 to 1½ in) in length, spotted with yellow and red, with green slips.
Veltheimia glauca
This plant is distinguished by its blue-green leaves which are at most 4 cm (1½ in) in width and more strongly undulate than those of the previous species. In addition the flowers are more pendent, forming narrow clusters. The flower stalks are only 2 to 3 mm (⅛ in) long. The flower tube itself is 2 to 3 cm (¾ to 1 in) long, red with yellow spots.

Veltheimia capensis

Vriesea

Bromeliaceae

Name Named after W. H. de Vriese, 1807–1862, Professor of Biology in Amsterdam.
Origin About 200 species occur in Central and South America.
Description Typical bromeliads with large, funnel-shaped rosettes and often very long and broad leaves, frequently beautifully marked. In their natural environment the plants usually grow as epiphytes on branches and rocks. Morphologically the genus is closely related to *Tillandsia*, but the species most frequently grown have much larger foliage than most cultivated tillandsia forms. The plants are cultivated on a large scale and many beautiful hybrids have been developed.
Position This depends on whether you want to grow the plant for its own sake or intend to propagate young specimens. In the former case almost any situation will do, but for propagation filtered sunlight, a high degree of humidity and a temperature of 18 to 20°C (64 to 68°F) are essential. All these conditions are of course more easily provided in a hothouse than in the living-room. It is sometimes possible, however, to cultivate young shoots of plants grown indoors and bring them into flower.
Care Some bromeliads, such as *Billbergia* and *Tillandsia* species, consist of a large number of smaller rosettes, a few of which flower one year, others the next. If all the rosettes grouped in a pot are treated as one plant it will continue to flower for several years on end if properly tended. The fact that the rosettes which have flowered inevitably die is not noticed, since there are always so many young rosettes to take their place.

In bromeliads like the vriesea and a number of others this does not apply. The plant we buy usually consists of one large rosette with a flower stalk in the centre which has already developed. And as you will know by now as soon as the flower has developed the rosette is doomed to die, for every rosette flowers only once. However, it may take a long time before the flower and the plant itself become unsightly, often as much as several months; if the plant is kept cool it may take even longer. There are bromeliads (such as the cryptanthus) which need not be watered at this stage and which proceed almost imperceptibly towards their eternal rest: when they become dry flowers they hardly change in appearance.

The flowering rosette therefore need not be treated with much consideration. It doesn't matter if you put it in a darker and cooler position than is prescribed for young plants and don't worry if the air is a little too dry.

The correct cultivation of young plants is a little more difficult. In the living-room the minimum temperature should be 18°C (64°F) both in summer and in winter. A little morning sun is tolerated, but after 10 or 11 a.m. the plants must be screened. An east-facing window would therefore be ideal. In addition the degree of relative humidity must be as high as possible; the foliage must be sprayed frequently, but the use of an electric humidifier is even better and more convenient.

The plants grow in spring and summer and during that period the tube may be filled with lime-free water. In winter it is advisable to empty the tube.

Young plants which have grown well for about three years may flower. In many cases the problem is that nothing happens. Fortunately there is a trick, although it only helps if the plants are large enough to produce a flower in the first place. A little acetylene gas can be blown into the tube, or put a small piece of carbide in the water in the funnel. Ripe apples exude acetylene gas and the entire plant can be wrapped in a plastic bag together with a few apples and left for a few days. Growers use a liquid called Ethrel, pouring a few drops into the tube. It often happens that a flower stalk will appear a few months after one of these treatments.

Species with predominantly green or grey-green foliage are easiest to cultivate. Species with marked foliage are often so beautiful that they need hardly flower at all to make an impression.
Watering In the period of active growth the compost must always be kept moderately moist. In winter a little less water can be given. Only lime-free water should be used, both for keeping the compost damp and for pouring into the tube. Unpolluted rainwater – always at room temperature – is best. This should also be used for spraying the foliage.
Feeding In summer the plants may be given measures of lime-free fertiliser. As a rule once a month is enough.
Repotting The compost must be practically lime free. A good mixture can be made of coarse peat lumps, sphagnum moss, rotted beech leaves and rotted manure. The bromeliads will also thrive in conifer needle compost, enriched with rotted or if necessary, dried, cow manure. Plastic pots should have a drainage layer of crocks an inch or two deep.

The plants can also be grown on tree trunks. The roots are tied together with a few tufts of sphagnum moss, a little osmunda fibre or some tree fern and are attached to the tree trunk by means of copper wire.
Propagation As the old rosette dies, new shoots usually develop. They are left in situ at first. After six months they can be carefully detached together with a few roots and potted up separately. Propagation from seed is a very lengthy operation and it will take many years before the plants are able to flower.

Vriesea splendens

Vriesea x poelmannii

Vriesea rodigasiana

Vriesea viminalis 'Rex'

Vriesea carinata
A tubular rosette of broad, tongue-shaped all-green leaves with smooth edges. There is a red flower stalk and the bracts are red, yellow towards the tips, with a green-tipped yellow flower.
Vriesea hieroglyphica
Large rosettes of 60- to 80-cm (24- to 32-in) long and 12-cm ($4\frac{1}{2}$-in) wide green leaves with almost black marking reminiscent of hieroglyphs. This species seldom flowers.
Vriesea × poelmannii
One of the numerous hybrids. It has pale green leaves, carmine-red and greenish-yellow bracts and yellow flowers.
Vriesea rodigasiana
This forms a very small rosette of dull green leaves, purple at the base. The flower stalk branches; the inflorescence consists of waxy lemon-yellow bracts and flowers.
Vriesea splendens
The best-known species. The rosettes are up to 40cm (16in) long and the leaves, 4cm ($1\frac{1}{2}$in) wide, have brown cross-banding. The inflorescence is long and narrow with bright red bracts. The small yellow flowers do not always appear. In the strains 'Major' and 'Flaming Sword' the inflorescence is larger.

Washingtonia filifera

Xantheranthemum igneum

Washingtonia
Palmae
Washington Palm

Name Named after George Washington, 1732–1799, first President of the United States.
Origin There are two species, both occurring in the southern part of the United States.
Description Relatively unknown palm species, whose leaves do not drop, but turn down to surround the trunk.
Position This palm may be kept in full sun nearly all day long; it should only be screened in the middle of the day. Plenty of fresh air is desirable and in winter the plants must be moved to a cool and drier environment.
Care Grown indoors these palms often lead to disappointment. In summer there is not enough ventilation and in winter the living-room, at any rate, is too warm. As soon as the plants have reached a certain size they can be kept in a sheltered position out of doors, possibly on a sheltered balcony. Brown leaf tips may be cut off, but always leave a narrow margin of brown, otherwise the cut edges will soon discolour again. Ideally the winter should be spent in an orangery. If cool, well-lit quarters are available, magnificent specimens may be cultivated. The minimum temperature is 5°C (41°F).
Watering Always keep the compost moderately moist in summer, a little drier in winter.
Feeding Feed every fortnight in the growing period.
Repotting Use tall, narrow plastic pots and wooden or plastic tubs at a later stage. Good drainage is essential. The ideal compost should consist of equal parts of clay granules, rotted beech leaves and rotted cow manure. In the first few years the plant should be repotted annually.
Propagation Fresh seed should be soaked for a few days and then sown at a soil temperature of 25 to 30°C (77 to 86°F). Germination may take a long time.

Washingtonia filifera
○ ◐ ⊜ ⓞ ⊛ ⊛ ▢
Young leaves are undivided, soon fused along half their length, and ravelled at the tip. The base of the leaf stalk is spiny.
Washingtonia robusta
Mature leaves lose the thread-like ravelled appearance. The leaf stalk is spiny along its entire length. This species needs slightly warmer conditions.

Xantheranthemum
Acanthaceae

Name From the Greek *xanthos*, yellow, and *Eranthemum*, generic name.
Origin Its native habitat is in the Andes range in Peru.
Description Low-growing little plants with recumbent stems and beautifully marked foliage. The various species and genera resemble each other and are often confused.
Position Particularly suitable for bottle gardens and glass cases. Naturally they will also thrive in a warm, humid greenhouse. In the open living-room these plants will usually disappoint you.
Care If in spite of this you want to make the attempt, the xantheranthemum should be grown in wide bowls or among other plants and the foliage should be sprayed several times a day with soft tepid water. Sunlight must be avoided, but a fair amount of light is needed to prevent the fine marking being lost. This is most likely to happen if the plant is grown in a bottle garden, which is often kept in a fairly dark spot and which itself does not let through much light. The most favourable temperature is between 18 and 22°C (64 and 71°F). In winter it may be a little lower.
Watering Rainwater is to be preferred, otherwise the water must be completely demineralised. It should always be tepid.
Feeding Give a feed every fortnight in the period of active growth.
Repotting A mixture of coarse lumps, leafmould and manure is ideal. A little pulverised clay or loam may be added.
Propagation Tip cuttings will root fairly readily in a heated propagator under glass or plastic. Young plantlets must be grown under glass.

Xantheranthemum igneum
◐ ⊜ ⓞ ⊛ ▢
Syn. *Chameranthemum igneum; Eranthemum igneum; Stenandrium igneum.* Small plants with short, recumbent stems. The leaves are arranged fairly close together; they are oval, 5 to 10 cm (2 to 4 in) long and 2 to 4 cm ($\frac{3}{4}$ to $1\frac{1}{2}$ in) wide. The upper surface is a velvety brown-green with white marking along the veins and the underside is reddish. It bears small white flowers with large bracts, arranged in spikes.

Xanthosoma
Araceae

Name From the Greek *xanthos*, yellow, and *soma*, body.
Origin About 30 species occur in humid forests in the tropical part of America.
Description Foliage plants with beautifully marked leaves, resembling the alocasia and the colocasia. The plant has underground rhizomes; a few species are tuberous rooted. When cut they exude a milky white sap.
Position Suitable for a hothouse with a high degree of humidity. The plants grow rather large so it is essential that there is plenty of room. In a warm living-room cultivation will rarely be successful.
Care Xanthosoma may be cultivated throughout the year in a warm environment, although in the case of most species the temperature may drop to a minimum of 15°C (59°F) in winter, that is, a little higher than is normal in a temperate greenhouse. Only the species *Xanthosoma lindenii* must be kept at least at 18°C (64°F), in other words, in a hothouse. Sunlight is absolutely forbidden; the greenhouse must always be well screened.

If you do, after all, want to make an attempt at growing this plant in the living-room, you would do well to place a large humidifier nearby, or to have your plant spray at the ready all day long.
Watering The use of unpolluted rainwater is recommended, and it should never be cold. In summer the plant may be watered generously; in the dormant season in winter the compost should be a little drier to the touch.
Feeding These plants are capable of extremely rapid growth and can therefore take a considerable amount of nourishment. Be generous in summer.
Repotting The best results will be achieved if the xanthosoma is planted out on the staging of the hothouse. Pots should be roomy and be provided with a deep layer of crocks in the bottom. Use a humusy mixture consisting of conifer needle compost, beech leaves, peat lumps, rotted cow manure and possibly some perlite. In an emergency the plant may be grown in standard potting compost. Use plastic pots.
Propagation The plants may be divided when they are repotted. Alternatively the stem may be cut into sections which will strike under glass in a certain degree of soil heat.

Xanthosoma lindenii
◐ ⊜ ⓞ ⊛ ▢
Syn. *Phyllotaenium lindenii.* A plant with fleshy, horizontally spreading, arrow-shaped leaves. The upper surface is bright green in colour, with white veining; the leaf stalk is pale green with two lengthwise black stripes. The flowers have creamy bracts.
Xanthosoma nigrum
Syn. *Xanthosoma violaceum.* This plant has edible rhizomes. The leaves are arrow shaped, up to 50 cm (20 in) long, dark green with a purple sheen. The leaf stalks are fleshy, brownish purple and coated with a blue bloom.

Yucca
Agavaceae

Name In Central America the name *yuca* is given to *Manihot esculenta*, the Tapioca or Cassava Shrub. The popular name later became the generic name of the present yucca.
Origin About 30 species are distributed over the southern part of North America and over Central America. Some of the species have been used as garden plants for a long time. The non-hardy indoor plants have been available in large quantities only since the 1960s.
Description The crisp or limp sword-shaped leaves are arranged in rosettes, at the top of brown-scaled trunks. In cultivation they rarely flower.
Position In a warm room these plants are often disappointing. A great deal of light, a well-ventilated position and cool

Xanthosoma nigrum

Yucca aloifolia, the Spanish Bayonet. If possible it should be grown out of doors in summer, but beware of the sharp leaf points

Yucca aloifolia 'Marginata'. This variegated form is rarer

winter quarters are essential conditions which cannot be provided in the living-room. On the other hand no problems will arise if the yucca is treated as a tub plant, but species with sharply pointed leaves must for safety's sake be kept out of the reach of children.

Care A yucca with more than one trunk is a magnificent sight, especially in a modern interior. In the early 1970s such plants demanded prices equal to those of a colour television set. Massive imports have made a difference, and in any case many people now dislike these plants because of their dangerous spines.

If such a 'palm' (it is not a true palm) is placed in a fairly dark corner of the living-room it will inevitably die, but since it is such a strong plant the process may take years. It has, in fact, such reserves that it will start into growth again, but the foliage will soon be infested by aphids. The grower usually gives only six months' guarantee (that is about the length of time the plant will certainly remain in good condition) and you will have made a poor investment.

Warned in advance you can give the yucca a spot on a sunny terrace. In winter it should be moved to a frost-free garage, and put as close to the window

Yucca elephantipes, the Spineless Yucca

as possible. The minimum temperature is 5°C (41°F). This method of cultivation is not ideal, but experience has shown that the plant will tolerate such treatment, provided it is able to assimilate sufficiently in summer. The end of May is the correct time to move the plant outside. During the first month it is advisable to provide some shade, otherwise the transition is too abrupt and the leaves will turn yellow. The lower leaves will turn yellow in any case; the trunk is formed from dead leaves, which should not be removed but left to dry out.

Watering In summer keep the plant moderately moist, but in winter withhold water if the plant is kept at 5°C (41°F).

Feeding If the yucca is repotted every year feeding is superfluous.

Repotting Always use pots with good drainage. Plastic containers are satisfactory. The potting compost must contain loam or clay, as well as some leafmould and fertiliser. Standard potting compost should preferably also be a soil-based one mixed with loam or clay.

Propagation The plants are nearly always imported. Sideshoots may be used as cuttings. They should be left to dry for several months, until roots are developed. Keep them out of the sun.

Pests and diseases Too warm conditions in winter will lead to pest infestation, especially scale insects.

Yucca aloifolia

○ ⊜ ⊙ ⊛ ⊡

Spanish Bayonet; Dagger Plant. The leaves grow in dense rosettes. They are up to 50 cm (20 in) long and 1.5 cm ($\frac{1}{2}$ in) wide, dull green with very sharp points. It has very decorative trunks, brown with foliage marking.

Yucca elephantipes

Spineless Yucca. The stem is thickened at the base. This has rosettes of dull green leaves, 60 to 80 cm (24 to 32 in) long, 5 to 8 cm (2 to 3 in) wide at the mid-line, only 3 cm (1 in) at the base. The lower leaves arch downward. The leaf tips are not sharp.

Yucca gloriosa

Not easily distinguished from the previous species. The stem is slightly shorter and unusually unbranched; the limp, grey-green leaves grow closer together. Of all the species this plant tolerates the lowest temperatures in winter.

Zantedeschia

Araceae

Arum Lily, Calla Lily

Name Named after Francesco Zantedeschi, 1773–1846, an Italian biologist and botanist. The plant is often called *Calla* or *Richardia*.
Origin Eight species occur in tropical parts of Africa and in South Africa in marshes which dry out in summer.
Description These are plants with fleshy rhizomes, large, succulent leaves and white or coloured sheathed flowers.
Position These plants cannot be grown in a warm living-room. In summer they may be put in the garden; in winter they must be kept in a cool environment.
Care The Arum Lily flowers in spring, until about the beginning of May. It must then be given a rest. Some people keep the plants indoors, giving so little water that nearly all the leaves drop. Others lay the zantedeschia on its side in the garden and forget about it for a month or so. The plant is repotted at the end of June and is then brought into growth once more, either in a sunny spot in the garden, where it must be kept sufficiently moist, or on a reasonably cool window-sill, where the compost must be kept very damp. A second dormant season follows in autumn. It is best not to water the plant at all then, so that all the foliage dies down. In winter the rhizome should be left in the pot at a minimum temperature of 10°C (50°F). The plant will start into growth early in the year, approximately at the end of January. It can now be moved to a warmer position.

Zantedeschia aethiopica

Watering Give a fair amount of water in spring and after the May–June dormant season. During the rest of the year water very moderately or not at all.
Feeding Feed every week in the period of growth in spring.
Repotting This is best done immediately after the summer resting period, or after the winter rest. The compost should preferably contain clay or loam.
Propagation When the plants are repotted the rhizomes may be divided.

Zantedeschia aethiopica
Long-stalked arrow-shaped leaves rise from tuber-shaped rootstock; they are green and glossy, fleshy, and up to 50 cm (20 in) long. The spathes, long stalked and white, are funnel shaped, and the spadix is yellow and fragrant.

Zantedeschia elliottiana
This has oval leaves, heart shaped at the base, with a few white patches. The flower spathe is bright yellow.
Zantedeschia rehmannii
Lanceolate leaves, to 4 cm (1½ in) wide, are spotted with white; they are wedge shaped at the base. The flower spathes are white, tinged with purple along the margins, and deep purple inside.

Zantedeschia aethiopica 'Green Goddess' growing in a greenhouse

Zebrina

Commelinaceae

Wandering Jew

Name The Latin word *zebrinus* simply means striped.
Origin Four species grow wild in Central America.
Description The plants closely resemble the *Tradescantia* with which they are regularly confused. It hardly matters, for they are cultivated in practically the same way. A characteristic of the zebrina is that the petals of the small flowers have coalesced into a tube. In other *Commelinaceae* the petals are free-standing or joined only at the base.
Position These are trailing plants for well-lit windows, or ground cover in greenhouses or flower windows. In winter the temperature should not be too high.
Care Easily grown plants which will thrive anywhere, as long as they are not placed in too dark a spot. Bright sunlight is not good for them, but if the light is poor the fine leaf marking disappears and the plants revert to green. If they are grown in the living-room you should try to keep the air as humid as possible. Plants which have grown unsightly can be drastically pruned in winter; they will start into growth again.

In winter the temperature may fall to 12°C (53°F). The plant ought to be kept in a cool environment at that time, since in a cool room the degree of relative humidity is higher and the plant will be less inclined to grow.
Watering In summer water moderately; ordinary tap water will do. Do not overlook your hanging plants!
Feeding Do not provide too much nourishment; this affects the marking.
Repotting It is advisable to repot every year in spring, at the same time removing all unsightly shoots. If the plant has been unattractive all through the winter you should take cuttings in good time. These can be potted in standard potting compost made somewhat more porous by adding extra sharp sand.
Propagation In many cases the shoots root spontaneously as soon as they touch the compost. They can then be cut off and potted separately. Tip cuttings also root very readily. Leave them to dry for a day or so (the stem is somewhat succulent) before inserting them in a mixture of sand and peat.

Even in a bottle of water the cuttings will soon develop roots. If you want to experiment with hydroponics this method has its advantages.

Zebrina pendula
A plant with creeping or trailing stems, pointed oval leaves, green with lengthwise purple stripes; the underside is purple. It bears small white or rose-red flowers. In 'Quadricolor' traces of rose-red appear in the foliage as well.
Zebrina purpusii
Distinguished from the previous species by its larger dimensions. The leaves are hairy at the base; the upper surface varies in colour, but is usually dark green to wine red, without white stripes.

The form 'Minor' has less red in the foliage colour and is smaller.

Zebrina pendula 'Quadricolor'

Zebrina purpusii

Zephyranthes
Amaryllidaceae
Zephyr Lily

Name From the Greek *zephyros*, zephyr or west wind, and *anthos*, flower.
Origin About 55 different species occur in Central and South America.
Description A fairly rare bulbous plant which flowers in summer or in the fall. It resembles the vallota to some extent.
Position Most species may be grown out of doors on a terrace or balcony in summer. In winter the bulbs are not kept completely dry.
Care The bulbs may be ordered in spring from a mail-order firm or a well-stocked garden centre. They are potted and started into growth in a modicum of warmth. In the second half of May the pots may be moved outside where they should be given a sunny and sheltered position. Flowering occurs in summer; in some species in autumn. The species *Zephyranthes candida* is so hardy that it may be used as a border plant and can spend the winter outside under light cover. The other species are best placed in a cool greenhouse, at a minimum temperature of 5°C (41°F); the compost should be kept slightly moist. The foliage will not die down entirely. In their natural habitat these plants grow in fairly damp places and so complete dryness must be avoided. In spring they can be brought into growth again.
Watering Water fairly generously in summer and keep slightly moist in winter.
Feeding The compost does not have to be renewed every year, but since the old compost becomes exhausted a fortnightly feed in the growing season is recommended.

Zephyranthes candida

Repotting Standard potting compost is satisfactory. Group several bulbs in wide, shallow pots and leave them there for a number of years. If necessary repot them after the dormant season.
Propagation Quite a few offset bulbs are developed and these will flower fairly soon. The zephyranthes is easily increased by dividing the plants when they are repotted. Propagation from seed, if available, is another possibility.

Zephyranthes candida
○⊜⊖Ⓜ⊛◙
These are dark-coloured bulbs with a long neck and four to six linear leaves, 2 to 5mm ($\frac{1}{8}$ to $\frac{1}{4}$in) wide, almost cylindrical. The flowers appear outside the leaf rosettes; they are 3 to 5cm (1 to 2in) long, clear white or slightly tinged with purple.
Zephyranthes citrina
This species produces sulphur-yellow flowers in summer. It should not be kept too cool.
Zephyranthes grandiflora
This has linear leaves, reddish at the base, and large rose-pink flowers with a yellow throat from May onwards.
Zephyranthes rosea
This species does not flower until the autumn, and the flowers are smaller and rose red in colour. It needs a little more warmth than the other species to be able to flower.

Zygocactus
Cactaceae
Christmas Cactus

Name From the Greek *zygos*, yoke, and *cactus*, cactus. It is still frequently called *Epiphyllum* or *Schlumbergera*. Note the differences between this plant and the Easter Cactus, *Rhipsalidopsis*.
Origin A number of species grow on trees in eastern Brazil.
Description Leaf cactus with winged joints and violet-coloured flowers which appear around Christmas.
Position In winter the plant may be brought indoors, but in summer it prefers to grow outside.
Care The plant will flourish only if the correct resting periods are observed. Suppose you have bought a flowering plant in December. At first a few flower buds may drop as a result of the change in the angle of the light. In the modern hybrids with pale pink, orange or white flowers this does not occur quite so often. In any case from now on they should always face the same way.

While it is in flower the Christmas Cactus may be kept in the warm living-room. From time to time the foliage should be sprayed lightly. After flowering the plant must be given a resting period of at least five or six weeks; it may last even longer. The temperature should now be lower, down to 15°C (59°F), and the water supply reduced, only just enough being given to prevent the joints from shrivelling.

In March–April the plants are repotted and once more moved to a slightly warmer position. At the end of May they should be put in a sheltered position out of doors; this is when the growing season starts.

In September the Christmas Cactus is brought indoors again, where it should be kept cool and dry until the pink flower buds appear. This phenomenon is stimulated by dryness and short-day treatment. Make sure that the plant is kept in the dark in the evening.
Watering In the period of active growth, that is, in summer, the compost must never dry out. While the plant is in flower it should be watered sparingly. For the rest of the year keep it as dry as possible. Use tepid rainwater.
Feeding In the growing period give it special cactus fertiliser every fortnight.
Repotting The plant is best repotted after the spring dormant season. It is often grown in plastic or clay pots, but will do much better if grown in lattice baskets or plastic hanging baskets. This is more in accordance with epiphytic habit. The ideal compost may consist of conifer needle compost and rotted cow manure, beech leaves with sphagnum moss and manure, and chopped fern roots. If the plants are grown in pots good drainage must be provided. Mature plants should be repotted only every third year.

Zygocactus truncatus, the well-known Christmas Cactus

A hybrid of a slightly different colour

Propagation In spring take cuttings of the previous year's growth which has not yet become woody, leave them to dry for a few days and root them with some degree of soil heat. Do not keep them too damp; this would cause them to rot.

In order to obtain an attractive standard plant the cuttings are grafted on stock, perhaps *Selenicereus hamatus*. The easiest method is cleft grafting, in which the scion is cut to a point and inserted in a cleft in the de-budded stock. The join is secured with a long cactus thorn and tied together with raffia until fusion has taken place.
Pests and diseases While the plant is left in the garden look out for slugs. Bud dropping may be due to one of the following causes: (a) too little nourishment in early summer; (b) the plants have been turned in relation to the light during bud formation; (c) too great a difference between day and night temperature during bud formation; (d) the compost has dried out during the growing season; (e) the water has been too cold.

Zygocactus truncatus
◐⊜Ⓜ⊛◙
A strongly branching cactus with arching stems. The flattened, winged segments are up to 6cm (2¼in) long. The areoles occur only along the somewhat undulate margins, especially at the tips of the segments, where they are bristly. Terminal flowers, 6 to 8cm (2¼ to 3in) long, are bright violet in colour; the petals curve back and are in two tiers.

The difference between the zygocactus and the rhipsalidopsis is that in the former the flowers are symmetrical along one line, while the petals are fairly broad.

In the rhipsalidopsis the flowers are symmetrical all round and the petals are smaller.

There are now quite a few hybrids on the market which are the results of crossing, either with each other or with *Schlumbergera* species. Their characteristics fall between the two progenitors. In many cases these plants are more vigorous. The colour of the flowers varies from white through orange to lilac.

Plant lists and tables

Plants for full sun and high temperature

Plants under this heading must be grown in full sun at a minimum summer temperature of 16 to 20°C (60 to 68°F). A south-facing windowsill is usually suitable. Some plants prefer an unscreened greenhouse. None of these plants can be moved outdoors in summer. Where only the generic name is mentioned the conditions of full sun and high temperature apply to all the species described. Where the specific name is also given the conditions apply only to the particular species.

Ananas
Anastatica
Canna
Cephalocereus
Cereus
Ceropegia
Chlorophytum
Cissus quadrangularis
Coleus
Echinocactus
Echinocereus
Epidendrum radicans
Espostoa
Eugenia myriophylla
Euphorbia fulgens
Ferocactus
Gloriosa
Hamatocactus
Haworthia cuspidata
Haworthia obtusa
Haworthia tessellata
Haworthia truncata
Heliconia
Hippeastrum
Jasminum sambac
Jatropha
Kalanchoe blossfeldiana
Kalanchoe longiflora
Kalanchoe manginii
Lithops
Musa
Opuntia
Pachypodium
Pachystachys
× *Pachyveria*
Parodia
Pereskia
Persea
Plectranthus fruticosus
Plectranthus parviflorus
Pyrrhocactus
Rebutia
Sansevieria
Senecio articulatus
Senecio citriformis
Senecio haworthii
Senecio herreianus
Senecio macroglossus
Senecio rowleyanus
Stapelia

Plants for full sun and moderate temperature

Plants under this heading must be grown in full sun at a minimum summer temperature of 10 to 16°C (50 to 60°F). An airy south-facing windowsill is suitable, but in summer the plants may also be grown in a sheltered position outdoors, provided they are not moved outside too early in the season and are brought indoors in good time. See the remarks in the first table concerning conditions referring to entire genera or particular species.

Adromischus
Aeonium
Agapanthus
Agave
Amaryllis
Aporocactus
Arachis
Borzicactus
Bougainvillea
Callistemon
Capsicum
Catharanthus
Citrus
Cleistocactus
Cocculus
Colletia
Conophytum
Cordyline
Corynocarpus
Cotyledon
Crassula
Crinum
Cuphea
Dasylirion
Datura
Dolichothele
Echeveria
Elisena
Erythrina
Euphorbia abyssinica
Euphorbia caput-medusae
Euphorbia coerulescens
Euphorbia globosa
Euphorbia grandicornis
Euphorbia lophogona
Euphorbia meloformis
Euphorbia milii
Euphorbia obesa
Euphorbia tirucalli
Faucaria
Gasteria
Gerbera
Graptopetalum
Haemanthus
Hibiscus
Homalocladium
Hoya australis
Hoya carnosa
Hymenocallis
Hypocyrta
Impatiens
Iresine
Jacobinia pauciflora
Jasminum mesnyi
Jasminum officinale
Jasminum polyanthum
Kalanchoe daigremontiana
Kalanchoe laxiflora
Kalanchoe marmorata
Kalanchoe tomentosa
Kalanchoe tubiflora
Lachenalia
Lampranthus
Lapeirousia
Lilium
Littonia
Malvastrum
Melocactus
Mikania
Myrtillocactus
Myrtus
Neoporteria
Nerium
Olea
Opuntia
Oreopanax
Oxalis carnosa
Oxalis vulcanicola
Pachycereus
Pachyphytum
× *Pachyveria*
Parthenocissus
Pelargonium carnosum
Pelargonium × *citrosum*
Pelargonium grandiflorum hybrids
Pelargonium garveolens
Pelargonium radens
Pelargonium zonale hybrids
Phoenix dactylifera
Punica
Rosa
Sandersonia
Scilla
Sedum
Setcreasea
Stenotaphrum
Strelitzia
Thunbergia
Trichocereus
Vallota
Washingtonia
Yucca
Zantedeschia
Zephyranthes

Plants for full sun and low temperature

Plants under this heading must be grown in full sun at a minimum summer temperature of 3 to 10°C (37 to 50°F). A sunny windowsill or a greenhouse is definitely too warm. From the end of May onward the ideal situation is outdoors on a balcony or terrace. The plants must be brought indoors before the first night frosts occur. See the remarks in the first table concerning conditions referring to entire genera or particular species.

Acacia
Aloe
Arequipa
Beaucarnea
Coryphantha
Eucomis
Eugenia paniculata
Euonymus
Harpephyllum
Hebe
Lagerstroemia
Laurus
Lobivia
Mammillaria
Nerine
Oreocereus
Oxalis deppei
Passiflora caerulea
Pelargonium peltatum hybrids
Phoenix canariensis
Pittosporum
Podocarpus
Saxifraga cotyledon
Sempervivum
Solanum
Veltheimia

Plants for half shade and high temperature

Plants under this heading require plenty of light, but between 10 a.m. and 5 p.m. direct sunlight must be avoided. The minimum summer temperature lies between 16 and 20°C (60 and 68°F), which means that these plants must be kept indoors throughout the summer, either in the living room or in a greenhouse. A screened south-facing window or an unscreened east or west-facing window is suitable.

Acalypha
Achimenes
Aechmea
Aerides lawrenceae
Aerides multiflorum
Aeschynanthus
Aglaonema
Alloplectus
Alocasia
Angraecum
Anthurium andreanum
Anthurium crystallinum
Anthurium magnificum
Aphelandra
Ardisia malouiana
Astrophytum
Begonia albo-picta
Begonia boliviensis
Begonia boweri
Begonia conchifolia
Begonia corallina
Begonia crispula
Begonia diadema
Begonia elatior hybrids
Begonia × *erythrophylla*
Begonia foliosa
Begonia fuchsioides
Begonia goegoensis
Begonia heracleifolia
Begonia hispida cucullifera
Begonia hydrocotylifolia
Begonia imperialis
Begonia incana
Begonia incarnata
Begonia limmingheiana
Begonia luxurians
Begonia maculata
Begonia manicata
Begonia masoniana
Begonia metallica
Begonia rajah
Begonia rex hybrids
Begonia serratipetala
Begonia socotrana
Begonia venosa
Billbergia
Brosimum
Caladium
Calanthe
Calathea
Calliandra
Celosia

Plants for half shade and high temperature (cont.)

Cissus discolor
Cissus gongylodes
Cissus njegerre
Clerodendrum
Coccoloba
Cocos
Codiaeum
Codonanthe
Coelogyne massangeana
Coffea
Coleus
Columnea gloriosa
Columnea hirta
Columnea linearis
Columnea microphylla
Columnea teuscheri
Columnea tulae
Costus
Crossandra
Cryptanthus
Ctenanthe
Cycnoches
Dendrobium chrysotoxum
Dendrobium superbiens
Dichorisandra
Dieffenbachia
Dipladenia
Dipteracanthus
Dracaena
Elettaria
Episcia
Eucharis
Euphorbia pulcherrima
Exacum
Ficus aspera
Ficus benghalensis
Ficus benjamina
Ficus buxifolia
Ficus cyathistipula
Ficus deltoidea
Ficus elastica
Ficus lyrata
Ficus macrophylla
Ficus montana
Ficus nekbuda
Ficus pumila
Ficus radicans
Ficus religiosa
Ficus triangularis
Fittonia
Gardenia
Guzmania
Gynura
Haworthia attenuata
Haworthia fasciata
Haworthia margaritifera
Haworthia reinwardtii
Hedera canariensis
Hemigraphis
Hoya bella
Hypoestes
Ixora
Jacobina carnea
Kohleria
Maranta
Medinilla
Microcoelum
Monstera
Murraya
Nautilocalyx
Neoregelia
Nepenthes
Notocactus
Oncidium altissimum
Oncidium kramerianum
Pandanus
Passiflora quadrangularis
Pavonia
Pedilanthus
Pellionia
Peperomia
Perilepta
Philodendron
Phlebodium
Phoenix roebelenii
Phyllanthus
Piper crocatum
Pisonia
Platycerium
Plectranthus oertendahlii
Plumbago indica
Polyscias
Polystichum
Pseuderanthemum
Rechsteineria
Rhaphidophora
Rhipsalidopsis
Rodriguezia
Scindapsus
Scirpus
Selenicereus
Siderasis
Sinningia
Smithiantha
Sonerila
Spathiphyllum
Stenandrium
Stephanotis
Stromanthe
Syngonium
Tillandsia cyanea
Tillandsia flabellata
Tillandsia leiboldiana
Tillandsia lindenii
Tolmiea
Vriesea
Xanthosoma
Zebrina

Plants for half shade and moderate temperature ◐ ⊜

Plants under this heading require plenty of light, but between 10 a.m. and 5 p.m. direct sunlight must be avoided. The minimum summer temperature is 10 to 16°C (50 to 60°F), which means that although the plants may be moved outside this should not be done too soon. A screened south-facing window which is opened in warm weather provides a suitable situation. Several of the plants must be cultivated in a screened, well-ventilated greenhouse.

Abutilon
Acanthus
Aerides japonicum
Aerides vandarum
Allamanda
Ampelopsis
Araucaria
Ardisia crenata
Arisaema
Asparagus
Aspidistra
Begonia (tuberous)
Begonia lorraine hybrids
Begonia schmidtiana
Begonia semperflorens hybrids
Bouvardia
Brassavola
Brassia
Browallia
Brunfelsia
Callisia
Carex
Cattleya
Chamaecereus
Chamaedorea
Chamaerops
Chrysanthemum
Chysis
Cissus antarctica
Cissus rhombifolia
Cissus striata
Cleyera
Clivia
Coelogyne cristata
Coelogyne flaccida
Columnea × banksii
Coprosma
Cycas
Cyperus
Dendrobium aggregatum
Dendrobium chrysanthum
Dendrobium fimbriatum
Dendrobium nobile
Dendrobium phalaenopsis
Dendrobium thyrsiflorum
Dendrobium wardianum
Dizygotheca
Duchesnea
Echinopsis
Epidendrum ciliare
Epidendrum cochleatum
Epidendrum radiatum
Epidendrum stamfordianum
Epidendrum vitellinum
Epiphyllum
× Fatshedera
Ficus rubiginosa
Ficus sycomorus
Fuchsia
Glechoma
Grevillea
Gymnocalycium
Haemanthus
Hatiora
Hedera helix
Howeia
Hyacinthus
Jacaranda
Laelia
× Laeliocattleya
Liriope
Lycaste candida
Miltonia
Mimosa
Narcissus
Nephrolepis
Odontoglossum bictoniense
Odontoglossum grande
Odontoglossum pulchellum
Odontoglossum schlieperianum
Oncidium cavendishianum
Oncidium ornithorhynchum
Oncidium sphacelatum
Oncidium varicosum
Oncidium wentworthianum
Ophiopogon
Oplismenus
Passiflora racemosa
Passiflora violacea
Pentas
Pilea
Piper nigrum
Pleione
Plumbago auriculata
Primula × kewensis
Primula malacoides
Primula obconica
Primula praenitens
Pteris
Rhododendron
Rhoeo
Rhoicissus
Rivina
Rochea
Saintpaulia
Saxifraga stolonifera
Schefflera
Selaginella
Senecio mikanioides
Soleirolia
Sprekelia
Streptocarpus
Tetraclinis
Tetrastigma
Tillandsia argentea
Tillandsia usneoides
Tolmiea
Torenia
Tradescantia
Trevesia
Vanda
Zygocactus

Plants for half shade and low temperature ◐ ⊖

Plants under this heading require plenty of light, but between 10 a.m. and 5 p.m. direct sunlight must be avoided. The minimum summer temperature is 3 to 10°C (37 to 50°F), which means that from the end of May onwards the plants may be moved outside, provided they are placed in a sheltered position well shaded by a tree or a building. Some species are better cultivated in a very cool screened greenhouse. If they are grown indoors a very cool environment is essential.

Acanthocalycium
Acorus
Aucuba
Begonia dregei
Begonia grandis
Begonia pearcei
Calceolaria
Camellia
Campanula
Colchicum
Convallaria
Crocus
Cussonia
Cyclamen
Cymbidium
Cytisus
Erica
Fatsia
Helleborus
Lycaste aromatica
Lycaste cruenta
Lycaste virginalis
Nertera
Odontoglossum cervantesii
Odontoglossum cordatum
Odontoglossum crispum
Odontoglossum maculatum
Odontoglossum oerstedtii
Odontoglossum rossii
Oncidium crispum
Oncidium marshallianum
Primula vulgaris
Sauromatum
Senecio cruentus hybrids
Skimmia
Sparmannia
Stenocarpus
Tolmiea

Plants for full shade and high temperature ●⊜

Plants under this heading will put up with little light (1000 lux is the minimum), but they usually do better in more light. A north-facing window is nearly always suitable, for direct sunlight is unnecessary; in fact it is often undesirable. The plants in this group need a mimimum summer temperature of 16 to 20°C (60 to 68°F) and must therefore never be moved out of doors. If cultivated in a greenhouse they will need adequate screening.

Adiantum
Aglaonema
Anthurium
Bertolonia
Billbergia
Brosimum
Calathea
Dieffenbachia
Didymochlaena
Dracaena
Ficus deltoidea
Ficus pumila
Ficus radicans
Hemigraphis
Howeia
Maranta
Microlepia speluncae
Monstera
Paphiopedilum niveum
Paphiopedilum sukhakulii
Phalaenopsis
Philodendron
Phlebodium
Phoenix roebelenii
Platycerium
Polystichum
Rhaphidophora
Sansevieria
Siderasis
Spathiphyllum
Syngonium
Zebrina

Plants for full shade and moderate temperature ●⊖

Plants under this heading will put up with little light (1000 lux is the minimum), but they usually do better in more light. A north-facing window is nearly always suitable, for direct sunlight is unnecessary; in fact it is often undesirable. The plants in this group need a minimum summer temperature of 10 to 16°C (50 to 60°F), which means that when the outside temperature is high enough they may be placed in a sheltered, shady spot out of doors.

Asparagus
Aspidistra
Asplenium
Blechnum
Chamaedorea
Chlorophytum
Cissus antarctica
Cissus rhombifolia
Cissus striata
Clivia
Cyrtomium
Dionaea
Doryopteris
× *Fatshedera*
Hypocyrta
Miltonia
Nephrolepis
Odontoglossum
Ophiopogon
Paphiopedilum callosum
Paphiopedilum spicerianum
Pellaea
Peperomia
Pteris
Rhoicissus
Schefflera
Selaginella
Soleirolia
Tetrastigma
Tradescantia

Plants for full shade and low temperature ●⊖

Plants under this heading will put up with little light (1000 lux is the minimum), but they usually do better in more light. A north-facing window is nearly always suitable, for direct sunlight is unnecessary; in fact it is often undesirable. The plants in this group need a minimum summer temperature of 3 to 10°C (37 to 50°F) and are therefore best grown out of doors in that season. If they are cultivated in a greenhouse good shading and practically constant ventilation are essential.

Aucuba
Calceolaria
Darlingtonia
Fatsia
Hedera helix
Hydrangea
Odontoglossum
Paphiopedilum insigne
Paphiopedilum venustum
Paphiopedilum villosum
Phyllitis scolopendrium
Skimmia

Plants requiring a high degree of atmospheric humidity ⊙

Plants under this heading require a degree of relative humidity of over 60 per cent. This means that they will present problems if grown indoors, especially in winter. Unless special measures are taken the degree of humidity in the home will drop as soon as the heating is turned on. They are therefore plants for the greenhouse, for glass cases, flower windows or glass bells. Several species can be successfully grown indoors in summer. The foliage should be sprayed as often as possible, unless this causes staining (for instance, in the case of hairy leaves).

Acalypha
Achimenes
Adiantum
Aerides
Aeschynanthus
Alloplectus
Alocasia
Ananas
Angraecum
Anthurium
Aphelandra
Araucaria
Ardisia malouiana
Asplenium
Brassavola
Caladium
Calanthe
Calathea
Cattleya
Clerodendrum
Cocos
Codiaeum
Coelogyne massangeana
Coffea
Coleus
Columnea gloriosa
Columnea hirta
Columnea microphylla
Columnea teuscheri
Columnea tulae
Costus
Crocus
Crossandra
Ctenanthe
Cycnoches
Cyrtomium
Darlingtonia
Dendrobium
Dichorisandra
Didymochlaena
Dieffenbachia
Dionaea
Dipladenia
Dipteracanthus
Dizygotheca
Doryopteris
Dracaena goldieana
Epidendrum
Episcia
Eucharis
Fittonia
Gloriosa
Guzmania
Heliconia
Hemigraphis
Hoya bella
Hypoestes
Ixora
Jacaranda
Jacobinia carnea
Jasminium sambac
Kohleria
Laelia
× *Laeliocattleya*
Lycaste
Maranta
Medinilla
Melocactus
Micrococlum
Microlepia
Mikania
Miltonia
Mimosa
Monstera
Murraya
Musa
Nautilocalyx
Neoregelia
Nepenthes
Nephrolepis
Odontoglossum cervantesii
Odontoglossum cordatum
Odontoglossum crispum
Odontoglossum maculatum
Odontoglossum oerstedtii
Odontoglossum rossii
Oncidium altissimum
Oncidium cavendishianum
Oncidium crispum
Oncidium kramerianum
Oncidium marshallianum
Oncidium sphacelatum
Oncidium wentworthianum
Pachystachys
Pandanus
Paphiopedilum
Passiflora quadrangularis
Passiflora racemosa
Passiflora violacea
Pavonia
Pellionia
Pentas
Perilepta
Persea
Phalaenopsis
Philodendron
Phoenix roebelenii
Phyllanthus
Phyllitis
Pilea
Piper crocatum
Pisonia
Plectranthus oertendahlii
Plumbago indica
Polyscias
Polystichum
Primula vulgaris
Pseuderanthemum
Pteris
Rechsteineria
Rhipsalidopsis
Rivina
Rodriguezia
Saintpaulia
Sandersonia
Scilla
Scindapsus
Scirpus
Selaginella
Siderasis
Sinningia
Smithiantha
Sonerila
Spathiphyllum
Stenandrium
Stromanthe
Tetraclinis
Tetrastigma
Tillandsia cyanea
Tillandsia flabellata
Tillandsia leiboldiana
Tillandsia lindenii
Trevesia
Vanda
Vriesea
Washingtonia
Xanthosoma
Zebrina

Plants requiring moderate atmospheric humidity ⊙

Plants under this heading need a degree of relative humidity of 50 to 60 percent. In winter it is not easy to provide this condition indoors. However, these plants can be grown in the living room provided they are frequently sprayed and placed over a bowl of water or near a humidifier. Plants that need a dormant season at a lower temperature should of course be transferred to winter quarters where sufficient relative humidity can be easily maintained.

Abutilon
Acacia
Acanthocalycium
Acanthus
Acorus
Aechmea
Agapanthus
Amaryllis
Ampelopsis
Arachis
Ardisia crenata
Arisaema
Asparagus
Aspidistra
Aucuba
Begonia
Billbergia
Blechnum
Bougainvillea
Bouvardia
Brassia
Brosimum
Browallia
Brunfelsia
Calceolaria
Calliandra
Callisia
Callistemon
Camellia
Campanula
Canna
Capsicum
Carex
Catharanthus
Celosia
Cephalocereus
Chamaedorea
Chamaerops
Chlorophytum
Chrysanthemum
Chysis
Cissus
Citrus
Cleistocactus
Cleyera
Clivia
Coccoloba
Cocculus
Codonanthe
Coelogyne cristata
Coelogyne flaccida
Colchicum
Columnea × banksii
Columnea linearis
Conophytum
Convallaria
Coprosma
Cordyline
Corynocarpus
Cotyledon
Crinum
Cryptanthus
Cuphea
Cussonia
Cycas
Cyclamen
Cymbidium
Cyperus alternifolius
Cyperus argenteostriatus
Cyperus diffusus
Cyperus gracilis
Cyperus haspan
Cyperus papyrus
Cytisus
Dasylirion
Datura
Dolichothele
Dracaena deremensis
Dracaena draco
Dracaena fragrans
Dracaena godseffiana
Dracaena hookeriana
Dracaena marginata
Dracaena reflexa
Dracaena sanderiana
Dracaena umbraculifera
Duchesnea
Echinocactus
Echinocereus
Elettaria
Elisena
Epiphyllum
Erica
Erythrina
Espostoa
Eucomis
Eugenia
Euonymus
Exacum
× Fatshedera
Fatsia
Faucaria
Ferocactus
Ficus
Fuchsia
Gardenia
Gasteria
Gerbera
Glechoma
Graptopetalum
Grevillea
Gymnocalycium
Gynura
Haemanthus
Harpephyllum
Hatiora
Hebe
Hedera
Helleborus
Hibiscus
Hippeastrum
Homalocladium
Howeia
Hoya australis
Hoya carnosa
Hyacinthus
Hymenocallis
Hypocyrta
Impatiens
Iresine
Jacobinia pauciflora
Jasminum mesnyi
Jasminum officinale
Jasminum polyanthum
Kalanchoe blossfeldiana
Kalanchoe longiflora
Kalanchoe manginii
Kalanchoe marmorata
Kalanchoe tomentosa
Lachenalia
Lagerstroemia
Lapeirousia
Laurus
Lilium
Liriope
Littonia
Malvastrum
Myrtillocactus
Myrtus
Narcissus
Nerine
Nerium
Nertera
Notocactus
Odontoglossum bictoniense
Odontoglossum grande
Odontoglossum pulchellum
Odontoglossum schlieperianum
Olea
Oncidium ornithorhynchum
Oncidium varicosum
Ophiopogon
Oplismenus
Opuntia
Oreocereus
Oreopanax
Oxalis
Pachycereus
Pachypodium
Parthenocissus
Passiflora caerulea
Pedilantus
Pelargonium × citrosum
Pelargonium grandiflorum hybrids
Pelargonium graveolens
Pelargonium peltatum hybrids
Pelargonium radens
Pelargonium zonale hybrids
Pellaea
Peperomia
Pereskia
Phlebodium
Phoenix canariensis
Phoenix dactylifera
Piper nigrum
Pittosporum
Platycerium
Plectranthus fruticosus
Plectranthus parviflorus
Pleione
Plumbago auriculata
Podocarpus
Primula × kewensis
Primula malacoides
Primula obconica
Primula praenitens
Punica
Rebutia
Rhaphidophora
Rhododendron
Rhoeo
Rhoicissus
Rochea
Rosa
Sauromatum
Saxifraga
Schefflera
Selenicereus
Senecio crunetus hybrids
Senecio mikanioides
Setcreasea
Skimmia
Solanum
Soleirolia
Sparmannia
Sprekelia
Stapelia
Stenocarpus
Stenotaphrum
Stephanotis
Strelitzia
Streptocarpus
Syngonium
Thunbergia
Tillandsia argentea
Tillandsia usneoides
Tolmiea
Torenia
Tradescantia
Trichocereus
Vallota
Veltheimia
Yucca
Zantedeschia
Zephyranthes
Zygocactus

Plants which tolerate dry air ⊙

Plants under this heading accept a degreę of relative humidity of under 50 percent. The group includes many succulents and cacti, plants which must be kept cool in winter. Most of these plants will tolerate the dry living room atmosphere. The leaves need not be sprayed. In summer most of the plants in this group will tolerate warm and dry air.

Adromischus
Aeonium
Agave
Aglaonema
Aloe
Anastatica
Aporocactus
Arequipa
Astrophytum
Beaucarnea
Borzicactus
Cereus
Ceropegia
Chamaecereus
Colletia
Coryphantha
Crassula
Echeveria
Echinopsis
Euphorbia
Hamatocactus
Haworthia
Jatropha
Kalanchoe daigremontiana
Kalanchoe laxiflora
Kalanchoe tubiflora
Lampranthus
Lithops
Lobivia
Mammillaria
Neoporteria
Pachyphytum
× Pachyveria
Parodia
Pelargonium carnosum
Pyrrhocactus
Sansevieria
Sedum
Sempervivum
Senecio articulatus
Senecio citriformis
Senecio haworthii
Senecio herreianus
Senecio macroglossus
Senecio rowleyanus
Zebrina

Plants which thrive in standard potting compost ◉

All the plants mentioned under this heading will flourish in a proprietary potting compost, but no harm will be done if you prefer to experiment with home-made mixtures. In that case use a standard compost with the addition of special ingredients such as peat, cow manure, and perlite.

Abutilon
Acacia
Acanthus
Adromischus
Alloplectus
Amaryllis
Ampelopsis
Ananas
Anastatica
Arachis
Ardisia
Aspidistra
Aucuba
Begonia dregei
Begonia elatior hybrids
Begonia × *erythrophylla*
Begonia foliosa
Begonia fuchsioides
Begonia goegoensis
Begonia pearcei
Begonia schmidtiana
Begonia semperflorens hybrids
Billbergia
Bougainvillea
Brosimum
Brunfelsia
Callisia
Campanula
Canna
Capsicum
Carex
Catharanthus
Celosia
Chrysanthemum
Cocculus
Cocos
Coleus
Coprosma
Cordyline
Crinum
Cuphea
Cytisus
Dipteracanthus
Duchesnea
Elettaria
Eucomis
Euonymus
Ferocactus
Glechoma
Hemigraphis
Hippeastrum
Impatiens
Iresine
Kalanchoe daigremontiana
Kalanchoe laxiflora
Kalanchoe tubiflora
Lapeirousia
Liriope
Malvastrum
Olea
Ophiopogon
Opuntia
Oreopanax
Pachystachys
Pandanus
Parthenocissus
Passiflora caerulea
Passiflora racemosa
Passiflora violacea
Pedilanthus
Pelargonium × *citrosum*
Pelargonium grandiflorum hybrids
Pelargonium graveolens
Pelargonium peltatum hybrids
Pelargonium radens
Pelargonium zonale hybrids
Pereskia
Perilepta
Phyllitis
Plectranthus
Primula
Rhoeo
Rhoicissus
Rivina
Rosa
Sansevieria
Sauromatum
Saxifraga
Schefflera
Scilla
Scirpus
Sempervivum
Senecio cruentus hybrids
Senecio mikanioides
Setcreasea
Siderasis
Solanum
Soleirolia
Sparmannia
Spathiphyllum
Sprekelia
Stenocarpus
Stenotaphrum
Streptocarpus
Tetrastigma
Thunbergia
Tolmiea
Torenia
Tradescantia
Trevesia
Trichocereus
Vallota
Zephyranthes

Plants requiring acid compost ◉

Plants under this heading like to grow in a light, humusy compost, for instance a mixture containing plenty of peat fibre, peat lumps or conifer needle compost. Standard compost contains a little too much lime for this group. Special ericaceous compost, occasionally available commercially, or pine needle compost, will be more satisfactory.

Achimenes
Aphelandra
Begonia albo-picta
Begonia boliviensis
Begonia boweri
Begonia conchifolia
Begonia corallina
Begonia crispula
Begonia diadema
Begonia grandis
Begonia heracleifolia
Begonia hispida
Begonia hydrocotylifolia
Begonia imperialis
Begonia incana
Begonia incarnata
Begonia (tuberous)
Begonia limmingheiana
Begonia lorraine hybrids
Begonia luxurians
Begonia maculata
Begonia manicata
Begonia masoniana
Begonia metallica
Begonia rajah
Begonia rex hybrids
Begonia serratipetala
Begonia socotrana
Begonia venosa
Blechnum
Calathea
Calceolaria
Calliandra
Callistemon
Camellia
Crossandra
Dizygotheca
Doryopteris
Erica
× *Fatshedera*
Hebe
Hydrangea
Jacaranda
Kohleria
Myrtus
Rhododendron
Saintpaulia
Sinningia
Skimmia

Plants requiring special mixtures ◎

For the plants under this heading it is best to mix your own compost. Sometimes special mixtures are commercially available, such as cactus or ericaceous composts.

In the plant descriptions the ingredients required for these special home-made mixtures are always indicated under the heading 'Repotting'. Further details may be found on page 62.

Acalypha
Acanthocalycium
Acorus
Adiantum
Aechmea
Aeonium
Aerides
Aeschynanthus
Agapanthus
Agave
Aglaonema
Alocasia
Aloe
Angraecum
Anthurium
Aporocactus
Araucaria
Arequipa
Arisaema
Asparagus
Asplenium
Astrophytum
Beaucarnea
Borzicactus
Bouvardia
Brassavola
Brassia
Browallia
Caladium
Calanthe
Cattleya
Cephalocereus
Cereus
Ceropegia
Chamaecereus
Chamaedorea
Chamaerops
Chlorophytum
Chysis
Cissus
Citrus
Cleistocactus
Clerodendrum
Cleyera
Clivia
Coccoloba
Codiaeum
Codonanthe
Coelogyne
Coffea
Colchicum
Colletia
Columnea
Conophytum
Convallaria
Corynocarpus
Coryphantha
Costus
Cotyledon
Crassula
Crocus
Cryptanthus
Ctenanthe
Cussonia
Cycas
Cyclamen
Cycnoches
Cymbidium
Cyperus
Cyrtomium
Darlingtonia
Dasylirion
Datura
Dendrobium
Dichorisandra
Didymochlaena
Dieffenbachia
Dionaea
Dipladenia
Dolichothele
Dracaena
Echeveria
Echinocactus
Echinocereus
Echinopsis
Elisena
Epidendrum
Epiphyllum
Episcia
Erythrina
Espostoa
Eucharis
Eugenia
Euphorbia
Exacum
Fatsia
Faucaria
Ficus
Fittonia
Fuchsia
Gardenia
Gasteria
Gerbera
Gloriosa
Graptopetalum
Grevillea
Guzmania
Gymnocalycium
Gynura
Haemanthus
Hamatocactus
Harpephyllum
Hatiora
Haworthia

Plants requiring special mixtures (cont.)

Hedera
Heliconia
Helleborus
Hibiscus
Homalocladium
Howeia
Hoya
Hyacinthus
Hydrangea
Hymenocallis
Hypocyrta
Hypoestes
Ixora
Jacobinia
Jasminium
Jatropha
Kalanchoe blossfeldiana
Kalanchoe longiflora
Kalanchoe manginii
Kalanchoe marmorata
Kalanchoe tomentosa
Lachenalia
Laelia
× *Laeliocattleya*
Lagerstroemia
Lampranthus
Laurus
Lilium
Lithops
Littonia
Lobivia
Lophophora
Lycaste
Mammillaria
Maranta
Medinilla
Melocactus
Microcoelum
Microlepia
Mikania
Miltonia
Mimosa
Monstera
Murraya
Musa
Myrtillocactus
Narcissus
Nautilocalyx
Neoporteria
Neoregelia
Nepenthes
Nephrolepis
Nerine
Nerium
Nertera
Notocactus
Odontoglossum
Oncidium
Opuntia
Oreocereus
Oxalis
Pachycereus
Pachyphytum
Pachypodium
× *Pachyveria*
Paphiopedilum
Parodia
Passiflora quadrangularis
Pavonia
Pelargonium carnosum
Pellaea
Pellionia
Pentas
Peperomia
Phalaenopsis
Philodendron
Phlebodium
Phoenix
Phyllanthus
Pilea
Piper
Pisonia
Pittosporum
Platycerium
Pleione
Plumbago
Podocarpus
Polyscias
Polystichum
Pseuderanthemum
Pteris
Punica
Pyrrhocactus
Rebutia
Rechsteineria
Rhaphidophora
Rhipsalidopsis
Rochea
Rodriguezia
Sandersonia
Scindapsus
Sedum
Selaginella
Selencereus
Senecio articulatus
Senecio citriformis
Senecio haworthii
Senecio herreianus
Senecio macroglossus
Senecio rowleyanus
Smithiantha
Sonerila
Stapelia
Stenandrium
Stephanotis
Strelitzia
Stromanthe
Syngonium
Tetraclinis
Tillandsia
Vanda
Veltheimia
Vriesea
Washingtonia
Xanthosoma
Yucca
Zantedeschia
Zygocactus

Flowering plants

The chief ornamental value of the plants under this heading is provided by the flowers.

The most normal flowering seasons are indicated, but often a plant will flower at other times as well. The figures represent the months: 1 = January, 2 = February, and so on.

Most flowering plants need a dormant season or other special treatment in order to flower for a second time. Refer to the instructions given under the heading 'Care'. For other flowering plants see Bulbous plants, Orchids, Succulents, Trailing and climbing plants and Tuberous plants.

Abutilon darwinii	1–12
Abutilon hybrids	5–10
Abutilon megapotamicum	1–12
Abutilon striatum	8–11
Acalypha hispida	1–10
Achimenes erecta	7–9
Achimenes grandiflora	7–9
Achimenes hybrids	7–9
Achimenes patens	7–9
Allamanda cathartica	5–9
Anthurium	1–12
Aphelandra aurantiaca	10–12
Aphelandra blanchetiana	7–8
Aphelandra chamissoniana	9–10
Aphelandra fascinator	9–10
Aphelandra liboniana	4–5
Aphelandra nitens	4–5
Aphelandra squarrosa	4–10
Begonia dregei	6–9
Begonia elatior hybrids	3–10
Begonia fuchsioides	7–8
Begonia hydrocotylifolia	6–8
Begonia incarnata	9–3
Begonia lorraine hybrids	11–1
Begonia maculata	6–10
Begonia manicata	11–1
Begonia schmidtiana	
Begonia semperflorens hybrids	6–9
Begonia socotrana	11–2
Begonia venosa	
Beloperone guttata	1–12
Bouvardia hybrids	7–11
Bouvardia longiflora	8–11
Browallia speciosa	1–12
Browallia viscosa	6–9
Brunfelsia hopeana	2–3
Brunfelsai pauciflora	2–3
Calathea crocata	
Caleolaria hybrids	4–5
Calceolaria integrifolia	5–9
Calliandra tweedyi	
Callistemon citrinus	6–7
Camellia japonica	1–4
Campanula fragilis	6–7
Campanula isophylla	7–9
Catharanthus roseus	3–10
Celosia argentea	7–9
Chrysanthemum indicum hybrids	1–12
Clerodendrum philippinum	1–12
Clerodendrum speciosissimum	6–9
Clerodendrum splendens	12–5
Clerodendrum thomsoniae	3–7
Clivia miniata	2–5
Clivia nobilis	8–11
Crossandra flava	12–4
Crossandra infundibuliformis	5–8
Crossandra nilotica	5–8
Cuphea ignea	5–9
Cytisus × *racemosus*	3–5
Dichorisandra thyrsiflora	9–10
Erica gracilis	9–12
Erica hiemalis	2–3
Erica × *willmorei*	4–5
Erica ventricosa	5–9
Euphorbia fulgens	9–3
Euphorbia pulcherrima	12
Exacum affine	7–9
Fuchsia	7–10
Gardenia jasminoides	7–10
Gerbera jamesonii	4–9
Hebe andersonii hybrids	9–10
Helleborus niger	12–3
Hibiscus rosa-sinensis	3–10
Hydrangea macrophylla	7–8
Hypocyrta glabra	7–9
Impatiens balsamina	6–9
Impatiens marianae	6–7
Impatiens walleriana	1–12
Ixora hybrids	5–9
Jacobinia carnea	6–8
Jacobinia pauciflora	12–2
Medinilla magnifica	2–8
Mimosa pudica	7–8
Pachystachys lutea	3–10
Passiflora caerulea	6–9
Passiflora quadrangularis	5–6
Passiflora racemosa	5–9
Passiflora violacea	8–9
Pavonia multiflora	9–5
Pelargonium grandiflorum hybrids	4–6
Pelargonium graveolens	6–8
Pelargonium zonale hybrids	4–10
Pentas lanceolata	9–1
Plumbago auriculata	6–9
Plumbago indica	6–11
Primula × *kewensis*	2–4
Primula malacoides	1–3
Primula obconica	1–12
Primula praenitens	12–4
Primula vulgaris	3–4
Saintpaulia	1–12
Senecio cruentus hybrids	2–4
Spathiphyllum floribundum	3–4
Streptocarpus hybrids	5–8
Streptocarpus wendlandii	8–9
Thunbergia alata	5–10
Torenia fournieri	6–9
Zantedeschia aethiopica	1–6
Zantedeschia elliottiana	6–8
Zantedeschia rehmannii	

Foliage plants

In the plants under this heading it is not the flowers, but rather the beautiful foliage which is the most striking feature. No distinction has been made between foliage plants for indoor cultivation and those which must be grown in a greenhouse.

Remember that variegated foliage plants always require more light than green forms of the same species. Palms and ferns, which are also regarded as foliage plants, are grouped under separate headings.

Abutilon
Acalypha
Acanthus
Acorus
Aeschynanthus
Agave
Aglaeonema
Alocasia
Aloe
Ampelopsis
Ananas
Anthurium
Aphelandra
Araucaria
Ardisia
Asparagus
Aspidistra
Aucuba
Beaucarnea
Begonia albo-picta
Begonia boweri
Begonia crispula
Begonia diadema
Begonia × *erythrophylla*
Begonia foliosa
Begonia goegoensis
Begonia heracleifolia
Begonia hispida
Begonia imperialis
Begonia incana
Begonia luxurians
Begonia masoniana
Begonia metallica
Begonia rex hybrids

Foliage plants (cont.)

Begonia serratipetala
Bertolonia maculata
Brosimum
Caladium
Calathea
Callisia
Carex
Chlorophytum
Cissus
Cleyera
Coccoloba
Cocculus
Codiaeum
Coffea
Coleus
Coprosma
Cordyline
Cryptanthus
Ctenanthe
Cussonia
Cycas
Cyperus
Dasylirion
Dichorisandra reginae
Dieffenbachia
Dionaea
Dizygotheca
Dracaena
Episcia
Eugenia
Euonymus
× Fatshedera
Fatsia
Ficus aspera
Ficus benghalensis
Ficus benjamina
Ficus buxifolia
Ficus cyathistipula
Ficus deltoidea
Ficus lyrata
Ficus macrophylla
Ficus religiosa
Ficus sycomorus
Ficus triangularis
Fittonia
Glechoma
Grevillea
Gynura
Harpephyllum
Hedera
Heliconia
Hemigraphis
Hibiscus
Homalocladium
Hypoestes
Iresine
Laurus
Liriope
Maranta
Mimosa
Monstera
Musa
Ophiopogon
Oplismenus
Pandanus
Parthenocissus
Pedilanthus
Pelargonium × citrosum
Pelargonium radens
Peperomia
Perilepta
Persea
Philodendron
Pilea
Piper
Pisonia
Pittosporum
Plectranthus
Podocarpus
Polyscias
Pseuderanthemum
Rhoeo
Sansevieria
Saxifraga
Schefflera
Scindapsus
Selaginella
Senecio
Setcreasea
Siderasis
Skimmia
Sonerila
Sparmannia
Stromanthe
Syngonium podophyllum
Tetrastigma
Tolmiea
Tradescantia
Xanthosoma
Yucca
Zebrina

Bromeliads

The following genera belong to the bromeliad family. The common factor of all these plants is that each rosette flowers only once and subsequently dies. In many cases the offsets developed at the base can only be brought into flower if cultivated in a greenhouse.

Aechmea
Ananas
Billbergia
Cryptanthus
Guzmania
Neoregelia
Tillandsia
Vriesea

Palms

The following foliage plants are members of the palm family.

Chamaedorea
Chamaerops
Cocos
Howeia
Microcoelum
Phoenix
Washingtonia

Ferns

These are the ferns described in this book.

Adiantum
Asplenium
Blechnum
Cyrtomium
Didymochlaena
Doryopteris
Nephrolepis
Pellaea
Phlebodium
Phyllitis
Platycerium
Polystichum
Pteris

Orchids

All orchids belong to the same family and are nearly always grown in a greenhouse by plant lovers specialising in these plants. Only a few species can successfully be cultivated in the living-room. Flowering seasons are indicated by the number of the month—1 = January, 2 = February, for example.

Aerides japonicum	6–8
Aerides lawrenceae	6–8
Aerides multiflorum	6–9
Aerides vandarum	2–3
Angraecum eburneum	12–1
Angreacum sesquipedale	12–2
Brassavola cucullata	11–12
Brassavola nodosa	10–12
Brassavola perrinii	5–6
Brassia maculata	6–8
Brassia verrucosa	4–6
Calanthe triplicata	4–5
Calanthe vestita	12–2
Cattleya bowringiana	10–11
Cattleya dowiana	7–9
Cattleya gaskelliana	7–9
Cattleya labiata	10–11
Cattleya mendelii	5–7
Cattleya mossiae	5–7
Cattleya skinneri	3–4
Cattleya trianae	12–2
Cattleya warscewiczii	7–8
Chysis aurea	5–6
Chysis bractescens	3–5
Coelogyne cristata	1–3
Coelogyne flaccida	3–4
Coelogyne massangeana	5–7
Cycnoches chlorochilum	5–6
Cymbidium lowianum	2–5
Cymbidium × tracyanum	10–1
Dendrobium aggregatum	3–5
Dendrobium chrysanthum	8–9
Dendrobium chrysotoxum	3–4
Dendrobium fimbriatum	3–5
Dendrobium nobile	3–6
Dendrobium phalaenopsis	8–12
Dendrobium superbiens	10–12
Dendrobium thyrsiflorum	3–5
Dendrobium wardianum	1–3
Epidendrum ciliare	11–1
Epidendrum cochleatum	11–2
Epidendrum radiatum	5–6
Epidendrum radicans	2–5
Epidendrum stamfordianum	3–4
Epidendrum vitellinum	10–12
Laelia anceps	12–1
Laelia cinnabarina	2–5
Laelia gouldiana	12–1
Laelia pumila	9–10
Laelia purpurata	5–6
× Laeliocattleya	
Lycaste aromatica	4–5
Lycaste candida	12–3
Lycaste cruenta	3–5
Lycaste virginalis	11–3
Miltonia candida	8–11
Miltonia phalaenopsis	8–11
Miltonia roezlii	10–11
Miltonia spectabilis	8
Odontoglossum bictoniense	9–10
Odontoglossum cervantesii	11–3
Odontoglossum cordatum	7–8
Odontoglossum crispum	2–4
Odontoglossum grande	11–3
Odontoglossum maculatum	3–4
Odontoglossum oerstedtii	2–5
Odontoglossum pulchellum	2–4
Odontoglossum rossii	2–4
Odontoglossum schlieperianum	7–9
Oncidium altissimum	4–6
Oncidium cavendishianum	4–5
Oncidium crispum	9–12
Oncidium kramerianum	1–11
Oncidium marshallianum	5–6
Oncidium ornithorhynchum	10–11
Oncidium sphacelatum	4–6
Oncidium varicosum	10–1
Oncidium wentworthianum	6–8
Paphiopedilum callosum	3–7
Paphiopedilum fairieanum	7–9
Paphiopedilum insigne	10–1
Paphiopedilum niveum	4–8
Paphiopedilum spicerianum	11–1
Paphiopedilum sukhakulii	10–11
Paphiopedilum venustum	11–1
Paphiopedilum villosum	12–4
Phalaenopsis amabilis	10–1
Phalaenopsis esmeralda	8–11
Phalaenopsis lueddemanniana	5–6
Phalaenopsis schilleriana	1–3
Phalaenopsis stuartiana	1–3
Phalaenopsis violacea	5–7
Pleione bulbocodioides	5
Rodriguezia decora	9–2
Rodriguezia secunda	9–11
Rodriguezia venusta	7–8
Vanda coerulea	9–11

Cacti

Practically all the succulents in this group bear thorns. In most cases successful cultivation depends on strict observance of a dormant season.

Acanthocalycium
Aporocactus
Arequipa
Astrophytum
Borzicactus
Cephalocereus
Cereus
Chamaecereus
Cleistocactus
Coryphantha
Dolichothele
Echinocactus
Echinocereus
Echinopsis
Epiphyllum
Espostoa
Ferocactus
Gymnocalycium
Hamatocactus
Hatiora
Lobivia
Lophophora
Mammillaria
Melocactus
Myrtillocactus
Neoporteria
Notocactus
Opuntia
Oreocereus
Pachycereus
Parodia
Pereskia
Pyrrhocactus
Rebutia
Rhipsalidopsis gaertneri
Rhipsalidopsis × *graeseri*
Selenicereus
Trichocereus
Zygocactus truncatus

Succulents

Cacti are excluded from the following list of succulents and semi-succulents; they are listed under a separate heading. All the plants mentioned are capable of storing moisture in their tissue. In semi-succulent plants this capacity is less obvious. The more moisture a plant can store, the stricter the dormant season it requires (usually in winter). In the case of species with fairly regular flowering seasons the normal months of flowering are shown as: 1 = January, 2 = February, and so on.

Adromischus	
Aeonium arboreum	1–2
Aeonium haworthii	4–5
Aeonium tabuliforme	7–8
Aloe arborescens	1–4
Aloe ferox	3–4
Aloe humilis	3–4
Aloe mitriformis	4–8
Aloe saponaria	5–6
Aloe striata	4–5
Aloe variegata	4–5
Ceropegia	
Cissus gongylodes	
Cissus quadrangularis	
Conophytum	
Cotyledon orbiculata	7–8
Cotyledon paniculata	
Cotyledon reticulata	
Cotyledon undulata	3–7
Crassula arborescens	6–7
Crassula barbata	1–5
Crassula columnaris	10–11
Crassula cooperi	3–5
Crassula cordata	6–8
Crassula falcata	7–9
Crassula lycopodioides	2–3
Crassula obliqua	4–7
Crassula perforata	4–5
Crassula pyramidalis	
Crassula rupestris	4–5
Crassula schmidtii	4–8
Echeveria agavoides	5–6
Echeveria carnicolor	1–3
Echeveria derenbergii	4–6
Echeveria elegans	3–7
Echeveria gibbiflora	9–10
Echeveria harmsii	5–7
Echeveria peacockii	4–7
Echeveria pulvinata	3–4
Echeveria secunda	4–5
Echeveria setosa	4–7
Euphorbia abyssinica	
Euphorbia caput-medusae	
Euphorbia coerulescens	
Euphorbia globosa	
Euphorbia grandicornis	
Euphorbia milii	1–12
Euphorbia obesa	
Euphorbia pseudocactus	
Euphorbia trigona	
Faucaria bosscheana	
Faucaria felina	
Faucaria tigrina	
Faucaria tuberculosa	
Gasteria angulata	
Gasteria armstrongii	
Gasteria caespitosa	
Gasteria liliputana	
Gasteria maculata	
Gasteria pulchra	
Gasteria verrucosa	
Graptopetalum amethystinum	7–8
Graptopetalum paraguayense	
Haworthia	
Hoya australis	9–11
Hoya bella	7–9
Hoya carnosa	5–9
Jatropha podagrica	5–6
Kalanchoe	
Lampranthus blandus	7–9
Lithops	
Pachyphytum bracteosum	4–6
Pachyphytum brevifolium	
Pachyphytum compactum	
Pachyphytum hookerii	4–5
Pachyphytum oviferum	5–6
Pachypodium	
× *Pachyveria*	
Pelargonium carnosum	5
Peperomia	
Phyllanthus	
Rochea coccinea	7–8
Sedum bellum	3–5
Sedum dasyphyllum	6–8
Sedum griseum	1–2
Sedum morganianum	
Sedum pachyphyllum	4
Sedum platyphyllum	
Sedum praealtum	
Sedum rubrotinctum	
Sedum sieboldii	9–10
Sedum stahlii	8–9
Sempervivum arachnoideum	6–7
Sempervivum tectorum	6–8
Senecio articulatus	
Senecio citriformis	
Senecio haworthii	
Senecio herreianus	
Senecio macroglossus	12–2
Senecio rowleyanus	
Stapelia variegata	

Bulbous plants

Most of the following bulbous plants flower in summer, a few in spring. As a rule the flowering and growing seasons alternate with strict dormant periods. Flowering seasons are shown as 1 = January, 2 = February.

Amaryllis belladonna	8–9
Crinum × *powellii*	7–9
Elisena longipetala	
Eucharis grandiflora	5–8
Haemanthus albiflos	7–10
Haemanthus × *hybridus*	7–9
Haemanthus katharinae	7–8
Haemanthus multiflorus	4–5
Hippeastrum hybrids	1–4
Hyacinthus orientalis	4–5
Hymenocallis narcissiflora	6–7
Hymenocallis speciosa	9–11
Hymenocallis × *festalis*	
Lachenalia aloides	1–3
Lachenalia bulbifera	1–3
Lilium Mid-Century hybrids	6–7
Narcissus	12–1
Nerine sarniensis	9–10
Oxalis deppei	8–10
Oxalis carnosa	
Oxalis vulcanicola	7
Scilla paucifolia	4–5
Scilla violacea	4–5
Sprekelia formosissima	4–5
Tulipa	12–1
Vallota speciosa	7–8
Veltheimia capensis	1–3
Veltheimia glauca	
Zephyranthes candida	7–10
Zephyranthes citrina	
Zephyranthes grandiflora	4–6
Zephyranthes rosea	9–10

Tuberous plants

These are plants with a stem or root tuber, flowering in spring or summer; a few flower in the autumn. Most tuberous plants have a dormant season during which part or all of the foliage dies. Flowering seasons are shown as 1 = January, 2 = February.

Achimenes erecta	7–9
Achimenes grandiflora	7–9
Achimenes hybrids	7–9
Achimenes patens	7–9
Agapanthus africanus	7–8
Agapanthus praecox spp. *orientalis*	7–8
Arisaema	
Begonia boliviensis	
Begonia grandis	
Begonia (tuberous)	
Begonia pearcei	
Caladium	
Canna indica hybrids	6–10
Colchicum autumnale	8
Crocus neapolitamus	3–4
Crocus speciosus	9–11
Cyclamen persicum	8–4
Eucomis bicolor	
Gloriosa rothschildiana	6–8
Gloriosa superba	6–8
Kohleria hybrids	7–9
Lapeirousia laxa	4–6
Littonia modesta	6–7
Rechsteineria cardinalis	3–4
Rechsteineria leucotricha	4–8
Sandersonia aurantiaca	7
Sauromatum	
Sinningia speciosa	6–8
Smithiantha cinnabarina	4–6
Smithiantha hybrids	7–9
Smithiantha multiflora	7–8
Zantedeschia aethiopica	1–6
Zantedeschia elliottiana	6–8
Zantedeschia rehmannii	

Trailing and climbing plants

There is of course an essential difference between the two, but since there are many marginal cases they have been grouped under one heading. Flowering seasons are shown as 1 = January, 2 = February.

Aeschynanthus boscheanus	6–8
Aeschynanthus javanicus	
Aeschynanthus lobbianus	6–7
Aeschynanthus marmoratus	
Aeschynanthus parasiticus	7–8
Aeschynanthus pulcher	6–8
Aeschynanthus speciosus	6–9
Ampelopsis	
Aporocactus	
Asparagus	
Begonia corallina	1–12
Begonia limmingheiana	
Begonia rajah	
Bougainvillea × *buttiana*	4–6
Bougainvillea glabra	4–6
Bougainvillea spectabilis	4–6
Callisia	
Campanula fragilis	6–7
Campanula isophylla	7–9
Ceropegia africana	
Ceropegia barkleyi	
Ceropegia radicans	6–8
Ceropegia sandersonii	7–9
Ceropegia stapeliiformis	7–10
Ceropegia woodii	1–12
Chlorophytum	
Cissus	
Clerodendrum philippinum	1–12
Clerodendrum speciosissimum	6–9
Clerodendrum splendens	12–4
Clerodendrum thomsoniae	3–7
Codonanthe	
Coleus	
Columnea	
Dipladenia atropurpurea	7–8
Dipladenia boliviensis	4–10
Dipladenia eximia	6–8
Dipladenia hybrids	5–10
Dipladenia sanderi	6–8
Dipladenia splendens	7–9
Duchesnea indica	6–9
Epiphyllum	
Euonymus	
× *Fatshedera*	
Ficus elastica	
Ficus montana	
Ficus pumila	
Ficus radicans	
Ficus rubiginosa	
Fuchsia	5–10
Glechoma	
Gloriosa rothschildiana	6–8
Gloriosa superba	6–8
Gynura	
Hedera	
Hoya australis	9–11
Hoya bella	7–9
Hoya carnosa	5–6
Jasminum mesnyi	3–4
Jasminum officinale	6–9
Jasminum polyanthum	6–9
Jasminum sambac	3–10
Lampranthus	
Littonia modesta	6–7
Microlepia	
Mikania	
Monstera	
Oplismenus	
Parthenocissus	
Passiflora caerulea	6–9
Passiflora quadrangularis	5–7
Passiflora racemosa	5–9
Passiflora violacea	8–9
Pelargonium peltatum hybrids	4–10
Pellaea	
Pellionia	
Philodendron	
Piper	
Platycerium	
Rhaphidophora	
Rhipsalidopsis gaertneri	4
Rhipsalidopsis × *graeseri*	3–4
Rhoicissus	
Saxifraga stolonifera	
Scindapsus	
Scirpus	
Senecio herreianus	
Senecio macroglossus	
Senecio mikanioides	
Senecio rowleyanus	
Setcreasea	
Soleirolia	
Stenandrium	
Stenotaphrum	
Stephanotis floribunda	6–9
Syngonium auritum	
Syngonium vellozianum	
Tetrastigma	
Thunbergia alata	5–10
Tradescantia	
Zebrina	
Zygocactus truncatus	10–12

Tub plants

Most species were or are grown in tubs because of the sizes they may attain. The essential factor is that these plants can be kept outdoors in the summer and must spend the winter in a cool but frost-free environment. They are sometimes called orangery plants. Practically all species mentioned are unsuitable for living room cultivation. Flowering seasons are shown as 1 = January, 2 = February.

Acacia armata	3–4
Acacia baileyana	3–4
Acacia dealbata	1–4
Agapanthus africanus	7–8
Agapanthus praecox ssp. *orientalis*	7–8
Agave	
Aloe	
Araucaria	
Aucuba	
Bougainvillea × *buttiana*	4–6
Bougainvillea glabra	4–6
Bougainvillea spectabilis	4–6
Callistemon citrinus	6–7
Camellia japonica	1–4
Citrus	
Cleyera	
Colletia cruciata	11–12
Corynocarpus	
Crinum × *powellii*	7–9
Datura candida	6–9
Datura sanguinea	1–3
Erythrina crista-galli	8–9
Harpephyllum	
Hibiscus rosa-sinensis	3–10
Jacaranda	
Jasminum mesnyi	3–4
Jasminum officinale	6–9
Jasminum polyanthum	6–9
Jasminum sambac	3–10
Lagerstroemia indica	8–10
Laurus	
Malvastrum capense	6–9
Myrtus communis	6–10
Nerium oleander	6–9
Olea europaea	7–8
Oreopanax dactylifolius	1–3
Passiflora caerulea	6–9
Passiflora quadrangularis	5–7
Passiflora racemosa	5–9
Passiflora violacea	8–9
Pittosporum eugenioides	7–8
Pittosporum tobira	3–5
Pittosporum undulatum	5–7
Plumbago auriculata	6–9
Podocarpus	
Punica granatum	7–8
Rhododendron	12–4
Rosa	6–9
Schefflera	
Skimmia	
Solanum	
Sparmannia africana	1–4
Stenocarpus sinuatus	7–8
Strelitzia reginae	12–1
Tetraclinis	
Trevesia	
Washingtonia	
Yucca	

Poisonous plants

It is essential to know which plants are poisonous to a greater or lesser degree, or which may cause irritations. This does not mean that they must be banned altogether, but you should be careful when there are children in the house, since many of them tend to put anything or everything in their mouths. In only a very few cases is the poison fatal.

Allamanda cathartica
Anthurium scherzerianum
Aucuba japonica
Capsicum frutescens
Catharanthus roseus
Clerodendrum
Clivia miniata
Codiaeum variegatum
Colchicum
Convallaria majalis
Cyclamen
Datura
Dieffenbachia
Euphorbia
Gloriosa superba
Hedera helix
Helleborus
Hoya
Hyacinthus orientalis
Monstera
Narcissus
Nerium oleander
Philodendron
Primula obconica
Rhododendron
Senecio
Solanum pseudocapsicum
Zantedeschia

Index

A
Abutilon darwinii 82
hybrids 82
megapotamicum 82
pictum 82
striatum 82
vexillarium 82
Acacia armata 83
baileyana 83
dealbata 83
decurrens dealbata 83
paradoxa 83
Acalypha hispida 83
sanderi 83
wilkesiana 83
Acanthocalycium spiniflorum 83
violaceum 82
Acanthus ilicifolius 84
montanus 84
acclimatising 64
Achimenes coccinea 84
erecta 84
grandiflora 84
hybrids 84
patens 84
pulchella 84
rosea 84
Achyranthes lindenii 185
verschaffeltii 185
acidity 62
Acorus gramineus 85
Adiantum caudatum 85
ciliatum 85
cuneatum 85
decorum 85
formosum 85
macrophyllum 85
raddianum 85
tenerum 85
Adromischus cooperi 86
festivus 86
trigynus 86
Aechmea bromeliifolia 87
calyculata 87
caudata 87
chantinii 87
coelestis 87
comata 87
fasciata 87
fulgens 87
lindenii 87
marmorata 87
miniata 87
tillandsioides 87
weilbachii 87
Aeonium arboreum 88
haworthii 88
tabuliforme 88
Aerides japonicum 88
lawrenceae 88
multiflorum 88
vandarum 88
Aeschynanthus boscheanus 88
grandiflorus 89
javanicus 89
lamponga 88
lobbianus 89
marmoratus 89
parasiticus 89
pulcher 89
speciosus 89
African Blood Lily 174
Hemp 256
Violet 146
Agapanthus africanus 89
orientalis 89
praecox ssp. *orientalis* 89
umbellatus 89
Agave americana 90
applanata 90
attenuata 90
ferdinandi-regis 90
ferox 90
filifera 90
geminiflora 90
ghiesbreghtii 90
parrasana 90
parryi 90
schnittspahnii 90
striata 90
stricta 90
victoriae-reginae 90
Aglaonema commutatum 91
costatum 91
crispum 91
pictum 91
roebelinii 91
treubii 91
air conditioning 59
air-layering 76
Allamanda cathartica 91
Alloplectus capitatus 92
lynchii 204
vittatus 92
Alocasia cuprea 92
lowii 92
metallica 92
plumbea 92
sanderiana 92
Aloe albo-cincta 93
arborescens 92, 93
disticha 93
ferox 93
humilis 93
mitriformis 93
x *principes*
saponaria 93
striata 93
supralaevis 93
umbellata 93
variegata 93
Amaryllis 180
Amaryllis belladonna 93
formosissima 257
hybrids 180
Amazon Lily 158
Ampelopsis aconitifolia 93
brevipedunculata 94
japonica 94
serjaniifolia 94
Ananas comosus 94
Anastatica hierochuntica 94
Ancistrocactus uncinatus 174
Angel's Wings 111
Angraecum eburneum 95
sesquipedale 95
Anhalonium williamsii 195
Anisdontea capensis 196
Aniseed Plant 184
annual corms 51
Anomatheca cruenta 192
anther 51
Anthurium andreanum 96
crystallinum 96
magnificum 96
scherzerianum 96
antique containers 33
ants 78
Aphelandra amoena 97
aurantiaca 97
blanchetiana 97
chamissoniana 97
fascinator 97
liboniana 97
nitens 97
punctata 97
squarrosa 97
aphids 78
Aporocactus flagelliformis 97
flagriformis 97
Arabian Jasmine 187
Arachis hypogaea 97
Aralia balfouriana 235
elegantissima 149
japonica 163
kerchovei 149
sieboldii 163
Araucaria excelsa 98
heterophylla 97, 98
Ardisia crenata 98
crenulata 98
malouiana 98
Aregelia carolinae 205
concentrica 205
Arequipa paucicostata 99
rettigii 99
Arisaema candidissimum 99
Arrowhead Vine 261
artificial fertiliser 61
light 47, 52
Artillery Plant 230
Arum cornutum 247
guttatum 247
venosum 247
Arum Lily 270
Asclepias carnosa 182
Asparagus asparagoides 100
crispus 100
decumbens 100
densiflorus 100
falcatus 100
medeoloides 100
myriocladus 100
plumosus 100
scandens 100
setaceus 100
Asparagus Fern 99
Aspidistra elatior 101
Aspidium caryotideum 143
falcatum 143
Asplenium bulbiferum 101
daucifolium 101
dimorphum 101
nidus 101
viviparum 101
assimilation 49
Astrophytum asterias 102
capricorne 102
myriostigma 102
ornatum 102
atmospheric humidity 58
Aucuba japonica 102
auraphotography 10
Australian Brake 239
Austrocylindropuntia 213
automatic watering systems 46
Avocado Pear 226
Aylostera deminuta 240
fiebrigii 240
pseudodeminuta 240
spinosissima 240
Azalea 242
Azalea indica 243

B
balcony greenhouse 60
Balsamina hortensis 185
Banana 202
Banyan Tree 165
Barbados Gooseberry 225
bark 51
Barrel Cactus 163
bast 51
bathroom plants 37
Bay Tree 192
Bead Plant 208
bedroom plants 37
Beaucarnea recurvata 103
stricta 103
Begonia 103
Begonia albo-picta 105
argyrostigma 107
boliviensis 105
boweri 105
conchifolia 105
corallina 105
crispula 105
diadema 105
discolor 106
dregei 105
elatior hybrids 105
× *erythrophylla* 106
foliosa 105
fuchsioides 106
goegoensis 106
grandis 106
heracleifolia 106
hispida cucullifera 106
hydrocotylifolia 106
imperialis 106
incana 106
incarnata 106
limmingheiana 107
lorraine hybrids 107
luxurians 107
maculata 107
manicata 107
masoniana 107
metallica 107
pearcei 107
rajah 107
rex hybrids 107
schmidtiana 107
semperflorens hybrids 107
serratipetala 107
socotrana 107
venosa 107
Bellflower 115
Belladonna Lily 93
Beloperone guttata 107
Bertolonia maculata 108
marmorata 108
Big Blue Lily-turf 193
Billbergia nutans 108
× *windii* 108
Bird of Paradise Flower 260
Bird's Nest Cactus 205
Fern 101
Bishop's Cap 102
Black-eyed Susan 262
Blechnum brasiliense 108
gibbum 108
occidentale 108
Blood Lily 174
Blue African Lily 89
Bolivicereus samaipatanus 109
bonsai 44
Borzicactus leucotrichus 99
samaipatanus 109
sepium 109
botany 49
Bo Tree 166
Bottle Brush Tree 114
bottle gardens 26
botrytis 78
Bougainvillea × *buttiana* 109
glabra 109
spectabilis 109
Bouvardia hybrids 109
longiflora 109
Bowstring Hemp 247
Brasilicactus graessneri 209
haselbergii 209
Brassavola cucullata 110
nodosa 110
perrinii 110
Brassia actinophylla 249
guttata 110
maculata 110
verrucosa 110
Brazilian Plume 187
bromeliads 40
cultivation 69
Broom 144
Brosimum alicastrum 110
Browallia major 111
speciosa 111
viscosa 111
brown patches 78
Brunfelsia hopeana 111
pauciflora calycina 111
Bryophyllum crenatum 189
daigremontianum 189
tubiflorum 189
Buffalo Grass 259
building regulations 22
bulb growing 68
bulbous plants 44, 51
bulbs in winter 68

burying plants 18
Busy Lizzie 184

C

cacti 42
cultivation 70
cambium layer 51
Caladium argyrites 111
bicolor hybrids 111
humboldtii 111
Calamondin Orange 123
Calanthe furcata 112
triplicata 112
veratrifolia 112
vestita 112
Calathea bachemiana 112
bicolor 197
crocata 112
insignis 112
lancifolia 112
leopardina 112
lietzei 112
lindeniana 112
louisea 112
makoyana 112
medio-picta 112
ornata 113
picturata 113
roseo-picta 113
rotundifolia 113
veitchiana 113
warscewiczii 113
zebrina 113
Calceolaria × herbeohybrida 113
hybrids 113
integrifolia 113
Calla Lily 270
Calliandra tweedyi 113
Callisia elegans 114
fragrans 114
Callistemon citrinus 114
lanceolatus 114
Callitris quadrivalvis 262
calyx 51
Camellia japonica 115
Campanula fragilis 115
isophylla 115
Canary Date Palm 229
Canna indica hybrids 116
Cape Jasmine 168
Leadwort 234
Primrose 260
capillary mat 25
capitulum 51
Capsicum annuum 116
capsicastrum 255
capsid bugs 78
Cardamom 154
Carex brunnea 116
elegantissima 116
Carpet Plant 157
Carrion Flower 258
Catharanthus roseus 117
Cattleya bowringiana 117
dowiana 117
gaskelliana 117
labiata 117
mendelii 117
mossiae 117
skinneri 117
trianae 117
warscewiczii 117
cell tension 51
Celosia argentea 118
Century Plant 90
Centrosolenia bullata 204
Cephalocereus chrysacanthus 118
guentheri 158
melanostele 158
senilis 118
Cephalophorus senilis 118
Cereus azureus 119
baumannii 124
chalybaeus 119
flagelliformis 97
flagriformis 97
grandiflorus 251
huntingtonianus 119
jamacaru 119
melanostele 158
peruvianus 119
silvestrii 120
strausii 124
validus 119
Ceropegia africana 119
barkleyi 119
radicans 120
sandersonii 120
stapeliiformis 120
woodii 120
Chamaecereus silvestrii 120
Chamaedorea elegans 120
metallica 120
Chamaerops humilis 121
Chameranthemum igneum 268
charcoal 62
Chenille Plant 83
Chestnut Vine 262
Chilenia nigrihorrida 205
Chinese Dwarf Orange Tree 123
Evergreen 91
Primula 237
chlorophyll 50
Chlorophytum capense 212
comosum 121
elatum 121
sternbergianum 121
chlorosis 78
choice of plants 27
Christmas Cactus 271
Cheer 250
Rose 178
Chrysanthemum 121
Chrysanthemum indicum hybrids 122
Chysis aurea 122
bractescens 122
Cigar Flower 139
Cineraria hybrids 253
Cissus antarctica 123
brevipedunculata 93
discolor 123
gongylodes 123
njegerre 123
quadrangularis 123
rhombifolia 123
striata 123
× Citrofortunella mitis 123
Citrus aurantium 123
limon 123
microcarpa 123
mitis 123
sinensis 123
Claret Cup Cactus 154
clay 62
granules 45
Cleistocactus baumannii 124
sepium 109
smaragdiflorus 124
strausii 124
Clerodendrum philippinum 124
speciosissimum 124
splendens 124
thomsoniae 124
Cleyera japonica 125
climbing plants 40
Clivia miniata 125
nobilis 125
Club Palm 132
Club Rush 249
Cob Cactus 195
Cobweb Houseleek 252
Coccoloba grandiflora 126
pubescens 126
uvifera 126
Coccolus laurifolius 126
cockroaches 78
Coconut Palm 126, 199
Cocos nucifera 126
weddelliana 199
Codiaeum pictum 127
variegatum pictum 127
Codonanthe crassifolia 128
Coelogyne cristata 128
flaccida 128
massangeana 128
Coffea arabica 129
Coffee Plant 128
Colchicum autumnale 129
Coleus blumei hybrids 129
fredericii 129
pumilus 129
rehneltianus 129
thyrsoideus 129
Colletia cruciata 130
Columnea × banksii 131
gloriosa 131
hirta 131
hybrids 131
linearis 131
microphylla 131
schiedeana 131
teuscheri 131
tulae 131
combinations 14, 35
Common Date Palm 229
Fig 166
Houseleek 252
compost 62
Cone Plant 131
conifer needle compost 62
Conophytum bilobum 131
calculus 131
mundum 131
scitulum 131
wettsteinii 131
conservatory 19
container planting 14
containers 15
Convallaria majalis 132
Coprosma baueri 132
repens 132
Coral Cactus 175
Moss 208
Tree 158
Cordyline australis 133
indivisa 133
rubra 133
stricta 133
terminalis 133
corm 51
corolla 5
Corynocarpus laevigatus 133
Coryphantha cornifera 133
elephantidens 133
pseudonickelsae 133
Corytholoma cardinale 241
Costus igneus 134
lucanusianus 134
malortieanus 134
speciosus 134
Cotyledon arborescens 135
fascicularis 134
orbiculata 134
paniculata 134
reticulata 134
undulata 134
Coxcomb 118
Crassula arborescens 135
argenta 136
barbata 135
bolusii 136
coccinea 244
columnaris 136
conjuncta 135
cooperi 136
cordata 136
falcata 136
impressa 136
lycopodioides 136
obliqua 136
perforata 136
perfossa 136
pyramidalis 136
rupestris 136
schmidtii 136
tetragona 135
Creeping Fig 166
Plant 157
Crinum × powellii 136
cristate formation 42
Crocus 136
Crocus neapolitanus 137
speciosus 137
vernus 137
Crossandra flava 137
infundibuliformis 137
nilotica 138
Croton 127
Croton variegatus 127
Crown Cactus 240
of Thorns 161
Cryptanthus acaulis 138
beuckeri 138
bromelioides 138
fosterianus 138
lacerdae 138
zonatus 138
Ctenanthe compressa 139
kummeriana 139
lubbersiana 139
oppenheimiana 139
cultivation systems 45
Cuphea ignea 139
platycentra 139
Curly Palm 181
Cussonia spicata 139
cut worms 78
cuttings medium 72
taking 74
Cycas revoluta 140
Cyclamen persicum 140
Cycnoches chlorochilum 141
pendadactylum 141
Cylindropuntia 213
Cymbidium lowianum 142
× tracyanum 142
Cyperus alternifolius 143
argenteostriatus 143
diffusus 143
gracilis 143
haspan 143
papyrus 143
Cyrtanthera carnea 187
magnifica 187
Cyrtomium caryotideum 143
falcatum 143
fortunei 143
Cytisus fragrans 144
× racemosus 144
× spachianus 144

D

Dagger Plant 269
damping off 78
Darlingtonia californica 144
Dasylirion acrotrichum 144
gracile 144
Date Palm 229
Datura candida 145
sanguinea 145
suaveolens 145
day length 53, 60
deficiency diseases 77
demineralisation 58
Dendrobium aggregatum 145
chrysanthum 145
chrysotoxum 145
fimbriatum 145
nobile 145
paxtonii 145
phalaenopsis 145
superbiens 145
thyrsiflorum 145
wardianum 145
Devil's Ivy 249
Pincushion 163
Tongue 163
Dichorisandra reginae 146
thyrsiflora 146
Didymochlaena truncatula 146
Dieffenbachia amoena 147
× bausei 147
bowmannii 147
humilis 147
imperialis 147
leopoldii 147
maculata 147
picta 147

reginae 147
seguine 147
Dionaea muscipula 147
Dipladenia atropurpurea 148
boliviensis 148
eximia 148
hybrids 148
sanderi 148
splendens 148
Dipteracanthus devosianus 148
makoyana 148
disease control 77
disposable plants 29
dissimilation 50
division 73
Dizygotheca elegantissima 149
kerchoveana 149
kerchovei 149
veitchii 149
Dolichothele camptotricha 149
longimamma 149
Dolomite limestone powder 62
Donkey's Tail 250
dormant seasons 60
Doryopteris palmata 150
pedata 150
double-lobed seed 49
downy mildew 78
Dracaena australis 133
cantleyi 151
concinna 151
deremensis 151
draco 151
fragrans 151
godseffiana 151
goldieana 151
hookeriana 151
indivisa 133
marginata 151
reflexa 151
rubra 133
sanderiana 151
stricta 133
terminalis 133
thalioides 151
umbraculifera 151
Dragon Tree 150
drainage 63
dried blood 62
drip watering 25
Drymonia punctata 157
Duchesnea indica 152
Dumb Cane 146
Dutch Wings 169
Dwarf Banana 202
Coconut Palm 199

E

ear 51
earwigs 78
Easter Cactus 242
Echeveria affinis 153
agavoides 153
carnicolor 153
derenbergii 153
elegans 153
gibbiflora 153
harmsii 153
leucotricha 153
peacockii 153
perelegans 153
pulvinata 153
purpusorum 153
secunda 153
setosa 153
Echinocactus acanthodes 163
andreae 172
baldianus 172
corniger 163
electracanthus 163
fiebrigii 240
gibbosus 173
grandis 153
grusonii 153
horizonthalonius 153
ingens 153
macrodiscus 163
mihanovichii 173
multiflorus 173
nidus 205
palmeri 153
quehlianus 173
senilis 205
stainesii 163
strausianus 239
villosus 205
Echinocereus berlandieri 154
knippelianus 154
pectinatus 154
pentalophus 154
procumbens 154
purpureus 154
reichenbachii 154
salm-dyckianus 154
scheerii 154
Echinopsis densispina 195
eyriesii 154
mamillosa 154
obrepanda 154
pygmaea 240
spiniflora 83
tubiflora 154
eelworm 78
Egyptian Paper Plant 143
Star Cluster 223
Elatostema pulchrum 223
repens 223
Elephant's Ear 174
Elettaria cardamomum 154
Elisena longipetala 155
Epidendrum ciliare 155
cochleatum 155
evectum 155
ibaguense 155
× *obrienianum* 155
radiatum 155
radicans 155
stamfordianum 155
vitellinum 155
epiphyte tree 16
epiphytic bromeliad 69
Epiphyllum crenatum 156
gaertneri 242
hybrids 156
Epipremnum aureum 241
Episcia cupreata 157
dianthiflora 157
fulgida 157
punctata 157
reptans 157
tessellata 204
Eranthemum igneum 268
sanguinolentum 184
Erica gracilis 157
hyemalis 157
ventricosa 157
× *willmorei* 157
Eriocactus leninghausii 209
Erythrina crista-galli 158
Espostoa guentheri 158
lanata 158
melanostele 158
Eucharis amazonica 158
grandiflora 158
Eucomis bicolor 159
Eugenia myriophylla 159
paniculata 159
uniflora 159
Euonymus japonicus 159
Euphorbia abyssinica 161
canariensis 161
caput-medusae 161
coerulescens 161
fournieri 161
fulgens 161
globosa 161
grandicornis 161
lophogona 161
meloformis 161
millii 161
obesa 161
pseudocactus 161
pulcherrima 161
tirucalli 161
trigona 161
evaporation 55
Exacum affine 162
excessive chlorine 78
eye cuttings 74

F

False Aralia 149
Fan Palm 120
× *Fatshedera lizei* 162
Fatsia japonica 163
Faucaria bosscheana 163
felina 163
tigrina 163
tuberculosa 163
feeding 61
hydro-plants 46
ferns 39
cultivation 71
Ferocactus acanthodes 163
latispinus 163
melocactiformis 163
recurvus 163
stainesii 163
fertiliser 61
Ficus aspera 165
australis 166
benghalensis 165
benjamina 166
buxifolia 166
cannonii 166
carica 166
cyathistipula 166
deltoidea 166
diversifolia 166
dryepondtiana 166
edulis 166
elastica 166
indica 166
lyrata 166
macrophylla 166
montana 166
nekbudu 166
nitida 166
pandurata 166
pumila 166
quercifolia 166
radicans 166
religiosa 166
repens 166
rubiginosa 166
sycomorus 166
triangularis 166
utilis 166
Fiddle Leaf Fig 166
Fig 164
Cactus 213
Finger Aralia 149
Fishhook Cactus 163
Fittonia gigantea 167
verschaffeltii 167
Flame Nettle 129
Violet 157
Flamingo Plant 95
flea beetle 78
flower pots 32, 63
windows 20, 66
flowering plants 38
Fly Trap 147
foliage plants 39
foliar feeding 61
forcing bulbs 69
Franciscea hopeana 111
free-standing plants 12
freezing 54
French Geraniums 222
Fruiting Myrtle 159
Fuchsia hybrids 168
fungus diseases 77

G

Gardenia florida 169
jasminoides 169
garden room 19
soil 62
Gasteria angulata 169
armstrongii 169
caespitosa 169
liliputana 169
maculata 169
pulchra 169
trigona 169
verrucosa 169
Genista fragrans 144
racemosa 144
Geranium 220
Gerbera jamesonii 170
German Ivy 253
germination 49
Gesneria cardinalis 241
cinnabarina 255
macrantha 241
Gladiolus laxus 192
glass cases 26
Glaziova martiana 199
Glechoma hederacea 170
Gloriosa rothschildiana 171
superba 171
Glory Lily 170
Gloxinia 254
Gloxinia speciosa 254
Golden Barrel Cactus 153
grafting 76
Graptopetalum amethystinum 171
paraguayense 171
greenhouse grasshopper 78
greenhouses 21
Grevillea robusta 171
grey mould 78
Ground Ivy 170
Groundsel 252
groups, indoor plant 38
growing medium 62
growth, watering for 55
Guernsey Lily 207
Guzmania angustifolia 172
hybrids 172
lindenii 172
lingulata 172
minor 172
monostachya 172
tricolor 172
zahnii 172
Gymnocalycium andreae 172
baldianum 172
bruchii 173
denudatum 173
gibbosum 173
lafaldense 173
mihanovichii 173
multiflorum 173
guehlianum 173
Gynura aurantiaca 173
procumbens 173
sarmentosa 173

H

Haemanthus albiflos 174
× *hybridus* 174
katharinae 174
multiflorus 174
puniceus 174
Hamatocactus hamatacanthus 174
setispinus 174
uncinatus 174
hanging plants 40
pots and baskets 16
Harpephyllum caffrum 175
hardening 64, 73
hard water 57
Hart's Tongue Fern 230
Hatiora cylindrica 175
salicornioides 175
Haworthia attenuata 176
cuspidata 176
fasciata 176
margaritifera 176
obtusa 176
reinwardtii 176
tessellata 176
truncata 176
head 51
Hearts Entangled 119
Heather 157

heating conservatory 19
greenhouse 24
Hebe andersonii hybrids 176
salicifolia 176
speciosa 176
Hedera canariensis 177
helix 177
Hedgehog Cactus 153
heel 75
Heimeriodendron brunonianum 231
umbellifera 231
Heliconia illustris-rubricaulis 178
indica 178
Hellebore 178
Helleborus niger 178
Helxine soleirolii 256
Hemigraphis alternata 179
colorata 179
repanda 179
Heptapleurum venulosum 249
Hibiscus rosa-sinensis 179
Hippeastrum × *hortorum* 180
hybrids 180
history of pot plants 9
holidays 67
Holly Fern 143
Homalocladium platycladum 180
Hortensia 182
Houseleek 252
Howeia belmoreana 181
forsteriana 181
Hoya australis 182
bella 182
carnosa 182
humidifiers 59
Hyacinth 182
glass 68
Hyacinthus orientalis 182
Hydrangea macrophylla 183
hydroponics 45
Hymenocallis calathina 184
× *festalis* 183
narcissiflora 184
speciosa 184
Hypocyrta glabra 184
Hypoestes phyllostachya 184
sanguinolenta 184
taeniata 184

I

Illicium verum 184
Impatiens balsamina 185
holstii 185
marianae 185
sultani 185
walleriana 185
Indian Shot 116
Strawberry 152
indoor plant groups 38
propagator 72
trees 41
insects 77
insulation of greenhouses 23
ion exchanges 46, 58
Iresine herbstii 185
lindenii 185
iron deficiency 78
Ismene calathina 184
× *festalis* 183
Isolepis gracilis 250
Isoloma hybrids 189
Ivy 177
Peperomia 224
-leaved Geraniums 222
Ixora hybrids 185

J

Jacaranda mimosifolia 186
ovalifolia 186
Jacobean Lily 257
Jacobinia carnea 187
pauciflora 187
Jacob's Ladder 220
Jade Tree 136
Japanese Aralia 162
Jasmine 187
Jasminum mesnyi 187
nudiflorum 187
officinale 187
polyanthum 187
primulinum 187
sambac 187
Jatropha podagrica 187
Jerusalem Cherry 255
Justicia carnea 187
rizzinii 187

K

Kalanchoe blossfeldiana 188
crenata 189
daigremontiana 189
grandiflora 189
laxiflora 189
longiflora 189
macrantha 189
manginii 189
marmorata 189
tomentosa 189
tubiflora 189
Kentia belmoreana 181
forsteriana 181
Kentia Palm 181
kitchen plants 37
Kleinia articulata 253
gomphophylla 253
tomentosa 253
Kohleria hybrids 189

L

Labisia malouiana 98
Lace Flower Vine 157
Lachenalia aloides 190
bulbifera 190
pendula 190
Ladder Fern 206
Lady's Eardrops 167
Laelia anceps 191
cinnabarina 191
gouldiana 191
pumila 191
purpurata 191
× *Laeliocattleya* 191
Lagerstroemia indica 191
Lampranthus blandus 191
brownii 191
Lapeirousia laxa 192
Laurus nobilis 192
Lawyer's Tongue 169
layering 73
Leadwort 234
leaf blotch eelworm 78
cuttings 74
fall 78
frog hopper 78
leafhopper 78, 79
leafmould 62
lean-to greenhouse 22
leaves 51
Lemon Geranium 222
Plant 123
length of day 53, 60
Libonia floribunda 187
lice 79
lie detector 10
light 47, 52
angle of 14
effect on flowering 53
intensity 52
measuring 52
Lilium auratum 193
longiflorum 193
Mid-Century hybrids 193
regale 193
speciosum 193
Lily 193
of the Valley 132
lime deposit 57
Liriope muscari 193
Lithops bella 194
optica 194
pseudotruncatella 194
ruschiorum 194
turbiniformis 194
Littonia modesta 194
Living Stone 194
Lobivia boliviensis 195
densispina 195
famatimensis 195
hertrichiana 195
pectinifera 195
pentlandii 195
pygmaea 240
long-day plants 53
Lophophora williamsii 195
Lucky Clover 214
lux measurement 47
Lycaste aromatica 195
brevispatha 195
candida 195
cruenta 195
skinneri 196
virginalis 196

M

Madagascar Jasmine 259
Maidenhair Fern 85
Malacocarpus apricus 209
concinnus 209
graessneri 209
haselbergii 209
leninghausii 209
mammulosus 209
napinus 205
scopa 209
strausianus 239
Malvastrum capense 196
Mammillaria bocasana 197
gracilis 197
hahniana 197
longimamma 149
magnimamma 197
multiceps 197
plumosa 197
prolifera 197
multiceps 197
rhodantha 197
spinossissima 197
vaupelii 197
verhaertiana 197
wildii 197
zeilmanniana 197
Mandevilla boliviensis 148
sanderi 148
splendens 148
Maranta bachemiana 112
bicolor 197
kummeriana 139
leuconeura 197
lietzei 112
makoyana 112
Meadow Saffron 129
mealy bug 79
scale 79
Medinilla magnifica 198
Mediolobivia aureiflora 240
ritteri 240
Medusa's Head 161
Melocactus bahiensis 198
intortus 198
maxonii 198
peruvianus 198
Melon Cactus 198
mice 79
Microcoelum martianum 199
weddellianum 199
Microlepia speluncae 199
Mikania apiifolia 200
scandens 253
ternata 200
mildew 79
Milkbush 161
Milkwort 160
millipedes 79
Miltonia candida 200
phalaenopsis 200
spectabilis 200
Mimosa pudica 201
Mimosa Tree 82
miniature trees 44
Miniature Wax Plant 182
Mistletoe Fig 166
mist-spraying 75
mites 79
moisture control 55
Monstera deliciosa 202
obliqua 'Leichtlinii' 202
Moreton Bay Fig 166
Moses in the Cradle 243
moss pole 64
Moth Orchid 226
Mother-in-law's Tongue 247
Mother of Thousands 248
moving 12
Muehlenbeckia platycladum 180
Murraya paniculata 202
Musa acuminata 202
cavendishii 202
ensete 202
nana 202
× *paradisiaca* 202
Myrtillocactus cochal 203
geometrizans 203
schenckii 203
Myrtle 203
Myrtus communis 203

N

Naegelia cinnabarina 255
Narcissus 203
Narcissus hybrids 203
natural fertilisers 61
Nautilocalyx bullatus 204
forgetii 204
lynchii 204
Neanthe bella 120
Neochilenia napina 205
Neoporteria napina 205
nidus 205
nigrihorrida 205
senilis 205
villosa 205
Neoregelia carolinae 205
concentrica 205
Nepenthes hybrids 206
Nepeta hederacea 170
Nephrolepis cordifolia 207
exaltata 207
tuberosa 207
Nerine sarniensis 207
Nerium oleander 208
Nertera depressa 208
granadensis 208
Never-never Plant 139
Nidularium acanthocrater 205
meyendorffii 205
Night Cactus 251
Nightshade 255
Nipple Cactus 196
nitrogen deficiency 79
Nolina recurvata 103
stricta 103
Norfolk Island Pine 97
Nothopanax guilfoylei 235
Notocactus apricus 209
concinnus 209
graessneri 209
haselbergii 209
leninghausii 209
mammulosus 209
scopa 209
nutrients 61
intake of 49

O

Odier Geranium 222
Odontoglossum bictoniense 210
cervantesii 210
cordatum 210
crispum 210
grande 210
maculatum 210
oerstedtii 210
pulchellum 210
rossii 210
schlieperianum 210
office gardens 36
plants 34
Old Man Cactus 118

Olea europaea 210
Oleander 208
Olive 210
Oncidium altissimum 211
cavendishianum 211
crispum 211
kramerianum 211
marshallianum 211
ornithorhynchum 211
sphacelatum 211
varicosum 211
rogersii 211
wentworthianum 211
Ophiopogon jaburan 212
japonicus 212
muscari 193
Oplismenus hirtellus 212
Opuntia basilaris 213
bergeriana 213
clavarioides 213
cylindrica 213
diademata 213
exaltata 213
ficus-indica 213
leucotricha 213
microdasys 213
phaecantha 213
scheerii 213
subulata 213
tunicata 213
orangery 60
plants 17
Orange Tree 123
Orchid Cactus 156
orchids 44
cultivation 69
Oreocereus celsianus 213
fossulatus 213
trollii 213
fossulatus 213
trollii 213
Oreopanax capitatus 214
nymphaeifolius 214
ornamental pots 32
osmosis 49
outdoor cultivation 17
ovule 51
Oxalis carnosa 214
deppei 214
purpurata bowei 214
vulcanicola 214

P

Pachycereus hollianus 214
pringlei 214
Pachyphytum amethystinum 171
bracteosum 215
brevifolium 215
compactum 215
hookeri 215
oviferum 215
Pachypodium brevicaule 215
geayi 215
lameri 215
succulentum 215
Pachystachys lutea 216
× *Pachyveria* 'Clavata' 216
'Clavifolia' 216
'Glauca' 216
palms 39
cultivation 70
Pancratium narcissiflorum 184
speciosum 184
Pandanus baptistii 217
sanderi 217
utilis 217
veitchii 217
Panda Plant 189
Panicum variegatum 212
Pansy Orchid 200
Paphiopedilum callosum 217
fairieanum 217
insigne 218
niveum 218
spicerianum 218
sukhakulii 218
venustum 218
villosum 218
Parlour Palm 120
Parodia aureispina 218
chrysacanthion 218
maassii 218
microsperma 218
mutabilis 218
nivosa 218
ritteri 218
suprema 218
Parthenocissus henryana 219
Passiflora caerulea 219
quadrangularis 219
racemosa 219
violacea 219
Passion Flower 219
Pavonia multiflora 220
Peace Lily 257
Peacock Plant 113
Peanut Cactus 120
Plant 97
peat fibre 62
pots 72
Pedilanthus tithymaloides 220
Peireskia 225
Pelargonium carnosum 222
× *citrosum* 222
cordatum 222
crispum 222
grandiflorum hybrids 222
graveolens 222
× *hortorum* 222
peltatum hybrids 222
radens 222
zonale hybrids 222
Pellaea rotundifolia 222
viridis 222
Pellionia daveauana 223
pulchra 223
repens 223
Pencil Tree 161
Pentas lanceolata 223
Peperomia argyreia 224
arifolia 224
argyreia 224
blanda 224
caperata 224
clusiifolia 224
fraseri 224
glabella 224
griseo-argentea 224
hederifolia 224
incana 224
magnoliifolia 225
metallica 225
nummulariifolia 225
obtusifolia 225
clusiifolia 224
prostrata 225
pulchella 224
puteolata 225
resediflora 224
rotundifolia 225
sandersii 224
scandens 225
serpens 225
velutina 225
verticillata 225
Pepper Plant 231
perennial plants 29
Pereskia aculeata 225
Perilepta dyeriana 225
perlite 62, 70
Persea americana 226
gratissima 226
pest control 77
petal 51
Phalaenopsis amabilis 226
buissoniana 226
esmeralda 226
grandiflora 226
lueddemanniana 226
schilleriana 226
stuartiana 226
violacea 226
Philodendron amazonicum 228
andreanum 228
bipinnatifidum 228
cannifolium 228
cordatum 228
cuspidatum 228
daguense 228
domesticum 228
dubium 228
elegans 228
erubescens 228
gloriosum 228
hastatum 228
ilsemannii 228
imbe 228
laciniatum 228
laciniosum 228
martianum 228
melanochrysum 228
micans 228
panduriforme 228
pedatum 228
pertusum 202
radiatum 228
sagittifolium 228
scandens 228
selloum 228
squamiferum 228
triumphans 228
verrucosum 228
Phlebodium aureum 229
Phoenix canariensis 229
dactylifera 229
roebelenii 229
Phormium aloides 190
phosphorus deficiency 79
photochemical reaction 50
Phrynium lubbersianum 139
Phyllanthus angustifolius 229
speciosus 229
Phyllitis scolopendrium 230
Phyllocactus crenatus 156
Phyllotaenium lindenii 268
Pick-a-back Plant 263
Pilea cadierei 231
globosa 231
involucrata 231
microphylla 231
muscosa 231
nummulariifolia 231
pubescens 231
serpyllacea 231
serpyllifolia 231
spruceana 231
Pilocereus chrysacanthus 118
lanata 158
Pineapple 94
Flower 159
Pink Periwinkle 117
Piper crocatum 231
nigrum 231
ornatum 231
Pisonia brunoniana 231
umbellifera 231
Pitcher Plant 206
Pittosporum crassifolium 232
eugenioides 232
revolutum 232
tobira 232
undulatum 232
plant containers 14, 66
cylinders 12, 32
plastic pots 12
Platycerium alcicorne 233
bifurcatum 233
grande 233
hillii 233
willinckii 233
Plectranthus australis 233
fruticosus 233
oertendahlii 233
parviflorus 233
Pleione bulbocodioides 234
formosana 234
henryii 234
limprichtii 234
Plumbago auriculata 234
capensis 234
coccinea 234
indica 234
rosea 234
plunging 56
Podocarpus macrophyllus 234
Poinsettia 161
Polypodium aureum 229
Polyscias balfouriana 235
filicifolia 235
guilfoylei 235
paniculata 235
Polystichum auriculatum 236
falcatum 143
tsus-simense 236
Pomegranate 239
pores 49, 51
porous threads 67
potassium deficiency 79
pots 32, 63
plastic 12
potting composts 62
Prayer Plant 197
pricking out 73
Prickly Pear 212
Primrose 236
Primula acaulis 237
× *kewensis* 237
malacoides 237
obconica 237
praenitens 237
sinensis 237
vulgaris 237
Princess of the Night 251
propagation 72
pruning 65
Pseuderanthemum atropurpureum 237
reticulatum 237
pseudobulbs 69
Pseudoespostoa melanostele 158
psyche, of plant 10
Pteris crenata 239
cretica 238
ensiformis 239
longifolia 239
multifida 239
quadriaurita 239
serrulata 239
tremula 239
umbrosa 239
vittata 239
public places 37
Punica granatum 239
Purple Passion Vine 173
Velvet 173
Pyrrhocactus strausianus 239

Q

Queen of the Night 251

R

Rabbit's Ears 213
raceme 51
rainwater 58
Rat's Tail Cactus 97
ray florets 51
Rebutia aureiflora 240
deminuta 240
pseudominuscula 240
fiebrigii 240
knuthiana 240
marsoneri 240
minuscula 240
grandiflora 240
minuscula 240
pseudodeminuta 240
pygmaea 240
ritteri 240
senilis 240
spinosissima 240
violaciflora 240
xanthocarpa 240
receptacle 51
Rechsteineria cardinalis 241
leucotricha 241
Red Cape Tulip 174
Ivy 178
Pepper 116
red spider mite 79

Red-hot Cat's Tail 83
relative humidity 58
repotting 62
reproductive organs 51
resistance, measuring 10
respiration 50
rest periods 60
Rhaphidophora aurea 241
Rhipsalidopsis gaertneri 242
× graeseri 242
rosea 242
Rhipsalis rosea 242
salicornioides 175
rhizome 51
Rhododendron obtusum 243
simsii 243
Rhoeo discolor 243
spathacea 243
Rhoicissus capensis 244
rhomboidea 122, 123
Ribbon Fern 238
Grass 212
river sand 62
Rivina humilis 244
Rochea coccinea 244
falcata 136
Rock Cactus 119
Rockfoil 248
Rodriguezia decora 245
secunda 245
venusta 245
room dividers 31
temperature 11
root 51
cutting 74
hairs 49
mealy bug 79
millipede 79
rot 79
rootstock 51
Rosa chinensis 'Minima' 245
lawrenceana 245
roulettii 245
Rose Geranium 222
Mallow 179
Pincushion 197
of Jericho 94
rosette 69
rotted turves 62
Rubber Plant 164, 166
Ruellia devosiana 148
makoyana 148
repanda 179
Rusty Fig 166

S

Sago Palm 140
Saint Augustine's Grass 259
Saintpaulia confusa 246
ionantha 246
salt damage 79
Sandersonia aurantiaca 246
Sansevieria trifasciata 247
sap movement 51
wood 51
Sauromatum guttatum 247
venosum 247
Saxifraga cotyledon 248
pyramidalis 248
sarmentosa 248
stolonifera 248
Saxifrage 248
scale insects 79
Scarborough Lily 266
Schefflera actinophylla 249
digitata 249
octophyllum 249
venulosa 249
Schlumbergera gaertneri 242
sciarid larvae 79
Scilla paucifolia 249
violacea 249
Scindapsus aureus 241
pictus 249
cernuus 250
Scirpus cernuus 250
scorching 79
screening 25, 53
Screwpine 216
Seaside Grape 126
Sea Urchin Cactus 102
Sedge 116
Sedum bellum 250
dasyphyllum 250
griseum 250
guatemalense 250
morganianum 250
pachyphyllum 250
platyphyllum 250
praealtum 250
rubrotinctum 250
sieboldii 251
stahlii 251
weinbergii 171
seeded plants 42
seedtrays 72
Selaginella apoda 251
kraussiana 251
lepidophylla 251
martensii 251
Selenicereus grandiflorus 251
pteranthus 251
self-watering systems 46
Sempervivum arachnoideum 252
tectorum 252
Senecio articulatus 253
citriformis 253
cruentus hybrids 253
haworthii 253
herreianus 253
macroglossus 253
mikanioides 253
rowleyanus 253
Sensitive Plant 200
sepal 51
Setcreasea purpurea 253
striata 114
sharp sand 62
short-day plants 53
Shrimp Plant 107
Sickle Plant 136
Siderasis fuscata 253
Silk Bark Oak 171
Silver Jade Plant 135
single-lobed seed 49
Sinningia speciosa 254
situation 11, 30
Skimmia japonica 254
slats 23
Slipper Flower 113
slugs 79
Smithiantha cinnabarina 255
hybrids 255
multiflora 255
zebrina 255
Snake's Beard 211
Solanum pseudocapsicum 255
Soleirolia soleirolii 256
Sonerila margaritacea 256
sooty mould 80
soul 12
sowing 73
medium 72
Sparmannia africana 257
Spanish Bayonet 269
Moss 263
Spathiphyllum floribundum 257
patinii 257
wallisii 257
Spear Fern 150
Flower 98
specimen plants 12
sphagnum moss 62
Spider Cactus 173
Plant 121
Spiderwort 264
Spindle Tree 159
Spironema fragrans 114
Spleenwort 101
spraying 59
sprays 59
Spreading Club Moss 251
Sprekelia formosissima 257
springtails 80
Spurge 160
St Augustine's Grass 259
stable manure 62
Stag's Horn Fern 232
staging 23
stairwells 37
stamen 51
Stapelia variegata 258
Star of Bethlehem 115
Starfish Flower 258
stem cutting 74
Stenandrium igneum 258
lindenii 258
Stenocarpus salignus 258
sinuatus 258
Stenotaphrum americanum 259
glabrum 259
secundatum 259
Stephanotis floribunda 259
stigma 51
stock 76
Stonecrop 250
stopping 65
Strawberry Cactus 174
Strelitzia reginae 260
Streptocarpus hybrids 261
wendlandii 261
Strobilanthes dyerianus 225
Stromanthe amabilis 261
sanguinea 261
succulents 42
cultivation 70
summer quarters 17
sun scorch 80
Swan Orchid 141
Sweet Flag 85
Swiss Cheese Plant 201
Syagrus weddelliana 199
Syngonium auritum 261
podophyllum 261
vellozianum 261
Syzygium paniculatum 159

T

Table Fern 238
tap root 51
tarsonemid mites 80
temperature 54
Temple Bells 255
Tephrocactus 213
terrarium 26
terrestrial bromeliad 69
Tetraclinis articulata 262
Tetrastigma voinierianum 262
Thorn Apple 145
thrips 80
Thuja articulata 262
Thunbergia alata 262
grandiflora 262
Tiger's Chaps 163
Tillandsia argentea 263
cyanea 263
flabellata 263
leiboldiana 263
lindenii 263
morreniana 262
usneoides 263
tip cuttings 73
Toad Flower 258
Tolmiea menziesii 263
Torch Thistle 118
Torenia fournieri 264
Tradescantia albiflora 264
blossfeldiana 264
fluminensis 264
sillamontana 264
Trailing Geraniums 222
Transvaal Daisy 170
Trevisia palmata 264
sanderi 264
Trevirana grandiflora 84
Trichocereus schickendantzii 265
spachianus 265
Trichosporum boscheanum 88
grandiflorum 89
javanicum 89
lobbianum 89
marmoratum 89
pulchrum 89
speciosum 89
tuberous begonias 106
plants 44, 51
cultivation 68
tub plants 17
tubular florets 51
rosettes 69
Tulip 265
Tulipa 265
turgor 51
Turk's Cap 198
Tydaea hybrids 189
tying 64

U, V

Umbrella Plant 142
Vallota speciosa 266
Vanda coerulea 266
variegated plants 28
Veltheimia capensis 266
glauca 266
ventilation 25
Venus Fly Trap 147
Venus's Slipper 217
Vinca rosea 117
vine weevil 80
Virginia Creeper 219
virus diseases 77, 80
Vitis dissecta 93
gongylodes 123
vinifera 93
voinierianum 262
Vriesea carinata 267
hieroglyphica 267
× poelmannii 267
rodigasiana 267
splendens 267

W

Wandering Jew 270
Wardian case 26
Wart Plant 176
Washington Palm 268
Washingtonia filifera 268
robusta 268
Watch Chain Crassula 136
water 55
filter 58
quality of 57
roots 45
softeners 58
watering can 50
Wattle 82
Wax Flower 181, 259
Vine 253
Weeping Fig 166
whitefly 80
White Lily-turf 212
wilting 80
window-sill 11, 66
wood core 51
lice 80
Wood Sorrel 214
worms 80

X, Y, Z

Xantheranthemum igneum 268
Xanthosoma lindenii 268
nigrum 268
violaceum 268
yellowing leaves 80
Yucca aloifolia 269
elephantipes 269
gloriosa 269
Zantedeschia aethiopica 269
elliottiana 269
rehmannii 269
Zebrina pendula 270
purpusii 270
Zephyr Lily 271
Zephyranthes candida 271
citrina 271
grandiflora 271
rosea 271
Zygocactus truncatus 271

Bibliography

Listed below are some of the books consulted in the compilation of this encyclopedia.

Baines, Jocelyn & Katherine Kay: The ABC of House and Conservatory Plants
Graf, Alfred B.: Exotica, 7th edition
Herwig, Rob & Margot Schubert: Complete Book of Houseplants
Hessayon, D. G.: Be Your Own Houseplant Expert
Hyams, Edward: A History of Gardens and Gardening
Kranz, Frederick & Jacqueline: Gardening Indoors Under Lights
Reader's Digest: Encyclopedia of Garden Plants and Flowers
Scott-James, Anne: Sissinghurst, The Making of a Garden
Seddon, George: Your Indoor Garden
Walls, Ian G.: The Complete Book of the Greenhouse
Wright, Michael: The Complete Indoor Gardener
Zander, c.s.: Handwörterbuch der Pflanzennamen, 10th edition

Photographic credits

With the exception of those mentioned below all the photographs in this book were taken by the author.
(a.r. = above, right; b.l. = below left; c.l. = centre left etc.)

Mr Ruys: 83 a.r., 133 b.r.
Mr Eisenheiss: 88 a.l., 211 a.l.
Mr J. F. M. Stampraad: 151 b.l.
Paul ter Straeten: 14, 14 b.l., 266 b.l.
Rijksmuseum voor Volkenkunde 8
Halls, England: 22 a.c.
Wolfram Stehling: 92 b.r., 16 a.l., 19 a.c., 27
Harry Smith: 19 b.r., 21, 22 a.l., 26 a.r., 31 a.l., 32 a.l., 32 c.l., 32 a.r., 40 b.r.
Georges Lévêque: 9 l., 11 a.r., 18 b.l., 22 c.l., 22 c.r., 22 b.l.
Mrs Buining: 11 a.l., 11 l.c., 11 b.l., 11 b.c.
Luwesa: 15 a.l., 41 b.l.
Grosfillex: 46 a.c.